DATE DUE

BRODART   Cat. No. 23-221

THE CARLETON LIBRARY SERIES

A series of original works, new collections and reprints of source material relating to Canada, issued under the supervision of the Editorial Board, Carleton Library Series, Carleton University Press Inc., Ottawa, Canada.

Ethnic Demography

Canadian Immigrant, Racial and Cultural Variations

Edited by Shiva S. Halli
Frank Trovato and Leo Driedger

Carleton University Press
Ottawa, Ontario
1990

© Carleton University Press Inc. 1990

ISBN   088629-108-9

Printed and bound in Canada

Carleton Library Series #157

Canadian Cataloguing in Publication Data

Main entry under title:
    Ethnic Demography: Canadian immigrant, racial
and cultural variations

(Carleton Library Series 157)
ISBN 0-88629-108-9

    1. Canada—Population—Ethnic groups. 2. Canada—Population—
Statistics. 3. Ethnicity—Canada. I. Halli, Shivalingappa S., 1952-
II. Trovato, Frank, 1951-   III. Driedger, Leo, 1927-   IV. Series.

    HQ3529.E84 1990   305'.8'00971   C90-090151-1

Distributed by: Oxford University Press Canada
                     70 Wynford Drive,
                     Don Mills, Ontario.
                     Canada. M3C 1J9
                     (416) 441-2941

Cover Design: Robert MacDonald/MediaClones

Acknowledgement

Carleton University Press gratefully acknowledges the support extended to its
publishing programme by the Canada Council and the Ontario Arts Council.

Contributors

T. R. Balakrishnan, University of Western Ontario, London
K. G. Basavarajappa, Statistics Canada
Roderic Beaujot, University of Western Ontario, London
Monica Boyd, Carleton University, Ottawa
Thomas K. Burch, University of Western Ontario, London
Neena Chappell, University of Manitoba, Winnipeg
Robert Choinière, University of Montreal, Montreal
John DeVries, Carleton University, Ottawa
Leo Driedger, University of Manitoba, Winnipeg
Carl F. Grindstaff, University of Western Ontario, London
Shiva S. Halli, University of Manitoba, Winnipeg
Warren E. Kalbach, University of Toronto, Toronto
John Kralt, Secretary of State, Ottawa
Karol J. Krotki, University of Alberta, Edmonton
M. J. Norris, Statistics Canada, Ottawa
Dave Odynak, University of Alberta, Edmonton
Bali Ram, Statistics Canada, Ottawa
J. Peter Rappak, University of Western Ontario, London
Madeline A. Richard, University of Toronto, Toronto
Anthony H. Richmond, York University, Toronto
Norbert Robitaille, University of Montreal, Montreal
T. John Samuel, Secretary of State, Ottawa
K. Selvanathan, University of Western Ontario, London
Shirley B. Seward, Institute for Research on Public Policy, Ottawa
Alan B. Simmons, York University, Toronto
Frank Trovato, University of Alberta, Edmonton

Table of Contents

Preface

This is the first volume written on ethnic demography in Canada. There is an extensive literature on immigrant, ethnic and racial studies in Canada, as the list of references clearly shows. However, a volume combining the two fields of demography and ethnicity has been lacking. The purpose of these contributions is to make available to students and policy-makers the very latest data on ethnic demography from the 1981 and 1986 censuses and recent social surveys. While some demographers have focused on ethnicity extensively, many have not, so this is our opportunity to involve the leading demographers in Canada in the ethnic demographic search. To facilitate this search a conference was held at the University of Manitoba in August 1988 where 25 demographers presented original papers. Twenty-one of those papers are published here.

Pioneering attempts such as this are always fraught with risks, but we have been helped in many ways which made the task easier. The census provides the best longitudinal data, but it is fraught with many problems of reliability; fortunately, half a dozen demographers involved in census gathering in Ottawa have contributed here. A number of demographers involved in ethnic research for several decades have also contributed, so we have the latest contributions from those on the cutting edge of the ethnic and demographic interface. There are many gaps where research is still needed, but we were able to get contributions covering most of the major demographic and social processes important to an ethnic demography. Many issues and problems have been raised if not answered, which we feel will generate more research.

Special thanks to the two Deans of Arts of the University of Manitoba who took a personal interest in the Ethnic Demography conference by their presence and help with funding. The Social Sciences and Humanities Research Council of Canada and the federal Multiculturalism Directorate also funded the project helping to make the conference and this publication possible. We also wish to thank the contributors who presented papers and were willing to revise to make *Ethnic Demography* possible.

Shiva S. Halli, Frank Trovato, Leo Driedger
Winnipeg, May 1989

1. THE SOCIAL DEMOGRAPHY OF ETHNIC GROUPS

Shiva S. Halli, Frank Trovato and Leo Driedger

The aim of this volume is to present a demographic overview of critical issues pertaining to immigrants and ethnic groups in Canada. Our orientation is social demographic: authors concern themselves with the analysis of demographic processes and their sociological implications with special reference to immigrants and ethnic groups.

Papers in this volume are organized into the conceptual frames of three general processes, each of which is an important influence in understanding multiethnic Canada. The first part deals with the basic demographic processes of fertility, mortality and migration. These basic plus and minus factors in plotting population growth will be applied to ethnicity in Canada. They will continue to provide the demographic foundation for all interpretations of Canada's ethnic history for more than a century.

Part two deals with ethnic cohesion and assimilation. An enormous literature has developed on ethnic identity and the survival of ethnic groups, as well as the decline of ethnicity through assimilation and amalgamation. In the United States Robert Park's assimilation theory has been influential so that American society is often described as a melting pot. In Canada the French fact, the aboriginals of the northlands, recent visible minorities, bilingual and multicultural policies have made Canada into a plural mosaic. Social demographers in part two focus on factors of pluralism such as language maintenance, ethno-religious identity, family cohesion and ethnic variations in aging.

Many studies have equated ethnicity with social class, but we see them as two distinct phenomena which may often converge but must be separated analytically. Social class is based on differences in power relations, stratification and socioeconomic status; ethnic relations by contrast are based on racial, religious, linguistic and cultural differences. The variety of ethnic characteristics and populations has enhanced interest in stratification, minority-majority power

1

relations and comparative investigations. In part three we focus on a few of these socioeconomic factors of inequality.

The first three parts clearly demonstrate the multiethnic challenge for demographers. The three processes and influences just reviewed combined with the scores of ethnic groups that can be compared lead us to close in part four with a challenge for demographers. Recent Third World immigrants will make the Canadian population increasingly more multicultural and multiracial. To add to the complexity, regionally and territorially this diversity of minorities is becoming more residentially segregated. The eighties have clearly shown this diversity with the 1981 and 1986 censuses trying to account for further fragmentation by language, intermarriage, assimilation and discrimination. Let us review these four parts in more detail and show how each contributor will add to the multiethnic demographic puzzle.

Finding Comparable Definitions

Our perception of ethnicity in Canada has been influenced to some degree by the way the censuses have recorded the ethnic questions. Every 10 years, the census paints a picture of our nation in this sense; ethnicity is partly a demographic construct of reality.

According to Kralt, the ethnic origin data in our censuses, from 1871 to 1971 had an impact on the way in which Canadian society was and is perceived by Canadians. By forcing all persons to report only one ancestry, or ethnic origin, the picture of our nation was characterized as being dominated by the two charter groups and a few others of relatively minor significance. Since 1981, the census has allowed the reporting of multiple ethnicities. In some respects this practice will give Canadians a more realistic picture of our heterogeneous multicultural and multiracial society.

From a statistical point of view, data concerning ethnic origin are valuable. They tell us the extent to which groups are changing in size and composition. Thus if accurate assessment of the growth patterns of sociocultural groups are to be made, it is all the more important that we have a clear understanding of ethnic origin statistics.

Definitions of ethnic origin discussed by Kralt provide a historical overview of the concepts used to measure ethnic origin in the Canadian censuses since 1871. One clear message that comes through in his analysis is that changes in the wording and coding of this variable reflect the societal conditions pertaining to race, ethnicity and immigrants at the time of the censuses. For example, around 1871 a time of substantial European immigration to Canada, the emphasis placed on the ethnic question was on country of birth or citizenship. In 1901 the census asked a question on racial origin, and by 1971 it was necessary to distinguish between race and ethnic origin; two questions were therefore included. By the time of the 1971 Census the established practice was to define

2

ethnicity in terms of paternal ancestry. By 1981, it had become clear to the statisticians in Ottawa that an appropriate question should allow for multiple ethnicities. Canada had changed over the decades. This new practice seems appropriate given that more intermarriage occurs between ethnic groups.

The various changes to the ethnic questions have been influenced by social context. The problem for users of ethnic statistics over time is comparability. However, multiple responses are difficult to analyse unless we have knowledge of the degree of importance each reported ethnicity has to the respondent. In order words, if a respondent gives three ethnicities, should we consider them as equally important to the respondent? Krotki and Odynak tackle this issue in a later section of this volume.

Basic Components of Population Change

Section one is concerned with the three basic components of population change: fertility, mortality and migration. Migration includes both internal and international migration. The six papers on fertility, mortality and migration offer both descriptive as well as substantive explanation for the observed variations among ethnic groups.

Norris sketches the basic demographic trends and patterns of Canada's aboriginal groups using primarily 1981 census data in a historical context. The fertility transition of this component of Canada's earliest population is characterized by patterns of traditionally high fertility.

Notwithstanding this overall picture of relatively high fertility, there are a range of differences amongst the aboriginals. For example, during the 1980s, Indians had a crude birth rate of 35 per 1000 population, but the Inuit fertility rate was only 15 per 1000. The total fertility rates of these two groups were 3 and 4 respectively, while for the general Canadian population the rate was 1.7.

The aboriginals share a life expectancy that is on average 10 years below that of the rest of Canada. Notwithstanding their higher mortality levels, their high fertility rate ensures them a very high rate of natural increase.

The aboriginal population of Canada is distinct in other demographic dimensions as well. Norris shows that native Indians, who are the largest segment of aboriginals (which also includes Inuit and Métis) share greater propensities for relocation than the total Canadian population. One outcome of the aboriginals' continued high fertility is their very young age structure, with an average age of 23 in 1986, as compared to 34 for Canadians as a whole. Approximately 68 percent of the aboriginal population is under the age of 30, compared to 47 percent of the total Canadian population.

Other ethnic groups in contemporary Canada may not be as demographically distinct as the aboriginal peoples. One clear indication of this view is that many groups do not show fertility levels that are radically different from the average.

The differentials across ethnic groups tend to be small. Halli presents an analysis of family size differences among six large ethnic groups in Canada (the British, French, Germans, Italians, Jews and Ukrainians) using data from the 1981 Census. Among women below the age of 30, the number of children ever born ranges from a low of .72 (Jews) to a high of 1.03 (British and Italians). For women aged 30 and above, the range is from 2.13 (Jews) to 3.17 (French). Clearly the differences among younger women is quite small in comparison to older ones.

The task facing social demographers is how to explain these differentials. The literature has identified two hypotheses: the effects of modernization or assimilation and the effects of minority group status. The main idea behind the modernization explanation is based on modernization theory; that is, over time, subgroup differences in social demographic action will converge due to the homogenizing effects of modernization. Observed differentials are thought to be a manifestation of cultural lag, and once equalization of social demographic characteristics takes place, differences in fertility will disappear. The minority status thesis predicts that fertility differences will persist even after social demographic characteristics have equalized.

The question pertinent to Halli's work is: are the small differentials among Canadian ethnic groups a sole function of differences in characteristics? Authors in North America have until recently discovered that fertility differences remain unaccounted for even after controls for ethnic characteristics have been considered in their statistical analyses. Substantive interpretations of this effect rest with either subcultural-normative sources or minority status effects. Thus in some cases, such as the Blacks in the United States, the group as a whole has above average fertility due to its disadvantaged status, not subcultural norms emphasizing large families. On the other hand, Catholics in the past had large families not because they were disadvantaged economically, but because of their pronatalist church doctrine. However, groups such as Japanese-Americans and Jews have always shown small family sizes. The main reason for their below average fertility is that they have always strived for economic acculturation, the groups do not possess norms discouraging the use of effective contraception, and they also share a history of prejudice and discrimination. Under these conditions upward mobility engenders feelings of insecurity which ultimately translate into a conscious limitation of fertility.

The Canadian situation as analysed by Halli supports the view that family size differences are largely a function of discrepancies in social demographic and compositional variables among ethnic groups. However, more research is necessary before the minority status thesis can be rejected altogether.

Trovato and Halli attempt to apply elements of the characteristics-assimilation and minority status explanations to study ethnic differences in geographic mobility. They hypothesize that differences in relocation are due to variations in social demographic variables. Any residual in the dependent variable they attribute to ethnic effects.

While the characteristics prediction is straightforward, the ethnic effects explanation requires elaboration. Trovato and Halli elaborate a number of mechanisms that are thought to be subsumed under ethnic effects. They propose that unexplained variations in mobility once characteristics differences have been controlled reflect group differences in ethnic cohesion, language assimilation, the importance of family and kin in the local area of residence, and insecurities about moving.

Their empirical results suggest that groups characterized by strong kinship and ethnic community affiliations are more likely to resist moving. Future research is needed to better ascertain the varied sources of migration decision-making among ethnic groups. A survey approach would be necessary as census data are very limited in this respect.

Canadian demography does not possess an established tradition of mortality analysis concerning ethnic groups. Trovato argues that this is rather peculiar given the importance of immigration and the emphasis social scientists have placed on the problems of adjustment of immigrants in their new society. He proposes that this state of affairs is largely a function of lack of suitable data. First, there are few variables coded on the death certificate. Secondly, there is much fluctuation in the extent to which ethnicity and nativity have been coded on the death certificate over the years. In some years these variables were not coded. Perhaps a further reason why so little study has been done may have to do with an implicit assumption that differentials in mortality are minimal. To a large extent this remains an empirical question. But it appears that an assumption of homogeneity in death rates is difficult to justify, especially with regard to differences in cause of death. Immigrant and ethnic groups are known to differ in their cultural traditions and lifestyles; it is therefore conceivable that differences in certain causes of death also prevail. Some immigrant groups share radically different migration experiences, predisposing them to certain health risks not shared by the general population.

Unfortunately, the available data are inadequate in demonstrating these kinds of sources of mortality variation. However, indirect evidence from a number of immigrant countries such as Canada, France, Australia and the United Kingdom, suggests there is a tendency for immigrants to approximate the morbidity and mortality experience of their host populations the longer they reside in their adoptive societies. Avenues for future work advocated by Trovato include more emphasis on health status and comparative analyses of the foreign-born with respect to cause of death differences.

The remaining two chapters in this section are also concerned with international immigrants in Canada, but they focus on their social and economic experience in Canada.

Beaujot and Rappak present a census analysis of immigration from the 1971 and 1981 censuses. They separate immigrants into two broad classes: those from traditional source areas, and those from new source countries, or ''new wave'' immigrants, as Simmons calls them in his paper later. Beaujot and Rappak study five dimensions of immigrants' experience in Canada: regional distribution, language transfer, education, labour force and earnings. Most foreigners are attracted to Ontario, Quebec and British Columbia, thus follow regional economic opportunity structures. As a whole, immigration contributes more to gains in the English language than to the French language. There are large differences in education with the new wave in general being better trained, but their earnings are generally not commensurate with their education. The predominant pattern suggests that the arrival status of immigrant cohorts largely determines their socioeconomic status from census to census.

What will be the impacts of the new wave immigration on Canadian society in the years ahead? According to Simmons, from a strictly numerical point of view, their present impact is small as they are too recent, too young, and many of them return home to their countries of origin. However, since the "mature" stream of immigrants (those from traditional source areas such as Europe and the U.S.) is aging, and approaching retirement, and fewer of them continue to come to Canada, the inevitable outcome will be a shift in multiculturalism policy toward Third World origin groups in the future.

Social Demography and Ethnic Cohesion

From the point of view of national populations it is the interplay of fertility, mortality and net migration that determine the size and growth of the population. This is of course also true of subpopulations, except for one important difference. Ethnic groups can gain or lose in numbers as a consequence of acculturation processes such as language transfer and exogamy. Social demography is principally concerned with the sociological analysis of demographic action which encompasses the basic variables of fertility, mortality and migration as well as other demographic phenomena that relate to the composition of groups in society (e.g., age-sex composition, marital status composition, occupational distribution, religious composition, etc.). The implied assumption is that sociological factors are determinants as well as consequences of demographic action.

The papers in this section all touch on social processes related to the interplay between ethnic cohesion and modernization including degree of language maintenance, ethno-religious identity, family solidarity, inter-marriage and variations in aging. Changes occur in all of these areas. What forms of adjustment and acculturation take place?

DeVries uses the idea of a balancing equation in formal demography to explain the change in the size of an ethnic or language community into three components: natural increase (the difference between births and deaths), net migration (the difference between in and out migration), and net language shift (the difference between gains and losses for a given ethno-language). The essential elements in the definition of language shift are the measurements of an individual's language behaviour at minimally two points in time. Language shift has occurred if the measurements do not produce identical values.

Of course, tracing language shifts over time becomes more complicated with the acknowledgment of multiple responses to the ethnic origin question. However, deVries finds that the tendencies for persons to declare more than one ethnicity is largely a native born phenomenon. Relatively few first generation immigrants give multiple responses.

Kalbach and Richards consider the problem of religious identification (a second social variable) and its relationship to ethnicity, generation, linguistic, and socioeconomic status for three broad categories of immigrants, the British, the non-British Europeans and the non-Europeans. They focus their attention on whether the degree of ethnic homogeneity of a religious denomination among non-Europeans is in any way related to economic status. They find that in comparison to groups of British and non-British European origin, the non-Europeans tend to do relatively well in terms of education and occupation, but are generally underrepresented in the above average income classes.

Concerning religion's association with economic status, the authors' analyses lead to the conclusion that religion is important in explaining language maintenance; that is, those belonging to distinctly ethnic religions are more likely to speak some language other than English or French in their homes. The effect of religion on socioeconomic status is weak, but they discovered that for many recent immigrants there is a strong tendency to report "no religion," and that such persons fare significantly better in economic terms than persons who identify with some religious denomination. Kalbach and Richards suggest that this association may indicate that the "secular" mobility path may offer the best opportunity for immigrants' status achievement in Canada.

The study of ethnic household and family structure (a third social factor) is largely underdeveloped in Canada. To a large extent family patterns of sociocultural groups must reflect variations in cultural values, acculturation tendencies, demographic patterns and ethnic cohesiveness.

Burch identifies the conceptual and methodological reasons for this gap in the literature. For example, he says that quite often, differentials are assumed to reflect normative-subcultural factors, but there is no clear cut way to test for these influences directly. This state of affairs has led some researchers into a tautological trap: the observed behaviour (e.g., high fertility) is used as evidence of a group's ideology (values) and their ideology is used to explain the behaviour. He identifies a number of valuable approaches to help overcome these problems, but recognizes that all such alternatives entail their own sets of difficulties. In the meantime, we should not abandon the analysis of ethnic differentials in family and household structure. We must try to tease out reliable substantial results from available sources and must combine statistical analysis with social and anthropological knowledge of specific ethnic groups.

Burch uses the 1985 General Social Survey to analyse ethnic differentials in family structure: the number of children in the household, siblings and relatives; the number of weekly visits by family and kin; the tendency to live alone as opposed to with one's family. His multivariate analyses reveal significant variations, but among the seven ethnic groups studied, the Italians and the French tend to stand out in demonstrating effects above and beyond the influence of control variables — a situation similar to the outcome in Halli's and in Trovato and Halli's studies discussed earlier. Why is it that Italians and Francophones are more likely to visit their fathers and relatives than other groups? Are their families more cohesive because ethnicity is important?

Bali Ram's analysis is closely related to ethnic family maintenance. He provides an analysis of intermarriage propensities among 40 immigrant groups in Canada using data from the 1981 Census of population. The percentage of foreign born husbands or wives living with Canadian-born spouses born in another foreign country is taken as the index of intermarriage, whereas the percentage of husbands or wives of the same origin is taken as the index of endogamy.

He discovered that the propensity for intermarriagee is somewhat higher for immigrant women than for foreign born men. Intermarriage is generally more frequent among those born in the United States, Australia and Northwestern Europe but less likely among those from Southern Europe, the Caribbean and Asia.

Why such differentials? Ram tests a number of hypotheses for the effect of group size, duration of residency in Canada, sex ratio imbalance and socioeconomic heterogeneity. His multiple regression results indicate that by and large the strongest determinant of immigrants having spouses who were born in Canada or are of the same origin, is period of immigration. The longer a group has been in Canada, the greater its exposure to interactions with persons from outgroups, and hence the greater the opportunities for exogamy.

Aging is an important part of the family cycle adding a fourth social demographic variable. The aging of the population has received much attention in recent years, but few have paid specific attention to this phenomenon from the perspective of ethnicity. Driedger and Chappell explore this topic by looking at demographic, regional, cultural and linguistic variations in eth-elders in Canada. An important contribution by these authors is their development of an eth-elder typology, which should prove useful for those interested in pursuing further study in this area of social demography.

Driedger and Chappell found striking differences in the ethnic distributions of elders. For example, the British group in Canada accounts for 40 percent of the total population but its proportion of eth-elders (age 65 +) is 49 percent. The French represent 27 percent of the population, but its proportion of the aged is only 23 percent. Clearly, such differences are largely a function of past fertility trends and population levels for these groups.

Canadian society will continue to age. Policies should not only be directed to the general population, but also to the various ethnic groups that make up this country. The needs of eth-elders may differ greatly from group to group.

Therefore, assimilationist policy approaches will not be successful. The ethnic communities must be involved in the provision of services.

The focus of Choinière and Robitaille is also on the aging of ethnic groups, but they restrict their study to Quebec. The question that drives their analysis is: what are the determinants of variation in aging among ethnic groups in Quebec over time?

From a purely demographic perspective the answer can only be mortality, fertility and migration. However, they also introduce the interesting idea that in addition to such processes, ethnic mobility explains the phenomenon of aging. By this they mean the tendency for some ethnic groups to give inconsistent declarations of their ethnicity from census to census. They find that groups who lose members due to this tendency experience significantly greater rates of aging. Gainers on the other hand enjoy an increasingly younger age structure. Thus, switchers are generally younger than those who consistently declare the same ethnic origin. This tends to vary by generation. Intergenerational shifts are greater than intragenerational ones, therefore reflecting a greater tendency for intermarriage among the native-born descendants of first generation immigrants.

Choinière and Robitaille's study is quite fascinating. In light of the work in the rest of Canada, or for the total country as a whole, discussed earlier in conjunction with intermarriage, and multiple ethnicities, it would be important to replicate their analysis for other provinces.

Socioeconomic Attainment and Inequalities

Research in Canada has often stressed that acculturation is related to success in economic performance among sociocultural groups. Also, it is frequently implied that the process involved in status attainment involves some loss of ethnic identity. For example, for the immigrants from non-English or non-French speaking countries, the ability to get ahead is largely contingent on their human capital including their ability to acquire the official languages of Canada. The question is: is such a process detrimental to ethnic identity?

An appropriate answer to this question necessitates the analysis of data at several points in time to adequately monitor changes in both economic status and ethnic identification for individuals. Unfortunately, these kinds of data are not readily available, therefore researchers confine their investigations to census data. While this may be a limiting feature much can be said for the use of statistics derived from the census: they are easily accessible and they allow for the statistical analysis of relatively small groups as well as large ones, which would likely be impossible with survey data.

It is clear that recent immigrants who have to learn either the English or French language are at a disadvantage in socioeconomic mobility. There are other disadvantages such as lack of education, being of female gender and being racially visible. In this section we focus extensively on the neglected link between gender and ethnicity.

Four chapters in this section deal specifically with the economic adjustment and/or attainment of immigrant women. They are particularly important because, as Grindstaff rightly contends, this area of investigation has generally been underdeveloped and more needs to be discovered. Gender intensifies the disadvantage immigrant women experience in the labour market. They carry a triple disadvantage: their sex, their immigrant status, and for many, physical visibility as a racial minority.

Boyd demonstrates the typical profile of immigrant women in Canada: a low level of educational attainment, low levels of employment and, among those who have jobs, occupations with low status in sectors service, food processing, accommodation and fabricating sectors. They also receive very low wages, particularly women from Southern Europe and Asia.

Boyd offers a number of policy suggestions to help ameliorate the situation for such women in Canada. Judicious implementation of language training coupled with educational and job training, child care services and employment equity programs in the private sector are necessary. Of course, such policies are not easy to implement nor are they free of difficulties themselves. Work in the area of policy analysis and evaluation along these lines will be necessary.

Basavarajappa and Verma compare the occupational distribution of the sexes by nativity using an index of dissimilarity for various occupational classes in the 1981 Census. They examine 15 immigrant groups classified by whether they belong to the ''traditional'' stream (U.K., U.S., other Western Europe, Central Europe, Southern Europe and East Europe) or nontraditional sources (Africa, South Asia, Southeast Asia, East Asia, West Asia, Oceania, Caribbean, South Central America).

They report that the occupational distribution of women differs more than for men, and although the index of dissimilarity for females tends to decrease with increased length of residency in Canada, it never converges with that of the native-born. The gender differential is considerably greater than by nativity. This, according to the authors, implies that the shift required for the Canadian-born women to achieve occupational similarity with Canadian-born men is much more than that required for the foreign-born women to achieve equality with foreign-born men.

Grindstaff proposes that economic status differences among immigrant women may be accounted for by not only structural factors such as those mentioned above, but also problems of credentialling in Canada for the foreigners, discrimination, lack of qualifications and subcultural factors such as socialization for achievement.

Following the role conflict hypothesis, Grindstaff predicts that among women aged 30-34 in 1981, the never married will have the highest levels of economic attainment followed by the widowed/divorced/separated and then the married. Presumably, the marital role is another constraining feature that conditions immigrant women's potential for economic success. In general, the hypothesis is supported. Concerning ethnicity, it appears that it may have an indirect effect on economic outcome through its influence on marital status and age at marriage.

There is need for an in-depth account of the occupational marginality of many immigrant women, who are largely found in the so-called job ghettoes. Seward takes a close look at one such job sector — the clothing industry — where immigrant females are concentrated in large numbers. This industry features a large percentage of women workers, a large proportion of immigrants, a very low education profile for its workers and low wages. Recently, a growing number of women in the Canadian clothing industry are from the Third World with very little, if any, knowledge of the official languages, hampering their prospects for economic advancement or job transfer.

Richmond focuses his observations on the Caribbean immigrants in Canada, a subgroup of non-Europeans. His aim is to analyse income differences within this immigrant group. The basis for selecting this group rests on the assumption that they are highly visible in physical and cultural characteristics and may therefore be subject to high levels of prejudice and discrimination.

A central hypothesis is that one's inability to converse in English or French hinders earning potential. Several of the subsequent papers in this volume deal in one way or another with this prediction. Richmond rejects the hypothesis. He contends that income from employment is largely a function of educational qualifications, length of residence in Canada and city of residence (Montreal vs. Toronto). This situation applies to both sexes, but in terms of levels, females do better than males, due mostly to their lower rates of unemployment.

The Multiethnic Challenge for Demographers

According to Samuel, the demographic effects of recent Third World immigrants may be difficult to predict at this stage because we do not know enough about their fertility and mortality patterns. Canada will face the challenge of avoiding racial tensions. As this class of immigrants continues to grow, the policy of multiculturalism will have to be modified to that of multiracialism. This would be justified as Canada has always been a multiracial society, and given its low levels of fertility, future population growth will depend on immigration, mostly from the Third World.

Balakrishnan and Selvanathan explore how changes in immigration to Canada since the early fifties and sixties have affected the largest cities in Canada. The authors confine their observations to one of several key aspects of this question: residential segregation in the 14 metropolises in this country.

Distinct patterns of segregation have developed for a number of reasons. City size may be positively related to segregation because larger cities may facilitate a minimum threshold of ethnic population size for residential segregation to develop. Also, it may be that more recent immigrants will tend to cluster in certain areas of the city due to their relatively low economic status and limited language fluency. Furthermore, new groups may cluster along social distance dimensions. Those who are relatively similar in culture and origins will tend to live in closer proximity than those who are culturally and racially distant.

Their empirical analysis provides limited or no support for these kinds of explanations, except for the social distance thesis which received strong support. Only qualified support was given for the idea that segregation decreases as socioeconomic status increases. The implication of this analysis is that cultural differences are perhaps more important than socioeconomic differences in explaining ethnic residential segregation. Residential segregation varies by ethnicity, adding another dimension to a multiethnic Canada.

Krotki and Odynak attribute the emergence of the multiethnic phenomenon to the differential processes of assimilation across ethnic groups over time, and more specifically to the reality of intermarriage. In essence multiethnicity is a natural outcome of the evolving ethnic structure of Canada — a movement toward cultural pluralism and varying degrees of accommodation.

These authors point out, however, that the tendency to exogamy and hence to report more than one ethnicity depends on a variety of sociological factors including the absolute and relative size of the ethnic group, the average length of residency in this nation, the degree of residential dispersion or concentration, and the degree of ethnic cohesion. They offer a list of hypotheses for future work. In addition, they develop a methodology suitable for the appropriate measurement of multiple ethnicity for individuals, which involves the assignment of different weights to each response. This is an appealing formulation, but it remains to be seen how effective it will be in future empirical study.

Krotki and Odynak show that with census data it is possible to identify two types of ethnic groups: the exogamous gainers, and the exogamous losers. Thus intermarriage implies a process of recruitment and loss. Prior to the advent of multiethnicities, most research in Canada has tended to support the notion that a loss of ethnic identity occurs through intermarriage. But now it becomes quite conceivable that as ethnicity becomes a random element in marriage selection, the biological basis for the preservation of ethnicity will become less important, unless racial distinctions will increasingly divide Canada by visible and nonvisible groupings as they have in the United States and South Africa.

The collection of papers in this volume reflects a variety of research orientations in sociological demography. The existing literature concerning immigrant ethnic and racial groups in Canada is mostly sociological. In offering a predominantly social demographic orientation, we hope that this volume will serve to complement and expand this research tradition in Canada by providing the best from the Canadian censuses and demographic research.

2. ETHNIC ORIGINS IN THE CANADIAN CENSUS, 1871-1986[1]

John Kralt

In every decennial Canadian census schedule since 1871, at least one question has been included which was intended to measure the mix of racial, ethnic or cultural origins within the Canadian population[2]. Originally, the rationale for the collection of these data was rooted in the political necessity to know the British/French racial mixture. While the ratio of these two ethnic groups to each other within today's population remains of concern to many Canadians, the more recent ethnic questions have also been concerned with the numbers of aboriginal or native persons and others whose origins exclude British or French. As a result of the arrival of large numbers of immigrants from Third World countries since the late 1960s, considerable interest has been shown in the data relating to persons reporting origins classified as *visible minorities* in the 1981 and 1986 censuses.

This paper will provide a historical overview of the concepts used to measure ethnic origin since 1871 and a context for interpreting these ethnic origin data. It should be emphasized from the outset that both the concept upon which the ethnic origin data are based and the collection and processing procedures used to prepare the data for the tabulation and publication are of almost equal importance. However, because very little information is available on processing procedures prior to 1971, the impact of these changes on the data will of necessity be limited to 1971-1986.

Many other factors that are not necessarily part of the enumeration process can have an impact on the final counts for a given ethnic origin. For example, if Statistics Canada implements specialized procedures to improve the enumeration of selected target groups, there may be a significant increase or decrease in the numbers of persons reporting specific origins. Similarly, whole groups within the population may refuse to cooperate with the census enumeration. This scenario in fact occurred with the enumeration of many Indian bands in

1986. An example of general societal conditions having an impact on the data is shown by the sharp decreases in the numbers of persons reporting German ethnic origin in the decennial censuses taken during or just after the two world wars.

The Early Censuses: 1871-1961

Over the past 115 years, there have been 13 different attempts to measure the ethnic origins[3] of the population, be these reflected in the instructions given to enumerators prior to 1961 or in the questions used in the 1961-1986 period. [See Appendix A for a complete listing of the enumerator instructions (1871-1951) and the questions (1961-1986) used to collect the data]. As there was a radical shift in the way in which the census was collected and the data were processed beginning in 1971, the discussion below will focus first on the ethnic data in the 1871-1961 censuses and then deal with the modern censuses starting with that of 1971.

Beginning in 1871, there was a desire to distinguish between *place of birth* or *citizenship* and *origins*. Exactly what was meant by the question was also considered to have been somewhat ambiguous from the beginning, especially for Canadians of mixed origin. The 1871 Census statisticians indicated to their users that the data had to be interpreted with some care as origin was not clear to all persons:

> [T]he enumerators had, of course, to record the answers given to them. Whenever no definite answer was obtained, the column was then filled with the word or sign not given, and this as a fact has occurred most particularly in families of mixed origin. It is in this way that only two half breeds have been reported. True again it is that the blood of the West, of whom there were very few settled within the four Provinces. (Kralt 1980, 19)

While the 1871 concept was retained for 1881, for unknown reasons, it was changed in 1891 to count only persons with French ancestry. The 1891 data were apparently unusable:

> An attempt was made ... to ascertain the number of French Canadians and French Acadians in the several provinces of the Dominion... It has been claimed, however, with much appearance of reason, that the columns headed French Canadians does not show the number of persons of French origin in Canada [in 1891]; that in the case of Acadians in the Maritime Provinces and the Half-breeds of Manitoba and the North-West Territories, the question was misunderstood and that in the province of Ontario, many persons of French Canadian origin have not so been enumerated.
>
> The fact is noted here so that persons, using the results published, may not be misled by supposing that the number of persons of French Canadian origin has been ascertained with precision or that the actual increases or decreases are such as a comparison with former Census returns might seem to show (Kralt 1980, 20).

14

The failure of the 1891 data probably was the key factor that led to the rein-troduction of *racial origin* in the 1901 Census. Persons with mixed aboriginal and European origins were enumerated as such. Canadians with mixture of other origins were to report the ancestry of their paternal ancestor. The procedure adopted in 1901 for the classification of persons with mixed aboriginal and European ancestries was apparently not too successful because in 1911 these persons were asked to report their maternal ancestry. Similar procedures were used in 1921 except that special emphasis was placed on not accepting answers *Canadian* or *American* as these referred to *citizenship* or *nationality*, not to a *race* or *people* (Kralt 1980, 41). It is with the 1921 Census monograph that the first clear attempt to distinguish between *origin* and *race* was made:

> [T]he term race signifies a subgroup of the human species related by ties of physical kinship. Scientists have attempted to divide and subdivide the human species into groups on the basis of biological traits, such as the shape of the head, stature, colour of skin, etc.
>
> The term origin, therefore, as used by the census usually has a combined biological, cultural and geographic significance. It suggests whence our people come and the implied biological strain and cultural background... Such usage is familiar to the public in general, and only when our origin classifications follow such lines, can they be collected by a Census, be understood by the people or have any significance from the practical stand-point of the development of a Canadian nation (Dominion Bureau of Statistics 1929, 12-13).

The authors of the 1921 monograph recognized there had been and continued to be considerable ethnic intermarriage. For groups such as the Chinese which they considered to be unassimilable, paternal ancestry was a good reflection of these origins. However, for ethnic groups whose members had inter-married to a large degree, paternal ancestry could be considered to have become mean-ingless for individual Canadians. They considered that this:

> may be accepted as true insofar as the individual is concerned. It remains true, however, that by the law of large numbers in the mass, the adoption of the practice followed in the census will yield approximately accurate measurements of the different infusions of blood that have gone up to make the total (Dominion Bureau of Statistics 1929, 4).

For the censuses between 1921 and 1941, the instructions given to enumer-ators were relatively similar with a gradual shift to the use of paternal ancestry to determine a single ethnic origin for all Canadians. The next major change was introduced in 1951 in which the:

> origin of the person ... was established by asking the language (i.e., native tongue) spoken by the person's paternal ancestor, or the person himself in the case of an immigrant, at the time of first arrival on this continent.
> ... In the event that a person's origin could not be determined by using the language criterion, they [the enumerators] were to ask a further question

such as: Is your origin in the male line English, Scottish, Ukrainian, ...
(Dominion Bureau of Statistics 1956, 132-133).

In 1961, the reference to language in the determination of ancestry was dropped. Unlike 1951 where aboriginal persons with mixed origins living on reserves were classified as aboriginal persons and those off reserves were to report their paternal ancestry, in 1961 aboriginal persons were divided into *Band (Treaty) Indians* and *non-Band (non-Treaty) Indians*.

The census-takers prior to 1971 realized that many Canadians had multiple ethnic origins. However the primitive computational devices available before 1971 meant it would be virtually impossible to try to deal with multiple ethnic origins. Even with today's high-speed computers and sophisticated software, the tabulation and interpretation of multiple ethnic origins is problematic.

It would appear that a major rationale for changing the question used to measure ethnic origins from 1871-1961 was to force single origins. At the same time, it would appear likely that the correction or modification of the instructions and procedures to correct one census led to additional problems in the next.

The Modern Censuses: 1971-1986

While the question and the concept seem to have remained relatively stable between 1961 and 1971, the procedures used to collect and process the data changed drastically with the large scale use of computers and the shift from enumerators to self-enumeration. The 1971 Census therefore can be considered as being the first of the truly modern censuses.

The shift to self-enumeration is the most visible of the changes in census methodology between 1961 and 1971. Instead of trained enumerators asking questions and recording the collected information, the vast bulk of 1971 questionnaires were filled in by individual respondents. While the impact of this change in enumeration on overall response rates was apparently examined by Statistics Canada, the impact of such a radical change in procedure has not, to the best of my knowledge, been quantified when dealing with the range or type of responses obtained for questions such as ethnic origin. This change would have had a major impact on the reporting of multiple origins. An enumerator going door to door in 1961 could be instructed to accept only one ethnic origin in response to this question. Even though respondents were instructed to provide only one answer, evidence from the 1976 Census mother tongue data suggests this instruction was often ignored (Kralt 1980).

A second change occurred in data capture methodology, i.e., the transfer of the data from the questionnaires to computer. In 1961, the data were transferred from the enumeration documents to computer (data capture) using a mark-sense device. It is probable that there were few multiple origins on the forms in that year as such multiple origins would probably have failed the quality control checks of the enumeration process.

This was not the case in the 1971 Census. As most questionnaires were filled in by individual householders, the quality control measures tended to be oriented towards ensuring that there was a response to each question on the questionnaire rather than insuring that there was only one response. For data capture Statistics Canada used a specialized optical scanner, which could be programmed to accept or reject more than one answer if such were reported. If multiple ethnic origins were reported, the decision was made at data capture which entries were to be retained. If the multiple response consisted of two answer categories given on the questionnaire (labelled as mark-ins), the darkest mark was retained and all other responses were dropped. If a response written in by the respondent (labelled as a write-in) was reported along with one or more mark-ins, then the write-in was always retained. For example, if *British* (a mark-in) and *French* (a mark-in) were reported, then the darkest of the two marks was retained. If *Norwegian* (a mark-in) and *Swedish* (a write-in) were reported, *Swedish* was always retained.

The assignment of data to the records of persons for whom no data was available also changed radically between 1961 and 1971. In censuses prior to 1971, persons for whom no data were available were assigned an origin by clerks using assignment tables. While there was no way of ensuring all assignments were done consistently, other data on the questionnaire, such as name, place of birth, language, etc. could be considered by the clerk in making the assignments. In 1971, a relatively simple set of rules was established to assign an ethnic origin if none had been reported. In part as a result of these changes, there appeared to be some interesting changes between 1961 and 1971 in the country's ethnic composition, at least insofar as these were reported.

Using the paternal ancestry criterion to determine ethnic origin, the total numbers of persons having a particular ethnic origin cannot decrease, unless there has been a large scale out-migration or other demographic phenomena that would lead to such a decrease. It is likely that, in order for a demographic change to have such an impact, it would be readily observable. However, a substantial number of ethnic origins were reported by fewer persons in 1971 than in 1961, even though there were no reasons for such declines. From the available 1961 and 1971 data, it seems reasonable to assume that self-enumeration led to gradual movement towards the reporting of *British* ethnic origins outside Quebec and a similar though smaller movement to the reporting of *French* origins in Quebec. As well, it is quite clear that the inclusion and position of a particular ethnic origin on the questionnaire had a definite impact on whether or not that ethnic origin was reported (Kralt 1977, 1-11).

Between 1901 and 1971 a trend emerged to gradually establish paternal ancestry as the only criterion to be used to force a single response to the ethnic origin question. Because of the limitations of data retrieval prior to 1971, it had not been possible to examine the adequacy of this criterion through an analysis of ethnic data within families to any great degree. With the computerization of the entire 1971 Census database in the early 1970s and the development of adequate data retrieval software, it was possible to examine the correlations between the origins of parents and their children living with these parents.

From these data, it was apparent that many children who should have the same origin as their fathers (i.e., their fathers should be their immediate paternal ancestors), did not in fact report the same ethnic origin. While a 100 percent correlation of ethnic origins of fathers to their children in these fathers' census families would be in error in the opposite direction due to such factors as adoption, remarriage, etc., the percentage of children whose origin was different than their fathers' was higher than could reasonably have been expected.

This discrepancy in turn raised questions about the accuracy of ethnic data based on paternal ancestry. If an unreasonably high proportion of children living with their fathers do not have the same ethnic origin as their fathers, it appears probable that the accuracy of the reporting of the ethnic, racial, or cultural origins of a long dead male ancestor is likely also to be suspect (Kralt 1980, 26-27).

The testing program carried out for the 1981 Census suggested very strongly that the reason for the lack of consistency between fathers and their children was due to the fact that only one origin was captured for these children. In the simplest case, if parents in a two-parent family reported different ethnic origins and both of these origins were reported for the children in that family, then a conflict would arise between the reported ethnic origins of at least some fathers and their children (Kralt 1980, 33-38).

After the 1971 ethnic data were released, much had been made of the fact that there was an undercount of about 10 percent between the number of Band or Treaty Indians enumerated in the 1971 Census and the number of Band Indians in Canada according to the Indian Register for the same reference date. Technically, given the traditional difficulties with the enumeration of reserves and other remote areas, as well as some of the known problems with the Indian Register, such a discrepancy between the two data sources is to be expected. Of equal concern was the fact that the 1971 Census enumerated only 64,000 non-Band Indians even though the estimates of the day ranged from 250,000 to 750,000 (Kralt 1980, 26).

The traditional ethnic origin data seem to assume that Canadian society is made up of a number of large and not so large groups having common ancestries or cultural backgrounds, much as it was identified in the 1921 Census monograph quoted above. In reality, the more appropriate observation about ethnic groups in Canada is that for many Canadians, ethnic origin has little significance because large scale ethnic intermarriage has made identification with specific cultural or ethnic groups extremely difficult if not impossible.

That there has traditionally been large scale ethnic intermarriage is indisputable in my view. In his monograph of 1961 Census data, Kalbach had shown that ethnic intermarriage was very extensive for the native-born component of most non-British/non-French ethnic groups. At the same time he showed the relatively high levels of intra-group marriage among the British and the French ethnic groups is probably a function of the sheer size of these groups (Kalbach 1970, 330-335).

Census data probably cannot distinguish between Canadians whose sense of ethnic awareness developed in Canada and those whose sense of ethnic awareness developed outside of Canada. There seems to be a general implicit assumption by many users of these data, that somehow or other, persons who report the same ethnic origin have more in common with each other than those who report other origins. In fact this is probably not the case. The vast bulk of the pre-World War II immigrants came prior to 1930 and the Depression. For these immigrants, the quest for self-identification or who they were, developed to a large extent in Canada or the United States. Voluntarily or involuntarily, many of these immigrants tended to associate themselves with persons who spoke similar languages or dialects, thereby creating for themselves a much wider sense of commonality than had hitherto been the case. For example, the sense of identity tended to change from a small hamlet in Prussia to a wider sense of German nationalism (Herberg 1955, 14).

Within Europe, the large scale population movements had a similar result. Local and regional allegiances, although still present, became secondary to the development of the sense of identity with the larger nation state. Evidence of this is shown in the severe agitation for independence by many linguistic groups from the Old European empires and the emergence of many countries whose basis was a common ethnicity based on language. The data from the 1971 Census seemed to support the hypothesis that there were in fact as many differences in socio-demographic characteristics within any given ethnic group as there were differences between different ethnic groups in 1971 (Kralt 1977, 23 ff).

While the preceding discussion has focused on the differences between the non-British/non-French immigrants coming prior to World War II and those coming after World War II, similar differences are found within the British and the French ethnic groups. Given the length of time since the British conquest of Quebec as well as the very different histories of Quebec and France, it seems reasonable to assume that the cultural ties between the French immigrant of the 1970s and the Quebecois of pre-conquest lineage are not necessarily that great, even though they speak the same language.

In general, the dissatisfaction with the data from the 1971 Census led to a review of the ethnic concepts proposed for the 1981 Census. During the course of this review, a number of data needs were identified which in turn required a significant change in the ethnic origin concept[4]. Although the 1981 Census question was meant to enumerate status Indians, the major reason for collecting the ethnic data in 1981 was to obtain an official estimate of the number of Métis and non-status Indians, as unofficial estimates towards the end of the 1970s varied anywhere from 350,000 to 1.5 million persons.

For the Band or registered Indians, it was felt that the terms *Band/non-Band* which had been used in 1971 were confusing. As a result, it was decided fairly early in the planning process to change the designation to *status or registered Indian*. At the same time, there was a general awareness that the term *Eskimo* should be replaced by *Inuit*. Finally, to improve the enumeration of aboriginal peoples and also to try to avoid erroneous reporting of an aboriginal origin by non-aboriginals, the location of the *Native* categories was separated from the *Other* origins.

These changes were minor compared to the conceptual implications of including *Métis* as an acceptable category. In 1971, data on Métis were not available as they were to report their paternal ancestor's origin. By definition, this origin was almost always either European or aboriginal. If a person reported *Métis* on the questionnaire, this answer was ignored. Instead, an origin was assigned to the record by the Statistics Canada computer during the edit and imputation process.

The changes to the ethnic concept required by the inclusion of *Métis* as an acceptable ethnic origin fit in nearly with the general desire to have the ethnic data reflect the actual origins of Canadians, not just paternal ancestry. In a response rate test of the questionnaire run in 1978, it was clear that a relatively large proportion of the population would report more than one ethnic origin. It was anticipated that most of these multiple responses would involve combinations of British and/or French and all other origins. Based in part on the testing program, and in part on discussions within and without Statistics Canada, there was a belief that if multiple origins were not permitted in 1981, a significant proportion of the population would report *Canadian* or *American* thereby defeating the purpose of the question.

In turn, the acceptance of multiples, required a complete reformulation of the computer processing procedures and the data set to handle multiple responses. These changes were possible in part because the specialized edit and imputation methodology required for such data was available and in part because it was anticipated that the computers available for the processing of the 1981 Census were fast enough to handle the complex editing and imputation for the processing of multiple responses. This probably would not have been the case in 1971.

In the years prior to the 1981 Census, there had been considerable pressure from a number of sources to collect data on *ethnic self-identification* rather than *ethnic roots* along the traditional lines. While no one disputes that there is a certain amount of self-identification with the roots option, the data are intended to measure what is primarily an ascribed characteristic. The major reasons for selecting the roots option rather than the self-identification option for the 1981 Census are summarized below:

- The interpretation of ethnic self-identification is problematic. What does it mean to be identified with ethnic origin X? Even if it could be determined for adults, the problem of interpreting these data for children whose sense of self-identity is still being developed would create a new series of disputes and debates.

- There is nothing to prevent a person reporting a strong ethnic self-identification of more than one origin, e.g., Italian and Slovenian and Canadian. Self-identification would not resolve the problem of multiple responses.

- For multicultural programming, it was considered important to know not only the numbers of persons who identify with a given ethnic group but also the numbers who could potentially identify with this origin.

- There is nothing to prevent a person from reporting *Canadian* or *American* in response to a self-identification question. If 20 percent of the population reported this answer, and it would seem that this would be a low estimate, then the usefulness of the ethnic data for 1981 would be seriously undermined.

- It was felt that self-identification would be a useful supplement to the roots question but that it should not replace it.

The paternal ancestry criterion to force the selection of only one ethnic origin was considered to be sexist by many staff and persons consulted during the development of the 1981 Census question. Given the concerted efforts being made to remove sexism from the census, it was considered inappropriate to retain paternal ancestry as the criterion to force one response to the ethnic origin question.

The detailed 1981 question with the answer options shown on the questionnaire as well the instructions are given in Appendix A. While multiple responses were expected, there was no explicit instruction on how persons with more than one origin were to respond to this question. In effect, while multiple responses were to be allowed, they were not to be encouraged. As a result, it was expected that the number of persons reporting more than one origin would be a low estimate of the total number of persons who actually had more than one origin.

Data processing refers to the process whereby write-in answers are coded (coding), the questionnaires are transferred to computer (data capture), and non-responses and inconsistencies (e.g., persons arriving in Canada as immigrants two years before they were supposedly born) are removed from the data (edit and imputation). In line with the decision to collect roots ethnic origin data, for the purposes of processing the 1981 data, ethnic origin was considered to be an ascribed characteristic (i.e., the respondent really has no choice in determining his or her ethnic origin).

It should be noted that a language was reported as mother tongue for every record at the time that the ethnic data were edited and imputed. If a language had not been reported as mother tongue, a language was assigned to the individual based on the mother tongue information of other family members, if such information was available. If not, a language was arbitrarily assigned as mother tongue.

If an ethnic origin was reported as a write-in, it was accepted without question, as long as it was given as one of the possibilities in either the code book or on the questionnaire. *Prussian*, for example, was coded to *German*.

Variations in spelling from those given in the code book was one common reason for referral. In most other cases, in making the decision to assign a referral as a given ethnic origin, information on language, place of birth and mother tongue, etc. were also examined. Strange responses such as *Klingon* and *Romulan* were left as a non-response.

The distinct ethnic or racial origins actually reported by Canadians in response to the Census question numbered in the thousands. Very early in the planning process, however, it was decided that only two digits would be allowed for coding, thereby limiting the number of possible write-ins to 100 (00-99). Consequently, the lack of data is the result of Statistics Canada's decision as to which groups are to be coded separately as one of the 100 categories and which are to be collapsed into other categories on the census database. For example, all ethnic groups originating in China were coded as *Chinese*. Similarly, the distinctions between varieties of Germans (Prussian, Bohemian, etc.), French (Breton, Normand, etc.), Dutch (Zeelands, Hollands, etc.), etc. are not maintained in the Canadian Census, even though these distinctions are very important in the countries of origin of various groups.

Unlike 1971 when multiple responses were resolved during the data capture process, in 1981 all responses given on the questionnaire were transferred to computer. However, as there was provision for only one write-in answer, the combinations of multiple origins were limited to two or more mark-ins or one or more mark-ins with a write-in answer.

After the data had been transferred to computer, the edit rules to check data acceptability were straightforward:

a) If a valid response was present, accept that response;
b) If a valid response was not present, mark that record for imputation.

In assessing the need for the edit rules required for these data, it was decided that obvious inconsistencies would be left in the data if they were reported as such. There was no procedure to determine whether a combination of data was a valid outlier or invalid (e.g., persons reporting combinations such as South Asian origins born in Yugoslavia, British origins born in China, etc.). The decision was taken however that such combinations of origins would not be imputed for non-responses.

The imputation procedures were also relatively straightforward:

Non-Census Family persons: If the person was not a member of a census family, a computer search was made for a record with a similar mother tongue. The ethnic origins reported for this donor record were assigned to the record in question.

Persons in Census Families: i. If the individual with the non-response was a member of a family in which ethnic data had been given by some members of that family, imputation of non-response was based on the assumption that the ethnic origin of the children should be the sum of the origins of the parents. Specific rules based on this assumption were then worked out. ii. If no data were captured for any family members, a computer search was made for the parent(s) of a similar family in which the same language was reported as mother tongue. The ethnic origins reported by the parents in the donor family were then assigned. The sum of the imputed parental ethnic origins were then assigned to the children in the family.

A series of constraints such as age of parents, place of residence, etc., were to be used to improve the fit of the donor family. These constraints were gradually lifted when a donor record matching the constraints could not be found. If a donor record or family could not be found, provision was made for a default assignment of an ethnic origin based on the mother tongue of the individual.

In 1981, a small number of Indian bands refused to cooperate with the 1981 Census. Data were arbitrarily assigned to all records. For example, for the Kahnewake reserve in Montreal, all persons were assigned *Iroquois* as mother tongue and home language, *Quebec* as place of birth, *status Indian* as ethnic origin, etc. In dealing with data for these reserves, caution should be used. (This imputation is also the reason why there are a relatively large number of persons with *Iroquoian* as mother tongue and as home language in Quebec in 1981.)

When the 1981 Census data for Métis and non-status origins were released, the counts were much lower than expected. Less than 200,000 persons reported having *Métis/non-status Indian* ethnic origins. An evaluation (Kralt et al., 1983) pointed to several reasons for the discrepancy between the data as reported and the estimates. In families in which one or both parents reported themselves as *Native Peoples*, often the children of such couples were not reported as *Native*. This reporting pattern ties in neatly with the observation made in Richmond and Rhyne, that as time passes, the aboriginal origin is gradually displaced by European origins, especially if the person's socioeconomic status improves (Richmond and Rhyne, 1982, 58). While it is not known if the data reflect the extent to which these children themselves will ultimately consider themselves as natives, if even a small proportion of children who have aboriginal and non-aboriginal parents no longer define themselves as native, then the numbers of natives will not grow to the extent expected.

A complaint of many native groups has been the removal of native children from the aboriginal community and their fostering and/or adoption by non-aboriginal persons. It is impossible to determine the extent to which aboriginal children are identified as such if they are in foster homes and to what extent they will still identify themselves as natives once they have become adults.

Non-status women who married status males are legally status Indians and are included in the Indian Affairs Register. However, the data from the 1981 Census suggest that many of these women did not report themselves as such in 1981, reporting their European or other origins instead.

Some felt the inclusion of the phrase *on first coming to this continent* in the question on the form probably caused many native peoples to report a European origin rather than an aboriginal origin. The Instruction Booklet that accompanied each questionnaire did contain a reference to the fact that the phrase did not apply to Canada's native peoples, but the extent to which the booklet was used is not known.

Until 1971, Statistics Canada always published data on the various components (Irish, Scottish, English and Welsh) which make up the origins usually identified as *British*. This practice was discontinued in 1971 and in 1981 but re-instituted in 1986. For 1971/81, it was felt that the data for individual groups made little sense when the historical trends were examined, especially with the decreases in all these groups except *English*. As well, for the 1981 Census, it was felt that so much intermarriage has occurred between these British groups over the past 100 years that it made little, if any, statistical sense to distinguish between them.

The ethnic data published in the census do not reflect the "population distribution by ethnic origin" but rather the "population distribution of persons reporting a given ethnic origin." While this may appear to be a minor distinction of concern only to purists, in reality the distinction is important. For many groups, the relatively narrow regional cultural identities are not reported in the census. Two of the more obvious examples of this type of reporting are persons reporting origins centred in Yugoslavia and from the South Asian subcontinent.

In 1981, 9,265 Canadians reported *Serbian* ethnic origin in Canada as part of either a multiple or a single response. However, among the 64,840 persons reporting *only Yugoslav not otherwise specified* (n.o.s.) (generally made up of Serbian, Croatian, Slovenian) as an origin many could in fact be Serbian. This type of misreporting of origins is even more clear for the South Asian population. The large numbers of persons who only reported themselves as *Indian n.o.s.* (63,690) or *East Indian n.o.s.* (74,950) indicates that the individual South Asian origins such as *Tamil* (685) and *Punjabi* (11,720), in 1981 are grossly underestimated.

By the time the ethnic data were released in 1983, the situation had changed to such an extent that, while there was still great interest in the aboriginal data, there was also a great demand for data on visible minorities. One indicator of the inadequacy of these data became evident when the counts of the number of Haitians in Montreal were acquired. A conservative estimate put the numbers enumerated in the 1981 Census at about two thirds of the estimated number of Haitians. Similar problems were identified for other Caribbean groups. In an evaluation a colleague and I did for Multiculturalism Canada in cooperation with Statistics Canada, we concluded that large numbers of persons who were expected to report their origins as *Black*, actually reported *British only* or *French only* (Kralt and Teitelbaum 1983).

In redefining the population that could be considered Black for statistical purposes, we assumed, and it is a debateable assumption, that persons who reported being born in the Caribbean and Guyana and who reported *British only* or *French only* as ethnic origin were considered to be Black, or as it was labelled, *Caribbean Assignments*. By making this correction, the number of Black

Canadians was estimated to be about 250,000 rather than the 150,000 originally published by Statistics Canada. In addition, we found that the persons who had misreported their origins had some 40,000 children born in this country, bringing the total Black population to approximately 300,000. However, these children were not reassigned in tabulations as virtually all of them were under the age of 15, a population for whom little other socioeconomic data was available from the census.

While the wording of the question remained relatively similar, a number of changes would have a dramatic impact on the data collected in 1986. The major changes to the question between 1981 and 1986 were:

- the dropping of the phrase *on first coming to this continent* to make the question more relevant to native peoples;

- the addition of *Black* as an answer category on the questionnaire in response to recommendations on the part of the Abella Commission and the Parliamentary report *Equality Now*;

- the encouragement of more than one answer if applicable; and

- the deletion of the distinction between *Status* or *Treaty* and *non-Status Indian* in the ethnic origin question. It was apparently felt at Statistics Canada that the term *North American Indian* was a better reflection of the ethnic concept than the distinction between Status and non-Status incorporated into the 1981 questionnaire (White 1987).

Statistics Canada also introduced a new question on aboriginal self-perception in the 1986 Census. In retrospect, it seems plausible that such data would be open to a wide range of interpretation by both respondents and users of the data. For example, by not linking self-identity to one's cultural and ethnic roots, there is no reason why an individual cannot consider him/herself to be an aboriginal person even though he/she is a recent immigrant.

While not stated as such by Hagey (1987) in her *Data Quality Note on Question 7 (Aboriginal Status)*, this question was likely to have been used to obtain reliable estimates of the numbers of status or registered Indians, non-status Indians, Métis, and Inuit in Canada. Again, even if all persons reporting themselves as aboriginal persons did in fact have such origins, the adequacy of these particular data on status Indians, non-status Indians and Métis is open to debate. An individual either has or does not have the legal status of registered Indian under the Indian Act regardless of self-identification. The problems with these data were of such magnitude that they will not be released as official counts of aboriginal persons.

The processing procedures used in the 1986 Census for ethnic origin data were relatively similar to those used in 1981. The major exceptions would appear to be an increase in the number of categories allowed as write-in answers, as well as an edit which did not allow the same individual to report South Asian languages, etc. and aboriginal origins[5].

Tables 1 and 2 in Appendix B show the numeric and percentage distribution of the combinations of *British, French* and *Other, (Other* is defined as persons not reporting *British* or *French* origins but who may be of mixed *Other* origins, e.g., *Ukrainian* and *Polish*) from the 1981 and 1986 censuses. As Kalbach's 1961 data would lead one to expect, for Canada as a whole, the 1981 data show that of all persons who reported British ancestry, 13.2 percent reported *British and one or more other* origins. The multiple response rate increased dramatically when respondents were encouraged to report all applicable origins in 1986 with the proportion of all persons reporting *British* who also reported one or more additional origins increasing to 32.1 percent. The increase in the multiple response rate for all persons reporting *French* is equally dramatic, from 9.8 percent in 1981 to 25.0 percent in 1986. For persons who did not report *British* or *French* origins, the proportion reporting multiple origins increased from 15.2 percent to 33.6 percent over the five-year period.

One additional impact of the change in the question for 1986 is a significant increase in the proportion of the total population who reported a given ethnic ancestry. While 45.8 percent reported *British* ancestry in 1981, this increased to 49.4 percent for 1986. *French* showed a similar increase, from 29.3 percent in 1981 to 32.5 percent in 1986 while *Other* increased from 32.0 percent to 37.5 percent over the five years.

The data for individual provinces show even more variation in the proportions reporting multiple responses. Among all persons reporting British origins, the proportion reporting more than one origin ranged from a low of 2.9 percent in Newfoundland to a high of 21.6 percent for the Yukon in 1981. The proportions reporting such answers increased dramatically for 1986 where the range of multiple responses was from a low of 7.4 percent in Newfoundland to a high of 46.4 percent for the Yukon. The tables also show that in the Atlantic region and Quebec, about 90 percent (1981) and 80 percent (1986) of persons who reported British multiple responses reported *French* as one of these responses. The proportion is considerably lower in Ontario and the western provinces.

The range of multiple origins for persons reporting *French* ranged from 1.9 percent in Quebec to 49.9 percent in the Yukon in 1981. With the exception of New Brunswick's 9.8 percent multiple response rate for French origins, in all the other provinces, the proportion of multiple origins for persons reporting *French* exceeded 25 percent. This changed dramatically for 1986. With the exception of Quebec's 5.5 percent and New Brunswick's 26.8 percent multiple response rates, in all other provinces more than 60 percent of all persons reporting *French* origins also reported one or more other origins. In most cases, *British* was one of these other origins.

Among persons who reported only *Other* origins, the proportion reporting multiple origins ranged from 7.4 percent in Quebec to 36.2 percent in Prince Edward Island in 1981. Using the 1986 data, the proportion who reported multiple responses involving *Other* origins ranged from the low of 16.2 percent in the Northwest Territories to 67.9 percent in Prince Edward Island. With the exception of Quebec (19.5 percent), in all other provinces, more than 25 percent of all persons reporting *Other* origins also reported *British* and/or *French* origins.

Tables 3 and 4 of Appendix B show the single and multiple response rates for a number of selected ethnic groups from 1981 and 1986 respectively for Canada and the provinces. These data are somewhat different than those of Tables 1 and 2 in that the multiple responses shown here also include *Other and Other* multiple answers, e.g., *German and Ukrainian*. For both censuses, the overall national multiple response rate for *Other* shown in Tables 1 and 2 masks rather wide variations in the extent to which multiple responses are reported for different origins at the national and the provincial levels. A cursory examination of these data shows quite clearly that the longtime European groups such as the Ukrainian, German and Scandinavian have high multiple response rates everywhere. More recent groups such as Portuguese, Italian and Chinese show much lower multiple response rates. Especially in the 1986 data, it is clear that the use of only single responses for a given ethnic group ignores a large proportion of the population which have reported a given ancestry.

Summary and Conclusions

Each census taken since Confederation has had at least one question on the ethnic or cultural origins of the Canadian population. As a result, there is a remarkably good historical data series which reflects the changes in the ethnic/cultural/racial composition of the Canadian population over the past 115 years.

In my view, the ethnic data collected in the censuses has had a very definite impact on the way in which Canadians have perceived their society. By forcing all Canadians to report only one ancestry or ethnic origin in the censuses prior to 1981, it was relatively easy for both the researcher and the general public to paint a picture of a Canadian society that consisted of four large, generally mutually exclusive ethnic or cultural groups. This image of society was reinforced every 10 years as new census results became available.

First and foremost, there were the *charter groups*, persons whose ancestors originated in either France or the British Isles. These two groups were dominant in their own areas, Quebec and the rest of Canada respectively. Then there were the *Others* — those whose ancestral and cultural ties were neither with the British Isles nor France. These *Others* were usually divided between those of European origin and the native peoples.

However, the problems census-takers have encountered over the past 115 years with the collection of ethnic data suggests that this rather static and simplistic view of Canadian society was and is simply not valid. In every census, the problem of how to deal with multiple origins surfaced again and again, until gradually paternal ancestry became the sole criterion for determining which ethnic origin was to be reported.

In his monograph on the 1961 Census data on immigrants released 20 years ago, Kalbach provided a measure of the extent to which ethnic intermarriage had taken place. It is surprising that the impact of such high rates of ethnic exogamy on Canadian society have apparently rarely been taken into account in studies of these ethnic data. An indication of the extent to which Canadians consider themselves to have multiple origins became clear from the 1981 Census (in which multiples were allowed but not encouraged) and is much clearer still from the 1986 Census data (in which the reporting of multiple origins was encouraged).

The 1981 and the 1986 Census data suggest very strongly that as a larger proportion of an ethnic group's members are born in Canada, a higher proportion of that group's members have more than one origin, usually including British and/or French. The relatively recent immigration of large numbers of other ethnic groups in Montreal is reflected in the relatively low multiple response rate for Quebec. To a lesser extent, large numbers of relatively recent immigrants probably also have depressed the multiple response rate for Ontario.

While the multiple response ethnic origin data are much more difficult to work with, and their interpretation is not always clear, there is little doubt that they provide a much fuller and realistic picture of the actual ethnic composition of the Canadian population than did the data collected prior to 1981. The collection and analysis of this type of data should be encouraged.

Notes

1. The views expressed in this paper are those of the author and do not necessarily represent the views of the Government.
2. In this paper, *ethnic origin* will be used to describe this concept, which in earlier censuses was generally referred to as *racial origin*.
3. For a more detailed description of the ethnic concept as well as more detailed information about the planning of the 1981 Census question, see John Kralt, ''Ethnic Origin in the Canadian Census, 1871-1981'' in Roman Petryshyn (Ed.) *Social Trends Among Ukrainian Canadians*. Edmonton: Canadian Institute of Ukrainian Studies, 1980.
4. The author was the officer at Statistics Canada in charge of the development of the 1981 Census question on ethnic origin and the related processing procedures. Much of the description of the changes to the 1981 question are based on the author's own notes and knowledge.
5. These observations are based on conversations with Pamela White at Statistics Canada.

I
FERTILITY, MORTALITY AND MIGRATION

3. THE DEMOGRAPHY OF ABORIGINAL PEOPLE IN CANADA[1]

Mary Jane Norris

Canada's aboriginal population consists of four major native groups: status Indians, who are registered under the Indian Act of Canada; non-status Indians, who have lost or never had status under the Indian Act; Métis, who are of mixed Indian and non-Indian ancestry; and, Inuit (Eskimo), northern natives, who reside mainly in Canada's arctic, in the Northwest Territories, northern Quebec and Labrador. Further distinctions can be made within some of these groups; for example the Métis of the prairies are historically different from those of mixed native ancestry elsewhere in Canada. But, overall, these major groups represent the main ethnic origins of Canada's aboriginal population.

This paper examines the demographic characteristics and trends of the aboriginal population. In addition to native and non-native comparisons, it focuses on differentials among the native groups themselves. To date, little attention has been paid to demographic differences among native groups, or between natives in rural and urban areas, or Indians on and off reserve. Native groups are not completely homogeneous: they differ not only in size and distribution, but in other respects such as their degree of urbanization, their level of fertility and types of migration.

Data Sources

The data presented in this demographic profile are compiled from a number of studies and sources, including census data, Indian Register data from the Indian and Northern Affairs Canada (INAC), and medical services data from Health and Welfare. The census, which is the most comprehensive source of aboriginal data, is used to examine native and non-native group differentials in age-sex structure, fertility, mobility and migration. Medical services and Register data provide information on trends in fertility and mortality for registered Indians and Inuit. Unfortunately, data collection systems for birth and death data, specifically the Métis and non-status Indian populations, do not exist.

All of the present data sources suffer from some limitations such as misreporting in the census or late reporting in the Register. Census data are based on self-reported counts and characteristics, and as such, can be at variance with other estimates of native population, especially for the Métis and non-status Indians. In the case of status Indians, the 1981 Census and Register populations differ not only in counts, but also in concept. The Register lists persons who are legally status Indians under the Indian Act, and this includes women of non-native origin who have gained status by marrying status Indian males.

Ethnic data from the most recent census, 1986, were not collected for status and non-status Indian origins, but rather for North American Indians as one group. Therefore most of the current analysis of native differentials is restricted to three ethnic groups: North American Indian, Métis and Inuit. Within these three groups, distinctions are also made between respondents with "single" origins only — those who report only native ancestry — and respondents with "multiple" or "mixed" aboriginal and non-aboriginal origins. Most of the comparative analysis among native groups is restricted "single" origins, and on-/off-reserve differentials are restricted to "single origin" North American Indians, who are more likely to be associated with reserves than those of multiple Indian and non-native origins.

Historical Background

At the time of the first European settlement in North America about four centuries ago, the Indian population probably numbered about 200,000 and the Inuit population around 10,000. The advent of the Europeans brought a sharp decline in the native population. The effects of war (both international and European) and disease (especially tuberculosis) took their toll: by the late 1870s, the Indian population had been reduced to some 80,000. In the several decades following, the native population was relatively stable, averaging about 120,000 during the 1901 to 1931 period.

It was not until the 1940s that the native population experienced a significant growth. By the 1960s the population had reached some 220,000, about the same size as it had been when the first Europeans had settled.

In the 1986 Census some 712,000 people in Canada reported themselves or their ancestors as belonging to at least one native group. Nearly one half of these reported multiple origins, that is, combinations of both aboriginal and non-aboriginal origins (e.g., North American Indian and French). Almost three quarters of these respondents (just over 525,000), reported a North American Indian origin, as either the only one (single) or in mixed combination with a non-aboriginal one, followed by 18 percent (128,000) with Métis origin (single and mixed), and about 5 percent (33,500) with Inuit. About 1 percent (5,960) of respondents gave a multiple aboriginal response; while the remaining 2 percent reported multiple aboriginal origins in combination with non-aboriginal ones (see Figure 1).

FIGURE 1

Distribution of Total Aboriginal
Population by Native Ethnic Origin
Canada, 1986

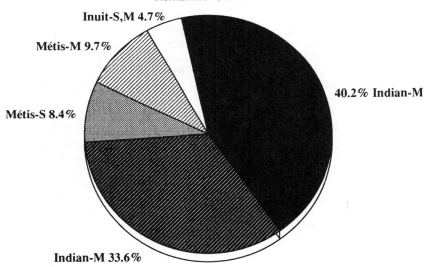

Remainder 3.4%

Inuit-S,M 4.7%

Métis-M 9.7%

Métis-S 8.4%

40.2% Indian-M

Indian-M 33.6%

Native Origin

S = Single Origin (Aboriginal Only)
M= Multiple Origin (Mixed, Aboriginal and Non-native)
Remainder = Multiple Aboriginal Origins with or without Non-native origins

Size and Growth, 1931-86

Tracing the size and growth of these native groups, as well as the overall native population, has been and remains a difficulty owing to problems of comparability in census data, changes in definitions and reporting problems. The census, which is the only source of population data for some native groups (Métis and non-status Indian), has differed over the years in its concepts and measurement of native groups, as well as of ethnic groups in general. (See Chapter 2 for an historical overview of Canada's census ethnic data.)

Population counts of native groups from 1931 to 1986, and cautionary notes on their degree of comparability are provided in Table 1. Even the two most recent censuses, 1981 and 1986, are not directly comparable, because in 1986, unlike 1981, respondents were encouraged to mark or specify as many ethnic groups as applied. Comparisons between 1981 and 1986 native population counts indicate a decline of single responses in 1986, from almost half a million in 1981 to 373,000, but a marked increase of multiple responses to almost 712,000.

In assessing growth of the native population, the 1941 and 1981 censuses are considered to be the most directly comparable since "...both made an explicit attempt to individually enumerate persons of mixed Native ancestry" (Statistics Canada 1983, 6). Overall, the aboriginal population increased by 205 percent from 161,000, during this period, compared to 109 percent growth for the total Canadian population. Among the different native groups, the Inuit (Eskimo) had the highest increase (252 percent), while the native Indian population grew by 210 percent. The Métis population (including only those who reported Métis as their only origin in 1981), grew by 177 percent, a rate lower than that of the other native groups, but higher than that of non-natives. Indian Register data also show that between 1971 and 1981 the registered Indian population grew twice as fast as the general population, increasing 27 percent, compared to 13 percent for Canada's total population (Perreault et al. 1985).

The "relative" growth rates provided by the census, albeit "crude," are corroborated by additional data sources on rates of natural increase (except for Métis, since birth and death data for this population are not available). The growth of the Inuit population, which is due solely to natural increase, has been the most rapid of the native groups. Census data show that between 1931 and 1981 the Inuit population more than quadrupled from 6,000 to 25,000 at an annual rate of 2.9 percent (Robitaille and Choinière 1985, 5). Recent estimates of crude birth and death rates by Robitaille and Choinière suggest a natural increase rate of 29 per 1,000 for 1981. The slower growth for Indians indicated by the census is also confirmed by INAC's data on registered Indians. Estimates of 1981 crude birth and death rates for registered Indians (Ram 1985; Rowee and Norris 1985) yield a lower rate of natural increase, of 23 per 1,000 (due largely to the higher Inuit crude birth rate of 35 per 1,000, versus the Indian birth rate of 29). In contrast, low rates of natural increase are responsible for the much slower growth of the Canadian population as a whole, despite the contribution by immigration. In 1981, the annual total growth rate for the Canadian population was 1.2 percent, while the rate of natural increase was less than 1 percent or 8.2 per 1,000.

Share and Distribution

Although native people make up a small proportion of Canada's total population, Table 1 shows that their share has been increasing, from 1.4 percent in 1941 to 2.0 percent in 1981. In 1986, the 712,000 persons who reported aboriginal origins (single or multiple) represented 2.8 percent of the population (3 percent if population estimates of incompletely enumerated reserves and settlements are included), while persons of single only aboriginal origins (373,000) represented 1.5 percent.

TABLE 1

Census Counts of Aboriginal and Total Canadian Populations, Canada, 1931 to 1986

Census Year	Total Canadian Population	Total Aboriginal Population	Aboriginal as % of Total Population	Population of Aboriginal Groups		
				Indian	Métis	Inuit
	(in millions)					
1931	10.4	128,900	1.2	n.a.	n.a.	n.a.[3]
1941	11.5	160,900	1.4	118,300	35,400	7,200
1951	14.0	165,600	1.2	155,900	n.a.	9,700
1961	18.2	220,100	1.2	208,300	n.a.	11,800
1971	21.6	312,800	1.5	295,200	n.a.	17,550
1981	24.1	491,500	2.0	367,800	98,300	25,390
1986[1,2]	25.3 Single Origins	373,260	1.5	286,230	59,745	27,290
	Multiple Origins	338,460	1.3	239,395	58,895	6,175
	Single & Multiple Combined	711,725	2.8	531,445	128,640	33,465

n.a. Not available or not published.

[1] Excludes inmates.

[2] Figures for 1986 exclude population of incompletely enumerated Indian reserves on settlements, estimated at 45,000.

[3] Estimate from Robitaille and Choinière (1985) of Inuit population from 1931 Census reported to be 6,000.

1931: Includes Native Indian, Inuit and persons of mixed native and non-native ancestry traced on the mother's side.

1941: Includes Native Indian, Inuit and persons of mixed native and non-native ancestry traced on the father's side.

1951: Includes Native Indian, Inuit and some persons of mixed native and non-native ancestry living on.

1961: Indian reserves or traced on the father's side.

1971: Includes Native Indian and Inuit only, traced on the father's side.

1981: Includes Native Indian, Inuit and self-reported Métis, traced through both parents.

Sources: 1931 to 1981: Data and notes from Statistics Canada *The Daily* Table 1, February 1, 1981. 1986 Census.

The native share of the population varies considerably across Canada. In 1986, people with native origins represented the majority (58 percent) of the population in the Northwest Territories and 21 percent of the Yukon population. As in 1981, the territories, followed by the western provinces, had the highest shares of native people. Among the provinces, Manitoba and Saskatchewan had the highest proportions of persons claiming aboriginal origins — around 8 percent. In Alberta and British Columbia, native people represented almost 5 percent of the population. In central and eastern Canada between 1 to 2 percent of the population reported native origins.

Ontario claimed the largest number of aboriginal people, followed by British Columbia and Alberta, in both 1981 and 1986[3]. In 1986, almost one in four Canadians who reported native origins (single or multiple)[4] resided in Ontario. Together, British Columbia and Alberta accounted for a third of Canada's native population, while another 23 percent resided in Manitoba and Saskatchewan. Quebec's share was almost 12 percent, while the territories and Atlantic region each had some 5 percent (see Figure 2).

FIGURE 2

Regional Distribution of Aboriginals
Canada, 1981 and 1986

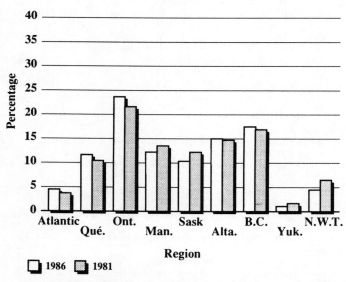

Region

□ 1986 ▨ 1981

*Including estimates for incompletely enumerated reserves and settlements.

Source: 1981-1986 censuses

The regional distribution among the native groups differs significantly: almost two thirds of North American Indians are concentrated in Ontario (40 percent) and British Columbia (22 percent); while two thirds of Métis are in the Prairies; and the majority (55 percent) of Inuit live in the territories, with large proportions in Quebec (21 percent) and the Atlantic region (Labrador, 12 percent).

Urban-Rural

The concentration of native people in rural and urban areas is much different from that of the general population. Table 2 shows that the majority (61 percent) of those with ''native only'' origins and nearly half (46 percent) of those of mixed (native and non-native) origins lived in rural areas in 1986 compared

TABLE 2

Population Distribution and Sex Ratios, by Urban and Rural Residence, Aboriginal and Total Canadian Populations, Canada, 1986

Populations	Percentage Distribution of Total Population		Sex Ratios		
	Urban %	Rural %	Total	Urban	Rural
			No. of Males per 1,000 Females		
Aboriginal					
• Single and Multiple Origins	54.3	45.7	964	898	1,047
• Single Origin Only	38.4	61.6	974	864	1,048
• Multiple Origins	72.4	27.6	952	920	1,043
North American Indian					
• Single and Multiple Origins	53.1	46.9	957	887	1,043
• Single Origin Only	35.8	64.2	965	831	1,048
• Multiple Origins	73.7	26.3	947	921	1,027
Métis					
• Single and Multiple Origins	64.9	35.1	965	918	1,058
• Single Origin Only	59.3	40.7	1,000	950	1,077
• Multiple Origins	69.7	30.3	936	895	1,036
Inuit					
• Single and Multiple Origins	25.8	74.3	1,025	957	1,050
• Single Origin Only	17.4	82.6	1,029	992	1,037
• Multiple Origins	63.0	37.0	1,008	916	1,187*
Total Canadian Population	76.4	23.6	977	952	1,063

* Small population = 2,300.

Source: 1986 Census, unpublished data.

to just 23 percent of the nation's population. Generally, most (70 percent) rural natives tend to have only aboriginal ancestry; in contrast, most urban natives (62 percent) are of mixed aboriginal and non-aboriginal origins.

Among the various native groups, the Inuit population was the most rural in 1986, with 82 percent of "Inuit only" respondents residing in rural areas. Those of "Indian only" origin were more likely than those of "Métis only" origin to live in rural areas, with six in every ten Indians being rural residents compared to four in ten Métis. For all native groups, those of mixed aboriginal and non-aboriginal ancestry were least likely to reside in rural areas, with rural populations at 26 percent for mixed native Indian, 30 percent for mixed Métis, and 37 percent for mixed Inuit. (Table 2).

On-off-Reserve

An important dimension of the geography of North American Indians is the distinction between residence on- and off-reserve. According to 1986 Census data, over half (53 percent) of North American Indians (single origins only), lived on reserves and settlements. This proportion rises to 59 percent if the estimated population of 45,000 residing on incompletely enumerated Indian reserves and settlements is included. This latter figure is similar to the proportion of status or registered Indians living on-reserve from the 1981 Census, at some 60 percent. Data from INAC's Register indicate higher proportions of registered Indians on-reserve, of about 70 percent, in both 1981 and 1986. However, INAC data are not directly comparable with census data and recent Register data for residence on- and off-reserve are not highly reliable, because of high non-response rates (Perreault, Paquette, George 1985).

Register data show a decline in residence on reserves since the 1960s and higher proportions of women than men living off-reserve. Proportions of registered Indians residing on-reserve declined from 85 percent in 1966[5] to 72 percent by the mid-1970s; and then remained relatively stable at around 70 percent during the late 70s and early 80s. (This stability might be partially explained by the high non-response rate.) The same data show that in 1981, 32 percent of women and 28 percent of men lived off-reserve.

Since 1985, a new factor has been introduced in the distribution of Indians on- and off-reserve: the reinstatement to Indian status of those Indians eligible under the amendment to the Indian Act. In 1986, almost 18,000 native people and twice as many in 1987, gained Indian status under these amendments. Practically all — 95 percent — of the reinstated population live off reserve and most were non-status Indian women (and their children)[6]. Females account for about 60 percent of the almost 55,000 people reinstated. Eventually some of these newly reinstated registered Indians could settle on reserves. In 1987, inclusion of the reinstated Indian women lowered the overall proportion of registered Indian women on-reserve from 69 to 62 percent.

Age-Sex Structure

Canada's aboriginal population has a much younger age structure than that of the general population in Canada, as the two contrasting pyramids in Figure 3 clearly demonstrate. In 1986, the average age of the native population was 23 compared to 34 for Canadians as a whole; and 68 percent of the total aboriginal population (multiple and single responses together) was under the age of 30, compared to 47 percent of Canadians overall. In contrast, the proportion of native people 65 years of age and over is much lower, only 3 percent, compared to 10 percent in the general population. Similarly, Table 3 shows that for the native population, the youth dependency ratio is twice as high as the Canadian ratio, while the elderly dependency ratio is about a third of the corresponding ratio.

Among native groups, the Inuit clearly have the youngest age structure and the Métis the oldest (based on single origins). In 1986, the average age of the Inuit population was 22.6, followed by 24.7 for North American Indians and 25.6 for Métis. Youth dependency ratios are highest for the Inuit, at 68 percent and lowest for the Métis at 53 percent (see Table 3).

Because of declining fertility, the native population is aging, like the Canadian population in general, but at a slower pace. The Inuit population, which like the Canadian population became younger between 1941 and 1961 and then older between 1961 and 1981, aged much less. Between 1961 and 1981 the average age was fairly consistent among the Inuit at about 22, but rose significantly among the total population from 29 to 33 (Robitaille and Choinière 1985). Median age data from INAC's Register indicate an aging trend among Indians, from 16.5 years in 1971 to about 19 in 1981, although still far below the corresponding overall Canadian levels of 26 and almost 30 (Perreault, Paquette, George 1985).

Generally young adults make up a higher proportion of the native population in urban areas, and off-reserve, than they do in rural areas and on reserves and settlements. Table 3 shows that in 1986, young adults aged 20 to 34 accounted for almost a third (32.2 percent) of the native people living in urban areas compared to just a quarter of natives in rural areas and of Indians on reserves. However, the concentrations of children (aged 0-14) were lower in urban areas (35 percent) and off-reserve (32 percent) compared to reserves and rural areas (39 percent). Because the working age group (15-64) constitutes a higher proportion of the aboriginal population in urban than in rural areas, both the youth and elderly dependency ratios are lower for urban populations.

Sex Ratios

As with the Canadian population in general, women outnumber men amongst native people as a whole, but not within each native group, particularly the Inuit.

TABLE 3

Selected Age Groups, Average Ages and Dependency Ratios, for Aboriginal and Total Canadian Populations, Canada, 1986

Populations	Percentage of Population Aged		Average Age			Dependency Ratio		
	0-14 %	20-34 %	Both Sexes	Male	Female	Total	Youth[1]	Elderly[2]
Total Aboriginal (Single & Multiple Origins)	36.5	28.7	23.6	23.3	24.0	65.0	60.2	4.8
• In Urban Areas	34.8	32.2	23.5	22.7	24.2	58.3	55.0	3.2
• In Rural Areas	38.6	24.6	23.8	23.9	23.7	73.8	67.0	6.8
North American Indian (Single Origins only)	35.4	27.1	24.7	24.3	25.1	65.1	58.5	6.6
• On-reserve	38.2	24.3	24.2	24.5	23.9	75.6	67.4	8.2
• Off-reserve	32.4	30.3	25.2	24.0	26.3	62.2	58.3	3.9
Métis (Single Origins only)	33.1	26.7	25.6	25.2	26.0	59.1	52.6	6.4
Inuit (Single Origins only)	39.5	25.0	22.6	22.3	22.9	72.9	68.3	4.6
Total Canadian Population	21.5	27.0	33.5	32.7	34.4	46.0	31.4	14.6

[1] Youth dependency ratio = (population aged 0-14/population 15-64) × 100.
[2] Elderly dependency ratio = (population aged 65+/population 15-64) × 100.

Source: 1986 Census, unpublished data.

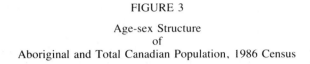

FIGURE 3

Age-sex Structure
of
Aboriginal and Total Canadian Population, 1986 Census

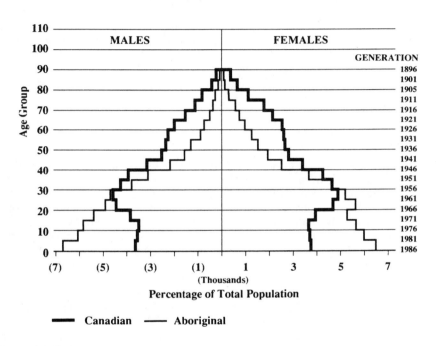

Source: 1986 Census

Overall, in 1986, for every 1,000 native women, there were 964 native men, slightly lower than the ratio of 977 for Canadians as a whole. But for Inuit, as shown in Table 2, men continue to outnumber women with a sex ratio of 1,029 in 1986 (based on single response), and 1,047 in 1981. In the case of Métis, the ratio between men and women was close to 1.0; while among Indians women outnumbered men, with 965 men per 1,000 women.

In a phenomenon that occurs among both native and non-native populations, men outnumber women in rural areas, while the opposite is true in urban areas, as shown in Table 2. In rural areas in 1986, for every 1,000 native women, there were 1,047 native men; while the ratio for the general population was

1,063. In contrast, in urban areas the sex ratio was 898 for natives and 953 for the general population. These differences between urban and rural sex ratios tend to reflect male-female differentials in migration. The situation is the same but more pronounced for Indians on- and off-reserve. In 1986 the sex ratio on reserve was 1,084 men for every 1,000 native women while off-reserve the ratio was a low of 846. Corresponding ratios in 1981 for status Indians were similar at 1,067 and 864. These ratios reflect the fact that women are much more inclined than men to leave reserves, particularly in the young adult ages. For every 1,000 Indian women aged 20 to 34 living off-reserve, there were only 747 men in the same age group.

Fertility

Trends

Over the past century, Canada's aboriginal people have undergone a transition in their fertility, from a traditional high to a modern low. Estimates of crude birth rates for Canadian Indians from 1900 to 1976 show that until the 1940s the birth rate remained relatively stable, at around 40 births per thousand population. After the outbreak of World War II, the rate rose rapidly to a peak of 47 births per 1,000 by 1960. Following this cycle of a rapidly increasing birth rate was a sharp downturn. Since the 1970s, the rate of decline has slowed.

For the Inuit of the Northwest Territories estimates of crude birth rates from 1931 to 1981 indicate a similar pattern. From 1941 rates rose sharply from about 30 births per 1,000 to a high of 60 per 1,000 by the 1960s. The rates dropped off sharply after the mid-1960s, plummeting to 35 births per 1,000 by the 1980s (Robitaille and Choinière 1985).

A number of factors have been considered in assessing the rise and fall in native fertility. The increase in native rates between 1941 and 1961 was due in part to improved health conditions, since more pregnancies went full term. At the same time, mothers had a better chance of surviving childbirth. The rise in the birth rate was seen as part of the early stages of modernization. As more native women shifted to bottle feeding, birth intervals shortened and the natural fertility rate increased (Romaniuc 1981).

The ensuing decline in fertility since the 1960s largely reflected the growing use of contraceptives among the native population. Birth control was implemented in terms of both family size and timing of childbearing. An analysis of age-specific fertility rates and parity-progression ratios for aboriginal women suggests that Canadian natives have been similar in their behaviour to European populations when the latter entered the demographic transition (Romaniuc 1987). Family size consideration was the dominant mechanism at the beginning of the demographic transition, augmented later by timing considerations of starting and spacing children. Census data indicate that not only is the size of the native family getting smaller, but that native women are having children later and spacing them out:

> For example the proportion of ever-married 20-24 year olds who had had
> their first child dropped from 80 percent in the 1961 Census to 74 percent
> in the 1981 Census. The proportion of those with at least two children in
> that age group went down from 78 percent to 61 percent respectively.
> (Romaniuc 1987, 78).

Factors such as smaller proportions getting married, later marriage and increased marital instability play a role in the fertility of native people, as for the population in general.

Group Differentials

Despite the decline in fertility, native birth rates remain about twice that of the non-aboriginal population. The crude birth rate for the Canadian population is about 15 births per 1,000, compared to about 28 and 35 per 1,000 for Indian and Inuit respectively. Comparisons based on the crude birth rates though, are difficult to interpret because the rate is affected by the age structure of the population, unlike total fertility rates.

Estimates of total fertility rates (TFR), for both the registered Indian and Inuit populations, as shown in Figure 4, indicate a declining trend in fertility over the past two decades, like that of the general population. The TFR for the Canadian population as a whole dropped from 3.8 in 1961 to 2.5 in 1968 to 1.7 by 1983. Corresponding to this drop, Inuit fertility started decreasing from a TFR of 9.2 in 1966 to 4.1 by 1983, while Indian fertility declined from a TFR of 6.1 in 1968 to 3.1 by the early 1980s. Between 1968 and 1981, the TFRs of Indians and Inuit declined at a much faster rate than for Canadians in general: both Indian and Inuit fertility rates dropped by 48 percent compared to 32 percent for the total population. These trends suggest a convergency in native fertility towards the overall Canadian fertility level. Some fluctuations exist in Inuit rates but generally, the rates are decreasing.

The comparison of total fertility rates indicates that Inuit fertility has been and remains higher than that of registered Indians. Data from the 1981 Census on "children born to ever-married women" clearly confirm this relation. In 1981 the average number of children born to ever-married women, was highest for Inuit, at 4.7, followed by 4.1 for status Indians, 3.6 for Métis, 3.0 for non-status Indians, and 3.9 for status and non-status Indians combined. The average number of children for Canadians in general was much lower at 2.5, compared to 3.9 for native people as a whole.

Data from the 1986 Census on children aged 0-4 as a percentage of total population also indicate that, among native people with single aboriginal origins, Inuit had the highest percentage of children (14 percent), followed by North American Indians (12 percent), and Métis (11 percent). Only 7 percent of the

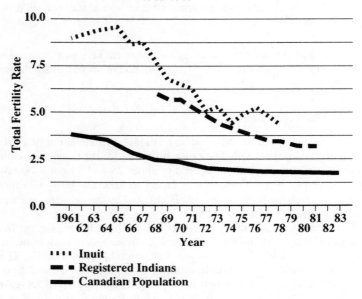

FIGURE 4

Total Fertility Rates, Canada
Inuit, Registered Indian and Canadians
1961-1983

Source: Inuit: Robitaille and Choinière, 1987
Registered Indians: Ram and Romaniuc, 1982
Canadian: Vital Statistics, Statistics Canada

total Canadian population is under the age of five. Child-woman ratios for 1986 also confirm the higher fertility of Inuit, with 566 children per 1,000 women aged 15-49, compared to 446 for Indian and 393 for Métis (see Table 4).

Geographic Differentials

Native fertility levels are significantly lower in urban than rural areas, especially among younger generations. The average number of births per ever-married woman, aged 15-19, in urban areas is less than half the number in rural areas; and in the case of women aged 20-29, the urban average is about two-thirds of the rural average. For example, according to the 1981 Census, ever-married native women aged 25-29 in rural areas have borne an average of 2.7 children compared to an average of 1.9 in urban areas. As well, the decline in fertility has been more rapid in urban than in rural communities. For women aged 15-29

TABLE 4

Child-Woman Ratios and Percentage of Population Aged 0-4 for
Aboriginal and Total Canadian Populations, Canada, 1986

Populations	Child-Woman Ratio No. of Children Aged 0-14 per 1,000 Women Aged 15-49	Population Aged 0-4 as Percentage of Total Population %
Aboriginal		
• Single and Multiple Origins	463	13.1
• Single Origin Only	449	12.3
• Multiple Origins	479	14.0
Aboriginal (Single & Multiple)		
• In Urban Areas	414	12.9
• In Rural Areas	536	13.3
North American Indian (Single Origins)	446	12.2
• On-reserve	571	13.4
• Off reserve	343	10.9
Métis (Single Origins)	393	10.9
Inuit (Single Origins)	566	14.4
Total Canadian Population	266	7.2

Source: 1986 Census, unpublished data.

as a group, the number of children ever born decreased by 29 percent in rural (non-farm) areas compared to 42 percent in urban areas (Romaniuc 1987, 81).

Similar differentials exist between status Indians[7] residing on and off reserves. Census data for 1981 show that the average number of children born to ever-married status Indian women is higher among those on-reserve, at 4.7, than the average 3.0 for those living off-reserve. Again, the differences between fertility levels on- and off-reserve are pronounced for the younger women. For example, women aged 20-24 living on-reserve had an average of 1.9 children compared to 1.2 among those living off-reserve.

Data from the 1986 Census on child-woman ratios indicate similar differentials, particularly between Indians on- and off-reserve. There were 571 children for every 1,000 women aged 15-49 living on-reserve compared to only 343 off-reserve. Similarly child-woman ratios were higher among native people in rural than in urban areas (see Table 4).

Census data also suggest that the fertility level of Inuit residing in southern Canada is lower than that of Inuit in the North (Robitaille and Choinière 1985).

Mortality

The mortality of Canada's native people remains much higher than for the general population. Current estimates of both registered Indians and Inuit life expectancy are comparable to overall Canadian levels during the 1940s, when life expectancies ranged between 65 and 69 years of age (for males and females combined). On average, life expectancies of these native groups are about 10 years less than for the overall population. In the case of Métis and non-status Indians, mortality data are not available. However, given that these two groups are more urbanized than registered Indians or Inuit, one might speculate that mortality levels of Métis and non-status Indians would be more similar to that of the general population, and, hence, lower than those of the other native groups.

Both Indian and Inuit life expectancies have risen over the past century as shown in Tables 5a and 5b. Indian life expectancies have increased from an estimated 33 years around the turn of the century, to some 62 years for males and 69 years for females by 1981. More recent estimates of status Indian life expectancies for 1982-85 are 64 and 73 years for males and females respectively. However, since there were no adjustments for late reporting or under-reporting of deaths these levels may be overestimated (Harris andMcCullough 1988). Available estimates for the Inuit indicate that life expectancy increased by some 30 years from 1940 to the present (1981) level of 62 (Northern Quebec) and 66 (Northwest Territories) years. By comparison, the life expectancy of the Canadian population as a whole increased by 10 years over the same period.

A large part of the increase in native life expectancy is attributable to the rapid decline in infant mortality. At the turn of the century, infant mortality rates (IMR) of registered Indians were estimated to be some 240 infant deaths per 1,000 live births, about 200 around World War II, and plummeting to around 30 by the late 1970s (Romaniuk 1981). Estimates based on data adjusted for late reporting from INAC's Register indicate a rapid decline in IMR during the 1971-81 period, from 42 to 15, a decrease of about 64 percent. Data from Health and Welfare's Medical Services Branch indicate a similar trend, but higher IMRs (22 in 1981). Because of under-reporting of infant deaths, additional adjustments were made to the Register-based data increasing the 1981 IMR from 15 to 27 (Rowe and Norris 1985). Nevertheless, the decline in infant mortality of registered Indians has been substantial. Over the same period Canadian rates decreased much more gradually from 17.5 to 9.6. These comparisons suggest a convergence of Indian rates to Canadian levels.

Declines of roughly the same magnitude have also occurred among the Inuit, although their levels of infant mortality have been and continue to be higher than those of registered Indians[8]. For example, infant mortality rates for Inuit in the mid-1960s were estimated to be about twice as high as Indian rates, with 100 deaths per 1,000 live births for Inuit compared to 50 for Indians (Webb

TABLE 5a

Estimated Life Expectancy at Birth for Registered Indians and
Total Canadian Populations, for Selected Periods and Years,
Canada, 1900-1981

Year/Period	Registered Indian		Total Canadian		
	Both Sexes		Year	Male	Female
1900	33		1921	58.8	60.6
1940	38		1941	63.0	66.3
1960	56		1961	68.4	74.2
	Males	Females			
1960-64	59.7	63.5			
1965-68	60.5	65.6	1966	68.7	75.2
1976	59.8	66.3	1976	70.2	77.5
1981	62.4	68.9	1981	71.9	79.0
1982-85	64.0	72.8	1984-86	73.0	79.8

Source: Registered Indian life expectancy: 1900, 1940, 1960 from Romaniuc, A.: 1981.
1960-64, 1982-85 Medical Services Branch, Health and Welfare.
1976, 1981, Rowe, G., Norris, M.J.: 1985.
Canadian Life Expectancy: Vital Statistics, Canadian Life Tables, Statistics Canada.

TABLE 5b

Estimated Life Expectancy at Birth for the Inuit and Total
Canadian Populations, Canada and Regions, 1940 to 1982

Inuit Population						General Population	
Labrador		Northern Quebec		Northwest Territories		Canada	
Periods	e_0	Periods	e_0	Periods	e_0	Periods	e_0
		1941-1951	35	1941-1950	29	1940-1942	65
		1951-1961	39	1951-1960	37	1950-1952	69
						1955-1957	70
		1961-1971	59	1963-1966	51	1960-1962	71
						1965-1967	72
1971-1980	60	1971-1981	62			1970-1972	73
						1975-1977	74
				1978-1982	66	1980-1982	75

Source: From Robitaille and Choinière, 1985, p. 23.

FIGURE 5

Age-Sex Specific Internal Migration
rates for Status Indians On- and
Off-Reserve & All Canadians,
Canada, 1976-1981

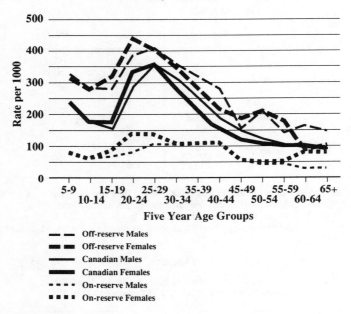

Off-reserve Males
Off-reserve Females
Canadian Males
Canadian Females
On-reserve Males
On-reserve Females

Source: 1981 Census unpublished data

1973). Since the 1950s, the infant mortality of Inuit has decreased substantially, from 300 per 1,000 to around 50 per 1,000 by 1981 (Robitaille and Choinière 1985).

While infant mortality rates of aboriginals have dropped significantly, declines in mortality at other ages are much less pronounced. An analysis of age-specific death rates of the registered Indian population for 1971, 1976 and 1981 indicated hardly any decrease for some ages over the period, or, in some cases, even slight increases in mortality (Rowe and Norris 1985).

This pattern of relatively little decline in mortality at older ages, compared to the great strides made in infant survival, reflects the fact that the major causes of death for registered Indians are not associated with disease, but rather with "accidents, poisoning and violence," and many of these deaths are alcohol-related (Jarvis and Boldt 1980). Because of improvements in health care, deaths from respiratory conditions, digestive disorders, infection and parasitic diseases as well as perinatal causes, decreased significantly since 1960. For almost 300 years, tuberculosis was a major threat to native health. Among Indians around Hudson Bay and James Bay, tuberculosis accounted for 30 percent of all deaths as early as 1885. In 1950, the incidence of tuberculosis among Indians and Eskimos was estimated to be 12 times the national rate (Graham-Cumming 1967). Today accidents, poisoning and violence are the leading causes of death. Rates increased dramatically from 139/10,000 in 1960 to 253/100,000 in 1978 (Murdock 1980). More recently, the rate dropped to 174/100,000 in 1983 (Siggner 1986) though still three times the rate for the Canadian population. Similarly, injuries and poisoning were the leading causes of death among the Inuit over the 1970-80 period: 21 percent in Northern Quebec; 34 percent in the Northwest Territories and 40 percent in Labrador, compared to only 9 percent among Canadians as a whole (Robitaille and Choinière 1985).

In the comparison between native and non-native mortality by death rates and cause, differences in age structure should be considered. Crude death rates of the status Indian population are lower than the rates for the general population because the Indian population is much younger. For 1981 the crude Indian rate was 6.1, compared to 7.0 for the overall Canadian population. However, the standardized death rate (adjusted to the age-sex structure of the Canadian population) is 9.5 (Rowe and Norris 1985). Similarly, causes of death associated mainly with young adults, such as accidents and injuries, are more liable to account for a higher proportion of deaths in the younger Indian population than in the older general population. When rates by cause from 1978-86 are standardized according to the Canadian age structure, diseases of the circulatory system become the leading cause of death among Indians, followed by injuries and poisonings (Harris and McCullough 1988).

At most ages, Indian death rates are higher than those of Canadians in general, with the exception of older ages when a crossover in mortality occurs. Male and female death rates based on INAC's Register were generally lower than Canadian rates after the age of 70. This crossover could simply be a function of poor data quality, more likely to occur with the extremes of older ages. But it is possible that such crossovers are real, as suggested by Trovato (1984) in his study of French, British and native Indian mortality differences, and by Markides (1983) in an American study of black, native American and Hispanic mortality. The explanation is based on a theory of selectivity (i.e., that those members of a disadvantaged minority who are able to survive through the high mortality years of infancy, youth and young adulthood would experience lower mortality at older ages than the population in general).

Mobility and Migration

According to the 1986 Census, native people changed residences and communities to a greater extent than Canadians in general. Over half (56 percent) of those with some aboriginal origins had moved (changed residences) over the past five years, compared to 44 percent of all Canadians; and, about 23 percent of natives had migrated (e.g., from one city to another) compared to 17.5 percent of Canadians.

Among the native groups (with "single only" origins) the Métis were the most mobile, with well over half, 57 percent of the population having changed residences at least once during the five years and 23 percent having changed communities. Just over half of both the Inuit and Indians[9] had moved, but the Inuit changed communities the least, with only 12 percent having lived in a different town or settlement five years earlier (Table 6).

Native groups (on single origin) not only differ in their propensity to move, but also in the type of moves: Inuit migrate mainly between rural areas, whereas Indians and Métis move most frequently between urban areas. Over the 1981-86 period, almost half (47 percent) of Inuit migrants had moved between rural communities compared to only 13 percent of North American Indians and 10 percent of Métis. In contrast, movement between urban areas accounted for 37 percent and 46 percent of Indian and Métis migrations, respectively. Migration from rural to urban areas also accounted for a larger share of Indian and Métis migrants: 25 percent compared to 14 percent for Inuit (Table 6). While Métis had a net loss of migrants from rural areas, urban-to-rural migration offset, or was greater than, the outflow from rural areas for Indians and Inuit.

Overall, rates of out-migration from rural areas are lower for aboriginals than for Canadians in general (72 per 1,000, compared to 115 for 1986). Among the native groups, rural out-migration was highest for Métis at 127 out-migrants per 1,000 rural residents, and lowest for the Inuit at 28 per 1,000.

Young adults, especially females, tend to be the most mobile in a population, and the native population is no different in that respect. Mobility rates follow the standard age pattern for both aboriginals and all Canadians, decreasing over the school age groups, peaking during the young adult years 25-29, and then declining fairly steadily thereafter. Young women, particularly in the 20-24 age group, move and migrate to a greater extent than their male counterparts (Norris 1985). For example between 1981 and 1986, 75 percent of native women in this age group had moved to a different dwelling compared to 64 percent of native men. Overall, aboriginal youth move to a greater extent than their non-native counterparts. The 1986 mobility rates for the general population aged 20-24, of 65 percent for women and 55 percent for men, were about 10 percentage points lower than the corresponding native rates. Similar findings were also reported with 1981 Census data, in a study which also found that Métis, non-status Indians and Inuit youth (in decreasing order) moved to a greater extent than either status Indian or non-aboriginal youth (Priest 1985).

Census data for 1981 indicate that while status Indians are less mobile as a group than Canadians in general, those that live off-reserve are highly transient, changing residences and communities to a much greater extent than the general population. It is the Indian population on-reserve that are less mobile than the

TABLE 6

Movers and Migrants by Type for Aboriginal and Total Canadian Populations, Canada, 1986

Populations	Movers as a Percentage of the Population Aged 5 + %	Migrants as a Percentage of the Population Aged 5 + %	Distribution of Migrants by Type of Move				Total No. of Internal Migrants
			Rural- to- Rural %	Urban- to- Urban %	Rural- to- Urban %	Urban- to- Rural %	
Aboriginal							
• Single and Multiple Origins	55.9	23.0	9.8	48.6	20.2	21.4	138,200
• Single Origin Only	51.4	18.6	13.8	37.9	24.3	23.9	60,485
• Multiple Origins	61.1	28.1	6.5	56.9	17.0	19.5	77,715
North American Indian (Single Origins)	50.2	18.5	12.9	37.3	24.7	25.1	44,960
Métis (Single Origins)	56.7	22.0	9.8	45.6	23.7	20.9	11,605
Inuit (Single Origins)	50.8	12.2	46.9	15.4	19.1	18.6	2,825
Total Canadian Population	43.7	17.5	5.8	61.4	15.4	17.3	4,049,945

Source: 1986 Census unpublished data

53

overall population (Norris 1985). For example, 44 percent of status Indian women, aged 20-24, living off-reserve, had changed communities over the 1976-81 period, compared to only 14 percent living on-reserve and 33 percent of all Canadian women (Figure 5). The 1986 Census data on mobility rates for North American Indians (single origins) also indicate that Indians living off-reserve move much more than those on-reserve: 84 percent of Indian women aged 20-24, residing off-reserve had changed dwellings over the 1981-86 period compared to only 52 percent of those on-reserve and 66 percent of all Canadian women.

In general, aboriginal people who live outside the regions of their native communities and settlements tend to be more transient than the general population, whereas within their own communities they are far less transient. Among the Inuit in northern regions, the rate of migration was low — between 10 and 15 percent in 1981 — but among the Inuit in the south the rate was higher, at 38 percent, than that of the general population at 23 percent (Robitaille and Choinière 1985). Another study based on 1981 Census data, showed that in the south, the native population had higher mobility rates than non-natives, while in the Far North, where mobility is high for both populations, non-natives were more mobile than natives (76 percent had moved compared to 54 percent of natives). In the mid-North, the native mobility rate was at its lowest, at 45 percent, but lower than the rate for non-natives of 49 percent. Most striking in the south, is the fact that 69 percent of the native population in metropolitan areas had moved, with 56 percent moving within or between metropolitan areas (Norris and Pryor 1985).

Movement to and from Reserves [10]

An important aspect of Indian migration is the movement to and from reserves. Reserves have always been a source of Indian migrants who leave in search of better social or economic opportunities. Cities, notably the large metropolitan ones, have become destinations for a growing proportion of migrants leaving reserves, with the result that more and more Indians moving back to reserves are coming from urban areas.

Since the early 1970s, the movement between reserves and urban areas has intensified. Data from the 1981 Census on status Indians show that about 86 percent of out-migrants from reserves moved to urban areas, compared to only 66 percent over the 1966-71 period. Similarly, 71 percent of in-migrants to reserves came from urban areas, compared to just 60 percent a decade earlier. As well, reserves attracted an increasing proportion of urban migrants during the 1976-81 period; 63 percent of all status Indians who had left urban areas moved to reserves, as opposed to just over half in 1966-71 (Norris 1985; Siggner 1977). Overall, 26 percent of all migrants in 1981 had moved to reserves, compared to 21 percent earlier on. Due in part to the growing stream of Indians

FIGURE 6a

Distribution of Out-Migrants
from Reserves by Type of Destination,
Canada, 1966-71 & 1976-81.

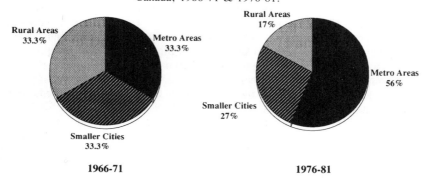

1966-71   1976-81

Source: 1971-81 Census of Canada

FIGURE 6b

Distribution of In-Migrants
to Reserves by Type of Origin,
Canada, 1966-71 & 1976-81.

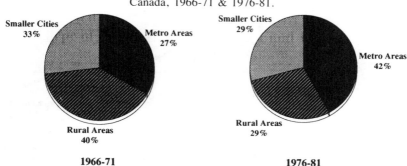

1966-71   1976-81

Source: 1971-81 Census of Canada unpublished census data

from urban areas, migrants to reserves outnumbered those leaving reserves over
the 1976-1981 period: 3,200 status Indians left reserves and settlements, while
10,700 moved in, yielding a net inflow of 7,500. Nearly two thirds of this net
gain to reserves was due to the flow from urban areas. (Data on out-migration
from reserves have not been derived from 1986 Census.)

While large metropolitan areas are attracting an increasing proportion of out-migrants from reserves, these cities are also becoming a rapidly growing source of migrants (back) to reserves. In 1981, 57 percent of out-migrants from reserves moved to metropolitan areas, compared to only a third earlier on. At the same time, 42 percent of in-migrants to reserves came from metropolitan areas compared to just 27 percent in 1971 (Figure 6). Over 1976-81, the slowdown in the economy along with high unemployment had probably forced many Indians to move back to reserves. Unlike most other migrants, especially immigrants, status Indians usually do have a "home" community — the reserve to which they can easily return in times of hardship.

Women predominate in the movement to and from reserves; they are far more mobile than men, especially in their out-migration from reserves. Studies by Gerber (1977) on Indian community characteristics and out-migration, and by Clatworthy (1980) in his study of Indian migrants in Winnipeg, have noted this

FIGURE 7a

Reserve out-Migration Rates, Status Indians, 1981
and Rural Out-Migration Rates, Aboriginals, 1986
by Age and Sex

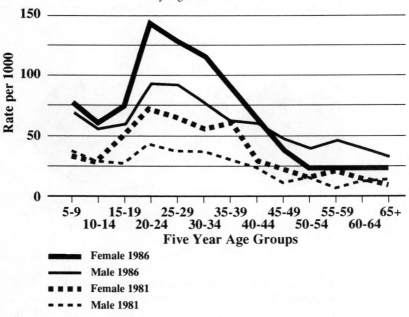

Female 1986
Male 1986
Female 1981
Male 1981

Source: 1981-1986 censuses unpublished data

higher incidence of migration among women. Census data for 1981 on status Indians show that among Indian youth aged 15-24, almost twice as many females than males had left reserves and settlements over the 1976-81 period. Out-migration rates are significantly higher among women than men, especially in the 15-35 age groups. For example, in the 20-24 age group 72 of every 1,000 Indian women residing on reserves or settlements, left over the five-year period, compared to a rate of 42 for men (Figure 7a). Overall, five-year out-migration rates for men and women are 28 and 42 per 1,000 respectively (Norris 1985).

Since more women leave reserves than men, they are also more likely to outnumber men as return migrants back to reserves; and even more so at older ages, due to sex differentials in life expectancy. (Most of the movement into reserves is probably return migration, especially at older ages.) In 1981, females dominated to some extent in the 20-29 age groups and notably, the older 55 + age group. At these older ages, two and a half times as many women than men moved back to reserves. But, relative to the outflow from reserves and settlements, males had higher rates of "return" than females. For every 10 men who had left reserves, 23 had moved in; compared to 18 for every 10 women who left.

Figure 7b

Rural Out-Migration Rates, by Age and
Sex, Canada, 1986
All Canadians

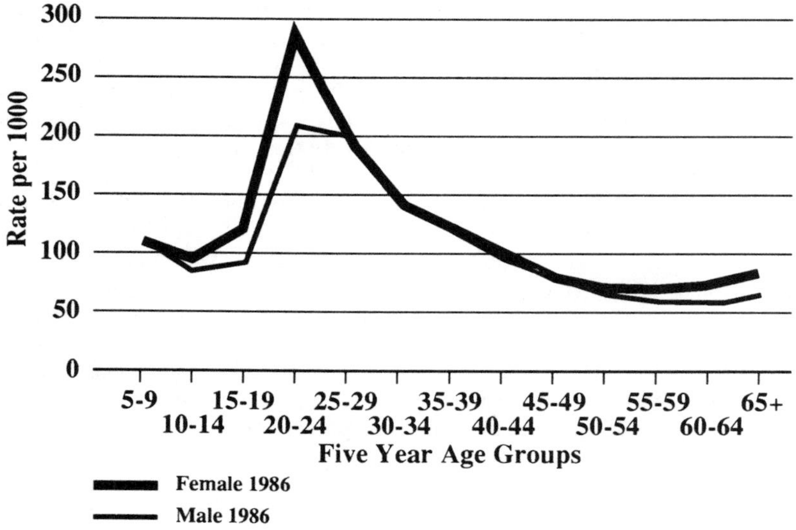

Source: 1986 Census unpublished data

57

The phenomenon of young Indian women leaving reserves to a greater extent than men is similar to, but much more pronounced than, the higher out-migration of women than men from rural areas among the general population. In the out-migration of Indians from reserves (1981) and native people from rural areas (1986) female rates were about twice those of males for ages 15 through to 39 (Figure 7a). For 1986, the effect of out-migration from reserves is reflected to some extent in native rural migration. In contrast, for rural out-migration among the general population in 1986 female rates were only about one and a third times greater than those of males for ages 15-24 (Figure 7b). Unlike non-native women in rural areas, native women, especially on reserves, experience different or additional push/pull factors in their moves. Until recently, the discrimination in the Indian Act against women, the high incidence of lone parenthood, compounded by economic conditions on reserves and opportunities in urban areas, are important influences in the decision to move.

Conclusion

The aboriginal population is demographically distinct from the total Canadian population. It is a much younger, faster-growing population, with fertility and mortality levels higher than the overall Canadian levels. Native fertility rates are about twice those of non-natives, while native life expectancies at birth are some 10 years less than those of the average Canadian. Unlike the rest of the Canadian population, the majority of aboriginal people live in rural areas. Aboriginal people who do not reside in native communities and settlements, but in urban areas and off reserves, tend to change dwellings and cities to a greater extent than the general population. In contrast, those who live within mainly native regions have moved considerably less than the average Canadian. Among natives, women are much more likely than men to move away from reserves and rural areas to cities.

Demographic differences exist among the native groups themselves. The Inuit are the youngest and fastest growing, most "rural" and least mobile of the aboriginal populations, with fertility and mortality levels higher than those of registered Indians. The Métis tend to be the closest in their demographic characteristics to the non-native population. North American Indians, particularly status Indians, are distinct from the other two groups in terms of settlement and migration patterns associated with reserves. However, all these major groups are similar in their urban-rural differentials, such that native populations in urban areas have higher concentrations of young adults, lower fertility and are highly transient.

Notes

1. The views expressed in this paper are those of the author and do not necessarily represent the views of Statistics Canada.
2. These figures for 1986 do not include estimates for incompletely enumerated reserves and settlements, totalling some 45,000 people.
3. Distributions based on single and multiple origins combined in 1986 are most similar to those in 1981.
4. The regional distribution of native people in 1986 differs between single and multiple origins. Over half of the respondents reporting mixed aboriginal and non-aboriginal origin in 1986 are concentrated in Ontario (33 percent), and British Columbia (20 percent). This is in sharp contrast to respondents with single origins, who are almost evenly distributed among the provinces, from Quebec westwards, with shares from between 14-16 percent.
5. INAC figures from 1966 to 1973 were adjusted to correspond to the definitions of "on-reserve" used from 1974 onwards.
6. Previously, under the Indian Act, a status Indian woman who married a man who was not status Indian lost her status. Any children from such a marriage did not have status either. This rule did not apply to status Indian men who retained their status regardless of who they married, as did their children.
7. Comparison of fertility levels between status Indian women on- and off-reserve may be somewhat limited because it is based only on the ever-married population. A high proportion (some 60 percent in 1981) of births to registered Indians occur outside of marriage, and the incidence of such births probably varies between status Indians residing on- and off-reserve.
8. Some caution must be used with estimates of infant mortality for both registered Indians and Inuit, owing to problems of registration and small numbers. For example, the range of estimates by Robitaille and Choinière (1985), for infant mortality rates of Inuit in different regions is very wide: in the Northwest Territories current (1981) rates were estimated to be between 26 and 42 per 1,000; in Northern Quebec (18 to 67 per 1,000); and in Labrador (49 to 82 per 1,000).
9. To some extent, this comparison for 1986 is limited particularly for the Indian population, because of the estimated 45,000 Indians living on incompletely enumerated reserves and settlements. Reserve populations tend not to be mobile. Their exclusion, therefore, may have produced an overestimate of native mobility and migration. For example, in 1981, status Indians and Canadians in general were equally mobile: about 48 percent had changed dwellings, while a lower proportion of Indians (20 percent) changed communities than Canadians (23 percent).
10. Discussion on migration to and from reserves is based on 1971 and 1981 census data only. Similar data have not yet been derived for 1986.

4. THE FERTILITY OF ETHNIC GROUPS

Shiva S. Halli

Differences in subgroup fertility have commonly been attributed to socioeconomic variations. Yet, when social change eliminates group differences in socioeconomic characteristics, or when such conditions are controlled statistically, discrepancies in family size still remain (Halli 1987). The persistence of this relationship has led to the consideration of ethnicity as an additional explanatory factor in the study of differential fertility. This paper provides a further extension of this issue, paying specific attention to the relationship between ethnicity and fertility in Canada during 1981.

Defining the term ethnicity is difficult since no universal definition has been established in the social sciences. As Balakrishnan et al (1979) asks, is ethnicity based on historical ancestry or is it more of a personal identification regardless of ancestry? This question is quite pertinent since ethnicity as a concept may refer to a variety of conditions. According to Anderson and Frideres (1980) the term ethnic group has been used more or less interchangeably with the terms race, culture, subculture, folk, people, nation, nationality, minority group, ethnic minority, ethno-linguistic group and ethnic-religious group. Based on a thorough examination of 65 sociological and anthropological studies published in scholarly journals, Isajiw (1985) concludes that the following attributes of ethnicity are mentioned most often: (a) common ancestral origin, (b) same culture, (c) religion, (d) race, and (e) language.

Incorporating the various forms of ethnicity that are commonly used is a difficult task. For instance, an ethnic group is often a minority group; but it is also a racial, cultural or religious group and therefore defining ethnicity as such must include a number of additional criteria to be complete. Yet, some kind of narrowing down must take place to make the term easily operational. In this paper the concept "ethnic group" will refer to "one's ethnic or cultural background traced through the father's side" (Richmond and Kalbach 1980, 31). This was the definition used by the census authorities to collect data on ethnicity in the 1971 Census. In the 1981 Census more than one ethnic origin response per individual was allowed. Since more than 90 percent of the respondents fall in a single response category instead of a multiple response category, we will consider only the single response ethnic origin, traced through the paternal ancestry.

The existence of a relationship between ethnicity and fertility in Canada has been well documented (Hurd 1937; Henripin 1972; Kalbach and McVey 1979; Trovato and Burch 1980; Trovato 1981; Basavarajappa and Halli 1984; Halli 1987). Despite evidence of a causal relationship, Sly (1970) and Johnson (1979) have argued that in contemporary society the ethnic concept is a "relic" with little behavioural significance. There is, however, a body of literature that emphasizes both the significance of ethnicity on the impact of human behaviour in general, and fertility behaviour in particular. Balakrishnan et al. (1975, 34) for example, in their study of fertility in Toronto advised that "it would be admissible in future fertility research to give the [ethnic] variable greater consideration." The authors stated that ethnicity may be a better predictor of fertility than the more commonly utilized socioeconomic characteristics. The importance of differentiating fertility by ethnicity is highlighted by Beaujot et al. (1977, 1) who state that because of high immigration, differences in reproduction have "obvious consequences on the future proportional representation of the sociocultural groups." Thus, in addition to ethnicity's importance in socioeconomic differentiation, it has significant relevance in terms of ethnic continuity. The larger the group, the greater the viability of the ethnic community. Fertility is clearly of importance in this relation.

Development of Hypotheses

The literature identifies three explanations for differences in fertility by ethnic affiliation. The first thesis claims that differences depend upon the extent to which ethnic populations have obtained access to and have been assimilated into the economic and political structures of the larger society (Frisbie and Bean 1978). These ethnic groups constitute "subpopulation" minorities or "groups whose members experience a wide range of discrimination and frequently are relegated to positions low in the status hierarchy" (Gittler 1956; quoted in Frisbie and Bean 1978, 3). This area of research, concentrating on structural differences, can be labelled as the "structural approach."

A second perspective is the "cultural approach." According to Frisbie and Bean (1978), this conceptualization encompasses Schemerhorn's (1970, 12) conception of an ethnic group: "a collectivity within a larger society having real or putative common ancestry, memories of a shared historical past, and a cultural focus on one or more symbolic elements defined as the epitome of peoplehood." Symbolic elements include kinship patterns, language, phenotypical features and religious affiliations. Of particular importance to fertility are the symbolic elements, or stated differently, its norms and values about family and reproduction.

The third explanation considers the possibility of an interaction effect between ethnicity, group ideology and minority status insecurities. Goldscheider and Uhlenberg's (1969) study of American ethnic groups proposed that the higher fertility rates of Catholics could be attributed to the pronatalist norms adhered to by the religion. On the other hand, the lower fertility experienced by Jews, higher status Blacks and Japanese Americans is a function of minority-group status. More explicitly, minority group membership engenders social-psychological insecurities that serves to decrease fertility when:

1) the acculturation of minority group members occurs in conjunction with the desire for acculturation;
2) equalization of social and economic characteristics occurs, particularly in middle and upper social class levels, and/or there is a desire for social and economic mobility;
3) there is no pronatalist ideology associated with the minority groups and no norms discouraging the use of efficient contraception (Goldscheider and Uhlenberg 1969, 272).

Consider the first of these assumptions. Where minority couples embrace the norms and values of society, particularly the goal of social mobility, but where full realization of these goals does not occur, assimilation will be experienced in part only. In other words, assimilation may occur in some dimensions, say education or occupation, but not in others. What then exists is a discrepancy which produces the social-psychological insecurities and minority couples limit their family sizes in an attempt to solidify their socioeconomic position. The effects on fertility should be experienced most severely by minority couples assimilated enough to feel socioeconomic insecurities (Bean and Marcum 1978).

In view of the explanations concerning ethnicity and fertility, in most cases, differentials are explained from the point of view of minority status insecurities or characteristics assimilation explanations because few groups today possess an identifiable explicit pronatalist ideology discouraging the use of contraception. Although the literature deals with both of these hypotheses, they are often subdivided resulting in a number of variations. For example, Johnson (1979) separated each of these two hypotheses into ''strong'' and ''weak'' forms in the context of black-white fertility differences in the United States:

The strong form of the characteristics hypothesis argues that once the differences in compositional factors between blacks and whites have been statistically controlled, race will retain no net relationship to number of children born to women at any level of educational achievement. In contrast, the weak form of the characteristics hypothesis posits that if the compositional factors are rendered similar for blacks and whites through social change, the most highly educated will be the first to depart from a radically distinct childbearing pattern. Consequently, in the early phase of social transition, controlling statistically for black-white compositional differences will remove the effect of race on fertility for the highly educated but not for the less educated. Whereas the strong form of the characteristics position

63

predicts no relationship between race and fertility at any educational level, the weak form predicts an interactive relationship among race, fertility and education.

The strong form of the minority-status hypothesis predicts that a net direct effect of race on fertility will exist at every level of education, although the direction of the effect is thought to vary with that level. On the other hand, the weak form of the minority-status hypothesis argues that minority-group membership is sensitively linked to fertility only for those who have sought and obtained upward mobility (i.e., the educated minority), for it is these who will encounter the barriers to full economic assimilation. Consequently, both forms of the minority-status hypothesis predict an interactive relationship among race, education, and fertility (Johnson 1979, 1397-98).

The forthcoming sections of the paper will examine fertility differentials in Canada based on the Johnson formulation above. In particular, an attempt will be made to answer the following two questions: Are ethnic family size differences a function of variations in social-characteristics levels? Do fertility differences persist after appropriate controls are introduced? The first stage in the exploration will consist of a series of bivariate analyses involving fertility and several socioeconomic characteristics. The second stage of the analysis consists of a multivariate evaluation of the minority-group status hypothesis.

Data and Methods of Analysis

The data for the analysis comes from the Public Use Sample Tapes of the 1981 Census. The unit of analysis is ever-married women aged 15 and over, classified on the basis of ethnic origin. Information on the husbands is not available since the individual file is used, which does not contain household information. Specific ethnic groups selected for the analysis are: British, French, German, Italian, Jewish, Ukrainian and an "other" residual category. All ethnic groups chosen constitute at least 2 percent of the total population with the exception of Jews. Besides being numerically large, these ethnic groups represent important cultural entities. While the French and British are two of the nation's founding groups, the others are known to be highly organized institutionally (Reitz 1980; Breton 1971).

The dependent variable is children ever born. In the census, ever-married females, 15 years of age and over, were asked to provide information as to the number of children to which they had given birth. Given this single question on fertility, it is not possible to calculate timing or spacing of births. Moreover, no information is provided on children born to unmarried women or girls under 15. Compositional variables have been selected on the basis of the importance attributed to them by previous studies in Canadian fertility (Balakrishnan et al. 1979; Beaujot et al. 1982; Henripin 1972). The selected variables are current age, age at first marriage, nativity, ethnic background, religion, education, family income and labour force participation. It is possible that these variables influence fertility behaviour directly and indirectly through other intermediate variables; however, this indirect link is omitted in the present analysis since the census data do not permit an explanation of this nature.

An important limitation of the study is that the dependent variable is a cumulative measure, while labour force status and family income reflect current status. In terms of causal order, it is difficult to verify whether any relationship among these variables is recursive or not.

The analysis will be performed in two stages. The first stage will provide descriptive statistics of the characteristics variables of all ethnic groups to indicate the socioeconomic inequality between ethnic groups. Next, the existence of ethnic differences in fertility-related behaviour will be demonstrated using bivariate analysis. The bivariate analysis is conducted for specific purposes: (1) to demonstrate the existence of ethnic differences in fertility behaviour; (2) to demonstrate the existence of fertility differences by the socioeconomic characteristics; and (3) to examine the patterns of socioeconomic differentials within each ethnic group in anticipation of possible interaction effects — that is, to demonstrate whether the socioeconomic characteristics have different kinds of influences on fertility behaviour for different ethnic groups.

In addition to the simple descriptive statistics (e.g., means and standard deviations) used to describe fertility patterns, multiple classification analysis and multiple regression will be used to disentangle some of the complex relationships between ethnicity and selected socioeconomic charateristics.

Multiple classification analysis is able to handle non-linear relationships between the independent and dependent variables. This technique allows the independent variables to be in either nominal, ordinal or interval scales, since the functional form of the relationship is not assumed in advance but is determined by the category coefficients of the variables as estimated from the data. In this way curvilinear relationships can be detected and postulated patterns of relationships easily checked. Another advantage of multiple classification analysis is that the coefficients of a variable are deviations from the overall mean, adjusted for the effects of the other predictors.

Finally, multiple regression is used to execute a direct test of the minority group status hypothesis. The test will be based on a race-education interaction for fertility (higher minority than majority fertility for those having primary schooling, lower minority than majority fertility for those having secondary and post-secondary education). The amount of difference in the explained variance in the dependent variable between equations with and without the interaction term would indicate the degree and significance of interaction involved. A significant increase in the explained variance due to the interaction term will be taken as support for the minority status hypothesis.

Multiple regression requires variables at interval or ratio level of measurement, and thus we must construct dummy terms for nominal variables such as ethnicity. Since the dummy variables have arbitrary metric values of 1 and 0, they may be treated as interval variables and inserted into a regression equation. Hence, it is necessary to exclude one of the dummies from the equation. The excluded category becomes a reference category by which the effects of the other dummies are evaluated and interpreted. In the present situation the British group is excluded from the equation and hence represents the reference category. Similarly, labour force status, religion and place of birth are also treated as dummy variables with appropriate reference classes.

In the interaction model, interaction terms are added to the basic additive model: ethnicity is a dummy variable form (e.g., being French or German with the British as the omitted category) combined with the socioeconomic variable, education. The significance of interaction terms has an immediate bearing on our hypotheses. Education when interacting with ethnicity should serve as an indicator to test the minority group status hypothesis to see whether the strong form or the weak form holds.

Discussion of Results

In Table 1, children ever born does not vary much by ethnicity. The national average is around 2.46 children. The French maintain the highest fertility followed by Italians and Germans, if we exclude the residual category. It is noteworthy that the French ethnic group also maintains the highest standard deviation (2.36). This may be explained by the fact that the recent cohorts in Quebec display much lower fertility than their older counterparts.

The remaining portion of Table 1 documents the ethnic difference in socioeconomic and demographic characteristics that we suspect are related to fertility. The average age of the sample is approximately 45 years, which indicates that a good portion of the respondents would have completed their childbearing. Age at first marriage is approximately 20 years for almost all ethnic groups with the exception of Jews which is slightly higher (21.80).

The religious differentiation among the ethnic groups is more distinct, with virtually 95 percent of the French and Italian women being Roman Catholics; nearly 100 percent of the Jews, non-Roman Catholics; and more than 80 percent of the British and Ukrainians, non-Roman Catholic. Given this wide overlap between ethnicity and religion, it may be possible to argue that religion per se may not have an independent effect on fertility.

The Jewish ethnic group is the most educated followed by the British. Italians are the least educated. Women's participation in the labour force varies little with ethnicity. The ethnic differential is most marked for family income. For example, the Jewish ethnic group has an average income of more than $11,500 as compared to the national average of $6,757.19. The French charter group is the poorest group on average, followed by Italians.

TABLE 1

Distribution of Means and Standard Deviations* of Study variables for Ever-Married women
by Major Ethnic Groups in Canada, 1981

Ethnic Groups	Family Size	Age	Age at First Marriage	Religion	Education	Labour Force Status	Family Income	Place of Birth
British	2.35	46.75	20.93	1.81	1.96	1.54	7121.41	1.17
	(1.88)	(17.33)	(6.45)	(0.39)	(0.54)	(0.50)	(7795.90)	(0.38)
French	2.65	43.67	20.19	1.05	1.73	1.60	5849.82	1.02
	(2.36)	(16.17)	(7.51)	(0.23)	(0.59)	(0.49)	(6952.17)	(0.15)
German	2.41	45.51	20.78	1.75	1.81	1.53	6678.50	1.33
	(1.94)	(16.70)	(6.12)	(0.43)	(0.56)	(0.50)	(7518.20)	(0.47)
Italian	2.49	44.60	20.55	1.05	1.49	1.52	6234.96	1.78
	(1.68)	(15.02)	(6.39)	(0.22)	(0.62)	(0.50)	(6660.11)	(0.42)
Jewish	1.95	50.63	21.80	1.99	2.02	1.51	11575.06	1.47
	(1.37)	(17.08)	(6.51)	(0.09)	(0.62)	(0.50)	(12599.10)	(0.50)
Ukrainian	2.35	47.84	20.41	1.84	1.74	1.52	7365.95	1.19
	(1.87)	(17.00)	(6.58)	(0.37)	(0.55)	(0.50)	(7667.62)	(0.39)
Other	2.48	43.73	20.31	1.63	1.81	1.50	6787.76	1.59
	(2.03)	(16.08)	(7.54)	(0.48)	(0.64)	(0.50)	(7621.92)	(0.49)
TOTAL	2.46	45.37	20.61	1.55	1.85	1.55	6727.19	1.23
	(2.04)	(16.78)	(6.93)	(0.50)	(0.59)	(0.50)		(0.42)

* Standard deviations are presented in parentheses.

Note: Religion, labour force status and place of birth are dichotomous variables.
Religion is coded as follows: 1 = Catholic and 2 = other.
Labour force status is coded as follows: 1 = employed and 2 = unemployed.
Place of birth is coded as follows: 1 = born in Canada and 2 = born outside Canada.
Education is coded as follows: 1 = primary, 2 = secondary and 3 = post-secondary.

Almost all of the French respondents are Canadian born, but the majority of the Italians are born outside Canada. The residual category, which includes Asians as well as other ethnic groups, is made up of a large number of immigrants to Canada.

Table 2 shows how some of the demographic and socioeconomic characteristics relate to fertility behaviour. Table 2 also shows whether taking these characteristics into account reduces, if not removes, the ethnic differences observed earlier with respect to the dependent variable. The purpose here is to look at the confounding effects of the demographic and socioeconomic factors on the bivariate ethnic differentials we observed in Table 1.

Concerning age, the sample is partitioned into two groups: 20-29 and 30 plus. The rationale for dividing the sample lies in the fact that the sample consists of all ever-married women 15 and over, and it is expected that the recent cohorts have different fertility patterns than their predecessors. The results are quite contrasting between the two age groups. For the older cohorts, French Canadians show exceptionally high fertility, but their younger counterparts are quite the opposite. This finding is consistent with recent fertility trends in Quebec.

Other variables such as religion, education and labour force status are all affecting fertility behaviour in the expected direction within each of the ethnic groups. Within each ethnic group, Roman Catholics maintain generally higher fertility. Education and labour force status have inverse relationships; that is, the higher educated and currently employed women tend to have lower family sizes.

For all the ethnic groups studied, family size decreases as income increases for income levels up to $30,000. Above this level of income, family size increases. This type of relationship resembles a reverse "J".

Based on the 1971 Census data, Balakrishnan, et al. (1979) found that foreign-born women have much lower fertility than native-born women. To some extent this statement seems to be true for the two charter groups and the residual category. For the remainder of the ethnic groups, foreign-born women have higher fertility than native-born women.

In summary, the crosstabular analysis has shown that the original ethnic differentials in fertility behaviour are maintained within each category of the various socioeconomic variables introduced as controls. There are no signs of convergence with higher education, higher income and current participation in the labour force.

A fuller understanding of the effects of socioeconomic variables on fertility is available from Table 3, which presents the results of the multiple classification analysis (MCA). It is interesting to note that the fertility patterns based on the MCA adjusted means vary substantially from the patterns discussed in Table 2, which utilized unadjusted means. Being employed, non-Catholic religion, and higher education are all inversely related to fertility. Most importantly, the income variable, which had shown a reverse "J" type relationship in an earlier table, shows an inverse relationship with fertility for both age groups. This

TABLE 2

Means and Standard Deviation* Reflecting the Relationship between Children ever Born and Ethnicity, Controlling for a Third Variable, for Ever Married Women, Canada, 1981

Ethnicity	Age 15-29	Age 30+	Religion Roman Catholic	Religion Other	Education Primary	Education Secondary	Education Post-Secondary	Labor Force Status Employed	Labor Force Status Unemployed	Family Income −50,000 9,999	Family Income 10,000 19,999	Family Income 20,000 29,999	Family Income 30,000+	Place of Birth Native Born	Place of Birth Foreign Born	Total
British	1.03 (1.06)	2.67 (1.90)	2.65 (2.18)	2.28 (1.80)	3.23 (2.39)	2.23 (1.72)	1.83 (1.56)	2.04 (1.72)	2.61 (1.97)	2.55 (1.92)	1.85 (1.67)	1.76 (1.65)	2.00 (1.66)	2.36 (1.91)	2.30 (1.74)	2.35 (1.88)
French	0.94 (0.99)	3.17 (2.40)	2.67 (2.38)	2.32 (1.96)	3.78 (2.71)	2.07 (1.89)	1.90 (1.88)	1.90 (1.86)	3.16 (2.51)	2.92 (2.43)	1.71 (1.82)	1.75 (1.67)	1.91 (1.77)	2.65 (2.36)	2.53 (2.20)	2.65 (2.36)
German	1.01 (1.10)	2.80 (1.95)	2.48 (2.07)	2.38 (1.90)	3.39 (2.33)	2.09 (1.66)	1.69 (1.41)	2.02 (1.74)	2.75 (2.05)	2.62 (1.98)	1.83 (1.72)	1.76 (1.59)	2.02 (1.78)	2.39 (1.96)	2.43 (1.90)	2.41 (1.94)
Italian	1.03 (0.98)	2.81 (1.63)	2.50 (1.68)	2.19 (1.70)	2.96 (1.69)	1.91 (1.43)	1.47 (1.40)	2.06 (1.44)	2.88 (1.79)	2.70 (1.72)	1.88 (1.41)	1.87 (1.35)	2.20 (1.56)	1.83 (1.58)	2.67 (1.66)	2.49 (1.68)
Jewish	0.72 (0.98)	2.13 (1.33)	1.60 (2.03)	1.95 (1.37)	2.28 (1.51)	1.94 (1.31)	1.68 (1.37)	1.78 (1.32)	2.11 (1.41)	2.02 (1.40)	1.84 (1.32)	1.72 (1.30)	2.02 (1.39)	1.86 (1.30)	2.04 (1.45)	1.95 (1.37)
Ukrainian	0.88 (1.01)	2.67 (1.86)	2.45 (1.92)	2.33 (1.86)	3.12 (2.16)	2.03 (1.61)	1.52 (1.43)	1.98 (1.67)	2.69 (1.98)	2.61 (1.92)	1.75 (1.58)	1.54 (1.55)	1.98 (1.51)	2.25 (1.79)	2.76 (2.14)	2.35 (1.87)
Other	1.14 (1.16)	2.86 (2.07)	2.51 (2.12)	2.46 (1.98)	3.40 (2.39)	2.14 (1.72)	1.68 (1.47)	2.04 (1.73)	2.91 (2.22)	2.72 (2.12)	1.87 (1.64)	1.66 (1.54)	1.94 (1.53)	2.55 (2.19)	2.43 (1.92)	2.48 (2.03)

* Standard deviations are presented in parentheses.

Note: Religion, labour force status and place of birth are dichotomous variables.
Religion is coded as follows: 1 = Catholic and 2 = other.
Labour force status is coded as follows: 1 = employed and 2 = unemployed.
Place of birth is coded as follows: 1 = born in Canada and 2 = born outside Canada.
Education is coded as follows: 1 = primary, 2 = secondary and 3 = post-secondary.

TABLE 3

Multiple Classification Analysis of Children Ever Born
for Ever-Married Women, Canada, 1981

Variable + Category	15 − 29 (Grand Mean = 1.01)				30+ (Grand Mean = 2.84)			
	Adjusted Mean	Beta	F-test	Significance Level	Adjusted Mean	Beta	F-Test	Significance Level
Ethnicity		.07	18.835	0.0000		0.05	37.136	0.000
British	0.04				0.03			
French	−0.10				−0.05			
German	0.00				0.06			
Italian	0.04				−0.36			
Jewish	−0.13				−0.25			
Ukrainian	−0.04				−0.14			
Other	0.09				0.11			
Birthplace		0.00	0.212	0.645		0.06	345.685	0.000
Native Born	0.00				0.07			
Foreign Born	0.01				−0.22			
Labour Force		0.26	1807.185	0.000		0.06	284.939	0.000
Employed	−0.23				−0.14			
Others	0.32				0.10			
Religion		0.01	2.640	0.104		0.08	457.414	0.00
Catholic	0.01				−0.20			
Others	−0.01				−0.15			
Education		0.15	359.468	0.000		0.17	1585.137	0.00
Primary	0.52				0.53			
Secondary	0.00				−0.21			
Post-Secondary	−0.25				−0.40			
Income		0.17	247.764	0.000		0.10	300.632	0.00
−50000 − 9999	0.12				0.12			
10000 − 19,999	−0.26				−0.31			
20000 − 29,000	−0.32				−0.49			
30,000+	−0.07				−0.37			
Age at First Marriage (Covariate)			373.018	0.000			4477.606	0.00

Variance Explained = R^2 = .19   Variance Explained = R^2 = 0.12

Multiple R = 0.430   Multiple R = 0.346

implies that the earlier relationship was not genuine and was contaminated by other factors. The MCA betas indicate the relative importance of the predictors in terms of their respective effects on fertility. The importance of variables included is not the same for younger and older cohorts. Labour force partic- ipation has the greatest effect on fertility for the younger age group (those under

30); while nativity and religion result in no significant effect. In contrast, fertility among the older age group is not at all affected by labour force participation but is influenced by nativity and religion as well as education and income. The MCA model explains 19 percent of the fertility variation for the younger cohort, compared to only 12 percent of the variation explained for the older age category.

Table 4 displays a comparison of partial regression coefficients for the additive and interaction model along with their levels of significance and standardized beta coefficients for the two age groups. The explained variance in the dependent variable for the two models can be seen at the bottom of the table. In addition, a formula is provided for an F ratio used to determine the significance of change in R^2 due to the addition of interaction terms to the additive model (Johnson 1979).

The key compositional variables, namely, education, labour force status and family income are all statistically significant. Their particular effects on family size are as expected. The negative effects of education and income imply that, as education and income increase, family size decreases. The relative importance of these variables is reflected in the observed beta coefficients. Among the younger age groups, in both models, family income and education have the greatest influence, whereas being Catholic and nativity have no influence on family size for these younger cohorts. The corresponding effect of religion and nativity on the older cohorts is significant.

The variable age at first marriage has an interesting effect on fertility. For older cohorts, the lower the age at first marriage, the higher the fertility, as would be expected. However, contrary to expectation, for the younger cohort, the higher the age at first marriage the higher the fertility.

The effect of ethnicity on fertility, based on the additive model, is weak and insignificant, particularly for the Germans in both the younger and older age groups, and for Italians and Ukrainians in the younger age groups. The precise interpretation of the regression coefficient for these groups is made in reference to the omitted category, the British. In other words, the German, Italian and Ukrainian ethnic groups are not significantly different from the British in the age group 15-29 whereas French and Jewish groups are significantly different from the British, at a 0.05 level of significance. The corresponding coefficients in the interaction model for the French and Jewish ethnic groups are similar for both age groups. However, for the German and Ukrainian ethnic groups, the coefficients are similar for the younger age cohorts, but not for the older groups. In other words, after accounting for the interaction effect of ethnicity and education, the effect of ethnicity on fertility is significant for Germans when considering the older age groups. This relationship was not significant for the Ukrainian group. The interaction effects on fertility are significant for both cohorts of the French and Jewish groups. They are also significant for the older German cohort. They are not significant for the Ukrainian group.

These interaction effects on fertility can be interpreted as structural. In other words, the significant interaction effects indicate that these ethnic groups suffer

TABLE 4

Multiple Regression of Children Ever Born on Ethnicity and Characteristics Variables:
Additive and Interaction Models, Canada, 1981

Independent Variables	Additive Model								Interaction Model							
	Age: 15-29				Age: 30+				Age: 15-29				Age: 30+			
	Slope	Beta	T-value	Sig. level	Slope	Beta	T-value	Sig. level	Slope	Beta	T-value	Sig. level	Slope	Beta	T-value	Sig. level
Age at Marriage	0.017	0.116	21.659	0.000	-0.059	-0.186	-64.546	0.000	0.017	0.118	22.041	0.000	-0.059	-0.188	-64.994	0.000
Education	-0.145	-0.186	-33.351	0.000	-0.190	-0.190	-60.833	0.000	-0.157	-0.201	-22.061	0.000	-0.156	-0.144	-30.363	0.000
L Force St.	0.423	0.197	31.241	0.000	0.253	0.060	18.206	0.000	0.424	0.198	31.352	0.000	0.249	0.059	17.966	0.000
Religion	-0.021	-0.110	-1.451	0.147	-0.337	-0.081	-20.488	0.000	-0.017	-0.008	-1.191	0.234	-0.337	-0.081	-20.507	0.000
Birthplace	-0.003	-0.001	-0.155	0.876	-0.258	-0.054	-16.196	0.000	-0.009	-0.003	-0.491	0.624	-0.254	-0.053	-15.838	0.000
Family Income	-0.0001	-0.207	-32.399	0.000	-0.0001	-0.076	-23.235	0.000	-0.0001	-0.208	-32.454	0.000	-0.0001	-0.076	-23.207	0.000
French	-0.143	-0.063	-8.454	0.000	-0.084	-0.018	-4.307	0.000	-0.479	-0.209	-8.543	0.000	-0.465	-0.099	-12.432	0.000
German	-0.013	-0.003	-0.512	0.609	0.018	0.004	1.310	0.190	0.004	0.002	0.075	0.940	0.179	0.039	5.425	0.190
Italian	-0.003	-0.001	-0.091	0.927	-0.413	-0.035	-10.826	0.000	-0.024	-0.004	-0.190	0.849	-0.277	-0.024	-4.133	0.000
Jewish	-0.129	-0.011	-2.013	0.044	-0.253	-0.014	-4.858	0.000	-1.221	-0.102	-3.512	0.000	-0.885	-0.049	-6.287	0.000
Ukrainian	-0.056	-0.008	-1.490	0.136	-0.185	-0.015	-5.091	0.000	-0.147	-0.021	-0.713	0.476	-0.072	-0.006	-0.881	0.379
Other	0.047	0.016	2.631	0.009	0.079	0.014	4.082	0.000	0.259	0.091	4.259	0.000	0.307	0.053	7.238	0.000
French × Education	—	—	—	—	—	—	—	—	0.064	0.154	6.341	0.000	-0.139	-0.124	-17.373	0.000
German × Education	—	—	—	—	—	—	—	—	-0.002	-0.004	-0.175	0.861	-0.036	-0.036	-5.038	0.000
Italian × Education	—	—	—	—	—	—	—	—	0.005	0.004	0.203	0.839	-0.017	-0.005	-0.876	0.381
Jewish × Education	—	—	—	—	—	—	—	—	0.186	0.093	3.211	0.0013	0.133	0.038	4.784	0.000
Ukrainian × Educa.	—	—	—	—	—	—	—	—	0.017	0.014	0.460	0.646	-0.019	-0.007	-1.033	0.302
Other × Education	—	—	—	—	—	—	—	—	-0.042	-0.079	-3.762	0.002	-0.050	-0.040	-5.626	0.000
Intercept	1.192	—	24.605	0.000	5.562	—	112.146	0.000	1.249	—	22.256	0.000	5.339	—	102.145	0.000

	Age Group: 15-29		Age Group: 30+	
	Additive Model	Interaction Model	Additive Model	Interaction Model
Explained Variance (R^2)	0.21	0.21	0.12	0.12
Difference in R^2		0.00		0.00

F-ratio[a] = 0.00 for both the age groups is not significant at 0.05 level of significance.

[a] A significance test of the change in R^2s due to the addition of variables to the additive model to obtain the interaction model:

$$F = \frac{(R^2I - R^2A)/(KI - KA)}{(I - R^2I)/(N-KI-1)} \qquad d.f. = KI - KA: N-KI-1$$

Where
R^2I = Percent of variance explained in an interaction model
R^2A = Percent of variance explained in an additive model
N = Total number of cases
K = Number of independent variables in the model

from feelings of insecurity and this may be taken as support for the minority group status hypothesis. However, overall, dummy variable interaction terms add nothing to the amount of variance explained by the additive model, and hence the application of the minority group status — insecurities hypothesis, beyond this limited set of ethnic groups, is in question. On the other hand, the strong effect of education and income provides convincing support for the characteristics-assimilation thesis.

Conclusions

The results derived from this analysis provide strong support for the characteristics-assimilation explanation. That is to say, the observed fertility differences between ethnic groups is largely a result of their differences in socio-economic conditions. This conclusion is particularly valid for younger women. Judging by the lack of conclusive results in support of the minority group status hypothesis, and the inadequacy of the characteristics hypothesis to explain a substantial amount of variation in family size, in future research it may be necessary to formulate an alternative theory of ethnic fertility differentials.

To conclude, we may argue that the relevance of ethnicity in fertility research, especially in Canada, is changing. To understand ethnic fertility behaviour, it is useful to recognize that there seems to be a strong overlap among the cultural, economic, social and psychological approaches. Failure to recognize this overlap in past research has led to inconsistent conclusions. Individual tastes are influenced by personal, psychological and group norms. Group norms are developed by groups to achieve their own objectives. On the other hand, a couple's motivations do not always follow either group taste, norms or calculations; what is rational for the group is not necessarily rational at the individual level.

5. ETHNICITY AND GEOGRAPHIC MOBILITY

Frank Trovato and Shiva S. Halli

The relationship between ethnicity and geographic mobility in Canada has received little attention from social demographers. This tendency is surprising given the multicultural nature of this nation and the growing importance of ethnicity and language in the sociopolitical context of Canadian society. In this paper, we seek to examine and compare the 1981 census levels and patterns of geographic mobility among seven major ethnic categories, and to test two competing hypotheses for the phenomenon of interest: the characteristics and ethnic effect explanations. We are interested in ascertaining whether there are ethnic and linguistic differentials in geographic mobility net of other social demographic variables. If there are differentials, how can they be explained? What is it about ethnicity and language that influence mobility propensities?

On a practical level, it is hoped that knowledge of ethnic differentials in mobility patterns will contribute toward a better understanding of ethnic continuity in the context of multiculturalism. A central assumption in this study is that differences in geographical relocation reflect ethnic group differentials in degree of community maintenance and viability. The more cohesive the ethnic community, the lower the propensity for its members to move away and hence the greater its continuity.

Ethnicity, Language and Geographic Mobility

The social demographic literature on ethnic and linguistic differentials in social demographic action encompasses two general hypotheses: The ethnic effect thesis posits that the observed variation in moving is due to ethnic variables, reflecting a wide range of normative and social psychological dimensions of ethnic social organization. In empirical research ethnic membership and language are often used as proxy measures of many unmeasurable aspects of ethnicity. The characteristics hypothesis (also referred to as the characteristics-assimilation thesis), explains observed differences in mobility on the basis of discrepancies in social demographic variables; it does not attribute any independent importance to ethnic factors. Rather, migration differentials are assumed to be a function of subgroup inequities in social economic variables such as education and income; and once discrepancies in social demographic variables are eliminated either through assimilation or statistical standardization, migration differences will disappear.

Concerning the characteristics explanation, Ritchey (1976) has reviewed the literature in this area of research, and with regard to Socio-Economic Status (SES) variables, he found that the rate of migration is generally directly related to socioeconomic status. Bogue (1959, 504), in his earlier review of the migration literature also affirmed that the lower the occupation rank of individuals, the lower the tendency to migrate. The underlying assumption concerning this relationship is that with higher levels of education and income, a person is more likely to have an occupation that predisposes him to a greater propensity to relocate due to a change in jobs and promotions. The better educated are usually more aware of opportunities for economic gains at places other than their areas of origin. The psychic and material costs of moving are generally lower for the more educated, thus facilitating migration and adjustment to new places.

Concerning the ethnic effect explanation, Ritchey (1976, 393) mentions the literature is rather scant. He reviewed a few studies pertaining to black-white differentials in the United States and concluded that in general: (1) minority groups have lower rates of migration and (2) there occurs a directional bias in the migration patterns of the minority group. The latter point refers to migration of group members toward large centres where other persons of the same ethnic group are located, suggesting that two important components of an ethnic effect on migration may be family ties and community affiliations. Research by Lansing and Mueller (1973) indicates support for this interpretation in that blacks are less migratory than whites in the southern region of the United States and they are more likely to want to remain at their place of origin vis-à-vis southern whites. "Blacks presumably, are more reluctant than whites to separate themselves from family through migration" (Ritchey 1976, 394).

Uhlenberg (1973) has shown that among certain groups social ties play an important role in migration considerations. He observed that during the period 1860-1920, very little out-migration from the southern part of the United States was noted for blacks even though many "push" factors at origin, and "pull" factors from the northern industrial centres were present. A similar phenomenon was documented for Japanese-Americans and residents of the Appalachian region, though under different circumstances. Uhlenburg (1973, 304) proposes the following explanation for such tendencies:

> The extent of integration into and dependence upon the local community
> is one social constraint on migration; the potential for assimilation into a

new community is another. This leads to the hypothesis that the stronger a person's ties with the local community and the more involved one is in a network of family ties the greater the constraints upon potential migration. Also the less cosmopolitan and less able to adjust to new environments, the less likely that motivation for migration will reach actual migration.

Later, he adds:

When migration is viewed within a social structure, dependence upon local community and potential for assimilation elsewhere appear as critical determinants ... Those with (1) deep roots in a community; (2) strong kinship ties in the local area; (3) large investments in the community and (4) an inability to assimilate easily into a new social environment are likely to resist migration (Uhlenburg 1973, 309).

Thus, ethnic and linguistic differentials in migration probably reflect group differences in the importance of family ties (Berardo 1967; Hendrix 1976), perceived ability to assimilate to place of destination (insecurity about conditions at destination), and degree of dependence to the local community (Toney 1976; Lansing and Mueller 1973; Kobrin and Goldscheider 1978; Kobrin and Speare 1983; Trovato 1988).

Clearly, the ethnic effect hypothesis subsumes many unmeasurable social, cultural and social psychological factors that may be associated with any given ethno-linguistic group (Trovato and Halli 1983; Mangalam and Schwarzweller 1970).

For many non-Anglo origin groups, the process of adjustment and integration into the new society involves the acquisition of a new language, and to some degree, the adoption of a new culture. It is not surprising therefore, to find that immigrants to Canada tend to form their own ethnic communities in large cities in order to be close to others of the same ethnic background and also to facilitate their economic adjustment in the host society (Balakrishnan 1978; Darroch and Marston 1984; Driedger and Church 1974; Duncan and Lieberson 1959; Macdonald and Macdonald 1964; Massey and Espana 1987; Trovato 1988).

The lower an ethnic group's degree of assimilation to the larger society, the lower the propensity of its members to migrate away from the ethnic community (Kobrin and Speare 1983), and the shorter will be the distance moved, should relocation occur. Some indirect evidence for this hypothesis may be found in the residential segregation literature in the United States and Canada (Darroch and Marston 1984; Duncan and Liberson 1959; Balakrishnan 1978): there is an inverse association between assimilation level and degree of residential segregation net of social class composition among ethnic groups. We propose that migration differentials among ethnic groups are partly explained by group differences in their levels of assimilation to the host society.

A number of authors have suggested that the viability of subcultural norms is highly dependent on the degree to which ethnic communities are institutionally complete (Darroch and Marston 1984; Trovato and Halli 1983; Driedger and

Church 1974; Breton 1973; Richmond 1969). In his study of Montreal ethnic communities, Breton discovered that the higher the degree of institutional completeness the greater the proportion of immigrants who have most social contacts with their "own" ethnic group members, and the greater the degree of "in-group" relations:

> [T]he ethnic group succeeds in holding its members' allegiance by preventing their contact with the native community. This is achieved by a process of substitution whereby ethnic institutions rather than those of the native community take hold in the immigrant's social life (Breton 1973, 58).

Some immigrant communities are more successful than others in maintaining institutional completeness (Reitz 1980). The greater the degree of institutional completeness, the greater the number of interactions by ethnic group members with others of the same group, and hence greater levels of ethnic consciousness. Highly associated with ethnic consciousness is the extent to which ethnic subcultural norms are observed and reinforced by its members (Kobrin and Goldscheider 1978, 57). There must be a strong correlation between institutional completeness, degree of ethnic solidarity, and maintenance of subcultural norms and values. The greater the degree of institutional completeness, therefore, the greater the extent to which ethnic members are tied to their community for jobs, family and social networks (Darroch and Marston 1984). In this regard Kobrin and Goldscheider (1978, 185) say that:

> Ethnic migration patterns are tied to the central question of ethnic identification which is reinforced at the family and community level by residential stability. The more ethnics change their place of residence, the weaker their ties not only to the local community and its institutions but also to the multiplicity of ethnic family relationships ... On the other hand extensive migration tends to break ethnic cohesiveness ... and may reduce the importance of ethnicity for migrants.

In the foregoing discussion of the ethnic effect hypothesis we proposed a number of mechanisms that may be subsumed under an independent effect of ethnicity on mobility. Ethnicity reflects many unmeasured sources of variation ranging from economic dependence on one's ethnic community and family ties to facility to assimilate. We also argued that to a large extent, the more institutionally complete the ethnic community, the greater its sense of ethnic continuity and its members would share low propensities to leave it.

We have no way of measuring all these effects directly because the data available to us is limited in the number of pertinent variables. Ideally, we would have liked to have measures of individuals' sense of attachment and dependence on their communities, their fluency in the official languages, their sense of insecurity about moving and other individual level characteristics. Also, it would be desirable to have community level measures such as degree of institutional completeness. Unfortunately, such a data set does not exist and we can only confine our analysis to the few variables available. In order to better ascertain the relative importance of ethnic factors on the propensity to relocate, we include language use and ethnic affiliation in our statistical analysis of the data. Both variables are interrelated, but to some extent, language use may be viewed as a proxy for subcultural effects such as extent of language maintenance, hence ethnic identification; ethnic origin may be considered as a residual factor subsuming all the sources of variation discussed earlier (e.g., the influence of institutional completeness). Our statistical methodology allows us to separate the independent effects of these two variables and their relative importance in explaining the dependent variable.

Hypotheses, Data and Methods

We test three hypotheses. The first two derive from the ethnic effect thesis; the third is a derivative of the characteristics-assimilation explanation.

1. Groups known to possess a relatively high level of ethnic cohesion, as reflected in their high degrees of institutional completeness, will demonstrate relatively low propensities to move or to make long distance moves such as interprovincial migration.
2. The greater an ethnic group's level of assimilation to the English language, the greater the group's propensities to change residence and to make long distance moves of the interprovincial type.
3. The effect of socioeconomic variables on mobility is positive; that is, the higher the level of completed education, the higher the tendency to move and to experience long distance migration.

The data for this analysis are taken from the 1981 Public Use Sample Tapes of the Canadian census. The units of analysis are individuals aged 20 and older classified by ethnic origin (British, French, German, Italian, Jewish, Ukrainian and Others), language of the home (English, French, Other), age (20-29, 30 +), and education (primary, secondary, post-secondary). Persons who entered Canada within the period 1976 to 1981 were deleted from the subsample because they could not, by the census definition, be considered as internal migrants, as their residence in 1976 was outside Canada.

The dependent variable in this analysis is based on the five-year mobility question in the census, which is a contrast of one's residence in 1976 with one's residence at the time of the 1981 Census. The variable is polytomous consisting of five categories: (1) non-movers (NM); (2) movers within the same census subdivision (MSCSD); (3) movers within the same census division (MSCD); (4) movers within the same province (MSP); (5) movers to a different province (MDP). In a crude sense, this classification reflects a measure of distance travelled for those who experienced relocation within the census interval, 1976-81.

Of the groups selected for this study, our first hypothesis predicts that Italians, Jews, French and Ukrainians would demonstrate relatively low propensities to change residence because these groups are known to possess high levels of ethnic cohesion and institutional completeness. We assume that their members share strong attachments to their ethnic communities. Members of these ethnic groups would move short distances if they do change residence. That is, given the necessity to move, their option would be to move in the same city as their ethnic community and in the same province rather than to a different province. The hypothesis also predicts that the British and the Germans would be more likely to move interprovincially. These two groups have been observed by researchers to be relatively more migratory than the other groups selected for this analysis (Trovato and Halli 1983). The Germans are known to have assimilated easily into Canadian society and therefore, we assume they are less insecure than those in other groups about moving to new places. Since the British represent the dominant sociocultural group in Canada, it is not surprising that they have relatively high migration levels in general (George 1970; Stone 1974).

The second hypothesis predicts that these who speak an ''Other'' language or French in their homes will demonstrate relatively low odds of moving, and that any relocation would be confined largely to within the same province. This hypothesis calls for an interaction effect of ethnicity with language use. For example, we wish to identify differences in mobility within ethnic groups on the basis of whether the language spoken in the home is English, French or ''Other.'' We anticipate that for any ethnic group, English language will be associated with increased odds of changing residence and long distance migration (interprovincial).

Hypothesis number three has been generally supported in previousu research and does not require further elaboration. The variable education is used as a proxy for socioeconomic status.

The data analysis consists of an examination of several crosstabulations followed by a multivariate logit analysis of the propensity to move during the census interval, 1976-1981. We restrict our statistical observations to only four predictor variables — age, education, ethnicity and language of the home — because larger tabulations required for the logit analysis contained many zero cells once the table was expanded to higher dimensions. Age is used as a demographic control variable since it is highly associated with mobility (Ritchey 1976).

Crosstabular Analysis

Table 1 displays a bivariate tabulation involving type of move and ethnicity. It is important to notice that in the recent census the categories of the dependent variable are not exactly the same as those included in the 1971 Public Use Sample Tapes; but they are highly comparable and should not pose any major limitation in the interpretation and comparison of results over time.

TABLE 1

Type of Move by Ethnicity in Canada, 1976-81

Type of Move		British	French	German	Italian	Jewish	Ukrainian	Other	Total
					ETHNIC GROUP				
NM	N	60,449	42,534	7,988	5,950	1,827	4,175	19,737	142,660
	%	50.8	51.8	52.0	61.7	55.4	56.1	48.4	51.4
MSCSD	N	30,678	22,178	3,887	2,545	1,025	1,803	12,093	74,209
	%	25.8	27.0	25.3	26.4	31.1	24.2	29.7	26.7
MSCD	N	6,165	4,794	844	386	123	137	2,231	14,860
	%	5.2	5.8	5.5	4.0	3.7	4.3	5.5	5.4
MSP	N	13,254	10,447	1,629	593	145	655	4,149	30,872
	%	11.1	12.7	10.6	6.1	4.4	8.8	10.2	11.1
MDP	N	8,486	2,194	1,025	175	176	486	2,539	15,081
	%	7.1	2.7	6.7	1.8	5.3	6.5	6.2	5.4
TOTAL	N	119,032	82,147	15,373	9,649	3,296	7,436	40,749	277,682
	%	100.0	100.0	100.0	100.0	100.0	100.0	100.0	100.0

Note: In this and subsequent tables, the categories of type of move are as follows: NM = Nonmovers; MSCSD = Movers within the same census subdivision; MSCD = Movers within the same census division; MSP = movers within the same province; MDP = Movers to a different province.

As we discovered in an earlier study (Trovato and Halli 1983), Italians (62 percent), Jews (55 percent), and Ukrainians (56 percent) are over-represented in the non-mover category. In terms of interprovincial migration, the British (7.1 percent), the Germans (6.7 percent) and the Ukrainians (6.5 percent) are most migratory. As expected, the French (12.7 percent) are most likely to move within the same province, undoubtedly in Quebec.

As a follow-up to Table 1, we attempted to ascertain whether nativity is an important conditioning variable in these relationships. Excluding a few minor exceptions, the inclusion of this variable did not confound the original relationship between ethnicity and mobility reported in Table 1.

With regard to language, Table 2 shows that the pattern of mobility conforms to our expectations: the English are the most mobile. Only 50 percent of those who speak English in the home did not change residence as compared to 53 and 60 percent of the French and "Others," respectively. The English are also more likely to change province.

A further extension of the crosstabular analysis was executed by computing Chi-square tests of significance associated with six alternative tabulations involving mobility, ethnicity and a third variable (e.g., education, age, nativity, language, etc.). Due to the large samples, all the values of Chi-square were substantial and highly significant, denoting that mobility may not be statistically independent of ethnicity. The next section of the analysis explores this aspect with greater rigour.

TABLE 2

Type of Move by Language of the Home in Canada, 1976-81.

Type of Move		English	French	Other	Total
		\multicolumn{4}{c}{Language of the Home}			
NM	N	92,089	38,971	11,600	142,660
	%	49.9	52.7	60.3	51.4
MSCSD	N	49,129	19,806	5,274	74,209
	%	26.6	26.8	27.4	26.7
MSCD	N	9,741	4,336	783	14,860
	%	5.3	5.8	4.0	5.3
MSP	N	20,204	9,616	1,052	30,872
	%	10.9	13.0	5.5	11.1
MDP	N	13,356	1,191	534	15,081
	%	7.2	1.6	2.7	5.4
Total	N	184,519	73,920	19,243	277,682
	%	66.45	26.6	6.9	100

Multivariate Logit Analysis

In Table 3, we test a number of alternative equations (models) by fitting them to a five dimensional crosstabulation involving mobility, education, age, language and ethnicity. For the purpose of hypothesis testing, model 2 reflects the ethnic-language effect equation; that is, both ethnicity and language have independent effects on mobility net of age and education. This model is analogous to a multiple regression equation with four main effects. If this emerges as the best fitting model, the implication would be that both ethnicity and language, as well as characteristics variables (age and education) are important predictors of relocation.

Model 18 represents a test of the characteristics hypothesis, which specifies only age and education as the predictors of mobility. Should this equation turn out to be the best fit to the data, the substantive interpretation would be that only characteristics variables, not language or ethnicity, explain variation in the dependent variable. Models number 6, 7 and 8 reflect two-variable equations: ethnicity and education, ethnicity and language, and ethnicity and age, respectively. None of these equations emerged as best fitting models. A number of other models in Table 3 contain interaction terms. For example, number 22 includes the interaction of ethnicity with language as well as all lower-order main effects.

Judging from the R^2 analogue measure and the L^2 statistic (the log-likelihood Chi-square), models 12 and 22 provide the best fit to our data, with 95 percent variance explained in mobility propensities. Since model 22 has the lowest L^2 value and the lowest number of degrees of freedom, it was decided to accept it as the best fitting equation.

The bottom panel in Table 3 shows a decomposition of model 22. Although all the terms in this equation are statistically significant, it is clear that age is the most important predictor, with a 60 percent proportionate reduction in error (PRE) in our dependent variable. Education is also quite important with a PRE of 22 percent. Ethnicity and the interaction term explain a small proportion of variance in mobility propensities (3 and 2 percent, respectively), but language shows a modest contribution of 13 percent. Thus, of the two ethnic variables, language is clearly the most important.

Concerning the general explanations of ethnic effect and characteristics-assimilation, these results provide strong support for the characteristics thesis, but only weak support for the ethnic effect perspective. But, the fact that language emerged as an important determinant of mobility, is indicative that sociocultural effects are relevant in explaining differences in the propensity to relocate. Insofar as language is an important dimension of ethnicity, this is an important finding.

From the intercepts in Table 4, it is evident that there is a strong tendency not to change residence within the 1976-81 intercensal period. If mobility does

TABLE 3

Specified Logit Models for the Analysis of Mobility
Propensities, Canada 1976-1981

	Model	D.F.	L^2	R^2 Analogue
1	M, EDLA (baseline)	500	36,223.77	–
2	ME, EDLA	476	32,490.18	.058
3	MD, EDLA	492	27,216.80	.236
4	ML, EDLA	492	30,794.19	.136
5	MA, EDLA	496	11,432.91	.680
6	ME, MD, EDLA	468	23,900.13	.290
7	ME, ML, EDLA	468	29,661.42	.125
8	ME, MA, EDLA	472	7,617.82	.770
9	ME, MDL, EDLA	444	21,617.69	.320
10	ME, MDA, EDLA	456	3,726.53	.880
11	ME, MDL, EDLA	444	21,617.69	.327
12	ME, ML, MDA, EDLA	448	1,711.13	.950
13	MED, EDLA	420	23,639.22	.220
14	ML, MED, EDLA	412	21,551.08	.278
15	MEL, EDLA	420	28,923.51	.049
16	ML, MEA, EDLA	440	4,934.71	.845
17	MD, MEA, EDLA	440	3,775.31	.880
18	MD, MA, EDLA	488	7,522.15	.780
19	MD, ML, EDLA	484	22,949.44	.345
20	MD, ML, MA, EDLA	480	3,268.2	.900
21	MA, ME, ML, MD, EDLA	444	2,193.50	.930
22	MA, ME, ML, MD, MEL, EDLA	408	1,588.59	.950
23	ME, ML, MD, EDLA	460	21,807.23	.346

Decomposition of Variance for Model 22

Effect Due To:	L^2	D.F.	P	PRE
Age: $(m_{21}\text{-}M_{23})$	19,613.73	16	$<.01$	.60
Education: $(m_4\text{-}m_{19})$	7,344.75	8	$<.01$	.22
Ethnicity: $(m_{20}\text{-}m_{21})$	1,074.70	36	$<.01$	.03
Language: $(m_{18}\text{-}m_{20})$	4,267.36	4	$<.01$	.13
Ethnicity $\times$ Language: $(m_{21}\text{-}m_{22})$	604.91	36	$<.01$	.02
TOTAL	32,300.54			1.00

Notes: R^2 ANALOGUE $= \dfrac{\text{Alternate Model/D.F.} - \text{Baseline Model/D.F.}}{\text{Baseline Model/D.F.}}$

PRE = Proportion Reduction in Error
m = Model (e.g., m_{19} = Model$_{19}$)
M = The Mobility Variable, E = Ethnicity, D = Education, L = Language, A = Age

take place, people are overwhelmingly predisposed to move within the same census subdivision (MSCSD), thus a short distance away from their place of original residence. The parameter values tend to get smaller for long distance moves such as between MSCDS and MDPS, but not in a linear fashion, as demonstrated by the increased value of the parameter corresponding to moving within the same province (MSP).

TABLE 4

Logit Parameters for Model 22 (Multiplicative Estimates)

EFFECTS	Mobility				
	NM	MSCSD	MSCD	MSP	MDP
Intercepts	3.173	2.495	0.479	0.783	0.288
ETHNICITY					
British	0.826	0.921	0.898	1.180	1.241
French	0.891	1.104	1.290	1.012	0.779
German	0.998	0.859	0.898	1.179	1.103
Italian	1.322	1.256	0.979	1.037	0.593
Jewish	1.189	1.469	1.087	0.590	0.892
Ukranian	1.134	0.593	0.904	1.121	1.467
Other	0.764	1.046	0.999	1.036	1.209
EDUCATION					
Primary	1.370	1.142	1.076	0.801	0.742
Secondary	0.849	0.973	1.047	0.979	1.182
Post-secondary	0.860	0.900	0.888	1.275	1.141
LANGUAGE					
English	0.896	0.915	0.807	0.947	1.592
French	0.908	0.965	1.247	1.386	0.660
Other	1.230	1.132	0.994	0.761	0.949
AGE					
15-29	0.592	1.101	1.102	1.142	1.210
30+	1.676	0.909	0.908	0.875	0.827
LANGUAGE *ETHNICITY					
ENGLISH					
British	1.166	0.949	1.102	0.958	0.857
French	0.836	0.820	0.798	1.902	1.674
German	0.924	1.014	1.182	0.958	0.943
Italian	0.978	0.987	1.072	1.051	0.919
Jewish	1.122	0.937	0.835	0.938	1.214
Ukrainian	0.896	1.551	1.013	0.924	0.769
Other	1.129	0.884	1.063	1.095	0.862

EFFECTS		Mobility			
	NM	MSCSD	MSCD	MSP	MDP
Intercepts	3.173	2.495	0.479	0.783	0.288
FRENCH					
British	1.033	1.051	0.958	1.058	0.909
French	1.367	0.963	0.703	1.163	0.929
German	1.046	1.422	0.846	0.959	0.828
Italian	0.874	1.017	0.786	1.024	1.400
Jewish	0.918	1.117	1.475	1.004	0.659
Ukrainian	0.883	0.567	1.434	0.960	1.451
Other	0.955	1.080	1.056	0.859	1.068
OTHER					
British	0.831	1.003	0.948	0.987	1.283
French	0.875	1.266	1.783	0.782	0.643
German	1.034	0.694	1.000	1.089	1.280
Italian	1.170	0.997	1.188	0.929	0.777
Jewish	0.971	0.955	0.812	1.062	1.251
Ukrainian	1.264	1.138	0.689	1.127	0.896
Other	0.927	1.048	0.891	1.063	1.086

Regarding the ethnic parameters, we have some support for our first hypothesis in that Italians, Jewish and Ukrainians are more resistant to a change in residence. For Italians and Jews, their most frequent type of mobility is intracity (MSCSD), thus reflecting an overall preference to confine their relocation tendencies to short distances in the vicinity of their communities of origin. The French are more inclined to move within the same census division (MSCD), but surprisingly, they do not predominate in moves within the same province (MSP). In fact, it is the British, the Germans and the Ukrainians who share increased odds of relocation within the same province (MSP). The Ukrainians, the British, and "Other," in that order are more likely to make interprovincial migrations than the remaining ethnicities in this analysis. We had anticipated that the British and the Germans would predominate in interprovincial migration.

The effect of education on geographic mobility is inverse, but it is not monotonic. While primary education is clearly associated with short distance moves, secondary school education increases the odds of interprovincial migration. Persons with post-secondary education lead in intraprovincial moves.

The pattern of effects for the language variable is consistent with the notion that "Other" linguistic groups in Canada are not as mobile as the English or the French. If they move, their tendency is to change residence within the same census subdivision, or short distance moves (MSCSD). In contrast to our earlier observation for French ethnicity, French language is now associated with an increased propensity to move within the same census district and within the same province. The English share a relatively greater likelihood of interprovincial migration.

With respect to age, younger persons are more mobile than persons above the age of 30 across all categories, and they are more likely to make long distance migrations of the interprovincial type.

The effect of language assimilation on geographic mobility is tested by the interaction term of language with ethnicity. If we examine the non-movers class (NM), we note that with the exception of Jews and "Other" ethnic groups, having English as a home language does not increase the odds of not moving which means that our hypothesis is partly supported. To further support the thesis of assimilation we need to demonstrate that in regard to interprovincial migration knowledge of the English language increases the odds. The evidence is not supportive of this notion. The only exception is the French who show that having English as the language of the home enhances propensities to change province. Beyond this ethnic group, the Jews come close to supporting the hypothesis in that the odds of changing province for Jews who speak English in the home are 1.21, while they are 1.25 for those who speak an "Other" language. It is interesting to note that for the "Other" and Ukrainian ethnic groups, the lowest odds of long distance moves is associated with English home language. Clearly, linguistic assimilation is not a major factor in the case of interprovincial migration propensities.

Discussion

To a large extent the situation concerning ethnicity and geographic mobility has not changed markedly since the 1966-71 intercensal period analysed by Trovato and Halli (1983). That is, ethnic groups found to be the most resistant to moving in the 1966-71 period, are also less inclined to do so in the 1976-81 censal interval, namely, Italians, Jews and Ukrainians. Although the Germans and the British were the most mobile interprovincially during 1966-71, in the most recent period the Ukrainians, along with the British and "Other" ethnic origins share the highest likelihood of relocating interprovincially (long distance moves). The fact that the Urkainians in 1976-81 are more inclined to change province in relation to the British may reflect a genuine change in this ethnic group's orientation to long distance migration, as in the 1966-71 period they were significantly below the British in the propensity for long distance migration. The underlying mechanisms for this reversal is a question worth pursuing in subsequent research. Perhaps an increasing number of Ukrainians are losing their sense of ethnic belonging; or perhaps their mobility may be largely confined to and from Ukrainian ethnic communities, which would in such a case pose no evidence of a decline in the importance of their ethnicity.

In the case of the French, our current results are similar to those derived in our analysis of the 1971 Census. That is, members of this ethnic-linguistic group tend to relocate mostly within their province of origin, presumably mostly in

Quebec; this effect emerged more clearly in the case of the language variable in our statistical analysis.

Concerning the ethnic effect and characteristics-assimilation explanations, we found strong support for the importance of characteristic variables and only weak support for the ethnic effect thesis, as ethnicity *per se* is relatively unimportant. This result implies that by and large, differentials in mobility are largely due to discrepancies in age composition and education. Language is a more relevant explanatory variable of mobility propensities than is ethnicity. To the extent that language and ethnicity are closely related, however, this result provides evidence for the importance of sociocultural factors in geographic mobility. We found support for the notion that French people tend to move mostly in Quebec and not so much to other parts of Canada. Also, we discovered that Italians and Jews are predominantly non-mobile and that for these groups, the tendency to make interprovincial migrations is quite low. We propose that this relationship is partly a function of the high degrees of ethnic community cohesiveness (Trovato and Jarvis 1986) and institutional completeness characterizing these groups. We had anticipated that similar tendencies would prevail among the Ukrainians. To some extent this notion is supported in that Ukrainians share a strong preference not to move, but we also found that this group leads (next to ''Others'') in interprovincial migration, suggesting that perhaps community ties may be eroding for some members of this ethnic group. This is only a speculative conclusion as we do not have the necessary data to test this idea adequately. We propose further inquiry on this question.

Concerning linguistic assimilation to the English, our results can only provide weak support for the idea that linguistic assimilation leads to increased chances of geographic mobility. First, our operationalization of this effect explains a very small amount of variance in mobility; secondly, in the case of long distance moves, English language within ethnic groups is not generally associated with increased odds. Only in the case of non-moving is there some support for the hypothesis in that within categories of ethnicity, English language is not generally associated with increased odds. Therefore, the notion that loss of ethnic identification, as operationalized by language transfer to English, may not be very pertinent in explaining mobility differentials. Clearly, a better operationalization of ethnic identification is needed before any definitive conclusions on this topic are possible.

In our earlier paper based on 1966-71 data (Trovato and Halli 1983), we argued that a comprehensive theory of ethnicity and migration is needed to better comprehend the mechanisms that underlie the so-called ethnic effect. The present investigation suggests that language is a more important factor than ethnicity *per se*. In future research we will need to reformulate the social demographic literature accordingly to include language as an important determinant of migration differentials. Language is perhaps a more sensitive index of ''ethnic effects'' than is ethnicity itself. If this is so, we will need to uncover in a more direct manner whether language effects are a reflection of group norms and values in relation to moving.

Future research in this area of study would benefit by the integration of language factors with emergent ethnicity factors (Yancey et al. 1976; Yinger 1985). That is, in a historical sense the tendency for ethnic groups to form viable ethnic communities in certain cities in the New World was largely due to the geographic location of large cities, and once the community became established in such "favoured" cities, the necessity to move away for social or economic reasons became minimal. In some cases, a city's "structural conditions," such as its location and its economic endowments, induce sociocultural groups to settle there permanently and to develop institutionally complete ethnic communities. This fact may, in turn, serve to reduce migration tendencies among ethnic members. This structuralist explanation complements the language effects hypothesis insofar that the more cohesive and institutionally complete the group the greater its ability to maintain its own language and unique culture, which may serve to provide members with few incentives to change residence, and at the same time offer strong inducements to stay in the ethnic community.

6. IMMIGRANT MORTALITY TRENDS AND DIFFERENTIALS[1]

Frank Trovato

Canadian demography does not possess an established tradition of migrant mortality studies. A great deal of attention, however, has been devoted to the social and economic adjustment of immigrants (Richmond 1967; Richmond and Kalbach 1980). What is needed is an eventual integration of migrant adjustment processes in Canada with their health status, morbidity and mortality patterns.

The paucity of research in this area of inquiry is partly associated with data accessibility and quality issues. First, there are a limited number of social demographic variables coded on the death certificate (age, sex, marital status, place of birth, cause of death). Secondly, there is considerable fluctuation in the extent to which nativity (country of birth) has been coded over the years. While this information was virtually fully complete during the early fifties, only 2 to 3 percent of the death certificates contained the decedent's country of birth for the 1960-63 period. This situation has been rectified since 1970, such that there is now virtually complete reporting of nativity on the official death records (Trovato 1985).

While this is a welcome change, the ethnic origin variable has followed a rather erratic pattern of completeness; and since 1973, it has been discontinued altogether (with the exception of Yukon and Northwest Territories). This imposes serious limitations for migrant mortality studies because it impedes analysis of native-born descendents of foreign parents in Canada. This is further complicated by extreme incompleteness in the recording of parents' place of birth on the decedent's death certificate.

This chapter provides a summary of research findings concerning immigrant mortality in Canada. Relevant work from other immigrant societies (Australia, England and Wales, France, and the United States) are also included in this survey of the literature. To a large extent foreigners in host nations experience common process and conditions that bear significantly on their adjustment and integration to their new society. The emphasis throughout most of this review is on the patterns of mortality differences between foreigners, their countries of origin and host society. In the closing segments of this review, I propose some directions for future research.

Typology of Research Designs Employed in the Analysis of Migrant Mortality

Most researchers in the literature are interested in determining the importance of genetic predisposition in the etiology of disease, the role of environment, and how self-selection may affect migrant mortality patterns (Marmot et al. 1983; 1984a; Kasl and Berkman 1985; Kmet 1970; Haenszel 1961; 1975; Fraumeni 1975; Haenszel and Kurihara 1968; Staszewski 1976; Staszewski and Haenszel 1965; Trovato 1985). The major difficulty of such studies lies in the inability of existing data and statistical applications to separate the independent effects of genetics, environment, selection and migration.

Table 1 displays 13 typical models for the analysis of migrant mortality patterns and differentials. Most applications in the literature focus on contrasting the immigrants (I), their country of origin (O), and the host country (H). In the first set of models in Table I, the immigrant population possesses lower death rates from some particular disease (or general mortality) relative to the host society. The origin population of the immigrants is either comparable or lower in risk vis-à-vis the immigrants' adoptive country.

The situation in (A) may be interpreted as a reflection of a genetic predisposition for low risk among immigrants and their national population. But full acceptance of this inference is hampered by several possible confounding factors. For example, immigrants may have low risk of disease as a function of early exposure to their environment of origin prior to migration. Thus age at immigration and length of residency in the host nation would be required information to control for this competing explanation. Moreover, the observed result in (A) may be an outcome due to foreigners not being exposed to the same set of environmental conditions prevailing in the receiving population. One could also surmise that the process of migration itself has had no deleterious effects on the health of migrants.

To a large extent, the same set of confounding sources are also characteristic of models (B), (C) and (D). For instance, the scenario in (B) is consistent with a "negative assimilation" experience (Trovato 1985) in the sense that foreigners seem to lose their superiority, as reflected in the lower risk in their society of origin, and "move" towards the higher risks of death that characterize the adoptive population. An alternative explanation (and it is a plausible one), is that migrants are negatively selected in both their demographic characteristics and their health status. Alternatively, it may also be hypothesized that the loss of

TABLE 1

Typology of Research Designs in Migrant Mortality Studies

CONDITION 1: Immigrant Population has lower Mortality Levels than the Host Population

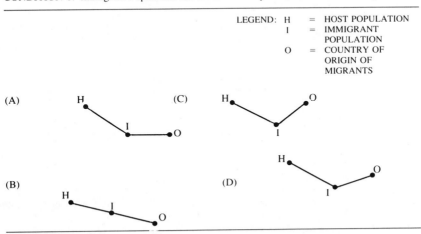

CONDITION 2: Immigrant Population has Higher Mortality Levels than the Host Population

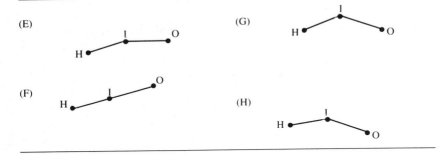

Explanations of Models

(A) = Genetic predisposition among origin and immigrant populations for lower relative risk of disease vis-à-vis the host population.

(B) = Negative assimilation of immigrant population toward higher risk of disease vis-à-vis the host population.

(C) = Positive selection of immigrants vis-à-vis origin population (and positive migration experience vis-à-vis host population?).

(D) = Variant of (C).

(E) = Genetic predisposition among origin and immigrant populations for higher relative risk of disease vis-à-vis the host population.

Models of Equality

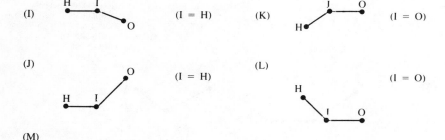

(I)	H I — O	(I = H)	(K) H — J — O (I = O)
(J)	O — H I	(I = H)	(L) H — I — O (I = O)
(M)	H — I — O	(I = O = H)	

(F) = Positive assimilation of immigrant population towards lower risk of mortality in the host population.

(G) = Negative selection of immigrants vis-à-vis origin population (and negative migration experience vis-à-vis host population?).

(H) = Variant of (G).

(I) = Complete negative assimilation to the risk level of host population.

(J) = Complete positive assimilation to the risk level of host population.

(K) = (E).

(L) = (A).

(M) = Model of no difference among the three populations.

their initial advantage is attributable to the life stresses associated with the migration experience itself.

The likelihood of positive selection among the foreign-born is exemplified in (C) and (D). But it is not certain whether the advantage possessed by immigrants represents health improvements as a consequence of immigration to a new society; and the possibility of positive selection and the migration experience interacting to diminish risk among immigrants cannot be discounted altogether.

The set of models under condition two denote situations characterized by higher death rates among immigrants than their host population. Model (E) is the compliment of (A); it suggests a genetic predisposition for elevated risk among the country of origin and its antipodes. A competing explanation would be that early exposure to deleterious "agents" in the environment of the origin country is "carried" by immigrants into the New World, hence migrants experience increased chances of mortality.

Model (F) represents the opposite to (B). In this case migrants may be viewed as assimilating the relatively low risk of death in the host population. The possibility of positive selection of foreigners cannot be easily rejected, however. It may be that those elements who left the country of origin are a select group in their demographic and health characteristics thus placing movers into an intermediate risk position vis-à-vis the receiving and origin countries.

The scenarios in (G) and (H), view immigrants as possessing increased odds of death in relation to both origin and host populations. Negative selection may be responsible for these effects, but the experience of migration, either by itself (as a stressful process), or in combination with negative selection, are also feasible hypotheses.

Five models in Table 1 depict equal risks among immigrants and host society ((I) and (J)), and immigrants with their origin nation ((K) and (L)). Model (M) is a perfect equality situation and would be of limited substantive utility. Notice that (K) and (L) are equivalent to (E) and (A), therefore will not be discussed further.

Model (K) may be referred to as a "complete negative assimilation" model if we assume that at some earlier point in time migrants had a risk of death that was similar to their country of origin (hence they had lower odds of mortality than the receiving society). Negative selection may be a confounding factor here in that migrants may have been originally negatively selected out of their population of origin.

We may term (J) a "complete positive assimilation model." Migrants are assumed to have started at a less advantaged position and eventually decrease their risk to the level of their adoptive country. However, one would need to control for the possible confounding effects of positive selection before accepting these postulated linkages.

The problems identified in all of the above models are confounded further by the lack of a control variable to monitor the effects of time, or migrants' length of exposure to the environments of the countries of origin and destination respectively. The effects of exposure to the host environment may be heightened when immigrants enter the country at an early age as opposed to when they migrate at more advanced ages, which would mean that most of their "exposure" had been in their homeland and not in their receiving society.

Length of residency and age at immigration (at least one of these variables is needed to derive the other) are essential control variables. Unfortunately, Canadian death records do not provide such information. The only country that codes such data routinely (to the knowledge of this author) is Australia (see Stenhause and McCall 1970; McMichael et al. 1980).

While knowledge of migants' age at immigration and length of residence in the adoptive country would enhance our capacity to make meaningful inferences, it is important to indicate that there are other related issues worth mentioning. A comprehensive analysis of foreigners' mortality experience would require knowledge of changing life circumstances after immigration, changing health habits, the extent of social, economic and psychological adaptation, and how the immigrant community conditions or "buffers" such processes by serving as a source of social support mechanisms (Marmot and Syme 1976; Trovato 1986; Trovato and Jarvis 1986).

Migrant Studies in Canada

Researchers in Canada have tended to confine their investigations to mortality in the total population without specific attention to national origin as a predictor or conditioning variable. Two Canadian studies are of particular interest to this review as they focus directly on the subject of immigrant mortality in Canada: Trovato (1983; 1985) and Kliewer (1979).

Kliewer's main findings are mostly consistent with models (B) and (F) in Table 1. Published mortality data were used to investigate factors that influence change in life expectancy at age 40 among immigrants in Canada and Australia. Although data for the years 1921 to 1950 are presented, the study concentrates primarily on the year 1941. The results suggest that the foreign-born generally experienced a more favourable level of longevity than the native-born population in Canada.

A comparison of mortality levels of the immigrants' countries of origin with the host country and the immigrants' life expectancies suggests that persons migrating from places where life expectancy was below Canada, actually improved their expectation of life and tended to approximate the levels of the Canadian-born population. In the case where immigrants emigrated from nations which showed a higher life expectancy than Canada, the migrants' levels at age 40 were found to be below the origin country and somewhat similar to Canada's average. Thus it seems that on one occasion immigrants improve their chances of living, while in the others they suffer a decline in their average length of life in relation to origin and host societies.

This "shifting" phenomenon does not necessarily constitute an assimilation of mortality patterns between foreign and native populations. Kliewer did not consider the possibility that migrants form a select group (Lee 1966). Therefore, as discussed earlier, the fact that immigrants appear to have average levels of mortality, which vary from their origin's population, may be due to a selection effect. The apparent shift toward a gain in life expectancy in the host country may be a function of positive selection on the part of the immigrants and not due to assimilation. Conversely, the observation that foreigners from countries of relatively high levels of longevity actually appear to decline in converging with the host country — but never decline below the host population — may actually reflect negative selection in the country of origin. By negative, I mean a process by which persons subject to poorer health are selected out. However, this kind of selectivity is very rare. In fact, due to the restrictive nature of immigrant laws and screening processes in recent decades, positive selection of immigrants is highly probable.

Kliewer's research suggests that: (a) migrants may reflect a select group which in turn exemplify a superior mortality experience; (b) there may be an assimilative phenomenon which operates upwardly or downwardly in aligning life expectation of immigrants with the indigenous host population. In the latter case, however, it seems more feasible to assume that if assimilation does indeed occur among immigrants, a convergence towards a host society with a superior life expectancy would seem reasonable as individuals improve their life conditions, but a trend in the opposite direction, from a group of foreigners who upon arrival initiate their experience possessing a more favourable life expectancy than the host population, would seem less feasible.

Since Kliewer's analysis involved a time frame when Canada was still largely a "pioneer" society, it would not be inconceivable that some groups originating from "advantaged" places might suffer elevated risk once confronted with the harsh environment of a largely "frontier" society. Early studies in the United States show evidence that conforms to this interpretation (e.g., Dublin and Baker 1920; Lombard and Doering 1929; Calabresi 1945; Buechley 1950; Jacobson 1963).

Trovato (1983; 1985) confined his analysis to the census periods between 1951 and 1971 to investigate mortality differences, general and cause-specific (four broad causes: neoplasms, cardiovascular, accidents-violence and all other), among several sociocultural groups in Canada (British native-born; British foreign-born; French native-born; Native Indians, Residual native-born, Other European foreign born; United States immigrants, and Other foreign-born). Due to numerous data problems (some of which were identified in the opening part of this paper), the only group that satisfies the minimum conditions in Table 1 to study the relative risk immigrants in relation to country of origin and destination is the British.

When the broad classification native-born and foreign-born was applied to study general mortality differences, crude rates for immigrants were at least twice as high as the host population. However, once differences in age composition were removed through the application of appropriate methodologies, it was found that being a foreigner tended to decrease slightly one's relative odds of death in 1951, but in 1964 and 1971, the situation reversed in favour of the native-born.

Concerning differences in causes of death, Table 2 shows age standardized death rates due to four broad causes of death among the native-born and foreign-born populations during three periods, 1951, 1964, and 1971. Among males, immigrants show a higher incidence of neoplasms mortality in 1951 and 1971. The foreign-born have always shared a lower risk of cardiovascular related deaths. In the case of accidents-violence, the rates were higher among foreigners in 1951 and 1964, but in 1971, they had a lower risk. With respect to "other causes," immigrant men in Canada have relatively lower levels of mortality in relation to the native born.

The situation for females is generally similar: foreigners have tended to die less from "all other" causes, more from accidents-violence complications, and with the exception of the 1964 period, they had lower odds related to neoplasms. The main difference lies in connection with cardiovascular mortality. In contrast to native-born women, the immigrant females suffered higher rates in 1951 and 1971, whereas for the same years, their male counterparts enjoyed lower death rates in relation to Canadian-born men.

Trovato's examination of the eight subgroups in his study revealed mixed results (probably due to the problematic nature of his data), but in general, native Indians have the lowest life expectancy and reflect a cause-of-death structure characterized by high odds of death from accidents-violence and "other" diseases, whereas, at the other extreme, the British native-born enjoyed the highest life expectancy.

TABLE 2

Standardized Death Rates* Due to Four Major Causes of Death among Native- and Foreign-Born Populations, Canada, 1951, 1964 and 1971.
(Rates per 10,000 population)

Sex and Year	Cause of Death and Nativity							
	Neoplasms		Cardiovascular		Accidents-violence		All other Causes	
	N-B	F-B	N-B	F-B	N-B	F-B	N-B	F-B
Males								
1951	12.48	14.58	46.45	45.58	7.20	10.48	33.91	29.31
1964	14.60	4.47	47.12	37.93	6.80	6.95	24.98	21.46
1971	15.40	17.62	40.30	39.52	8.72	6.99	23.25	21.10
Females								
1951	13.20	13.37	39.96	40.84	2.90	3.60	28.69	22.10
1964	12.94	10.87	34.51	28.14	2.40	2.48	17.60	14.51
1971	11.91	12.52	26.64	27.55	2.63	3.18	14.98	13.70

* 1964 Age-sex population of Canada used as the standard; directly standardized rates.
Source: Trovato (1983).

A contrast involving British immigrants, their descendants in Canada, the British Isles, and Canada's population (less all British), showed support for the hypothesis that immigrants share intermediate odds of mortality and that the second generation and beyond descendants would demonstrate the most advantaged position in the face of death. British immigrants experience lower odds of death than their population of origin. British born in Canada also fare better than the British Isles, and Canada. In total, although the differentials are not very large, the British born in Canada demonstrate the lowest risk, Canada is second-lowest, followed by the British immigrants; and British Isles is highest in the relative odds of death. These findings conform to positive assimilation and positive selection models of mortality: immigrants originate from a relatively "high" risk society, and are intermediate vis-à-vis the host country's lower rates, but their descendants in the host country eventually benefit, partly from positive selection of the parental generation and partly from other social and economic improvements, in sharing a relatively low mortality risk.

In a recent investigation of mortality differences among Portuguese in Canada, Portugal and the Canadian-born in this country for 1971 and 1981, Loh (1986) noted that although the migrants do not display an advantaged socio-economic status in Canada, their mortality ratios are appreciably lower than Portugal and the receiving population. Furthermore, although migrants experienced some increases in their mortality risk over time, they remained below the level of their host nation. Thus, the evidence suggests that immigrants from Portugal may be positively selected in health characteristics, and that with increasing residency in Canada, their advantage tends to erode somewhat, but their rates remain below the host nation. Loh (1986) examined cause-specific mortality between the Portuguese immigrants and the native-born (cardiovascular, degenerative, neoplasms, accidents-violence, and all other causes). In all cases, the foreigners were observed to share a risk that is two to three times below the host population.

The Portuguese situation in Canada offers some evidence that is not directly typified by any of the models in Table 1. Essentially, the native-born Canadian population is an intermediate mortality level in relation to Portugal (highest level) and Portuguese immigrants (lowest level). None of the models in the table entertain this possibility. In the majority of studies reviewed, this pattern occurs infrequently (see Locke and King 1980; King and Locke 1980, for a similar case for Chinese and Japanese in the United States; see also Rosenwaike 1984; Rosenwaike and Shai 1986, for Puerto Ricans in New York).

A number of other works in Canada, mostly from an epidemiological perspective, have focused on specific causes of death, mostly cancer sites and heart-related diseases. As is true with the majority of epidemiological studies of migrant groups, the main emphasis is on isolating environmental, and genetic causes of the observed differentials. The basic idea is to identify diseases that are known, or thought to have either a genetic basis (e.g., sickle cell anemia) or an environmental genesis (e.g., diet), and then to examine how mortality patterns differ among immigrants in relation to their country of origin and the population in the receiving country.

Coy et al. (1968), investigated the association between birthplace and lung cancer mortality during the time interval 1931 to 1965. These authors analysed data collected by the Vital Statistics Division of British Columbia in Victoria.

99

TABLE 3

Predicted Death Rates Due to Five Major Causes of Death for the Portuguese Immigrant and Native-Born Populations of Canada, 1971 and 1981 (Rates per 10,000 Population).

Population By Period	Cause by Sex														
	Neoplasms			Cardiovascular			Certain Degenerative			Accidents-Violence			All Other Causes		
	Male	Female	Total	Male	Female	Total	Male	Female	Total	Male	Female	Total	Male	Female	Total
1971															
Portuguese Immigrants	7.0	4.6	5.8	9.5	6.3	8.0	1.7	1.1	1.4	4.8	3.2	4.0	3.2	2.2	2.7
Native-Born	22.0	14.8	18.3	48.6	32.8	40.6	4.4	3.0	3.7	10.6	7.1	8.8	13.8	9.3	11.5
1981															
Portuguese Immigrants	7.3	5.0	6.2	10.0	6.9	8.5	1.8	1.2	1.5	5.0	3.4	4.2	3.4	2.3	2.9
Native-Born	20.5	14.3	17.3	45.3	31.5	38.3	4.1	2.8	3.5	9.9	6.9	8.3	12.9	9.0	10.9

Source: Loh, 1986.

In addition, they provided a comparative study of lung cancer deaths between British Columbia, Ontario and Saskatchewan for 1950-52 and 1960-62, paying special attention to male decedents who were born in Canada and the United Kingdom.

Their results suggest that over time the intensity of death due to lung cancer has increased. Moreover, it was found that men of United Kingdom origin had much higher age-specific rates than Canadian-born men, while men born in other parts of the world had intermediate rates. In the three provinces surveyed both foreign-born classes showed mortality rates that surpassed those of the native-born.

Two relevant features of the above study are that they demonstrate the greater mortality risk from lung cancer among foreigners, and secondly, that they inferred lifestyle differences and habits — what they call familial and personal factors — along with environmental conditions, as mainly responsible for the results (e.g., smoking, air pollution and lifestyle). It is unfortunate that no substantive discussion of "environmental effects" was offered by the analysts.

The study by Abu-Zeid and his associates (1978), attempted to deal partly with this issue. They were interested in ascertaining the relationship between mortality from ischemic heart disease (IHD), ethnicity and nationality, in Manitoba during 1960-62. They reasoned that the population of this province is ethnically diverse and would therefore provide an opportunity to investigate the extent to which the occurrence of IHD is determined by genetic or environmental factors. To achieve this task the analysis measured mortality differences between ethnic groups of migrant populations and their descendants. They argued that a lack of significant differentials between a particular nationality group and its ethnic native-born descendants would indicate a genetic predisposition common to both native and foreign-born affinities to a specific nationality. Conversely, substantial differences in this regard would be interpreted as an environmental effect. In general, they concluded that both environmental and genetic factors operate in the development of IHD, but the environmental factors seem to be more important.

Experts have noted the difficulties in separating these two sources of disease (Kitagawa 1977). A significant number of researchers take the position that environmental causes are most relevant. For example, Choi and colleagues (1971, 2081) asserted that dietary habits and other related environmental agents are more important factors than genetic ones in the etiology of stomach and intestinal cancers in Canada. With particular reference to nativity, they presented the following results: (1) foreigners have a higher risks of cancer than the native-born; (2) there is a general gradient of risk, with immigrants possessing the most heightened odds, followed by their descendants, and finally, the native-born.

Most of the studies that include the British, generally conclude that people of British ethnic origin (England, Wales, Scotland, Ireland) have an elevated risk of death due to a number of specific diseases in comparison to most, but not all, other sociocultural groups in Canada. Choi (1968) included English,

Scottish and Welsh, as part of the category "British Isles." When he inspected deaths due to gastrointestinal disease by place of birth, the British Isles had standardized death ratios generally below others (Scandinavian, France, Italy, Netherlands, U.S.S.R., Poland, Austria, Czechoslovakia, Hungary, Rumania, other European and other foreign-born); but when deaths from cancer of the colon or rectum were observed, the pattern generally reversed to the disadvantage of the British.

Abu-Zeid et al. (1978) found that among many different ethnic groups Scottish and English ranked very high in death rates from ischemic heart disease. Among foreigners, Irish, Scottish and English ranked highest, while females from these groups showed an irregular ranking pattern. Among the native-born, Scottish, English and Irish males had the highest risks of dying next to Finnish origin men but the rates for females belonging to these groups were relatively low and hence ranked below most other groups.

Kliewer (1979) found that the life expectancy at age 40 among males and females was lowest for Irish immigrants — 30.79 and 32.89 respectively; however English and Welsh men had the highest life expectancies at age 40, with 32.63 years of life remaining, on the average. It must be reiterated that Kliewer's study was based on 1941 data and may not be an accurate assessment of the situation today. Other evidence, although limited, suggests that among major ethnic groups in Canada in 1951 and 1961, British males ranked fourth and third highest in standardized death ratios, respectively; their female counterparts for the same periods, ranked sixth and third, respectively (Kalbach and McVey, 1979, 83)

Migrant Studies Outside Canada

Many studies involving the relationship between nativity and mortality take place in the United States, but some excellent analyses outside North America exist and are worth reviewing briefly.

Using statistics from 1974-75, Brahimi (1980) discovered that immigrants tend to experience a longer life expectancy than the native-born French population. This may be surprising because most foreign-born groups residing there originate from countries where overall life expectancy is lower. Brahimi maintains that if the below average mortality "des étrangers" is not due to data errors, a likely explanation for this fact is migration selectivity.

Migration selectivity, as it relates to lower mortality among foreigners, can be tested indirectly by investigating the age patterns of mortality of recent and earlier immigrant groups against the native-born. The author classified Portuguese, Moroccans and Tunisians as falling into the former category; Italian, Polish and Spanish were assigned to the latter grouping. He determined that the different nationality groups (except Poland), exhibit lower risks of dying; and furthermore, the more recent immigrants have even lower rates than the native-born. The superior life expectancy of foreigners may be largely a function of self-selection; immigration "bring in" the most healthy, and tends to "leave behind" the least healthy.

Brahimi's analysis of death by cause shows that foreign-born males have a more favourable mortality experience than indigenous males due to cardio-vascular disease, cancer, alcoholism, suicide, depression and senility. The more recent immigrants fare even better than their more established counterparts. In some cases, foreign males were observed to have excess deaths due to accidents (including work related and motor vehicle), and violent deaths.

A different situation emerged with regard to foreign-born females. They die more of cardiovascular heart disease, cerebrovascular complications, respiratory ailments (ages 25-64 only), and accidents involving motor vehicles. However, they have lower death rates than native-born females due to cancer of the diges-tive system, cirrhosis of the liver and suicide.

Brahimi's conclusions in connection with causes of death among immigrants are suggestive of another important phenomenon associated with nativity and mortality. Causes of death mostly associated with life stresses (e.g., suicide, alcoholism) are generally less prevalent among foreigners. Thus, it is possible to infer, on the basis of this evidence, that immigrants are also better able to cope with life stresses in the host nation.

Migrant studies in Australia have produced results that contradict some of Brahimi's findings in France. Burvill and colleagues (1973) studied deaths from suicide, motor vehicle accidents and all forms of violent deaths among migrants in Australia and the host population during 1962-66. Generally, death rates were higher for immigrants than either country of origin and native-born Australians.

Moreover, they found that immigrant women had higher suicide rates than Australian-born women. In general, the ratio of migrant suicide rates to their country of origin tends to be larger for women than it is for men (Kliever and Ward, 1988), suggesting that life in the new society may be more stressful for migrant women than their male counterparts. Stenhouse and McCall (1970), in their analysis of differential mortality from cardiovascular disease among immigrants from England-Wales, Scotland and Italy, contrasted to native Australians, established that: (1) in general, immigrants have lower death rates than their countries of origin and destination; (2) the longer the duration of res-idence in the host society, the more their death levels rise to those of the host country; (3) overall, females had lower rates than males. The implications of a connection between nativity, selection and life stresses (as implied by assim-ilation of native death rates over time), were stated as follows by Stenhouse and McCall (1970, 430):

> "It appears that death rates in migrants tend towards those of the country of their adoption ... The death rate is lowest for those migrants resident in Australia for short periods of time and rises progressively with increasing length of residence. The effect appears to be more pronounced in persons resident in Australia from an early age than in those who may have come

> to Australia late in life. The particularly low rates for migrants ... resident
> in Australia for less than 7 years, is probably due either to selection for
> personal reasons or as a result of medical screening, since these rates are
> significantly lower than those of their countries of origin. ... These data
> provide ... support for ... the proposition that environmental and cultural
> factors are of major importance in the genesis of coronary heart disease.''

Like Brahimi (1980), these authors agree that selection accounts for lower risks of dying from cardiovascular disease; and also, like Burvill et al. (1973), they found a gradient in mortality on the basis of recency (duration) in the host country. These facts imply two propositions: (1) migrants are initially positively selected, but (2) the longer they live in the host country the more they assimilate the mortality experience (levels) of the indigenous population (McMichael et al. 1980; McMichael 1982; Dunt 1982).

This last proposition is troublesome from the point of view of empirical analysis because it contains two possible effects: (1) the influence of lifestyle and health habits, and (2) the influence of life stresses — the sum effects of coping in a foreign environment, which range from socioeconomic to social psychological stresses in the process of adjustment and adaptation. The question is whether the increasing mortality of the foreign-born in relation to increasing duration of stay in the host nation is due to assimilation or life stresses, or both? The lack of data makes it especially difficult to disentangle these effects in a statistical sense.

It is known that ''modern'' immigrants generally do well economically and that they experience a certain degree of upward mobility (Richmond 1967; Richmond and Kalbach 1980). It may be that one of the costs associated with these processes is an increase in mortality due to life stresses (Hull 1979).

At the turn of the century, and up until the early part of the 1950s, foreigners in the United States had lower life expectancy than the resident-born white population (Dublin and Baker 1920). Recent evidence suggests that contemporary immigrants in general have a superior mortality condition (Kestenbaum 1986; Rosenwaike 1984; Rosenwaike and Shai 1986; Nasca et al. 1981; King and Locke 1980; Locke and King 1980), or not appreciably different than the host population (Kitagawa and Hauser 1973). Of course, generalizations become more difficult when many specific causes of death are investigated rather than general mortality (Kmet 1970; Haenszel 1961; Sauer 1962; Krueger and Moriyama 1967).

Vallin (1985), in reviewing the work of Marmot, Adelstein and Bulusu (1984) in England and Wales, proposes that there are a variety of forces that explain immigrant mortality: the life conditions of migrants (stresses associated with adaptation and adjustment to new work, settings and environment) factors in the country of origin; factors in the country of destination; self-selection; and assimilation to the behavioural patterns of the host nation.

Marmot and colleagues have published a number of reports based on their large-scale study of 17 immigrant categories in England and Wales during the period 1970-78 (Marmot et al. 1984a; 1984b; 1983). During 1970-72, these analysts found that standardized mortality ratios (SMRs) for overall mortality (England-Wales = 1.0) were below 1.00 for males and females from Spain, Italy, New Zealand, France, U.S., Australia, Canada, West Germany, and Mediterranean Commonwealth countries (the latter is one class). On the other hand, men from Ireland, Scotland, and African Commonwealth (one class) had risks above England and Wales. Men from the Caribbean Commonwealth (one class), the Indian subcontinent, U.S.S.R., and Poland had SMRs below 1.00; and immigrant women from these areas had reduced risks as well.

An analysis of circulatory diseases, neoplasms, and all causes combined, revealed a somewhat better risk experience for migrants from Australia and New Zealand than the United Kingdom-born, but not for Canadians and South Africans. Italian migrants (as in most other countries where they comprise an immigrant class), have considerably lower overall mortality than that of their new country, particularly for ischemic heart disease, diabetes mellitus, and cancers of the breast and of the colon. Overall, the worst mortality levels are experienced by immigrants from the African Commonwealth.

Among men, the lowest SMRs for neoplasms were found among New Zealanders and Americans, while the highest were associated with the Scottish and the Irish. For women, Spaniards and New Zealanders share relatively low risks, while the highest rates are among South Africans, U.S.S.R., Scottish, and Irish, with respect to the SMRs for neoplasms.

Deaths from accidents and violence were found to be high across all immigrant groups, but suicide is notably higher among migrants from Poland, Germany and U.S.S.R., while for Italians, Spaniards and French (all of Catholic background), the suicide rates are very low. The Irish stand out for having high mortality from accidents and violence vis-à-vis Ireland and England-Wales.

In relation to countries of origin and England-Wales (receiving society), it was found that male mortality is lower in migrants from Italy, Caribbean and Poland than in their countries of origin. For the Irish, the opposite is true.

Among migrants from the Indian subcontinent and Ireland, the low risk of ischemic heart disease prevailing in the homeland appears to have been "carried over" by the migrants into their new country. For this cause of death, persons from Spain, Scotland, U.S. and South Africa, have intermediate risk in relation to the origin and destination areas.

We may reach a number of generalizations based on the work of Marmot, Adelstein and Bulusu in England and Wales. First, the significantly poorer mortality condition of the African Commonwealth migrants may reflect negative selection, or a number of other interrelated "forces" such as the "importation" of poorer health status from the origin, and the possible stresses and "shocks" associated with being a visible minority in a new environment characterized by a very different culture than that which is common to the immigrant's country of origin. However, as is true with all other immigrant studies, the data themselves do not allow for a direct determination of the influence of conditions in the host environment as opposed to ''origin'' effects, selection and life stresses associated with migration itself.

A second feature of this research is suggestive of an assimilation process. In general, immigrants appear to be in an intermediate position (relative to countries of origin and destination), but they also demonstrate a general tendency to adopt the cause-of-death patterns and levels of the receiving population.

Concerning self-selection, the overall evidence suggests that migration is a selective process with respect to mortality. The Irish case may be used as an example: because Ireland is proximate to England and Wales in geography and culture, and there are no immigration ''screening'' restrictions, there is little difference between the risk in Ireland and its immigrants in England-Wales. Thus, no selection occurs. On the other hand, appreciable differences emerge when the migrants originate from countries outside the British Isles, suggesting that some degree of ''screening'' and self-selection occurs for immigrants from varied cultural and national origins. Therefore, as a general principle, it would seem that the greater the geographic and cultural distance between the migrants country of origin and the receiving society, the greater the degree of positive self-selection in health and social demographic characteristics.

Summary of the Literature Reviewed

What follows is a brief synthesis of the literature reviewed. There are four major limitations:

1) Most research has not provided the inclusion of a duration control variable thus hampering a more definite analysis of the relationship between length of residence in a host country and immigrant mortality.
2) In most instances, authors do not test specific hypotheses, but confine themselves to observational type studies. When they do test specific theses, they are mostly interested in answering whether immigrants' mortality experience is a response to environmental conditions in the host or origin country, or due to genetic predispositions.
3) Beyond age and sex, virtually no other control variable is introduced into the analysis. Hence it is not possible to determine whether the relationship between nativity, ethnicity and longevity may be a function of other social or economic factors.
4) Most studies suffer from a general lack of theoretical foundations and do not attempt to progress beyond mere observational research. The linkage of empirical results to a social demographic theory of migration and mortality is still missing.

Following these problems, the main generalizations from the literature may be summarized as follows:

1) Within the context of North America, the relationship between nativity and mortality has changed. In the pre-World War II era, foreigners

were generally observed as possessing higher risks of dying than the native-born; in recent decades the opposite seems to be occurring.

2) In both Canada and the United States, ethnic and racial differentials in mortality exist and have been documented over the decades. Generally, Blacks in the U.S.A., Native Indians and French-Canadians in Canada appear to be most disadvantaged in the face of death.

3) Outside Canada and the United States, contemporary immigrants tend to experience a more favourable mortality experience than natives of the host countries, but variations by cause of death exist, suggesting the influences of both country of origin effects (e.g., diet) exposure to the host environment (e.g., life stresses) and possibly selection effects.

4) The available evidence (mostly indirect), seems to suggest that the longer an immigrant group resides in a host country, the more likely it is to adopt the general morbidity and mortality experience of the host population. In most cases, however, immigrants have intermediate risk levels between their country of origin and the host nation.

5) There exists an implicit assumption that by examining the life expectancy of migrants in relation to their countries of origin and destination, one is able to ascertain the relative impact of genetics versus environment to account for the mortality experience of the foreign-born population. However, this kind of contrast is hampered by the inability to separate the independent effects of selection, migration effects, and exposure to countries of origin and destination, prior to and after migration.

Immigrant Mortality in the Host Nation: a Look Ahead

What has been identified in this review is a number of tendencies, problems and deficiencies in the existing literature concerning migrant mortality. Of particular interest is the fact that migrant studies *do not* deal primarily with the way the migration process and life experiences in the new society interact to affect mortality conditions among foreigners (Kasl and Berkman 1985). The recommendation put forth here is that it is now time to redirect our focus, away from the approaches exemplified in Table 1, and move toward the investigation of immigrant's health status, adaptation, social supports and other attributes important in understanding what happens to the newcomers once they settle in their adoptive land. There is now some convincing evidence, based on controlled follow-up studies of immigrants, that factors such as acculturation to the new society (e.g., diet, lifestyle), degree of traditionalism (maintenance of ethnic traditions), and the extent of social support systems in the immigrant community have a significant bearing on the incidence and prevalence of diseases such as elevated blood pressure and coronary heart disease (Cassel 1974; Barrera 1986; Ulman and Abernethy 1975; Kasl and Berkman 1985; Marmot and Syme 1976; Reed et al. 1982).

Such work has been carried out by Marmot and Syme (1976) among Japanese in Hawaii, California and Japan. Their study is exemplary in this respect in that it contributes toward specifying under what conditions migrants in a new society experience reduced or increased risk of disease and disability in comparison to the native-born population. It was found that acculturation, traditionalism and social support are important "agents" which serve to condition the risk of coronary heart disease among immigrants. Respondents who manifested high levels of acculturation possessed an increased risk of heart disease, but maintenance of traditional ways and maintaining contacts with "supports" in the ethnic community served to reduce the odds of morbidity.

A similar argument has been proposed recently by Trovato (1986) and Trovato and Jarvis (1986) in the case of immigrant suicide in Canada. Their research suggests that immigrant groups that are known to possess high degrees of ethnic community integration, are generally more "sheltered" from committing suicide than those immigrants who do not belong to highly cohesive ethnic communities.

Future research should focus specifically on how adjustment processes in their entirety (this includes many components, such acculturation, life stresses, community integration, social supports, kin contacts, etc.) affect immigrant health status, morbidity and mortality in their host country. The evidence available in the literature suggests the following working hypothesis: the greater the extent of social support mechanisms in an immigrant community in a host nation, the lower the immigrants' mortality risk from "life stress" related causes such as accidents, violence, suicide and cardiovascular complications. A corollary hypothesis is that this relationship is conditioned by length of residency in the host nation. These hypotheses are also applicable to the analysis of morbidity and health status. It becomes more difficult to apply these hypotheses in a straightforward manner to causes of death that do not have obvious "life stress" related geneses, such as certain cancers and other degenerative diseases that may have little, if any, relationship to social support factors.

Notes

1. This is a revised version of a paper originally written for Phase I of the National Demographic Review sponsored by Health and Welfare Canada, 1987.

7. THE EVOLUTION OF IMMIGRANT COHORTS

Roderic Beaujot and J. Peter Rappak

In their immigration monograph based on the 1971 Census, Richmond and Kalbach (1980) paid special attention to the post-war immigrants and their adaptation over the period 1961-71. In particular, when the 1946-60 immigrant cohort was observed in the 1961 Census, most age-sex categories had lower median total earnings than the Canadian-born. However, the immigrants made greater progress over the following decade. When this same cohort was considered in the 1971 Census, the majority of age-sex categories now had higher median incomes than the Canadian-born.

This is an interesting result in several ways. It would imply that immigrants have initial disadvantages, possibly related to problems of settlement, recognition of credentials and the shock of immigration. However, after a certain period, immigrants could be expected to have relative advantages, based on their selectivity for education and skills, and possibly because of their self-selection for inner drive and achievement orientation. These results are also interesting from a policy perspective. They would imply that one need not worry about the disadvantages of immigrants; time will take care of things.

The question of the adjustment of immigrants deserves further attention. In particular, have subsequent cohorts of immigrants experienced patterns similar to the 1946-60 arrivals, and do the patterns also apply to the new immigrant group from Asia, Latin America and Africa?

The purpose of this chapter is to analyse the evolution of given immigration cohorts over the censuses of 1971, 1981 and 1986. In particular, we wish to see if the arrival status of given cohorts predominantly determines their subsequent evolution, or if given cohorts can be said to move from a position of relative disadvantage (or difference) to a position of relative advantage (or similarity) compared to the Canadian-born. Further, we wish to determine whether these trajectories are the same or different for the new immigrant group from

Asia, Latin America and Africa compared to the traditional immigrant group from Europe and the United States. These trajectories will be analysed with respect to geographic distribution, language, education, labour force status and income. Immigration has fluctuated considerably over the decades of this century. Starting from a high of 1,550,000 arrivals in 1901-11, the numbers decreased to 149,000 in 1931-41 and subsequently increased to 1,543,000 in 1951-61. In each of 1961-71 and 1971-81 the figures have been 1,429,000 arrivals per decade, and an additional 500,000 arrivals in 1981-86 (Beaujot et al. 1988, 2). Return and re-migration are high for immigrants, some 30 percent of the 1951-70 immigrant cohorts and 20 percent of the 1971-80 cohorts had left by 1986 (Beaujot and Rappak 1988). We will pay attention here to the characteristics of the immigrants who stay in Canada, and their change over time.

Throughout the analysis, the immigrants are separated into two groups: the traditional immigration group defined as persons born in Europe and the United States, and the new immigrant group defined as persons born in other areas of the world. Both immigrants born in Canada and Canadian citizens born abroad are classified as Canadian-born. The next chapter provides information on the arrival of new immigrant groups to Canada. As for the survivors in the 1986 Census, the new immigrants made up 5.0 percent of pre-1961 arrivals, compared to 50.3 percent of the 1970-74 cohort and 65.1 percent of the 1980-86 arrivals. Altogether, the new immigrants amounted to 11.1 percent of the total foreign-born Canadian population in the 1971 Census, and 30.6 percent in the 1986 Census.

Geographic Distribution

The first two tables show the geographic distribution of the Canadian-born and the various immigration cohorts over the period 1961-86. It is noteworthy how little the distribution of the Canadian-born has changed over the period: 12 to 10 percent are in the Atlantic provinces, 32 to 28 percent in Quebec, 32 to 33 percent in Ontario, 17 to 18 percent in the Prairie provinces and 8 to 11 percent in British Columbia (Table 1).

In general, compared to the Canadian-born, the immigrants are more concentrated in Ontario and British Columbia and less concentrated in the Atlantic provinces and Quebec. The immigrants who arrived before 1946 are an exception in the sense that they are more concentrated in the Prairie provinces. As of 1986, only 9.5 percent of pre-1946 immigrants were in Quebec compared to 17.5 percent of the 1985-86 arrivals. The immigrant cohorts that are most concentrated in Ontario arrived in 1946-74. Those most concentrated in the Prairie provinces arrived either before 1946 or in 1975-86. The concentration in British Columbia has been decreasing since the 1970-74 cohort. The differential distribution patterns of the various cohorts clearly follows historical trends in the economic prominence of the various regions of Canada. In particular,

TABLE 1

Geographic Distribution of Canadian-born and Given Immigration Cohorts, 1961-1986

	Canadian-Born				Arrived Before 1946		
Census Year:	1961	1971	1981	1986	1971	1981	1986
Atlantic	11.9	10.3	10.9	10.3	2.8	3.1	3.2
Quebec	31.6	30.7	28.9	28.,1	10.2	9.7	9.5
Ontario	31.7	33.2	32.2	32.8	39.8	41.4	42.2
Prairies	16.7	16.5	17.8	18.0	27.4	25.7	25.0
British Columbia	8.0	9.3	10.3	10.8	19.7	20.0	20.1
Total	100.0	100.0	100.0	100.0	100.0	100.0	100.0

	1946-60				1961-69		
Census Year:	1961	1971	1981	1986	1971	1981	1986
Atlantic	2.1	1.9	1.8	1.8	2.1	2.1	1.9
Quebec	16.3	15.0	12.8	12.3	18.0	16.0	15.5
Ontario	55.4	56.9	57.4	57.4	55.5	55.5	57.0
Prairies	14.1	12.6	12.8	12.5	11.3	11.3	10.8
British Columbia	12.0	13.6	15.2	15.9	13.0	15.1	14.8
Total	100.0	100.0	100.0	100.0	100.0	100.0	100.0

	1970-74			1975-79		1980-84		1985-86
Census Year:	1971	1981	1986	1981	1986	1981	1986	1986
Atlantic	2.7	2.5	2.1	2.3	2.1	2.2	1.9	2.0
Quebec	15.8	13.1	12.2	15.3	14.9	15.0	15.7	17.5
Ontario	53.9	54.3	56.1	48.5	49.8	44.0	47.6	49.0
Prairies	13.2	12.8	12.4	17.7	17.0	21.2	19.0	17.8
British Columbia	14.4	17.3	17.2	16.2	16.3	17.7	15.8	13.7
Total	100.0	100.0	100.0	100.0	100.0	100.0	100.0	100.0

Territories are included with British Columbia in 1961 and 1986 and with Atlantic in 1981.

Source: Richmond and Kalbach (1980:88) for 1961, public use sample for 1971 and 1981, special tabulations for 1986.

Ontario and British Columbia presented advantages throughout the century, but especially in 1946-74, while the Prairie provinces had some advantages before 1946 and in 1975-86.

The change in geographic distribution over time is slight, both for the Canadian-born and the given immigration cohorts. For the Canadian-born and the immigration cohorts arriving after 1945, the changes in distribution tend to be to the disadvantage of Quebec and the Prairie provinces and to the advantage of Ontario and British Columbia.

TABLE 2

Geographic Distribution of Traditional Immigrant Groups and New Immigrant Groups
for Given Immigration Cohorts, 1971-1986

Arrived Before 1946

Census Year:	1971		1981		1986	
Immigration Group	TIG	NIG	TIG	NIG	TIG	NIG
Atlantic	2.8	4.0	3.1	3.2	3.2	3.4
Quebec	10.2	10.1	9.6	13.3	9.4	13.1
Ontario	40.2	28.4	41.6	35.3	42.3	37.9
Prairies	27.6	19.4	26.1	12.9	25.3	14.5
British Columbia	19.1	38.1	19.6	35.3	19.8	31.0
Total	100.0	100.0	100.0	100.0	100.0	100.0

1946-60

Census Year:	1971		1981		1986	
Immigration Group	TIG	NIG	TIG	NIG	TIG	NIG
Atlantic	2.0	1.7	1.8	1.8	1.7	2.2
Quebec	14.7	20.2	12.7	14.4	12.2	15.2
Ontario	57.6	44.4	58.5	40.3	58.3	42.5
Prairies	12.7	11.4	12.7	15.0	12.4	14.0
British Columbia	13.0	22.3	14.4	28.5	15.3	26.2
Total	100.0	100.0	100.0	100.0	100.0	100.0

1961-69

Census Year:	1971		1981		1986	
Immigration Group	TIG	NIG	TIG	NIG	TIG	NIG
Atlantic	2.2	1.8	2.2	1.7	2.1	1.6
Quebec	16.7	22.8	14.6	20.0	14.5	18.7
Ontario	57.6	48.4	57.7	49.2	58.9	50.8
Prairies	11.5	10.8	11.6	10.5	10.7	11.1
British Columbia	12.1	16.3	13.9	18.6	13.8	17.8
Total	100.0	100.0	100.0	100.0	100.0	100.0

1970-74

Census Year:	1971		1981		1986	
Immigration Group	TIG	NIG	TIG	NIG	TIG	NIG
Atlantic	3.8	0.7	3.8	1.2	3.3	0.9
Quebec	15.8	15.9	12.1	14.0	11.6	12.7
Ontario	53.5	54.5	54.9	53.8	56.8	55.5
Prairies	13.9	12.0	12.5	13.1	12.3	12.5
British Columbia	13.0	16.9	16.6	17.9	16.0	18.3
Total	100.0	100.0	100.0	100.0	100.0	100.0

1975-79

Census Year:	1981		1986	
Immigration Group:	TIG	NIG	TIG	NIG
Atlantic	4.0	1.1	3.9	0.9
Quebec	13.5	16.6	12.7	16.3
Ontario	49.8	47.6	50.8	49.1
Prairies	17.8	17.6	17.2	16.9
British Columbia	14.9	17.1	15.4	16.8
Total	100.0	100.0	100.0	100.0

1980-84

Census Year:	1981		1986	
Immigration Group:	TIG	NIG	TIG	NIG
Atlantic	3.6	1.3	3.6	1.0
Quebec	11.1	17.4	12.0	17.7
Ontario	48.7	41.1	50.6	46.0
Prairies	19.4	22.3	19.6	18.7
British Columbia	17.2	18.0	14.2	16.6
Total	100.0	100.0	100.0	100.0

1985-86

Census Year:	1986	
Immigration Group:	TIB	NIG
Atlantic	4.3	1.0
Quebec	13.6	19.3
Ontario	52.8	47.2
Prairies	16.6	18.3
British Columbia	12.7	14.2
Total	100.0	100.0

Table 2 separates these data into the traditional immigrant group and the new immigrant group. Among those who arrived before 1946, the two groups are rather different, with the new group being more concentrated in British Columbia, and less likely to be in Ontario or the Prairie provinces. Many of these older generations are the long-established Asian groups of British Columbia.

In subsequent cohorts, the new immigrants are more likely to be in Quebec and British Columbia, and their distribution largely plays to the advantage of British Columbia and the disadvantage of Quebec. Overall, except for the cohorts arriving before 1946, the distribution and redistribution patterns of traditional and new immigrant groups are not particularly different. The distribution of given cohorts of new immigrants changes more over time. Except for the 1970-71 cohort in 1971, the new immigrants are less likely to be in Ontario. Essentially all cohorts of new immigrants are more likely to be in Quebec and British Columbia.

In conclusion, immigration has played a significant role in the redistribution of Canada's population over the period 1961-86. For instance, the Canadian-born of Ontario were only 3 percent more than the Canadian-born of Quebec in 1961 and 17 percent more in 1986. However, the total population of Ontario was 19 percent larger than Quebec in 1961 and 39 percent larger in 1986. In comparison, the difference between new immigrant and traditional immigrant groups is rather small, especially since the new immigrants are less likely to be in Ontario and more likely to be in Quebec and British Columbia. The distribution and redistribution patterns of immigrants have largely followed the differential opportunity structures across the regions, and their change over time. Departures from Quebec probably also reflect the fact that immigrants have largely not integrated into the French-language majority of this province.

Language

Our analysis of language will focus on the extent to which immigrants speak the two official languages. The concept of predominant language has been used, combining the responses on home language and knowledge of official languages. Those speaking one of the official languages at home have been coded as "predominantly" associating with that language. Those speaking a third language at home have been classified as English or French "predominant language" respectively if they know only English or only French among the official languages. The remainder who speak a third language at home (or speak both official languages at home) and know either "both" or "neither" of the official languages are classified as "other." This classification reduces the "other" category to 3.2 percent of the entire population in 1986, thus it is not differentiated further by specific languages.

TABLE 3

Predominant Language of Canadian-born and Given Immigration Cohorts, Showing Traditional and New Immigrant Groups, Quebec and Rest of Canada, 1971-1986

	Quebec			Rest of Canada		
	English	French	Others	English	French	Others
Canadian-born						
1971	13.1	86.0	0.9	94.2	5.2	0.7
1981	11.3	87.8	1.0	95.0	4.5	0.5
1986	9.7	86.7	3.6	94.8	3.7	1.6
Arrived before 1946						
1971	67.8	26.4	5.8	97.0	0.6	2.4
TIG	67.6	26.9	5.5	97.4	0.7	2.0
NIG	75.0	10.7	14.3	85.6	0.0	14.4
1981	66.5	29.7	3.8	97.8	0.7	1.4
TIG	66.4	29.9	3.6	98.0	0.7	1.2
NIG	70.3	21.6	8.1	89.6	1.2	9.1
1986	62.1	29.5	8.4	97.9	0.5	1.6
TIG	62.2	29.8	8.0	98.2	0.5	1.3
NIG	58.7	22.8	18.6	88.0	0.3	11.8
Arrived 1946-60						
1971	50.4	27.2	22.3	93.4	0.5	6.1
TIG	49.1	27.4	23.4	93.8	0.5	5.7
NIG	65.8	25.0	9.2	86.0	0.8	13.1
1981	49.9	28.6	21.4	95.4	0.5	4.2
TIG	49.2	28.9	21.9	95.6	0.5	3.9
NIG	61.0	24.1	14.9	90.7	0.6	8.7
1986	46.6	29.2	24.2	95.7	0.4	4.0
TIG	45.9	29.4	24.7	96.0	0.4	3.7
NIG	56.2	26.4	17.4	90.2	0.5	9.4
Arrived 1961-69						
1971	43.7	33.0	23.3	85.5	1.4	13.1
TIG	41.1	32.6	26.3	84.9	1.3	13.8
NIG	50.1	34.3	15.6	87.9	2.0	10.1
1981	38.8	36.0	25.2	91.2	0.9	7.8
TIG	36.5	34.3	29.2	90.7	0.8	8.4
NIG	43.7	39.6	16.7	92.7	1.3	6.0
1986	36.9	36.3	26.8	92.4	0.7	7.0
TIG	34.7	36.5	28.8	92.4	0.6	7.1
NIG	42.4	36.0	21.6	92.4	1.0	6.7
Arrived 1970-74						
1971	48.8	29.4	21.8	77.2	2.2	20.6
TIG	42.2	32.3	25.5	73.4	2.3	24.3
NIG	60.4	24.2	15.4	84.1	1.9	14.1
1981	41.7	38.5	19.8	91.3	0.9	7.8
TIG	41.3	35.1	23.6	89.5	1.3	9.2
NIG	42.0	41.3	16.7	93.1	0.6	6.4
1986	37.1	39.5	23.5	92.2	0.7	7.0
TIG	34.8	37.9	27.4	90.8	1.0	8.2
NIG	39.1	40.9	19.9	93.7	0.5	5.9

TABLE 3 (cont.)

	Quebec			Rest of Canada		
	English	French	Others	English	French	Others
Arrived 1975-79						
1981	31.8	48.6	19.5	88.0	1.3	10.7
TIG	34.4	47.7	17.9	89.4	1.7	8.8
NIG	30.4	49.2	20.4	87.0	1.0	12.1
1986	27.0	47.0	26.0	90.2	0.9	8.9
TIG	29.6	45.0	25.5	91.4	1.2	7.4
NIG	25.8	48.0	26.3	89.4	0.6	10.0
Arrived 1980-84						
1981	25.0	46.8	28.2	75.1	1.3	23.6
TIG	39.3	42.1	18.6	85.1	1.3	13.6
NIG	19.5	48.6	31.9	68.5	1.3	30.2
1986	24.9	49.7	25.5	86.1	0.8	13.1
TIG	31.6	44.2	24.3	91.5	1.0	7.5
NIG	22.4	51.7	25.9	83.0	0.7	16.4
Arrived 1985-86						
1986	34.4	35.9	29.7	72.7	1.3	26.0
TIG	34.9	39.4	25.7	78.3	2.0	19.8
NIG	34.2	34.8	31.0	70.0	1.0	29.1

Sources and notes: See Appendix.

The data are shown in Table 3, separately for Quebec and the rest of Canada. For Canada outside of Quebec, the results are simple: immigration contributes overwhelmingly to the English language. Among the Canadian-born in this area, 5.2 percent were predominantly French in 1971 and 3.7 percent in 1986. Among immigrant cohorts, the proportion speaking French is considerably lower and it tends to decline between 1971 and 1986 for given immigration cohorts. By 1986 the highest proportion of French speaking immigrants is 1.3 percent for the 1985-86 cohort. The difference between traditional and new immigrant groups is small; in 1986 the new immigrant group arriving before 1970 were slightly more French and those arriving later were slightly less French than the traditional immigration group.

The immigrant trends in Quebec are more complex with regard to their association with the official languages. For the Canadian-born in Quebec, 86.0 percent were predominantly French in 1971 and 86.7 percent in 1986. The immigrant groups were much less French, with the highest percentage occurring among the more recent cohorts. The cohorts that arrived before 1970 are in fact more likely to associate with the English language. For instance, in the cohort arriving before 1946, 62.1 percent were predominantly English and 29.5 percent were predominantly French in 1986. It is only for the 1970-86 cohorts that we see more French than English; for instance 49.7 percent French and 24.9 percent English for the 1980-84 cohort.

The change over time for given immigrant cohorts in Quebec favours French, especially for the later cohorts. This is partly a function of the greater departure of English groups (Lachapelle and Henripin 1980). The traditional immigrant group is more English than the new immigrant group for cohorts preceding 1961, but for subsequent cohorts the new immigrant group is more French.

In Quebec, a reasonable proportion of the population cannot be assigned one of the official languages as their predominant language by the procedure adopted here. This especially applies to 1986 where the census procedures allowed for more than one home language. A total of 3.0 percent of Quebec's population (5.3 percent of immigrants) declared using both official languages at home, compared to 1.1 percent for the rest of Canada. Quebec is more likely to receive persons classified as neither English nor French, and these are also more likely to retain their "other" language in Quebec. For example, the proportion "other" in the 1961-69 immigrant cohort in Quebec actually increased from 23.3 percent in the 1971 Census to 26.8 percent in 1986. For the rest of Canada, the equivalent proportion decreased from 13.1 to 7.0 percent.

In general, for Canada as a whole, immigration contributes mostly to the English group. in 1986, 27.0 percent of the Canadian-born were predominantly French, compared to 5.6 percent of immigrants. The proportion French increases for more recent immigrants, but only reaches 8.5 percent for the 1980-84 cohort. In Canada outside of Quebec, immigrants contribute overwhelmingly to the English language. In Quebec, immigrants arriving before 1970 are more likely to be English and those since 1975 are more likely to be French. Especially for the more recent cohorts, the change over time for given cohorts in Quebec favours French, and the new immigrant group is more likely to be French than the traditional immigrant group. However, the immigrants are far from reaching the French predominance of the Canadian-born population in Quebec. Altogether, only 37.6 percent of immigrants are predominantly French compared to 86.7 percent of the Canadian-born in 1986 making Quebec's population 82.7 percent predominantly French. Therefore, taken as a whole, immigrants reduce the proportion French both in Quebec and in the rest of Canada.

Education

Two sets of tables on education are presented. The first set shows proportions with low levels of education, that is less than nine years education for the population 25 years and over (Tables 4a and 4b).

The pre-war immigrant males have higher proportions at low levels of education, but the proportion with less than nine years education declines with recency of immigration to reach its lowest level among the 1975-79 arrivals. Within given age groups, the differences are smaller. In the 66 comparisons that can be made for men in age groups 25-64, there are only 18 cases (three in 1971, six in 1981 and nine in 1986) where an immigrant cohort has higher proportions

TABLE 4a

Proportion with less than nine years of education, by age, for Canadian-Born and Given Immigrant Cohorts, showing Traditional and New Immigrant Groups, Ages 25 and over, Males, 1971-1986

	Total	Age				
		25-34	35-44	45-54	55-64	65+
Canadian-born						
1971	41.9	23.4	38.9	45.8	53.2	70.6
1981	27.8	6.9	17.1	30.7	38.5	52.6
1986	16.2	4.8	11.2	24.7	36.1	47.4
Arrived before 1946						
1971	56.3	12.1	30.0	33.1	54.7	65.1
TIG	56.4	13.5	30.4	33.6	54.6	65.2
NIG	52.7	–	–	16.7	57.6	62.8
1981	46.5	–	8.8	23.0	30.7	54.2
TIG	46.4	–	9.0	23.4	31.0	53.9
NIG	50.0	–	–	9.1	21.4	61.5
1986	43.0	–	7.5	15.1	29.9	48.6
TIG	43.0	–	7.4	14.8	30.1	48.6
NIG	41.0	–	–	18.2	24.8	48.0
Arrived 1946-60						
1971	37.1	24.0	38.0	38.0	46.7	51.2
TIG	37.6	24.2	38.1	39.1	47.5	50.6
NIG	27.6	20.3	36.7	10.7	25.0	–
1981	24.8	3.3	17.3	27.3	31.4	42.9
TIG	25.3	3.3	17.6	27.9	31.8	42.9
NIG	16.7	3.1	13.9	20.4	20.2	39.5
1986	24.7	2.0	7.6	26.3	30.9	39.3
TIG	25.1	1.9	7.5	26.5	31.5	39.7
NIG	17.8	3.3	8.2	24.3	18.9	26.3
Arrived 1961-69						
1971	29.4	23.0	31.1	37.5	53.5	61.7
TIG	35.1	28.3	38.2	41.5	56.4	66.2
NIG	10.9	6.3	10.3	18.4	42.3	43.8
1981	19.4	11.5	16.4	25.4	31.6	44.8
TIG	24.0	14.4	20.6	31.8	36.1	49.4
NIG	6.7	4.0	5.4	7.8	15.9	23.5
1986	16.6	4.9	16.3	21.5	30.5	45.0
TIG	19.7	5.4	19.7	26.7	35.9	50.4
NIG	6.5	3.4	5.6	5.9	12.6	26.4
Arrived 1970-74						
1971	19.3	15.6	24.7	33.3	26.7	25.0
TIG	24.4	18.8	30.4	41.2	40.0	27.3
NIG	11.9	11.7	14.8	–	–	–
1981	15.6	10.0	15.8	22.7	33.8	45.6
TIG	23.4	18.1	23.7	29.0	30.7	54.4
NIG	9.2	3.7	8.8	17.4	37.9	36.8
1986	12.0	8.8	11.2	18.8	27.2	38.8
TIG	17.2	14.7	18.0	26.5	33.3	43.4
NIG	7.0	4.2	5.2	11.5	20.3	33.9

TABLE 4a (cont.)

| | Total | Age | | | | |
		25-34	35-44	45-54	55-64	65+
Arrived 1975-79						
1981	13.8	9.2	8.7	15.2	33.1	51.1
TIG	14.8	13.7	8.0	13.6	21.9	52.1
NIG	12.9	5.8	9.3	16.3	40.2	50.4
1986	11.0	10.0	7.8	12.1	26.1	41.3
TIG	12.4	14.9	9.4	11.2	23.4	40.1
NIG	10.2	7.3	6.7	12.7	28.0	41.9
Arrived 1980-84						
1981	20.2	13.6	11.8	30.0	38.8	42.4
TIG	10.7	6.5	2.6	12.1	30.3	30.3
NIG	27.0	18.5	19.6	42.6	42.9	54.6
1986	13.9	9.6	9.2	17.0	35.8	41.2
TIG	9.1	6.6	4.8	9.4	19.5	31.1
NIG	16.3	11.1	12.8	22.3	41.3	45.4
Arrived 1985-86						
1986	16.4	11.1	11.6	22.0	38.9	35.1
TIG	12.8	8.8	9.0	11.2	23.3	32.1
NIG	17.9	12.2	13.1	27.2	43.5	36.4

Source and Notes: See Appendix.

In 1986 the total is for 15 and over.

TABLE 4b

Population with Less than Nine Years of Education, Females, 1971-1986

| | Total | Age | | | | |
		25-34	35-44	45-54	55-64	65+
Canadian-born						
1971	37.7	21.7	33.2	40.9	48.1	59.0
1981	23.8	6.9	17.0	28.9	37.5	47.0
1986	15.7	4.0	10.8	22.4	33.8	43.3
Arrived before 1946						
1971	54.8	25.6	25.8	34.2	49.8	64.9
TIG	55.1	25.3	25.5	34.3	49.9	65.1
NIG	45.1	–	30.8	30.8	46.4	53.9
1981	48.3	–	12.5	22.7	32.4	55.5
TIG	48.5	–	11.8	22.5	32.6	55.5
NIG	42.5	–	18.2	–	23.1	53.3
1986	44.2	–	7.1	16.1	28.7	49.6
TIG	44.3	–	7.2	15.7	28.8	49.8
NIG	36.7	–	–	21.8	22.9	43.1

TABLE 4b (cont.)

	Total	Age				
		25-34	35-44	45-54	55-64	65 +
Arrived 1946-60						
1971	40.3	31.9	39.9	36.9	51.6	58.6
TIG	40.5	32.2	40.8	37.2	50.8	57.8
NIG	36.1	27.3	27.0	29.1	63.2	69.2
1981	29.9	4.4	23.9	34.1	33.1	51.7
TIG	30.0	4.3	24.1	34.7	33.3	50.9
NIG	27.2	6.1	20.7	25.8	24.7	62.6
1986	29.5	2.4	9.9	34.0	34.4	45.2
TIG	29.8	2.4	9.9	34.8	34.8	44.8
NIG	24.6	2.8	8.6	23.9	25.2	52.8
Arrived 1961-69						
1971	36.1	26.6	38.2	50.8	59.2	64.5
TIG	39.7	31.1	41.4	53.3	56.8	63.3
NIG	24.2	13.9	26.4	39.6	66.7	70.0
1981	28.3	19.4	22.0	32.1	46.9	63.0
TIG	33.0	23.8	27.3	37.4	51.0	62.6
NIG	15.5	7.4	9.3	17.4	32.6	64.2
1986	23.1	6.7	23.0	27.3	41.3	57.1
TIG	26.4	7.6	28.3	32.6	45.9	58.1
NIG	12.9	3.8	7.8	11.9	25.2	54.0
Arrived 1970-74						
1971	29.6	23.7	23.3	31.0	65.2	69.6
TIG	34.7	30.2	20.0	31.3	61.1	75.0
NIG	31.5	14.7	28.6	30.8	–	–
1981	23.2	13.2	22.3	39.8	43.1	59.6
TIG	29.3	20.3	29.5	45.7	40.6	53.9
NIG	17.9	7.2	16.4	33.9	45.9	65.5
1986	17.7	14.3	14.5	27.9	40.9	56.1
TIG	21.9	23.9	20.2	34.2	40.8	53.1
NIG	13.5	5.6	9.5	22.0	41.0	59.5
Arrived 1975-79						
1981	22.2	10.9	18.5	32.7	48.0	57.5
TIG	18.7	11.6	13.4	21.6	40.9	46.7
NIG	24.7	10.5	22.5	39.9	51.3	67.1
1986	17.6	11.0	12.2	24.3	48.6	58.0
TIG	15.9	14.4	10.7	18.8	36.9	47.3
NIG	18.7	9.1	13.2	28.3	54.4	64.4
Arrived 1980-84						
1981	32.4	13.4	17.8	50.8	60.2	63.8
TIG	17.0	5.0	8.8	29.4	28.6	52.0
NIG	42.6	19.9	26.9	58.3	70.0	74.6
1986	21.1	11.2	14.1	35.1	55.6	56.8
TIG	11.2	5.2	6.0	14.4	29.7	40.7
NIG	26.3	14.7	20.7	45.8	63.4	66.7
Arrived 1985-86						
1986	22.1	12.7	15.1	39.5	54.3	55.9
TIG	12.5	5.9	8.2	17.0	35.7	37.8
NIG	26.4	16.1	19.2	47.2	59.5	66.8

with less than nine years of education than the Canadian-born. For cohorts arriving in the period 1946-74, the new immigrant group has significantly lower levels with less than nine years education than the traditional immigrant group. Among the 1980-86 cohorts, the traditional immigrant group has lower proportions with less than nine years education.

For women, the immigrant cohorts tend to have higher proportions with less than nine years education than the Canadian-born. In the 66 comparisons that can be made for women in age groups 25-64 in 51 cases (11 in 1971, 18 in 1981 and 22 in 1986) an immigrant cohort has higher proportions with less than nine years education than the Canadian-born. There are significantly lower levels with less than nine years education among new immigrant women arriving in the period 1961-74. In the 1980-86 cohorts, the new immigrant group has higher proportions with less than nine years of education. As a consequence, there are significant proportions of women among the more recent immigrants, especially at ages 45-65, with low levels of education.

The other end of the educational spectrum is measured through proportions with some university education (Tables 5a and 5b). In all but 2 of the 66 comparisons at ages 25-64 for men, the immigrants have higher education than the Canadian-born. At these same ages 25-64, the new immigrant cohorts arriving before 1980 have considerably higher proportions with some university education than the traditional immigrant group. Of the 49 comparisons among arrivals before 1980, there are only two cases in 1971, two in 1981 and one in 1986 where the traditional immigrant group has more education than the new immigrant group. For persons arriving in 1980 or later, 10 of 12 comparisons show lower education for the new immigrant group.

For women, the immigrant cohorts again tend to have higher levels of education than the Canadian-born. In the 66 comparisons, only 10 cases show higher education on the part of the Canadian-born than the immigrants. For the arrivals preceding 1980, in 44 of 51 comparisons, the new immigrant group has more education on average than the traditional immigrant group. For the more recent arrivals, all 12 comparisons show lower education for the new immigrant group.

Measured both through low and high levels of schooling, the immigrant cohorts tend to have more education than the Canadian-born. The main exception to this is that immigrant women as well as new immigrant group men arriving since 1980 tend to have higher proportions than the Canadian-born at both high and low levels of education. Compared to the traditional immigrant group, the new immigrant group tends to have higher proportions at high levels of education, and lower proportions at low levels of education. However, for the 1975-79 arrivals the new immigrant group tends to have higher proportions at both high and low levels of education, and for the 1980-86 arrivals the new immigrants have less education. Stated differently, there is more diversity in levels of education on the part of immigrant women and on the part of recent cohorts of new immigrants. Considering all persons aged 25 and over, immigrants comprise 21.4 percent of the total Canadian population in 1986, 24.3

TABLE 5a

Proportion with Some University Education, by Age, for Canadian-Born and Given Immigration
Cohorts, Showing Traditional and New Immigrant Groups, Ages 25 and over, Males, 1961-1986

	Total	25-34	35-44	45-54	55-64	65 +
Canadian-born						
1971	8.3	10.0	9.1	7.3	6.8	5.1
1981	12.2	18.7	12.1	10.2	8.6	5.2
1986	19.2	26.6	22.8	14.3	12.3	9.0
	19.1	25.0	27.1	17.9	13.5	10.2
Arrived before 1946						
1961	6.1	16.5	11.6	6.7	5.1	4.5
1971	7.1	29.3	16.2	13.7	6.1	4.9
TIG	6.8	30.8	16.2	12.9	5.9	4.5
NIG	15.8	–	–	38.9	12.1	12.8
1981	9.8	–	30.8	22.2	14.0	6.8
TIG	9.4	–	30.3	21.4	13.0	6.6
NIG	22.2	–	–	45.5	50.0	12.8
1986	11.1	–	32.2	31.5	16.8	8.2
TIG	10.7	–	31.5	30.2	16.1	7.9
NIG	23.0	–	55.6	45.5	40.7	15.6
Arrived 1946-60						
1961	13.4	12.4	14.4	14.0	13.8	12.0
1971	16.3	22.4	15.1	15.6	13.0	13.2
TIG	15.7	21.9	14.4	14.9	12.7	13.3
NIG	26.9	30.4	24.2	33.9	21.4	–
1981	20.4	39.8	24.6	15.4	15.0	13.5
TIG	19.6	38.7	24.4	14.4	14.2	13.2
NIG	34.4	55.4	27.8	27.5	41.7	23.7
1986	21.4	36.6	37.6	16.3	15.7	14.7
TIG	20.5	35.4	36.8	15.4	14.8	14.2
NIG	35.8	50.7	50.5	25.9	34.7	30.1
Arrived 1961-69						
1971	28.2	30.8	30.6	22.5	13.4	2.5
TIG	21.8	24.4	21.3	19.9	13.9	1.5
NIG	49.1	51.0	57.7	34.7	11.5	6.3
1981	30.1	29.9	33.3	28.5	24.2	16.6
TIG	23.0	22.2	26.2	21.0	20.3	12.6
NIG	49.7	49.8	52.2	49.5	38.1	35.3
1986	29.1	32.4	29.6	29.6	24.6	18.3
TIG	23.0	27.3	23.0	21.4	18.8	15.4
NIG	49.1	49.8	50.5	54.2	43.5	27.9
Arrived 1970-74						
1971	36.7	41.0	30.1	37.5	13.3	16.7
TIG	35.0	41.4	28.3	29.4	10.0	18.2
NIG	39.1	40.5	33.3	–	–	–
1981	36.2	40.4	37.0	28.9	24.1	11.4
TIG	26.4	28.2	26.7	25.3	25.3	7.0
NIG	44.5	49.8	46.0	31.8	22.4	15.8

TABLE 5a (cont.)

	Total	Age				
		25-34	35-44	45-54	55-64	65 +
1986	31.7	33.2	40.5	32.6	28.4	18.6
TIG	23.8	21.5	31.8	25.0	27.4	15.3
NIG	39.3	42.1	48.2	39.7	29.5	22.1
Arrived 1975-79						
1981	35.4	38.2	39.5	34.2	18.7	14.4
TIG	32.1	31.5	37.8	32.7	31.3	11.0
NIG	38.0	43.2	40.9	35.3	10.8	16.5
1986	31.0	33.0	42.5	36.1	26.4	17.3
TIG	27.1	25.0	37.1	33.7	29.9	15.4
NIG	33.4	37.3	46.4	37.9	23.9	18.3
Arrived 1980-84						
1981	31.7	34.4	38.8	25.0	23.3	18.2
TIG	32.0	30.6	39.7	27.3	39.4	18.2
NIG	31.6	37.0	38.0	23.4	15.7	18.2
1986	30.5	37.4	43.2	34.3	19.1	18.0
TIG	33.4	37.8	45.2	37.5	26.7	20.3
NIG	29.1	37.3	41.5	32.1	16.4	17.1
Arrived 1985-86						
1986	30.3	40.3	42.8	32.9	20.4	19.4
TIG	33.5	39.1	45.0	42.2	34.1	19.3
NIG	28.9	40.9	41.3	28.1	16.2	19.2

Source: Kalbach, 1970: 195-196; see also Appendix.

In 1986 the total is for 15 and over.

TABLE 5b

Proportion with Some University Education, by Age, for Canadian-born and Given Immigration Cohorts, Showing Traditional and New Immigrant Groups, Ages 25 and over, Females, 1961-1986

	Total	Age				
		25-34	35-44	45-54	55-64	65 +
Canadian-born						
1961	4.8	5.7	4.9	5.2	4.6	3.1
1971	7.4	10.5	8.0	6.1	5.9	4.0
1981	14.1	21.9	15.4	10.5	7.8	6.8
1986	16.2	23.2	21.5	13.0	9.0	12.1
Arrived before 1946						
1961	3.7	8.9	5.6	4.4	3.2	2.7
1971	4.5	16.7	13.3	6.7	5.0	2.7

TABLE 5b (cont.)

	Total	Age				
		25-34	35-44	45-54	55-64	65 +
TIG	4.3	14.5	13.6	6.7	4.7	2.6
NIG	11.5	–	7.7	7.7	17.9	5.8
1981	5.9	–	27.1	12.1	7.8	4.4
TIG	5.7	–	25.9	11.1	7.3	4.4
NIG	17.5	–	36.4	–	30.8	6.5
1986	6.7	–	25.5	19.3	9.2	5.4
TIG	6.5	–	24.9	18.4	8.9	5.2
NIG	15.7	–	44.4	27.7	22.5	11.5
Arrived 1946-60						
1961	7.0	7.2	7.5	7.0	5.2	4.1
1971	8.0	10.5	8.1	7.7	7.1	2.9
TIG	7.6	10.2	7.5	7.5	6.7	3.1
NIG	13.7	15.2	18.0	10.9	13.2	0.0
1981	12.5	28.5	14.4	9.1	8.7	5.4
TIG	12.1	27.8	14.3	8.6	8.5	5.4
NIG	18.6	38.6	15.7	18.2	13.6	5.6
1986	13.8	31.0	26.1	10.1	8.9	7.6
TIG	13.3	29.9	25.3	9.5	8.5	7.6
NIG	22.6	43.6	39.1	17.7	18.6	7.4
Arrived 1961-69						
1971	16.4	21.0	15.9	6.4	6.8	4.1
TIG	13.2	16.5	14.0	5.3	5.4	4.3
NIG	26.8	33.7	22.9	11.3	11.1	3.3
1981	18.8	20.9	23.0	16.1	11.5	3.6
TIG	14.6	16.5	17.6	12.7	10.1	3.8
NIG	29.8	33.0	35.8	25.7	16.3	3.0
1986	21.5	27.9	22.1	19.8	12.6	6.7
TIG	17.9	23.7	17.5	15.0	10.4	6.6
NIG	33.0	42.1	35.3	33.4	20.1	6.9
Arrived 1970-74						
1971	23.1	29.5	20.6	6.9	4.4	8.7
TIG	20.2	27.1	22.2	0.0	5.6	0.0
NIG	27.8	32.6	17.9	15.4	–	–
1981	24.2	28.7	26.2	15.3	8.8	8.4
TIG	20.0	23.7	21.7	11.7	10.4	9.6
NIG	27.9	32.9	29.9	18.8	7.1	7.3
1986	23.6	24.9	32.0	20.0	13.5	7.2
TIG	19.5	17.5	28.5	17.1	14.9	7.3
NIG	27.6	31.6	35.2	22.7	12.1	7.0
Arrived 1975-79						
1971	25.2	32.8	26.8	15.1	9.3	5.9
TIG	24.0	30.7	23.9	17.6	9.1	7.4
NIG	26.0	34.2	29.0	13.4	9.3	4.6
1981	23.0	28.1	32.3	20.4	8.8	6.5
TIG	21.9	25.6	29.3	22.8	11.5	7.5
NIG	23.8	29.6	34.3	18.7	7.4	5.9

TABLE 5b (cont.)

	Total	Age				
		25-34	35-44	45-54	55-64	65 +
Arrived 1980-84						
1981	18.0	27.0	21.5	10.8	6.8	3.8
TIG	22.9	29.2	23.5	23.5	17.9	4.0
NIG	14.8	25.2	19.4	6.3	3.3	3.6
1986	22.7	32.2	31.1	17.8	7.7	6.8
TIG	27.2	35.9	36.1	24.9	13.6	8.3
NIG	20.4	30.2	27.0	14.2	5.9	5.9
Arrived 1985-86						
1986	24.1	36.1	30.9	16.8	9.2	6.7
TIG	32.2	46.0	40.7	29.7	17.0	10.9
NIG	20.5	31.1	24.9	12.7	7.1	3.2

percent of those with some university education and 26.2 percent of those with less than nine years of education. This again suggests that there is more diversity among immigrants since they are more likely to be at the more extreme parts of the educational distribution.

Labour Force

As a measure of labour force involvement, we have chosen to present the proportion working mostly full-time for 40 or more weeks in the year preceding the 1986 Census (Tables 6a and 6b). The comparisons here exclude the groups that have arrived in the year and a half before a given census.

Immigrant men are more likely to be working full-time in 66 of the 78 age-specific comparisons shown in Table 6a. The main exception involves 1980-84 immigrants who are less likely to be working full-time at ages 25-64. The difference between traditional and new immigrant groups is small, but the new immigrant group is less likely to be working full-time than the traditional immigrant group in 45 of the 76 comparisons. It is especially among cohorts arriving in 1975-84 that the new immigrant group is less likely to be working full-time.

For women, the 1946-79 immigrant cohorts are significantly more likely to be working full-time than the Canadian-born. Altogether, in 60 of 78 comparisons, the immigrant women have higher proportions working full-time. In 1986, it is mostly the 1980-84 arrivals that are less likely to be working full-time. The new immigrant group is more likely to be working full-time than the traditional immigrant group in 55 out of 76 comparisons. It is especially at ages 25-64 that the new immigrant group women are more likely to be working full-time.

126

TABLE 6a

Proportion Working Full-Time by Age, for Canadian-born and Given Immigration Cohorts, Showing Traditional and New Immigrant Groups, Males, 1971-1986

	Total	Age					
		15-24	25-34	35-44	45-54	55-64	65 +
Canadian-born							
1971	56.1	24.5	77.7	80.3	77.8	66.8	16.5
1981	55.5	28.1	75.6	80.7	77.2	60.9	10.6
1986	63.9	29.0	71.8	80.9	80.0	70.4	38.1
Arrived before 1946							
1971	40.8	–	74.1	80.2	84.2	70.0	14.9
TIG	40.9	–	76.9	80.1	84.1	70.1	14.9
NIG	38.2	–	–	–	88.9	66.7	15.7
1981	24.5	–	–	80.2	82.6	64.7	6.3
TIG	24.5	–	–	80.9	82.6	64.5	6.3
NIG	24.7	–	–	–	81.8	71.4	7.7
1986	58.3	–	–	85.3	81.7	70.8	34.1
TIG	58.2	–	–	85.2	82.3	70.8	34.1
NIG	61.6	–	–	88.9	76.5	72.8	33.8
Arrived 1946-60							
1971	73.0	30.4	83.2	85.7	83.6	77.7	28.7
TIG	73.1	31.4	83.0	85.7	83.3	77.8	27.7
NIG	70.2	19.3	85.5	85.2	92.9	75.0	–
1981	73.1	53.7	82.3	87.8	84.8	75.2	13.3
TIG	72.6	54.7	82.4	87.5	84.5	75.2	13.2
NIG	81.0	40.0	80.8	91.4	87.9	75.0	18.4
1986	79.4	–	80.1	85.9	83.4	78.0	42.4
TIG	79.3	–	80.3	86.1	83.3	77.8	41.9
NIG	81.3	–	76.9	83.6	84.6	81.0	52.2
Arrived 1961-69							
1971	68.3	38.8	79.5	81.1	79.0	59.8	13.6
TIG	70.3	44.4	81.0	81.3	78.0	64.4	13.9
NIG	61.8	21.2	74.5	80.4	83.7	42.3	12.5
1981	66.8	23.4	78.3	84.5	80.0	72.3	14.8
TIG	65.8	25.8	78.4	83.3	78.3	71.9	15.5
NIG	69.6	15.0	77.9	87.6	84.1	73.5	11.8
1986	74.9	34.0	75.3	84.5	83.2	80.0	46.9
TIG	74.4	36.3	75.9	83.8	82.4	79.2	45.1
NIG	76.5	24.5	73.3	86.5	85.8	82.6	52.6
Arrived 1970-74							
1971	31.5	17.1	37.7	54.8	50.0	0.0	25.0
TIG	33.1	19.7	42.1	52.2	47.1	0.0	18.2
NIG	29.1	12.7	32.4	59.3	–	–	–
1981	66.3	23.7	76.6	83.3	79.3	66.9	13.2
TIG	66.2	27.0	77.6	81.4	81.5	69.0	10.5
NIG	66.5	20.5	75.7	85.0	77.4	65.5	15.8
1986	69.8	22.8	76.0	82.1	81.2	77.0	46.3
TIG	68.0	26.4	76.0	81.3	79.8	75.1	43.3
NIG	71.4	17.7	75.9	82.9	82.5	79.3	48.6

TABLE 6a (cont.)

	Total	15-24	25-34	35-44	45-54	55-64	65+
				Age			
Arrived 1975-79							
1981	62.5	30.2	77.2	83.1	75.3	56.0	12.2
TIG	68.6	36.6	78.8	87.9	79.1	65.6	5.5
NIG	58.5	27.1	75.9	79.0	72.6	50.0	16.5
1986	67.8	24.5	74.2	81.7	80.6	74.4	47.6
TIG	70.3	26.3	77.8	83.0	81.6	77.8	47.8
NIG	66.1	23.3	72.1	80.7	79.9	71.6	47.3
Arrived 1980-84							
1981	21.1	11.7	29.1	35.3	20.0	17.5	1.5
TIG	34.7	27.2	42.4	43.6	30.3	36.4	0.0
NIG	13.5	6.8	19.8	28.3	12.8	8.6	3.0
1986	62.0	35.0	68.3	75.2	72.3	56.8	45.0
TIG	68.2	32.8	73.8	79.4	78.2	64.4	39.7
NIG	58.6	35.9	65.5	71.5	68.1	53.8	46.6
Arrived 1985-86							
1986	27.2	14.3	28.4	37.3	36.8	30.9	23.5
TIG	36.5	20.7	35.2	46.9	51.0	42.9	37.5
NIG	22.6	12.0	24.9	31.2	29.3	26.7	11.1

Source and notes: See Appendix.

TABLE 6b

Proportion Working Full-Time, by Age, for Canadian-born and Given Immigration Cohorts, Showing Traditional and New Immigrant Groups, Females, 1971-1986

	Total	15-24	25-34	35-44	45-54	55-64	65+
				Age			
Canadian-born							
1971	22.3	21.0	26.7	23.8	27.5	24.1	5.2
1981	26.7	23.3	38.0	33.8	31.9	20.5	3.1
1986	45.3	26.9	52.7	52.7	53.2	49.2	27.1
Arrived before 1946							
1971	13.3	–	25.6	30.7	29.6	23.8	3.9
TIG	13.0	–	22.9	30.2	29.3	23.4	3.8
NIG	26.6	–	–	38.5	46.2	39.3	7.7
1981	8.2	–	–	49.0	34.2	20.5	2.0
TIG	8.1	–	–	51.8	34.0	20.6	1.9
NIG	11.7	–	–	27.3	–	15.4	5.2
1986	41.9	–	–	53.2	55.3	48.9	23.0
TIG	41.7	–	–	53.2	55.5	48.6	23.1
NIG	47.9	–	–	53.3	54.8	56.1	19.6

TABLE 6b (cont.)

	Total	Age 15-24	25-34	35-44	45-54	55-64	65+
Arrived 1946-60							
1971	28.3	27.7	28.5	30.5	32.8	27.1	5.6
TIG	28.1	28.4	28.2	29.9	32.5	26.8	5.7
NIG	30.4	17.9	33.3	39.0	38.2	31.6	3.9
1981	31.7	47.0	44.3	38.5	37.8	26.7	3.2
TIG	31.2	46.0	44.2	37.6	37.3	26.4	2.9
NIG	40.1	64.3	45.6	50.7	47.0	37.0	6.5
1986	54.0	–	55.9	54.8	56.5	53.0	29.8
TIG	53.7	–	55.9	54.8	55.8	52.7	29.6
NIG	58.6	–	56.7	55.1	63.9	58.3	32.5
Arrived 1961-69							
1971	32.2	30.2	35.2	36.4	34.7	17.7	6.5
TIG	30.1	32.1	31.3	32.6	34.4	17.1	5.0
NIG	38.9	24.5	46.0	50.7	35.9	19.4	13.3
1981	36.9	21.1	42.5	45.1	46.0	33.3	4.0
TIG	33.7	21.9	39.5	40.0	42.0	30.8	4.3
NIG	46.0	17.8	50.6	57.5	57.4	41.9	3.0
1986	55.6	34.4	57.9	59.4	61.6	59.9	35.5
TIG	53.5	36.1`	57.4	56.3	58.6	58.2	33.0
NIG	61.6	26.7	59.7	67.5	69.2	64.4	42.9
Arrived 1970-74							
1971	14.4	17.8	14.7	12.3	3.5	0.0	13.0
TIG	14.0	19.1	13.2	13.3	0.0	0.0	10.0
NIG	14.9	15.6	16.8	190.7	7.7	–	–
1981	40.0	20.9	47.8	49.6	47.7	24.3	2.7
TIG	33.4	23.8	37.1	41.8	43.2	24.0	2.6
NIG	45.4	18.1	56.8	56.0	52.1	24.7	2.7
1986	53.1	22.3	58.2	61.4	63.9	59.4	30.4
TIG	47.8	24.5	54.0	54.3	58.5	57.2	24.8
NIG	58.0	19.5	61.7	67.1	68.6	62.0	35.6
Arrived 1975-79							
1981	32.0	24.3	40.6	41.2	36.2	16.0	2.8
TIG	30.8	25.6	37.0	36.3	36.8	23.9	3.0
NIG	32.8	23.6	43.1	45.1	35.8	12.4	2.6
1986	50.2	22.9	54.9	58.3	62.3	51.5	37.0
TIG	46.2	22.4	50.5	52.0	60.5	50.5	38.1
NIG	52.6	23.2	57.2	62.4	63.5	52.0	36.3
Arrived 1980-84							
1981	10.1	10.0	14.2	17.0	6.9	0.9	1.0
TIG	12.5	17.0	14.9	13.2	2.9	3.6	0.0
NIG	8.5	6.1	13.6	20.9	8.3	0.0	1.8
1986	45.1	30.6	49.9	51.9	50.7	41.1	34.7
TIG	43.7	31.5	46.6	45.8	51.5	48.4	33.7
NIG	45.9	30.3	51.7	56.6	50.3	38.7	34.9
Arrived 1985-86							
1986	23.6	17.4	28.1	25.6	23.6	22.6	23.7
TIG	26.2	21.7	29.9	26.0	30.1	17.8	12.5
NIG	22.2	15.0	27.1	25.2	21.2	24.2	18.2

Source and notes: See Appendix.

Overall, the immigrants comprise 18.4 percent of the population aged 15 and over but 20.4 percent of persons working full-time in 1986. Also, within age categories, both immigrant men and women are more likely to work full-time. The main exception involves the 1980-84 arrivals, who are less likely to do so. New immigrant men are less likely to be working full-time than their traditional immigrant group counterparts, but for women the new immigrant group is more likely to be working full-time.

Total Income

Average total incomes, were calculated for persons with positive incomes in the year preceding the 1986 Census (Tables 7a and 7b). Once again, persons who arrived in the year and a half preceding the census are excluded from the tables.

For men at ages 25-64, the average income of immigrant cohorts is above the Canadian-born in 32 out of 54 comparisons. The 1971, 1981 and 1986 income averages are all above the Canadian-born average among cohorts that arrived before 1961 for both traditional and new immigrant groups. In the 1961-69 cohort, incomes are typically below the Canadian-born in 1971 but above in 1981 and 1986. This progress applies to both traditional and new immigrant groups. In the 1970-84 cohorts, incomes are below the Canadian-born in 1981 and 1986. In the 1970-79 arrivals, average incomes of the traditional immigrant group are above that of the Canadian-born in five of eight comparisons in 1981 but in all cases in 1986. For the new immigrant group in these same cohorts, average incomes are below the Canadian-born in all eight comparisons in 1981 and in seven cases in 1986. For the 1980-84 arrivals, the income averages of both traditional and new immigrant groups are below the Canadian-born. Average incomes are higher for the traditional immigrant group in 31 out of the 51 comparisons that can be made at ages 25-64. Typically, incomes are higher for the traditional immigrant group in 31 out of the 51 comparisons that can be made at ages 25-64. Typically, incomes are higher for new immigrant groups that arrived before 1970 but higher for traditional immigrant groups that arrived since 1970. It is especially for the 1975-84 arrivals that the new immigrant group is at a significant disadvantage.

For women at ages 25-64, average total incomes are higher for immigrants than Canadian-born in 35 of 54 comparisons. Typically, average incomes are higher for immigrants who arrived before 1970 and lower for those who arrived in 1975-84. It is only at ages 45-64 that females who arrived in 1961-69 follow the male pattern of having lower incomes in 1971 and higher incomes in 1981 and 1986. At ages 25-44 the 1961-69 cohort already has an average income above that of the Canadian-born in 1971. For the arrivals preceding 1970, the income averages of the new immigrant group are above the traditional immigrant group in 28 of 32 comparisons. In the 1970-74 arrivals, the new immigrant group

TABLE 7a

Average Total Income, by Age for Canadian-born and Given Immigration Cohorts, Showing Traditional and New Immigrant Groups, Males, 1971-1986

		Age					
	Total	15-24	25-34	35-44	45-54	55-64	65 +
Canadian-born							
1971	6,508	2,999	7,324	8,733	8,562	7,276	4,052
1981	16,503	7,863	18,175	23,006	22,491	19,151	11,413
1986	22,933	8,795	23,437	31,436	31,804	27,330	19,245
Arrived before 1946							
1971	5,885	–	7,704	9,779	10,255	7,637	3,885
TIG	5,839	–	7,870	9,572	10,008	7,613	3,868
NIG	7,081	–	–	–	17,801	8,414	4,287
1981	14,298	–	–	25,067	26,360	22,650	10,604
TIG	14,225	–	–	25,197	26,231	22,304	10,589
NIG	16,554	–	–	–	30,393	35,208	11,060
1986	20,791	–	–	34,823	39,812	31,222	21,257
TIG	20,680	–	–	34,798	39,775	30,810	21,209
NIG	23,876	–	–	35,592	40,208	44,414	22,778
Arrived 1946-60							
1971	7,988	3,353	8,055	9,392	9,268	8,087	4,215
TIG	7,963	3,431	8,072	9,362	9,082	8,114	4,179
NIG	8,420	2,468	7,814	9,816	14,193	7,367	5,213
1981	21,088	10,764	20,822	24,780	24,128	21,028	10,811
TIG	21,002	10,966	20,929	24,732	24,131	20,935	10,770
NIG	22,550	7,572	19.353	25,390	24,088	24,128	12,450
1986	29,340	–	27,892	35,570	33,159	29,864	19,587
TIG	29,144	–	27,829	35,497	33,212	29,583	19,463
NIG	32,547	–	28,640	36,752	32,574	35,545	23,701
Arrived 1961-69							
1971	7,033	3,889	7,301	8,498	9,733	5,829	3,096
TIG	7,077	4,115	7,392	8,333	9,882	6,205	2,790
NIG	6,882	3,032	7,009	8,990	9,030	4,006	–
1981	19,005	6,808	18,940	23,495	23,082	19,553	10,294
TIG	18,545	7,076	18,678	23,088	22,584	19,260	10,291
NIG	20,341	5,793	19,616	24,575	24,457	20,575	10,311
1986	27,647	9,786	23,700	33,164	33,953	29,052	17,298
TIG	26,847	10,152	23,529	32,466	32,854	27,692	17,055
NIG	30,293	8,269	24,301	35,374	37,279	33,498	18,091
Arrived 1970-74							
1981	17,030	6,797	17,930	20,810	19,085	16,596	10,080
TIG	18,370	7,697	19,652	22,069	21,548	18,481	11,227
NIG	15,868	5,879	16,588	19,702	17,105	13,964	8,829
1986	24,859	7,209	24,200	31,149	30,312	25,994	15,260
TIG	25,522	7,873	24,727	32,850	32,104	27,447	17,348
NIG	24,224	6,305	23,793	29,638	28,623	24,270	13,087
Arrived 1975-79							
1981	15,507	7,290	16,644	20,177	21,846	14,329	7,240

TABLE 7a (cont.)

		Total	Age					
			15-24	25-34	35-44	45-54	55-64	65+
	TIG	18,601	8,431	18,678	24,181	26,365	19,396	8,915
	NIG	13,312	6,719	15,109	16,749	18,744	10,752	5,970
1986		22,358	7,425	22,435	30,357	28,976	22,423	10,535
	TIG	26,280	8,010	25,868	35,293	33,395	28,327	12,882
	NIG	19,808	7,050	20,560	26,686	25,683	18,265	9,386
Arrived 1980-84								
1986		17,800	8,244	18,787	25,395	23,727	15,460	10,463
	TIG	23,703	9,349	23,755	30,982	30,562	24,363	14,493
	NIG	14,631	7,853	16,241	20,814	18,905	12,054	8,698

Source and notes: See Appendix.
In 1986: 65+ is 65-74.

TABLE 7b

Average Total Income, Females, 1971-1986

		Total	Age					
			15-24	25-34	35-44	45-54	55-64	65+
Canadian-born								
1971		2,908	2,277	3,474	3,319	3,360	3,282	2,338
1981		8,329	5,663	10,066	10,176	9,919	8,330	7,126
1986		12,527	6,904	14,520	15,980	14,895	12,435	11,131
Arrived before 1946								
1971		2,515	–	2,913	3,357	3,335	3,469	2,124
	TIG	2,491	–	2,815	3,366	3,328	3,432	2,108
	NIG	3,483	–	–	3,241	3,584	4,607	2,997
1981		7,464	–	–	10,537	10,260	8,598	6,997
	TIG	7,443	–	–	10,980	20,204	8,584	6,974
	NIG	8,544	–	–	7,039	–	9,354	8,260
1986		11,997	–	–	16,834	16,456	13,316	11,966
	TIG	11,961	–	–	16,809	16,164	13,248	11,946
	NIG	13,375	–	–	17,609	19,544	15,941	12,760
Arrived 1946-60								
1971		3,150	2,562	3,511	3,395	3,625	3,352	1,819
	TIG	3,137	2,615	3,435	3,341	3,597	3,407	1,834
	NIG	3,325	1,900	4,431	4,088	4,247	2,719	1,623
1981		9,564	8,157	11,219	10,657	10,280	9,213	6,455
	TIG	9,454	8,096	11,199	10,508	10,075	9,137	6,419
	NIG	11,287	8,995	11,495	12,728	13,146	11,275	6,973
1986		14,088	–	16,522	17,387	15,486	13,199	10,765
	TIG	13,942	–	16,376	17,349	15,246	13,043	10,693
	NIG	16,375	–	18,283	18,014	18,278	16,303	12,290

TABLE 7b (cont.)

				Age			
	Total	15-24	25-34	35-44	45-54	55-64	65 +
Arrived 1961-69							
1971	3,299	2,716	3,660	3,701	3,236	2,515	1,427
TIG	3,151	2,780	3,498	3,393	3,136	2,398	1,388
NIG	3,709	2,514	4,030	4,536	3,704	2,929	1,612
1981	9,523	5,251	10,440	11,228	11,242	9,951	5,758
TIG	8,925	5,322	9,887	10,339	10,559	10,004	5,839
NIG	11,045	4,977	11,767	13,075	12,892	9,791	5,506
1986	14,530	8,207	15,234	16,912	16,793	13,881	9,757
TIG	13,712	8,351	14,815	15,939	15,521	13,066	9,519
NIG	16,947	7,551	16,593	19,469	20,050	16,329	10,449
Arrived 1970-74							
1981	8,957	5,195	10,065	10,538	9,179	6,527	4,613
TIG	8,522	5,464	9,574	10,168	8,494	6,585	5,300
NIG	9,308	4,935	10,407	10,812	9,870	6,460	3,774
1986	13,651	6,232	14,732	16,769	15,344	12,544	9,723
TIG	12,994	6,325	13,768	16,459	15,024	12,551	10,111
NIG	14,256	6,108	15,531	17,021	15,621	12,537	9,355
Arrived 1975-79							
1981	7,891	5,797	8,866	8,920	9,253	6,352	5,001
TIG	8,237	5,763	9,399	8,635	10,347	8,724	5,612
NIG	7,668	5,816	8,546	9,129	8,601	4,912	3,917
1986	12,105	6,290	13,324	15,372	14,105	9,815	7,269
TIG	12,336	6,142	13,526	15,648	14,742	12,320	7,418
NIG	11,968	6,389	13,221	15,201	13,673	8,520	7,186
Arrived 1980-84							
1986	9,955	6,766	11,262	12,083	10,878	8,127	7,289
TIG	11,149	7,222	12,462	12,896	12,624	10,667	8,408
NIG	9,296	6,576	10,610	11,484	9,961	7,224	6,364

Source and notes: See Appendix.

In 1986: 65 and over is 65-74.

is above in six out of eight comparisons. The predominant pattern in this cohort, for both groups, is to be below the Canadian-born average in 1981 but above in 1986. For the 1975-84 arrivals, average incomes are below the Canadian-born in both 1981 and 1986. Also, the average incomes of the traditional immigrant group are above the new immigrant group in 11 out of 12 comparisons for these cohorts.

It should be noted that for the older immigration cohorts, a majority of the immigrants recorded here were children at the time of arrival. For instance, in the cohort arriving before 1946, 88.5 percent of those aged 35-64 in 1981 were less than 15 when they arrived. Similarly, the majority of the 1946-60 arrivals who were aged 15-34 in 1981, and of the 1961-69 arrivals who were aged 15-24 in 1981, arrived as children. However, by using controls for age, the cells tend not to confuse the immigrants who arrived as children with those who arrived as adults. That is, most cells apply to only one of these two categories. For those cells involving both categories (in particular the 1946-60 cohort who were aged 35-64 in 1981) those who arrived as children had higher average total incomes in 1981 than those who arrived at older ages and also higher incomes than the Canadian-born (data not presented).

In general, 1986 average total incomes are above that of the Canadian-born for immigrant men who arrived before 1970 and for immigrant women who arrived before 1975. For men, the 1961-69 cohort is below the Canadian-born in 1971 but above in 1981 and 1986. For women, the 1970-74 cohort is below the Canadian-born in 1981 and above in 1986. Compared to the traditional immigrant group, the new immigrant group is typically at an advantage for men arriving before 1970 and for women arriving before 1975. For the most recent cohorts, both men and women new immigrants are at a relative disadvantage.

Employment Income

Table 8a presents comparisons over the 1971-86 censuses of average employment incomes for men working full-time for 40 or more weeks. As with Table 7, the cohorts (both the traditional and new immigrant groups) arriving before 1961 have higher mean incomes than the Canadian-born. In the 1961-69 cohort, two (out of five) age groups are above the Canadian-born in 1971, three in 1981 and four in 1986. The progress over censuses applies to both the traditional and new immigrant groups. For the 1971-74 cohort, all age groups are below the Canadian-born in 1981 but two are above by 1986. For the 1975-79 arrivals, the traditional immigrant group shows four of five cases above the Canadian-born in both 1981 and 1986. However, the new immigrant group is constantly below the Canadian-born average. In the 1980-84 arrivals, all but two cases (both involving the traditional immigrant group) are below the mean employment income of the Canadian-born. Thus the intercensus comparisons show some progress for the 1961-74 cohorts, otherwise groups tend to be above or below the Canadian-born at each census.

In the case of women, the 1946-60 cohort is the most advanced in average employment income, compared to the Canadian-born (Table 8b). In the 1961-69 cohort, no age groups are above the Canadian-born in 1971 but two age groups are above in 1981 and two in 1986. In this cohort, the new immigrant group is most likely to be above the Canadian-born. The employment income for cohorts arriving since 1970 are uniformly below the Canadian-born average, for both the traditional and new immigrant groups.

In general, average employment incomes tend to be above the Canadian-born for immigrant cohorts that arrived before 1960. The 1961-69 cohort is the one most likely to make progress from below to above the Canadian-born average

TABLE 8a

Male Average Employment Income For Persons Working Full Time, 40 or Over Weeks Per Year,
Ages 15-64, Canada 1971, 1981, 1986

Males	Total	Age				
		15-24	25-34	35-44	45-54	55-64
Canadian-born						
1971	8,146	5,265	7,927	9,217	9,032	8,117
1981	20,784	13,492	19,950	24,208	23,688	21,352
1986	29,790	16,486	26,970	34,118	34,972	32,249
Arrived before 1946						
1971	9,036	–	8,735	10,466	10,381	7,912
TIG	8,918	–	8,678	10,253	10,223	7,842
NIG	12,647	–	–	–	15,001	10,404
1981	24,776	–	–	26,761	26,325	23,821
TIG	24,600	–	–	26,708	26,483	23,468
NIG	30,389	–	–	–	–	34,428
1986	36,306	–	–	36,975	41,847	35,111
TIG	35,786	–	–	37,077	41,586	34,519
NIG	48,511	–	–	34,135	44,843	52,018
Arrived 1946-60						
1971	8,901	5,483	8,446	9,444	9,499	8,614
TIG	8,846	5,505	8,472	9,421	9,299	8,623
NIG	9,845	5,075	8,064	9,759	14,087	8,346
1981	22,971	13,366	21,770	24,705	23,728	21,792
TIG	22,964	13,584	21,832	24,701	23,789	21,701
NIG	23,076	–	20,934	24,750	22,981	24,794
1986	33,987	–	30,490	36,981	34,307	32,438
TIG	33,901	–	30,299	36,868	34,448	32,189
NIG	35,213	–	32,845	38,877	32,790	37,128
Arrived 1961-69						
1971	8,058	5,548	7,825	8,939	10,628	6,897
TIG	8,009	5,527	7,849	8,730	10,866	7,164
NIG	8,242	5,692	7,743	9,559	9,560	5,186
1981	22,162	13,024	20,125	23,384	24,346	21,704
TIG	21,680	12,980	19,757	23,419	24,077	21,281
NIG	23,480	13,307	21,078	24,876	25,037	23,160
1986	32,257	16,588	26,665	34,406	35,886	32,760
TIG	31,199	16,670	26,232	33,543	34,718	31,384
NIG	35,645	16,084	28,254	37,051	39,253	36,881
Arrived 1970-74						
1981	19,748	11,870	19,536	21,520	20,152	19,172
TIG	21,278	12,704	21,185	23,083	22,142	22,550
NIG	18,429	10,790	18,229	20,204	18,416	14,575
1986	30,466	15,817	27,044	33,042	32,603	20,696
TIG	31,655	16,134	27,159	34,962	34,803	31,998
NIG	29,379	15,168	29,956	31,363	30,574	37,134
Arrived 1975-79						
1981	18,569	11,772	18,159	21,346	22,925	16,040

Ethnic Demography

TABLE 8a (cont.)

| Males | Total | Age | | | | |
		15-24	25-34	35-44	45-54	55-64
TIG	21,457	12,868	20,290	24,819	26,928	21,911
NIG	16,277	11,089	16,519	18,085	19,796	11,365
1986	28,243	15,290	25,275	32,492	31,233	25,996
TIG	32,347	16,507	27,988	37,437	33,851	30,908
NIG	25,351	14,398	23,666	28,676	27,612	21,894
Arrived 1980-84						
1986	23,198	14,048	22,093	28,644	26,919	16,702
TIG	29,046	16,598	27,014	34,055	33,539	30,370
NIG	19,218	13,187	19,235	23,571	21,342	14,681

Sources and notes: see Appendix.

TABLE 8b

Female Average Employment Income For Persons Working Full time, 40 or Over Weeks Per Year, Ages 15-64, Canada 1971, 1981, 1986

| Females | Total | Age | | | | |
		15-24	25-34	35-44	45-54	55-64
Canadian-born						
1971	4,795	4,011	5,176	5,212	4,982	5,097
1981	13,284	10,237	14,232	14,679	14,200	13,677
1986	19,506	13,381	19,893	22,015	20,785	19,798
Arrived before 1946						
1971	5,014	–	4,566	5,098	4,633	5,321
TIG	5,026	–	5,048	5,157	4,646	5,278
NIG	4,790	–	–	–	–	6,279
1981	13,398	–	–	14,293	14,053	12,933
TIG	13,333	–	–	14,384	13,913	12,884
NIG	15,861	–	–	–	–	–
1986	20,536	–	–	22,423	21,402	20,078
TIG	20,464	–	–	22,571	21,131	20,033
NIG	22,048	–	–	17,938	24,236	21,264
Arrived 1946-60						
1971	4,843	4,286	5,101	4,926	4,959	4,809
TIG	4,798	4,288	4,990	4,884	4,942	4,747
NIG	5,514	4,239	6,492	5,402	5,312	5,663
1981	13,891	10,824	14,985	14,161	13,255	13,931
TIG	13,795	10,958	14,890	14,036	13,069	13,958
NIG	15,206	–	16,357	15,559	15,480	13,261
1986	20,954	–	22,037	22,847	19,801	19,769
TIG	20,859	–	21,899	22,772	19,696	19,642
NIG	22,187	–	23,675	24,086	20,857	21,745

TABLE 8b (cont.)

Females	Total	Age				
		15-24	25-34	35-44	45-54	55-64
Arrived 1961-69						
1971	4,552	3,905	4,773	4,829	4,329	4,214
TIG	4,385	3,782	4,717	4,556	4,135	3,975
NIG	4,957	4,377	4,878	5,473	5,261	–
1981	13,548	10,271	13,696	14,260	13,441	14,505
TIG	13,094	10,288	13,266	13,679	13,131	14,778
NIG	14,494	10,194	14,615	15,223	14,086	13,777
1986	20,032	13,939	19,667	21,174	21,108	19,458
TIG	19,105	13,827	19,251	20,308	19,933	18,531
NIG	22,402	14,632	20,992	23,084	23,630	21,730
Arrived 1970-74						
1981	12,245	9,622	12,586	12,986	11,521	10,089
TIG	12,281	9,214	12,735	13,690	11,310	10,512
NIG	12,221	10,147	12,505	12,556	11,690	9,626
1986	19,156	13,347	18,604	20,817	18,623	17,730
TIG	19,167	13,038	18,039	21,658	19,039	18,863
NIG	19,148	13,868	19,019	20,264	18,314	16,721
Arrived 1975-79						
1981	11,107	9,472	11,645	10,946	12,499	10,278
TIG	12,125	9,303	13,145	11,603	13,706	12,877
NIG	10,502	9,570	10,812	10,524	11,706	8,005
1986	17,505	12,942	17,318	19,342	17,267	14,761
TIG	18,696	12,638	18,301	21,088	18,619	17,779
NIG	16,883	13,140	16,864	18,427	16,372	13,138
Arrived 1980-84						
1986	14,446	11,680	15,092	15,713	14,367	11,818
TIG	16,822	12,391	17,632	18,273	16,554	15,409
NIG	13,208	11,364	13,821	14,113	13,037	10,347

over the period 1971 to 1986, especially for males. For male arrivals since 1975 and since 1970 for women, the new immigrant group has average incomes that are uniformly below the Canadian-born, by age groups.

Conclusion

In summary, the predominant pattern appears to be that the arrival status of immigrant cohorts largely determines their evolution on given socio-demographic characteristics from census to census. While the geographic distribution of immigrants changes somewhat from census to census, this change is small compared to the overall impact of arriving cohorts on the distribution of the Canadian population. For cohorts since 1946, immigration has largely been to the advantage of the relative size of the population of Ontario and British Columbia and to the disadvantage of the Atlantic provinces and Quebec. The immigrants who arrived in Quebec since 1970 are more likely to contribute to the French than the English language of that province, but in general immigration reduces the predominance of the French over the English language in Quebec. For the rest of Canada, immigration largely contributes to the English language and increases the predominance of English over French.

As can be expected, the educational characteristics of adult immigrants does not change extensively over time. The immigrant cohorts tend to have more education than the Canadian-born. However, immigrant women, as well as new immigrant group men arriving since 1980 tend to have higher proportions at both high and low levels of education. Except for the 1980-84 arrivals as measured in 1986, immigrants, both men and women, are more likely to be working full-time than their Canadian-born counterparts. In contrast to their advantages on education and labour force status, immigrant men arriving since 1970 and women arriving since 1975 tend to have lower average total incomes. On average employment incomes, the men arriving since 1975 and women arriving since 1970 have lower average incomes. Earlier immigrants tend to have higher incomes than the Canadian-born of the same age and sex groups. It would appear that, compared to the Canadian-born, the more recent immigrants, especially of the 1980-84 period, are less selective on characteristics of education, labour force status and income.

As of the 1986 Census, the traditional immigrant group from Europe and the United States comprised 95 percent of the pre-1961 immigrants; however the complement of new immigrants amounted to 65 percent of the 1980-86 arrivals. While they are different in terms of recency of arrival and place of origin, these two immigrant groups are rather similar on other characteristics. Their geographic distribution is similar except that the new immigrant group is slightly less likely to be in Ontario and more likely to be in Quebec and British Columbia. They are also similar on linguistic characteristics except that the recent cohorts of new immigrant groups in Quebec are more likely to be oriented toward the French language. Among cohorts preceding 1975, the new immigrants have more average education, but the opposite holds for the 1980-86 cohorts. New immigrant men are less likely to be working full-time than their traditional immigrant group counterparts, but for women the new immigrant groups are more likely to be working full-time. Regarding average total income, the new immigrant group is typically at an advantage for men who arrived before 1970 and for women who arrived before 1975. On average employment income, it is in the male cohorts before 1975 and the female cohorts before 1970 that the new immigrant group is most likely to be at an advantage. Among the most recent cohorts, both male and female new immigrants are at a relative disadvantage on both of these income measures.

The lower income of the 1980-84 new immigrant cohort would partly follow from their lower education (and the lower labour force status of men). For the cohorts preceding 1970, the higher education and labour force status of new immigrant groups is reflected in their higher average incomes. The 1970-79 cohorts are at an intermediate position. The new immigrant group in these cohorts sometimes has advantages on education and/or labour force status but lower average total and/or employment incomes.

This analysis has not documented many cases of the transitions over time that Richmond and Kalbach (1980) had found when they considered the change in the 1946-60 immigrant cohort between 1961 and 1971. On geographic distribution, immigration accentuates the regional inequalities in terms of proportionate share of the population. On language, immigration both to Quebec and the rest of Canada plays to the disadvantage of the relative size of the French population. However, in the cohorts since 1970, the immigrants who stay in Quebec are more likely to transfer to the French than to the English language. Regarding education and labour force participation, there are very few transitions; in the overwhelming majority of comparisons, given immigrant cohorts are either above or below the Canadian-born at each of the 1971, 1981 and 1986 censuses. There are some transitions in average incomes: men who arrived in 1961-69 are below the Canadian-born in 1971 but above in 1981 and 1986 (for both total employment income), women who arrived in 1970-74 had lower total income than the Canadian-born in 1981 but higher in 1986. Otherwise, the majority of specific age groups, for given cohorts, are either above the Canadian-born figures on average income at each census or below the Canadian-born at each census.

This lack of transitions in the relative position of immigrants implies that their status at the time of arrival is key to their subsequent situation, at least in the medium term. Therefore, the relative selectivity of immigrants, along with the receptivity of the host society, are important to their subsequent progress. This points to concerns regarding the 1980-84 cohort, who have disadvantages not only on income, as we would expect, but also on education and labour force participation. This cohort starts with more disadvantages relative to the Canadian-born cohort than did the earlier immigrant cohorts analysed here. The greater importance of the family and refugee classes in this cohort must be contributing to their weak relative situation on these socioeconomic characteristics.

Notes

1. *Sources*
   The sources of the 1971 and 1981 data shown in Tables 1 to 7 are the Census Public Use Sample Tapes. The 1986 data are from special tabulations derived from the 1986 Census.

2. *Immigrant groups*
   TIG: traditional immigrant group (persons born in Europe or the United States).
   NIG: new immigrant group (persons born in other parts of the world).
   The Canadian-born in 1981 and 1986 includes persons who were born abroad but were Canadian citizens at birth. In each of 1971, 1981 and 1986, the Canadian-born also includes persons who were born in Canada but who subsequently immigrated to Canada.

3. *Immigration cohorts*
   Due to categories in the Public Use Sample Tapes, in 1981 the cohort labelled 1961-69 is really the 1961-70 cohort and the cohort labelled 1970-74 is really the 1971-74 cohort.
   Obviously, in 1971 the 1970-74 cohort is really the 1970-71 cohort (arriving before the census) and in 1981 the 1980-84 cohort is the 1980-81 cohort.

4. *Small cells*
   All results involving less than 10 cases are deleted in the tables.

5. *Specific tables*
   Tables 1 and 2: The Territories are included with British Columbia in 1961 and 1986, and with the Atlantic provinces in 1981. In 1971 the Territories and Prince Edward Island are excluded.
   Table 3: Predominant language is measured through official languages and home language, giving priority to English and French (see text).
   Table 6: Working full-time is defined as working 40 or more weeks in the year preceding the census, *and* working mostly full-time in this period.
   Tables 7 and 8: Average incomes are calculated for persons with incomes higher than zero.

8. "NEW WAVE" IMMIGRANTS: ORIGINS AND CHARACTERISTICS

Alan B. Simmons

This paper concerns the characteristics of the "new" immigration wave to Canada, which began after the adoption of major changes to the immigration law in 1968. Prior to this date Canadian policy had been based on a nationality preference system which was racist in tone and which favoured immigrants from Europe. In contrast, the revised law opened the door to people of all national origins by eliminating preferences for particular national groups. To be accepted as an Independent Class immigrant, an applicant from any country had to gain a fixed number of "points" based primarily on occupation, education, language skills and age.[1]

Since 1968, some 2.8 million immigrants have arrived in Canada. As one would expect, the total inflow has come increasingly from new origin countries, particularly from Africa, Asia and Latin America. In fact, immigration from Third World origins now constitutes two-thirds of the inflow to Canada. Of course, the racial, ethnic and cultural characteristics of Third World origin immigrants are distinctive. At the same time, their age, gender and educational characteristics (which are determined in large part by the points selection system) fall within a narrower range and are less different from those of immigrants arriving from Europe. Within this restricted range of variation, however, immigrant streams from particular countries and regions do reveal important differences in age, gender and educational characteristics.

The paper argues that the "new wave" of immigration has various implications for the changing ethnic character of the Canadian population. Actual impacts to date have been fairly modest but are accelerating in pace; the future implications of current trends are significant indeed.

Background

Canada is a country of relatively recent settlement and, correspondingly, the number of immigrants arriving over the past 100 years has been high relative to world flows and also high in terms of social, economic and demographic impact, particularly in the earlier period of settlement when the Canadian population was smaller. Inflow levels over the 20th century up to the present averaged around 150,000 arrivals per year, with very wide fluctuations from one year and decade to the next.

As Table 1 shows, there was a boom in immigration during the early years of the century prior to World War I as the Canadian West was settled. In dramatic contrast, scarcely any new immigrants came during the Depression. After World War II there was a return to higher inflows (150,000/year) associated with relative prosperity and a labour shortage, particularly in the burgeoning construction industry in large cities during the 1950s. These higher levels continued on the average through the 1960s to the end of the 1970s. The first half-dozen years of the 1980s were characterized by low average annual inflows, followed by an upward shift to the historical average in 1987.

TABLE 1

Impact of Immigration on Canadian Population, 1861-1986

Period	Population at end of period	Population growth over period	Immigrant arrivals over period	Annual arrivals as a % of Cdn. pop (average)
1861-71	3,689	–	183	0.5
1871-81	4,325	636	353	0.8
1881-91	4,833	508	903	1.9
1891-01	5,371	538	326	0.6
1901-11	7,207	1,836	1,759	2.4
1911-21	8,788	1,581	1,612	1.8
1921-31	10,377	1,589	1,203	1.2
1931-41	11,507	1,130	150	0.1
1941-51	14,009	2,502	548	0.4
1951-61	18,238	4,229	1,543	0.8
1961-71	21,568	3,330	1,429	0.7
1971-81	24,083	2,515	1,447	0.6
1981-86	25,400	1,317	496	0.4

Sources: Data for 1861 to 1981 from *Employment and Immigration Canada, Immigration Statistics, 1984*. (Ottawa: Minister of Supply and Services, 1986. Table G-1) Data for 1981-86 from Statistics Canada, 1986 Census, and from special runs of Employment Immigration data on arrivals. Intercensal estimates are from mid-year to mid-year.

From 1951 to the present, as the population of Canada grew and as immigration levels fell (in the early to mid-1980s), the ratio of immigrants to the resident population has tended to decline: whereas annual arrivals represented about 0.8 percent of the Canadian population in any given year during the 1950s, this proportion fell by half to only 0.4 percent in the first half of the 1980s.

A more detailed assessment of recent trends in inflow (see Figure 1) shows wide annual fluctuations in total arrivals and arrivals by class after 1967. The inflow level dropped gradually (from 180,000/year to 120,000/year) over the first four years after the new legislation was introduced. The level then rose over the next four years (peaking at 218,000 in 1974), only to then drop quickly to around 85,000 by 1978. Over an eight year period from 1978 to 1986 levels stayed generally low, although there was a very small rise (peaking in 1981) and subsequent fall during this period. Between 1983 and 1986 arrivals were at their lowest since the end of World War II, with 85,000 or fewer immigrants arriving each year. In 1987, the tail end of the series shown, arrivals rose back to 151,000 that is, to the Canadian historic average over the 20th century. Current policy statements suggest that the target level will be in the range of 125,000 to 135,000 for 1988 and may rise thereafter.[2]

Recent fluctuations in total inflow stem largely from Canadian policy considerations:

a)   The decline in inflow during the late 1970s and again during the mid-1980s reflected official concern with stagflation and unemployment levels (i.e., immigration targets in these periods appear to be part of a delayed Canadian adjustment to the first oil crisis in 1975 and the second in 1979). Correspondingly, the rise and fall of immigration levels over this period takes place almost entirely through fluctuations in the number of Independent Class immigrants — that is workers whose entry is geared to labour market conditions. The number of Family Class (i.e., sponsored) immigrants, whose freedom to enter Canada is determined not by labour market considerations but by statutory right (they have a right to enter because they are spouses, children or parents of previous immigrants or Canadian-born citizens).

b)   The modest rise in inflow in the early 1980s was in good part a response to pressure to admit Indochinese and other refugees, despite tight economic circumstances. In 1980, nearly as many refugees entered Canada as did Family Class immigrants, while the number of Independent Class immigrants was miniscule.

c)   The upward shift in 1987 reflected in good part official targets concerning the desirability of admitting more investors and workers, in addition to simply admitting higher levels overall, as part of a new official concern with Canada's need for immigrants to compensate for long-term fertility decline.

FIGURE 1

Immigrant Arrivals by Entry Class

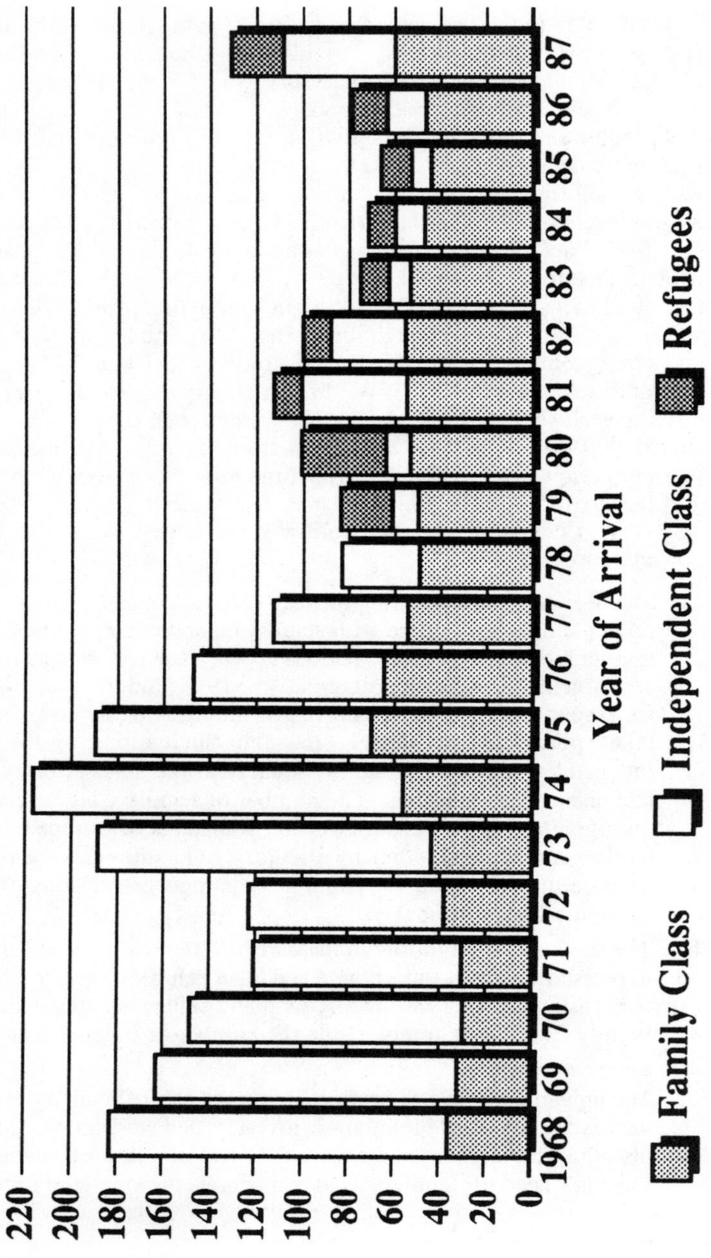

Year of Arrival

■ **Family Class**   □ **Independent Class**   ▨ **Refugees**

Canada in the "world system"

Trends in the origin of immigrants to Canada are not unique. Several other immigrant-receiving nations are following a similar trajectory toward increasing levels of immigrants from Third World origins. As Table 2 indicates, the other major immigrant-receiving developed nations (namely Australia, New Zealand and the U.S.) have similar patterns: all show rapidly accelerating proportions of immigrant arrivals from Third World nations after 1966, and corresponding decreases in the proportion of immigrants arriving from Europe. In the case of the U.S., the trend began earlier, reflecting significant Hispanic and Caribbean immigration in the 1950s. The Asian component in the new Third World movement alone reached more than one third of the total inflow to Australia, Canada and the U.S. by the 1976-80 period.

These four more developed nations shown in Table 2 are the only more developed nations still receiving significant numbers of migrants from the Third World. This said, the number of migrants involved appears large in absolute terms (in total, around 600,000 Less Developed Country (LDC) residents leave each year to these four developed nations), but it is very small relative to the total population of the receiving countries. In the 1976-1980 period, relative to its own population, Canada received the highest proportion of Third World immigrants. Annually, over this period, Third World immigrants constituted about one half of one percent of the Canadian population in any given year of arrival; cumulatively, over the five-year time span the new arrivals totalled about 2.6 percent of the Canadian population at the start of the period.

The remarkable transition from European to Third World origin immigration experienced by Australia, Canada and the U.S. over recent decades is part of a restructuring of the international migration system in the world as a whole. We may analyse this transition by examining how the international migration system functioned prior to World War II and how it has begun to function since then.

Historical studies show that subsequent to the rise of national states in various parts of the world large peaceful international resettlements have taken place. International migration has often been the result of massive forced expulsions (as regional and ethnic minorities are pushed out by dominant groups as nation states emerge) or part of forceful conquest and settlement of new lands by imperial powers in an expansionist phase. Excluding the early years of forceful conquest of Europe's new frontiers in North America and Australia, the period from the mid-19th century onward has been characterized by an historically unusual period of massive, peaceful, planned, international family resettlement from Europe to Australia, Canada and the United States. The flow took on this large and peaceful character because the sending and receiving nations involved were all part of the same interconnected economic and cultural system (the so-called North Atlantic economy, with its links to Oceania), and because the new frontier

TABLE 2

Number and Region of Origin of Immigrants Admitted to Australia, Canada, New Zealand and
the United States between 1956 and 1980

Region of Origin	Receiving Country	1956-1960	1961-1965	1966-1970	1971-1975	1976-1980
Numbers in Thousands						
World	Total	2826.6	2713.6	3748.3	3404.7	3095.8
	Australia	500.0	594.2	807.0	494.7	402.7
	Canada	782.9	498.8	910.8	834.5	605.9
	New Zeal.	115.9	170.3	159.1	139.2	60.8
	U.S.A.	1427.8	1450.3	1871.4	1936.3	2026.4
MDCs	Total	2292.9	1951.9	2340.7	1495.0	945.2
	Australia	470.0	550.6	697.2	368.4	234.6
	Canada	738.1	437.8	722.7	470.4	263.4
	New Zeal.	105.2	153.9	144.5	124.2	44.7
	U.S.A.	979.6	809.6	776.3	532.0	402.5
LDCs	Total	533.7	761.7	1407.6	1909.7	2150.6
	Australia	30.0	43.6	109.8	126.3	168.1
	Canada	44.8	61.0	188.1	364.1	342.5
	New Zeal.	10.7	16.4	14.6	15.0	16.1
	U.S.A.	448.2	640.7	1095.1	1404.3	1623.9
Percent from LDCs						
	Total	18.9	28.1	37.6	56.1	69.5
	Australia	6.0	7.3	13.6	25.5	41.7
	Canada	5.7	12.2	20.7	43.6	56.5
	New Zeal.	9.2	9.6	9.2	10.8	26.5
	U.S.A.	31.4	44.2	58.5	72.5	80.1
Percent from ASIA						
	Total					
	Australia	n.a.	4	8.3	15.6	32.2
	Canada	2.7	5.5	11.3	22.6	36.9
	New Zeal.	3.1	2.8	3.3	3.1	10.9
	U.S.A.	7.8	7.8	17.8	31.6	38.8

Source: United Nations, International Migration Statistics. Modeled on Kritz (1987) Table 2.1

Note: More Developed Countries (MDCs) include Australia, Canada, Japan, New Zealand, the U.S.S.R., the United States, and all of Europe. Less Developed Countries (LDCs) include all other countries.

countries were short on capital and labour (for producing food, raw material later industrial exports to Europe) while Europe had excess capital and labour (but needed food, raw materials, etc.).[3]

The basic dynamics of the North Atlantic migration system were played out by the early part of the 20th century (as the new frontier nations, particularly the U.S., became industrial powers in their own right, and as birth rates and relative surplus labour declined in Europe). However, the conflict, chaos and economic collapse of Europe associated with World War II followed by economic prosperity in the new frontier nations in the post-war period led to a resurgent flood of families from Europe to Australia, Canada and the United States between 1945 and 1965. The conditions for this post-war flood from Europe no longer exist: Europe has recovered economically and after two decades of very low birth rates it no longer has a relative surplus population to export.

The relationship between major metropolitan receiving nations and the Third World has also changed dramatically within the international migration system. Prior to World War II, potential migrants in Third World nations had only limited prospects of moving to developed countries. Racism and cultural preferences built into national immigration quotas or targets in the new frontier countries largely restricted entry to individuals of European background. The availability of large numbers of Europeans willing to work at "entry level" and other positions unattractive to the native-born in the new frontier countries also reduced opportunities for the Third World immigrants who did come. Citizens in most Third World nations were isolated culturally from the metropolitan nations, their population growth rates were still low (mortality having not yet declined), and travel costs were very high. After World War II, the situation changed dramatically. Third World population growth exploded; education, mass media and consumerism spread; shifts in international business led to greater contacts between developed and Third World nations; travel costs plummeted in relative terms. In addition, economic trransformation and the development of nation states in the Third World have been accompanied by class struggle (for example, that arising as peasants have been pushed off their lands by expanding plantations and agro-business) and ethnic/regional conflict (for example, Tamils versus Sinhalese; Sikhs versus Hindus) which has created pressure for massive refugee flows. Combining all these factors has led to an enormous potential for Third World emigration.

Canada's current position in the international migration system is similar to that of Australia and the United States, and it is for this reason that all three countries show some major parallel trends in immigrant origin. All three countries were settled through massive immigration, hence they have multi-ethnic populations and a relative openness (compared to the largely single ethnic states of Europe) to ethnically diverse immigration from the Third World. All three still see themselves as nations in the building phase hence are open to sizeable immigration. International economic and political links with the Third World have expanded and are responded to in all three nations by efforts to develop non-racist policies and show humanitarian concern for refugees, particularly those streams composed of people with similar political aspirations (for example, Vietnamese fleeing a communist regime). Gradually a bridgehead of "pioneer" immigrants from the Third World has built up in all three countries and now exerts internal political pressure for the admission of ethnic kin. Last but not least, the high levels of education in these developed nations means that there are labour shortages for a number of less skilled or low paid jobs (clerking in stores, washing dishes in restaurants, picking fruit, etc.) which Third World immigrants are pleased to fill.

In addition to similarities between the new frontier nations, there are differences as well. While all three receiving nations admit few Africans and large numbers of Asians (particularly from countries such as India, the Philippines, Korea and Hong Kong, where English is widely spoken), the United States has been distinctive in also receiving large numbers of people from the Caribbean and Latin America. Yet, as the following section indicates, Canada is now beginning to show movement toward the U.S. pattern, as the inflow of Caribbean and Latin American immigrants becomes more important.

Origins of "New Wave" Immigrants to Canada

Table 3 shows a detailed portrayal of shifting origin patterns among immigrants to Canada. The decline in European immigrants from 1968 to 1987 is impressive: whereas European migrants constituted two thirds of the inflow at the start of the period, by 1987 they provided less than one quarter of the total. An examination of the sub-components reveals that the greatest decline was in immigrants from North-west Europe and South Europe. The small stream from East Europe (mostly refugees) has fluctuated up and down at low levels (5 to 10 percent of the total inflow) without any clear trend.

Among Third World immigrants, those from Asia have shown the most spectacular increases, moving from 13 percent of the total inflow in 1968 to 45 percent in 1987. The Asian stream is currently more or less equally divided between those from East Asia (major inflows from Hong Kong, including both older people born in China but living in Hong Kong and younger people born in Hong Kong), South-east Asia (Vietnam, the Philippines), and South Asia (India, Pakistan). During the early 1980s the Asian inflow was dominated by refugees from Indochina (Indochinese and other South-east Asians constituted 30 percent of all immigrants to Canada in 1980).

Caribbean immigrants rank second in terms of inflow levels. The Caribbean provided about 5.5 percent of the total inflow in 1968; immediately after implementation of the new legislation the Caribbean inflow leaped to twice this level (just above 10 percent in 1969) where it has remained ever since. Very few Caribbean immigrants come from the Hispanic islands; nearly all come from the Commonwealth Caribbean and Haiti.

Latin American immigrants rank in third place. Whereas in 1968 they constituted less than 1 percent of all arrivals, this total has climbed gradually to between 7 and 8 percent of the inflow. Growth took place in a wave-like fashion

A Portrayal of Shifting Origin Patterns Among Immigrants to Canada

	1968	1969	1970	1971	1972	1973	1974	1975	1976	1977	1978	1979	1980	1981	1982	1983	1984	1985	1986	1987
Europe N.W.	31.05	28.48	25.54	19.49	20.69	18.53	21.20	22.27	19.96	22.29	20.25	17.37	17.45	21.96	20.45	12.40	10.72	10.12	9.49	9.56
Europe S.	21.71	16.88	17.10	17.64	15.78	15.21	14.00	10.51	9.05	8.60	9.31	6.84	5.40	5.42	4.35	3.57	3.57	3.50	4.16	6.37
Europe E.	11.57	8.92	8.29	6.07	5.22	4.09	3.87	4.61	4.45	4.95	5.41	4.99	5.20	7.33	12.03	10.99	9.38	8.73	9.38	8.46
Europe-Oth	0.01	0.00	0.00	0.00	0.00	0.00	0.00	0.00	0.00	0.00	0.00	0.00	0.00	0.01	0.01	0.00	0.00	0.00	0.00	0.00
EUROPE-total	64.34	54.28	50.93	43.21	41.70	37.83	39.08	37.38	33.47	35.84	34.97	29.21	28.05	34.72	36.84	26.96	23.67	22.35	23.03	24.39
U.S.A.	9.32	12.05	14.24	17.24	15.79	11.73	10.43	9.22	9.64	9.48	9.65	7.09	5.75	6.89	6.63	7.09	6.72	6.86	6.32	4.43
Canada	0.57	0.71	0.78	1.01	0.92	0.72	0.62	0.60	0.61	0.65	0.65	0.53	0.41	0.44	0.44	0.46	0.47	0.48	0.40	0.25
N. America-Oth	0.01	0.01	0.01	0.02	0.01	0.01	0.02	0.02	0.02	0.04	0.04	0.03	0.01	0.01	0.01	0.01	0.00	0.01	0.01	0.00
Oceania	0.06	0.09	0.17	0.17	0.17	0.12	0.17	0.22	0.27	0.21	0.22	0.21	0.24	0.27	0.33	0.21	0.25	0.22	0.39	0.43
MDCs-Total	74.31	67.14	66.12	61.64	58.58	50.42	50.31	47.44	44.01	46.22	45.54	37.07	34.46	42.33	44.26	34.73	31.12	29.91	30.15	29.49
Africa N.	2.67	1.77	1.46	1.28	1.25	1.26	1.26	1.41	1.49	1.48	1.27	1.10	1.15	1.46	1.57	1.41	1.30	1.43	1.59	1.53
Africa W.	0.09	0.12	0.19	0.22	0.25	0.38	0.29	0.34	0.33	0.32	0.43	0.23	0.23	0.27	0.19	0.19	0.35	0.45	0.48	0.91
Africa E.	0.33	0.35	0.37	0.59	4.91	3.23	3.37	3.49	2.48	1.52	1.50	1.20	1.19	1.51	1.42	1.99	2.17	2.15	2.06	2.04
Africa S.	0.09	0.10	0.08	0.09	0.11	0.10	0.14	0.22	0.55	0.68	0.52	0.37	0.31	0.35	0.31	0.19	0.21	0.17	0.26	0.30
Africa C.	0.04	0.03	0.04	0.03	0.04	0.05	0.29	0.19	0.10	0.08	0.10	0.07	0.06	0.07	0.03	0.13	0.12	0.12	0.04	0.18
Africa-Sabel	0.01	0.01	0.02	0.01	0.01	0.02	0.02	0.02	0.03	0.03	0.03	0.04	0.03	0.02	0.03	0.03	0.03	0.04	0.04	0.05
South Africa	0.59	0.51	0.55	0.64	0.43	0.41	0.50	0.76	0.95	1.73	1.52	0.98	0.86	0.98	0.78	0.48	0.34	0.41	0.82	1.09
Africa-Oth	0.00	0.01	0.01	0.01	0.02	0.04	0.01	0.01	0.01	0.01	0.00	0.01	0.00	0.01	0.00	0.00	0.01	0.00	0.00	0.00
AFRICA-total	3.82	2.91	2.73	2.87	7.02	5.49	5.87	6.44	5.95	5.82	5.39	4.01	3.82	4.68	4.40	4.52	4.53	4.78	5.38	6.10
Asia East	5.79	6.79	5.49	7.39	8.24	10.84	8.93	10.22	11.41	9.31	9.09	10.38	10.88	13.46	11.58	13.49	14.57	14.82	11.14	16.11
Asia S.E.	1.97	2.56	2.94	4.30	4.14	4.56	5.44	5.32	5.50	6.93	7.91	26.67	30.01	14.30	12.60	15.89	20.73	19.53	14.36	11.51
Asia South	3.01	4.94	5.73	6.30	6.95	8.04	8.94	8.92	7.66	7.60	8.86	6.16	7.70	8.59	8.78	10.29	9.23	7.35	10.86	11.26
Asia West	2.37	1.80	1.95	1.92	2.14	1.77	1.96	2.37	6.15	4.62	3.32	2.72	2.36	2.99	2.76	2.23	2.79	4.01	5.02	4.99
Asia Gulf	0.04	0.04	0.05	0.07	0.09	0.09	0.15	0.15	0.10	0.12	0.13	0.18	0.24	0.28	0.28	0.19	0.21	0.25	0.39	0.61
Asia-Oth	0.01	0.01	0.01	0.03	0.01	0.07	0.05	0.02	0.03	0.01	0.01	0.02	0.00	0.01	0.10	0.00	0.08	0.00	0.00	0.04
ASIA-total	13.19	16.15	16.17	20.01	21.57	25.37	25.46	27.00	30.85	28.58	29.32	46.13	51.19	39.63	36.10	42.10	47.61	45.95	41.77	44.51
Caribbean	5.46	9.92	10.62	11.35	9.06	13.86	13.21	12.79	12.67	12.81	12.48	8.24	6.79	9.29	10.30	11.29	8.78	10.27	12.98	11.48
Caribbean-sp.	0.06	0.08	0.07	0.10	0.09	0.07	0.07	0.05	0.07	0.07	0.07	0.05	0.27	0.11	0.10	0.24	0.25	0.28	0.47	0.41
CARIB.-total	5.52	10.00	10.68	11.45	9.15	13.93	13.28	12.84	12.74	12.87	12.56	8.29	7.06	9.40	10.49	11.54	9.03	10.55	13.45	11.89
Mexico	0.13	0.22	0.29	0.30	0.51	0.37	0.31	0.44	0.49	0.66	0.63	0.35	0.29	0.31	0.43	0.59	0.62	0.54	0.70	0.56
America Central	0.04	0.08	0.11	0.12	0.17	0.26	0.28	0.31	0.36	0.36	0.39	0.26	0.23	0.40	0.96	3.61	4.14	5.42	5.42	4.02
America South	0.71	1.30	1.52	1.79	1.65	3.08	3.60	4.67	4.65	4.47	5.06	2.93	2.10	2.43	2.73	2.46	2.45	2.36	2.65	3.06
Americas-Oth.	0.00	0.00	0.00	0.00	0.00	0.00	0.00	0.00	0.00	0.00	0.00	0.00	0.00	0.00	0.00	0.00	0.00	0.00	0.00	0.00
L.A.-total	0.88	1.60	1.92	2.21	2.33	3.71	4.18	5.42	5.50	5.49	6.08	3.54	2.62	3.15	4.12	6.66	7.21	8.32	8.77	7.64
Australia	2.27	2.20	2.37	1.82	1.36	1.08	0.90	0.86	0.95	1.01	1.12	0.97	0.86	0.81	0.64	0.46	0.50	0.49	0.47	0.37
LCDs-Total	25.69	32.86	33.88	38.36	41.42	49.58	49.69	52.56	55.99	53.78	54.46	62.93	65.54	57.67	55.74	65.27	68.88	70.09	69.85	70.51
Total Arrivals	100.00	100.00	100.00	100.00	100.00	100.00	100.00	100.00	100.00	100.00	100.00	100.00	100.00	100.00	100.00	100.00	100.00	100.00	100.00	100.00

corresponding to add-on inflows of refugees, from Chile (in the mid-to-late 1970s) and El Salvador (after 1983). In fact, immigrants from the latter two countries constitute approximately forty percent of all arrivals from the region. The rest of the total flow comes from many smaller streams, of which those from Argentina, Colombia, Ecuador and Peru are somewhat larger.[4]

Immigrants from Africa rank in last place, although their inflow has been growing steadily (from 3.8 percent to 6.1 percent of total arrivals) and is now approaching that from Latin America. Of this, the proportion coming from North Africa (mostly Jews from Arab states in North Africa) has been small but constant, while all other flows have increased from miniscule levels to still very small but higher proportions. It should be noted that the data in Table 3 refer to place of birth, hence they under-represent the number of former residents of South Africa arriving to Canada, since many of these were born in Europe.

The levels and trends in national origin of immigrants to Canada reflect in large part the overall structure of the global international migration system. Africa is in general still largely isolated within the world migration system (though flows from North Africa to Europe did become appreciable in the 1960s and 1970s), hence few Africans come to Canada. As the community of Africans in Canada expands and as international links between Africa and the world migration system improve, the proportion coming from that region should continue to rise gradually. Far more Asians than Latin Americans come to Canada for various reasons: the Asians who come (excepting the Vietnamese) are predominantly English-speaking, hence are favoured by Canadian policy and culture. Not only has Canada not had a large Spanish-speaking ethnic minority in the past, but the United States has a huge one going back over a very long period. In effect, the United States (with its large population, wealthy economy and huge hispanic cultural minority) constitutes a preferred destination for Latin American emigrants, to the point where until recent years few had any awareness of Canada as a possible destination. This structure is changing in good part due to the presence of a growing population of Latin American refugees, changes in United States legislation which threaten undocumented Latin American immigrants in that country, and generally expanding communications links between Canada and the Third World.

As Figure 2 indicates, the dramatic decline in immigrant arrivals from Europe (and the United States) and the corresponding rise in arrivals from the Third World has not been constant over time. Rather, the downward shift seems to have taken place in somewhat of a step-wise fashion, with the most rapid shift occurring between 1968 and 1976, where it levelled off for three years. The last four years (1984 to 1987, inclusive) have similarly shown an unchanging pattern: roughly two thirds coming from the Third World and one third from developed nations.

Most immigrants come from a relatively small number of specific countries within their region.

TABLE 4

Selected Characteristics of Immigrants Arriving to Canada Between 1968 and 1987, Controlling
for Region of Origin (Birth)

	Europe	Africa	Asia	Carib.	Latin Am.
Percent Distribution by Arrival Class (for immigrants aged 20-44 only)					
Family	18.7	21	29.3	33.1	26.8
Refugee	5.6	7.2	12.6	0.3	16.7
Independent	75.7	71.8	58.1	66.6	56.5
TOTAL	100	100	100	100	100
Precent age distribution					
0 to 14	22	20	19	23	29
15 to 44	64	68	62	65	62
45 to 64	9	10	14	9	7
65 and over	5	2	5	3	2
TOTAL	100	100	100	100	100
Dependency ratio [1]	0.37	0.28	0.32	0.35	0.45
Sex ratio [2]	100.4	118.9	99.1	85.8	97.4
Percent immigrants aged 20-44 with University Education	10.9	20.1	22.4	4.3	10.8

Source: Special tabulations of CEIC data on Landed Immigrants

Notes: [1] Dependency ratio calculated as population under age 15 and over age 64 as a proportion
of population aged 15-64.
[2] Sex ratio calculated as males per 100 females.

Characteristics by Region

Immigrant characteristics vary from one origin stream to another. We may distinguish the following streams:

1.   The "Mature" Stream (from Europe).

Immigrants from Europe continue to flow into Canada, although in declining
numbers. The European stream is characterized by a balanced sex ratio and a
relatively high proportion of children, suggesting that young families with children form a large block among those moving. The percentage of young adult
immigrants with university level education is high by world standards (10.0
percent have completed university), but only intermediate in terms of levels
found in two of the "new" streams (namely those from Asia and Africa).

151

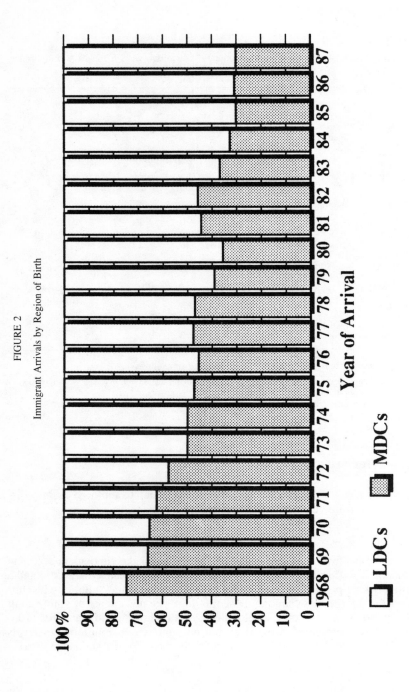

FIGURE 2

Immigrant Arrivals by Region of Birth

2. The "New" Wave

Immigrant streams from the Third World differ in important ways from one another as well as from the Mature Stream.

a) *Africa.* The small stream coming from Africa is rather distinctive. It is disproportionately composed of well-educated young-adult males. Relatively few adult females come and, similarly, relatively few children are found in the arrival stream. There are very few elderly African immigrants.

The high average educational level of adult African immigrants deserves further comment. The very high proportion (20 percent) with university education is rather surprising in one sense, since Africa has the lowest levels of schooling of all world regions. Yet in another sense, the pattern fits with explanatory models of migration: only those Africans with considerable relative financial resources and educational skills (in a region where most people are poor and have little schooling) are likely to attempt to migrate a long distance to another country where there are as yet few relatives, kin or others from the same ethnic groups to help them.

b) *Caribbean* immigrants are also distinctive. Women predominate in the overall stream; separate tabulations (not shown) indicate that the women particularly predominate in the young adult stream (ages 20-24) and in the older adult stream (ages 35-44) — in the latter women outnumber men by three to one in some arrival years during the early 1970s.[5] In addition, the proportion of children is somewhat higher than in other origin groups. Educational levels are the lowest of all incoming streams.

The age-gender pattern conforms to previous research findings showing that Caribbean migration to Canada is, in contrast to most other streams, led by young adult females who later sponsor their own children and frequently also their own mothers as well as their spouses.[5] Low educational levels in this group also conform to the fact that women immigrants from the Caribbean often come first as domestic workers (a privileged entry class). Many Caribbean women also work in skilled jobs requiring technical training (nursing, office work) but not a university degree. Census tabulations show that the Caribbean-born population resident in Canada eventually achieves rather high levels of schooling:[7] this may in large part be the result of the fact the inflow from the Caribbean includes a large number of adolescents who come to Canada in good part to continue their education.

c) The immigrant stream from *Latin America* includes a slightly larger proportion of children; virtually no older people; and relatively few with a university education. These characteristics reflect, by and large, the fact that a high proportion (40 percent) of those coming from Latin America originate in Chile and El Salvador; these streams started with refugee flows and now include other Family Class immigrants from similar social backgrounds. Many of the Salvadorian refugees are from rural areas; the Chilean refugees include both industrial workers and skilled professionals.

d)   The stream from Asia has the highest proportion of adults over age 44 and particularly over age 64. Educational levels are extremely high, with more than 22 percent of young adults having university education.

Implications

Important changes in the origin of immigrant streams to Canada over the past 20 years will have a gradual, cumulative impact on the racial, ethnic and cultural composition of Canadian society.

The effects of "new wave" immigrants have to date been relatively minor, for several reasons: (a) the recency of the "new immigration," (b) the fact that many who come later return home (or migrate elsewhere) such that even the total number of arrivals is perhaps 40 percent greater than the number who stay over the longer term,[8] and (c) the fact that the absolute inflow of immigrants to Canada has been, in recent years, small relative to the overall size of the Canadian population.

Table 5 shows the changing birth-place composition of the Canadian population. Third World immigrants constituted a miniscule proportion (less than 1 percent) of the Canadian population up to 1961; even by 1971 (three years after the new legislation) levels had changed only slightly (to 1.6 percent). The 1981 and 1986 census data show larger, but still small (4.0 and 4.6 percent respectively) proportions of Third World origin immigrants in Canadian society.

The future impact of past and continuing trends in immigration on Canada's population will depend on a number of other changes which are taking place or which can be anticipated. The following consequences seem probable:

1.   The European-born population of Canada is large and aging. It is composed largely of those who arrived as adults in the 1950s and 1960s and who are now approaching retirement, and it is not being renovated by a sufficient number of new, younger arrivals to ensure its replacement. As a result, the absolute number of European-born in Canada peaked in 1971 and has declined subsequently. Over the next decade, and even more rapidly thereafter, this population will diminish and the ethnic communities and cultural groups the European wave established will weaken. The focus of multiculturalism will shift dramatically to the Third World origin groups who by then will still be larger, relatively young, while at the same time growing through new arrivals. The Third World origin immigrant population, by 1986, constituted 30 percent of the total foreign-born in Canada.

2.   The shift in focus to new ethnic communities will not be evenly felt across Canada. Rather, it will be concentrated in Canada's major cities: Montreal, Toronto and Vancouver. These cities were built with heavy inflows of post-World War II immigrants from Europe; they are also the cities where most Third World migrants settle.

Date of Census / Place of Birth	1921	1931	1941 (4)	1951	1961	1971	1981	1986
Canada (1)	6,855,327	8,095,671	9,513,095	11,949,518	15,393,984	18,272,780	20,216,335	21,445,914
United Kingdom (2)	1,025,119	1,138,942	960,125	912,482	969,715	933,040	884,915	793,075
Rest of Europe	459,325	714,462	653,705	801,618	1,468,058	1,684,515	1,701,343	1,642,364
Total Europe	1,484,444	1,853,404	1,613,830	1,714,100	2,437,773	2,617,555	2,586,343	2,435,439
United States	374,022	344,574	312,473	282,010	283,908	309,640	312,015	282,025
Australia	2,855	3,565	2,813	4,161	6,663	14,335	14,800	13,585
South Africa (3)							15,860	18,780
Rest of Africa (5)							86,860	95,645
Africa (3)	1,760	2,235	2,109	2,057	4,025		102,720	114,425
Carribean	4,270	4,537	4,134	3,888	12,363	55,145	212,200	244,260
Latin America (5)							64,345	96,975
Asia	57,484	65,280	48,819	41,079	66,789	163,080	534,525	692,595
Other Countries	7,787	7,520	7,887	12,616	32,742	135,775	40,212	28,846
Total Foreign-born	1,932,622	2,281,115	1,992,065	2,059,911	2,844,263	3,295,530	3,867,160	3,908,150
Total	8,787,949	10,376,786	11,505,160	14,009,429	18,238,247	21,568,310	24,083,495	25,354,064
Of Total Population, Percent:								
Foreign-born	22.0	22.0	17.3	14.7	15.6	15.3	16.1	15.4
Europe-born	16.9	17.9	14.0	12.2	13.4	12.1	10.7	9.6
U.S.-born	4.3	3.3	2.7	2.0	1.6	1.4	1.3	1.1
Third World	0.8	0.8	0.5	0.4	0.6	1.6	4.0	4.6
Of Foreign-born, Percent								
Third World	3.7	3.5	3.2	2.9	4.1	10.7	24.7	30.1

Sources: Data from 1921 to 1971 from Census of 1971, Table 33
Other data from 1981 Census (Place of birth... Table 1B) and special tabulations of the 1986 Census.

Notes: (1) Newfoundland included since 1921
(2) Includes Republic of Ireland prior to 1951
(3) Included with Other Countries in 1971
(4) Birth place not stated – 1945 persons – not included in the total
(5) Included with "other countries" prior to 1981.

TABLE 6

Estimated Components of Canadian Annual Population Growth

Year	Population Growth (00)	Natural Increase (00)	Net Migration (00)	Immigration Rate (00)	Emigration Rate (00)	% Growth due to Migration	Efficiency of Migration
1955	2.69	2.06	0.63	0.7	−0.07	23.42	0.90
1956	2.44	1.99	0.45	1.03	−0.58	18.44	0.44
1957	3.29	2.05	1.24	1.7	−0.46	37.69	0.73
1958	2.83	2.01	0.82	0.73	0.09	28.98	1.12
1959	2.36	1.96	0.40	0.61	−0.21	16.95	0.66
1960	2.21	1.94	0.27	0.58	−0.31	12.22	0.47
1961	2.06	1.90	0.16	0.39	−0.23	7.77	0.41
1962	1.89	1.80	0.09	0.4	−0.31	4.76	0.22
1963	1.87	1.75	0.12	0.49	−0.37	6.42	0.24
1964	1.90	1.66	0.24	0.58	−0.34	12.63	0.41
1965	1.83	1.52	0.31	0.75	−0.44	16.94	0.41
1966	1.89	1.29	0.60	0.97	−0.37	31.75	0.62
1967	1.81	1.16	0.65	1.09	−0.44	35.91	0.60
1968	1.59	1.05	0.54	0.89	−0.35	33.96	0.61
1969	1.45	1.03	0.42	0.77	−0.35	28.97	0.55
1970	1.41	1.02	0.39	0.69	−0.30	27.66	0.57
1971	1.27	1.02	0.25	0.57	−0.32	19.69	0.44
1972	1.07	0.90	0.17	0.56	−0.39	15.89	0.30
1973	1.10	0.83	0.27	0.84	−0.57	24.55	0.32
1974	1.45	0.82	0.63	0.98	−0.35	43.45	0.64
1975	1.48	0.83	0.65	0.83	−0.18	43.92	0.78
1976	1.29	0.84	0.45	0.65	−0.20	34.88	0.69
1977	1.21	0.84	0.37	0.49	−0.12	30.58	0.76
1978	1.04	0.82	0.22	0.37	−0.15	21.15	0.59
1979	0.97	0.83	0.14	0.47	−0.33	14.43	0.30
1980	1.24	0.84	0.40	0.6	−0.20	32.26	0.67
1981	1.24	0.83	0.41	0.53	−0.12	33.06	0.77
1982	1.18	0.82	0.36	0.49	−0.13	30.51	0.73
1983	1.02	0.81	0.21	0.36	−0.15	20.59	0.58
1984	0.96	0.80	0.16	0.35	−0.19	16.67	0.46
1985	0.93	0.80	0.13	0.33	−0.20	13.98	0.39
1986	0.91	0.76	0.15	0.40	−0.25	16.48	0.38

Sources: Estimates of Natural Increase and Net Immigration Rates taken from Statistics Canada, *Current Demographic Analysis: Report on Demographic Situation in Canada, 1986* (Ottawa, Minister of Supply and Services, 1987), Tables 1, A1 and A2. Immigration rates for 1985 and 1986 estimated from preliminary results of 1986 Census showing a total population of 25,400,000 from special runs of employment and immigration data on immigrant arrivals in these two years.

Notes: Efficiency of migration is Net Migration/Immigration × 100.

3.   Canadian society will continue to face a major challenge in seeking ways to avoid conflict between racial, linguistic and cultural groups as the total number of Third World immigrants and their descendants rise. As growth will be gradual and fit in with existing institutional patterns, there is no reason to believe that problems in this area will become worse and good reason to hope that multi-cultural programs and the very fact of new ethnic diversity will lead to improving relations between communities.

4.   The demographic consequences of current patterns of immigration are more difficult to assess: these depend on various factors, including fertility levels in Canada and emigration from Canada.

Table 6 shows historical trends in the components of Canadian population growth. The findings confirm previous analyses: Canada's population growth is slowing due to two factors: declining fertility (leading to lower natural increase) and immigration levels which have been declining relative to Canada's overall population size. Of these two trends, the fall in fertility has had the greatest impact, such that the proportion of total population growth brought about by immigration has been rising, even in the early 1980s, a period when immigration levels were relatively low. Correspondingly, fertility and natural increase among Third World origin immigrants, once they have arrived, is also a rising proportion of Canadian natural population growth, primarily because they are a rising proportion of the Canadian population but also because their fertility is higher than that of the Canadian-born.[9]

Under the current level of natural population growth and emigration, in order for the Canadian population not to decline in the early part of the next century, immigrant admissions must rise quickly to 175,000 per year and stay at this level.[10] Under current immigration targets (rising from a maximum planned intake of 125,000 in 1987 to a maximum of 135,000 in 1988 and possible gradual growth thereafter) we may anticipate:

- a sustained high proportion of immigrants arriving from the Third World. In fact, any major increases in inflow targets would likely lead to an increased proportion of Third World immigrants, on the assumption that streams of European origin are declining for reasons of population aging and relative affluence in Europe.

- a further increase in the Third World origin immigrant contribution to total population growth in Canada (both directly through immigration and indirectly through their fertility in Canada).

- an amplification of the anticipated impacts on the size and growth of the ethnic and racial minorities described above.

Notes

1. The 1968 legislation basically recognized two categories of immigrants:
    Independent Class migrants (essentially workers admitted because they met labour
    force criteria of being young adults, having job skills relevant to Canadian demand,
    speaking either English or French, etc.) and Family Class migrants (spouses and
    dependent children or parents of an independent migrant or another family class
    migrant). Subsequently, the legislation has been modified, most notably in 1978
    to give explicit recognition to the need to give special treatment to refugees, and
    in 1988 to allow parents to sponsor unmarried children over age 21. Other important
    changes in legislation — governing particularly the right to seek asylum from within
    Canada —- are to be implemented in early 1989.
2. See *Annual Report to Parliament on Future Immigration Levels, 1967.* (Ottawa:
    Minister of Supply and Services Canada, 1987). It should be noted that policy tar-
    gets proposed by the federal government are only general indicators of intent; actual
    arrivals may fall below targets (as they did in 1984 and 1985) or exceed them (as
    was the case in 1987 when the proposed target of 125,000 was surpassed by approx-
    imately 25,000).
3. See B. Thomas, *Migration and Urban Development.* (London: Methuen, 1972)
    for an analysis of economic growth and international migration in the North Atlantic
    economy during the late 19th and early 20th century.
4. For a more detailed review of Latin American immigration to Canada see Fernando
    Mata, ''Latin American Immigration to Canada: Some Reflections on the
    Immigration Statistics,'' *Canadian Journal of Latin American and Caribbean
    Studies* 10: 27-42, 1985.
5. For more details on the characteristics on Caribbean immigrants, see Jean E. Turner
    and Alan B. Simmons, ''The Caribbean and Canadian Family: Change, Stress and
    Adaptive Strategies.'' Paper presented to Conference on Caribbean Migration and
    the Black Diaspora. Institute of Commonwealth Studies, University of London.
    June 1987.
6. See reference in previous footnote for details.
7. See A.H. Richmond, *Caribbean Immigrants in Canada.* (Ottawa: Statistics
    Canada, forthcoming in 1989).
8. For recent estimates of re-emigration for different communities of immigrants in
    Canada, see R. Beaujot and P. Rappak (1987).
9. It would appear that the foreign-born in Canada have clearly higher fertility levels
    than the Canadian-born population, although nowhere near as high as those found
    in many Third World countries of origin. Overall, immigrant women have a Total
    Fertility Rate between 0.3 and 0.5 higher than those of native-born women (e.g.,
    2.06 versus 1.62 in 1981; 1.93 versus 1.57 in 1986). See Anne H. Gauthier,
    ''Quand les différences sont négligées... Fécondité différentielle et projection de
    population''. Communication présentée au troisième colloque international de l'AI-
    DELF, Montréal, juin 1988. Mimeo Statistics Canada.
10. This projection assumes a Total Fertility Rate (TFR) stabilizing at the 1981 level
    of 1.7 and emigration stabilizing at 50,000 per year, the level estimated for the
    early 1980s [see Statistics Canada, *Current Demographic Analysis: Report on the*

Demographic Situation in Canada, (Ottawa, 1986, p. 51]. It should be noted that the 1986 Census suggests that the TFR may have fallen to 1.64 (see Gauthier, ibid., p. 5). If this preliminary indication of a trend in fertility is confirmed, then the number of immigrants required to stabilize Canada's population at its current level would naturally have to rise above 175,000/year. Current levels of fertility combined with current proposed immigration targets suggest that Canada's population will begin to decline in number sometime in the early 21st century.

II

DEMOGRAPHIC PROCESSES
AND ETHNIC COHESION

9. ETHNIC LANGUAGE MAINTENANCE AND SHIFT

John DeVries

This paper contains several sections. I begin with a set of definitions; such terms as "language maintenance," "language shift" and associated concepts need at least some discussion. The next section reviews the notion of demographic "balancing equations," introduces the effects of language shift into these equations and hints at measurement approaches based on these balancing equations; the analogy with the analysis of internal migration will be evident. The measurement issue will be discussed in greater detail in the next section.

While these "introductory" sections are deliberately cast in general terms (and thus could be applied to multilingual or multiethnic societies anywhere in the world), the next sections focus on the Canadian situation. One discusses, briefly, the nature of Canadian census data, their utility for the study of ethnic minorities in Canada, as well as conceptual and empirical problems associated with their use. The other provides some data from the 1971 and 1981 censuses of population. I attempt to generalize on the basis of these data, not only to the situation in Canada, but also to the broader issue of minority language relations.

Definitions and General Comments

Several terms have been used in the theoretical and empirical literature dealing with the language characteristics of ethnic minorities. For the sake of simplicity, I will use two basic terms throughout this paper: language shift and language maintenance.

Language Shift

The basic definition of language shift goes back to the linguist Uriel Weinreich, who defined it as "... the change from the habitual use of one language to that of another..." (1953, 68). Most of the studies of minority language behaviour, by sociologists and linguists alike, use this definition, or one that closely resembles it.

The essential elements in the definition are the measurements of an individual's language behaviour at minimally two points in time; language shift has occurred if these measurements do not produce identical values. Conversely, language shift has not occurred in cases where two measurements for the same individual produce identical responses.

The definition, though intuitively clear, does beg a few important questions:

(i)   how does one operationalize "habitual"?

(ii) does the definition imply a change in language behaviour in all possible settings or only in one?

(iii) to what degree is such a process, or transition, final, to what degree is it temporary? (e.g., how do we classify the tourist who, during a vacation, uses the language of the country being visited? What about guest workers, foreign students, others whose language use has changed temporarily?).

This is not the proper place to address all of these issues. Subsequent sections of this paper will deal with the first two to some extent; the third question falls outside the scope of this paper.

Language Maintenance

If we assume, for the moment, that we can develop useable operational definitions of language shift, then language maintenance is easily defined (and eventually measured) as the *absence* of language shift.

Domains

The question about the "generality" of language shift (and, by implication, of language maintenance) is often addressed by means of the concept of "domains" — a term used by linguists to indicate what sociologists usually call "social institutions." Examples are: the work place, educational institutions, the family, places of religious worship. One generally orders such domains from "public" (e.g., various levels of government, labour unions) to "private" (e.g., the immediate family, personal friends). A common finding is that members of ethnic minorities use one language in the more public domains, a different language (usually the minority language) in the private domains. It should be noted that, in Canada and other officially bilingual or multilingual societies, such differentiation by domains is not only a characteristic of ethnic minorities created by international migration, but also of "regional" or "autochtone" minorities. In Canada, we do find evidence of this pattern for Francophones outside Quebec, as well as Anglophones in Quebec.

Bilingualism

A pattern in which an individual uses two or more languages, either in different domains or in the same domain (e.g., speaking Italian at home with parents, English with siblings) indicates that the individual is *bilingual*. Linguists have had lengthy discussions about the possibility of bilingualism as "native-like" fluency in two languages (probably impossible to attain); the more common position, held by most social scientists and some linguists, is that bilingualism is indicated by an individual's ability to have meaningful communications in more than one language. It should be obvious that a process of language shift (from language A to language B) must include a period of time during which an individual is bilingual in both languages. It is equally obvious that such bilingualism (and the associated process of second language acquisition) is a necessary, but not sufficient, condition for language shift.

A Continuous Process

The preceding comments make it clear that language shift, when it occurs, is really a summary measure of a continuous process of individual adaptation. For most people, the process begins with the acquisition of one language, the mother tongue. In a next phase, one or more languages are acquired. After — or for some people during — this phase, the individual begins to use this second language in one or more domains. Eventually, the second language may be used in all domains. A possible final stage in the process is that the individual ceases to understand the mother tongue. It should be noted, incidentally, that the process is reversible, e.g., that one can forget the second language and return to unilingualism.

The Double Nature of Language

There are two possible views of language:

(i) one can see language as a symbolic system (de Saussure's *langue*) with intrinsic characteristics. Language shift (or maintenance) could be studied from this linguistic perspective, e.g., in terms of lexical interference, maintenance or acquisition of accent, and so forth. Linguists generally consider these aspects in their research;

(ii) language can also be seen as a social characteristic or resource, which may be acquired, cultivated, developed, applied, or neglected or lost. As such, one can study language characteristics as a function of other characteristics such as age, sex and place of birth. Social scientists tend to use this approach almost exclusively. This paper will consider language maintenance and shift from the social science perspective.

165

Language Shift as Element in Demographic Balancing Equations

A typical demographic approach to the study of change in populations is by means of the so-called balancing equations, summarized as $P_2 - P_1 =$ (Entries) $-$ (Exits).

For ordinary populations, "Entries" equal the sum of immigrants and births, while "Exits" equal the sum of emigrants and deaths. Demographers use the approach to estimate processes for which data are either unavailable or unreliable (e.g., emigration, or net internal migration). Moreover, such approaches may be applied to total populations (e.g., all of Canada; or all inhabitants of Newfoundland) or to cohorts (e.g., all persons born in 1941-1946).

One refinement introduced in this approach to analysing change is the idea of a *quasi-population*. This can be seen as a proper subset of an overall population; the extra defining characteristic ought to be a reasonably permanent one (such as place of birth, gender or ethnic origin) *and* should produce a human group that can reproduce itself (thus, gender or age are not applicable as definers of a quasi-population; ethnicity or place of residence are).

When we consider a language community (or an ethnic group defined by language) as a quasi-population, we can set up a basic balancing equation as follows:

$$P_2 - P_1 = (\text{Births} - \text{Deaths}) + (\text{Immigrants} - \text{Emigrants}) +$$
$$(\text{Net language shift})$$

Thus, the balancing equation allows us — at least in principle — to decompose the change in the size of an ethnic group or language community into three components: the net effects of natural increase, the net effects of international migration (i.e., moves across international boundaries) and the net effects of language shift (if you will, moves across language boundaries).

The practical problems of this approach should be obvious. For a complete description of change in the size of a particular group, we need to address the following issues:

(i)   births must be recorded in such a way that they can be allocated to the proper group;

(ii) the model assumes that mother, father and baby belong to the same group. A simplifying assumption, often made, is that the child belongs to the same group as either the mother or the father, but not necessarily both;

(iii) deaths must be recorded in such a way that they can be allocated to the proper group;

(iv) international migrants must be recorded in a consistent way, to enable us to allocate them to the proper group;

(v)   language shift, both into and out of a particular group, must be measured reliably.

In practice, these conditions are not met by *any* data collection system in the world. Thus, applications have generally invoked simplifying assumptions (e.g., stating that intercensal mortality by age-group and sex was equal for all language groups). Generally, ''net language shift'' is then taken as a *residual* in an equation in which all other elements are either known or may be estimated with acceptable reliability. The analogy with a well-known approach to the study of internal migration should be obvious. As in that approach, all of the errors of measurement, estimation and model design are loaded onto the residual component. The greater the difference between ''real'' and ''measured'' values for the known elements in the equation, the greater the error in the residual element.

I am not aware of any complete ''residual analysis'' of language shift on Canadian data. Some illustrations may be found in DeVries and Vallee (1980, 46-50) pertaining to ''official bilingualism'' (i.e., the self-reported ability to speak English and French) in Canada for 1961 and 1971. A more pertinent application of the residual method was the study of intercensal language shift among Swedish-speakers in Finland for 1951-1960 and 1961-1970 (DeVries 1974; 1977).

While the practical application of these balancing equations is generally not realistic, given the nature of available data, such equations help us to consider the future of ethnic or linguistic minorities. A variety of empirical studies has suggested that the magnitude of the ''net language shift'' component is usually so high that differential fertility and mortality are insufficient factors to help a minority group maintain its size (let alone its share of an overall population). For immigrant groups, only substantial net immigration is capable of sustaining a group's size; for autochtone minorities (e.g., Francophones outside Quebec), only policies that reduce the intensity of language shift towards the majority language may have the effect of sustaining the minority. Lachapelle and Henripin (1982, 163-164) suggest that differential fertility *might* compensate for the effects of net language shift for Francophones; such compensation would be hard to attain for native people and biologically impossible for immigrant groups.

General Approaches to Measurement of Language Shift

It should be clear, by now, that language maintenance and shift require a measurement approach in which the same individuals or groups are measured at two points in time. We can distinguish the following measurement approaches:

Direct Measurement

In this approach, individuals are classified, in terms of some language characteristic, at two points in time (t_1 and t_2). The measurement at time t_1 gives us a classification by ''quasi-population'' (put differently, it gives us an indication of the number of people exposed to the risk of shifting out of a given language or ethnic group). The cross-classification of the characteristics at t_1 with those at t_2 allows us to measure what proportion of a given group has shifted away from a group (and how many people the group gained by means of language shift). Obviously, the complement of language shift is language maintenance. We can distinguish two approaches to direct measurement:

(i) *panel studies*, in which we select a sample of individuals at t_1 (and obtain data on these respondents), then conduct repeat observations at later times (t_2, possibly t_3 and so forth). Given the near prohibitive costs of panel studies, and the need for very large samples in the study of slow processes, panel studies of language use do not exist. An approximation to the panel study is the approach in which individual census records are linked across more than one census. The Swedo-Finnish Mobility Project developed a longitudinal database starting with a multistage sample of Swedish-speaking households, drawn from the census of 1950; individual records were then located, where possible, in the censuses of 1970 and 1975 (see Sandlund 1980, for a description of the project; Finnäs 1986, for an analysis based in part on this database). Another database offering this kind of possibility is the British Longitudinal Data Base, which provides an adequate number of cases for Welsh-speakers in Wales and Gaelic-speakers in Scotland.

(ii) *retrospective approaches* involve the selection of a sample at t_2 and then "reconstructing" the language characteristics of individuals at an earlier time (ideally, but not always, t_1). Generally, respondents are asked to describe their language use in early childhood (mother tongue), as well as at other crucial stages in the life cycle (e.g., at various levels of schooling, on entry into the labour market, at marriage, at current job). The familiar difficulties with this retrospective approach are: the declining reliability of responses with increases in time lapsed; selection and truncation biases in sample design; difficulties in establishing satisfactory populations exposed to the risk of language shift; disentangling the effects of age, period and cohort. Despite these messy methodological problems, retrospective survey data are generally the most accessible source of information on language maintenance and shift. The language module of the 1986 General Social Survey will eventually provide a wealth of information of this nature pertaining to language maintenance and shift in Canada (note: this file was not yet available for public use in June, 1988).

Indirect Measurement

The most common approach is to distinguish birth cohorts and use the component method to estimate net language shift. As I already indicated, such a measure loads all errors onto the residual component. The approach works best if we have several measures (t_1, t_2, t_3, etc.) on narrowly defined cohorts which may be mapped exactly from one census to the next. Moreover, the approach requires *identical* measurement instruments at all points in time (e.g., question wordings, response categories, procedures for editing or imputing inconsistent or missing responses) and low (and identical) propensities for respondent error. Some of the analyses of the ethnic origin data in the Canadian census suggest that the last condition is not met for all ethnic origins categories (see Ryder 1955; DeVries 1985, for some illustrations pertaining to the German, Dutch, Austrian and Ukrainian ethnic origins).

Canadian Census Data on Ethnic Origins and Language

Most of the sociological and demographic analyses of ethnic language maintenance and shift in Canada have used data from the censuses of population. Four questions have been used; they require some discussion.

Ethnic Origin

Canadians have been asked to indicate their ethnic origin by naming the group, or groups, to which they or their ancestors belonged on arrival in North America. The initial versions of the census question restricted this ancestral ethnic origin to the paternal line; however, starting in 1981, all lines of descent could be mentioned. Until 1971, respondents could therefore report only *one* ethnic origin. Beginning with the 1981 Census, respondents could legitimately report multiple ethnic origins, as a consequence of the omission of the restriction to the "paternal ancestry."

There is ample evidence, from a variety of sources, that a large proportion of Canadians will report multiple ethnic origins when offered the possibility. Driedger et al. report on data collected in Edmonton and Winnipeg in 1980. In these two cities, about 10 per cent of the respondents identified themselves as "hyphenated" Canadians (e.g., Italian-Canadian, Ukrainian-Canadian). In Winnipeg, an additional 30 per cent reported their ethnic preference to be "Canadian"; the corresponding percentage in Edmonton was 49 (1982, 65). Krotki and Odynak have analysed the responses to the ethnic origin question in the 1986 Census. His findings show many ethntic groups where multiple responses are more frequent than the single responses (e.g., Welsh, Irish, Scottish; all the Scandinavian groups; Austrian) (Krotki and Odynak, this volume). Such predispositions to report multiple ethnic ancestry are largely a function of nativity: those born in Canada have far higher proportions reporting two or more ethnic origins than do immigrants.

The Driedger et al. study also attempted to deal with potential contrasts between "paternal" and "maternal" ethnic ancestries. Their respondents were asked to indicate the "ethnic preferences" for their mother and father. The data reported in this article suggest that the differences between the parents of these respondents were very slight (Driedger et al. 1982, 65).

There is ample evidence that the census question on ethnic origin confounds two logically separate dimensions of ethnicity, "descent" and "identification" (see DeVries, 1985, for a detailed discussion). Take, for example, the Canadians of German ethnic origin discussed in Ryder's 1955 paper. It has been shown that understatements of German ethnic origin occurred, especially during the years when Germany was at war with Canada. This "self-identification" as something other than German was probably stronger for those individuals who had been in Canada for a long time than for relatively recent arrivals. The latter category is much more likely to speak German than the former. Thus, the bias introduced by self-identification has most likely (artificially) increased the estimated German-language maintenance above its true value.

There are other methodological problems associated with the analysis of language maintance or shift on the basis of the ethnic origin data. For the censuses prior to 1981, the "paternal" ethnic ancestry data tell us that X generations ago (where $X \geqslant O$), some male settled in this country whose ethnic origin was German, or Ukrainian or Greek. In some cases (Belgian, Swiss, Jewish are examples), the link between ethnic origin and language was imprecise, but in most cases, the link was quite clear. For respondents with $X = O$ (the foreign-born), such data do allow us to produce meaningful and probably valid statements about language maintenance and shift; for respondents with $X = 1$ (i.e., the respondent had a foreign-born father, but was born in Canada), we can also make meaningful statements about language shift. The 1971 Census, which did contain a question on the place of birth of the respondent's parents, has indeed yielded some analyses of the impact of nativity on ethnic language maintenance (see Richmond and Kalbach 1980; deVries and Vallee 1980. For those Canadians for whom $X > 1$, the ethnic origin data provide an unreliable basis for the analysis of ethnic language maintenance, even when we are restricted to the male ancestral line.

Life becomes much more complicated with the acknowledgment of multiple ethnic origins in 1981, in particular when this is combined with the disappearance of the question on the place of birth of the respondent's parents. Except where $X = O$, we do not know which of the several ethnic origins pertain to relatively recent arrivals. Moreover, respondents may well have selected one of the more salient ethnic categories from a larger number for which they qualified by descent. Thus, the self-identification component may have increased as a consequence. We really do not have sufficient evidence on the processes and conditions which led Canadians to select a particular configuration of ethnic origins in the censuses of 1981 and 1986.

Mother Tongue

In the Canadian census, mother tongue has been operationalized as the language first learned in childhood and still understood. Exact question phrasings have changed between 1941 and 1986, but the differences are not extensive. In principle (though not always in practice) the question determines the *earliest* language environment for the respondent. Note that there is no requirement that the person ever *spoke* the language; the ability to (still) understand it is sufficient. As such, "mother tongue" is — with minor exceptions — an inherited characteristic. The exceptions are, generally, cases where a respondent no longer understands the language he or she learned first in early childhood. There is some evidence that such "mother tongue drift" does indeed occur, in particular among persons who immigrated to Canada at an early age.

In analyses of language maintenance and shift prior to 1971, mother tongue data have been used as the "terminal" measure of language use, with ethnic origin as the initial one (see, for example, R.C.B.B. 1970, 117-136). The earlier comments on the ethnic origin data already suggest that this application of the census data on mother tongue and ethnic origin is of dubious validity, especially when we are dealing with Canadian-born respondents.

If we use the mother tongue data as the basis for the measurement of *current* language shift or maintenance, we are on safer grounds. In principle, the earliest language acquired may be used as an indicator of an individual's exposure to the risk of language shift (usually to English or French). The problem of "mother tongue drift," mentioned above, needs to be tackled separately. It may be argued that this phenomenon represents a final stage in language shift (i.e., the stage during which a respondent ceases to understand the language first learned in childhood). Unfortunately, these very extreme cases of language shift are not easily identified; to make matters worse, the extent to which mother tongue drift occurs is directly related to the level of *understatement* of language shift for a particular language community.

In recent censuses, analysts have identified a non-trivial number of cases where more than one language was mentioned as mother tongue. Such cases are relatively common among the children of immigrants (who, in many cases, learned the language of their parents and the language of the host society simultaneously), and among residents of the "Bilingual Belt" (the zone of contact between the English- and French- language communities). The number of individuals reporting two mother tongues amounted to about 955,000 in 1986, or 3.8 percent of the total population. Very little is known, at this time, about detailed characteristics of individuals who report more than one mother tongue. Moreover, the analytical problems generated by these multiple responses have not been solved yet.

Home Language

In 1971, a new question was introduced in the census in which respondents were asked to indicate the language spoken most often in the home. The question was repeated, with minor modifications, in 1981 and 1986. The original phrasing was ambiguous, in the sense that respondents could interpret the question to ask for *individual* language use, or for "*collective*" language use in the household (neither the English "you," nor the French "vous" make that distinction).

The revisions for 1981 and 1986 make it clear that the individual characteristic is measured (by the use of "you yourself" and "vous vous-même").

One can regard this measure as a possible indicator of current language use in one domain. As such, the data obtained by this question do not tell us anything about a respondent's "total" language use pattern (at work, at school, with friends, etc.). However, it is reasonable to assume that, for individuals shifting from one language to another, the home is the domain in which the original language is used most frequently, and from which it disappears last. As such, the use of an ethnic language at home may be taken as indicating at least some degree of ethnic language maintenance; conversely, the absence of an ethnic language from the home may be taken as a valid indicator of shift towards the language of the host society.

Several problems may be noted with this question and the interpretation of the responses. As with the responses to the mother tongue question, multiple responses were given to the question on home language. Such multiple responses may indicate a stage of partial language shift (i.e., an individual could be halfway between the use of language A and language B). Alternatively, they could reflect the linguistic composition of the respondent's household. A common pattern in many minority families is for the parental generation to use a minority language as well as an official language; the younger generation (the children) will use the official language almost exclusively; the older generation (grandparents) may be unable to speak either official language and use the minority language exclusively. Driedger and Hengstenberg (1986) provide some relevant data from a national survey of Mennonites. In their sample, 48 percent of the respondents used their traditional mother tongue (High German, Low German or Pennsylvania Dutch) with their parents while only 28 percent of the respondents did so with their children.

Other evidence for this type of intergenerational shift is given in Veltman's studies on the Greeks and Portuguese in Montreal (Veltman 1986). It should be obvious that census data, even with the allowance for multiple responses, cannot give an accurate picture of such complicated patterns of interaction.

Official Language(s) Spoken

Data on the individual's ability to speak one or both of Canada's official languages have been collected since the census of 1901. While these data only measure the self-reported *ability* to use English and/or French, they may be used to refine the measurement of the "exposure to the risk" of language shift. It is obvious that someone who is unable to speak English must acquire the ability to use that language before language shift to English can occur. Thus, the ability to speak English or French is a necessary condition for language shift (though not a sufficient one).

To summarize: with the Canadian census data on ethnic origin and language, we can distinguish the following processes:

1. ancestral language shift, indicated by the relation between one's ethnic origin and one's mother tongue;
2. current language shift, indicated by the relation between one's mother tongue and one's home language. This latter process may be subdivided into:
    a) official language acquisition, indicated by the relation between mother tongue and the ability to speak English and/or French; and
    b) language shift, narrowly defined as the proportion (of those able to speak one of the official languages) reporting the official language as the one spoken most often in the home.

Some Evidence

The censuses of 1971 and 1981 have yielded a fair number of analyses of ethnic language maintenance and shift. As I indicated before, censuses for 1961 and earlier had to use the data on mother tongue and ethnic origin, in the absence of the question on home language. Although it was possible to analyse the propensities of various groups to acquire English or French, very little work was conducted on this aspect of current language shift.

To illustrate some of the processes discussed in preceding sections of the paper, I compiled some data on four ethnic groups: Ukrainians, Italians, Finns and Greeks. This choice was by no means a random one: the first two are large groups, the last two somewhat smaller. Ukrainians and Finns settled in Canada earlier than did the Greeks and Italians. Finally, each of these groups has been studied fairly extensively. The accompanying tables summarize the salient aspects of ethnic language maintenance and shift for these groups.

Table 1 gives data on "ancestral" language maintenance, by the percentage of the members of an ethnic group who learned the associated language in early childhood. Note that the 1981 data are not strictly comparable with those from the earlier censuses as a result of the rephrased question on ethnic origin. Aside

TABLE 1

Mother Tongue Maintenance as Percentage of Ethnic Origin, 1941-1981

	1941	1951	1961	1971	1981[1]
Finns	87.7	70.4	67.8	56.0	61.2
Greeks	74.8	57.5	71.6	78.3	79.4
Italians	70.6	50.9	73.6	70.4	69.2
Ukrainians	92.1	73.5	64.4	48.9	55.2

[1] Data are based on single ethnic origins.

from this "methodological" aberration, we note that ancestral language shift progresses as larger proportions of an ethnic group are Canadian-born; the process appears to reverse itself during periods of heavy immigration (this is, of course, a compositional effect — most recent immigrants are likely to maintain their language for several years after settling in Canada). Even for the Greeks, more than half of whom were born outside Canada in 1981 (see Table 4), ancestral language shift amounted to about 20 percent.

Table 2 documents the propensity of the ethnic groups to have acquired the ability to speak English. Recall that these propensities are indicators of the exposure to the risk of shifting to English. As with ancestral language shift, these data are somewhat sensitive to fluctuations in immigration. As an example, the Italian ethnic origin category increased from around 150,000 in 1951 to about 450,000 in 1961 and about 730,000 in 1971. The proportion able to speak English declined, in 1961 and 1971, to values well below those for 1941 and 1951. With the decline in Italian immigration in the period 1971-81, the proportion able to speak English increased again.

TABLE 2

Percentage of Ethnic Origin Group Acquiring English, 1941-1981

	1941	1951	1961	1971	1981[1]
Finns	94.8	95.0	94.7	95.1*	97.5
Greeks	–	–	–	79.6	88.6
Italians	92.4	86.8	75.8	77.4	86.7
Ukrainians	93.0	93.1	97.2	97.8	98.8

Table 3 shows the magnitude of "current" language shift as the proportion of those who had acquired the ability to speak English-indeed reporting it as the language spoken most often at home. While the ability to speak English may only be seen as a *necessary* condition for language shift, but not a *sufficient*

TABLE 3

Percentage of Those Who Acquired the Ability to Speak English
Reporting English as Home Language, 1971-1981

	1971	1981
Finns	73.6	77.4
Greeks	35.4	41.8
Italians	48.0	55.6
Ukrainians	77.8	83.9

one, the data for the oldest immigrant groups suggest that there are strong tendencies to shift to English, once the ability to speak it has been acquired. For long-settled groups such as the Finns and the Ukrainians, this current shift has affected over three quarters of the group; the more recently settled Greeks and Italians only host about half of those exposed to the risk of shifting.

Table 4 provides some information about the situation in 1981. I already mentioned the fact that respondents could report multiple ethnic origins in 1981; the first row in the table shows that the tendency to report multiple origins varied widely among the four groups. Quick inspection of the first and third row of the table shows that the propensity to report multiple ethnic origins is associated with the percentage born in Canada.

The middle row of the table indicates the group's propensity to report multiple mother tongues. The range here is much narrower; it may be argued that only the Ukrainian ethnic group is strongly affected by multiple mother-tongue reporting.

TABLE 4

Various Methodological Aspects of 1981 Census Data

	Finns	Greeks	Italians	Ukrainians
% Single Ethnic Origin (Based on Reported Totals)	75.8	94.3	85.8	70.2
% Single Mother Tongue (Based on Reported Totals)	95.0	94.8	94.1	90.7
% of Group Born in Canada	68.8	42.6	54.0	89.0

TABLE 5

Percentage of Ethnic Origin Group Maintaining Ethnic Mother Tongue, by Age at Immigration, 1981

	Born in Canada	Age at Immigration		
		Under 20	20-44	45 and over
Finns	26.2	82.3	89.8	87.6
Greeks	50.2	85.0	93.3	92.7
Italians	32.2	86.2	95.2	96.5
Ukrainians	29.0	79.4	89.7	88.6

Tables 5 and 6 are both derived from unpublished tabulations from the 1981 Census, based on "total" ethnic origin; that is, both single mentions *and* multiple ones including the specific group. Table 5 shows the effects of nativity and of the age at immigration on ancestral language shift. It is quite obvious that this process primarily affects those born in Canada. Among immigrants, those who arrived as children (under age 20) are affected much more strongly than those who came as adults. Table 6 reports on the effects of the same background factors on current language shift. It is important to note that these effects are much more pronounced than they were for ancestral shift. Ethnic language maintenance is extremely low for the Canadian-born members of the oldest immigrant groups (Finns and Ukrainians), for whom the majority will have Canadian-born parents. The process works about equally intensively for persons who immigrated as children, but much less so for those who arrived as adults.

To get a full appreciation of the impact of language shift on ethnic group maintenance, we should keep in mind that the values in Tables 5 and 6 may be multiplied. Recall that Table 5 gave the propensity for a given language to be used as mother tongue by members of a particular ethnic origin, and that Table 6 gives the propensity for a given language to be used most often at home by persons reporting that language as mother tongue. (In formulas, Table 5 gives the ratio MT/EO, Table 6 gives HL/MT. Multiplying these gives HL/EO). Thus, for example, only 5 percent of Canadians of Finnish ethnic origin, born in Canada, used Finnish most often at home (.262 × .182). At the other extreme, almost 94 percent of Italians who arrived in Canada at ages 45 or over were using Italian most often at home.

TABLE 6

Percentage of Mother Tongue Group Using Ethnic Language Most Often at Home, by Age at Immigration, 1981

	Born in Canada	Age at Immigration		
		Under 20	20-44	45 and over
Finns	18.2	29.7	68.5	75.8
Greeks	63.9	66.8	80.6	95.5
Italians	46.8	52.1	84.4	96.9
Ukrainians	20.7	42.9	80.3	91.6

Summary

It is worth it, at this stage, to stand back and review the major points made in this paper. In contrast to the main demographic processes of fertility, mortality and migration, language shift is a transition process which affects ethnic minorities in a unique fashion. While majority groups gain members by virtue of the acquisition of a majority language by members of minority groups, such gains are proportionately small in comparison with the gains due to net migration and natural increase. Especially for groups which were established in Canada several generations ago (e.g., Scandinavians, Ukrainians), net migration makes only an insignificant contribution, while natural increase may well be negative as a consequence of the age structure in such groups. Language shift then further accelerates the decline of these groups.

The discussion in this paper has hinted at the difficulties in arriving at reliable estimates of language shift on the basis of the stock data from censuses of population; flow data are non-existent. Such difficulties are in part of a conceptual nature, partly of the practical variety. Many of the lower level hypotheses about ethnic language maintenance and shift cannot be tested using census data, but require reliable data from surveys.

The rather brief illustrations of data analysis at the end of this paper demonstrate the impact of language shift on such early immigrant groups as the Finns and the Ukrainians. They also show the relation between a minority group member's acquiring the ability to speak English and the (subsequent) use of English as the language spoken most often at home. Especially for the older immigrant groups, this association is quite common. The consequence is, of course, that the descendants of the persons who shifted to the use of English are very likely to grow up with English as mother tongue. Thus, in such cases, language shift occurs both *within* and *between* generations.

The final issue to be raised is this: for most ethnic groups, language is a very important "marker" of ethnic identity. To the extent that language shift erodes the strength of a minority language community, the ethnic identity of the community's members will be diluted; many people will become "hyphenated" Canadians or even deny having a distinct ethnicity (see Driedger et al. 1982, and Driedger and Hengstenberg 1986, for some evidence). As a consequence, all demographic analyses of ethnic minorities should consider the magnitude of language shift, and the consequences of this process for group size and composition.

10. ETHNO-RELIGIOUS IDENTITY AND ACCULTURATION

Warren E. Kalbach and Madeline A. Richard

The establishment of an official "multiculturalism" policy for Canada in 1971, which states that "diverse groups and communities are free to retain their respective identities while joining one another as equal partners in a united country" (Department of the Secretary of State of Canada, 1987) was a significant achievement. While it set an idealistic goal, it did not necessarily ensure the elimination of racial, ethnic or religious discrimination and prejudice within the population. Inequalities and differential treatment of ethnic minority groups have existed in the past and continue to exist today. French Canadians have not generally thought of themselves as equal partners with the British origin population since losing political control to the British in 1763, nor have most of those belonging to other ethnic minority populations who have immigrated to Canada. With few exceptions, success in the past meant not only hard work, but becoming less visible as a foreigner and more Canadian. "Classical" theories of assimilation and urban growth, developed on the basis of the U.S. experience, incorporated the assimilation process as one of the basic mechanisms by which immigrants achieved the social and economic status mobility necessary to move from initial reception areas into the higher status neighbourhoods of the larger community. Persistence of ethnic behaviour patterns was generally regarded as an obstacle preventing equal access to the community's opportunity structure and economic status mobility (Porter 1965). Traditional dress, foreign tongues, different religions, and unfamiliar customs have provided barriers to social acceptance by the dominant cultural groups. Over the years, interaction between new immigrants and the established and dominant cultural group has contributed to the emergence of a latent hierarchical structuring of the various ethnocultural groups in terms of favourable characteristics and their general desirability as co-workers, neighbours, friends, relatives and as close kin through marriage (Berry, et al. 1977). Immigrants who have been in Canada the longest and who came from cultural backgrounds most similar to the two charter groups have always been favourably regarded as well as those more recent immigrants who have been quick to assimilate with respect to language, social and economic behaviour and have been able to diminish their "visibility."

Assessing the Consequences of Ethnic Identity Retention

Given Canada's historical record of ethnic group relations, and the significant changes that occurred during the 1960s and '70s, it seems important to determine the extent to which ethnic identities, and their concomitant values and behaviours affect the individual's social and economic status in a society that has officially proclaimed itself "multicultural". Past research on the significance of ethnic differentials in social and economic status in Canadian society has been handicapped not only because of the ambiguity and confusion surrounding the definition and meaning of such terms as "ethnic origin," "ethnicity," and "nationality" (Ryder 1955), but also because of the difficulty of employing such concepts as "ethnicity" and "ethnic origin" in research in a manner consistent with their theoretical conceptualization as multidimensional phenomena. Only recently have census data become readily accessible in a form permitting the greater flexibility of data manipulation required to incorporate additional dimensions such as religion and birthplace in the identification of ethnocultural groups.

Previous analyses using multiple regression techniques, after controlling for major demographic variables have left very little variation for the "ethnic origin" variable to explain (Boyd et al. 1985). The degree of religious heterogeneity within immigrant populations, as defined by the standard census categorization of ethnic origins, may be part of the problem underlying the lack of success in establishing the significance of ethnic origin in social and economic status mobility studies. Distributions of religious preferences, based on the 1981 Census of Canada for the populations of British, non-British European and non-European origins, provide some notion of the degree of religious diversity that exists within Canada's immigrant population (Table 1). Yet, these too are gross simplifications of the extent of variation in religious heterogeneity to be found for the specific ethnic origin subgroups that comprise these rather broad categories of non-British origin populations.

However, with the availability of the Public Use Sample Tapes, it has become possible to take into account the basic multidimensional nature of ethnocultural groups and variations in religious heterogeneity by identifying and disaggregating their ethnoreligious components for separate analysis. Recognizing ethnoreligious combinations as the more meaningful and distinctive basic cultural entities permits an examination of the significance of the religious component of the group's cultural base for its survival or demise in an Anglo-Saxon dominated society, as well as its link to individual status mobility.

TABLE 1

Religious Composition, Population 15 Years and Over,
British, Other European and Non-European Ethnic Origin Groups
Canada, 1981

Religious Denomination	British		Other European		Non-European	
	Number	Percent	Number	Percent	Number	Percent
Roman Catholic	36,350	21.5	125,133	72.3	9,665	32.6
Other Catholic	152	0.1	2,921	1.7	126	0.4
Anglican	34,228	20.2	2,801	1.6	2,209	7.5
Baptist	8,049	4.8	1,918	1.1	830	2.8
Lutheran	2,412	1.4	7,379	4.3	1,695	5.7
Mennonite-Hutterite	231	0.1	2,477	1.4	250	0.8
Pentecostal	3,046	1.8	1,174	0.7	566	1.9
Presbyterian	11,492	6.8	1,353	0.8	593	2.0
United Church	49,098	29.0	7,919	4.6	2,422	8.2
Other Protestant	8,042	4.8	4,520	2.6	1,454	4.9
Eastern Orthodox	198	0.1	4,427	2.6	1,067	3.6
Jewish	312	0.2	4,444	2.6	112	0.4
Eastern Non-Christian	374	0.2	139	0.1	3,853	13.0
No Religion	14,446	9.1	6,481	3.7	4,772	16.1
Total	169,430	100.0	173,086	100.0	29,614	100.0

Source: Statistics Canada, 1981 Census of Canada, 2 Percent Public Use Sample, Individual File.

Social scientists have long pointed to the pervasiveness and conservative influence of traditional religions that have helped to maintain traditional family values, influenced political orientations and accounted for differences in socioeconomic status (Tomes 1983; Hertel and Hughes 1987). However, the same strengths that contribute to the survival of religious institutions often force those persons most strongly motivated towards status improvement to leave their church (Simpson and Yinger 1972, 545). Overall, few studies of ethnoreligious differentials in relation to immigrant assimilation have been done. One recent, but marginally relevant, longitudinal analaysis of socioeconomic achievement of five white religio-ethntic subgroups in the United States, found only limited evidence of ethnoreligious effects on socioeconomic achievement (Featherman 1971). This paper considers the problem of religious heterogeneity in some of Canada's more visible ethnic minority immigrant populations, and examines the significance of religious identity for the individual's accculturation and socioeconomic status achievement.

Data Sources and Variables

Data used in this analysis are from the 2 percent Individual File of the 1981 Census of Canada Public Use Sample Tapes; and special tabulations from the 1981 Census Master File purchased from Statistics Canada with funds provided by Health and Welfare Canada as part of Phase II of its Demographic Review Project. The major variables are defined in the *1981 Census Dictionary* (Statistics Canada 1982), but some additional comment is required concerning definitional changes which may affect the comparability of the findings with earlier analyses based on the 1971 Census Public Use Sample Tapes.

Ethnic Origin: The 1981 Census is the first census in which the respondents were not specifically instructed to trace their ancestry on the paternal side of their families. To the question "To which ethnic or cultural group did you or your ancestors belong on first coming to this continent?" respondents could report either their paternal or maternal ancestry, or both without having to indicate which one they felt to be most important to them. For this research, the population for analysis was limited to those reporting single origins to ensure greater comparability with earlier studies. Given that most multiple responses involved British and other European origins, and that the focus of this paper is on non-European populations, the effects of excluding multiple origins are thought to be negligible. At most, exclusion of multiple origins would tend to underestimate the extent of acculturation and social and economic status achievement of those groups with high proportions of multiple origins.

Religion: The question "What is your religion?" permits the respondent to make a "stated identification with a specific religious group, body, sect, cult, community or individual belief system (Statistics Canada 1982, 43). It does not reflect active membership, nor the degree of affiliation with or commitment to a given religious group. It is used in this research as a crude indicator of the general conservative or liberal nature of the respondents' philosophical or moral stance as reflected in their religious affiliation or identity. The literature suggests that on a traditional-conservative-liberal continuum, those identifying with ethnic churches would tend to be most conservative, followed by those with preferences for Canadian churches, and those with no preference (Hertel and Hughes 1987).

Generation: Generational Status is generally defined in terms of place of birth. Members of the first generation — the foreign-born — include all those who were not Canadians at birth. All others comprise the second and subsequent generations. Earlier research based on the 1971 Census data was able to identify and distinguish the second generation composed of those born in Canada of foreign-born parents, from the third and subsequent generations, i.e., those born of Canadian-born parents. Studies using the generational status data from the 1971 Census have shown the second generation to be a key group for understanding the degree of acculturation and the social and economic status achieved by ethnic minority populations (Richmond and Kalbach 1980). As the question on birthplace of parents was not included in the 1981 Census, this useful distinction was not possible in this research.

Home Language: The language reported as being spoken in the home by the respondent is utilized as a more sensitive index of acculturation than mother tongue. It is interpreted as reflecting purposive behavior on the respondent's part either to preserve one's cultural heritage (by maintaining the mother tongue in the home) or to deliberately improve "official language skills" through everyday use in order to facilitate social and economic adjustment in the immigrant's new sociocultural setting.

Highest Level of Schooling: Refers to the highest grade or year of elementary or secondary school attended, or the highest year of university or other non-university completed. The percentage of respondents reporting some university or degree is used as an index of educational status.

Occupation: Refers to the kind of work persons were doing the week prior to the census enumeration, or if they did not have a job that week, the job of longest duration since the first of the year in which the census was taken. The percentage of respondents reporting managerial, administrative, professional and related occupations is used as an index of occupational status attainment.

Total Family Income: The total reported income of all members of a census family. The percentage of respondents reporting family total incomes of $50,000 or more is included in this analysis as an additional index of relative economic status achievement to reflect the adaptive capabilities of the family unit.

Data Analysis

A relatively simple comparative analysis is employed based on computer-produced crosstabs from the Public Use Sample Tapes, as well as customized crosstabulations, produced by Statistics Canada for selected ethnic origin subgroups of the population. Log-linear modeling would ordinarily be the more appropriate procedure for analysing complex relationships among discrete variables for relatively small populations. However, the Public Use Sample Tapes only provide individual level data for a limited number of the larger ethnic origin groups. Similar analyses of the more recent and smaller of Canada's ethnic minority populations cannot be disaggregated from the combined or residual categories, thus special customized crosstabulations were required. The relative efficacy of three distinctive ethnoreligious mobility paths for members of the various ethnic minority groups is judged by the method of percentage differences. Only gross effects are examined in this paper. The possible effects of differences in age and sex composition with respect to occupational status and income achievement levels will be examined using period of immigration and age at immigration as controls in a subsequent analysis of male and female subgroups.

Ethnic Church, Language Retention and Educational and Economic Status Achievement Among Ethnic Minority Populations

Earlier research has explored the relationship between ethnic church identity and ethnic contacts for retention of ethnic-related behaviour over successive generations (Kloss 1966; Gibbon 1938; Anderson, et al. 1981; Gordon 1964). An earlier study of Ukrainians in Canada, using data from the 1971 Census Public Use Sample, showed interesting lateral patterns of language attrition within generations associated with non-Ukrainian church preferences, which were also associated with higher levels of educational attainment and occupational status (Kalbach and Richard 1980). Even though all immigrant minority populations are exposed to the pressures of acculturation and assimilation in the host society, those who retain a preference for, or affiliation with an "ethnic" church appear to experience less ethnic language loss and social and economic assimilation than that experienced by their ethnic counterparts whose preferences are for the mainline Canadian churches, or who report no religion. The differences tend to be greatest within the foreign-born generations. For the Canadian-born, variations between religious subgroups appear to be minimal with the exception of those with "no religion" who tend to retain their educational and economic status advantage (Kalbach and Richard 1987, 1988).

The significance of the religious heterogeneity of ethnic origin groups for language assimilation and social and economic status attainment was originally demonstrated with data from the 1971 Census for populations of German and Ukrainian origin (Kalbach and Richard 1981). It was later shown to apply beyond these specific minority ethnic groups on the basis of an analysis of samples of a larger number of ethnic groups in the Toronto CMA using a measure of ethnic connectedness based on religious preferences and church attendance (Kalbach and Richard 1987). A subsequent replication of the analysis using data from the 1981 Public Use Sample Tapes for the combined non-British origins produced similar results (Kalbach and Richard 1988). Increases in the religious diversity of ethnic groups resulting from intra- and inter-generational shifts in religious distributions that have favoured the main Canadian churches, and increases in those having no religious preference, suggest that acculturation and social and economic assimilation can be expected to continue, at least insofar as the minority groups of European origins are concerned.

With the changing ethnic composition of immigrants to Canada since the liberalization of immigration regulations during the 1960s, the proportion of non-European immigrants has increased dramatically (Taylor 1987). Questions arise as to the extent to which these more recent and more "visible" immigrants will have the same experience as their European predecessors in achieving access to the social, economic and political structures of their host society. The greater religious homogeneity of non-European origin immigrants and the presence of larger numbers of Eastern Non-Christian religions raises questions as to the relative viability of the alternative mobility paths open to them, and the extent to which their religious orientations may impede or facilitate their efforts to successfully adjust to life in Canada.

The Non-British Origin Population

The populations of interest for this research have been those ethnic origin groups other than the British or French whose decade rates of growth during the post-war period have been responsible for the declining dominance of Canada's two founding charter groups. As previously noted, the results of research based on the 1971 Census reflected the experience of European ethnic minority groups in general and the German and Ukrainian populations specifically. There was little reason to believe that their experiences would necessarily be valid for the more recent non-European immigrants.

In 1971, the population of British or French origin comprised 73 percent of Canada's total; other European origins, 23 percent; and, non-Europeans, 4 percent. While the reporting of multiple origins in the 1981 Census makes it difficult to derive comparable figures, single origin data suggested a continuing decline of the British and French origin component, approaching 67 percent, and increases in other European and non-European origins that would have probably brought their proportionate size to 27 and 6 percent respectively (Statistics Canada 1987).

Because of relative size differences, the analyses of the 1981 data would mainly reflect the experience of the non-British European ethnic subgroups. Further disaggregation of the population was required to determine the relevance of earlier findings for the rather small but rapidly increasing non-European subgroups. This has been done for the population 15 years of age and over reporting single ethnic origins. Because of the significantly higher proportion of foreign-born for the non-European component — 55 percent, compared to 14 and 19 percent respectively for the British and non-British European origins — data are analysed for both foreign- and native-born components (Table 2). These data provide the basis for a gross comparison of the three subgroups with respect to the major dependent variables, i.e., measures of accculturation and social and economic status achievement.

The expected pattern of convergence in the characteristics of the non-British European and non-European origin populations with those of the British, indicative of acculturation and assimilation, is apparent in Table 2, but only for the language characteristics. For education and the economic status variables, non-Europeans exceed the combined non-British European origins group in every case, as well as the British origins, with respect to educational attainment. For a plausible explanation, that when ethnic and racial restrictions were removed from the criteria for landed immigrant status in Canada, a point system favouring high educational attainment and professional and skilled occupational experience was implemented. It would appear that only the most highly educated of the

TABLE 2

Selected Social and Economic Characteristics for the Foreign- and Canada-born Population of
British, Non-British European and Non-European Origins 15 Years of Age and Over
Canada, 1981

Characteristic	Foreign-born			
	British	Non-British European	Non-European	Total Pop. 15 +
Percent Professional and Managerial	31.5	20.1	26.1	25.0 (49,833)
Percent Total Family Income >$50,000	12.3	8.9	8.4	9.9 (58,346)
Percent Some Univ. or Univ. Degree	19.5	13.7	30.2	19.3 (72,019)
Percent Non-English/ French in Home	1.3	46.1	51.8	32.8 (72,019)
Percent Non-English/ French Mother Tongue	3.9	83.1	71.0	54.7 (72,019)
	Canadian-born			
Percent Professional and Managerial	23.8	22.4	22.1	23.1 (213,440)
Percent Total Family Income >$50,000	11.2	9.1	10.2	10.2 (247,002)
Percent Some Univ. or Univ. Degree	17.3	12.9	15.4	15.2 (300,111)
Percent Non-English/ French in Home	0.1	1.9	14.5	1.6 (300,111)
Percent Non-English/ French Mother Tongue	0.4	7.9	29.5	5.2 (300,111)
	Total Population 15 +			
Percent Professional and Managerial	24.8	22.0	24.4	23.5 (263,273)
Percent Total Family Income >$50,000	11.4	9.1	9.2	10.1 (305,348)
Percent Some Univ. or Univ. Degree	17.6	13.1	23.6	16.0 (372,130)
Percent Non-English/ French in Home	0.2	10.2	35.0	7.6 (372,130)
Percent Non-English/ French Mother Tongue	0.9	22.0	52.3	18.6 (372,130)

Source: Statistics Canada, 1981 Census of Canada, 2 Percent Public Use Sample, Individual File.

non-European origin applicants were accepted under the independent worker category.

Preferential selection in terms of educational criteria becomes even more apparent in the case of foreign-born non-Europeans. The possible effects of discrimination against visible minorities in Canada may be reflected in the fact that non-Europeans have the highest proportions with some university or degree (30 percent), yet the lowest proportion of individuals reporting total family incomes of $50,000 or more. That these status inconsistencies are not equally evident among the Canadian-born suggests that economic status is more consistent with educational and professional status among the more acculturated groups, at least insofar as language behaviour is concerned. Given the greater visibility of non-European origins in general, and the evidence of convergence for their Canadian-born generations, the question arises: which of the alternative mobility paths explored in earlier research on non-British European populations in general is likely to be the most viable path for the more visible non-European ethnic minority populations?

Religious and Generational Differences in Language Use, Education and Economics Status Characteristics for Non-European Origin Populations

A review of the data for language use, educational attainment, and total family income for the combined non-British European population, presented in Table 3, reveals the same general patterns of intra- and inter-generational ethnoreligious variations as reported previously for the population of non-British origins (Kalbach and Richard 1988a). As a negative index of acculturation, the use of language in the home other than English or French, by the foreign-born, was most likely to be reported by those with ethnic church identities, e.g., Eastern Orthodox and Other Catholic religions. Conversely, those with Anglican and United Church preferences were most likely to report the use of either English or French in the home. Those identifying with the Roman Catholic Church (which can represent either an ethnic or a Canadian church), were intermediate to the above groups, as were those indicating no preference. Levels of use of languages in the home other than English or French are significantly lower for all native-born, but remain highest for the ethnic churches and lowest for two of the main Canadian churches, followed closely by Roman Catholics and those with no preference. Similar religious differentials may be observed with respect to educational attainment and total family income as indexes of social and economic status. Again, the religious differentials are least for the native-born.

Table 4 presents similar data for the non-European origins including the more recent visible minority immigrant groups. The non-European origin population is of particular interest because of the presence in some groups of significant numbers of individuals with Eastern Non-Christian religious preferences.

TABLE 3

Characteristics of the Non-British European Population, 15 Years of Age and Over, by Native- and Foreign-born For Selected Religions, Canada 1981

Generation	Lutheran	Eastern Orthodox	Other Catholic	Roman Catholic	Presbyterian	United Church	Anglican	No Religion	Total 15+
				Percent With Non-English, Non-French Home Language					
Foreign-born	28.3	69.5	72.2	54.8	26.2	13.0	10.9	20.3	46.1
Native-born	1.5	22.1	17.0	1.0	1.2	0.6	0.2	1.1	1.9
Total Population 15+	12.1	49.7	31.6	8.7	9.4	2.2	1.5	6.0	10.2
N	7.379	4.427	2.921	125.133	1.353	7.919	2.801	6.481	173.086
				Percent Not Attending School With Some University or University Degree					
Foreign-born	12.6	9.4	13.1	10.5	17.4	20.3	22.7	33.8	13.7
Native-born	11.4	16.0	15.3	11.4	13.2	14.0	14.2	25.6	12.9
Total Population 15+	11.9	12.1	14.7	11.3	14.5	14.9	15.2	27.6	13.1
N	7.379	4.427	2.921	125.133	1.353	7.919	2.801	6.481	173.086
				Percent in Families With Total Family Income of $50,000+					
Foreign-born	10.2	5.9	6.6	7.3	13.9	13.1	11.1	13.8	8.9
Native-born	11.3	9.8	10.0	8.2	9.0	11.1	10.1	11.3	9.1
Total Population 15+	10.8	7.5	9.2	8.1	10.6	11.4	10.2	12.0	9.1
N	6.064	3.694	2.305	105.161	1.100	6.695	2.323	4.764	144.158

Source: Statistics Canada, 1981 Census of Canada, 2 Percent Public Use Sample, Individual File.

Questions are raised as to whether the same three mobility paths offer realistic alternatives for achieving higher socioeconomic status. Changing one's religious preference or disaffiliating from non-Christian religions may involve a different magnitude of difficulty than that required to shift preferences from one Christian ethnic church to one of the major Canadian churches. On *a priori* grounds, it would seem that the path of least resistance would be either the retention of the traditional ethnoreligious orientation that has been brought to Canada, or the gradual disengagement or disaffiliation suggested by those who no longer express a religious preference.

An examination of the data for the non-European population reveals that a surprisingly higher proportion of the foreign-born report some university or degree, in comparison to the native-born than was reported for the non-British Europeans in Table 3. Higher proportions for Roman and other Catholic church preference groups suggest that educational attainment may have less relevance as an indicator of status achievement in Canada, than as an indicator of the success of immigration regulations in allowing only the most educated to come to Canada. This interpretation is supported by the fact that ''above average'' levels of educational attainment tend to be associated with below average values for economic status indicators, e.g., proportions of individuals 15 years of age and over reporting family total incomes of $50,000 or more (Table 4), or proportions in managerial, administrative, professional and related occupations (Kalbach and Richard 1988b). With the removal of the more overt discriminatory aspects of immigration regulations, the criteria for selecting immigrants may have shifted from the ''perceived potential for adjustment'' of various ethnic origin groups to evidence of competence in English or French and educational achievement or proven skills in professional and entrepreneurial occupations as evidence of social and economic assimilation.

It is quite possible that the persistence of discrimination and prejudice in Canadian society against some ethnic subgroups is a factor in the inconsistent relationships between language assimilation, educational attainment, occupational status and economic rewards. Insofar as these data are concerned, inconsistencies are most apparent for the foreign-born of non-European origin. Differences between religions within ethnic subgroups for the Canadian-born are much less apparent. The fact that those reporting ''no preference'' tend to show achieved status characteristics as high, or higher, than those reporting ethnic or Canada church preferences, suggests that the ''secular'' mobility path may offer the best opportunity for status achievement in Canadian society for non-Europeans. However, the high degree of cultural heterogeneity for the combined non-European origins requires a closer examination of the data before assuming that the relationships observed in Table 4 are equally valid for specific ethnic minority groups.

TABLE 4

Characteristics of the Non-European Origin Population, 15 Years of Age and Over, by Native- and Foreign-born For Selected Religions, Canada 1981

Generation	Lutheran	Eastern Orthodox	Other Catholic	Roman Catholic	Presby-terian	United Church	Anglican	No Religion	Total 15+
	Percent With Non-English, Non-French Home Language								
Foreign-born	59.9	62.2	43.8	41.6	38.4	41.1	11.0	70.5	51.8
Native-born	22.0	9.3	17.2	11.6	7.6	6.0	27.0	8.5	14.5
Total Population 15+	57.7	48.4	30.4	27.1	25.5	14.2	22.5	48.2	35.0
N	3,853	1,067	9,665	1,454	593	2,422	2,209	4,772	29,614
	Percent Not Attending School With Some University or University Degree								
Foreign-born	32.5	25.0	34.1	28.2	33.7	28.2	28.0	28.5	30.2
Native-born	18.9	16.5	11.6	15.3	13.6	17.4	10.0	25.7	15.4
Total Population 15+	31.7	22.8	22.8	22.0	25.3	20.0	15.0	27.5	23.6
N	3,853	1,067	9,665	1,454	593	2,422	2,209	4,772	29,614
	Percent in Families With Total Family Income of $50,000 +								
Foreign-born	7.0	7.0	9.1	6.9	9.4	9.0	11.2	9.1	8.4
Native-born	17.5	14.4	8.5	9.3	11.6	11.6	6.1	14.3	10.2
Total Population 15+	7.6	8.9	8.8	8.1	10.3	11.0	7.5	11.0	9.2
N	3,222	1,831	7,777	1,179	477	1,972	1,777	3,653	23,725

Source: Statistics Canada, 1981 Census of Canada, 2 Percent Public Use Sample. Individual File.

Specific Non-European Origins and Mobility Paths

Data for the same language, education and economic variables shown in Table 4, are presented in Tables 5-8 for four of the larger non-European ethnic subgroups, specifically the Chinese, Indo-Pakistanis, Blacks and Caribbeans, and Middle-Eastern Arab/Asians. While these four populations are fairly similar with respect to their recency of immigration, proportion foreign-born and the age composition of the population 15 years of age and over, they differ considerably with respect to their ethnoreligious composition. The Chinese, for example, while exhibiting an intermediate level of religious heterogeneity, have the highest proportion claiming no religious preference, i.e., 57 percent compared to the second highest, 7 percent, reported by Blacks and Caribbeans. The Indo-Pakistanis, in contrast to the Chinese, are the most homogeneous in terms of their religious composition, with 82 per cent indicating a preference for Eastern Non-Christian religions. The Blacks and Caribbean subgroup contrasts with the others in that they have the highest proportions reporting English or French both as their mother tongue and the language they speak in the home. The Middle-Eastern Arab/Asian origins differ significantly from the others mainly in terms of their excess of males, with a sex ratio of 117. There are other differences among these groups, but the ones central to this analysis are the difference in religious composition, the amount of change that occurs between first and subsequent generations, and whether these differences are associated with acculturation and status achievement in the same way that they have been shown to be related for the major non-British European origin subgroups.

Intergenerational Shifts in Religious Composition

There have been questions as to the extent to which non-European origin subgroups with significant numbers of Eastern Non-Christians would show intergenerational changes in their religious composition. In this case, three of the four subgroups show changes in the direction of the distribution for the native-born population of British origins, albeit small ones. The only exception was for the Black and Caribbean origin subgroup. They showed no significant difference between their distributions for the foreign- and Canadian-born. With Indexes of Dissimilarity of 34, their religious distributions were, by far, more similar to that of the British native-born than any of the others.

Slightly lower Indexes of Dissimilarity for the Canadian-born, in comparison to the foreign-born Chinese, Middle-Eastern Arab/Asians and Indo-Pakistanis, suggest at best only a slight convergence of their religious composition with that of the Canada-born population of British origin. In all four cases, the proportions of Canadian-born with Eastern Non-Christian religions were less than that for the foreign-born, while the reverse was true for the main Canadian churches. The only exception was for the Blacks and Caribbeans which already had the highest proportion of Canadian-born with a preference for the major

191

TABLE 5

Characteristics of the Chinese Origin Population, 15 Years of Age and Over,
by Native- and Foreign-born For Selected Religions, Canada 1981

Generation	Percent With Non-English, Non-French Home Language					
	E. Non-Christian	Roman Catholic	Other Protestant	Main Protestant	No Religion	Total Pop. 15+
Foreign-born	84.9	54.5	75.6	61.6	82.6	75.7
Native-born	51.3	29.0	35.1	16.9	41.5	34.4
Total Population 15+	82.0	49.5	65.8	42.3	72.3	65.2
N	18,240	42,810	25,255	35,280	164,315	289,225

	Percent Not Attending School With Some University or University Degree					
Foreign-born	16.2	38.8	39.7	29.2	23.3	27.4
Native-born	29.0	30.2	32.3	36.4	31.6	33.1
Total Population 15+	16.6	38.3	38.8	31.7	24.3	28.2
N	14,755	32,485	20,045	28,360	123,790	222,095

	Percent in Families With Total Family Income of $50,000+					
Foreign-born	4.9	13.3	9.6	11.7	7.5	8.8
Native-born	8.6	13.5	14.8	18.8	13.3	14.3
Total Population 15+	6.1	13.4	12.0	16.5	10.2	11.4
N	10,885	27,440	16,330	23,575	99,350	179,680

Source: Statistics Canada, 1981 Census of Canada, Special Tabulations.
Total includes population 15 years and over for all religious denominations.

Protestant churches, i.e., 24 percent, or just 2 percentage points less than for
the foreign-born. As expected, all groups but the Chinese, showed intergenerational increases in the proportion indicating "no religious preference." The
exceptionally high percentages of both foreign- and native-born Chinese (57
and 56 percent), claiming no religious preference was quite unexpected. Its significance for acculturation and status mobility remains to be examined.

On the basis of earlier analysis of European origin populations, preferences
for major Canadian churches, or no church, as opposed to an ethnic church,
have been shown to be associated with one form of acculturation, e.g., the use
of English or French in the home and higher educational attainment and eco-

TABLE 6

Characteristics of the Indo-Pakistani Origin Population, 15 Years of Age and Over,
by Native- and Foreign-born For Selected Religions, Canada 1981

Generation	E. Non-Christian	Roman Catholic	Other Protestant	Main Protestant	No Religion	Total Pop. 15 +
Percent With Non-English, Non-French Home Language						
Foreign-born	56.1	5.9	20.3	11.1	23.5	48.3
Native-born	39.8	4.6	5.0	1.8	10.8	32.8
Total Population						
15 +	52.4	5.6	16.3	8.7	18.8	44.7
N	160,390	16,995	4,890	6,555	6,000	196,405
Percent Not Attending School With Some University or University Degree						
Foreign-born	36.3	38.3	42.4	45.1	52.4	37.4
Native-born	21.8	13.2	15.0	14.0	28.8	20.4
Total Population						
15 +	35.9	37.2	39.9	42.1	48.2	36.8
N	110,565	12,265	3,380	4,755	4,070	136,130
Percent in Families With Total Family Income of $50,000 +						
Foreign-born	7.9	11.5	10.8	14.2	17.9	8.7
Native-born	7.2	10.1	5.4	14.1	14.5	7.8
Total Population						
15 +	7.5	10.9	7.8	14.1	15.8	8.3
N	96,595	10,325	2,815	3,960	3,075	117,730

Source: Statistics Canada, 1981 Census of Canada, Special Tabulations.
Total includes population 15 years and over for all religious denominations.

nomic status achievement. If intergenerational shifts can occur in religious composition away from the ethnic church and in the direction of Canadian churches, or disaffiliation from ethnic religions for the more visible immigrants, it would seem that Canada's more recent immigrant groups could expect increased access to the more viable mobility paths that have been available to the non-British European populations in the past.

Ethno-Religious Variations in Acculturation

It has been suggested that those with no religious preference would not only tend to be the most acculturated with respect to language behaviour for the

TABLE 7

Characteristics of the Black and Caribbean Origin Population, 15 Years of Age and Over, by Native- and Foreign-born For Selected Religions, Canada 1981

Percent With Non-English, Non-French Home Language

Generation	E. Non-Christian	Eastern Orthodox	Roman Catholic	Other Protestant	Main Protestant	No Religion	Total 15+
Foreign-born	15.1	45.8	9.3	3.8	1.6	4.2	6.0
Native-born	6.8	5.3	1.3	0.5	0.3	1.0	1.0
Total Population							
15+	13.7	35.2	7.4	2.7	1.2	3.2	4.7
N	10,295	725	40,960	42,625	36,225	9,545	142,125

Percent Not Attending School With Some University or University Degree

Generation	E. Non-Christian	Eastern Orthodox	Roman Catholic	Other Protestant	Main Protestant	No Religion	Total 15+
Foreign-born	18.8	34.1	22.6	13.5	23.4	31.5	20.8
Native-born	16.1	13.0	20.6	12.3	19.9	23.1	16.5
Total Population							
15+	18.7	29.8	22.5	13.2	23.0	30.2	20.3
N	7,685	570	28,895	29,920	27,170	6,955	102,455

Percent in Families With Total Family Income of $50,000+

Generation	E. Non-Christian	Eastern Orthodox	Roman Catholic	Other Protestant	Main Protestant	No Religion	Total 15+
Foreign-born	5.0	0.0	5.7	3.5	8.3	7.5	5.8
Native-born	3.1	0.0	7.1	3.3	8.7	11.1	6.3
Total Population							
15+	4.2	0.0	6.5	3.4	8.6	9.8	6.1
N	6,410	360	21,865	22,945	21,490	4,705	78,715

Source: Statistics Canada, 1981 Census of Canada, Special Tabulations.
Total includes population 15 years and over for all religious denominations.

foreign-born, but for the Canadian-born as well. This was, in fact the case only for the Middle-Eastern Arab/Asians (see Table 8). Their next most accculturated group, in terms of language usage, was the one composed of those with preferences for the major Canadian churches. However, in no other case were those with no preference most likely to use English or French at home. In fact their language behaviour was closer to that of Eastern Non-Christians for Chinese and Indo-Pakistani origins. In most cases, the foreign-born of these groups with Catholic church, or the native-born with major Canadian church preferences, showed the most evidence of (language) acculturation. Some variation from this pattern can be seen for the Blacks and Caribbeans (Table 7). In their case, where the use of English or French in the home is generally most prevalent,

TABLE 8

Characteristics of the Middle Eastern Arab-Asian Origin Population, 15 Years of Age and Over, by Native- and Foreign-born For Selected Religions, Canada 1981

Generation	E. Non-Christian	Eastern Orthodox	Roman Catholic	Other Protestant	Main Protestant	No Religion	Total 15+
Percent With Non-English, Non-French Home Language							
Foreign-born	51.4	67.8	44.9	75.6	44.7	24.6	55.1
Native-born	31.8	26.6	14.3	47.6	5.6	2.6	22.3
Total Population							
15+	46.8	57.6	34.0	69.1	21.0	15.4	45.5
N	30,755	26,385	28,370	6,685	4,415	2,300	101,590
Percent Not Attending School With Some University or University Degree							
Foreign-born	38.3	28.8	32.2	24.5	33.1	62.9	33.2
Native-born	12.6	22.8	26.9	27.5	21.5	42.4	24.8
Total Population							
15+	37.1	28.0	30.9	24.9	26.5	56.0	31.8
N	21,585	21,070	22,100	5,350	3,835	1,865	77,845
Percent in Families With Total Family Income of $50,000+							
Foreign-born	6.3	7.8	12.3	4.7	13.8	15.6	8.8
Native-born	6.3	14.5	15.8	8.6	13.7	13.7	12.2
Total Population							
15+	6.3	11.0	14.4	6.3	13.7	14.3	10.6
N	17,770	16,985	18,085	4,425	3,130	1,190	63,330

Source: Statistics Canada, 1981 Census of Canada, Special Tabulations.
Total includes population 15 years and over for all religious denominations.

the most acculturated were those with major Canadian church preferences for both foreign- and native-born generations, followed by Other Protestants. For the Chinese, who appear to be least likely to use English or French in the home, language assimilation is greatest for those with preference for the Catholic church, followed by those who identify with one of the major Canadian churches.

Education and Economic Status Achievement for Non-European Ethnoreligious Subgroups

Historically, the potential for acculturation has been regarded as one of the prime requisites for educational and economic status achievement for immigrants coming to Canada. Among post-war immigrants, variations in acculturation have been observed for major ethnic origin populations (Richmond and Kalbach 1980), as well as for their ethnoreligious subgroups that are associated with differentials in educational attainment and economic status. Recall that for the foreign-born of non-British European origins, those identifying with one of the major Canadian churches, or having no religion, tended to have the highest proportions with some university or degree and economic status either in terms of proportions reporting managerial and professional occupations (Kalbach and Richard 1988b), or belonging to census families whose total incomes were $50,000 or more (as shown in Table 2). For the Canadian-born, only those with "no religion" appeared to retain their status advantage over the other ethnoreligious subgroups of the same generation. Differences generally disappeared between those still identifying with ethnic churches or the other major Canadian churches in generations following the foreign-born.

This does not seem to be the case for the particular non-European ethnoreligious subgroups included in this analysis. In the one case where the percentage of Eastern Non-Christian individuals reporting family incomes of $50,000 or more actually increased from the first generation to the next (i.e., for the Chinese), the increase was insufficient to bring them in line with any of the other ethnoreligious subgroups. While it appears that the selective immigration criteria generally leads to higher proportions of the more visible immigrant groups having high educational status, it obviously does not ensure them as high an income as found for non-British European ethnoreligious groups. Or, more importantly, not even to the same degree that individuals of the same origin, but of different religious preferences, are rewarded. The best examples of apparent status inconsistencies are for native-born Indo-Pakistanis with Eastern Non-Christian religions (Table 6) and for the foreign-born Middle-Eastern Arab/Asians (Table 8). In the latter, Eastern non-Christians have the second highest proportion with some university or degree (38 percent), but the second lowest proportion (6 percent) reporting total family incomes of $50,000 or more. Similarly, the native-born Eastern Non-Christian Indo-Pakistanis have the second highest proportion with some university or degree (22 percent) but the second lowest proportion (7 percent) of any of the native-born Indo-Pakistani religious subgroups reporting total family incomes of $50,000 or more. Similar types of inconsistencies between educational attainment and family income can be noted between foreign- and native-born for the Main Protestant and No Religion groups of Black/Caribbean origins, and Other Protestants of Chinese origins. However, inconsistencies notwithstanding, non-ethnic churches in general, and more specifically the main Protestant groups, appear to present more viable mobility paths vis-à-vis higher economic status attainment.

Of the four non-European origin populations analysed here, those of Chinese origin are clearly atypical both in the proportions claiming to have no religion, and in their relatively low levels of acculturation, educational attainment and socioeconomic achievement. Why this is the case for the Chinese is not clear from the data available for this analysis. In any event, it is clear that a declaration of having no religion or no religious preference (during a Canadian census enumeration) by those of Chinese origin cannot be assumed to reflect any kind of weakening of the influence of the ethnoreligious church because of the secularization of Canadian society in general, or a more conscious attempt to become more acculturated and assimilated through changes in reference or membership groups.

Summary Comments

Although the methodology is essentially descriptive and comparative and the operational definitions of such concepts as ethnic origin, religious preference, ethnic church and acculturation are constrained by the nature and availability of census data, religion emerges as a meaningful dimension of ethnocultural groups. A strong case is made for the necessity of studying ethnocultural groups, not solely in terms of "ethnic origins" but in terms of their "ethnoreligious" character.

Ethnoreligious patterns of acculturation and socioeconomic status achievement by generation, observed for those of the more established non-British European origin groups highlight three general mobility paths by which members of Canada's ethnocultural groups can become acculturated and achieve socioeconomic status mobility, i.e., with the ethnic church, a main Canadian church, or with no church. The patterns observed for the non-British Europeans in general and the German and Ukrainian origins in particular, suggest that ethnic church affiliation tends to be associated with less acculturation and lower socioeconomic status achievement for the first generation (foreign-born) than is the case for those expressing preference for mainline Canadian churches or expressing no religious preference or affiliation. Ethnoreligious differentials tend to be of minimal significance after the first generation, except for those who appear to be on the "secular" no religion path to continuing acculturation and socioeconomic achievement and assimilation.

The previous experience of European origin populations has some validity for understanding the ethnoreligious and generational differences in patterns of acculturation and socioeconomic achievement observed for some of the larger and more recent non-European origin populations immigrating to Canada in increasingly large numbers since the early 1960s. However, the shift to more selective immigration policies and procedures emphasizing criteria known to be positively associated with acculturative behaviour and status mobility has produced some inconsistencies in the relationships between acculturation, educational attainment and socioeconomic status achievement for some of the non-European origin immigrant cohorts and their native-born generations. Still, for the four selected non-European origin groups (Chinese, Indo-Pakistani, Black/Caribbean, and Middle-Eastern Arab/Asian), those with "ethnic church" preferences tend to be less acculturated, have lower levels of education, and exhibit lower levels of socioeconomic achievement. Those with main Canadian church preferences, as well as no church preferences, do relatively better, with the possible exception of those of Chinese origins. Furthermore, the ethnoreligious differences within the ethnocultural groups tend to remain significant for the native-born generations of these more recent and more visible non-European immigrant groups.

The appearance of some status inconsistencies between levels of educational attainment and socioeconomic achievement for several of the more visible non-European ethnoreligious subgroups should attract the interest of those supporting a multiculturalism model for Canadian society in which no one is consciously denied opportunity on the basis of ethnic origin, race, place of birth or religion. There are obvious differences between as well as within ethnocultural groups, that are associated with differences in potential for the minimal levels of acculturation required for social and status mobility. These should be given serious consideration by those formulating immigration policy and regulations.

The differences reported in this paper reflect gross effects in that little control for age differences was possible beyond the fact that recent immigrants to Canada generally exhibit similar age and sex characteristics. However, further analyses of income and occupational status differentials for males and females, incorporating controls for period of immigration, and age at immigration should permit additional refinement of the analyses presented in this paper.

11. FAMILY STRUCTURE AND ETHNICITY

Thomas K. Burch

While it is easy to document and describe ethnic differentials in demographic behaviour in Canada — including family formation, household and kinship behaviour — the explanation of those differentials in causal terms remains problematic. In particular, it is difficult to assess the precise causal role of ''ethnicity'' as such. Conceptual, theoretical, methodological and empirical problems stand in the way of such an assessment.

This chapter begins with a general discussion of some of the theoretical and methodological issues involved, with focus on the challenge of rigorous research on the behavioural effects of ideational factors, including ethnic subcultures. Next it reviews data sources available in Canada for research on ethnicity and the family. Then it provides some exploratory results on family structure and the family, gleaned from a major new data source, Statistics Canada's 1985 General Social Survey. Finally, it suggests a multi-equation approach to the explication of ethnic effects, with an illustration from the General Social Survey.

Ideational Culture and Behaviour

After decades of relative neglect, cultural variables have gained acceptance in mainstream demography. A major finding of the European Fertility Study (Coale and Watkins 1986), for example, is the extent to which region, religion, language and ethnic group accounted for variation and change in fertility, over and above that accounted for by more traditional, ''hard'' variables such as mortality, urbanization, income and industrialization (Anderson 1986). International regression analyses by Lutz (1986) and Burch (1988) have yielded a similar result for contemporary data. Recent theoretical writings on fertility have assigned a prime causal role to culture (see, for example, Preston 1986; Cleland and Wilson 1987; Caldwell and Caldwell 1987).

Determining the precise role of cultural factors in demographic and family dynamics, however, remains a formidable scientific challenge (Burch 1987). There are problems of conceptualization and measurement (e.g., finding indicators independent of the behaviour to be explained), problems of interpretation (e.g., what does it mean to say that "region" affects fertility; what does "region" stand for apart from geographical location?), and problem of causal ordering (e.g., does ideology have a life and force of its own, or is it largely derivative of social and economic structure?).

The difficulties of demonstrating and explaining cultural effects on behaviour are nowhere better illustrated than in the research tradition on ethnic differences in fertility in North America (for a comprehensive summary of this research see Trovato and Burch 1980; Halli 1987). Three lines of explanation have been developed to deal with these differences: 1) the minority-group hypothesis, which attributes low fertility to a disadvantaged minority's wish for upward social mobility; 2) the particularized ideology hypothesis, which attributes characteristic ethnic group fertility levels to a distinctive subculture — norms and values; 3) the characteristics hypothesis, which attributes distinctive behaviour to the group's socioeconomic characteristics such as education, income, occupation or residence. The statistical implication of the last hypothesis is that ethnic differences may disappear once other characteristics are properly controlled for. The theoretical implication is that often there is no "pure" ethnic or cultural effect at all.

A problem with this last approach is that it seems to empty the concept of ethnic group of its usual meaning. What does it mean, for example, to speak of the the effect of French origin in Quebec, with a control for religion? To be Quebecois traditionally was to be Catholic; one might argue that the two are inseparable. Similarly, in the context of U.S. fertility studies, is it sensible to discuss Irishness, with religion and urban residence held constant, when being Catholic and urban were part and parcel of history for the bulk of American Irish? Some resolution is needed of this apparent conflict between attention to concrete social phenomena and the demands of abstract analytic science. A resolution suggested and exemplified below is to avoid one-equation models in this context.

The minority-group hypothesis may be seen as a special case of the social mobility/fertility hypothesis, which in turn is a special case of a microeconomic model of fertility behaviour. In that sense, its theoretical underpinnings are well-developed and reasonably secure, and it is not difficult to give a reasonable account of the mechanisms at work.

The case of the particularized ideology hypothesis is more difficult. Its explanation often involves one or both of the problems identified by Becker (1976) in his discussion of explanations invoking "tastes" or "preferences." The first problem is that ethnic differences in behaviour are cited to demonstrate the existence of a distinctive ethnic ideology, and then the ideology is used to explain the behavioural differences — in essence, circular reasoning. In specific instances, this trap has been avoided. For example, in the study of Catholic fertility, it has not been too difficult to document a distinctive ideology relating to fertility, completely independently of the survey or census data on religious fertility differentials. But in many other instances, the main basis for asserting a distinctive subculture is the differential behaviour itself.

The second problem is that the cultural or ideological explanation remains *ad hoc*, with no prior theoretical reasoning as to why a subpopulation has a distinctive subculture that would lead to observed behavioural differences. Both the origins of the ideology and the mechanisms by which it affects behaviour are left obscure; one explanation is that demography has yet to tap systematically the long tradition of research and theorizing on culture by anthropologists.

An illustration of the potential value of anthropological work can be found in a recent book by Todd (1985), *The Explanation of Ideology: Family Structures and Social Systems*, a work with great relevance to the study of ethnic differentials in family structure in Canada. Todd's work does three things:

1) It develops a typology of family types that is somewhat more detailed than that commonly used in demography or in comparative family studies by sociologists. Essentially he expands on the LePlay typology of *stem, extended* and nuclear to arrive at a sevenfold classification of traditional family systems (that is, at least up to the beginning of this century). The classification is based on: a) equality/inequality of inheritance; b) liberty/authority in regard to residence and father-son relationships; c) patterns of exogamy/endogamy.

2) Todd advances the extravagant but carefully reasoned claim that a society's family system *determines* its political and religious ideology.

3) Finally, he offers an essentially psychoanalytic mechanism to explain the above determinism, vis-à-vis the subliminal learning by the child of fundamental values and attitudes relating to authority, equality and strangers or outsiders.

The relevance of Todd's work to ethnic differences in family structure is twofold. First, Todd's mapping of family types emphasizes the diversity of family types of origin of the largely immigrant-derived population of Canada. The diversity is apparent even if one looks at persons of European origin, and of course becomes even greater when one considers persons of Asian, African or Latin American ancestry. According to Todd, for example, the family systems of the British and Dutch (absolute nuclear) are far different from those of Germans or Irish (authoritarian, LePlay's stem) or from those of the populations of southern France and northern Italy (exogamous community, a form of extended family). Even within European nations, Todd asserts, one finds great variation in traditional family types — four different types in France and two in Italy, for example.

Based on this mapping and on his psychoanalytic theory of the transmission of family structures and values, one would expect distinctive differences in family structure among Canadian national origin groups. Substantial theoretical work is needed to derive specific predictions from Todd's theory, but some fairly

201

straightforward implications come to mind. One might expect persons from an authoritarian family background, with its emphasis on inequality among siblings and stern authority relationships between father and son, to exhibit less frequent interaction with siblings and parents (see below for some relevant data).

Todd's propositions are not proven and are best viewed as hypotheses, a good example of so-called "strong theory," which can provide new insights and research leads. Nor are his ideas without problems when applied to Canada. A recent paper by Kerr (1988), for example, shows that Todd is correct in his classification of the traditional Quebec family as authoritarian, but that the majority of Quebecers derive from regions of France Todd characterizes as having egalitarian nuclear family systems. Either the original settlers of Quebec were highly atypical of their regions of origin (selective migration) or the process of migration and resettlement somehow broke the subliminal transmission of basic family values.

In light of our earlier discussion of hypotheses to explain ethnic fertility differences, it is worth noting that Todd's thesis might be viewed as turning the particularized ideology hypothesis on its head: it is not ideology or subculture that determines family structure but family structure that determines ideology (this point needs further clarification since Todd's definition of *family structure* includes cultural elements; for example, norms relating to endogamy, inheritance, residence and so forth).

Canadian Data Sources

The empirical study of the ethnic factor in Canadian family and household structure faces all the theoretical and conceptual challenges reviewed above, plus the problem of the lack of available data. To begin with, Canada's political geography — with only ten provinces and two territories — hampers effective ecological regression analysis, a technique that proved so fruitful in the European Fertility Study and is readily applicable to the United States, with its 50 states. The resort to analysis at the sub-provincial level in Canada increases the number of cases, but sharply limits the variables for which data are readily available.

Turning to micro-data, one must choose — at the national level — between the census and national sample surveys. The census can provide more or less adequate-sized samples of many ethnic groups of interest. Special tabulations are more helpful in this respect, since even the largest Public Use Sample Tapes tend to generate frustratingly small N's for many ethnic groups. Problems of coding sometimes arise, for example, the merger of English, Irish and Scottish into "British" in the 1981 tape. Finally, variables that have been shown to be important correlates of family and household structure commonly are not collected in the census (e.g., physical disabilities, at least until 1986; numbers of kin; attitudinal variables).

National sample surveys such as the Quality of Life survey or the General Social Survey typically contain a much richer selection of variables, including attitudinal variables, but provide small samples of all but the largest ethnic groups. The 1985 Family History Survey provided unique family event-history data, but did not ask ethnic background.

Clearly no existing data source is adequate to the job. A national survey with overall N and sampling design aimed at producing adequate numbers of all important ethnic groups would be desirable. In the meantime, the researcher must try to tease out reliable substantive results from existing sources, used singly and in combination, and must combine statistical analysis with social historical and anthropological research of specific ethnic groups.

Data and Measurement

The present paper explores ethnic differences in Canadian household and family structure using the 1985 General Social Survey (GSS). The exploration is guided by the theoretical and methodological issues discussed earlier, but is meant more to illustrate these issues than to test specific hypotheses.

The 1985 GSS involved a national sample of 11,200 respondents age 15 and over. It contains items on religion and language (first language, language spoken in home), and identifies the following specific national origin groups: English, Irish, Scottish, French, German, Italian and Ukrainian. The home language item also allows identification of persons who speak Chinese, but only 20 respondents in the total sample so identified themselves (see Statistics Canada 1985).

To the student of household and family structure, the most attractive feature of this survey is the inclusion of questions on living relatives, whether or not resident in the same household as respondent — unique data for Canada and still fairly rare anywhere. Respondents were asked whether their mother and father were still living, and the number of living siblings, children and grandchildren, along with the frequency of face-to-face and other contacts. They also were asked about the number of other relatives they had contacted in the last three months, and the number of persons considered close friends. The household roster was used to indicate whether the respondent lived with (i.e., in the same household) one or more relatives or close friends.

Data also are included on the usual socio-economic variables such as education and income, and on a variety of physical limitations that might affect living arrangements.

The question on ethnicity — ''To what ethnic or cultural group do you or did your ancestors belong?'' — specifically allowed for multiple responses, but the coding permits identification of those who indicated a unique background. Respondents could indicate ethnic backgrounds other than those mentioned on the schedule, but these are coded as ''other'' in the Public Use Tape.

The results presented below focus on respondents who reported a unique ethnic background. Given limitations of time and space, no attempt has been made to look also at persons reporting multiple origins or to integrate the ethnic background data with that pertaining to religion or language.

Descriptive Results

Tables 1 and 2 give descriptive results from the survey, showing a variety of measures of household and family status for two broad age groups: 15 through 39; and 40 and over. This particular age categorization is not ideal, but the use of finer age groups yields impossibly small cell sizes. Even with age dichotomized, many of the cells are below what is generally needed for statistical reliability, so that the results must be taken as provisional. Males and females are treated separately when sex differentials seemed likely. For example, data on

TABLE 1

Household and Family Status by Ethnic Group
Respondents 40 and over

	Ethnic Group				
	French	English	Irish	Scottish	German
N	1,153	834	252	314	266
# of children	3.1	2.6	3.0	2.9	2.7
# of grandchildren	3.1	2.8	3.0	3.3	2.7
Grandchildren per child	0.7	0.9	0.7	1.1	0.8
# of siblings	5.0	2.9	3.6	2.7	3.9
# of other relatives	8.5	7.7	10.6	7.1	11.0
# of close friends	3.4	5.6	5.7	5.2	6.3
Mother living [%]	37.3	36.5	28.4	26.5	34.1
Father living [%]	16.5	16.1	11.3	17.9	19.8
See at least once/wk [%]					
Mother	48.6	42.1	39.3	33.8	36.0
Father	44.0	35.8	40.7*	31.6*	25.0*
Siblings	30.4	24.5	30.3	19.4	23.2
Total adult kin	17.3	13.7	17.6	13.1	18.1
Living alone [%]					
Male	9.7	8.9	12.6*	12.8	8.7*
Female	16.3	20.8	11.5*	22.3	17.9
Currently married [%]					
Male	80.5	84.1	82.8	82.3	88.9
Female	66.2	65.4	72.7	64.0	70.7

*Refers to cell with weighted frequency of less than 20.

TABLE 1 (cont'd)

Household and Family Status by Ethnic Group
Respondents 40 and over

	Ethnic Group				
N	Italian 158	Ukrainian 132	Other 817	Don't know 111	Total 4,037
# of children	2.6	2.6	2.7	3.4	2.8
# of grandchildren	1.8	2.6	2.5	2.9	2.8
Grandchildren per child	0.6	0.8	0.7	0.7	0.7
# of siblings	3.6	3.4	3.3	4.6	3.8
# of other relatives	10.3	7.8	7.2	7.8	8.3
# of close friends	5.4	7.4	5.2	5.1	5.0
Mother living [%]	54.2	37.1	42.8	27.5	37.0
Father living [%]	21.4	11.7	22.5	19.0	17.8
See at least once/wk [%]					
Mother	36.3*	44.4*	38.6		40.8
Father	46.7*	40.0*	39.1		38.2
Siblings	29.0*	22.4	21.3		24.2
Total adult kin	17.2	14.3	13.8	16.3	15.4
Living alone [%]					
Male	2.4*	9.6*	8.6	11.4*	9.4
Female	6.7*	24.4	15.4	19.5*	17.3
Currently married[%]					
Male	94.5	90.0	85.6	83.4	84.2
Female	88.8	63.3	70.7	67.4	68.1

*Refers to cell with weighted frequency of less than 20.

parental survival is given for the two sexes combined, since it is largely independent of sex. But data on living alone must be presented separately, since the two sexes generally differ in this regard.

No attempt will be made here to discuss all these data except to note that they suggest substantial variation among Canadian ethnic groups in family structure and behaviour, some of it systematic (e.g., Scots appear less apt to be married, more apt to live alone, and less apt to see kin frequently).

As is apparent, subsample sizes sometimes are small so that the issue of statistical significance arises. A convenient procedure for testing significance in this context is to estimate logit parameters within a loglinear procedure for a saturated model involving a particular family variable and a multiple category variable for ethnicity. This allows ethnicity to be treated as one variable rather than as a series of eight or more dummy variables, and yields coefficients for each category of ethnic group, along with t-scores for judging significance.

TABLE 2

Household and Family Status by Ethnic Group
Respondents 15 to 40

	Ethnic Group				
	French	English	Irish	Scottish	German
N	1,399	867	257	270	237
# of children	0.8	1.0	0.9	0.8	0.9
# of grandchildren	–	–	–	–	–
Grandchildren per child	–	–	–	–	–
# of siblings	4.1	3.2	3.7	3.1	3.4
# of other relatives	11.2	12.5	14.6	12.8	15.9
# of close friends	3.9	5.7	5.4	5.7	6.2
Mother living [%]	91.8	91.9	88.9	95.6	93.3
Father living [%]	79.8	83.2	78.3	76.4	89.1
See at least once/wk [%]					
Mother	55.5	47.1	45.0	49.0	45.1
Father	56.4	41.9	50.3	47.5	47.2
Siblings	46.8	41.2	46.2	37.9	43.8
Total adult kin	17.0	17.5	20.0	17.6	21.1
Living alone [%]					
Male	7.9	7.7	8.3*	7.8*	9.7*
Female	4.5	6.5	11.0*	6.6*	9.3*
Currently married [%]					
Male	49.6	55.8	41.1	48.2	44.4
Female	61.8	58.5	51.3	58.2	56.1

*Refers to cell with weighted frequency of less than 20.

Table 3 shows results relating to living alone by ethnicity for men and women in the two broad age groups in Tables 1 and 2, using the SPSS-X procedure LOGLINEAR.

For males 40 and over, there appear to be significant ethnic effects for Scots and Italians (at the .05 level using a conservative two-tailed test on the grounds that any "predictions" from Tables 1 and 2 are not really *a priori*, but are based on the same data used for the logit analysis), while that for the Irish approaches significance with a t-score of 1.7.

For females over 40, there are significant positive effects for English, Scottish and Ukrainian, and a significant negative effect for Italian, plus a nearly significant negative effect for Irish. For females 15-39, the logit analysis shows a nearly significant [t = 1.9] effect for Italian women, and reveals a significant negative effect for women of French background (in Table 2, the proportion of French women living alone is only slightly smaller than average; significance

TABLE 2 (cont'd)

Household and Family Status by Ethnic Group

Respondents 15 to 40

	Ethnic Group				
N	Italian 182	Ukrainian 99	Other 1,091	Don't know 266	Total 4,668
# of children	0.7	0.9	0.9	0.6	0.8
# of grandchildren	–	–	–	–	–
Grandchildren per child	–	–	–	–	–
# of siblings	2.6	3.2	3.6	3.8	3.6
# of other relatives	17.1	11.7	11.6	9.0	12.2
# of close friends	4.4	6.3	5.2	4.6	4.9
Mother living [%]	93.3	93.3	92.5	92.2	92.2
Father living [%]	87.3	81.0	80.0	82.8	81.2
See at least once/wk [%]					
Mother	64.9	53.0	42.6		46.8
Father	60.7	47.7	40.2		45.1
Siblings	65.1	40.7	40.1		42.2
Total adult kin	21.5	16.6	16.9	14.6	17.5
Living alone [%]					
Male	4.5*	10.7*	8.5	6.2*	7.9
Female	1.3*	12.5*	6.9	2.3*	6.0
Currently married [%]					
Male	45.0	50.0	34.3	50.3	48.8
Female	56.3	59.5	57.4	54.1	58.0

*Refers to cell with weighted frequency of less than 20.

is obtained primarily because of the large N for this subgroup). Positive effects for Irish [t = 1.6] and Ukrainian [t = 1.8] approach significance.

None of the effects for males 15-39 is significant, with the largest t-value (for Italians) at 1.0.

Apart from the effect of specific backgrounds, the logit analysis reveals a small overall association between ethnicity and living alone; that is, generally speaking, ethnicity is only a weak predictor of living alone in the bivariate case, with proportionate reduction of error measures close to zero. In addition, as the example of French women 15-39 shows, significance and substantive importance are not the same.

TABLE 3

Ethnic Background and Living Alone: A Logit Analysis

Ethnic Background	Logit Coefficient	t-Value
Females 40 + :		
French	− 0.016	− 0.271
English	0.136	2.256
Irish	− 0.203	− 1.786
Scottish	0.187	2.227
German	0.050	0.521
Italian	− 0.474	− 2.606
Ukrainian	0.251	2.099
Males 40 + :		
French	0.047	0.573
English	− 0.012	− 0.136
Irish	0.206	1.692
Scottish	0.213	1.916
German	− 0.023	− 0.167
Italian	− 0.592	− 2.233
Ukrainian	0.070	0.407
Females 15-39:		
French	− 0.216	− 1.989
English	− 0.027	− 0.243
Irish	0.269	1.644
Scottish	0.033	0.187
German	0.196	1.269
Italian	− 0.660	− 1.867
Ukrainian	0.387	1.804
Males 15-39		
French	− 0.034	− 0.365
English	− 0.030	− 0.227
Irish	0.031	0.205
Scottish	0.007	0.042
German	0.121	0.744
Italian	− 0.249	− 1.034
Ukrainian	0.120	0.536

Testing the Characteristics Hypothesis: An Illustration

All of the ethnic effects presented above are essentially zero-order effects since no other variables have been introduced into the tables or analysis. Clearly, one might not want to speak of an ethnic effect in the proper sense of that term unless some controls are introduced. Indeed the thrust of the characteristics hypothesis described earlier is that many of these apparent effects are not due to ethnicity at all but to other factors. In the case of living alone, for example, in a loglinear analysis not reported here, after the introduction of controls for age, sex, marital status, income, education, physical disabilities, and number of close kin, only the French (negative) and Ukrainian (positive) effects remain significant.

A more complete illustration will be given for the variable relating to the frequency with which the respondent sees his/her father. This variable is of particular interest because national data on kin interaction are novel and unique to the General Social Survey, and because the item is relevant to the Todd hypothesis. As noted above, one might expect persons of French/Quebecois, Irish, Scottish and German background — groups which Todd assigns to the authoritarian family category — to have less interaction between a father and his children, and similarly for persons of English descent (absolute nuclear family, which minimizes relationships between the generations). By contrast, one would expect more contact for persons of Italian (exogamous community or egalitarian nuclear family). More refined hypotheses are both possible and necessary but will require much more theoretical work.

Table 4 presents some relevant data. The fivefold categorization of the variable on frequency with which the respondent sees her/his father has been treated as an arbitrary scale and used as the independent variable in a multiple regression analysis (Note: Broadly similar results were obtained using a dichotomous dependent variable in a logit analysis; regression is preferred for present purposes because it more easily yields measures of the relative importance of variables vis-à-vis betas).

Table 4 presents results from four models. The first regresses frequency of seeing father on ethnicity only. The second adds controls for age, sex and marital status (dummy variables for single and for previously married). The third adds further controls for respondents' income from all sources and educational achievement (less than secondary school graduate/secondary school graduate or more). The final equation adds a variable pertaining to the migrant status of the respondent: he/she is classified as a migrant if born outside Canada, or if born in Canada, if living outside province of birth. Otherwise, he/she is classified as a non-migrant. The analysis pertains to persons 25 years and older to avoid complications associated with younger persons — the fact they are less apt to have finished schooling or to have left the parental home.

As is apparent in column one of Table 4, there are only two ethnic effects, both positive — for persons of French or Italian background. These two effects persist when controls are added for age, sex and marital status (column two) and for income and education (column three). The French effect is much the stronger of the two, with a metric coefficient nearly twice as large and a beta five times as large as for the Italians.

The introduction of migrant status to the model (column four) does not obliterate either of the previously identified ethnic effects. In fact, the Italian effect becomes much more significant and somewhat stronger as measured by beta.

TABLE 4

Regression of How Often Respondent Sees Father
On Ethnicity, With Various Control Variables

Variables**	Model			
	#1	#2	#3	#4
		Standardized Coefficients		
Ethnic background				
French	.18*	.17*	.17*	.08*
English	.03	.02	.02	.00
Irish	.00	.00	.00	− .03
Scottish	.00	.00	.00	.00
German	.02*	.02	.02	.02
Italian	.04*	.04*	.04*	.05*
Ukrainian	.00	.00	.00	− .01
Age group	−	.02	.02	.03
Sex	−	.02	.02	.01
Marital status				
Never married	−	− .20*	− .20*	− .21*
Widowed/divorced	−	− .07*	− .07*	−0.07
Income	−	−	.01	.01
Educational level	−	−	−0.01	− .02
Migration status	−	−	−	− .28*
Adjusted R ^{2}	.03	.07	.07	.14

* Significant at 0.05 level.
** Frequency respondent sees father: arbitrary scale, 5 = daily, 4 = at least once a week, 3 = at least once a month, 4 = less than once a month, 5 = never. Ethnicity: dummy variables, 1 = member of group (single responses only), 0 = not a member, Age: 0 = 25-59, 1 = 60 and over. Sex: 1 = male, 0 = female. Never married = 1, other marital statuses = 0. Widowed or divorced = 1, other = 0. Income: 0 = up to $ 15 000 per year, 1 = $ 15 000 or over. Education: 0 = less than secondary graduate, 1 = secondary graduate or more. Migration status: 0 = neither immigrant nor lifetime interprovincial migrant, 1 = immigrant or lifetime interprovincial migrant.

An obvious interpretation is that, given the large proportion of Italians who are immigrants to Canada and/or who have migrated (interprovincially) within Canada if born here, they have a relatively high frequency of contact with their fathers.

The French effect remains in the final model but is greatly attenuated (Note: In a logit analysis using a dichotomized version of the frequency of contact variable, the French effect disappears, but the result depends in part on the cutting point chosen). Both the metric coefficient and the beta are cut in half with the introduction of migrant status as a control, and French ethnicity becomes only

210

the third most important predictor after migrant status and whether or not the respondent is single, i.e., never married. (Note: A positive French effect on frequency of seeing father is at odds with our prediction from the Todd theory. Either our inference from his theory is incorrect, or there is some problem with the characterization of the contemporary Quebec family as authoritarian, or the empirical analysis is faulty. The positive effect of Italian background is as predicted.)

According to an uncritical application of the characteristics hypothesis, one might argue that some of the original difference in frequency of contact with father attributed to French ethnic background should instead be attributed to migrant status. But a somewhat more concrete approach to the meaning of ethnic background suggests a different interpretation and a different statistical model. To be of French background in Canada means for the most part to be a descendant of the original settlers in New France, most of whom live in Quebec (The French populations in New Brunswick, Manitoba and other provinces are not being dismissed, but discussion of them would not change the basic argument). There has been relatively little migration to Canada from France in modern times. At the same time, the structure of Canadian society is such as to discourage interprovincial migration of persons of French background to provinces other than Quebec (or New Brunswick). In other words, French background plays a causal role in regard to migrant status, a fact not reflected in Table 4.

A more adequate statistical model would acknowledge this indirect effect of French background on frequency of contact with father *through* migration status. Figure 1 suggests a relevant path model. For simplicity of exposition, only three variables are included. It is apparent that the positive indirect effect of French ethnicity on contact with father is almost as large $[-.286 \times -.268 = +.077]$ as the direct effect of French on contact $[+.091]$. The total effect of French background is approximately twice as great as one would have concluded from Table 4.

Discussion

The above example provides strong support for the view that an adequate statistical assessment of the role of ethnic subcultures in shaping family structure (or other behaviours) cannot rely on single-equation models. Some of the effects of a particular ethnic background may be indirect — through the very variables that are "netted out" in such a model — thereby obscuring the full influence of ethnicity. This implies the need for further theoretical work to provide an adequate basis on which to construct more complex, multi-equation models. It is possible and even likely that suitable models for the various ethnic groups may take different forms, each one reflecting the specific historical experience and social and ecological circumstances of a particular group. Such a modelling approach would seem to answer a need for statistical rigour while at the same

FIGURE 1

Path Diagram of How Often Respondent Sees Father
in Relation to Ethnicity and Migration Status
[Standardized coefficients]

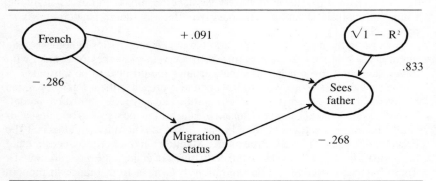

Note: All coefficients are significant at less than .001.

time respecting the concrete realities of specific ethnic groups. It is less apt to lead to either a dismissal of ethnicity as a causal factor or to its treatment as a source of statistically — but not theoretically — explained variance.

12. INTERMARRIAGE AMONG ETHNIC GROUPS[1]

Bali Ram

It has often been suggested that intermarriage is an important indicator of assimilation. Milton Gordon (1964, 80) considers intermarriage or marital assimilation as an "inevitable by-product of structural assimilation." In a multicultural society such as Canada, intermarriage occupies a place of special importance. With 16 percent of its population of foreign-born origin as of the 1981 Census, Canada provides a unique laboratory for studying trends and patterns of intermarriage among various immigrant groups. This study explores the propensity for intermarriage among immigrants originating from 40 countries, using as its base statistics from census tabulations that show the number of husbands and wives who had the same or different countries of birth.

An attempt is also made to examine how variations in the structural background of immigrant groups relate to their tendency to intermarry. Much of the inspiration for this study derives from Blau's research on the impact of social-structural variables on social relations. Taking a slightly modified approach, this study examines the importance of population size, period of residence in Canada, the sex ratio, sex segregation in the labour force and occupational heterogeneity in influencing intermarriage.

Census Data and the Current Scene

Intermarriage statistics for this study are based on the 1981 Census tabulations of the number of husbands and wives according to their country of birth. The percentage of foreign-born husbands or wives living with Canadian-born spouses or spouses born in another foreign country is taken as the index of intermarriage, whereas the percentage of husbands or wives of the same origin is taken as the index of inmarriage. Thus, in total, six measures concerning inmarriage or intermarriage are derived:

WSAME   = % of foreign-born husbands married to wives of the same origin.

WCANADA   = % of foreign-born husbands married to wives of Canadian origin.

WOTHER   = % of foreign-born husbands married to foreign-born wives (of origins other than their own or Canadian).

HSAME   = % of foreign-born wives married to husbands of the same origin.

HCANADA   = % of foreign-born wives married to husbands of Canadian origin.

HOTHER   = % of foreign-born wives married to foreign-born husbands (of origins other than their own or Canadian).

The above variables are crude proxies of intermarriage. They suffer from numerous conceptual and operational limitations. First of all, they are based on husband-wife families, and exclude persons whose marriages have been dissolved. Secondly, they cannot distinguish between intermarriages that occurred before spouses' arrival in Canada and marriages that have taken place in Canada. Thirdly, the differential in the age distribution and the duration of residence in Canada makes problematic the comparison of the rate of intermarriage for one group with that of another. Some immigrant groups have arrived in Canada earlier than others and therefore have been more exposed to the risk of intermarriage. (The effect of this latter factor is controlled, however, by introducing a proxy for the length of residence (PERIOD) in the analysis of determinants of intermarriage.)

Perhaps a more serious problem is the use of country of birth as the unit of analysis. The conceptual boundary of this variable overlaps with numerous other concepts such as ethnicity, religion, language, race or visibility. Therefore the marriage between members of two different countries of birth may not strictly be intermarriage when the couple is from the same ethnic, religious or linguistic origins. For example, marriage between men from Taiwan and women from Hong Kong or between Moslem men born in India and Moslem women born in Pakistan confuses the true picture of the prevalence of intermarriage among numerous immigrant groups. Similarly, marriage between a Japanese born in Japan and a Japanese born in Canada may be more properly classified as an inmarriage than an intermarriage. The effect of this limitation is particularly pronounced when small numbers are involved. Thus, variables WOTHER and HOTHER, which are based on small numbers of cases, should be used with caution when drawing inferences. WSAME and HSAME may be used with confidence as they involve larger numbers, while WCANADA and HCANADA are also relatively reliable.

In Table 1, 40 nationalities are arranged according to their propensity for inmarriage evidenced by the 1981 Census data. The propensity is higher among

TABLE 1

Rank Positions of 40 National Origins (Countries of Birth) According to the Incidence of Inmarriage, Canada, 1981

Rank	Wife's Country of birth	% married to husband of the same origin	Rank	Wife's country of birth	% married to husband of the same origin	Rank	Husband's country of birth	% married to wives of the same origin	Rank	Husband's country of birth	% married to wives of the same origin
1	Australia	16.8	21	Netherlands	66.9	1	Australia	19.4	21	Netherlands	58.4
2	U.S.	21.0	22	Egypt	69.0	2	Norway	21.0	22	Hong Kong	59.9
3	Sweden	30.7	23	Trinidad & Tobago	69.4	3	Sweden	21.1	23	Finland	60.9
4	Ireland, Rep. of	35.3	24	U.S.S.R.	69.8	4	U.S.	24.4	24	Japan	62.1
5	Norway	35.7	25	Hungary	69.9	5	Austria	30.8	25	Pakistan	63.5
6	Austria	37.6	26	Malta	70.3	6	France	33.1	26	Lebanon	65.7
7	Belgium	37.8	27	Jamaica	76.8	7	Switzerland	33.2	27	Trinidad & Tobago	66.4
8	France	38.7	28	Lebanon	76.9	8	Belgium	34.4	28	Yugoslavia	67.8
9	Germany	43.5	29	Guyana	78.6	9	Denmark	35.8	29	China	70.5
10	Switzerland	43.5	30	China	78.7	10	Ireland, Rep. of	36.1	30	Taiwan	73.6
11	Japan	48.8	31	Taiwan	79.2	11	Romania	41.8	31	Guyana	76.7
12	U.K.	49.3	32	Philippines	79.7	12	Germany	42.6	32	India	77.4
13	Romania	50.6	33	Yugoslavia	81.3	13	U.K.	47.6	33	Italy	77.6
14	Denmark	51.3	34	India	86.3	14	Czechoslovakia	49.0	34	Jamaica	77.7
15	Hong Kong	52.1	35	Vietnam	89.7	15	Poland	51.0	35	Greece	82.6
16	Finland	59.7	36	Haiti	90.2	16	Hungary	52.5	36	Haiti	84.6
17	Czechoslovakia	62.0	37	Italy	92.0	17	U.S.S.R.	54.6	37	Portugal	91.1
18	Poland	62.4	38	Greece	92.1	18	Spain	55.6	38	Vietnam	92.0
19	Spain	63.1	39	Korea, S.	92.8	19	Malta	57.1	39	Philippines	95.4
20	Pakistan	63.5	40	Portugal	93.9	20	Egypt	57.6	40	Korea, S.	96.6
				Total	63.5					Total	57.7

the foreign-born women (62.5 percent) than among the foreign-born men (57.7 percent), implying that a foreign-born woman is more likely to have a husband of the same origin than a foreign-born man is to have a wife of the same origin. In 24 cases, 60 percent or more of the wives were married to husbands of the same origin, while only 18 observations could be found in which a similar proportion of husbands were married to wives of the same origin. Similar findings have been observed in the studies based on U.S. data (Besanceney 1970, 38-39).

The above observation is further reinforced by the data presented in Table 2, which show that the incidence of the foreign-born husbands having Canadian-born wives is higher (30.1 percent) than that of foreign-born wives having Canadian-born husbands (24.3 percent). This table shows that compared to 9 origins in which 40 percent or more of the foreign-born husbands had Canadian-born wives, there were only 4 origins in which foreign-born wives had Canadian-born husbands. Also, in the case of 22 observations the propensity for intermarriage involving foreign-born husbands and Canadian-born wives was 20 percent or more, whereas the comparable propensity for intermarriages between foreign-born wives and Canadian-born husbands was observed for only 15 observations.

Because in any given period more single males than females tend to immigrate from a particular country, single male immigrants are at greater risk of intermarriage than females. This risk further increases when women of equal or of better social backgrounds origin are available in the host country.

In some cases immigrants are a selected group and therefore may represent a higher overall socioeconomic level than many of the host country's eligible males. For some Canadian women, marrying an immigrant may be an avenue for upward mobility, whereas marrying a Canadian-born man may not provide the same advancement to foreign-born women. Also, a foreign-born man can more afford to marry a Canadian-born spouse without diminishing his social status than can a foreign-born woman, since it is usually the male's socioeconomic status which is a major factor in determining the status of the immediate family. This observation is consistent with the hypothesis that "men tend to marry down and women tend to marry up" (Burchinal 1964; 54).

Tables 1 and 2 also show that intermarriage is usually most prevalent among those born in the U.S., Australia and Western and Northern European countries and least prevalent among those born in Southern European, the Caribbean and Asian countries. This finding is consistent with previous research on intermarriage (Kalbach 1983; Carter and Glick 1976, 132-135). However, it does not hold true when the data on intermarriage between spouses born in two different foreign countries, presented in Table 3, are examined. To take an example, the incidence of intermarriage is higher for those born in Hong Kong and Pakistan than for those born in the U.K. or U.S. But as we mentioned earlier, this measure of intermarriage suffers from various limitations and should not be used as a reliable guide to draw inferences. In the following section, therefore, the emphasis is on the results based on data on intermarriage between a foreign-born person

TABLE 2

Rank Positions of 40 National Origins (Countries of Birth) According to the Incidence of Intermarriage between Foreign-born and Canadian-born Persons. Canada. 1981

Rank	Wife's Country of birth	% married to husbands of Canadian origin	Rank	Wife's country of birth	% married to husband of Canadian origin	Rank	Husband's country of birth	% married to wives of Canadian origin	Rank	Husband's country of birth	% married to wives of Canadian origin
1	U.S.	65.3	21	U.S.S.R.	13.0	1	U.S.	65.4	21	Romania	24.9
2	Australia	52.3	22	Trinidad & Tobago	10.2	2	Norway	58.0	22	Spain	21.0
3	U.K.	41.5	23	Egypt	9.8	3	Sweden	57.7	23	Egypt	19.3
4	Norway	40.0	24	Philippines	8.9	4	Australia	52.1	24	Lebanon	18.6
5	Belgium	39.7	25	Spain	8.1	5	Belgium	50.3	25	Italy	17.2
6	Sweden	35.5	26	Jamaica	7.8	6	France	49.5	26	Trinidad & Tobago	16.8
7	Japan	34.8	27	Guyana	6.7	7	Denmark	48.1	27	Yugoslavia	16.2
8	Denmark	33.4	28	Yugoslavia	6.5	8	U.K.	44.8	28	Haiti	12.0
9	France	33.2	29	Lebanon	6.2	9	Switzerland	40.4	29	Greece	10.9
10	Ireland, Rep. of	30.1	30	Haiti	6.1	10	Germany	37.5	30	Jamaica	10.2
11	Germany	28.8	31	Hong Kong	5.8	11	Ireland. Rep. of	36.1	31	Pakistan	10.1
12	Finland	24.3	32	Italy	5.1	12	Austria	35.7	32	Guyana	9.2
13	Netherlands	23.8	33	Pakistan	4.8	13	Netherlands	33.0	33	Hong Kong	7.1
14	Austria	23.4	34	China	4.2	14	Finland	30.4	34	India	6.5
15	Switzerland	20.6	35	India	4.1	15	Malta	28.6	35	Portugal	6.2
16	Malta	18.9	36	Taiwan	4.1	16	Japan	28.5	36	China	6.1
17	Poland	18.2	37	Portugal	3.2	17	Poland	28.2	37	Taiwan	5.0
18	Romania	14.7	38	Greece	3.1	18	Hungary	27.5	38	Vietnam	2.8
19	Czechoslovakia	13.7	39	Korea. S.	2.4	19	U.S.S.R.	26.8	39	Philippines	2.5
20	Hungary	13.2	40	Vietnam	1.4	20	Czechoslovakia	25.6	40	Korea. S.	0.7
		Total 24.3					Total 30.1				

TABLE 3

Rank Positions of 40 National Origins (Countries of Birth) According to the Incidence of Intermarriage between spouses born in Different Foreign Countries, Canada, 1981

Rank	Wife's Country of birth	% married to husbands born in a different country	Rank	Wife's country of birth	% married to husbands born in a different country	Rank	Husband's country of birth	% married to wives born in a different country	Rank	Husband's country of birth	% married to wives born in a different country
1	Hong Kong	42.1	21	China	17.1	1	Austria	33.5	21	Denmark	16.1
2	Austria	39.0	22	Hungary	16.9	2	Romania	33.3	22	India	16.1
3	Switzerland	35.9	23	Lebanon	16.9	3	Hong Kong	33.0	23	Yugoslavia	16.0
4	Romania	34.7	24	Taiwan	16.7	4	Australia	28.5	24	Lebanon	15.7
5	Ireland, Rep. of	34.6	25	Jamaica	15.4	5	Ireland, Rep. of	27.6	25	Belgium	15.3
6	Sweden	33.8	26	Denmark	15.3	6	Pakistan	26.4	26	Malta	14.3
7	Pakistan	31.7	27	Guyana	14.7	7	Switzerland	26.4	27	Guyana	14.1
8	Australia	30.9	28	U.S.	13.7	8	Czechoslovakia	25.4	28	Jamaica	12.1
9	Spain	28.8	29	Yugoslavia	12.2	9	China	23.4	29	U.S.	10.2
10	France	28.1	30	Philippines	11.4	10	Spain	23.4	30	Japan	9.4
11	Germany	27.7	31	Malta	10.8	11	Egypt	23.1	31	Finland	8.7
12	Czechoslovakia	24.3	32	India	9.6	12	Taiwan	21.4	32	Netherlands	8.6
13	Norway	24.3	33	Netherlands	9.3	13	Sweden	21.3	33	U.K.	7.6
14	Belgium	22.5	34	U.K.	9.2	14	Norway	21.0	34	Greece	6.5
15	Egypt	21.2	35	Vietnam	8.9	15	Poland	20.8	35	Italy	5.2
16	Trinidad & Tobago	20.4	36	Greece	4.8	16	Germany	20.0	36	Vietnam	5.2
17	Poland	19.4	37	Korea, S.	4.8	17	Hungary	20.0	37	Haiti	3.4
18	Finland	17.8	38	Haiti	3.9	18	U.S.S.R.	18.6	38	Korea, S.	2.7
19	U.S.S.R.	17.2	39	Italy	2.9	19	France	17.4	39	Portugal	2.7
20	China	17.1	40	Portugal	2.9	20	Trinidad & Tobago	16.8	40	Philippines	2.1
				Total	13.1					Total	12.1

and a Canadian-born spouse or on inmarriage between spouses of the same origin.

Structural Determinants of Intermarriage

From the above discussion, an important question arises: why are members of certain origins more likely to intermarry than members of other origins? Blau's macrosociological theory, which focuses on the effects of social structure on intergroup relations, may be used to answer this question. Blau and his colleagues (Blau et al. 1982, 1984) have developed a rather clearly articulated position on the impact of the relative size of different racial and ethnic groups and the degree of heterogeneity in the community on the rate of intermarriage. They compared the 125 largest metropolitan areas of the United States and found support for various theorems derived from Blau's theory of social structure. Also, in the examination of intermarriage in Hawaii from 1950 to 1983, Labov and Jacobs' (1986) findings were largely consistent with Blau's hypotheses concerning structural determinants of intermarriage.

Blau and his associates have argued that group size and the rate of intermarriage are inversely related. "Members of the smaller group have on the average more outgroup friends than those of the larger group, and the proportion of outgroup marriages in the small group exceeds that in the large group" (Blau et al. 1982, 46). The smaller group provides fewer possibilities for finding a suitable match inside the group and therefore some of its members are forced to find a compatible spouse outside the group. Previous research has generally supported the group size-intermarriage hypothesis (Burma 1963; Schmitt 1965; Labov and Jacobs 1986; Alba and Golden 1986).

The relevance of group size in explaining intermarriage is usually confounded by the length of residence in the host country (Alba and Golden 1986). The longer the duration of residence in the host country, the greater the opportunity for intergroup relations and consequently the greater the probability of intermarriage.

Sheer numbers need not always be a strong predictor of intermarriage. Some social scientists have found an unbalanced sex ratio combined with a relatively small group size to be associated with higher rates of intermarriage between groups (Parkman and Sawyer 1967; Tinker 1982). It has been argued that a radically unbalanced sex ratio in a group forces some members to go outside the group to find suitable partners and consequently encourages intermarriage (Guttentag and Secord 1983, 23-225).

It is also reasonable to argue that even if there is a numerical balance between the sexes, members of a group are likely to outmarry because of an imbalance between the sexes of socioeconomic characteristics. This last hypothesis is reinforced by the fact that, by and large, women tend to marry at the same or a higher social level.

A central theorem of Blau's theory is that hetergeneity promotes intergroup relations. The greater the heterogeneity in a group, the greater the chances that some of its members will make social contacts involving members of different groups. Thus, it has been argued, "Much heterogeneity increases the likelihood that members of different groups have the opportunity to get to know each other, which is expected to increase the probability of intermarriage" (Blau et al. 1982, 47). Blau and his colleagues have used a number of measures of heterogeneity based on national origin, mother tongue, birth region, industry and occupation, and found empirical support for their direct impact on the rate of intermarriage.

The above hypotheses have been tested in this study using data from the 1981 Census of Canada. The units of analysis for the study were the 40 national origins (countries of birth) mentioned earlier, for which data on the independent and dependent variables were obtained. As noted earlier, six measures concerning inmarriage and intermarriage (WSAME, WCANADA, WOTHER, HSAME, HCANADA and HOTHER) were used as dependent variables. The independent variables were as follows:

POP = Population 15 years and over (the natural logarithmic form of this variable has been used in the model).

PERIOD = Percentage of population which immigrated to Canada before 1945.

SEX RATIO = $\dfrac{M}{F} \times 100$, where M was the number of males who immigrated to Canada at age 20 and over, and F was the number of females who immigrated to Canada at age 20 and over.

DISSIMILARITY = $\dfrac{\Sigma\,|M_i - F_i|}{2}$, where M_i was the percentage of males engaged in occupation i and F_i was the percentage of females engaged in occupation i. This index which was based on 10 occupational categories varied from 0 to 100, indicating the range of minimum and maximum sex imbalance in occupations. The occupational categories used were: (1) managerial, (2) professional and technical, (3) clerical, (4) sales, (5) service, (6) processing, machining and fabricating, (7) construction, (8) transport, (9) farming and other primary occupations, and (10) other occupations. The computational procedure was based on the "index of dissimilarity."

HETEROGENEITY = $1 - [\Sigma\, x^2/(\Sigma\, x)^2]$, where x was the number of persons in each of the 10 occupational categories stated above. This index measured the *occupational heterogeneity* of a group. The computational procedure was based on Gibbs and Martin's (1962) index of "division of labour."

At the zero-order level, the relationships between POP, SEX RATIO and the six dependent variables were small and inconsistent (Table 4). However, PERIOD, DISSIMILARITY and HETEROGENEITY had moderately high associations (r's being between .50 and .70 with WCANADA, WSAME, HCANADA and HSAME) but somewhat weaker associations, though in expected directions, with WOTHER and HOTHER. Some of these associations may be spurious or weak when other variables in the model are controlled, and therefore the results of a multivariatie analysis need to be examined.

The results of the regression analysis are presented in Tables 5 and 6. In each table there are six equations, each of which utilizes only four independent variables. Because of a high correlation (r = .786) between them, DISSIMILARITY and HETEROGENEITY are not included simultaneously. The strongest determinant of immigrants having spouses born in Canada or of the same origin is PERIOD, suggesting that the longer a group resides in Canada, the greater are the chances of its members marrying outside the group. This observation is quite consistent with the hypothesis that longer duration of residence in a host country promotes interaction between immigrants and the native-born population and therefore increases their chances of getting married to a native-born partner.

The second significant determinant of intermarriage (immigrants marrying a Canadian-born partner) and inmarriage was DISSIMILARITY. If an imbalance exists between the sexes of a group in terms of socioeconomic background, their members are more likely to marry outside the group. The imbalance between sexes in terms of sheer numbers does not seem to matter, as suggested by an insignificant regression coefficient for SEX RATIO. Population size also does not appear to be an important variable in explaining inmarriage or intermarriage (marriage between persons born in Canada and those born outside Canada). However as expected, population size exerts a negative impact on intermarriage between the members of two foreign-born populations.

Coefficients for HETEROGENEITY suggest that occupational differentiation in a group promotes its members' outmarriage. A group's greater occupational heterogeneity implies a greater diversification of its members in terms of socio-economic background. Greater heterogeneity in a group encourages its members to establish contact with members of other groups and therefore provides more opportunity for them to marry outside the group. It also reduces their chances of marrying within their own group.

Discussion and Conclusion

This study analysed the prevalence of intermarriage and its structural determinants among 40 immigrant groups, using data from the 1981 Census of Canada. Several observations are consistent with the theory and previous research and therefore are useful in understanding intergroup relations. Intermarriage is most

TABLE 4

Means and Standard Deviations for the Independent Variables and Selected Zero-Order Correlations

	POP(LN)	PERIOD	SEX RATIO	DISSI-MILARITY	HETERO-GENEITY	MEAN	STANDARD DEVIATION
POP(LN)	1.000					10.65	1.08
PERIOD	-.009	1.000				11.87	14.32
SEX RATIO	-.308	.255	1.000			103.05	24.84
DISSIMILARITY	.053	.580	.238	1.000		35.28	9.11
HETEROGENEITY	-.008	.639	.214	.786	1.000	.84	.03
WCANADA	0.055	.667	.261	.617	.645	25.69	17.66
WOTHER	.339	.231	.224	.209	.329	16.83	8.88
WSAME	.184	-.639	.304	-.589	-.661	57.48	21.64
HCANADA	-.001	.573	-.015	.512	.531	18.17	15.53
HOTHER	-.427	.278	.156	.274	.397	19.20	10.58
HSAME	.213	-.562	-.069	-.516	-.593	62.55	21.11

TABLE 5

Regression Analysis of Measures of Husbands' Intermarriage. 1981

Independent Variable	WCANADA (1)	WOTHER (2)	WSAME (3)	WCANADA (4)	WOTHER (5)	WSAME (6)
POP (LN)	-.91 (-.45)	-2.70 (-2.02)	3.61 (1.45)	-.45 (-.22)	-2.63 (-2.03)	3.09 (1.29)
PERIOD	.56 (3.16)	.08 (.72)	-.64 (-2.94)	.51 (2.73)	.01 (.11)	-.53 (-2.34)
SEX RATIO	.03 (.36)	.02 (.34)	-0.5 (-.47)	.05 (.54)	.02 (.34)	-.07 (-.63)
DISSIMILARITY	.67 (2.40)	.13 (.70)	-.80 (-2.32)			
HETEROGENEITY				193.61 (2.41)	80.54 (1.55)	-274.17 (-2.85)
Constant	1.69	37.86	60.30	-143.17	-25.02	268.06
R^2 (adjusted)	.48	.09	.47	.48	.14	.50

TABLE 6

Regression Analysis of Measures of Wives' Intermarriage, 1981

Independent Variable	HCANADA (1)	HOTHER (2)	HSAME (3)	HCANADA (4)	HOTHER (5)	HSAME (6)
POP (LN)	-1.20 (-.61)	-4.54 (-3.07)	5.71 (2.20)	-.84 (-.43)	-4.39 (-3.10)	5.19 (2.06)
PERIOD	.49 (2.82)	.12 (.94)	-.61 (-2.69)	.47 (2.54)	.04 (.29)	-.51 (-2.15)
SEX RATIO	-.14 (-1.61)	-.03 (-.52)	.18 (1.51)	-.13 (-1.46)	-.03 (-.51)	.16 (1.41)
DISSIMILARITY	.53 (1.93)	.26 (1.25)	-.79 (-2.19)			
HETEROGENEITY				139.04 (1.75)	119.93 (2.10)	-261.40 (-2.59)
Constant	21.35	60.65	18.65	-81.89	-35.85	216.32
R^2 (adjusted)	.35	.21	.39	.34	.27	.42

prevalent among persons originating from the U.S., Australia and Western and Northern European countries, and least prevalent among those originating from Asian, the Caribbean, and South European countries. This observation, which has been documented before, raises the question as to why this distinction has persisted. In future research one may be tempted to re-examine the hypothesis which finds intermarriage a most important indicator and an "inevitable by-product" of assimilation. It may also be interesting to examine the role of the multicultural policy as it relates to higher prevalences of intermarriage among certain immigrant groups.

Drawing upon Blau's theory of social structure, this study involved a multiple regression analysis using five structural determinants of intermarriage — population size, sex ratio, period of residence in Canada, sex dissimilarity in occupational structure and heterogeneity. From this analysis, a number of conclusions followed. Population size was found to be a relatively weak predictor of intermarriage, although it did exert a positive impact on inmarriage and a negative impact on intermarriage as expected. Intermarriage in the 1981 Census was high among some larger immigrant groups (e.g., persons from the U.S. and U.K.) and some smaller groups (e.g., those from Australia and Sweden). Similarly, intermarriage was low among certain larger groups (e.g., from Italy and Portugal) and smaller groups (e.g., immigrants from South Korea and Pakistan).

Another conclusion resulting from this study was that the sex ratio appeared to be the weakest predictor of intermarriage. This may have happened due to the crude operationalization of the sex ratio variable. A sex ratio calculated by taking an appropriate difference between the ages of spouses may prove to be a stronger predictor of intermarriage. However, sheer numbers without taking into account other socieconomic factors are not of much significance when their impact on intergroup relations is examined. In terms of social background, sex imbalance (measured by occupational status) in this study proved to be an important predictor of intermarriage. One of the reasons that immigrants from Asia, the Caribbean, and Southern Europe exhibit a lower propensity for intermarriage is probably the greater similarity between the social backgrounds of men and women from these parts of the world.

The duration of residence in Canada was very strongly associated with intermarriage, suggesting that one of the reasons why the propensity to intermarry is lower among persons originating from Asia, the Caribbean and Southern Europe than from the U.S., Australia, and Western and Northern Europe, is the fact that immigrants from the former group of countries are more recent arrivals and therefore are less exposed to intergroup relations. Once they have lived longer in Canada, their rate of intermarriage is likely to increase.

Occupational heterogeneity proved to be another powerful predictor of intermarriage. The heterogeneous nature of certain groups pushes their members outside to seek marriage partners. Immigrant groups differ markedly in their dispersion among social backgrounds, for example, in their occupational status. To take just one example, persons of Scandinavian origins were the most heterogenous group in terms of their occupations, while those from Haiti, Vietnam and Greece were the most homogenous groups. Such disparity may have exposed people to differential opportunity for intergroup contact and therefore to a differential propensity to intermarry.

One finding that emerges very clearly is that foreign-born women are less likely to intermarry than foreign-born men. Data in this study do not lend support to the hypothesis that the sex ratio is an important factor in intermarriage, but the significant predictors discussed above (i.e., sex imbalance in social background, duration of residence in Canada and heterogeneity) provided stronger explanatory power for the likelihood of intermarriage among immigrant men, than among immigrant women. Why this is the case is not clear, although foreign-born women are probably less exposed than foreign-born men to persons from origins other than their own. Perhaps they are unable to find suitable partners from other origins, who can provide them with a better social status than they are able to attain by marrying a person of their own group. Perhaps again, foreign-born men marry persons of other origins, who would not otherwise find a suitable spouse. These are merely some of the questions that need further investigation.

Because of the weakness in operationalizing the concept of intermarriage, and the cross-sectional nature of the analysis, the findings of this study are tentative and suggest the need for future research. This research could be extended along various dimensions. Perhaps the most important task would be to develop more refined measures of intermarriage than currently exist in Canada. This could be done in several ways. Firstly, census-dependent measures should be based exclusively on marriages that occurred in Canada. Dates of marriage and immigration can be utilized to produce tabulations of husbands and wives by country of birth. Another improvement would be the application of a control for ethnic origin. The 1981 Census did allow for this type of analysis.

A second approach that would enhance measures of intermarriage would be to turn to the registration (vital statistics) data which contain information on the country of birth of couples. These data, which can be derived for every year, refer to marriages that took place in Canada.

Another dimension along which future research could proceed would be to examine the propensity of intermarriage within smaller geographic communities, such as municipalities. This approach would be particularly meaningful if intermarriage were to be studied in terms of intergroup relations. Obviously, the social interactions which lead to intermarriage between members of different cultural groups are often governed by the geographic proximity of couples' places of residence.

Notes

1. The views expressed in this paper are those of the author and not necessarily the views of Statistics Canada.
2. I would like to acknowledge with thanks the technical assistance provided by Susan Ingram, Gerry Ouellette and Suzanne Paulin. I am also grateful to M.J. Norris, Frank Trovato and an anonymous reviewer for commenting on an earlier draft of the paper, to Lawrence Wise for editorial assistance, and to Dorothy Goyette for typing the manuscript. The views expressed in this paper are those of the author and should not be interpreted as reflecting those of Statistics Canada.

13. VARIATIONS IN AGING AND ETHNICITY

Leo Driedger and Neena Chappell

While ethnic studies received an enormous boost 25 years ago, with the publication of the Bilingual and Bicultural Commission reports and John Porter's classic *Vertical Mosaic* (1965), studies on aging in Canada have emerged only during the past 10 years. Studies combining the two fields of aging and ethnicity are sparse. The volume *Aging and Ethnicity: Toward an Interface* (1987), was the first attempt in Canada to do so in monograph form. Consequently, this field of research is underdeveloped. This paper presents a demographic review of the very diverse and varied eth-elder phenomenon in Canada, using mostly census data.

This paper has been ordered into four general categories, beginning first with the Canadian demographic and ecological context, dealing with the demographic range of eth-elders showing the provincial, regional, cultural and linguistic variations. Next, factors of modernization are presented, of considerable concern to scholars of gerontology. These factors include variations in education, occupation and urbanization, by eth-elderly status. Third, there is a focus on such ethnic identification factors as language and religion, to assess the importance of linguistic and cultural factors for the ethnic elderly. And finally, three eth-elder patterns are summarized. A traditional-modern continuum of ethnic variety is discussed; a status-urbanization model is presented; and six eth-elder types illustrate the variety of elderly people in Canada.

Demographic and Ecological Variations

The enormous diversity of the Canadian ethnic population has been amply demonstrated in other papers in this volume. However, the extent to which the population over 65 years is typical of the general demographic patterns has not been explored. How do eth-elder demographic patterns vary by province and region,

Ethnic Demography

and what implications do these demographic and regional patterns have for gerontological policy and programs?

Population Comparisons

In 1981 elderly persons (65 plus) comprised 9.1 percent of the total Canadian population; projections indicate that by the year 2001 the proportion will be considerably larger, around 12 percent. By 2031 it will exceed 20 percent. Canada's population is aging, but it varies enormously by ethnic group. In Table 1 ethnic groups are compared for older (65 plus) and younger (under 65) age groups. There are important differences when controlling for ethnicity.

Almost half (49.3 percent) of Canada's elderly are British, while the British represented only 40 percent of the total population in 1981. The British elderly are over-represented, but the French charter elderly are under-represented (23.0

TABLE 1

Elderly and Non-elderly Populations by Ethnicity,
Canada, 1981

Ethnicity	Per 100 of age group		Per 100 of total	
	0-64	65+	0-64	65+
British	39.3	49.3	88.9	11.1
French	27.1	23.0	92.2	7.8
British/French*	1.9	0.8	96.0	4.0
Jewish	1.0	2.0	83.5	16.5
Polish	1.0	1.7	85.5	14.5
Ukrainian	2.1	3.3	86.3	13.7
German	4.7	5.4	89.7	10.3
Dutch	1.7	1.4	92.5	7.5
Chinese	1.2	0.9	93.3	6.7
Italian	3.2	2.3	93.3	6.7
All other	14.7	9.2	94.1	5.9
Native peoples	2.2	0.8	96.5	3.5
Total	100.0	100.0	90.9	9.1

* Multiple response

Note: This table includes British, French and British/French, plus the eight ethnic origins (single response) with the largest counts for the total population. These latter ethnic origins are arranged here by descending proportions of the aged population (last column).

Source: Statistics Canada. *The Elderly in Canada*. Ottawa: Minister of Supply and Services, 1984, Table 8, p. 16.

percent) compared with their total in the population (27 percent). The much larger families of French Canadians in the past is reflected in the smaller proportion of French elderly. However, since French Canadian families have declined recently, the French eth-elder population will rise in the future. The Quebec population will be aging increasingly. The Jewish eth-elders (2 percent of all elders in Canada) even more than the British are over-represented, which reflects the aging Jewish population in Canada. The Ukrainian (3.3 percent), Polish (1.7 percent), and German (5.4 percent) elders reflect the British pattern. On the other hand, native elderly (0.8 percent), even more than the French, under-represent persons over 65 years of age. Native Indian fertility is among the highest in Canada, and their life expectancy is among the lowest, so that relatively few reach the elderly stage. Italians (2.3 percent), and Chinese (0.9 percent) and all others (9.2 percent) follow the native Indian and French Canadian pattern. Recent immigrants are heavily represented here, and fertility tends to be high, so that the elderly proportion is under-represented.

A comparison of each ethnic group internally shows that the Jews (16.5 percent) have the largest proportion of elderly, and the native peoples (3.5 percent) the smallest. Five groups have a disproportionate number of elderly (exceeding the 9.1 Canadian average): Polish, Ukrainian, British, German and Jewish; and seven groups are under the average: French, Dutch, Chinese, Italian, All other, British/French and Native peoples.

Provincial Distributions

While the proportions of eth-elders in the different ethnic groups vary enormously, the distribution of eth-elders also varies considerably by province. In Table 2 it is clear that British eth-elders (55 years plus) dominate in Newfoundland (94.3 percent) and Nova Scotia (75.8 percent), while in Quebec French Canadians (76.6 percent) dominate. In these three provinces the two charter groups are clearly the major ethnic focus. They could be called uni-ethnic provinces, two British and one French.

New Brunswick is clearly a bilingual eth-elder province with two thirds British (62.6 percent) and one third French (31.3 percent). However, no other province conforms to such a bilingual and bicultural pattern.

The eth-elderly contrast to the uni-charter and bi and bi examples is found in the Prairies where no ethnic group is in the majority. While the British are the largest ethnic group (ranging from 44 to 48 percent), there are large groupings of German (10-18 percent), Ukrainian (10-14 percent), Scandinavian (4-6 percent) and French (4-6 percent) eth-elders. Ontario and British Columbia rank in the middle of the uni-ethnic and pluralist range, with a majority who are British (61-62 percent) and large numbers of others but growing in the pluralist direction.

It is fairly obvious that the provinces have different tasks ahead if they wish to serve their eth-elders well. Newfoundland can concentrate on the British,

TABLE 2

Distribution of Ethnic Elderly (55 years plus) by Province, Canada, 1981

Ethnic Origin	Nfld.	N.S.	N.B.	P.Q.	Ont.	Man.	Sask.	Alta.	B.C.	N.W.T.¹ P.E.I.	Total Canada
British	94.3	75.8	62.6	11.3	61.0	44.4	43.5	48.3	61.8	73.1	47.5
French	2.5	9.9	31.3	76.6	6.6	6.4	4.0	4.4	3.0	11.2	24.2
African	.0	.4	.1	.2	.3	.1	.0	.1	.1	.2	.2
Chinese	.0	.0	.0	.2	.9	.4	.3	1.1	2.4	.0	.7
Dutch	.1	2.2	.6	.2	1.9	2.9	2.0	3.2	2.1	.8	1.6
German	.1	4.7	1.2	.7	5.1	10.3	17.5	11.4	7.2	.3	5.3
Greek	.0	.1	.0	.4	.4	.0	.1	.1	.2	.0	.3
Italian	.1	.3	.2	2.5	4.5	.7	.1	.1	1.8	.2	2.6
Jewish	.1	.4	.2	2.7	2.2	2.8	.2	.6	.5	.0	1.8
Polish	.0	.4	.0	.6	2.3	4.8	2.7	2.8	1.5	.0	1.8
Portuguese	.0	.0	.0	.2	.8	.4	.2	.1	.2	.0	.4
Scandinavian	.2	.0	.5	.1	.7	3.6	6.8	6.0	4.4	.3	1.8
Ukrainian	.0	.3	.1	.5	2.5	13.8	11.2	9.7	2.8	.2	3.1
Other Single	1.1	1.6	.5	2.7	7.8	7.4	8.7	8.4	8.9	9.7	6.1
Multiple Origins	1.5	3.5	2.7	1.1	3.0	2.0	2.4	2.7	3.1	4.0	2.6
Totals %	100.0	100.0	100.0	100.0	100.0	100.0	100.0	100.0	100.0	100.0	100.0

Source: 2 Percent Sample Tape of the 1981 Census, Aged 55 and Over, Canadian Association on Gerontology (Association Canadienne de Gérontologie).

1. A residual category dominated by P.E.I. numerically.

but it may be more difficult to ensure other minority ethnic needs are not neglected. However, in the prairies a great diversification is warranted.

Modernization and Aging

Modernization theory is one of the more comprehensive conceptual developments in the area of aging. Cowgill (1974) suggests that as industrial modernization progresses, the social status and social integration of the elderly declines. Modernization is the transformation of a total society from a relatively rural way of life based on animate power, limited technology, relatively undifferentiated institutions, and parochial and traditional outlook and values. It becomes a predominantly urban way of life based on inanimate sources of power, highly developed scientific technology, highly differentiated institutions matched by segregated, segmented individual roles, and a cosmopolitan outlook that emphasizes efficiency and progress (Cowgill 1974, 127).

To help understand modernization, Cowgill (1974) has isolated four of the most significant and salient changes in modern society that affect the conditions of the elderly: 1) scientific technology; 2) urbanization; 3) literacy and mass education; and 4) health technology which he presented in a modernization model. Each of these is discussed briefly to help focus the discussion on the extent to which ethnicity is an important factor to consider when discussing elderly populations in part three of this paper. Economic status may not be the only or the major determinant of life satisfaction, prestige or quality of life, especially for the ethnic elderly. More research is needed to explore the alternatives and explanatory power of theories that are beginning to emerge.

Like modernization theory in aging, assimilation theory in ethnicity also assumes loss of status as a central focus. Modernists assume that with occupational retirement, income will drop, and compared to younger Canadians, the elderly will fall behind in educational preparedness. With the advance of new technology and urbanization the elderly lose social status, perhaps even before retirement. Assimilationists assume that unless immigrants coming into Canada shed some of their ethnic distinctiveness, they will not be able to compete in the larger society and attain the status of native-born Canadians. This paper looks first at some of the indicators of modernization by ethnicity and then turns to some indicators of assimilation (ethnic identity) and ethnicity.

Health Technology

According to Cowgill (1974), greater proportions of elderly people in the population brings with it greater generation competition for jobs and concomitantly increased pressures toward early retirement. With elderly people staying healthy longer and capable of good work, but feeling pressures to retire early, many find themselves in a meaningless stage of life. They lack goals and feel they are not carrying out recognized productive activity. Many elderly people may be pushed out of their jobs prematurely, especially as they find it difficult to change with the new technology. National morbidity data are not available in Canada by ethnicity but they are available for Cowgill's other three major changes accompanying modernization.

Educational Training

Premodern societies depend largely on oral tradition, so the aged have an important role in perpetuating and interpreting past traditions. The elderly act as a repository of the past in a preliterate environment (Driedger and Chappel 1987, 22). This is still the case in many northern aboriginal settings and to some extent on farms. With urbanization and formal education, literacy, mass education and technical training are necessary. Children are often more educated than their parents, especially in the beginning stages of the modernization process. Thus the elderly do not have a monopoly on knowledge, indeed, youth have the advantage in greater specialization and more recent knowledge. There is often an inversion of educational status. These differences vary by ethnic group, and for important reasons.

Table 3 presents a comparison of 15 ethnic groups and their educational attainment. There is considerable variation. For example, the French (37.7 percent), Italian (8.6 percent), Ukrainian (6.5 percent) and Portuguese (2.0 percent) elderly are disproportionately represented in the less-than-grade-five category. On the other hand, Jewish (3.4 percent) and British (56.2 percent) eth-elders are disproportionately represented in the highest B.A.-degree-or-more category. Interestingly, the Chinese are U-shaped with disproportionate numbers at both ends, early Chinese "bachelors" are located in the lower end and recent professional immigrants at the higher end, with fewer in between.

Recent immigrants such as the Portuguese and Italians came from rural areas where they had little opportunity for education, and French and Ukrainian elderly often came from poorer rural settings as well where education was less important. On the other hand, Jewish elderly have lived in cities extensively and have valued education through many generations. The British as the dominant group have also had more opportunities for more education. These enormous differences in eth-elder education illustrate that Jewish elders require quite different services in the cities, for example, than less-educated food gathering native Indians in the North. The value of education in their respective urban and northland environments varies also, so it is difficult to assess which of the eth-elders are better off.

Occupational Status

Cowgill designated economic technology as his third modernization factor, which centred largely around work. He proposed a sequence in which the chang-

TABLE 3

Education Level of Canada's Elderly (55 years and over)
by Ethnic Groups

Ethnic Origin	% of Total Canadian Population	Education Level				
		Less than Grade 5	Grade 5-8	Grade 9-13	High School Graduate	B.A. Degree or more
British	45.4	20.8	38.1	62.1	50.0	56.2
French	23.2	37.7	31.8	14.1	29.9	16.2
African	.2	.3	.1	.2	.2	.2
Chinese	.7	2.6	.5	.5	.6	1.2
Dutch	1.5	.8	1.9	1.2	1.1	1.2
German	5.1	4.0	6.6	4.9	3.1	3.8
Greek	.3	.7	.4	.2	.1	.2
Italian	2.5	8.6	3.2	1.2	1.2	.5
Jewish	1.1	1.5	1.1	2.3	2.8	3.4
Polish	1.7	2.8	2.2	1.3	.9	1.4
Portuguese	.4	2.0	.2	.1	.1	.1
Scandinavian	1.7	.6	1.8	2.1	1.1	1.8
Ukrainian	3.1	6.5	3.9	2.7	1.6	1.8
Other Single	4.1	8.3	4.3	3.6	3.6	5.8
Other	9.0	2.8	3.9	3.6	3.7	5.0
Totals	100.0	100.0	100.0	100.0	100.0	100.0

Source: Two Percent Sample Tape of the 1981 Canadian Census Aged 55 and over, Canadian Association on Gerontology/Association Canadienne de Gérontologie.

ing economic system requires many new jobs which youthful pioneers are able to learn more easily, so that the jobs of older citizens become obsolete. Thus, many are forced or encouraged to retire earlier which results in a loss of status for the elderly, since occupation is one of the important indicators of status in a modern society.

Table 4 lists some of the 1981 Census occupational categories, roughly beginning with higher status jobs (akin to the Blishen scale) and ending with occupations which require less education and often receive less pay. Again, the various ethnic elderly (55 years and over) in 1981 cluster quite differently. While the British elderly represent 49 percent of the total Canadian elderly population, they represent more than half of the participants in the top eight managerial to sales positions. As was the case in education, only the Jews follow the same pattern, but more so, especially in sales, managerial, artistic, social services and medical occupations.

TABLE 4

Occupational Status of Ethnic Groups in Canada (aged 55 and over) in 1981

	British	French	Chinese	Dutch	German	Italian	Jewish	Polish	Portuguese	Scandinavian	Ukrainian	Other Single	Multiple Mixed	N	Total %
Managerial	54.7	18.0	.3	1.5	4.5	1.8	5.3	1.1	.1	1.5	2.5	6.0	2.6	3,452	100
Engineering	55.2	13.5	1.0	3.4	5.0	1.0	1.4	2.6	.1	2.4	1.7	9.3	3.4	765	100
Social Services	56.5	17.1	.4	1.3	5.4	.6	3.6	1.5	.0	1.5	3.2	5.8	3.4	467	100
Teaching	50.6	23.5	.3	2.0	5.9	.8	2.2	1.4	.1	2.0	2.8	6.0	2.4	1,005	100
Health, Med.	53.4	20.6	.3	1.5	4.4	.6	3.1	1.3	.2	.9	2.4	7.2	4.1	1,237	100
Artistic, Ent.	51.6	20.2	.2	2.0	4.2	2.0	4.2	.5	.0	2.0	1.2	8.1	3.3	401	100
Clerical	56.9	18.5	.4	1.2	3.9	1.6	3.0	1.4	.2	1.5	2.7	5.5	3.4	5,090	100
Sales	52.0	18.8	.6	1.8	4.7	1.7	6.1	1.3	.2	1.9	3.0	4.7	2.7	3,502	100
Service	41.3	22.3	.5	1.6	6.0	4.4	.7	3.0	1.1	1.6	5.0	8.5	2.5	4,807	100
Farming	46.3	12.8	.3	3.6	12.3	1.0	.1	2.2	.3	4.3	7.1	8.1	1.8	2,584	100
Primary, other	48.8	31.4	.2	.8	2.5	1.6	.0	2.3	.2	2.0	3.3	11.5	1.4	488	100
Processing	32.6	30.9	.8	1.5	5.8	5.9	1.1	3.5	.8	1.5	4.1	9.3	2.2	1,233	100
Machining	36.0	23.7	.5	1.7	6.8	7.3	1.9	3.8	.7	1.4	3.6	9.8	2.8	3,229	100
Construction	39.3	25.4	.1	3.1	6.8	7.1	.5	1.7	1.1	2.7	3.4	7.2	1.7	2,119	100
Transport	49.8	29.5	.0	1.6	4.2	1.2	1.3	1.5	.2	1.8	2.8	4.4	1.7	1,278	100
Other	42.5	26.6	.6	1.7	4.8	3.9	.5	3.0	.4	1.5	3.8	7.6	2.9	1,877	100
TOTAL % Population	45.4	23.2	.7	1.5	5.1	2.5	1.7	1.7	.4	1.7	3.1	6.4	2.4	33,534	100

Source: 2 Percent Sample Tape of 1981 Canadian Census aged 55 and over Canadian Association on Gerontology/Association Canadienne de Gérontologie.

As in education, recent immigrants like the Portuguese and Italians are more heavily represented in the lower rankings, especially construction, machining, processing and service. The French are heavily located in primary and processing occupations. Older European groups such as the Germans, Scandinavians and Ukrainians are heavily into farming, and rank more in the middle of the occupational hierarchy.

Clearly, the Jews and British rank highest, Northern Europeans next, followed by the French and recent Southern Europeans at the bottom. Native Indians, who are not listed separately, would rank at the very bottom. Social status as measured by occupation is an important factor in differentiating eth-elders, where some reveal life-long higher status; others lower status.

Urbanization

In Table 5 the various ethnic groups are compared by urbanization, Cowgill's fourth modernization factor. Generally (not shown here) Jews, Chinese, Italians and Portuguese tend to be almost entirely urban, while native Indians, Germans, Dutch, Scandinavians and Ukrainians tend to be mostly rural. The British and French charter groups usually rank in the middle. In Table 5 it is clear that the types of eth-elders in the 10 cities presented tend to follow the provincial ethnic clustering examined earlier.

British eth-elders (55 years and older) are very heavily represented in the Maritime cities of St. John and Halifax, while French Canadians are most heavily located in Montreal. Ottawa is the most bilingual and bicultural urban centre, and Winnipeg and Edmonton on the Prairies follow the prairie pattern of greatest cultural pluralism. Toronto is fast following the prairie pluralist pattern, although this does not show up as much in 1981 with eth-elders as it will increasingly when recent immigrants age. Kitchener is unique in that it has a very large German eth-elder population.

Cities generally tend to follow their respective provincial ethnic patterns. Jewish eth-elders and recent immigrants such as the Italians, Greeks and Portuguese are almost all urban. Since the last three groups represent young recent immigrant populations they will become a larger part of the eth-elder population increasingly, especially in larger cities like Toronto, Montreal and Vancouver.

Three of Cowgill's salient changes which typify the process of modernization were used to examine ethnic diversity within Canada. It is evident that the characteristics of modernization examined here differ considerably depending on which ethnic group is being examined. The educational and occupational levels of the elderly in the eighties are lower than non-retired citizens but this varies enormously by ethnic group. Jewish and British elderly tend to rank the highest, and native Indians and recent immigrants the lowest in educational and occupational status. On the other hand, recent immigrants are the most urban while older European agriculturalists are mostly rural.

TABLE 5

Percentage of Ethnic Elderly (55 years and older)
in 10 Metropolitan Centres of Canada, 1981

Ethnic Origin	St. Johns	Halifax	Quebec	Montreal	Ottawa	Toronto	Kitchener	Winnipeg	Edmonton	Vancouver
British	91.0	73.3	3.7	15.2	48.6	53.8	44.1	40.6	41.7	56.8
French	2.4	8.7	89.4	58.7	30.8	1.8	2.5	6.4	5.5	3.2
Chinese				.4	.6	1.8	.3	.5	1.8	4.2
Dutch	.1	2.7	.2	.2	.7	1.0	1.8	1.7	2.9	1.3
German	.1	3.6	.1	1.2	2.0	3.0	29.3	8.7	8.8	5.7
Italian	.1	.1	.1	5.0	1.9	7.4	.9	1.3	1.2	2.0
Jewish	.1	.7	.1	5.5	1.5	5.6	.2	4.8	.9	.9
Polish		.3	.1	1.1	1.2	2.7	2.8	5.2	3.4	1.6
Portuguese				.4	.3	1.5	2.4	.5	.3	.2
Scandinavian	.2	.3		.1	.4	.4	.3	3.1	4.2	4.2
Ukrainian		.2		1.0	1.1	2.9	2.0	13.7	14.2	2.8
Other Single	1.0	2.4	.7	5.4	3.6	11.9	5.7	7.1	7.3	9.0
Multiple	1.4	4.5	.6	1.7	3.0	2.4	3.6	2.3	2.7	2.8
Other	3.6	3.2	5.1	4.1	4.3	3.8	4.1	4.1	5.1	5.3
Total:	100.0	100.0	100.0	100.0	100.0	100.0	100.0	100.0	100.0	100.0

Source: 2 Percent Sample Tape of the 1981 Canadian Census. Aged 55 and Over. Canadian Association on Gerontology/Association Canadienne de Gérontologie.

As Rosenthal (1983) has argued, high ethnic identity families are assumed to fall at the traditional end of a traditional-modern continuum. The ethnic family has been characterized by respect for elderly members, high degree of familism, cohesion and continuity between the generations, providing much support and integration for aged members. This is contrasted with the white or Anglo-Saxon (supposedly non-ethnic) family which is assumed to fall at the modern end of the continuum. Assumptions about ethnic families and the traditional way of life are consistent with the modernization theory of aging but also with the assimilation theory of ethnicity. Assimilation theory was popular for some 50 years in ethnic studies, particularly in the United States. Basically, assimilation theory argues that all ethnic groups will change, losing their original language, culture and values, and adopting values, norms and structures of their host society (Hughes 1950; Gordon 1964). However, pluralism has been more popular in Canadian ethnic studies than assimilation. Pluralists argue that many groups retain a separate identity and do not assimilate. They live side by side, many of them in relatively harmonious co-existence (Newman 1973; Reitz 1982). Assimilation and pluralism can be viewed as two polarities, each representing an opposite ideal polar type. Ethnic groups can be viewed as leaning more towards one or the other. The next section examines the extent to which various ethnic groups still maintain ethnic identity.

Variations in Ethnic Identity

While an important literature has developed in Canada on ethnic identity (O'Bryan et al. 1973; Driedger 1975; Isajiw 1981; Reitz 1980) in the last 15 years, very little has focused on eth-elder identity. Driedger and Chappel (1987) reviewed the literature and were forced to rely mostly on census data. Factors such as choice of friends, extent of parochial education, participation in ethnic organizations and use of ethnic media, as well as the salience of identity and symbolic features of identity are not available. Unfortunately, language competence and use, and religious affiliation are the only ethnic identity factors available in the 1981 Census. Cowgill maintains modernization tends to undermine the status of eth-elders but data in the preceeding section suggests this varies by ethnic group. Does ethnic identification also vary?

Language Ability and Use

Language knowledge and use is considered by many (Lieberson 1970; Joy 1972; de Vries and Vallee 1980) a highly important feature of ethnic identification. For eth-elders who may not yet have learned English, their own mother tongue is a salient form of communication with which they feel comfortable, part of their enrichment of life. A special run of the 1981 Canada census data of elderly persons (65 years plus) shows the extent to which the mother tongue of their ancestors was learned and the extent to which it is still being used. It was expected elderly people would use their ethnic languages more than the young, because the elderly would not be as assimilated. That is, language was expected to be strongly related to generational status (immigrant, second and third generation, etc.). This would also provide some indication of the extent to which ethnic languages are an important part of dealing with the aged in Canada.

Table 6 shows that a majority (less for the Jews) had learned their respective mother tongues. Such knowledge was especially strong among the elderly representing the charter groups, the British (97.9 percent) and the French (92.8 percent). Most of the Chinese (93.6 percent), Greeks (93.2 percent), Portuguese (90.4 percent) and Italians (89.6 percent) could also use their mother tongues because a majority are foreign-born.

TABLE 6

Mother Tongue by Ethnic Groups and Their Home Language Use,
Aged 65 and Over in Canada, 1981

Ethnic Origin	Mother Tongue	Home Use of Mother Tongue	Home Use of English
British	97.9%	99.0	99.0
French	92.8	88.4	11.4
African	83.3	83.3	83.3
Chinese	93.6	86.4	12.2
Dutch	53.6	23.3	70.2
German	62.3	24.7	73.8
Greek	93.2	76.3	18.6
Italian	89.6	72.4	23.1
Jewish	45.2	18.1	77.5
Polish	68.7	40.0	49.9
Portuguese	90.4	86.4	12.8
Scandinavian	57.0	5.5	94.5
Ukrainian	89.3	52.6	46.5
Other Single	60.9	42.5	49.0

Source: 2 Percent Sample Tape of the 1981 Canadian Census Aged 55 and over, Canadian Association on Gerontology/Association Canadienne de Gérontologie.

To what extent do the current cohorts of ethnic elders still use their ethnic mother tongue? Almost all of the elderly of charter group origin use their mother tongue at home and so do more recent immigrants such as the Portuguese and Chinese. However, Scandinavian, Jewish, Dutch and German elders (mostly

Northern Europeans who came earlier) have shifted extensively to English (de Vries and Vallee, 1980, 98, 107, 116, 122). This illustrates that while most eth-elders still speak their respective mother tongues, it varies as to which tongue they would most prefer to use at home.

Religion as Elderly Support

In addition to language, which is a major means of communication, religion is also considered an important support system ideologically and socially. In Table 7, 14 religious denominations are listed. Except for the Chinese (54.3 percent who preferred no religion), almost all eth-elders claimed affiliation with a religious denomination. However, the ethnic clustering varies enormously.

French (96.3 percent), Portuguese (96.0 percent), Italian (95.9 percent) and Polish (78.9 percent) elders are almost all Roman Catholics. Greeks (94.1 percent) and Jews (97.3 percent) are affiliated with Eastern Orthodox and Jewish religions respectively. While the elders of these six ethnic groups belong predominantly to one religion, the others tend to be more plural in their affiliations. The British prefer both United Church (35.1 percent) and Anglican (25.0 percent) denominations; the Germans are both Lutheran (31.2 percent) and Roman Catholic (23.5 percent); the Scandinavians belong to both the Lutherans (51.8 percent) and the United Church (21.5 percent); and the Ukrainians divide between the Ukrainian Orthodox (37.8 percent) and Eastern Orthodox (31.5 percent).

This diversity of religious preference shows once again eth-elders live in a plural Canada and their needs are varied and complex. Unfortunately data are not available to measure salience of religiosity for eth-elders, using only census data. Recently Reginald Bibby (1987) illustrated salience of religiosity in Canada, but he did not control for age.

Language and religion are but two indicators of ethnic identification, and this discussion has suggested that for many eth-elders both are important for their identity. Future research needs to explore the extent to which ingroup friendships, use of the ethnic media such as radio, television and newspapers, participation in ethnic organizations, and educational preparation in ingroup schools differentiates those over and under age 65. It is expected that all these means of ethnic identity maintenance are more important to the elderly than to youth but that this also varies by ethnic group depending on socio-economic status, recency of immigration, exposure to modernization, spatial segregation and the like.

In other words, the theory of assimilation, like the theory of modernization, is too deterministic in stating loss of identity. Ethnic identity is still an important factor for many in the Canadian mosaic. That is, modernization and assimilation processes are multidimensional, complex, and not necessarily related to one another. The next section attempts to establish order out of the enormous ethnic variations just discussed.

TABLE 7

Affiliation of Ethnic Elderly (age 65 and over) with Religious Denominations

Ethnic Origin	Roman Catholic	Ukrainian Catholic	Anglican	Baptist	Lutheran	Mennonite	Pentecostal	Presbyterian	United Church	Other Protestant	Eastern Orthodox	Jewish	Eastern non-Christian	No Religion
British	13.4%	.0	25.0	5.8	.8	.1	1.3	10.1	35.1	4.8	.1	.2	.1	3.3
French	96.3	.0	.5	.4	.1	.0	.1	.2	1.2	.5	.0	.1	.0	.6
African	21.2		18.2	15.2			10.6	3.0	9.1	1.1	3.0		4.5	3.0
Chinese	6.4		2.5	5.0	.6	.3	1.4	3.4	14.1	2.8		.6	8.3	54.3
Dutch	15.0		7.3	4.6	1.8	12.4	2.1	5.0	18.6	26.2		.2		6.8
German	23.5	.0	3.6	5.2	31.2	10.9	2.0	2.6	12.7	4.8	.1	.1		3.3
Greek	1.7		.8					.8		2.5	94.1		.0	.6
Italian	95.9		.3	.1	.2		.7	.4	1.2	.5	.1			1.7
Jewish	.3		.1					.1	.1	.1		97.3		
Polish	78.9	2.9	1.9	.4	2.5		.1	.6	3.3	1.5	2.3	2.6		2.9
Portuguese	96.0		.8		.8			.8	.8	.8				
Scandinavian	1.8		4.4	4.4	51.8		2.1	2.0	21.5	7.4	.1		.1	4.4
Ukrainian	11.5	37.8	1.8	1.4	.7	.2	1.1	.6	5.8	2.7	31.5	.3		4.8
Other Single	31.5	.6	7.1	2.1	16.5	1.1	1.0	2.1	9.6	5.0	8.6	1.1	8.8	5.0

Source: 2 Percent Sample Tape of the 1981 Canadian Census aged 55 over. Canadian Association on Gerontology/Association Canadienne de Gérontologie.

FIGURE 1

Emerging Eth-elder Types Plotted on a Traditional-Modern Continuum

		Germans		
	Inuit	Scandinavians	Jews	
	Indians	Ukrainians	Chinese	
Traditional				Modern
	Food	Agriculturalists	Urban	
	Gathering		Industrial	

Eth-Elder Social Patterns

Two examples of ordering and summarizing this information into types or clusters is presented. First, the ethnic groups are ordered along a traditional-modern continuum. Secondly, they are plotted using rural, urban and socio-economic status axes. Both alternatives result in a similar clustering of ethnic groups. Finally, five eth-elder types are discussed and depicted on a regional map.

Traditional-Modern Continuum

In Figure 1 a traditional-modern continuum is presented to summarize the discussion of modernization in part two. The assumption is that ethnic groups begin at the traditional end of the continuum, and as urbanization sets in some move along the continuum toward increased modernization as they are exposed to new experiences and greater technological diversity, from gemeinschaft to more gesellschaft social relations. Some groups stay at the traditional end longer, while others modernize faster.

The Inuit and Indians of Canada, many of them in the northlands still food-gathering, are closest to the traditional end of the modernization process. North and East Europeans already came to Canada as agriculturalists, many established themselves on farmlands, and these eth-elders still feel close to the land even though many have now moved to the city. Their general values and norms have been shaped by the land. The Jews and Chinese, most entrepreneurs for generations, have lived in the city all their lives and feel at home in the city. They are less oriented to the land and more oriented to business, and more open to a changing technological society. The aspirations of the Inuit and Indians are vastly different than those of the Jews and Chinese. Their service needs also vary greatly.

A Status-Urbanization Model

While modernization is an important factor in ordering the Canadian ethnic diversity, socio-economic status (SES) and rural-urban residence are also important dimensions of organization. In Figure 2 both of these dimensions are incorporated in a model. Not all ethnic groups can be neatly placed in the four cells created by an intersection of the rural-urban and high and low SES continua, but some have been placed in each to symbolically illustrate tendencies toward four types.

FIGURE 2

Eth-elder Types by Socio-economic Status and Degree of Urbanization

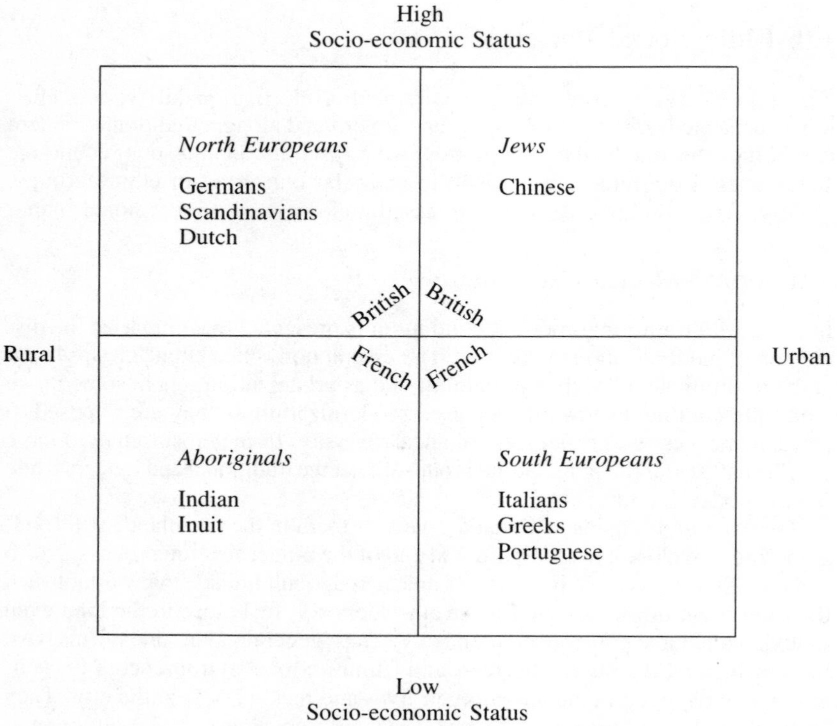

High
Socio-economic Status

North Europeans Germans Scandinavians Dutch	*Jews* Chinese
Aboriginals Indian Inuit	*South Europeans* Italians Greeks Portuguese

Rural — British / British — French / French — Urban

Low
Socio-economic Status

The British elderly are placed in the middle of the upper socio-economic status end, and the French in the middle of the lower end. They are located in the middle because as charter groups these eth-elders represent almost three-fourths of the elderly in Canada and they live in both rural and urban places.

North Europeans were originally located heavily in agricultural areas. While many have moved to the cities since, their elderly have often stayed behind to live their last years comfortably in small rural towns and villages, especially on the prairies and in agricultural Ontario.

Canada's Indian and Inuit aboriginal eth-elders are still located mostly in the Northwest Territories and northern parts of the six most westerly provinces, where urbanization has not yet developed extensively. They are poor, and many of them are illiterate. The aboriginals clearly fit in the rural low socio-economic cell.

More recent South European immigrant eth-elders such as the Portuguese, Greeks and Italians are small in number, and located mostly in the cities of Toronto, Montreal and Vancouver. They are mostly urban with limited education and economic resources and occupational skills. Other recent immigrants, visible minorities like Blacks and East Asians, tend to fall in this category as well. While not all ethnic groups fit this model as well as the ones discussed, most of them have been ordered to provide a guide as to what their social needs and aspirations might be. We turn next, in the last part, to plotting some of these eth-elders regionally.

Regional Eth-Elder Types

Provincial diversity among eth-elder populations calls for some attempt at classifying Canada's ethnic population into regions, so some holistic view can be presented of the task practitioners and politicians are faced with when they seek to serve the needs of an ever-growing aging population where grey power will increasingly become part of the political, economic and social agenda in the future.

In Figure 3 six regions of Canada are plotted which represent very different eth-elder types. Traditional aboriginals, European prairie agriculturalists, French charter Canadians, the multi-British majority and urban Jewish elderly as eth-elder types are discussed by region.

Northlands: Traditional Aboriginals. The 413,000 native people of Canada are composed mostly of Native Indians; only about 20,000 are Inuit (Frideres 1983). The basic homeland of these aboriginals is the Northlands, representing about four fifths of the Canadian land area (Figure 3). While many are still located in their preindustrial aboriginal habitat, more and more are moving to the mining and logging settlements and some are coming south. Only 3.5 percent are elderly because early deaths tend to wipe out high birth rates: very few enter old age. Thus, there are relatively few who are 65 years plus scattered in the northlands in the food-gathering setting. Edwards (1983, 75-76) found that over half of these elderly lived below the poverty line, over half the women were

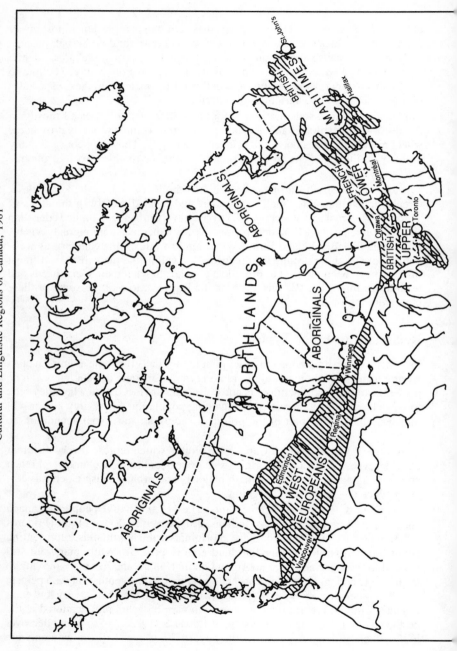

FIGURE 3

Cultural and Linguistic Regions of Canada, 1981

widowed, and housing was inadequate and crowded. They often live with their extended families in a native cultural setting where they speak their mother tongue and follow their traditions. These few scattered native elderly are usually far away from modern services, but in a familiar gemeinschaft social context with their people. They are segregated from most modern influences, definitely a Traditional Aboriginal Northlands eth-elder type.

The Prairies: European Agriculturalists. When the Prairies opened up for settlement a hundred years ago, they were settled very heavily by North Europeans such as the British, French, Germans, Dutch, Scandinavians, and later Poles and Ukrainians who were agriculturalists. Anderson (1972) studied the variety of farmers in Saskatchewan and found that all perpetuated their own languuages, cultures, institutions and folklore. The North European eth-elders are fairly well off financially and large numbers moved into small villages and towns near their farming communities close to their children and grandchildren. They are fairly independent and the various ethnic groups have built homes for elderly people who need them. Socio-economically they are quite well to do and their ethnic communities frequently can provide for the needs of their elderly. They are a distinct North European Prairies Farm type.

French Québecois: A Charter Minority. The French were the first Europeans to settle permanently in New France, what is now southern Quebec along the St. Lawrence, some 350 years ago (Rioux 1971). Most of the elderly in Quebec are francophone and French Canadian culturally. Since birth rates in Quebec were high until recently, only 7.8 percent of the population are 65 years plus in 1981 compared to 9.1 percent nationally. However, now that birth rates have declined dramatically and industrialization is increasing, the proportion of elderly will climb steadily in the future, especially since new immigrants have been slow to enter Quebec. The French elderly in Quebec come out of the habitant rural setting so that 37.7 percent of all Canadian elderly with grade five or less reside in Quebec. They have retained a strong French Canadian identity and prefer to speak French. They are spatially segregated along the St. Lawrence River in a French Canadian world. These French Québecois eth-elders are a distinct third type, quite different from the Northland Aboriginals and Prairie Agriculturalists.

The Multi-British Plurality. The British are the largest charter group in Canada, representing 40.2 percent of the population in 1981. One hundred years ago the British were indeed a majority, but no ethnic group is now a majority, though British elders over 65 years of age represent almost half (49.3 percent) of Canada's elderly. In the future the British elderly will decline proportionately. Well over half of all elderly in Canada with Bachelor degrees are British; and they are disproportionately represented in the higher status occupations; English is their dominant language; and they belong to the higher status Anglican and United Church denominations. While of high status, the British elderly are not a homogeneous group. Large numbers are located in industrial urban southern Ontario, the heartland of the original Empire Loyalists, part of the economic and political power magnet of Canada to which recent immigrants are attracted. However, British fishermen on the periphery of the Newfoundland coastlines are definitely a contrast, representing economic struggle for survival. In Quebec they are a minority and on the Prairies the British fit well with the North European agriculturalists. Thus, the British elderly are quite plural, with their needs in southern Ontario and Newfoundland varying considerably. They are not homogeneous, but are a Multi-British Plural type (English, Scottish, Irish and Welsh), quite different than assimilationists have been prone to portray them. British political dominance has been clear, but British economic and cultural status is varied. This will become more apparent in the future.

Urban Jewish Elderly. Earlier it was suggested that the Jewish elders represented an urban polar type quite the opposite of native aboriginals. The Jews are an aging population (16.5 percent 65 years plus), they are almost all urban, highly segregated in Montreal, Toronto and Winnipeg, where most of them live, they rank highest on education, occupational status and income, and on most indicators of ethnic identity, they score higher than all other ethnic groups (Driedger and Chappell 1987, 53, 54). The Jews are definitely an Urban High Status eth-elder type, with high ethnic and religious identity, an enormous contrast to the Northlands Aboriginal type.

We have summarized by presenting five eth-elder types which live in distinct areas of Canada. The Northland Aboriginals, the Prairie European Agriculturalists, the French Québecois, the British Pluralists and the Jewish Urbanites are quite distinct groups of eth-elders located in their respective regions. The needs and aspirations of these eth-elder types vary enormously and those who wish to relate to and serve them will need to take careful note as to what needs are increasing. Politicians and economists might do well to design their appeals to this dynamic plurality of Grey Power.

Implications for Social Policy

The data presented suggest that the degrees and types of assimilation vary from one ethnic group to another. In addition, social and economic mobility, and therefore high social status in the sense used in modernization theory, is not necessarily associated with assimilation. That is, it is not necessarily related to a loss of ethnic identity. A major example here are the Jews. They have achieved high status while maintaining high ethnic identity. The Germans and Chinese also rank relatively high on three standard indicators of socio-economic status — occupation, income and education. The explanation for how groups who attain high status within the society can also maintain their ethnic identity might be found in primary group relations. Ethnic culture is a source of ethnic identity and a major determinant of behaviour. It is within primary group relations that people interpret the world around them. Indeed the importance of this subjective level has been recognized in suggested revisions to the modernization theory (see for example, Rhoads 1984). Furthermore, the extent to which factors related to modernization and socio-economic status are important to the elderly in evaluating prestige, especially after they are retired, is not known. Nor is the extent to which this status varies by ethnicity known. It is doubtful that Hutterite elders worry much about their status in the larger society; whether they are valued within the colony — and evidence suggests that they are (Hostetler and Huntington 1967) — is more important to them. Much more research is needed to understand the extent to which elders desire status within their immediate peer and ethnic group and the extent to which status in the larger society is important to them.

The discussion so far has confirmed ethnic diversity on a number of variables. Indeed there is much literature that recognizes the special needs of different ethnic groups, stemming from their unique ethno history, language and culture, and the importance of incorporating these elements into service delivery systems (Cuellar 1981). Even reports from the Canadian government (Begin 1982) recognize that "familiar cultural surroundings" may be important in the provision of services.

The paramount importance of language is unmistakable in MacLean and Bonar's (1983) study of elderly residents of long-term care institutions in Montreal. That study describes residents who could not speak English or French; no one else could speak their language and the mental and physical devastation which resulted. The role of culture is evident in Ujimoto's (1986) study of Japanese elders. He tells how they tend not to express pain and suffering because it is a sign of weakness; elderly Asians regard doctors as authority figures and consequently seldom question doctors directly. Strong's (1984) study comparing Indian and White caregivers of elderly natives also emphasizes cultural differences. The Indians' greater belief in passive forbearance (together with a cultural dictum forbidding interference) differ dramatically from the White group.

While an overall policy may recognize ethnic differences, implementation does not necessarily follow easily. Many advocate that services be delivered by members of the ethnic group (Krickus 1980). If this is not possible, agency personnel can work with members of that community. Grassroots social service programs designed, based and implemented in and by the community are often mentioned. Informing ethnic individuals about services is clearly insufficient. Providing services within their cultural context is of major importance. This applies to both short- and long-term care. Morrison (1983), for example, notes that utilization of nursing homes by minority aged is higher if facilities are located within ethnic neighbourhoods. However, neighbourhood location is insufficient by itself if culturally accustomed patterns of eating, socializing and living in general are not taken into consideration. That is, cultural congruence is important where ethnic culture is sufficiently distinct to warrant attention.

Many charge that the insensitivity of agency personnel to cultural nuances is one of the reasons members of ethnic groups underutilize agency services (Kim 1983; Lum 1983; Wesley-King 1983). It is not known whether this insensitivity stems from the belief on the part of agency personnel that members of ethnic groups are well cared for by their families, from ignorance, from prejudice, or from ethnocentrism on the part of the personnel. It need not result from prejudice and discrimination. However lack of knowledge about a culture and/or an insensitivity to cultural nuances can be as devastating in their consequences as prejudice and discrimination.

It is important to remember that many of the recommendations found in the literature on the ethnic elderly would be equally welcome among other elderly. For example, in relation to eth-elders, Gelfand and Kutzik (1979) recommend that family therapy be a more integral part of mental health services. Especially in the mental health area, diagnostic labels and standardized norms have been criticized as being culturally biased. Blau and associates (1979) argue for strategies to encourage the elderly to replenish and restore informal social networks of support as their social resources become depleted. The recommendation that transportation be provided not merely to visit doctors in hospitals, nutrition centres and community centres, but also to visit friends, libraries, museums, classes and hobby groups would be welcome by most groups of elderly persons.

Indeed, the similarity of recommendations made by both ethnic scholars and gerontological scholars is striking. A common theme is that services should be designed to enable elderly persons to remain in their own homes, in their own neighbourhoods, in familiar environments as long as possible. The fact that this similarity is evident need not mean that ethnic culture should be ignored in the provision of services. Rather, it can mean that providing services that are familiar within our own system of beliefs will require attention to ethnic culture for some people. Elderly persons are a heterogeneous group and ethnicity is an important dimension to be taken into account in service delivery. Eth-elders want continuity and familiarity throughout their old age, as do those of us for whom ethnicity is not as salient.

Summary

This paper began with some eth-elder population comparisons and their provincial distributions. To assess ethnic variation in modernization, three of Cowgill's four factors which, he argues, tend to lower the status of the elderly were discussed. Measures of the maintenance of ethnic identity were not optimal; nevertheless, extensive ethnic language ability and use, and adherence to religious denominations did show that these forms of identification varied among ethnics groups.

To summarize, a dozen ethnic groups were plotted on a tradition-modern continuum to show that in Canada there are eth-elders represented on the entire traditional to modern range. The demographic data were further summarized showing aboriginal, North European, South European and Jewish types, which illustrated differential rural-urban and socio-economic eth-elder diversity. Five eth-elder types emerged which were plotted regionally into the traditional aboriginals in the northlands, the European agriculturalists on the prairies, the French Québecois along the St. Lawrence, the plurality of the British, and finally the Jewish elderly as urban eth-elder types.

The data presented here clearly demonstrate the diversity among eth-elders in Canada. Their own means of providing for themselves also vary. Finally, a brief discussion of the provision of services for eth-elders was presented.

14. THE AGING OF ETHNIC GROUPS IN QUEBEC

Robert Choinière and Norbert Robitaille

The population of Quebec, like that of the rest of Canada and other industrialized countries, has aged rapidly since the early sixties. Between 1966 and 1986 the average age in Quebec went from 24 to 32 years. The main reason for this aging is the decline in the fertility rate, which has resulted in a decrease in the relative proportion of young people in relation to adults and old people (Desjardins and Légaré, 1977). Mortality played a less significant role, since it basically decreased for young people, which had the effect of making the population younger rather than older. The fertility rate in Quebec is currently one of the lowest in the world. We can therefore expect that the population of Quebec will continue to age rapidly.

But what about the different ethnic groups that make up the population of Quebec? Is the aging process the same for all of them? Is the declining fertility rate the main cause of aging?

This study will attempt to answer these questions by examining the evolving aging patterns of the main ethnic groups in Quebec, and related demographic phenomena.

Selecting the Ethnic Groups to be Studied and the Concept of Ethnicity

Any study based on statistical measures of population is limited by the available data. The Census of Canada is the main source of data about ethnic groups. The researcher who uses this source must however take two major limitations into account: the ethnic groups included in the available data, and the methodology used to classify the population according to ethnic group.

The decision about which ethnic groups to include in the census data is often a function of their relative numeric weight in terms of the total Canadian population. So in studying the main ethnic groups in a particular province, it often happens that those groups do not exactly correspond to the categories for the country as a whole. Similarly, the less important groups — numerically speaking — may be of special interest due to their particular characteristics. Taking these considerations into account, we selected the ethnic groups in Table 1 for inclusion in this study:

TABLE 1

Number of Individuals in Selected Ethnic Groups[1] in Quebec, 1981

Ethnic Group	Number
French	5,105,670
British	487,385
Italian	163,735
Jewish	102,355[2]
Greek	49,420
German	33,770
Haitian	30,000[3]
Portuguese	27,370
Polish	19,755
Chinese	19,260
Ukrainian	14,640
Inuit	5,047[4]
Other origins and residual	310,687[5]
Total Population	6,369,070[5]

Source: Census of Canada, 1982.
       Bernèche, 1983
       Choinière and Robitaille, 1988.

Notes: [1] Numbers based on individuals who declared a single origin.
     [2] Population professing the Jewish faith.
     [3] Numbers based on Bernèche, 1983
     [4] Numbers based on the Register of the Inuit Population of New Quebec.
     [5] Single and multiple origins.

Of the groups included, only the Inuit are not among the 13 largest groups in Quebec. Status Indians and Spaniards, who are respectively ranked 7th and 12th, were not selected for inclusion because of the lack of information about these two groups. The Inuit were included because of the particular demographic characteristics of this population (young in age, absence of ethnic mobility, geographic isolation, etc.) and because of the abundance of sources available to us (the special tables from the 1981 Census, the Register of the Inuit Population of New Quebec).

The criteria used to define an individual's ethnic origin have changed considerably from census to census. In the 1931 and 1941 censuses, the term used to define ethnicity was racial origin, and enumerators were instructed to not confuse racial origin with nationality, country of birth or country of nationality. In 1951, the term origin replaced racial origin and was determined by the language spoken by the paternal ancestor on arrival in the country. If this question could not be answered, people were asked to specify their origin on the paternal side. In 1961 and 1971, the term became ethnic or cultural group and the procedure was reversed, since people were first asked about their paternal ancestor's origin, then, in cases that were hard to decide, what language they spoke. Finally, in 1981, origin was determined by the group adherence of the individual or his or her ancestors. The reference to paternal or maternal lineage was abandoned. The person being enumerated could thus declare more than one ethnic origin.

These changes make it difficult to compare total ethnic group membership from census to census. Therefore we have tried to only use relative frequencies in this study, so that we could more easily compare membership over time. Our assumption is that the distribution of different ethnic groups by characteristics studied is not significantly affected by changes in the definition of ethnicity in each census.

Evolution of Aging

Using the various censuses, we shall first examine the evolution of aging in the different ethnic groups. The index chosen for studying these changes is the proportion of people aged 65 or more compared to the population as a whole. This index is based on the legal age of retirement. It can be used to quickly estimate the proportion of people who have finished their working life and who live on various pensions (retirement plans, old age pensions, etc.). An increase in this index is the result of an aging in the population, since the proportion of older people increases in relation to those of other ages.

There appear to be major disparities among ethnic groups with regard to aging. In the 1981 Census, we find Ukrainians, Jews and Poles among the oldest groups, with the percentage of individuals aged 65 and over higher than 15 percent. At the other extreme, the Inuit, Haitian, Portuguese and Greek groups are the youngest ethnic groups, with the percentage of people aged 65 and over being under 5 percent.

There are also important variations over time. For most of the groups for which we have data from more than one census, the percentage of people aged 65 and over has increased sharply. Differences between recent censuses show that this increase is on the rise. For the British and French groups, though they are also affected by the recent acceleration in aging, the percentage of people aged 65 and over has increased at a more steady pace than for other groups.

TABLE 2

Evolution in the Percentage of People Aged 65 and over, by Ethnic Group, Quebec, 1931 to 1981

Ethnic Group	1931	1941	1951	1961	1971	1981
Ukrainian	0.3	1.3	3.4	5.8	10.9	19.9
Jewish	2.5	4.7	6.4	8.0	12.0	18.9
Polish	0.8	2.0	3.5	4.8	9.2	17.1
British	6.2	8.0	9.6	9.7	10.1	13.1
German	4.3	5.6	6.7	4.0	6.2	10.4
Italian	2.0	3.0	5.2	3.4	4.2	7.8
French	4.7	4.9	5.2	5.4	6.4	7.7
Chinese	0.8	6.4	12.6	n.a.	n.a.	6.5
Greek	n.a.	3.3	n.a.	n.a.	n.a.	4.4
Portuguese	n.a.	n.a.	n.a.	n.a.	n.a.	4.0
Haitian	n.a.	n.a.	n.a.	n.a.	n.a.	3.3[1]
Inuit	4.1	1.7	1.5	1.6	2.5	2.5
All of Quebec	4.8	5.3	5.7	5.8	6.9	8.3

Sources: Census of Canada, 1931, 1941, 1951, 1961, 1971 and 1981. Choinière and Robitaille, 1988.

Note: [1] Percentages calculated based on sample tapes from the 1981 Census.

The evolution in the relative proportion of people aged 65 and over inside each ethnic group shows there are different thresholds in the aging process in these groups. Some groups are further along in this process than others.

To what phenomena should we attribute these disparities in the aging process of the various groups? If, when compared to another group, a current population shows accelerated signs of aging, it is because the components of growth have undergone modifications in such a way as to produce this aging. In ethnic groups, as in all sub-populations, we find the following growth components: fertility rate, mortality and migration. In considering ethnic groups, however, we must take another phenomenon into account: ethnic mobility. Some individuals are not consistent in their declaration of ethnic origin (Ryder, 1955). This mobility can also be intergenerational. Children can ascribe themselves a different origin than that of their parents.

The decrease in mortality does not play a significant role in the recent aging of the Quebec population. On the contrary, its impact is to make the age structure of the population younger, since there is an increase in very young children.

We can assume that the situation is similar for individual ethnic groups. There is no question that the group with the sharpest decrease in mortality, the Inuit,[1] has been the least affected by population aging. We will therefore leave aside the study of mortality and will focus on other demographic phenomena involved in the aging of ethnic groups: fertility rate, migration and ethnic mobility.

Fertility Rate

Data on the marital status of individuals in ethnic groups did not become available until 1951. In subsequent years, only the information provided by Quebec organizations lets us follows some ethnic groups up to 1975. We must therefore use census data to examine the evolution of fertility in these groups. However, census data only provides us with summary and indirect indices of change, such as the child/women ratio and the ratio of children to the population as a whole, which compare respectively to the general rate of fertility and to the gross birthrate.

The child/women ratio is obtained by dividing the number of children aged 0 to 4 years old by that of the female population aged 15 to 44. We decided to use this measure since it only requires the breakdown of the population by age, sex and ethnic group, and is less affected than the child-population ratio by variations in the age structure of the different groups.

TABLE 3

Evolution of the Child-women Ratio,[1] by Ethnic Group, Quebec, 1931 to 1981

Ethnic Group	1931	1941	1951	1961	1971	1981
French	117.3	95.9	122.1	123.5	91.1	59.9
British	69.4	58.2	91.9	100.9	64.3	44.9
Italian	131.5	70.3	80.6	120.0	88.6	43.4
Jewish	51.5	48.1	88.7	77.0	58.2	56.2
Greek	n.a.	76.2	n.a.	n.a.	n.a.	70.0
German	71.0	74.0	87.4	85.9	57.7	23.8
Haitian	n.a.	n.a.	n.a.	n.a.	n.a.	53.0[2]
Portuguese	n.a.	n.a.	n.a.	n.a.	n.a.	64.9
Polish	82.3	57.0	80.7	89.6	46.0	31.5
Chinese	217.7	146.2	114.1	n.a.	n.a.	58.1
Ukrainian	84.4	55.0	73.2	88.11	47.2	28.1
Inuit	119.9	100.5	136.3	182.4	211.2	150.7
All of Quebec	107.5	88.8	116.3	119.2	70.2	58.8

Sources: Census of Canada, 1931, 1941, 1951, 1961, 1971 and 1981. Choinière and Robitaille, 1988.

Notes: [1] Ratio calculated per 1,000 women, divided by 5, to be comparable to the overall rate of general fertility.

[2] Ratio calculated based on sample tapes from the 1981 Census.

In general, the fertility rate for different ethnic groups appears to have followed the same pattern. There was a decrease between 1931 and 1941, which corresponded to the economic crisis, followed by an increase between 1941 and

1961, which was linked to the post-war baby-boom, which was then followed by another decrease between 1961 and the present.

However, despite the increase in fertility observed between 1941 and 1961, in most ethnic groups the percentage of people over 65 continued to increase. The increase in fertility was apparently not sufficient to increase the relative proportion of younger generations and, therefore, to decrease that of the older ones.

Only the Germans and Italians — between 1951 and 1961 — and the Inuit — between 1931 and 1951 — show a decrease in the percentage of people aged 65 and over. Immigration may have had a major impact on this decrease for the German and Italian groups. For the Inuit, the variations observed between 1931 and 1951 may have been caused by a distinct under-enumeration of young children in the 1931 Census, compared to the rest of the population. The very low level of the aging index is thus due primarily to the strong Inuit rate of fertility. The other factor that played a role in making the Inuit population younger was a decrease in infant mortality.

The recent decrease in fertility seems to have accelerated the aging of the different ethnic groups. The values obtained for the German, Ukrainian and Polish groups in the 1981 Census seem very low, and could also reflect ethnic mobility. In the 1981 Census the young children would have been attributed an origin other than that of their parents or parent of German origin. This phenomenon could also come into play in the calculation of the child-women ratio for other ethnic groups. It appears that ethnic mobility has an aging effect on the groups who lose members and results in a younger age structure for those who gain members.

The high indexes observed for the Chinese in the first censuses are due to the age and sex structure particular to that population at that time. We thus find a population that is primarily male and adult, which implies a female population in which the proportion of married women would be particularly high.

In 1981, with the exception of the Inuit, no group shows a higher ratio than the one observed for Quebec as a whole in 1971. Even the very young groups, such as the Haitians, the Portuguese and the Greeks, usually show relatively low values compared to those for most of the other groups in preceding censuses.

The evolving fertility rate does not in and of itself explain ethnic group aging. An examination of migration will perhaps allow us to provide an additional explanation for this phenomenon.

Migration

It is possible, using the different censuses, to determine the breakdown of the immigrant population by period of immigration to Canada. If we assume that the proportion of international immigrants coming from other provinces is negligible, we can then locate the main arrival periods for the different ethnic groups in Quebec. Though this method does not allow us to directly measure the volume of immigration, we nonetheless obtain a picture of the importance of migration in the evolution of ethnic groups. For the French and British groups, given the strength of their numbers, immigration has a negligible effect on the growth of their populations. They will therefore not be included in Table 4.

Table 4 shows disparities among the ethnic groups with regard to the period of arrival in Quebec and the importance of immigration.

The Italians arrived predominantly between 1951 and 1971. The Jewish migration occurred in two separate periods: the first wave, from 1901 to 1921, corresponded to the Jews coming from the U.S.S.R., fleeing the pogroms; the second wave, between 1946 and 1961, was due to the upheaval caused by World War II.

TABLE 4

Relative Weight (%) of Immigrants in Overall Population, by Period of Immigration and Ethnic Group, Quebec, 1931 to 1981

Periods	Italian	Jewish	Greek	German	Haitian[1]	Portuguese	Polish	Chinese	Ukrainian
1931 Census									
Before 1901	3.3	4.2		4.3			0.8		0.2
1901-10	12.2	16.5		4.5			7.6		7.6
1911-20	15.1	14.1		5.7			13.3		17.1
1921-25	6.0	9.6		5.4			5.7		6.9
1926-31	5.6	11.0		29.5			39.7		33.5
% Immigrants	42.0	55.4		49.4			67.1		65.3
% Non-immigrants	58.0	44.6		50.6			32.9		34.7
Total	100.0	100.0		100.0			100.0		100.0
1941 Census									
Before 1931	32.8	43.1		31.9			45.1	79.3	46.2
1931-35	1.3	2.2		4.2			4.9	1.8	3.8
1936-41	1.0	2.8		4.4			3.7	1.0	2.5
% Immigrants	35.0	48.2		40.5			53.6	82.0	52.3
% Non-immigrants	65.0	51.8		59.5			46.4	18.0	47.7
Total	100.0	100.0		100.0			100.0		100.0
1951 Census									
Before 1941	23.4	27.8		20.4			23.1		27.7
1941-45	0.5	0.8		1.4			2.2		0.5
1946-51	13.7	11.8		13.4			32.1		21.4
% Immigrants	37.5	43.6		40.8			62.1		53.7
% Non-immigrants	62.5	56.4		49.2			37.9		46.3
Total	100.0	100.0		100.0			100.0		100.0
1961 Census									
Before 1951	9.7	27.4		11.4			34.1		30.2
1951-55	20.6	7.7		24.2			15.8		12.0
1956-61	31.0	8.0		21.9			8.9		2.7
% Immigrants	61.4	43.2		57.4			58.7		44.9
% Non-immigrants	38.6	56.8		42.6			41.3		45.1
Total	100.0	100.0		100.0			100.0		100.0

TABLE 4 (Cont'd.)

Periods	Italian	Jewish	Greek	German	Haitian[1]	Portuguese	Polish	Chinese	Ukrainian
1971 Census									
Before 1961	33.3	29.1		30.8			39.5		34.6
1961-65	11.1	4.3		3.9			5.3		1.0
1966-71	10.0	6.3		6.9			5.0		1.0
% Immigrants	54.4	39.7		41.6			49.7		36.6
% Non-immigrants	45.6	60.3		58.4			50.3		63.4
Total	100.0	100.0		100.0			100.0		100.0
1981 Census									
Before 1955	12.7	18.1	4.8	20.2	0.5	2.2	31.5	5.9	32.1
1955-64	25.4	6.3	24.7	15.5	1.9	16.4	11.1	3.1	3.1
1965-69	10.5	5.3	15.1	5.0	7.1	19.4	5.2	12.1	0.9
1970-74	3.2	3.4	10.0	2.5	31.5	24.2	3.7	13.3	0.6
1975-81	2.2	4.9	6.2	4.0	45.4	14.5	4.7	34.2	0.8
% Immigrants	54.0	37.9	59.8	47.2	86.3	75.7	56.2	73.7	37.5
% Non-immigrants	46.0	62.1	40.2	52.8	13.7	24.3	43.8	26.3	63.5
Total	100.0	100.0	100.0	100.0	100.0	100.0	100.0	100.0	100.0

Sources: Census of Canada, 1931, 1941, 1951, 1961, 1971 and 1981.

[1] Percentages calculated based on sample tapes from the 1981 Census.

The arrival of individuals of Greek origin was concentrated during the period 1955-69; before then, there were few Greek immigrants in Quebec. The migration of the Germans corresponds to the 1951-61 period and, to a lesser degree, between 1926 and 1931.

The Haitians are recent immigrants. The vast majority arrived in Quebec after 1970. The Portuguese came to Quebec at the end of the 1950s through to the mid-1970s.

Both the Poles and the Ukrainians, like the Jews, migrated to Quebec during two very distinct periods, first between 1926 and 1931, then between 1946 and 1955. If we exclude the low levels of immigration before 1931, the migration of the Chinese started in 1965 and increased during the 70s and early 80s with the arrival of "boat people" immigrants from Indochina.

Between 1951 and 1961, immigration was particularly important for the Italians and the Germans, since the proportion of immigrants in the total population increased significantly. Also, for these two groups, there was a decrease in the relative proportion of people aged 65 and over during this period (Table 2).

Given the younger age structure of the immigrants compared to the host population, the effect of extensive immigration would be to slow down the aging of the population. As is shown in Table 5, and since knowing the breakdown by age of the immigrants admitted to Canada with Quebec as their destination, the immigrant age structure has varied little over time and is younger than that of all ethnic groups included in the study, with the exception of the Inuit.

TABLE 5

Relative Weight (%) of Immigrants Admitted to Canada with Quebec as Their Destination, by Age, from 1958 to 1980, and Ethnic Groups by Age, Quebec, 1981

Periods	0-14 years	15-29 years	30-44 years	45-64 years	65 years +	Total
Immigrants admitted to Canada with Quebec as their destination						
1958-60	20.1	45.9	21.7	10.4	1.9	100.0
1961-65	21.3	44.9	22.7	8.8	2.3	100.0
1966-70	20.1	48.5	21.5	7.6	2.3	100.0
1971-75	20.9	47.0	20.9	8.0	3.1	100.0
1976-80	23.9	40.5	19.4	11.7	4.5	100.0
Ethnic Group 1981 Census						
French	22.2	29.5	21.5	19.0	7.7	100.0
British	17.3	26.4	20.6	22.6	13.1	100.0
Italian	19.5	26.4	21.6	24.7	7.8	100.0
Jewish	16.7	21.6	18.5	24.2	18.9	100.0
Greek	27.4	23.1	24.7	20.4	4.4	100.0
German	10.9	25.0	24.2	29.5	10.4	100.0
Haitian[1]	23.5	30.4	34.7	8.1	3.3	100.0
Portuguese	25.6	28.0	24.5	17.9	4.0	100.0
Polish	9.9	22.4	20.1	30.5	17.1	100.0
Chinese	23.5	31.3	22.0	16.7	6.5	100.0
Ukrainian	7.3	21.1	18.6	33.0	19.9	100.0
Inuit	45.8	28.2	13.0	10.6	2.5	100.0
All of Quebec	21.9	28.9	21.5	19.4	8.3	100.0

Sources: Employment and Immigration Canada, Immigration Statistics, 1958 to 1980. Census of Canada, 1981.
Note: [1] Percentages obtained from sample tapes from the 1981 Census.

Nearly 65 percent of immigrants are under 30 years old when they arrive. By comparison, in the youngest ethnic groups, except for the Inuit, about 54 percent of the population is under 30.

Assuming that the distribution of immigrants by age does not vary greatly among ethnic groups, one would conclude that immigration had a negative effect on aging.

There is, however, a phenomenon that acts in the opposite direction: emigration. If immigration characteristically recruits a young population, the same can be said of emigration. Unfortunately, given the sources available to us, it is not possible for us to study this phenomenon. However, it seems reasonable to believe that in cases where the migratory balance is negative, migration would have a positive role to play in population aging.

The available sources do not give us enough information to determine the migratory balances of the different ethnic groups. We can however calculate the balances of linguistic groups for the 1976-1981 period. The French-speaking group shows a slightly negative balance, the English-speaking group a very negative balance, and the group of people speaking languages other than French and English a clearly positive balance (Tremblay, 1983).

This information leads us to believe that the British and older immigration groups, whose main mother tongue is often English, would show a trend towards emigration similar to that of Anglophones as a whole, whose total migratory result is negative. Migration would thus accelerate the process of aging in these groups. The Jewish, Ukrainian, Polish and German groups are all in this situation. On the other hand, ethnic groups whose main period of immigration is more recent, and of whom only a small proportion use English or French (Haitian, Chinese, Portuguese) would have positive migratory balances and migration would play a negative role in the aging of their populations.

If we are to judge by the rates of migratory increase obtained by Tremblay for Francophones, migration has had little impact on population aging for individuals of French origin.

Ethnic Mobility

Another phenomenon that affects the aging of ethnic groups is ethnic mobility. An ethnic group loses members because they move from one ethnic group into another. This change in allegiance can be accomplished in the life of one individual — intragenerational mobility — when this individual declares a different origin in two censuses. But ethnic mobility can also occur from one generation to the next — intergenerational mobility — when the children declare a different origin than that of their father or mother. In this case, mobility causes aging in the ethnic groups who lose members, by decreasing the relative weight of the numbers of young people in relation to the older ones. The opposite phenomenon occurs for the groups who gain members.

One of the main causes of ethnic mobility is probably exogamy, which implies that in the census the children would be attributed the origin of one of their parents and not the other. Ethnic mobility can also arise inside endogamous couples if an origin is declared for the children that is different from that of both parents.

It is not possible to study intragenerational mobility directly through census data. We cannot follow, from census to census, the changes in an individual's declaration of origin. And when it comes to comparing the ethnic origin of children to that of their parents (intergenerational mobility), this can only be done using special tables that are not presently available to us.

The study of linguistic mobility, however, can give us some idea of the importance of ethnic mobility in the evolution and aging of ethnic groups. We can assume that the progressive abandon of the mother tongue in favour of a different home language would represent an important stage in changing an individual's allegiance to a given origin. The breakdown of ethnic groups by mother tongue and home language will thus give us a picture of the linguistic assimilation of the two main cultural communities in Quebec.

In Table 6, we notice first of all that for the Inuit, Greeks, Portuguese, Italians and Chinese, a high percentage of individuals speak other mother tongues. On the other hand, less than 50 percent of Jews, Germans and Haitians possess a mother tongue other than English or French. The importance of the French language as a mother tongue for the Haitians is no doubt explained by the fact that a large number of respondents in this group associated Creole with French.

For the two dominant ethnic groups, the French and British, there is a certain difference in the percentage of individuals who claim the vernacular as their mother tongue. Almost all those of French origin (98 percent) have French as their mother tongue, while only 80 percent of British immigrants have English as their mother tongue.

When we compare the ethnic groups' mother tongues to the home language, we note an increase in the abandon of the vernacular in favour of English. Among the Jews, Germans, Ukrainians and Poles, more than 50 percent of their members use English as the home language. Only the Portuguese and the Haitians favour French. These last two groups spoke French before they arrived

TABLE 6

Breakdown (%) of Ethnic Groups by Mother Tongue and Home Language, Quebec, 1981

Ethnic Group	Mother tongue			Home language			Total[1]
	English	French	Other	English	French	Other	
French	1.6	98.2	0.2	2.3	97.6	0.1	100.0
British	80.4	18.2	1.3	78.9	20.5	0.6	100.0
Italian	11.2	10.4	78.4	23.2	17.1	59.7	100.0
Jewish	63.8	9.7	26.5	78.6	9.9	11.5	100.0
Greek	10.7	2.7	86.7	21.7	3.5	74.8	100.0
German	24.8	27.2	48.0	50.7	31.2	18.1	100.0
Haitian[2]	2.2	79.4	18.4	3.2	75.1	21.7	100.0
Portuguese	5.6	9.1	85.3	11.5	16.7	71.7	100.0
Polish	26.7	7.9	65.4	49.7	13.6	36.6	100.0
Chinese	18.2	4.8	77.1	29.3	5.5	65.3	100.0
Ukrainian	27.7	6.2	66.1	51.1	11.3	37.5	100.0
Inuit[3]	1.8	0.2	98.1	2.1	0.2	97.7	100.0
Total	10.9	82.4	6.7	12.7	82.5	4.8	100.0

Sources: Census of Canada, 1981.

Notes: [1] Due to the rounding of percentages, the sums do not always total 100.0
     [2] Individuals born in Haiti.
     [3] Data taken from 1981 Census special tables.

in Quebec, so this is not linguistic assimilation toward French. We note also that for the French, British and Haitian ethnic groups, the breakdown by mother tongue is about equivalent to that by home language.

Table 7 shows the rates of stability and linguistic mobility for the various groups, from the point of intersection of the mother tongue and language of use. The stability rates are weakest for the Poles, Germans and Ukrainians and highest for the Inuit, French and British. The Jewish population has a relatively high rate of stability since a great majority already have English as a mother tongue.

TABLE 7

Rates of Stability and Linguistic Mobility by Ethnic Group, Quebec, 1981

Ethnic Group	Rate of Linguistic Stability[1]	Rate of Linguistic Mobility			Total
		Towards English[2]	Towards French[3]	Towards Other Languages[4]	
French	97.2	1.6	1.1	0.1	100.0
British	93.4	2.5	4.0	0.1	100.0
Italian	72.6	15.2	8.9	3.4	100.0
Jewish	78.8	16.4	2.3	2.5	100.0
Greek	79.8	14.1	2.1	4.1	100.0
German	65.9	27.9	5.2	1.0	100.0
Haitian[1]	76.2	2.3	9.4	12.1	100.0
Portuguese	76.9	7.6	10.8	4.7	100.0
Polish	64.2	25.9	6.9	3.0	100.0
Chinese	75.1	15.2	2.7	7.0	100.0
Ukrainian	66.3	26.0	6.0	1.7	100.0
Inuit[2]	98.0	1.0	—	0.9	100.0
Total	94.2	3.3	2.0	0.5	100.0

Source: Census of Canada, 1981.
Special 1981 Census table.

Notes: [1] Home language is the same as the mother tongue.
[2] Home language is English and the mother tongue is different from home language.
[3] Home language is French and the mother tongue is different from the home language.
[4] Home language is neither French nor English and the mother tongue is different from the home language.

The linguistic characteristics of the different groups lead us to believe that ethnic mobility could be important for the Germans, Ukrainians, Poles and Jews.

In Table 8, the breakdown of ethnic groups by home language and age shows that, in general, linguistic assimilation is stronger for individuals under 40 years old. The percentages of "other" home languages are not as high for groups

TABLE 8

Breakdown (%) of Ethnic Groups by Language of Use, for Different Age Groups, Quebec, 1981

Ethnic Group	0-19 years			20-39 years			40-59 years			60 years and over			Total
	Eng.	Fr.	Oth.	Eng.	Fr.	Oth.	Eng.	Fr.	Oth.	Eng.	Fr.	Oth.	
French	1.9	98.0	0.1	2.3	97.6	0.1	2.8	97.1	0.1	2.7	97.2	0.1	100.0
British	79.8	19.4	0.8	69.8	29.5	0.7	80.0	19.6	0.4	87.1	12.6	0.3	100.0
Italian	32.5	12.4	55.1	30.5	21.2	48.3	9.0	16.3	74.7	10.8	15.3	73.9	100.0
Jewish	78.2	15.1	6.7	80.2	13.6	6.2	75.3	13.8	10.9	73.5	6.7	19.8	100.0
Greek	32.5	3.9	63.6	17.9	3.3	78.8	16.3	4.5	79.3	15.0	6.7	78.3	100.0
German	54.6	33.8	11.6	44.7	48.5	6.8	56.7	24.3	19.0	49.6	17.3	33.1	100.0
Haitian	0.7	91.3	8.0	3.1	76.6	20.3	4.2	83.3	12.5	0.0	75.0	25.0	100.0
Portuguese	18.7	16.4	64.9	11.9	16.9	71.2	2.4	12.0	85.6	2.9	2.9	94.2	100.0
Polish	63.6	5.5	30.9	65.3	20.3	14.4	41.2	21.1	27.2	34.4	4.2	61.4	100.0
Chinese	38.5	3.3	58.2	32.6	7.6	59.8	17.9	4.5	77.6	5.7	2.9	91.4	100.0
Ukrainian	61.1	13.9	25.0	63.7	6.6	29.7	58.2	11.9	29.9	28.9	4.8	66.3	100.0
Total	12.1	83.7	4.3	11.7	84.2	4.1	13.1	80.8	6.1	17.2	77.0	5.8	100.0

Source: Sample tapes from the 1981 Census.

aged 0 to 19 years and 20 to 39 years as they are for those aged 40 to 59 and 60 and over.

The data in Table 8 come from the sample tapes from the 1981 Census, for 1/50th of the total population. The numbers in this table for the numerically less important groups are therefore small, so we can only draw general conclusions.

As with linguistic mobility, it appears that ethnic mobility is also important for individuals under age 40. So ethnic mobility, since it mainly affects the younger groups, would tend to accelerate the aging process of the groups that are most affected by it.

Ethnic mobility, like migration, does not operate in one direction only. Certain ethnic groups increase their numbers through this phenomenon. Judging by Tables 6 and 7, and based once again on the linguistic characteristics of ethnic groups, it would appear that ethnic mobility benefits the British, has no effect on the French and is unfavourable for other ethnic groups, in particular the Germans, Ukrainians, Poles and the Jews.

A final measure — the proportion of exogamous unions — will give us a more precise image of ethnic mobility. In the various censuses, the children of such couples must often declare the origin of one parent and not the other. This was particularly true before 1981, when only one origin was accepted on the questionnaire, while reference was made to the origin or language spoken by the first paternal ancestor upon arrival in America. Starting with the 1981 Census, it was no longer necessary to select one ancestor over the other in determining origin and it was possible to indicate more than one origin.

Marriage data based on spousal origin are available from the published data for the 1951 and 1961 censuses and the sample tapes from the 1981 Census. Since the sample for the 1981 Census is small, we can only speculate about general trends.

Exogamy seems very high for the Germans, Ukrainians, Poles and British. In 1981, more than 75 percent of Germans married a person of another origin. In 1961 this percentage was a little under 50 percent (Table 9).

The difference between the sexes observed, in particular, for the Italians, Germans and Poles can no doubt be explained by an imbalance in the matrimonial market inside these groups, where there are more men than women.

The French, Jewish, Chinese and Inuit groups have low percentages of exogamous marriages. For the first group this situation is explained by the high numbers involved; the possibilities of finding a spouse from the same ethnic group are good. With regard to the Jews, one of the main characteristics of this group is adherence to the Jewish religion. Judaism does not proselytize but rather encourages marriage with other Jews. The Chinese are an old ethnicity with a fairly recent presence in Quebec, and for the most part their marriages have been made before arrival in Quebec. Finally, the Inuit, due to their geographic isolation, have fewer possibilities for exogamous marriages.

TABLE 9

Relative Weight (%) of Exogamous Marriages, by Ethnic Group, Quebec, 1951, 1961 and 1981

Ethnic Group	1951		1961		1981	
	Men	Women	Men	Women	Men	Women
French	3.5	4.6	3.6	5.2	4.8	6.2
British	22.0	20.3	26.3	24.0	43.1	43.2
Italian	n.a.	n.a.	23.5	13.3	27.5	12.2
Jewish	5.1	3.4	7.1	5.7	4.5	4.1
Greek	n.a.	n.a.	n.a.	n.a.	n.a.	n.a.
German	66.6	60.8	47.9	47.5	72.8	62.7
Haitian	n.a.	n.a.	n.a.	n.a.	n.a.	n.a.
Portuguese	n.a.	n.a.	n.a.	n.a.	n.a.	n.a.
Polish	36.6	29.8	42.1	32.6	57.8	25.0
Chinese	n.a.	n.a.	n.a.	n.a.	0.0	0.0
Ukrainian	28.3	27.1	40.8	34.7	51.4	61.4
Inuit	n.a.	n.a.	n.a.	n.a.	2.4	5.9

Sources: Census of Canada, 1951 and 1961
Sample tapes from the 1981 Census
Register of the Inuit Population of New Quebec

Exogamy could also play a role in the aging of the British, German, Polish and Ukrainian groups. The difficulty would be to determine which group is favoured by these exogamous marriages. For example, in the case of a marriage between a woman of German origin and a man of British origin, what origin would one attribute to the children? Does the origin of the father overrule that of the mother or is it the origin of the group with the most influence that should determine the children's origin? Does the home language have an important influence?

It seems reasonable to think that the British group, due to its social and economic influence, would benefit from marriages that combine two different origins, while the German, Polish and Ukrainian groups would be disadvantaged.

According to the data presented in Table 9, the Jews, though strongly assimilated into the English language, would be very little affected by ethnic mobility.

Discussion

Ethnic groups in Quebec have very different degrees of aging. The ethnic groups can be classified into three categories (Table 10). In the first category, with a very high degree of aging, are the Ukrainians, Jews, Poles, British and Germans: the percentage of individuals aged 65 and over is higher than 10 percent. The Italians, French and Chinese fall into the category of groups whose aging is not yet very high. The third category is made up of the young groups — the Greeks, Portuguese, Haitians and Inuit — where the percentage of individuals aged 65 and over is lower than 5 percent.

Table 10 summarizes the evolution of aging for Quebec ethnic groups, including related demographic phenomena. If we exclude the British, French and Inuit, it appears that the classification of ethnic groups by degree of aging reached in 1981 depends predominantly on the time of major period of immigration. Older immigrant groups have higher proportions of people aged 65 and over while more recent immigrant groups have lower proportions.

Similarly, in censuses done immediately after the major periods of immigration, the groups that have high degrees of aging in 1981 had very low percentages of people aged 65 and over. This is true of the Ukrainian, Jewish and Polish groups in the 1931 Census and the German group in the 1961 Census.

Immigrants are mainly young adults and children. A newly arrived ethnic group, or a group that has a large proportion of recent immigrants, will thus show a younger age structure.

But the earlier the major period of immigration, the more the aging of the groups increase, due to the combined effects of the decrease in fertility and ethnic mobility.

Since 1961, groups have been affected by the decrease in fertility, but to different degrees. It is, however, difficult to determine the role of each demographic phenomenon in the aging of the various ethnic groups. It may however be assumed that for the French and Inuit, for whom migration and ethnic mobility have little effect, the change in fertility is the main factor in aging. The very young age structure of the Inuit comes from the high rate of fertility, while the aging of the population of French origin is due essentially to a decrease in fertility.

For the other groups who are not recent arrivals, it is clear that the decrease in fertility played an important role, as is shown in Table 10. However, the major emigration to other provinces of English-speaking people in the period from 1976-1981 certainly accelerated the aging process of the British as well as other highly anglicized groups, such as the Jews, Germans, Ukrainians and Poles.

Similarly, judging by the data on language and exogamy, ethnic mobility — which like migration appears to recruit relatively young people — plays a role in the aging of the German, Ukrainian and Polish groups. It could, however, have the opposite effect on the British, who would gain members from this phenomenon.

The decrease in fertility seems to be the main factor in the aging of the Italian group. We do not know if the 1976-81 emigration affected this group. Ethnic mobility for the Italians would be relatively low.

From our observations of groups with a high degree of aging, who immigrated early, we can predict a similar evolution for the more recent immigrants — Chinese, Greek, Portuguese and Haitian.

TABLE 10

Summary of Phenomena Related to Aging of Ethnic Groups in Quebec

Ethnic Group	% of those aged 65 and over			Child/women ratio			Main period of immigration	% of English or French language of use 1981	% of exogamous marriages 1981	
	1931	1961	1981	1941	1961	1981			Men	Women
Groups with a high degree of aging										
Ukrainian	0.3	5.8	19.9	84.4	88.1	28.1	1926-31, 1946-55	62.5	51.4	61.4
Jewish	2.5	8.0	18.9	51.5	77.0	56.2	1901-21, 1946-61	88.5	4.5	4.1
Polish	0.8	4.8	17.1	82.3	89.6	31.5	1926-31, 1946-55	63.4	57.8	225.0
British	6.2	9.7	13.1	69.4	91.9	44.9	does not apply	20.5¹	43.1	43.2
German	4.3	4.0	10.4	71.0	85.9	23.8	1926-31, 1951-61	81.9	72.8	62.7
Groups with a middle degree of aging										
Italian	2.0	3.4	7.8	131.5	120.0	43.4	1951-71	40.3	27.5	12.2
French	4.7	5.4	7.7	117.3	123.5	59.9	does not apply	2.3²	4.8	6.2
Chinese	0.8	n.a.	6.5	217.7	n.a.	58.1	after 1965	34.7	0.0	0.0
Groups with a low degree of aging										
Greek	n.a.	n.a.	4.4	n.a.	n.a.	70.0	1955-69	25.2	n.a.	n.a.
Portuguese	n.a.	n.a.	4.0	n.a.	n.a.	64.9	after 1955	28.3	n.a.	n.a.
Haitian	n.a.	n.a.	4.0	n.a.	n.a.	53.0	after1970	78.3	n.a.	n.a.
Inuit	4.1	1.6	2.5	119.9	182.4	150.7	does not apply	2.3	2.4	5.9

Sources: Tables 2,3,4, 6 and 9.

Notes: ¹ Percentage of French home language.
      ² Percentage of English home language.
      n.a. not available

Once the number of immigrants starts to drop, immigration is no longer sufficient to maintain a low percentage of individuals aged 65 and over, when combined with the decrease in fertility and ethnic mobility. As the main period of immigration recedes, assimilation into the French group, or more often the English group, increases. Ultimately, this could lead to a change in cultural identity. However these changes are slow and can require more than a generation before being completed. They are not very apparent in the short term.

We have seen in this study that changes in demographic phenomena — the decrease in fertility, immigration and ethnic mobility — have resulted in the aging of various ethnic groups. These changes are in turn related to the social, economic and hygienic conditions of these groups. It would be interesting to examine the conditions that, through the intermediary of demographic phenomena, result in the aging of ethnic groups.

We have noted that for Quebec as a whole the aging of the population and the decrease in fertility have occurred simultaneously with an improvement in social and economic conditions: higher incomes, an increase in life expectancy and more schooling (Bourbeau 1983; Bureau de la Statistique du Québec 1986; Duchesne and Lavoie 1975; Dufour and Péron 1979; Mathews 1974; Robitaille, Bourbeau and Trembly 1985; Roy 1974).

It remains to be seen whether the same phenomenon will be observed among ethnic groups in Quebec. The groups with the most evidence of aging would likely be those with the most favourable social and economic conditions.

Notes

1. The life expectancy of the Inuit increased by 95 percent between 1951 and 1981, while that of the overall population in Quebec increased by 14 percent over the same period (Choinière, Levasseur and Robitaille, 1988).

III
IMMIGRANT SOCIOECONOMIC STATUS

15. Immigrant Women: Language, Socioeconomic Inequalities and Policy Issues

Monica Boyd

Introduction

The migration of women represents a significant share of migration flows to Canada during the 20th century. Between the end of World War II and the present, at least four out of ten permanent residents age 15 and older have been female. Since the 1960s the percentages of these permanent residents who are female steadily rose to over 50 percent by the 1970s (Table 1). Although the percentage of elderly among female and male permanent residents is increasing over time (Boyd 1988, 1989), over 90 percent of these "adult" permanent residents are between the ages of 15 and 64 (Table 1, columns 4-9).

The geographical origins of both foreign-born females and males shifted dramatically during the post-war period. These shifts reflect the changed criteria of admissibility which appeared first in the 1962 and 1967 immigration regulations and then in the Immigration Act, 1976. The previous criterion of national origins, which heavily favored the entry of European origin groups was replaced with those of family reunification, labour maket skills and, more recently, refugee status[1]. The removal of national origin restrictions meant increasing numbers of migrants from areas other than the United States, the United Kingdom and Europe. In the 1950s and 1960s, most immigrants came from these source areas; by 1987 only 30 percent were from these areas with the remaining 70 percent from Africa, Asia, the Caribbean and Latin and South America (Boyd and Taylor, 1989). Census data also indicate the changing origin composition of foreign-born men and women over time. Table 2 shows that of the foreign-born age 15 and older who were enumerated in the 1981 Census, the majority immigrating prior to the 1970s came from the United States, the United Kingdom and European regions. But immigrants entering Canada in the 1970s increasingly

TABLE 1

Permanent Residents Entering Canada, Age 15 and Older by Sex and Age Groups, 1946-1985

| | Total 15 plus | | Age 15 plus Females as a Percentage of Total | Age Distribution | | | | | |
| | Female | Male | | Females | | | Males | | |
	(1)	(2)	(3)	Total (4)	15-64 (5)	65+ (6)	Total (7)	15-64 (8)	65+ (9)
1946-1950	174,385	167,500	51.0	100.0	97.8	2.2	100.0	98.6	1.4
1951-1955	265,860	351,896	43.0	100.0	97.7	2.3	100.0	98.9	1.1
1956-1960	290,273	314,920	48.0	100.0	97.2	2.8	100.0	98.6	1.4
1961-1965	199,479	182,073	52.3	100.0	95.6	4.5	100.0	97.8	2.2
1966-1970	346,731	356,163	49.3	100.0	96.2	3.8	100.0	97.8	2.2
1971-1975	318,938	317,040	50.1	100.0	95.0	5.0	100.0	96.9	3.1
1976-1980	243,489	221,544	52.4	100.0	92.2	7.8	100.0	93.9	6.1
1981-1985	218,989	195,246	52.9	100.0	91.2	8.8	100.0	92.7	7.3

Source: For 1946-1960: Parai (1965-Table A3). For 1961-1984: Employment and Immigration Canada, *Immigration Statistics*, annual reports. For 1985, unpublished tabulations, Research Division, Immigration, Employment and Immigration Canada, January 14, 1988.

TABLE 2

Country/Region of Birth for the Foreign-born[1] Population Age 15 and Over by Sex and by Period of Immigration, Canada 1981

	Total	<1946	1946-1955	1956-1965	1966-1970	1971-1975	1976-1981[2]
Female	100.0	100.0	100.0	100.0	100.0	100.0	100.0
U.S.A	8.3	20.0	3.1	5.0	7.4	8.2	8.2
U.K.	24.7	44.3	29.6	22.2	20.9	13.2	12.9
Western Europe[3]	11.5	4.4	26.5	15.8	6.8	3.6	4.3
South Europe[4]	15.4	2.1	13.3	29.8	21.6	12.8	5.8
East Europe, U.S.S.R.[5]	12.5	21.4	19.0	11.0	9.2	5.3	4.9
Other Europe	4.0	5.9	4.6	4.4	3.2	2.2	2.7
Asia	13.0	1.1	2.2	5.6	14.6	28.6	39.8
Africa	2.4	0.2	0.2	1.8	3.6	6.1	4.6
South America, Caribbean	7.3	0.6	1.1	3.7	11.4	18.3	15.0
Other[6]	0.9	0.2	0.4	0.7	1.5	1.6	1.7
Male	100.0	100.0	100.0	100.0	100.0	100.0	100.0
U.S.A.	6.7	16.7	2.2	4.0	7.4	7.4	5.7
U.K.	21.9	40.2	21.1	22.1	20.2	13.3	13.5
Western Europe[3]	12.2	5.8	26.8	14.7	7.4	3.8	4.6
South Europe[4]	17.6	2.9	17.3	31.7	22.0	14.1	6.6
East Europe, U.S.S.R.[5]	13.6	23.3	22.6	12.2	9.2	4.3	4.8
Other Europe	4.6	8.0	5.4	4.7	3.0	2.5	3.8
Asia	13.5	2.1	3.3	5.4	15.3	29.6	41.3
Africa	2.7	0.2	0.3	1.9	3.9	6.6	5.7
South America, Caribbean	6.3	0.6	0.8	2.7	9.8	16.6	13.2
Other[6]	1.0	0.3	0.4	0.7	1.7	1.8	1.6

[1] Excludes persons born outside Canada but who are Canadian citizens by birth.
[2] First five months of 1981.
[3] Persons born in Belgium, Luxembourg, France, German Democratic Republic, Federal Republic of Germany, Netherlands, Austria.
[4] Persons born in Greece, Italy and Portugal.
[5] Persons born in Czechoslovakia, Hungary, Poland and the U.S.S.R.
[6] Persons born in Australia, Oceania and countries not included in other regions captured above.

Source: Statistics Canada. 1981 Census of Canada. Public Use Sample Tape of Individuals, full count.

came from other areas, particularly Asia, Central and South America and the Caribbean.

The sizeable presence of women in immigration flows and their changing geographical origins has increased interest in the socioeconomic position of foreign-born women, vis à vis Canadian-born women and vis à vis foreign-born men. Two dominant factors underlying this interest are the concern over inequalities associated with ethnicity/birthplace and the recognition of extensive sexual inequality in Canada. Adult immigrants generally bring with them the imprint of their former society. Thus immigrants from different regions that are characterized by differences in educational systems (type, coverage and level), and in economic structure (agrarian or nonagrarian) can be expected to vary with respect to education and labour market skills. However, their experiences in Canada are conditioned not just by the characteristics associated with a region of origin but also by the economic and social conditions in Canada. The demand for certain kinds of labour and not for others, and the existence or nonexistence of ethnic/birthplace stereotypes are formidable forces which can differentiate the experiences of people with similar outlooks and labour market skills.

To summarize, socioeconomic inequalities between groups can reflect both supply and demand side factors. Which is more important has enormous implications for immigrant integration and for analysis and formulation of social policy.[2] Understandably, a growing body of research now exists which has one or more objectives: to document socioeconomic inequalities by birthplace and ethnicity, to assess various explanations for such inequalities, and/or to develop various models of Canada's stratification system and the position of immigrants in that system (for examples see: Beaujot, Basavarajappa, and Verma 1988; Rao, Richmond and Zubrzycki 1984; Richmond and Verma 1978).

Sexual inequality is another dimension of inequality in Canada. Women's responsibilities in the home often are not accorded the same importance as paid labour. Often they cause women to either curtail labour force participation or to experience the double day/double burden syndrome that results from the combination of domestic and paid labour. In the labour force, women as a group earn less than two thirds the earnings of men, and they concentrate in different industries and occupations than men. For example, in the early 1980s, over three fourths of all female employees in the labour force worked in five occupational groups—clerical, service, sales, medicine, health and teaching compared to one-third of the employed males. Less than 20 percent of women were employed in primary industries or in manufacturing or construction industries compared to nearly 40 percent of the employed men (Statistics Canada 1985: Tables 5 and 6).

Sexual inequalities combine with ethnic/country of origin inequalities to create disadvantages for immigrant women. Labour force participation in an economy characterized by sex segregated occupational and industrial structures and by unequal pay for work of equal value means that foreign-born women, like

Canadian-born women, are likely to have lower incomes and different sites of employment compared to foreign-born men. But, inequalities associated with country of origin also mean that foreign-born women may earn less or hold different jobs than do Canadian-born women. These inequalities characterize certain birthplace groups more than others, leading to the observation that foreign-born women are triply disadvantaged by their status as female, as foreign-born and by their origins or race. As a result, certain groups of foreign-born women may be at the bottom of the socioeconomic hierarchy, at least compared to native-born women and their foreign-born male counterparts (Boyd 1975; 1985; 1986).

Analyses of census and survey data confirm the disadvantaged socioeconomic positions of immigrant women, particularly those who are recent arrivals or who are from Asian and Southern European countries (Beaujot 1986; Beaujot, Basavarajappa and Verma 1988; Boyd 1985; 1986; 1987; McLaughlin, 1985; Ornstein 1983; Ornstein and Sharma 1983; Rao, Richmond and Zubrzycki 1984; Richmond 1981; Richmond and Kalbach 1984; Samuel and Woloski 1985). These analyses are reviewed elsewhere (Boyd 1987; Boyd and Taylor 1989) but in general they show that lower education, higher unemployment rates, concentration in service and processing occupations and lower earnings are more likely to characterize foreign-born women who are recent arrivals or who are from selected Third World countries compared to Canadian-born women and foreign-born males.

Research also shows the disadvantaged position of foreign-born women with respect to knowing English and/or French. In 1981, only 6 percent of the foreign-born age 15 and older indicated that they did not know English or French well enough to carry on a conversation (Beaujot, Basavarajappa and Verma 1988). But this figure hides differences by length of residency, birthplace and sex. Recently arrived immigrant groups are the least likely to know English or French well enough to carry on a conversation with percentages ranging from nearly 10 percent to over 20 percent for persons born in Southern European and Asian countries (Beaujot, Basavarajappa and Verma 1988: Figure 10). Foreign-born females enumerated in the 1981 Census are twice as likely as foreign-born males not to know one or both of the official languages (Boyd 1987: Table 13).

Knowing the language of the host society is important for accessing information about employment opportunities and for performing most jobs. However, most Canadian research assumes a link between language knowledge and the socioeconomic positions of immigrants. Knowing one or both of the official languages is assumed to mean lower unemployment, a higher position in the occupational structure and higher income compared to not knowing an official language. In this paper, the association is explicitly documented. Since foreign-born women are less likely to know English or French and more likely to experience socioeconomic disadvantage, emphasis is placed on the correlates of language knowledge for immigrant women. The following section presents data on the language characteristics of Canadian-born and foreign-born women and men. Following a discussion of these data, policy issues that emerge from the association between language ability and labour market position of these women are reviewed.

Language Knowledge and Socioeconomic Inequalities

The extent of language familiarity and fluency of the resident foreign-born population can be examined from several questions in the 1981 Census. These questions requested information on mother tongue, language spoken in the home, and ability to converse in French and/or English. Since English and/or French are the predominant languages of the workplace, this paper analyses responses to the latter question on the ability to converse in French or English.[3]

Since 1971, Statistics Canada has released representative samples of individual records in the form of Public Use Sample Tapes (PUST). The 1981 PUST of individuals is based on a 1-in-50 sample of the population answering the long form. It is used in this paper to construct information on the language ability of the foreign-born population. The age group 15-64 is examined because this group is most likely to be in the labour force where language knowledge is expected to be strongly correlated with socioeconomic status.

As shown in Table 3, not knowing one or both of the two official languages is highest for recent arrivals, and for persons born in Asia and the Southern European countries of Greece, Italy and Portugal. In many instances, foreign-born women are more than twice as likely as their male counterparts not to know an official language well enough to carry on a conversation. These sex differences in language ability most likely reflect sex differences in the opportunities to learn languages in area of origin, the existence of institutionally complete communities in Canada for numerically large and geographically concentrated birthplace groups (Breton 1968) which reduces the need to gain extensive familiarity with the language of the receiving society, and the difficulties experienced by immigrant women in accessing language training programs. These difficulties are discussed in the subsequent section of the paper.

Immigrants' knowledge of English or French is important for understanding the socioeconomic inequalities which exist among foreign-born women as well as between foreign-born women and Canadian-born women and foreign-born men. Not knowing the language spoken in the workplace and used in social conversations means that many jobs are forfeit. As a result, workers who are not able to converse in English or French may be less likely to find employment. When employed, such workers may be located in ethnically segmented labour markets and/or in menial occupations in which extensive verbal exchanges are not a requirement for doing the work. Such employment conditions usually are characterized by low wages.

Data from the 1981 Census PUST show the association between not knowing English or French and socioeconomic status for persons age 15-64[5] (Table 4).

TABLE 3

Percentage Not Knowing English and/or French[1] by Birthplace, Period of Immigration, of Population Age 15 and Over, and Age Group, Canada 1981

	Percentage Not Knowing English or French[1]					
	Female			Male		
	Total (1)	15-64 (2)	≥65 (3)	Total (4)	15-64 (5)	≥65 (6)
Birthplace						
Native-born	0.1	0.1	0.3	0.1	0.1	0.3
Foreign-born	7.3	6.0	12.8	3.7	3.2	6.4
U.S.A.	0.1	0.1	0.0	0.0	0.0	0.0
U.K.	0.0	0.0	0.0	0.0	0.0	0.0
Western Europe[2]	1.0	0.2	5.8	0.3	0.1	1.8
Southern Europe[3]	22.3	17.6	62.8	11.6	9.0	40.8
East Europe, U.S.S.R.	7.3	3.4	14.7	2.3	1.2	4.7
Other Europe	2.7	1.9	5.0	1.3	1.3	1.2
Asia	18.9	14.7	61.8	8.2	7.0	27.6
Africa	2.8	1.8	17.0	0.5	0.3	5.3
South America, Caribbean	3.1	2.7	9.9	1.8	1.8	3.4
Other	1.8	1.6	7.1	0.0	0.0	0.0
Foreign-born, Year of Immigration						
<1946	1.8	0.5	2.4	0.5	0.1	0.6
1946-1955	3.4	1.5	12.5	1.5	0.7	5.8
1956-1965	7.6	5.2	35.7	3.5	2.4	22.6
1966-1970	8.5	5.6	50.0	3.7	3.0	28.1
1971-1975	9.2	7.2	43.5	4.9	3.9	36.2
1976-1981	17.1	14.8	44.6	10.8	9.4	35.6

[1] Well enough to carry on a conversation.

[2] Includes Belgium and Luxembourg, France, German Democratic Republic, Republic of Germany, Netherlands, Austria.

[3] Includes Greece, Italy and Portugal.

Compared to their Canadian-born counterparts and to the foreign-born who do know English or French, immigrants who do not know English and/or French are older, immigrated to Canada after 1965, are more likely to be born in Southern Europe or Asian countries, or to have lower mean years of schooling. They are characterized by lower rates of participation in the 1981 labour force, by higher unemployment rates, by distinctive occupational and industrial locations and by lower average 1980 weekly earnings.

Foreign-born women who do not know English or French well enough to carry on a conversation are the most socioeconomially disadvantaged group.

As shown in Table 4, foreign-born women not knowing English or French in 1981 have an average of 5.7 years of schooling compared to 6.5 for their foreign-born male counterpart and over 11 years of schooling for all other groupings. Less than half of these women are in the 1981 labour force, and over 20 percent indicate no labour force experience. Although their unemployment rate is lower than the rate for native-born women, it is higher than the rates observed for Canadian-born and foreign-born men and for foreign-born women with a conversational knowledge of English or French. Foreign-born women who cannot converse in English or French are more likely than other women to work longer hours on a weekly basis, to be employed full-time, and to have lower average weekly earnings in 1980 (Table 4).

TABLE 4

Selected Social, Demographic and Economic Characteristics of Ages 15-64, for Foreign-born by Sex and Knowledge of Official Language and for Native-born by Sex, Canada, 1981

	Foreign-born[1] Knows English and/or French well enough to carry on a conversation				Native-born Total[1]	
	Female		Male			
	Yes (1)	No (2)	Yes (3)	No (4)	Female (5)	Male (6)
Total N	26,411	1461	27,457	724	41,729	134,278
Percent Distributions						
Age	100.0	100.0	100.0	100.0	100.0	100.0
15-24	13.8	4.3	13.5	4.4	30.9	31.7
25-34	25.5	14.0	23.6	15.7	25.7	25.9
35-44	24.1	21.4	24.8	20.7	16.6	16.8
45-54	19.4	29.3	21.8	29.7	14.1	13.9
55-64	17.1	31.0	16.2	29.4	12.7	11.7
Mean Age	39.5	46.5	39.8	45.9	34.6	34.1
Year of Arrival	100.0	100.0	100.0	100.0	n.a.	n.a.
<1946	6.2	0.5	5.2	0.3	n.a.	n.a.
1946-1965	21.9	6.1	23.0	6.1	n.a.	n.a.
1966-1970	45.2	47.5	46.0	47.0	n.a.	n.a.
1971-1975	17.3	24.4	17.2	26.2	n.a.	n.a.
1976-1979	9.4	21.6	8.6	20.4	n.a.	n.a.
Birthplace, Foreign-born	100.0	100.0	100.0	100.0	n.a.	n.a.
U.S.A.	7.7	0.1	6.3	–	n.a.	n.a.
U.K.	23.5	0.2	20.3	–	n.a.	n.a.
Western Europe[2]	13.4	0.5	13.4	0.3	n.a.	n.a.
Southern Europe[3]	15.5	58.4	18.7	67.3	n.a.	n.a.

Table 4 (cont'd)

	Foreign-born[1] Knows English and/or French well enough to carry on a conversation				Native-born Total[1]	
	Female		Male			
	Yes (1)	No (2)	Yes (3)	No (4)	Female (5)	Male (6)
East Europe U.S.S.R.[4]	10.8	5.8	11.9	4.0	n.a.	n.a.
Other Europe	3.8	1.2	4.2	1.4	n.a.	n.a.
Asia	12.5	29.1	13.5	23.2	n.a.	n.a.
Africa	2.9	0.8	3.1	0.3	n.a.	n.a.
South America, Caribbean	8.9	3.5	7.4	3.6	n.a.	n.a.
Other[5]	1.1	0.3	1.2	–	n.a.	n.a.
Mean Education[6]	11.6	5.7	12.3	6.5	11.3	11.4
Labour Force Activity 1981, Reference Week[6]	100.0	100.0	100.0	100.0	100.0	100.0
In the labour force	63.7	49.8	90.6	85.6	59.1	84.3
Not in the labour force	36.3	50.2	9.4	14.4	41.9	15.7
Last worked 1981	3.5	2.2	1.9	2.2	3.9	2.6
Last worked 1980	4.3	4.1	1.8	2.3	5.0	3.0
Last worked before 1980	20.7	20.7	2.8	8.4	19.7	3.8
Never in labour force	7.9	23.2	2.9	1.4	13.3	6.3
Labour Force Status, Reference Week[6]	100.0	100.0	100.0	100.0	100.0	100.0
Employed	93.8	92.2	96.2	95.2	90.8	93.0
Unemployed	6.2	7.8	3.8	4.8	9.2	7.0
Occupation, Reference Week[6]	100.0	100.0	100.0	100.0	100.0	100.0
Managerial, Administrative	5.4	1.0	12.2	1.6	5.1	10.7
Other White Collar	18.1	0.9	15.8	1.9	19.4	11.4
Clerical	32.0	3.8	6.1	1.6	36.7	7.4
Sales	8.6	1.8	7.2	2.3	10.0	8.9
Service	17.5	30.0	10.5	24.2	16.4	9.5
Farming, Fishing, Forestry	2.0	4.6	3.9	2.8	2.7	8.9
Processing	2.4	9.8	5.2	10.5	2.3	5.6
Machining and Product Fabrication	10.2	39.9	18.6	17.7	4.0	13.1
Construction	0.4	0.2	11.1	29.9	0.3	10.9
Transport	0.4	0.0	3.6	1.2	0.7	6.7
Other	3.1	8.0	5.8	6.4	2.4	6.9
Industry, Reference Week[6]	100.0	100.0	100.0	100.0	100.0	100.0
Agriculture and Other Primary	2.8	5.1	4.8	1.9	3.7	10.4
Manufacturing	18.5	54.7	28.3	28.5	11.5	21.9

283

TABLE 4 (Cont'd.)

| | *Foreign-born*[1] Knows English and/or French well enough to carry on a conversation | | | | Native-born Total[1] | |
| | Female | | Male | | | |
	Yes (1)	No (2)	Yes (3)	No (4)	Female (5)	Male (6)
Construction	1.6	0.6	11.0	29.0	1.5	9.8
Transportation, Communication, Utilities	3.6	0.5	8.5	1.7	4.9	10.8
Wholesale	3.6	2.3	5.1	2.9	3.4	5.7
Retail	13.6	5.5	8.6	7.0	15.5	10.7
Finance	8.3	2.0	4.0	1.2	7.8	3.2
Education	8.6	1.1	5.8	2.5	9.5	4.5
Health	14.1	3.6	3.8	2.0	14.4	3.0
Recreation	1.1	0.2	1.0	0.5	1.5	1.3
Business Service	4.6	0.9	4.8	1.7	4.3	3.7
Personal Service	3.4	4.4	1.0	1.4	2.7	0.6
Accommodation and Food	8.6	11.4	5.9	14.7	9.6	3.5
Miscellaneous Service	2.6	7.5	2.1	4.0	2.2	2.1
Public Administration and Defence	5.1	0.2	5.5	0.9	7.4	8.9
Mean Hours Worked in Reference Week[6]	34.8	37.6	43.0	41.4	33.4	42.4
Full-time — Part-time in 1980[8]	100.0	100.0	100.0	100.0	100.0	100.0
Full-time	72.2	84.6	93.6	97.8	68.5	88.9
Part-time	27.8	15.4	6.4	2.2	31.5	11.1
Weeks Worked in 1980[9]	40.1	39.6	44.4	41.9	37.2	41.3
Mean Weekly Earnings in 1980[9]	242	205	431	344	232	386

n.a. = not applicable

[1] Excludes persons born abroad but who are Canadian citizens by birthright. Excludes all other foreign-born immigrating in 1980 or later.
[2] Persons born in Belgium, Luxembourg, France, German, Democratic Republic, Federal Republic of Germany, Netherlands, Austria.
[3] Persons born in Greece, Italy and Portugal.
[4] Persons born in Czechoslovakia, Hungary, Poland and the U.S.S.R.
[5] Persons born in Australia, Oceania and countries not included in other regions captured above.
[6] The reference week refers to the week prior to the census (June 3, 1981).
[7] Coded to approximate years of schooling including post-secondary education.
[8] Excludes persons who were not employed in 1980.
[9] Excludes persons with zero weeks worked in 1980.

Some of the anomalies in the socioeconomic characteristics of women by language may be related to the importance of language in allocating workers to the formal and informal sectors of the Canadian economy. The lower participation rate of women who do not know English or French may be an accurate portrayal of participation in the formal economy but it may not measure all income-generating activity. This would be true if substantial numbers of these women find employment in the invisible economy as domestic workers, office cleaners and seamstresses. The selectivity of the informal economy for non-French or English speaking persons, especially on a part time basis, also would serve to increase the percentages of these women in full-time employment in the formal economy. By its very nature, the size of employment in the invisible economy remains unknown. But several studies have documented the employment of immigrant women as domestic workers and as piecework seamstresses in the home (Cohen 1986; Johnson 1982; Ng and Neale 1987; Ng and Ramirez 1981).

Language knowledge is a powerful factor in determining labour market location. Women who cannot speak English or French are absent from occupations performed primarily in the host language. In contrast to nearly four-fifths of the Canadian-born women and two thirds of the foreign-born women who know English or French, less than 4 percent of those without such knowledge are in clerical, sales or other white collar occupations (including managerial and administrative). Seven out of ten foreign-born women without knowledge of English or French are employed in service, or processing and fabrication occupations. Likewise, over half of the foreign-born women who do not know English or French well enough to carry on a conversation are in the manufacturing, or accommodation and food preparation industrial sectors of the Canadian economy — compared to approximately one-quarter of the native-born women and foreign-born women who know one or both of the official languages. These distributions capture the extensive employment of immigrant women, particularly from Asia and Southern Europe in seamstressing occupations/textile industries and as chambermaids in hotels and kitchen service workers (Boyd 1986: 56; Gannage 1986; Johnson 1982).

Immigrants born in Asia and in Southern Europe are the least likely of the major birthplace regions to know English or French. Approximately nine out of ten immigrants who do not know English or French well enough to carry on a conversation are born in South European or Asian countries (Table 4). Table 5 focuses on these two birthplace groups, showing the correlates of not knowing the language. The general conclusions drawn from Table 4 remain substantiated. But the data in Table 5 generate three additional observations. First, birthplace is an important factor underlying the socioeconomic position of immigrants. Regardless of language knowledge, women who are born in Southern Europe are less well educated than are the Asian-born, less likely to be in the labour force, more likely to be unemployed and, when in the labour force, to be employed in machining occupations and in manufacturing industries. Southern

TABLE 5

Selected Social and Economic Characteristics for Southern Europe[1] and Asian-born Groups by Sex and by Knowledge of Official Language, Canada 1981

	Knows English and/or French Well Enough to Carry On a Conversation							
	Female				Male			
	South Europe		Asia		South Europe		Asia	
	Yes (1)	No (2)	Yes (3)	No (4)	Yes (5)	No (6)	Yes (7)	No (8)
N. PUST	4099	853	3291	425	5130	487	3715	168
Mean Education [2]	8.3	4.8	12.9	6.8	9.0	5.6	13.9	8.3
Labour Force								
Participation Rate	62.3	49.4	72.0	51.8	92.5	89.1	89.1	77.4
Labour Force Status,								
Reference Week	100.0	100.0	100.0	100.0	100.0	100.0	100.0	100.0
Employed	93.7	91.9	94.4	92.3	96.5	95.6	96.0	93.1
Unemployed	6.3	8.1	5.6	7.7	3.5	4.4	4.0	6.9
Occupation, Reference Week	100.0	100.0	100.0	100.0	100.0	100.0	100.0	100.0
Managerial, Administrative	2.8	0.4	5.7	1.6	6.5	1.3	10.0	3.0
Other White Collar	5.9	0.4	20.4	1.2	5.2	0.9	23.0	5.3
Clerical	23.6	3.0	32.7	4.9	4.8	0.7	3.2	3.0
Sales	6.4	1.1	5.7	4.1	5.6	2.0	7.6	3.8
Service	22.8	29.4	16.8	32.8	16.2	18.5	14.7	43.1
Farming, Fishing, Forestry	1.3	3.6	1.1	5.3	2.5	2.9	1.5	3.8
Processing	5.3	10.1	2.6	9.4	6.8	10.1	6.1	12.0
Machining and Product Fabrication	26.7	42.7	11.6	34.4	21.3	17.8	17.1	11.3
Construction	0.7	0.4	0.1	0.0	21.5	39.4	3.6	1.5
Transport	0.1	0.0	0.1	0.0	3.4	1.3	3.2	0.0
Other	4.4	8.9	3.2	6.6	6.1	5.1	5.1	8.3
Industry, Reference Week	100.0	100.0	100.0	100.0	100.0	100.0	100.0	100.0
Agriculture, Other Primary	1.7	3.8	1.9	5.7	1.7	1.3	1.7	3.8
Manufacturing	36.5	59.4	18.4	47.5	30.0	28.0	28.1	25.3
Construction	2.6	0.8	0.6	0.4	21.6	38.1	3.8	3.0

	Col 1	Col 2	Col 3	Col 4	Col 5	Col 6	Col 7	Col 8
Transportation, Communication, Utilities	2.3	0.2	3.4	1.2	6.3	1.5	8.8	0.0
Wholesale	3.2	1.9	4.4	2.5	4.0	2.9	5.1	4.5
Retail	12.9	4.7	12.0	7.0	9.5	6.4	9.8	7.5
Finance	6.4	2.3	9.4	0.8	2.5	1.5	4.3	0.8
Education	4.6	1.3	5.7	0.8	2.7	2.6	4.8	3.0
Health and Welfare	6.9	2.7	16.2	4.1	2.2	1.8	5.4	2.3
Recreation	0.4	0.4	0.7	0.0	0.6	0.4	0.6	0.8
Business Service	2.4	0.8	4.7	0.8	1.9	1.3	6.5	0.8
Personal Service	5.0	3.8	2.7	5.3	2.4	1.8	0.9	0.8
Accomodation and Food	10.1	7.4	11.7	21.3	9.6	7.3	12.7	43.6
Miscellaneous Service	3.3	10.1	2.1	2.0	2.3	3.7	1.8	2.3
Public Admin. and Defence	1.7	0.2	6.1	0.4	2.7	1.3	4.7	0.0
Mean Hours Worked in Reference Week [3]	35.9	36.9	37.1	39.0	43.1	41.0	42.0	42.1
Full-time/Part-time in 1980 [4]	100.0	100.0	100.0	100.0	100.0	100.0	100.0	100.0
Full-time	77.7	84.7	79.8	87.0	95.5	97.5	90.8	98.5
Part-time	22.3	15.3	20.2	13.0	4.5	2.5	9.2	1.5
Weeks Worked in 1980 [5]	40.4	40.5	39.8	37.5	43.7	41.1	43.3	44.1
Mean Weekly Earnings in 1980 [5]	212	217	255	184	383	356	389	309
Median Weekly Earnings in 1980 [5]	195	171	218	169	354	313	345	220

[1] Consists of persons born in Greece, Italy or Portugal who are not Canadian citizens by birth.

[2] Coded to approximate years of schooling including post-secondaray schooling.

[3] The reference week refers to the week prior to the census (June 3, 1981).

[4] Consists of occupations in the social and physical sciences, medicine, health, artistic and literary occupations (standard occupational classification #21, 23, 25, 27, 31, and 33).

[5] Excludes all persons with zero weeks worked in 1980.

Source: Statistics Canada. 1981 Census of Canada. Public Use Sample Tape of Individuals, full count.

European-born men are more likely than Asian-born men to have lower education and to be employed in construction occupations and industries. These patterns exist regardless of language knowledge although linguistic ability can minimize or increase the pattern.

Second, not knowing English or French more sharply differentiates among the Asian-born compared to the Southern European-born with respect to educational, occupational, industrial and income characteristics. Especially noteworthy is the high percentage of Asian-born men and women who do not converse in English or French but who are employed in the service occupations and in the accommodation and food industries. This contrasts with the very high percentages of the Asian-born who do speak English and/or French and who are employed in white collar occupations and for women, in health and welfare industries. The Asian-born who can converse in English and/or French are highly educated, and earn high mean incomes, even more than the Canadian-born men and women (Table 4, columns 5 and 6). Why these sharper differentials by language knowledge occur for the Asian-born population is not ascertainable from the data, but it probably reflects the three sources of variation between the two groups: 1) recency of arrival; 2) the heterogeneous nature of Asian migration (refugees, economic or independents, migrants and family class migrants) and; 3) the more numerous and diverse countries comprising the Asian-born group compared to the Southern European group, which consists of persons born in Greece, Italy and Portugal, many of whom immigrated in the 1960s.

Table 5 also points out the disadvantages faced by Southern Europeans. Of all the various groups formed by combining the categories of Southern Europe/Asian-born with female/male and yes/no on language, Southern Europe-born women who do not know English well enough to hold a conversation have the lowest levels of education, the lowest labour force participation rates, and the greatest amount of occupational and industrial concentration. They and their Asian-born female counterparts have the lowest 1980 weekly earnings of all groups.

While slightly less pronounced than that of women born in Southern Europe, the socioeconomic situation of Asian-born women who do not know English or French well enough to converse also merits attention. Over time, Asian migration is increasing its share of total migration to Canada, accounting for nearly 40 percent of all immigration in 1987. Such trends mean substantial increases in the size of the resident Asian-born population in Canada. Yet it is this group that is the most strongly socioeconomically bifurcated on the basis of French or English knowledge. Asian-born women who cannot converse in English or French are relegated to processing and fabrication occupations largely as seamstresses while their male counterparts are heavily concentrated in service occupations. Although not knowing one of the official languages is associated with a high degree of occupational and industrial concentration for both men and women, it is the women who bring home the lower wages and who have higher unemployment rates.

Policy Issues

Socioeconomic profiles indicate that the inability to converse in English or French generally is associated with lower labour force participation rates (for women), higher unemployment, occupational and industrial concentration and lower weekly wages. Immigrant women, especially those born in Southern Europe or in Asia particularly handicapped by not knowing one of Canada's official languages. Strong interventionist measures are required to eradicate these socioeconomic inequalities experienced by many immigrant women. Extensive provision of language training services is a major requirement for improving the status of immigrant women. But equally important ingredients are education and literacy programs, skill retraining programs and childcare services. Affirmative action policies, designed to remove discriminatory employment practices, also are essential.

A number of reports review the various language training policies and programs in Canada and outline their shortcomings (Boyd 1986, 1987; Burnaby et. al. 1987; Estable 1986; Giles 1987; Ng and Ramirez 1984; Paredes 1987; Seward and McDade 1988; Seydegart and Spears 1985). Three main categories exist: the Language Training Program, funded by Canada Employment and Immigration Commission (CEIC); 2) the language instruction programs funded by the Secretary of State (funding for these programs was terminated in 1989 federal budget); and 3) specific programs which either are pilot programs such as the Settlement Language Training Program (SLTP), funded by CEIC (Burnaby, et. al. 1987) or are offered by local voluntary associations (Estable 1986: 44; Giles 1988). In October 1988, Employment and Immigration Canada announced a new three-part initiative directed at immigrant women. This initiative includes: 1) funds to allow the overseas delivery of basic language skills training in refugee camps; 2) the expansion of SLTP; and 3) a new program under the Canadian Job Strategies Program which provides subsidies to employers for language and skills upgrading of women in the workplace. However, it will take several years to implement and assess these new programs. At the moment, Canada does not have a comprehensive, integrated and universally accessible language training policy for immigrants.

Compared to their male counterparts, foreign-born women are less likely to access the language programs funded by CEIC and Secretary of State. The Canada Employment and Immigration language training program is part of the job entry component of the Canadian Job Strategies Program, Employment and Immigration. The program is directed at persons who are destined for the labour market. To be eligible for language training in this program, persons must acquire French or English language skills in order to find employment in their usual occupation, or if unskilled, their lack of language skill must prevent them from obtaining employment. Although this program does not explicitly discriminate on the basis of sex, three features of the program curb its accessibility to immigrant women. First, persons not destined for the labour force are not eligible for language training under the CEIC program. Yet foreign-born women who cannot converse in English or French are most likely not to be in the labour force (Tables 4 and 5) and thus not to be eligible for the program.

Second, if the ability to speak English or French is not necessary for employment, persons may not qualify for CEIC language training. Many jobs held by women in the service and processing sectors of the Canadian economy can be performed without knowing one of the official languages. In particular, seamstresses, hotel maids and domestics are likely not to be eligible for CEIC language training (Axworthy 1981).

Third, the program does provide five types of income support: living allowances — called a basic training allowance — dependent care allowance, commuting allowance, living away from home allowance and (long distance) transportation allowances. In general, the sum of the allowances is not large.[6] Paredes (1987) finds that women in her study had to supplement the allowances by working part time, which reduced the learning process. Furthermore, the basic training allowance may be eliminated by the proviso that sponsored immigrants in the family and assisted relatives classes are not eligible for the basic training allowances, the argument being that sponsors have agreed to economically provide for these immigrants. Because women more than men are sponsored immigrants (Boyd 1987: Table 21), they are more likely than men not to be receiving basic training allowances even if they are eligible to participate in the CEIC program. This curtailment of income increases the likelihood that sponsored immigrant women will not participate in the program (Boyd 1987; Giles 1987; Paredes 1987).

The second language instruction program is funded by the Secretary of State. It arises from two long-standing federal-provincial agreements collectively known as CILT (Citizenship Instruction and Language Training). The intent of this program is to help prepare permanent residents for citizenship. Under the auspices of the provinces, courses are offered, usually part-time, in the evening and through the facilities of local school boards. These courses represent another way of learning English or French, particularly for immigrant women who do not participate in the CEIC language training program. However, attending part-time classes, working long hours and caring for a family can make participation difficult for immigrant women (Axworthy 1981; Paredes 1987).

In addition to the issues of accessibility and use, the instructional organization and content of the CEIC and Secretary of State programs can be a barrier for learning English or French for two reasons. First, the use of unilingual instructors in total immersion formats may cause discomfort among the participants and retard learning (Estable 1986: 45). An assessment of a government pilot study found that in situations of low literacy a bilingual mode of instruction was more effective (Burnaby et. al. 1987). Second, critics also note the cultural insensitivity of language training programs. The organization of classroom instruction and the use of textbooks means that language learning is not always pertinent to the daily reality of many participants. These criticisms elicit two recommendations. First, the content of English and French language instruction should be more sensitive to the practical situations in which immigrants find themselves. Second, language training should function more than it does as a hands-on introduction to Canadian institutions, and to practices regarding job searches and employment which exist in Canada and which may be quite different from those in the origin country (Burnaby et. al. 1987; Paredes 1987; Seydegart 1985: 42). However, to have relevancy for immigrant women, the implementation of these recommendations requires the recognition that foreign-born women often have different skills and experiences than foreign-born men (Paredes 1987). In particular, they are more likely to need language instruction not only for employment situations but also for interacting with schools, medical services and stores.

The assumptions of literacy is another criticism levied at the existing language training programs in Canada (Burnaby, et. al. 1987; Estable 1986). For participants with low levels of education, emphasis on published text and reading and writing increases program drop-outs (Burnaby et. al. 1987). The previous analysis shows that foreign-born women who cannot converse in French or English have lower levels of education than foreign-born men or than Canadian-born women (Tables 4 and 5). These data indicate that matching the mode of instruction to the literacy levels of participants is particularly important if immigrant women are to benefit from language training programs.

The lower educational levels of foreign-born women without English or French speaking ability also is the basis for formulating policies and programs directed at educational upgrading and job retraining. From a human capital perspective, the low status of immigrant women in the labour force not only reflects their inability to speak either English or French but also their low levels of literacy in a labour market where completion of high school is increasingly expected by employers. In this case, education is responsible for the creation of an underclass, because education is a criterion used to allocate people to lower wage and less skilled jobs and because its presumption in language training courses is inconsistent with the educational characteristics of clients. Amelioration of sex/birthplace inequalities thus requires not only the redesign of language curriculum to better suit the clientele, but it also requires programs directed at upgrading education and related job skills. This requires the development of adult education courses which are aimed at immigrant groups, including immigrant women, and which are designed to facilitate access. Upgrading job related skills may be achieved through design of the Canadian Job Strategies program, which currently does not offer courses that would benefit many immigrant women except those of the language training program, job re-entry and more recently the Severely Employment-Disadvantaged Option (Seward and McDade 1988; also see Boyd 1987). The National Action Committee on Immigrant and Visible Minority Women, which is a recently formed umbrella organization (see Action Committee on Immigrant and Visible Minority Women, n.d.; Boyd 1987) observes that even these programs may not reach many immigrant women. Designating immigrant women as specific targets is needed for these programs to significantly affect immigrant women.

Language training, educational upgrading and improved job related skills are potential mechanisms for improving the socioeconomic position of immigrant women who currently are not conversant in either English or French. However, unless support facilities exist, the domestic responsibilities of these women will depress participation in any future programs. As with instructionally oriented programs, child care programs must be devised which elicit participation of immigrant women. At the moment, child care provisions are the responsibility of the parents and existing training programs lack on-site care. Yet, in a CEIC funded pilot program (Settlement Language Training Program), designed to meet the language needs of adult immigrants not expected to join the labour force, baby sitting support for language training was critical to the success of the program. Assessors observed that such babysitting services can be developed to include language work with the children (Burnaby et. al. 1987). By minimizing linguistic gaps between parent and children, this one-stop-shopping model may have benefits beyond providing childcare. At the same time, culturally sensitive childcare is important not only for the confidence and increasing learning ability of the child (Seward and McDade 1988) but for other reasons including parental-child relationships and the preservation of a multicultural society. Overall, the provision of on-site culturally sensitive child care facilities are essential for immigrant women to fully benefit from language, educational upgrading or job skill upgrading programs.

Finally, policies and programs directed at providing language training, education and literacy and job skills are human capital enriching strategies. Successful participants of these programs still must contend with labour markets which recruit and allocate on the basis of sex, colour and race. In general, current equity employment programs are restricted to the labour force under federal government jurisdiction or employed by provincial and municipal governments. Many immigrant women are employed in other sectors of the economy, where affirmative action programs are not in place and where the likelihood of their voluntary implementation is low.

Overall, improving the socioeconomic status of immigrant women requires both supply side and demand side policies. Not knowing one of the official languages is associated with socioeconomic disadvantages for the foreign-born population. Since foreign-born women are more likely than foreign-born men not to know English or French, a language training policy that offers extensive culturally sensitive instruction in an applied setting with funded childcare would be influential in ameliorating some of the socioeconomic disadvantages experienced by immigrant women. However, this alone is not sufficient. Other conditions are necessary if women, especially those born in Southern Europe and Asia are to leave job ghettos with poor working conditions and low pay. Educational upgrading and job retraining are two important conditions facilitating improved socioeconomic well-being of these women. And, affirmative action programs aimed at increasing the proportionate share of visible minority and foreign-born women are necessary to break down barriers due to systemic discrimination.

None of these interventions are easy. But the geographic origins of current and future immigrants, the near equal numbers of men and women in those flows, and the socioeconomic disadvantages associated with language ability, sex and origins are evidence of their importance.

Notes

1. A general overview of the various classes of immigrants and the criteria for admissibility is found in Employment and Immigration Canada, 1986.
2. For example, if a group is shown to earn less than another group because of lower education attainments and if the objective were to eradicate inequality, one policy response might be to focus educational upgrading at that group. Alternatively, the lower incomes of a group might have little to do with education but rather reflect employer job assignment practices. Again, assuming the objective of eradicating such inequalities, affirmative action would be an appropriate policy. Finally, a group might earn less than another because they were recruited only for certain kinds of employment (e.g. domestic work, seasonal agricultural labour) or were hired in secondary labour markets. If such practices were judged to meet the needs of a capitalist economy, no remedial policy action need occur. Ng and Das Gupta (1981) argue that in fact immigrant women, particularly non-English-speaking women, are a supply of cheap labour in Canada's capitalist economy.
3. Replies probably provide a conservative estimate of the inability to speak English or French. The 1981 Census question asks whether the enumerated person knows English and/or French well enough to carry on a conversation with the census guide indicating the intention to tap the ability to carry on a lengthy conversation on several topics. But whether or not the intention was actually realized is dependent on the reading of the guide and the proxy responses. Several researchers (Noivo 1984; Veltman 1984) note the tendency of survey respondents to inflate their ability to speak the language of the receiving society. This tendency could mean that some respondents, particularly if the guide book was not consulted, would indicate an ability to speak English and/or French when in fact they were unable to undertake a sustained conversation on various topics. At the same time, this tendency might be curtailed (or enhanced) by the procedure in which one member of the household usually fills out the form for all members. In such cases of proxy recording the conversational ability of the respondent would be determined not by the respondent but by the judgments of an observer, who also may or may not consult the guide book.
4. The percentages differ slightly from those discussed in Beaujot, Basavarajappa and Verma, 1988. The differences can be attributed to the use of public sample tape material and the restriction of the population to age 15-64 in this study compared to the analysis of the full one-in-five household data, the use of more detailed regional groupings and the selection of the population age 15 and over in the Beaujot, Basavarajappa and Verma study.
5. The foreign-born population that immigrated in 1980 or in the first five months of 1981 is excluded from the remaining analysis (Tables 4 and 5). Including these recent arrivals confounds the analysis of income differentials since persons immigrating in 1980 were instructed to report only their Canadian income. Persons immigrating in 1981 were assigned an 1980 income of zero dollars.
6. In 1987, the training allowance was $1.75 per hour of training (a minimum of 10 hours and a maximum of 40 hours per week) if the participant lived in a household maintained by a parent or spouse whose weekly income is greater than $210. If the

person was self-supporting with no dependents or if the parent/spouse has a weekly income of $210 or less, the allowance was $3.50 per hour. With one dependant and the preceding conditions the allowance rises to $4.20 with $0.35 per additional dependant. The dependant care allowance provides an hourly rate of $3.50 with up to a maximum of $16.00 per day for the first dependant; $16.00 for the second dependant; $10.00 for the third dependant and $5.00 for the fourth dependant. Under these two provisions, a woman who had one dependant child requiring full time care and a spouse with a weekly income under $210 would be receiving $248.00 for a 40 hour instructional week. A woman with one dependant child and a spouse with a weekly income over $210 would receive $150.00 maximum from the training allowance and dependant care allowance. If a sponsorship agreement was in effect, a woman with one dependant would receive only a maximum of $80.00 from the dependancy care allowance.

16. OCCUPATIONAL COMPOSITION OF IMMIGRANT WOMEN[1]

K.G. Basavarajappa and Ravi B.P. Verma

Country of birth and sex are of interest not only as demographic characteristics but also as variables associated with occupational stratification across the globe. It has been asserted that immigrant women experience a "double negative" in the Canadian labour force, as "immigrants" and "women" (Armstrong and Armstrong 1975; Boyd 1982). However, this paper explores the notion that there is a "triple negative" for immigrant women who are members of "visible minorities." For this purpose occupational distribution of immigrant women by birthplace is analysed. The distribution of immigrant women is compared with that of immigrant men as well as with those of Canadian-born men and women. Also, the immigrant groups are compared with each other and with a Canadian-born group with respect to representation (or proportion) of women in various occupations.

Review of Literature

A brief analysis of occupational distribution of immigrant women presented in a recently published report *Income of Immigrants in Canada* (Beaujot, Basaavarajappa and Verma 1988) showed that immigrant women were less likely than were immigrant men, or the Canadian-born population, to be in managerial and professional occupations. Immigrant women were more likely than their Canadian-born counterparts to have been in service occupations, especially processing (32.5 percent vs. 22.7 percent). While the clerical occupations were the largest single category for women, immigrant women seemed to have been less concentrated in this category (29.9 percent) than were Canadian-born women (36.8 percent). The index of dissimilarity[2] between the occupational distributions of Canadian-born and immigrant women was 10.3 percent, which was similar to that between the distributions of Canadian-born and immigrant men, 10.5 percent Boyd (1986) observed roughly the same levels of difference, 12.5 percent for men and 11.7 percent for women. Boyd used slightly different occupational categories. In contrast, the index of dissimilarity between the occupational distributions of men and women was much higher. For example, between Canadian-born men and women, it was 45.3 percent and between immigrant men and women, it was 33.9 percent. Thus the gender differences in occupational distributions were greater than those among birthplace groups. Also, the gender difference among the Canadian-born population was much greater than that among the immigrant populations.

The imbalance between the socioeconomic achievements of female workers and their male counterparts has been examined by several other researchers (Abella 1984; Almquist 1977; Armstrong et al. 1987; Arnopoulos 1979; Richmond et al. 1980; Simon and Brettell 1986; Boyd et al. 1985, 1989). Women's lower socioeconomic status is largely explained by the roles they play — those of wives and mothers, and consequently allocating less time to the labour force. But gender also influences location *within* the labour market, in combination with birthplace and class origin. Gender may intensify the disadvantaged workplace experience of some immigrant women. When this occurs, immigrant women are said to be the recipients of multiple negative status (Boyd 1986, 1989). Immigrant women can be doubly or triply disadvantaged as immigrants, women and by given country of origin. Country of origin can operate as a source of advantage or disadvantage with respect to labour market location due to differences in educational attainment, training and other work-related skills, including language of work; and the extent of labour-market discrimination for members of given birthplace groups (Boyd 1986).

Many immigrants do not achieve employment in their intended occupations (Richmond 1974). This analysis, as well as the earlier ones, has shown that immigrants are involved in various parts of the economy (McInnis 1980). After reviewing several studies, Richmond and Zubrzycki (1984) concluded that "the most striking feature of the distribution of the foreign-born in the labour force is the degree of similarity to the native-born." On the other hand, a more detailed breakdown of the foreign-born population by length of residence in Canada might show a different picture; that is, higher concentrations in certain occupations.

Educational attainment and knowledge of official languages have an important bearing on occupational attainment. Analysis of 1981 Census data on educational attainment showed that in general, while foreign-born men had an advantage with regard to education when compared with Canadian-born men, immigrants from non-traditional source regions had a particular advantage in terms of university education (Beaujot et al. 1988). In contrast, foreign-born women did not have the same educational advantage when compared with Canadian-born women. However, proportions with university education were higher among groups from Asia, Africa, Oceania and the United States. The proportion with only elementary education was highest (60.7 percent) among immigrant women from Southern Europe. Further, immigrant women were also found to be in a disadvantaged position in terms of knowledge of English or French. According to the 1981 Census, more than 10 percent of persons born in Southern Europe, Southeast Asia and East Asia knew neither official language — English or French. It would be interesting to see how these differences relate to occupational attainment.

In particular, we examine the following questions/issues:

- Do immigrant women differ from Canadian-born women much more than immigrant men from Canadian-born men?
- Do immigrants from non-traditional sources differ from the Canadian-born more than those from traditional sources?
- Do occupational distributions of immigrant women vary by length of residence in Canada?
- With increasing length of residence in Canada, do the occupational distributions of immigrant women tend to converge with that of Canadian-born women?
- Are the gender differences in occupational distributions more than those of the birthplace differences?
- Do Canadian-born women differ from Canadian-born men much more than immigrant women from immigrant men?
- Are immigrant women the recipients of multiple negative status?
- How do educational attainment and knowledge of official languages impact on occupational attainment of immigrant women?

In this study, immigrants and foreign-born are used synonymously.

Data and Methods

Occupation classifications from the 1981 Census were derived from a two-part question:

(a)   What kind of work were you doing?
(b)   In this work, what were your most important activities or duties?

A two-part question is asked to ensure there is enough information to place people who do similar kinds of work in the same occupational group. The occupational details refer to the job held during the last week prior to the Census. If a person held no job, the information required was for the job of longest duration since January 1, 1980. If a person held more than one job in the last week, the information required was for the job at which the person worked the most hours.

It should be noted that the occupations reported by a large number of unemployed people actively looking for a job, and for part-time workers (especially women) could be misleading. In fact, for the first few years after arrival, the occupational status of immigrant men and women may be quite unsettled. As well, in some cases, where immigrants are engaged in many part-time jobs, there may be problems reporting the precise type of occupation. All these factors could cause greater gender differences than birthplace differences in occupational distributions.

To make the comparisons more valid, only the employed population aged 15 years and over working full-time and working for 40 weeks or more in 1980 is considered. Consequently, the following categories of population are excluded:

    i) the population who did not work in 1980 or who worked before 1980 only, or never worked;
   ii) the population who worked in 1981, but not in 1980;
  iii) the population who worked part-time (1-52 weeks); and,
   iv) the population who worked full-time 1-39 weeks.

It should be noted that in the census, no specific definition was given to respondents because of the varying number of hours considered as full-time in different occupations and industries. For this reason, full-time data should not be interpreted as specifying a certain number of hours. Part-time work is that work which is less than the normally scheduled weekly hours of work performed by persons doing similar work. Some 73.8 percent of foreign-born males and 50.7 percent of foreign-born females worked full-time, according to the 1981 Census. The corresponding percentages for Canadian-born males and females were 66.4 and 45.1, respectively.

Fifteen immigrant groups are considered. The immigrants came from two broad sources: (i) "traditional sources" included seven regions — the United States, United Kingdom, Other Western Europe, Central Europe, Southern Europe, Eastern Europe and Northern Europe; and (ii) "non-traditional sources" or new immigrant sources included eight regions — Africa, South Asia, Southeast Asia, East Asia, West Asia, Oceania, Caribbean, and South and Central America.

The method of analysis is simple and straightforward. First, proportional distributions by occupation of various immigrant groups are compared. Second, the differences in occupational distributions are summarized by the index of dissimilarity. The index is also used for purposes of comparison.

Analysis of Data

Birthplace Differences in Occupational Distributions

The indices of dissimilarity between the occupational distributions of Canadian-born men and foreign-born men and those between the occupational distributions of Canadian-born women and foreign-born women are presented in Tables 1

TABLE 1

Index of Dissimilarity Between the Occupational Distributions of Canadian-born Men and
Foreign-born Men, by Period of Immigration and Birthplace, 1981

Place of Birth	Total*	Period of Immigration				
		Before 1960	1960-1964	1965-1969	1970-1974	1975-1979
All foreign-born	6.1	4.9	6.2	9.0	8.2	9.5
Traditional Sources	4.8	3.7	7.3	8.4	9.5	9.3
United States	20.6	12.3	18.0	29.3	29.1	29.5
United Kingdom	14.6	14.4	16.8	14.9	13.6	15.4
Other Western Europe	6.0	5.5	7.4	13.2	17.0	14.7
Central Europe	6.4	5.7	6.2	10.5	10.3	11.3
Southern Europe	21.8	16.9	21.0	25.4	29.1	28.2
Eastern Europe	7.8	7.3	10.1	8.7	15.6	23.9
Northern Europe	8.7	7.5	12.8	16.7	12.7	12.7
Non-Traditional Sources	14.2	26.7	24.4	19.3	11.2	11.7
Africa	25.7	34.2	30.1	32.7	24.2	18.6
South Asia	13.0	15.5	37.0	28.4	10.2	9.9
Southeast Asia	17.5	32.4	44.7	35.5	19.2	16.4
East Asia	28.6	33.3	36.2	33.0	25.5	24.7
West Asia	12.7	33.1	23.4	13.2	9.7	11.5
Oceania	11.4	26.6	21.9	17.2	8.5	8.3
Caribbean	9.5	28.0	21.9	11.5	13.8	17.5
South and Central America	8.2	12.2	11.9	6.5	11.0	16.3

* Computed from Appendix Table A. The indices for period of immigration cohorts are calculated from the detailed unpublished occupational distribution of foreign-born men by period of immigration and birthplace.

TABLE 2

Index of Dissimilarity Between the Occupational Distributions of Canadian-born Women and
Foreign-born Women, by Period of Immigration and Birthplace, 1981

Place of Birth	Total*	Period of Immigration					
		Before 1960	1960-1964	1965-1969	1970-1974	1975-1979
All foreign-born	14.7	13.2	17.5	13.7	17.8	20.6
Traditional Sources	15.8	13.3	21.1	19.4	23.6	16.2
United States	14.4	8.1	7.6	22.9	21.2	18.8
United Kingdom	5.5	5.9	6.9	4.4	5.2	6.1
Other Western Europe	11.6	11.1	9.8	12.6	18.3	13.1
Central Europe	15.0	14.9	15.7	13.3	16.4	24.3
Southern Europe	45.9	38.1	43.1	48.1	58.2	60.7
Eastern Europe	18.5	19.8	18.9	21.3	19.5	28.8
Northern Europe	12.2	14.3	8.3	18.6	6.7	11.2
Non-Traditional Sources	12.4	11.0	12.8	12.9	13.3	23.1
Africa	4.7	7.5	16.4	7.4	7.3	12.6
South Asia	14.2	14.1	14.1	9.3	15.9	27.6
Southeast Asia	20.2	22.6	45.8	41.7	14.0	21.0
East Asia	22.0	35.9	28.9	14.9	15.5	28.2
West Asia	16.9	13.7	17.2	17.1	18.6	26.7
Oceania	9.8	15.0	18.6	12.1	12.9	10.7
Caribbean	15.9	14.6	26.9	13.7	18.9	25.1
South and Central America	19.9	7.8	6.2	9.4	22.5	30.3

* Computed from Appendix Table B. The indices for period of immigration cohorts are calculated from the detailed unpublished occupational distribution of foreign-born women by period of immigration and birthplace.

and 2 respectively. Considering the foreign-born as one group, the index is considerably greater for women than for men — 14.7 percent vs. 6.1 percent — meaning that the occupational distributions of women differed much more than those of men. This is true for all cohorts of immigrants arriving in Canada at different periods. However, this does not hold true for some of the birthplace and period of immigration cohorts.

For the foreign-born group as a whole, the index exhibited a tendency to decrease as the length of residence in Canada increased. This is true for both males and females. Does it mean that as the length of residence in Canada of the foreign-born increases, they and the Canadian-born converge with respect to occupational distribution? This did not appear to be so because such convergence was not observed for all birthplace groups. A similar finding was observed by Richmond and Kalbach earlier (1980). It may be mentioned that the immigrants arriving from various sources and at various periods differed with respect to socioeconomic characteristics not only among themselves but also from the Canadian-born group. For example, persons coming from developing countries during the 1970s contained much higher proportions of family class immigrants compared with those from traditional source regions. Higher numbers of conventional refugees and designated classes arrived during the 1975-79 period. Consequently, occupational differences tended to persist rather than decrease with increasing length of residence in Canada for many groups.

As mentioned earlier, the index of dissimilarity measures the degree of similarity between the two distributions compared. The index could also be interpreted as representing the proportion that one of the groups would have to shift (occupational categories) in order to become identical with the other group. Let us choose an arbitrary level of 25 percent for the index as representing substantial differences in the occupational distributions. By this criterion, for women, there were 6 cases out of a possible 35 cases (5 periods of immigration × 7 birthplace groups), or 17.1 percent, that differed substantially from the Canadian-born group among the traditional source groups. These groups differed substantially were Southern European and Eastern European. In contrast, there were 9 cases out of 40, or 22.5 percent among the non-traditional source groups that showed substantial differences. Except African and Oceanian, all non-traditional groups differed substantially. The percentages for men were 17.1 among traditional source groups (the same as for women) and 37.5 among non-traditional source groups. The groups that differed substantially were U.S. and Southern European among traditional sources and all except South and Central American among the non-traditional sources. Thus both among men and women, the non-traditional source groups differed more from the Canadian-born group than did the traditional source groups. The reasons are probably those mentioned above, i.e., higher proportions of family class immigrants and higher proportions of refugees among the non-traditional sources.

Gender Differences in Occupational Distributions

Table 3 presents indices of dissimilarity between the occupational distributions of males and females among the Canadian-born and foreign-born persons by place of birth and period of immigration. The indices show that the gender differences are significant and indeed much more so than the birthplace differences. Canadian-born male and female populations differed much more (45.6 percent) than did immigrant populations from traditional (32.6 percent) as well as non-traditional (27.8 percent) sources. This means that the shift required for the Canadian-born women to achieve occupational similarity with Canadian-born men is much more than that required for the foreign-born women to achieve similarity with foreign-born men.

Gender differences among the Southern European and East Asian populations seemed to be the lowest. The two populations with similar gender differences to the Canadian-born population were North European and Oceanian. Generally speaking, the gender differences among the immigrants from non-traditional sources were lower than those among immigrants from traditional sources.

No uniform pattern in gender differences by length of residence was observed for birthplace groups.

The association of educational achievement with occupational attainment is examined by calculating Spearman's rank correlation coefficient.[3] In fact the rank correlation for females (0.67) was significant at the 5 percent level and for males (0.79) at the 1 percent level, indicating that educational achievements and occupational attainments are positively related. If some of the groups are underrepresented in managerial and professional occupations, their lower educational achievements explain at least part of those differences.

Representation of Women in Various Occupations

Table 4 presents women workers as a proportion of total workers in various occupational categories for the Canadian-born and the two broad immigrant groups by period of immigration. Representation of women in all occupations was roughly of the same order: 33.2 percent among the Canadian-born and 32.8 percent among the foreign-born. However, the non-traditional source groups had higher representation than the traditional source groups, 38.6 percent vs. 30.8 percent, and especially of those from non-traditional sources (24.7 percent) were particularly high when compared with that of the Canadian-born women (10.0 percent).

Representation of immigrant women in the managerial category was roughly of the same magnitude as that of the Canadian-born women. However, it was considerably lower in the professional and technical category, 32.7 percent among traditional and 38.1 percent among non-traditional source groups as compared with 45.6 percent among the Canadian-born women. Women's represen-

TABLE 3

Index of Dissimilarity Between the Occupational Distributions of Males and Females
Among Canadian-born and Foreign-born Persons by Place of Birth and Period of Immigration, 1981

Place of Birth	Total*	Period of Immigration				
		Before 1960	1960-64	1965-69	1970-74	1975-79
Total	42.7					
Canadian-born	45.6	n.a.	n.a.	n.a.	n.a.	n.a.
All Foreign-born	31.8	34.9	29.6	30.2	29.9	33.3
Traditional Sources	32.6	35.8	29.9	29.8	28.7	33.2
United States	34.4	40.1	35.6	24.9	30.3	30.7
United Kingdom	39.9	37.5	39.6	40.6	44.5	48.8
Other Western Europe	39.5	40.0	43.6	35.0	35.9	33.6
Central Europe	38.9	39.9	41.0	35.7	38.3	36.1
Southern Europe	19.9	22.6	21.4	20.1	15.9	14.7
Eastern Europe	35.3	36.4	28.6	34.9	32.6	27.4
Northern Europe	43.8	44.7	50.5	54.2	51.5	50.9
Non-Traditional Sources	27.8	24.8	25.7	33.9	30.4	26.7
Africa	37.3	38.0	28.9	34.4	37.1	42.6
South Asia	34.3	45.6	34.2	37.9	33.5	30.3
Southeast Asia	29.3	30.2	27.5	26.8	31.1	26.1
East Asia	22.6	23.7	29.2	23.2	27.2	22.2
West Asia	26.1	33.6	31.4	27.7	30.8	22.3
Oceania	40.1	38.4	32.4	39.8	40.0	50.1
Caribbean	37.5	28.6	37.6	42.0	37.4	35.9
South and Central America	33.0	38.6	39.3	40.5	31.6	29.3

n.a. = Not Applicable.

* Computed from Appendix Tables A and B. The indices for period of immigration cohorts are calculated from the detailed unpublished occupational distribution of foreign-born men and women by period of immigration and birthplace.

TABLE 4

Women as Percentage of Total Number of Persons Working Full-time¹ by Occupation Among Canadian-born and Foreign-born Persons by period of Immigration and Source Regions, 1981

Occupational Group	Canadian-born	Period of Immigration					
		Total	Before 1960	1960-1964	1965-1969	1970-1974	1975-1979
Foreign-born from All Sources							
All Occupations	33.2	32.8	28.4	36.8	34.8	37.1	36.3
Managerial	21.9	21.0	19.0	25.2	22.7	23.9	20.9
Professional and Technical	45.6	34.4	32.3	37.9	35.8	35.7	34.2
Clerical	74.0	73.1	70.5	77.2	76.0	73.2	73.5
Sales	28.4	31.0	29.4	35.0	32.5	31.3	31.4
Service	39.5	41.2	37.0	43.5	43.0	46.4	43.5
Processing and Other	10.0	18.5	13.5	22.7	20.3	23.6	23.6
Foreign-born from Traditional Sources							
All Occupations	33.2	30.8	28.3	35.9	32.8	34.7	31.7
Managerial	21.9	20.5	19.1	24.8	23.2	23.3	19.2
Professional and Technical	45.6	32.7	32.5	36.6	32.0	33.0	30.6
Clerical	74.0	73.8	70.6	77.8	77.1	77.6	80.3
Sales	28.4	31.6	29.7	34.9	33.8	33.9	33.5
Service	39.5	40.7	38.0	42.7	41.5	46.8	44.7
Processing and Other	10.0	16.9	13.3	22.6	20.1	23.0	17.7

Foreign-born from Non-Traditional Sources

All Occupations	33.2	38.6	29.9	41.3	39.7	39.1	39.6
Managerial	21.9	22.6	18.0	26.4	21.7	24.5	22.9
Professional and Technical	45.6	38.1	29.1	40.9	40.7	37.9	37.8
Clerical	74.0	71.6	69.0	74.4	74.0	71.0	70.5
Sales	28.4	29.1	24.5	35.7	29.6	29.1	29.6
Service	39.5	42.6	27.4	49.6	47.5	45.9	42.9
Processing and Other	10.0	24.7	19.4	24.2	21.4	24.2	27.9

[1] Working full-time includes only those who worked full-time and who worked for 40 weeks or more in 1980.

Source: Statistics Canada, Special Tabulations, 1981 Census of Canada.

307

tation in clerical, sales and service categories was roughly of the same magnitude both among Canadian-born and immigrant groups.

Generally speaking, immigrant women's representation in managerial, pro- fessioinal and technical, clerical and sales categories increased with increasing length of residence in Canada for cohorts arriving in Canada after 1960. On the other hand, in service and processing and other occupations, it generally decreased with increasing length of residence in Canada. It appears that immi- grant women soon after their arrival join service, processing and other occu- pations and gradually move into professional, technical and clerical jobs as length of residence in Canada increases.

Much higher levels of participation of immigrant women in lower paid pro- cessing and other occupations give support for double or triple negative status for at least some groups. Detailed occupational distributions for women (not presented here) show that Southern Europeans and some of the non-traditional immigrant groups who are also visible minorities — East Asians, West Asians, South Asians and people from the Caribbean — and South and Central Americans may well be the recipients of triple negative status. This is further supported by an examination of income of immigrant groups arriving in Canada at various periods.

Among the more recently (1975-79) arrived immigrant women, mean incomes of all immigrant groups were less than for Canadian-born women. Among those who arrived during the 1970-74 period, the only exception was the group from Central Europe. Incomes of groups from the Caribbean and Southern Europe never surpassed those of Canadian-born women (Beaujot et al. 1988).

Although the broad occupational categories used for the analysis did not indi- cate the existence of labour market segmentation, such segmentation is known to exist for some groups of immigrant women (Seward et al. 1988).

It has been found that immigrant women from Southern Europe and Asia form the backbone of the machine garment industry. Working conditions for these sewing-machine operators were found to be the least rewarding. They were the least well-paid and the most unprotected in terms of job security (Arnopoulos 1979; Johnson 1982; Boyd 1986). Using the data from the 1979 Quality of Life Survey, Boyd found that "immigrant women are more likely to be working in small size firms. And, compared to Canadian-born women, immigrant women are more likely to be supervised several times a day. They are more likely to be required to produce a specific quota and to be physically and mentally tired at the end of the day. They had relatively more problems with the hours worked, the work schedule, and the overtime arrangements."

Summary

Using the 1981 Census data on occupational status of the population working full-time in 1980, the occupational composition of immigrant women was compared with those of the Canadian-born women and immigrant men. The index of dissimilarity between the occupational distributions of immigrant and Canadian-born women was 14.7 percent and that between immigrant and Canadian-born men was 6.1 percent meaning that women differed much more than did men. For the immigrant group as a whole, the index exhibited a slight tendency to decrease as the length of residence in Canada increased. This held good for both immigrant men and women. However, this did not mean that the foreign-born groups converge to the Canadian-born group with respect to occupational distribution because it was not observed for all immigrant groups. The reason seems to be that the immigrants arriving from various sources and at various periods differed with respect to socioeconomic characteristics not only among themselves but also from the Canadian-born group.

Immigrant women from non-traditional sources differed from the Canadian-born women less than those from traditional sources. However, men from non-traditional sources differed from the Canadian-born men more than those from traditional sources.

It was observed that the gender differences were significant and indeed much more so than the birthplace differences. The index of dissimilarity between the occupational distributions of Canadian-born males and females was 45.6 percent. The corresponding difference for the traditional source group was 32.6 percent and for non-traditional source group 27.8 percent. This means that the shift required for the Canadian-born women to achieve occupational similarity with the Canadian-born men is much more than that required for immigrant women to achieve occupational similarity with immigrant men.

Although the representation of women in all occupations was roughly of the same order — about 33 percent both among Canadian-born and immigrant populations — there were considerable differences in specific occupations. While immigrant women's representation in professional and technical occupations was lower than that of Canadian-born women, it was considerably higher in processing and other occupations. Generally speaking, immigrant women's representation in managerial, professional and technical, clerical and sales categories increased with increasing length of residence while it decreased in processing occupations, indicating that immigrant women, soon after their arrival, join service, processing and other occupations and gradually move into professional, technical and clerical jobs as length of residence in Canada increases. Southern Europeans and some of the non-traditional groups who are also visible minorities — East Asians, West Asians, South Asians and people from the Caribbean — and South and Central Americans may well be the recipients of multiple negative status.

Immigrant women's lower educational levels and lack of knowledge of official languages seem to have affected their occupational attainments. The higher indices of dissimilarity among women (Canadian-born vs. immigrants) than among men and the higher proportions of immigrant women than Canadian-born women in lower paid processing and other occupations show this impact.

Notes

1. The views expressed in this paper are those of the authors and not necessarily those of Statistics Canada. The authors wish to thank Dave Broad and Ron Van Moerkerke for their assistance in preparing this paper.
2. For the method of computing the index of dissimilarity, refer to Shryock and Siegel (1973). This index measures the extent to which two distributions differ, and its magnitude varies between 0 and 100. The lower the value, the greater is the similarity in the distributions compared. This also shows the percentage by which one of the groups would have to shift the categories to achieve similarity with the other group.
3. A brief description of the method of calculating Spearman's rank correlation coefficient follows:
   The immigrant groups were first ranked according to the proportions with post-secondary education from the lowest to the highest. Next they were ranked according to the proportions in managerial and professional occupations given in Appendix Tables A and B, again from the lowest to the highest. The correlation coefficient is calculated as:

$$r_s = 1 - \frac{6 \sum_{i=1}^{n} Di^2}{n(n^2 - 1)}$$

where Di is the difference between the ith pair of ranks and n the number of groups (15). For the method of calculating r_s and testing for its significance see Blalock, H.M. (1960).

APPENDIX TABLE A

Occupational Distribution of the Canadian-born and Foreign-born Male Population Working Full-time [1], 1981

Place of Birth	Total Number	Occupation					
		Managerial	Professional and Technical	Clerical	Sales	Services	Processing and Other
		Percent					
Total	5,148,805	14.2	13.6	7.0	8.9	8.4	47.9
Canadian-born	4,085,255	14.3	12.7	7.3	9.4	8.0	48.3
Foreign-born	1,063,550	13.8	16.8	5.7	7.2	9.9	46.5
Traditional Sources	821,390	14.2	15.3	4.9	7.2	9.4	49.1
United States	56,170	19.1	28.6	4.6	9.4	5.5	33.0
United Kingdom	226,640	20.1	21.6	6.1	8.7	7.1	36.5
Other Western Europe	82,830	16.2	16.8	4.4	7.9	6.8	47.8
Central Europe	153,045	14.7	15.9	4.3	7.3	6.7	51.2
Southern Europe	247,720	6.9	5.6	4.4	5.1	15.6	62.5
Eastern Europe	35,065	11.8	17.1	5.1	7.0	7.2	51.7
Northern Europe	19,920	15.1	13.8	3.5	6.9	5.5	55.3
Non-Traditional Sources	242,155	12.6	21.9	8.6	7.3	11.7	37.9
Africa	29,645	21.4	27.8	9.4	10.9	6.8	23.8
South Asia	40,190	12.6	24.8	8.2	6.1	5.3	43.0
Southeast Asia	26,920	8.1	25.9	10.4	4.2	9.1	42.3
East Asia	51,445	13.4	23.8	6.3	7.9	25.5	23.1
West Asia	17,105	14.7	16.9	5.6	13.7	11.8	37.3
Oceania	10,655	14.5	23.9	6.6	6.5	7.7	40.7
Caribbean	40,830	8.7	16.5	11.1	5.4	8.4	49.8
South and Central America	25,365	10.1	13.5	9.5	5.4	9.1	52.3

[1] Working full-time includes only those who worked full-time and who worked for 40 weeks or more in 1980.

Source: Statistics Canada, Special Tabulations, 1981 Census of Canada.

APPENDIX TABLE B

Occupational Distribution of the Canadian-born and Foreign-born Female Population Working Full-time[1], 1981

Place of Birth	Rank	Total Number	Occupation					
			Managerial	Professional and Technical	Clerical	Sales	Services	Processing and Other
			Percent					
Total		2,551,235	8.0	20.8	39.8	7.3	11.2	13.0
Canadian-born		2,033,100	8.1	21.4	41.8	7.5	10.4	10.8
Foreign-born		518,135	7.5	18.1	31.8	6.6	14.3	21.6
Traditional Sources		366,000	8.3	16.7	30.8	7.4	14.5	22.4
United States	15	30,640	11.5	32.2	31.9	7.8	8.5	8.2
United Kingdom	10	112,220	10.9	19.6	43.7	8.2	9.3	8.3
Other Western Europe	12	27,830	10.2	24.5	30.2	8.9	11.9	14.3
Central Europe	7	63,485	9.3	18.3	29.9	9.1	15.8	17.6
Southern Europe	1	110,970	3.4	6.0	18.7	4.9	20.7	46.3
Eastern Europe	6	13,555	7.5	20.0	25.2	9.0	17.5	20.7
Northern Europe	11	7,300	11.3	20.3	30.7	9.5	10.0	12.3
Non-Traditional Sources		152,145	5.9	21.5	34.3	4.7	13.8	19.8
Africa	8	15,220	9.2	18.6	44.7	8.1	8.7	10.6
South Asia	4	16,100	5.9	18.4	36.3	4.0	11.5	23.9
Southeast Asia	14	23,435	4.9	34.4	31.2	2.4	9.1	18.0
Esat Asia	3	31,445	6.7	14.5	28.8	6.8	21.2	21.9
West Asia	5	5,855	9.1	15.5	30.9	9.2	12.5	22.7
Oceania	13	6,195	8.6	28.3	37.0	4.0	13.0	9.1
Caribbean	9	38,115	4.0	25.4	34.3	3.1	14.0	19.2
South and Central America	2	15,780	4.5	12.2	37.9	4.3	13.8	27.4

[1] Working Full-time includes only those who worked full-time and who worked for 40 weeks or more in 1980.

Source: Statistics Canada, Special Tabulations, 1981, Census of Canada.

17. ETHNIC, MARITAL AND ECONOMIC STATUS OF WOMEN

Carl F. Grindstaff

While there is a great deal of research published on such ethnic marital issues as intermarriage, marital instability among certain groups and illness (both physiological and emotional) incidence and prevalence in particular ethnic marriages, there is very little in the literature that documents the relationship between ethnicity and marital status on the one hand and economic situation on the other. This paucity of research is especially evident when the focus of studies is on women. This paper provides some information concerning several indices of economic outcome for women by three categories of marital status (single, currently married, and widowed, divorced, separated) and various ethnic identifications. Women aged 30-34 in Canada in 1981 are the focus of the research. It is not the intent of this paper to use exhaustive multiple controls or to determine variance explained in the economic dependent variables. Rather, an elaboration approach is adopted that examines both the dependent and independent variables in detail with an extensive range of categories within variables. Thus, this paper attempts to determine which of the two variables (marital status or ethnic identity) is more important in differentiating economic outcome. Along with marital status, age at marriage will also be examined.

Theoretical Development

The role-conflict model suggests that there are fewer family constraints on single women compared to those who are married, with more alternatives in the life course for unmarried females (Houseknecht et al. 1987). It is contended that marriage is not only a demographic status, but also an institution that reflects the cultural and normative framework of a society. In Canada, historically, it was (and to a large extent is) the husband's role to provide and create social position, and it was (and to a large extent is) the wife's role to contribute to that creation, but to remain more in the background, tending more to the affairs of the family and household (Veevers 1977; Grindstaff 1988; Grindstaff and Trovato 1988).

The earlier a woman enters the family system, the less likely she is to receive training for other roles outside her familial responsibilities. If a woman marries at an older age, this would usually allow her time to attain credentials that would qualify her for a wider range of jobs outside the home. Thus, age at marriage is an important factor in outcomes for women other than those associated with marriage/family. The economic penalties for early marriage have increased as more and more education is required for advancement in the world outside the family system (Weeks 1987). As one recent article began: "The rate at which men and women enter the married state is one of the most sensitive barometers of social, economic and demographic change" (Trovato 1988, 507).

All of the evidence shows that the age at marriage has been increasing rapidly for both men and women over the past generation. In 1966 in Canada, the average age at first marriage for women was 22.6 years. In 1985, this number was 24.6 (Statistics Canada 1985). This two year increase marks by far the largest change in any 20-year period in Canadian history. In addition, for women age 20-24, the percentage never married has climbed from 38 percent in 1961 to 67 percent in 1986. These changes in marriage rates may reflect a widespread dissatisfaction with the roles and opportunities available for women within the formal family structure (Beaujot 1986, 1988). These changes may also be indicative of a rise in individualism among women with a corresponding decrease in the importance of marriage (Trovato 1988). In an article concerning data from the United States, Ball and Robbins (1986) indicate that among Black Americans, there was no relationship between marriage and life satisfaction for women, while men reported less satisfaction among the married group.

Particular groups of women, for example females with particular ethnic affiliations, who may not have taken part in this changing marriage pattern may find themselves with fewer economic alternatives available to them. In an article written in the 1970s, DeRuyter (1976) found some ethnic variation in age at first marriage in Canada, most of which was explained by residence, religion, language and occupation. However, in general, neither the ethnic literature in Canada (Anderson and Frideres 1981; Goldstein and Bienvenue, 1980; Gardner and Kalin 1981; Driedger 1987) nor the family research (Ishwaran 1980; Eichler 1983; Ishwaran 1983; Nett 1988) discuss variations in ethnic marriage patterns or economic outcomes associated with differential patterns.

There is a great deal of research focusing on economic outcome associated with ethnic group membership. Rather wide differentials have been found relating to educational, occupational, income and educational achievement among various ethnic groups, especially when concerning sex differences (Denis 1978; Trovato and Grindstaff 1986; Kalbach and McVey 1979; Boyd 1982, 1984). Generally speaking, the factors accounting for observed differentials can be categorized under subcultural or structural theories, often determined by norms and values on the one hand and by discrimination and lack of opportunity on the other. For example, the foreign-born in Canada are often the best educated, but do not have high status jobs, probably due to problems of credentialing and timing of immigration (Boyd 1984; Trovato and Grindstaff 1986). Ethnicity by itself may have an important impact on the socioeconomic position of women in the society. It might be that women from substantially different racial or cultural backgrounds would be less well integrated into an economic system, in effect, subjects of racism and discrimination.

Hypotheses

Following the role-conflict model, it is hypothesized that never-married women will have the highest levels of economic achievement, followed by separated/divorced/widowed females and then currently married women. When considering only the married women, it is hypothesized that the younger the women at their age of first marriage, the less well placed they are economically. When women marry relatively late, near age 30, they are more likely to approach the economic situation of never-married females, particularly in terms of educational attainment and occupational achievement.

Among ethnic groups, two competing hypotheses could account for observed differences. The first explanation of ethnic variation in economic standing is related to discrimination and lack of opportunity, a structural outcome. In this scenario, the host society, especially the British/English combination, should be ranked highly on economic variables while different racial, ethnic and language groups would be consistently less advantaged economically.

The second hypothesis of ethnic variation can be cast within a subcultural framework. In this explanation, there may be economic differences between ethnic groups, but there are no consistent racial or ethnic differences compared to the "host" group. Rather, the norms and values of certain groups result in a varied commitment to economic success. Thus, different ethnic groups might be either higher or lower in economic attainment depending on their internal group dynamics.

Methodology

The 1981 Canadian Census two percent Public Use Sample Tapes (PUST) provides an excellent data source for examining patterns of marriage, ethnic identification and economic outcome for women. The data are aggregate in nature, and thus this paper will focus on an elaboration approach for each outcome under consideration rather than a multivariate analysis to sort out amount of variance explained. The interest here is a detailed examination of economic outcome in terms of the two variables of ethnic identification and marital status. For data management purposes, it was decided to limit the analysis to women age 30-34 because they are likely to have had ample opportunity to marry and at the same time to have had extensive economic experience. The data set has a total of 2,168 never-married women (11 percent of the total), 1,937 divorced, widowed or separated women (9 percent of the total), and 16,392 currently married women.

Variable Definitions

There has been a great deal of debate in the literature over an appropriate definition of ethnicity that takes into account all of the demographic and psychological aspects of the status (Anderson and Frideres 1981; Isajiw 1980; Simpson and Yinger 1983). It is well beyond the scope of this paper to enter that debate. Rather, the census variables related to religion, language, national origin and ancestral identification will be employed as reasonable indices of the concept. Unfortunately, there is no information on the PUST concerning the native peoples of Canada.

Due to possible problems of mixing somewhat dissimilar groups (e.g., Baptists and Hutterites, German and Dutch) it is not a particularly desirable practice to collapse ethnic, national, linguistic or religious categories. However, because of some rather severe sample size problems in some of the tabular analyses, it was necessary to make some groups larger by combining certain categories. This type of reconstruction from the census data was kept as parsimonious as possible.

Ethnic Origin: Refers to the ethnic or cultural group to which the respondent or the respondent's ancestors belonged on first coming to this continent. A person may now report more than one ethnic origin. The 1981 ethnic origin question attempts to trace the roots of the population of Canada (Statistics Canada 1981, 120). The census PUST reports on the total population, excluding inmates. There are 22 ethnic categories listed in the file, but due to small sample size, these were collapsed into the following 10 groups: British, French, Italian, Other Western Europe, Eastern Europe, Jewish, African, Chinese, Other Single Response and Multiple Response.

Place of Birth: For those born outside Canada, it refers to the specific country of birth according to boundaries at the census date. Twenty foreign countries are listed in the documentation, which were reduced to the following countries or continents: Canada, U.S., Europe, Asia, Africa, South America and the Caribbean, and Other.

Mother Tongue: Refers to the first language learned in childhood and still understood by the individual... it does not necessarily indicate language usage by a given individual at the time of the census. Mother tongue can perhaps best be thought of as the language of childhood socialization. The census reports 11 mother tongue categories which were reduced to the following seven:

English, French, Italian, German/Dutch, East Europe, Chinese, Other. The census designations do not allow for finer breakdowns.

Religion: Refers to specific religious groups or bodies, denominations, sects, cults or religious communities. Respondents were instructed to report a specific denomination even if they were not necessarily active members of the denomination. Thus, the issue of commitment or degree of affiliation is not addressed. The census has 14 religious categories, which were reduced to six: Catholic, Protestant (eight sub-categories included), Jewish, East Orthodox, Eastern Non-Christian, and Other/None. It is estimated from other aggregated census data that about 80 percent of this last classification consists of people responding no religion.

Age at Immigration: Refers to the age at which the respondent first immigrated to Canada and acquired the official status of a permanent resident. These foreign-born women account for about 20 percent of the total sample, and this variable is arranged in four age groups: 0-4, 5-12, 13-19, and 20 and older.

The marital status variable consists of three categories: never-married (single), currently married, and currently divorced, widowed or separated. When analysing age at marriage, those women who are in a cohabiting situation are excluded. To obtain reasonable numbers in cells, age at marriage was collapsed into six categories: 17 and under, 18-19, 20-22, 23-25, 26-29 and 30 and over.

The dependent variables in this study relate to economic outcome, plus age at marriage and number of children ever-born. Five economic variables were developed from the census tape: employment status (working/not working), weeks worked, years of education, percentage in professional occupations, and personal income.

Findings

Never-married Women

Table 1 presents information for never-married (single) women age 30-34. These women account for about 11 percent of the total number of women in the study. Compared to women who have other marital statuses (See Tables 2 and 3), they are clearly more likely to be in the economic mainstream. Single women are more likely to be employed (88 percent), to earn higher wages ($9,000), to have more years of formal education (13 years) and to be in professional types of occupations (39 percent). Being single is associated with substantial economic accomplishment. This is understandable in Canadian society given that these women must, by and large, depend only on themselves for economic solvency.

Table 1 also shows some differences in economic outcome by the various indices of ethnic status among never-married women, but generally the differences are within 10 percent of the average values for the particular indices. There are some significant outliers in the data: Women who came to Canada as adults

TABLE 1

Economic Situation for Never-married Women Age 30-34, by Ethnic Characteristics, Canada, 1981

Ethnicity	Economic Outcome				
	Percentage Employed	Personal Income	Years of Education	% Professional Occupation	Weeks Worked
1. *Age at Immigration* (N = 404)	92.3	$ 8,530	13.6 yrs	35.7	43.5
0-4 (N = 70)	94.3	9,971	14.3	44.3	47.6
5-12 (N = 68)	88.2	9,897	14.0	39.7	47.2
13-19 (N = 48)	95.8	8,543	13.3	41.7	41.1
20+ (N = 218)	92.2	7,628	13.3	28.4	41.6
2. *Ethnic Group* (N = 2124)	88.0	$ 8,878	13.1	38.5	44.1
British (N = 812)	91.1	9,211	13.4	40.6	44.2
French (N = 638)	82.6	8,546	12.1	35.0	44.3
African (N = 37)	89.2	7,784	11.9	29.7	42.1
Chinese (N = 45)	95.6	8,578	14.2	37.8	42.2
Eastern Europe (N = 90)	91.1	9,322	13.5	40.0	43.6
Western Europe (N = 105)	98.1	9,713	13.7	49.1	46.9
Italian (N = 46)	89.1	8,456	13.5	37.0	47.1
Jewish (N = 29)	89.7	9,482	15.9	58.6	44.9
Other Single Response (N = 159)	76.7	7,226	13.2	27.7	40.5
Multiple Response (N = 160)	95.6	9,678	14.2	43.8	44.7
3. *Place of Birth* (N = 2124)	88.0	$ 8,878	13.1	38.5	44.1
Canada (N = 1717)	87.0	8,952	13.0	39.3	44.2
U.S.A. (N = 18)	100.0	7,611	15.0	55.6	38.8
Europe (N = 189)	92.6	9,376	13.7	40.2	45.5
Asia (N = 100)	90.0	7,920	14.7	32.0	41.9
Africa (N = 10)	90.0	10,500	13.3	20.0	47.2
South Amer. and Caribbean Islands (N = 83)	92.8	7,337	11.9	24.1	41.7
Other (N = 7)	100.0	9,857	14.7	42.9	45.9

Foreign-born (N = 407)	92.4	8,560	13.6	35.1	43.6
4. *Mother Tongue* (N = 2168)	86.3	$ 8,677	13.1	37.7	44.1
English (N = 1265)	89.6	8,958	13.5	40.0	44.2
French (N = 658)	80.9	8,395	12.2	34.8	44.0
Chinese (N = 36)	94.4	8,639	14.1	33.3	43.3
German (N = 42)	90.5	8,262	12.7	42.9	43.7
East Europe (N = 44)	88.6	8,841	13.4	36.4	44.0
Italian (N = 28)	82.1	7,893	13.1	28.6	49.3
Other (N = 95)	74.7	7,242	13.9	30.5	42.6
5. *Religion* (N = 2124)	88.0	$ 8,878	13.1	38.5	44.1
Catholic (N = 1056)	85.2	8,727	12.6	35.6	44.5
Protestant (N = 760)	90.8	8,843	13.1	38.7	43.8
East Orthodox (N = 24)	83.3	8,542	13.0	29.2	37.6
Jewish (N = 36)	88.9	9,111	16.2	58.3	43.7
East Non Christian (N = 20)	80.0	6,350	15.4	25.0	37.6
Other and None (N = 228)	93.0	9,908	14.8	50.4	44.6

earned $2,300 less than women who came to the country as children. There are most likely linguistic and credentialling problems for these adult immigrants (Trovato and Grindstaff 1986). Women of African ancestry had four years less education and were only half as likely to be in a professional occupation compared to women from a Jewish background. Women born in the U.S. have the highest rates of education and professional occupation, but work the fewest weeks and have the lowest incomes, compared to women born elsewhere. These particularistic findings may relate to issues of need, culture and even discrimination. Care should be exercised in interpreting some of the associations due to small numbers in some of the cells.

Generally, women of Jewish ancestry or the Jewish faith are the best educated in terms of the index and they are the most highly placed in the occupational structure. Women of European origin (other than French) also do well on these measures. The women of French origin and women from African and the "other" categories are more likely to have below-average economic situations. The women of French origin are heavily concentrated in Quebec where the general economic climate in the early 1980s was poor. The ethnic groups associated with the largest numbers of women, British/French, English/French, Catholic/ Protestant, indicate that the British/English/Protestant do better economically, but rarely do any of the major groupings have the highest levels of economic outcome among the never-married women. While there are some ethnic differences, the patterns are not always consistent and most often the differentials are small. The major gaps in economic situation are across marital status.

Currently Married Women

Currently married women comprised approximately 80 percent of all women 30-34 years of age in Canada in 1981. Two thirds of these married women are employed outside of the home, with the average female working about 36 hours per week and earning just under $5,000.They are the least likely of the three marital status groupings to be well placed in the economic structure. Again, lack of economic necessity may be a factor because of the other potential wage earners in the household. On average, these women have nearly two children which undoubtedly is related to having fewer alternatives to get a job because of family responsibilities. It must be remembered that the majority of these women are in the paid work force which is difficult.

The economic patterns around the various ethnic indices are similar to those observed in the previous section on never-married women, only the levels of economic activity and achievement are lower. For example, in comparison to others, Jewish married women have higher incomes ($6,000), are well educated (15 years), are in the professional work category (40 percent), and have few children (1.65). The same generally advanced pattern is reflected among the currently married women of Chinese ancestry and language, with the exception of occupational position. These two groups of women come from cultural back-

TABLE 2

Socioeconomic Situation for Currently Married Women Age 30-34, by Ethnic Characteristics, Canada, 1981

Characteristics	Percentage Employed	Personal Income	Years of Education	Economic Outcome Percentage Professional Occupation	Weeks Worked	Age at 1st Marriage	No. of Children Ever born
1. *Age at Immigration* (N = 3473)	73.7	$ 5,265	12.4	19.8	37.2	21.2	1.87
0- 4 (N = 404)	72.2	5,126	13.0	26.7	36.6	21.0	1.86
5-12 (N = 501)	73.4	5,446	12.3	20.1	37.3	20.7	1.93
13-19 (N = 602)	73.4	4,887	10.9	10.8	38.2	19.4	2.13
20+ (N = 1966)	75.6	5,358	12.8	21.0	37.0	21.9	1.77
2. *Ethnic Group* (N = 16392)	67.9	$ 4,709	12.1	21.7	36.3	20.5	1.90
British (N = 6465)	69.6	4,730	12.4	23.5	35.9	20.6	1.90
French (N = 4520)	61.2	4,267	11.4	19.6	36.1	20.1	1.85
African (N = 116)	93.1	6,991	11.8	25.0	39.7	22.4	1.93
Chinese (N = 284)	83.8	7,215	13.0	19.4	39.5	22.8	1.58
Eastern Europe (N = 1013)	70.6	4,983	11.7	18.1	37.6	20.5	1.92
Western Europe (N = 1145)	69.9	4,583	12.3	21.1	36.7	20.5	2.04
Italian (N = 502)	62.9	4,410	10.5	10.6	36.8	20.0	2.12
Jewish (N = 181)	69.6	6,033	15.3	40.3	38.5	21.5	1.65
Other Single Response (N = 1134)	71.0	4,922	13.0	22.5	36.3	20.7	2.06
Multiple Response (N = 1032)	73.7	5,140	12.9	26.0	35.9	20.5	1.85
3. *Place of Birth*	67.9	$ 4,709	12.1	21.7	36.3	20.5	1.90
Canada (N = 12905)	66.3	4,558	12.0	22.2	36.0	20.3	1.91
U.S.A. (N = 254)	67.3	4,197	14.7	27.9	31.9	21.0	1.87
Europe (N = 2093)	69.7	4,831	11.7	17.9	37.0	20.6	1.89
Asia (N = 631)	81.4	6,414	13.9	22.2	38.4	22.3	1.77
Africa (N = 120)	84.1	6,542	13.7	25.8	37.7	22.4	1.71
South Amer. and Caribbean Islands (N = 334)	85.0	6,129	11.8	18.6	39.8	22.1	1.93

323

TABLE 2 (Cont')

Characteristics	Percentage Employed	Personal Income	Years of Education	Economic Outcome Percentage Professional Occupation	Weeks Worked	Age at 1st Marriage	No. of Children Ever born
Other (N = 55)	80.0	5,636	12.3	23.6	32.4	22.2	1.76
Foreign-born (N = 3487)	73.8	5,267	12.4	19.9	37.2	21.2	1.87
4. *Mother Tongue* (N = 16392)	67.9	$4,709	12.1	21.7	36.3	20.5	1.90
English (N = 9764)	70.4	4,855	12.5	23.6	36.2	20.6	1.90
French (N = 4339)	60.6	4,261	11.4	19.7	36.2	20.1	1.84
Chinese (N = 228)	85.5	7,211	13.1	21.5	39.3	23.1	1.59
German (N = 419)	68.0	4,055	11.9	18.1	36.3	21.3	2.12
East Europe (N = 472)	72.2	4,892	10.8	14.6	37.9	20.5	1.98
Italian (N = 395)	65.3	4,430	10.1	9.9	36.5	19.7	2.19
Other (N = 775)	71.6	5,007	13.1	21.6	36.4	20.7	2.05
5. *Religion* (N = 16392)	67.9	4,709	12.1	21.7	36.3	20.5	1.90
Catholic (N = 7716)	64.8	4,586	11.6	19.7	36.6	20.4	1.92
Protestant (N = 6778)	69.3	4,587	12.3	22.5	35.7	20.6	1.94
East Orthodox (N = 259)	76.4	5,290	11.1	14.7	38.3	20.5	1.96
Jewish (N = 207)	69.5	5,981	15.3	37.7	37.0	21.7	1.63
East Non Christian (N = 271)	74.9	5,221	13.5	15.9	36.6	21.6	1.86
Other and None (N = 1161)	76.3	5,761	13.6	30.9	37.0	20.5	1.60

grounds and norms that, within the Canadian mosaic, emphasize and place high value on economic achievement (Anderson and Frideres 1981; Li 1980; Verma, et al. 1980). Women of French and Italian ancestry and mother tongue are less likely to have achieved high levels of economic position. The Italian married women have the most children, the least number of years of education, one of the lowest average incomes and the fewest women in professional occupations. It may be that there are structural and discriminatory factors in operation here, but it is more likely that cultural factors relating to the role of women in families are important in this profile (Sturino 1980; Sidlofsky 1969; Kalbach and McVey 1979). Canadian-born women, and those of British/English/Protestant background fall basically in the middle economically, although they are somewhat more likely to be professionals.

While there are certainly variations by ethnic criteria in economic outcome, the distance of most individual categories from the overall means of the economic measures are small. Marital status provides a more discriminating feature in the analysis. In comparison to married females in 1981, single women, both on average and even across most of the ethnic designations, (1) earn $4,000 more, nearly twice as much income; (2) have one more year of formal education; (3) are almost twice as likely to be employed in a professional occupation (39 percent compared to 22 percent); and to work eight weeks longer in the year (44 to 36). For all of the reasons of need, opportunity, training and availability — marital status matters for economic position. The hypothesis concerning the role-conflict model is generally supported by the data presented from the census.

Separated, Widowed or Divorced Women

Table 3 provides the data for women who, in 1981, were divorced, separated or widowed. About nine percent of the total number of women 30-34 were previously married. In the economic indices, these women fall roughly in between the situations cited above in the description of the never-married and currently married females.

This group is very much like the currently married women group in education and occupation, but they were married, on average, one year younger (19.4 compared to 20.5) and they have fewer children. They are also significantly more likely to be in the labour force and they earn substantially higher incomes. The previously married women are similar to the single females on these two economic indices. Clearly, these women are more likely to be on their own economically, and they need to be employed and to have an income that allows them some level of economic independence. They may also receive income from other-than-employment sources.

The ethnic differentials in economic outcome follow the patterns already reviewed for the married and the single females. British/English do better economically than their French counterparts while the Jewish women have relatively

TABLE 3

Economic Situation for Widowed, Separated or Divorced Women Age 30-34, by Ethnic Characteristics, Canada, 1981

Characteristics	Percentage Employed	Personal Income	Years of Education	Percentage Professional Occupation	Weeks Worked	Age at 1st Marriage	No. of Children Ever born
				Economic Outcome			
1. *Age at Immigration* (N = 291)	87.6	$8,567	13.1	29.6	40.9	19.9	1.31
0- 4 (N = 46)	86.9	9,717	13.4	23.9	43.5	20.8	1.33
5-12 (N = 61)	88.5	8,836	13.2	39.3	41.6	19.4	1.46
13-19 (N = 33)	81.8	9,636	13.4	27.3	42.2	19.3	1.24
20+ (N = 151)	88.7	7,874	12.8	27.8	39.6	20.0	1.26
2. *Ethnic Group* (N = 1937)	79.8	7,927	12.0	23.3	39.1	19.4	1.60
British (N = 874)	82.9	7,950	12.0	24.0	39.8	19.4	1.57
French (N = 495)	70.7	7,180	11.1	17.0	36.7	19.6	1.64
African (N = 20)	85.0	8,450	13.1	20.0	40.4	20.8	1.70
Chinese (N = 8)	100.0	8,375	11.6	12.5	38.5	18.1	1.13
Eastern Europe (N = 90)	78.8	8,200	12.5	22.2	39.8	18.1	1.39
Western Europe (N = 109)	84.4	9,312	12.7	28.4	43.0	19.7	1.60
Italian (N = 20)	75.0	7,050	13.7	35.0	37.3	19.3	1.35
Jewish (N = 23)	86.9	9,652	15.4	47.8	36.6	21.4	1.00
Other Single Response (N = 125)	74.4	10,456	12.0	26.4	37.6	18.4	2.20
Multiple Response (N = 173)	89.5	9,000	12.9	30.0	40.4	20.1	1.35
3. *Place of Birth* (N = 1937)	79.8	$ 7,927	12.0	23.3	39.1	19.4	1.60
Canada (N = 1645)	78.4	7,811	11.8	22.2	38.8	19.4	1.65
U.S.A. (N = 33)	93.9	8,333	14.8	33.3	37.9	20.0	1.24
Europe (N = 165)	86.6	9,024	12.9	32.1	41.7	19.5	1.30
Asia (N = 28)	92.8	7,286	13.8	28.6	40.2	19.9	1.29
Africa (N = 10)	90.0	10,300	15.4	40.0	46.1	23.5	.80

South Amer. and Caribbean Islands (N = 50)	82.0	7,720	11.6	16.0	41.7	20.2	1.54
Other (N = 6)	100.0	7,833	12.7	33.0	28.5	20.7	.67
Foreign-born (N = 292)	87.6	8,575	13.0	29.5	40.9	19.9	1.30
4. *Mother Tongue* (N = 1938)	79.8	$ 7,922	12.0	23.3	39.1	19.4	1.60
English (N = 1326)	83.5	8,150	12.2	24.7	39.9	19.4	1.59
French (N = 466)	69.3	7,169	11.1	18.4	37.1	19.8	1.61
Chinese (N = 5)	100.0	7,400	11.8	0.0	40.2	19.4	1.20
German (N = 26)	80.7	9,462	12.7	19.2	42.7	20.4	1.38
East Europe (N = 30)	76.6	8,833	12.4	23.3	39.0	18.4	1.50
Italian (N = 13)	69.2	6,615	13.3	38.5	35.0	17.7	1.54
Other (N = 71)	80.2	7,943	12.4	29.6	36.6	18.3	1.73
5. *Religion* (N = 1937)	79.8	7,927	12.0	23.3	39.1	19.4	1.60
Catholic (N = 840)	74.4	7,539	11.4	19.5	38.9	19.3	1.68
Protestant (N = 833)	81.7	8,076	11.9	23.7	39.3	19.5	1.63
East Orthodox (N = 16)	68.7	6,688	11.9	18.8	38.1	20.9	1.69
Jewish (N = 24)	91.6	9,875	15.9	50.0	40.2	21.5	1.08
East Non Christian (N = 19)	94.7	8,368	12.7	26.3	39.7	20.9	1.11
Other and None (N = 205)	92.1	8,737	13.7	34.6	39.5	19.3	1.20

high economic stature in comparison to other groups. Protestants and Catholics have approximately the same economic profile.

Age at Marriage

This paper has shown that marital status is an important indicator of economic status, independent of various ethnic indices. Married women have the fewest economic resources, but it may be that those resources are differentially available depending on the age at which the women are married. Tables 4 and 5 show three selected economic indicators (employment, education and income) along with two selected ethnic indices (mother tongue and religion) for six different ages at first marriage (17 and under, 18-19, 20-22, 23-25, 26-29, and 30-34) for all currently married women 30-34.

Mother Tongue

Table 4 provides the economic data for mother tongue and age at first marriage. There are substantial differences in age at marriage across the seven categories of language first learned as a child and still understood. Over 40 percent of the Italian women were married as teenagers, compared to only 10 percent of the Chinese-speaking females. The Italian women married on average at least one year earlier than any other group. These are important statistics in that educational attainment is associated with age at first marriage in a systematic way. The relationship is generally linear; the older the age at marriage, the higher the education, and this is apparent for every ethnic group as defined by mother tongue. For Italian-speaking women it is especially crucial in that so many of the women were married as adolescents, and even in that category of marital age, the Italians had the lowest educational achievement. The highest number of years of schooling completed is among the Chinese and ''other'' mother tongue groups. The overall range between the ethnic groups is about three years. Women with the two ''founding'' languages, French and English, are in the middle in terms of educational achievement, but the English-speaking women acquire about one year more schooling on average.

At the same time, there are important educational variations by age at marriage. Women who marry as adolescents average between 9 and 10 years of education, independent of mother tongue, while those who first wed at age 23 or older have completed between 12 and 14 years of school. A key age level seems to be about 23. When married before that age, the educational attainment for all of the seven mother tongue groups is below the mean, while after that age the educational level is much higher than the mean. Overall, it would appear that marriage age is the more important factor, but it is also true that the ethnic groups vary substantially in the age at which they marry for the first time. The educational range by age at marriage within ethnic groups is from approximately 9 to 14 years, while across the ethnic groups it is from 10 to 12 years.

The proportion of women who are in the employed labour force varies more by mother tongue than by a systematic difference in age at first marriage. Only 60 percent of the French-speaking married women are employed compared to 86 percent of the Chinese, with the other five ethnic groups within those extremes. With the exception of the French, the various ethnic women are about as likely to be employed independent of marriage age. There is a slight tendency for women who married after age 30 (a very small number) to be proportionately more engaged in outside-the-home employment. It is probable that the differences observed along the ethnic dimension are related more to normative and value systems within the groups rather than to any systematic structure factors such as discrimination.

The personal income variable is quite linear with a later age at marriage being associated with higher income for all ethnic groups, especially when considering the age at first marriage occurring after 25. Within the mother tongue categories, except for the Chinese (over $7,000), the range for income is between $4,300 and $5,300. Except for the Chinese, there is more range of income within the ethnic groups across age at marriage than within the ethnic groups controlling for age at marriage. The women with English as their mother tongue provide a good example, with an income that changes from $4,500 for women who married at 17 and under to $7,800 for those who were first wed at age 30 or older. The widest range is found among the Italian women, with a difference of over $4,000. It is likely that much of the income differential is related to rural-urban residence and percentage employed.

Religion

Type of religious affiliation has been an important differentiating variable for a number of social and economic outcomes in the past, but seems to have been declining in importance recently (Bibby 1979; Balakrishnan and Chen 1988). Religious commitment seems to provide explanatory power, but this type of information is not available on the census variable.

The economy findings relating to the religious factor are much the same as those reported in the mother tongue section. The major differences in economic outcome are accounted for by age at marriage, although there are some significant differences by religious affiliation. Jewish women have the highest education by a rather wide margin (14.7 years) and they earn the most income ($6,500). Catholics, the single largest religious group, are at the lower end of each distribution, with 11.6 years of education and $4,800 in income. Compared to the Catholic women, Protestants, the next largest numerical category, have slightly higher achievements on income and education. Again, across the religious groups, it would appear that the economic differences noted would be cultural in origin rather than structural.

The data clearly suggest that age at marriage is the critical factor in differentiating these women, with age 23 a seemingly critical point, especially for

TABLE 4

Selected Economic Outcomes (Years of Education, Percent Employed and Personal Income) for Currently Married Women Age 30-34, by Mother Tongue and Age at Marriage, Canada, 1981

AGE AT FIRST MARRIAGE	MOTHER TONGUE AND YEARS OF EDUCATION						
	English	French	Chinese	German	Italian	East Europe	All Other
17 and Under	10.24 (906)	9.28 (257)	9.14 (7)	9.56 (18)	8.82 (63)	9.59 (44)	10.16 (56)
18-19	11.35 (2,475)	10.25 (832)	9.94 (16)	11.08 (92)	9.28 (101)	9.95 (93)	11.20 (122)
20-22	12.84 (4,154)	11.42 (1,901)	11.47 (49)	11.96 (192)	10.52 (146)	10.82 (193)	12.84 (265)
23-25	13.55 (1,932)	12.03 (912)	14.09 (76)	12.31 (78)	11.84 (55)	12.23 (99)	14.59 (174)
26-29	13.61 (894)	12.31 (425)	14.31 (62)	13.77 (43)	12.60 (20)	11.55 (42)	14.68 (129)
30-34	13.18 (264)	12.29 (107)	12.92 (12)	12.31 (13)	11.83 (6)	11.57 (7)	14.33 (30)
Total	12.47 (10,625)	11.31 (4,434)	13.05 (222)	11.92 (436)	10.22 (391)	10.90 (478)	13.15 (776)
Mean Age at First Marriage	21.3	21.7	24.1	21.7	20.4	21.3	22.3
% Married as Teens	32%	25%	10%	25%	41%	29%	23%

330

TABLE 4 (Continued)

AGE AT FIRST MARRIAGE	MOTHER TONGUE AND PERCENT EMPLOYED						
	English	French	Chinese	German	Italian	East Europe	All Other
17 and Under	34.5 (666)	32.6 (144)	43.7 (7)	40.6 (15)	35.4 (39)	33.1 (35)	25.0 (45)
18-19	36.1 (1.739)	34.1 (491)	32.8 (14)	32.3 (68)	38.4 (67)	39.2 (69)	36.8 (77)
20-22	36.2 (2.901)	35.6 (1.087)	36.9 (40)	39.7 (124)	37.65 (92)	37.7 (139)	36.7 (200)
23-25	37.1 (1.381)	37.5 (582)	44.5 (65)	35.7 (53)	31.6 (38)	37.0 (70)	36.1 (119)
26-29	38.8 (714)	37.4 (297)	36.6 (53)	34.1 (28)	38.8 (15)	43.0 (30)	36.8 (104)
30-34	40.3 (219)	37.7 (82)	37.3 (12)	37.9 (10)	28.8 (6)	39.0 (6)	39.9 (25)
Total	36.6 (7.620)	35.8 (2.683)	39.4 (191)	36.8 (298)	36.4 (257)	37.9 (349)	36.6 (570)

TABLE 4 (Continued)

AGE AT FIRST MARRIAGE	MOTHER TONGUE AND PERCENT EMPLOYED						
	English	French	Chinese	German	Italian	East Europe	All Other
17 and Under	73.5 (666)	56.0 (144)	100.0 (7)	83.3 (15)	61.1 (39)	79.5 (35)	80.3 (45)
18-19	70.2 (1,739)	59.0 (491)	87.5 (14)	73.9 (68)	66.3 (67)	74.1 (69)	63.1 (77)
20-22	69.8 (2,901)	57.1 (1,087)	81.6 (40)	64.5 (124)	63.0 (92)	72.0 (139)	75.4 (200)
23-25	71.4 (1,381)	63.8 (582)	85.5 (65)	67.9 (53)	69.0 (38)	70.7 (70)	68.3 (119)
26-29	79.8 (714)	69.8 (297)	85.4 (53)	65.1 (28)	75.0 (15)	71.4 (30)	80.6 (104)
30-34	82.9 (219)	76.6 (82)	100.0 (12)	76.9 (10)	100.0 (6)	85.7 (6)	83.3 (25)
Total	71.7 (7,620)	60.5 (2,683)	86.0 (191)	68.3 (298)	65.7 (257)	73.0 (349)	73.4 (570)

Note: Sample Sizes in Parentheses.

TABLE 4 (Continued)

AGE AT FIRST MARRIAGE	MOTHER TONGUE AND PERSONAL INCOME						
	English	French	Chinese	German	Italian	East Europe	All Other
17 and Under	4,562	3,159	5,714	3,833	3,889	4,977	5,018
18-19	4,639	3,666	6,125	3,837	4,505	5,054	4,728
20-22	4,923	3,968	6,020	4,302	4,438	4,731	5,373
23-25	5,742	5,291	7,974	4,397	4,746	5,293	5,046
26-29	6,720	5,911	7,661	5,047	6,250	6,548	6,326
30-34	7,830	6,911	8,167	4,923	8,167	6,286	6,933
Total	5,198	4,395	7,261	4,294	4,560	5,115	5,321

educational achievement. Delaying marriage, continuing in school and earning power all seem to go hand in hand, independent of religious conviction. For all ethnic groups, later age at marriage is associated with economic advancement.

While later age at marriage improves the economic situation of currently married women, they do not "catch up" to the levels achieved by never-married females, and this finding is applicable to all of the ethnic groups, no matter what index of ethnicity is employed. Even those women who marry as late as age 30 are employed less, earn less, and they even have slightly fewer years of education completed. Age at marriage, marital status, and ethnicity all contribute to our understanding of the economic position of women in Canada. The importance of the contribution is probably most apparent in age at marriage.

Summary and Discussion

This paper examines the association of marital status and various indices of ethnicity with several measures of economic outcome for women age 30-34 in Canada in 1981. In addition, age at marriage is used as a control variable.

The ethnic group data associated with the largest numbers of women, British/ French (ancestry), English/French (language), and Protestant/Catholic (religion), indicate that the British/English/Protestant women do better economically, but rarely do any of the major groupings have the highest levels of economic outcome among single or married women. Women with Jewish or Chinese ethnic associations seem to have the overall highest levels of economic achievement while those of Italian ancestry have some of the lowest economic profiles. It does not appear that women from different racial or cultural backgrounds are particularly disadvantaged in the economic sphere. While there are some specific major ethnic differences, the patterns are not always consistent across ethnic groups, and most often the differentials are small. The major gaps in economic situation are across marital status and age at marriage.

In comparison to married females age 30-34, single women, both on average and even across most of the ethnic designations, earn nearly twice the level of income, have more than one year of additional formal education, are almost twice as likely to be employed in a professional occupation and work up to eight weeks longer in the year. For all of the reasons of need, opportunity, role compatibility, training and availability — marital status matters for economic position. Divorced, widowed and separated women usually are in between the never-married and the currently married females.

The data also clearly suggest that age at marriage may be the critical factor in distinguishing economic outcome among married women, rather than ethnicity. While there are some major economic differences by religion and mother tongue (the selected ethnic indices), the major variance in economic measures is accounted for by age at marriage. On both the education and income variables, the range of difference is greatest across the age at marriage in comparison to

TABLE 5

Selected Economic Outcomes (Years of Education, Percent Employed and Personal Income) for Currently Married Women Age 30-34, by Religion, Canada, 1981

AGE AT FIRST MARRIAGE	RELIGION AND NUMBER OF CHILDREN EVER BORN					
	Catholic	Protestant	East Orthodox	Jewish	East Non-Christian	Other and None
17 and Under	2.74 (554)	2.73 (650)	2.50 (22)	2.43 (7)	2.79 (14)	2.42 (104)
18-19	2.29 (1,615)	2.22 (1,747)	2.48 (56)	2.52 (25)	2.85 (26)	2.01 (262)
20-22	1.98 (3,271)	1.93 (2,900)	2.02 (97)	1.75 (92)	1.82 (78)	1.57 (462)
23-25	1.59 (1,593)	1.60 (1,263)	1.61 (66)	1.35 (62)	1.73 (91)	1.24 (251)
26-29	1.21 (778)	1.14 (596)	.94 (17)	.77 (30)	1.22 (51)	.90 (143)
30-34	.87 (198)	.75 (174)	.60 (5)	.33 (6)	.40 (10)	.80 (46)
Total	1.92 (8,009)	1.92 (7,330)	1.96 (263)	1.58 (222)	1.77 (270)	1.56 (1,268)
Mean Age at First Marriage	21.6	21.2	21.4	22.5	23.1	21.8
% Married as Teens	27%	33%	30%	14%	15%	29%

TABLE 5 (Continued)

AGE AT FIRST MARRIAGE	RELIGION AND PERCENT EMPLOYED					
	Catholic	Protestant	East Orthodox	Jewish	East Non-Christian	Other and None
17 and Under	62.8 (348)	74.0 (481)	90.9 (20)	71.4 (5)	85.7 (12)	81.7 (85)
18-19	65.4 (1,057)	68.6 (1,200)	71.4 (40)	60.0 (15)	57.6 (15)	75.5 (198)
20-22	62.3 (2,041)	68.3 (1,982)	75.2 (73)	67.3 (62)	82.0 (64)	78.1 (361)
23-25	66.9 (1,067)	70.1 (886)	78.7 (52)	79.0 (49)	72.5 (66)	74.9 (188)
26-29	73.3 (571)	79.5 (474)	70.5 (12)	76.6 (23)	82.3 (42)	83.2 (119)
30-34	78.2 (155)	84.4 (147)	80.0 (4)	66.7 (4)	90.0 (9)	89.1 (41)
Total	65.4 (5,239)	70.5 (5,170)	76.4 (201)	71.1 (158)	77.0 (208)	78.2 (992)

TABLE 5 (Continued)

AGE AT FIRST MARRIAGE	RELIGION AND NUMBER OF WEEKS WORKED					
	Catholic	Protestant	East Orthodox	Jewish	East Non-Christian	Other and None
17 and Under	35.3 (348)	33.3 (481)	30.1 (20)	28.2 (5)	29.8 (12)	39.0 (85)
18-19	35.6 (1,057)	35.7 (1,200)	40.1 (40)	39.4 (15)	37.3 (15)	35.6 (198)
20-22	36.0 (2,041)	36.0 (1,982)	39.8 (73)	36.0 (62)	40.0 (64)	37.2 (361)
23-25	37.7 (1,067)	36.4 (886)	36.5 (52)	38.1 (49)	35.9 (66)	38.8 (188)
26-29	39.0 (571)	38.2 (474)	39.9 (12)	43.1 (23)	34.0 (42)	34.9 (119)
30-34	37.5 (155)	40.5 (147)	50.8 (4)	48.0 (4)	39.1 (9)	39.7 (41)
Total	36.6 (5,239)	36.1 (5,170)	38.3 (201)	38.1 (158)	36.8 (208)	37.2 (992)

TABLE 5 (Continued)

AGE AT FIRST MARRIAGE	RELIGION AND YEARS OF EDUCATION					
	Catholic	Protestant	East Orthodox	Jewish	East Non-Christian	Other and None
17 and Under	9.5 (554)	10.2 (650)	8.9 (22)	11.9 (7)	11.2 (14)	11.1 (104)
18-19	10.5 (1,615)	11.3 (1,747)	10.0 (56)	13.9 (25)	10.7 (26)	12.2 (262)
20-22	11.7 (3,271)	12.6 (2,900)	11.0 (97)	14.8 (92)	13.5 (78)	13.9 (462)
23-25	12.4 (1,593)	13.4 (1,263)	13.2 (66)	14.9 (62)	14.2 (91)	14.3 (251)
26-29	12.8 (778)	13.5 (596)	12.1 (17)	16.1 (30)	14.1 (51)	14.2 (143)
30-34	12.6 (198)	13.0 (174)	13.2 (5)	14.0 (6)	14.3 (10)	13.9 (46)
Total	11.6 (8,009)	12.3 (7,330)	11.2 (263)	14.7 (222)	13.6 (270)	13.5 (1,268)
Mean Age at First Marriage	21.6	21.2	21.4	22.5	23.1	21.8
% Married as Teens	27%	33%	30%	14%	15%	29%

TABLE 5 (Continued)

AGE AT FIRST MARRIAGE	RELIGION AND % IN PROFESSIONAL OCCUPATION					
	Catholic	Protestant	East Orthodox	Jewish	East Non-Christian	Other and None
17 and Under	8.5	9.9	4.6	14.3	0	12.5
18-19	10.1	11.7	10.7	32.0	11.5	17.9
20-22	19.2	25.1	10.3	37.0	16.7	36.2
23-25	27.6	30.7	28.8	33.9	17.6	32.7
26-29	27.6	35.1	17.7	53.3	21.6	39.2
30-34	31.8	35.1	20.0	50.0	10.0	50.0
Total	19.4	22.6	15.2	37.4	16.3	30.6

TABLE 5 (Continued)

AGE AT FIRST MARRIAGE	RELIGION AND PERSONAL INCOME					
	Catholic	Protestant	East Orthodox	Jewish	East Non-Christian	Other and None
17 and Under	$3,868	$4,425	$4,273	$1,286	$4,143	$5,952
18-19	4,261	4,313	5,240	6,120	4,000	5,580
20-22	4,383	4,651	5,052	5,326	6,256	6,073
23-25	5,466	5,484	6,046	7,532	5,506	6,116
26-29	6,363	6,609	5,353	8,467	5,412	6,420
30-34	7,005	7,736	9,400	9,167	6,800	7,978
Total	4,796	4,926	5,380	6,432	5,537	6,087

differences by ethnicity (mother tongue and religion). For example, the educational range by age at marriage within ethnic groups is approximately 9 to 14 years, while across the various ethnic categories it is 10 to 12 years. Early marriage, and the child-bearing/childrearing usually associated with it, restricts the nonfamilial roles and thus limits other opportunities. At a time when the resource of youth could be invested in personal development, it is directed primarily toward her new family role (Grindstaff 1988).

Age at marriage, marital status and ethnicity all contribute to our understanding of the economic position of women in Canada. The importance of the contribution is probably most apparent in age at marriage. Later age at marriage is associated with an improved economic situation for currently married women, but never-married females are always at the top of the economic scale. This undoubtedly relates to role incompatibility involved with marriage (along with fertility) and employment (Terry 1975; Yeung 1988).

The variations in economic position relating to ethnicity may well be indirect, through age at marriage, with marital age differing according to cultural norms for the various ethnic groupings. For example, married women with Italian mother tongue have the lowest level of educational achievement (10.2 years), and the highest rate of adolescent marriage (41 percent married as teenagers). Although few Italian women marry after the age of 25, when they do marry later their educational attainment is higher than the women with a French or Eastern European mother tongue. In general, it is probable that economic differences observed along the ethnic dimension are related to normative and value systems within the group rather than to any structural inequities in the social system. The analysis presented here would seem to lend support to the subcultural hypothesis. This type of subcultural interpretation is in contradiction to the vertical mosaic concept, but it has been supported by other research (Darroch 1979; Trovato and Grindstaff 1986). In such an argument there is a danger of being caught in the "blaming the victim" trap. However, given the range of economic outcomes across the various ethnic measures, the specific cultural interpretation seems most appropriate.

18. IMMIGRANT WOMEN IN THE CLOTHING INDUSTRY[1]

Shirley B. Seward

Introduction

A growing body of research on the role and status of immigrant women in the Canadian labour force has observed that disproportionate numbers of immigrant women — especially from Southern Europe and Asia — are in low-skill, low-wage jobs in the economy (Arnopoulos 1979; Boyd 1987, 1986, 1984, 1975; Estable 1986; Seward and McDade 1988).

The classic example is, of course, the clothing industry. In 1986, almost one-half of the female labour force in the clothing industry were immigrants. This over-representation is substantial, given that immigrant women represent only 18.2 percent of the total economy-wide female labour force (Seward and Tremblay 1989, Table 10.3). Furthermore, the analysis in this paper suggests that a high proportion of these immigrant women were born in Southern Europe and Asia.

The concentration of Southern European and Asian immigrant women in the clothing industry is not surprising. Previous research as well as the detailed analysis in this paper reveals that women from these two areas are most disadvantaged in terms of English or French language ability. This, together with limited work-related skills and education, forces many Southern European and Asian immigrant women to take employment in the low-skill clothing industry where language skills are not necessary. The result is that they may have little opportunity to learn an official language or other job skills. It is frequently argued that once in these job ghettos, immigrant women's occupational mobility may be very limited (Arnopoulos 1979; Boyd 1987, 1986, 1984; Estable 1986; Gannagé 1986; Johnson and Johnson 1982; Ng and Das Gupta 1981; Seward and McDade 1988).

The purpose of this paper is to develop a better understanding of the demographic characteristics of immigrant women workers in the clothing industry,

343

to assess their labour adjustment difficulties, and to discuss policy options for improving the effectiveness of governmental labour adjustment programs. While the focus will be on the clothing industry, reference will be made as appropriate to the broader clothing and textile sector. This is useful from a public policy perspective, since a number of labour adjustment programs developed in the past have been applied to this broader sector.

The limited occupational mobility of immigrant women in sectors such as the clothing industry is one aspect of a broader concern regarding the labour adjustment problems associated with "demographically fragile" labour forces in "vulnerable" industries which are threatened by international trading patterns, technological change and other pressures. A demographically fragile labour force is one with various combinations of the following characteristics: relatively low levels of education; a predominance of women — especially married women; a high percentage of older workers; and disproportionate numbers of immigrants with limited official language skills. It is argued that these demographic characteristics militate against the capacity of the labour force to adjust and adapt to economic change. This problem is especially severe in industries that are regionally concentrated in areas where alternative employment opportunities are limited (Akyeampong 1987; Industry, Trade and Commerce, Canada 1979; Cohen 1987; Economic Council of Canada 1988; Langdon 1978; Miles 1975; North-South Institute 1985; Ontario Ministry of Labour 1984; Picot 1986 and 1987; Picot and Wannell 1987; and Statistics Canada 1986).

Research on Canadian industrial adjustment in response to import competition from developing countries has signalled the fragility of the labour force of a range of vulnerable industries, including the textile and clothing sectors. Langdon (1978) utilized 1971 Census data to analyse the regional concentration as well as select demographic characteristics (gender, marital status, level of education and age) of the Quebec labour force in vulnerable industries. The study revealed that in the case of textiles and clothing, employment was much more concentrated in Quebec, compared with the pattern for all manufacturing. It also demonstrated that the textile and clothing labour force was characterized by a higher proportion of married women — particularly in the clothing industry — and lower levels of education than were evident in manufacturing as a whole in the province. With respect to age, there were significant variations within the textile and clothing industry. The presence of older workers was most marked in the predominantly female labour force in women's and children's clothing (Langdon 1978, 5-6 and Table 1).

A study by the North-South Institute (1985) included a brief discussion of the demographic characteristics of the labour force in the textile, clothing, knitting and leather sectors, as well as other vulnerable industries, based on published 1981 Census data. Key findings can be summarized as follows:

- about 30 percent of the female labour force in the leather, textile, clothing and knitting industries were over 45 years of age, as compared to 24 percent of the total Canadiaan female labour force;

- there was a larger proportion of married women in these industries (70-72 percent) than in the general labour force (63 percent), and the women were more likely to be married than the men;

- "...in the clothing industry, 46.9 percent of all women workers, and 43.7 percent of the men, were born outside Canada (14.8 and 11.8 percent in Southern Europe and Asia respectively), and 41.0 percent claimed a mother tongue other than the two official Canadian languages" (North-South Institute 1985, 31 and Table 4.3); and

- education levels were lower in the vulnerable industries than for the labour force as a whole. For example, almost 42 percent of women in the clothing industry did not proceed beyond grade 9, compared to only about 10 percent of females in the Canadian labour force (North-South Institute 1985, Table 4.4)

For nearly 30 years, Canadian governments have recognized the difficulties faced by the textile and clothing industries, and have maintained a range of protectionist import measures in the form of high tariffs (in the 20 percent range) and non-tariff barriers to imports from low-cost sources, mainly in Asia. The rationale for this protection was to prevent injury to Canadian firms and workers, and to provide a "breathing space" during which firms could revitalize themselves and become internationally competitive. With this objective in mind, government protection of the textile and clothing sectors has been accompanied, especially during the first half of the 1980s, by programs designed to assist with such revitalization, with a view to being able, ultimately, to decrease the reliance on protectionist measures. These programs have included labour adjustment assistance for displaced workers, consisting of pre-retirement income support for older workers, as well as training and mobility assistance designed to help workers find new employment. As will be seen in Part 2 below, the extent to which these adjustment assistance programs have been utilized is related, at least in part, to the demographic characteristics of the workers. (For a full description and critique of government adjustment assistance to the clothing industry, see Seward 1989; see also: Ahmad 1988; Canada, Textile and Clothing Board 1986 and 1987; Canadian Industrial Renewal Board 1982, 1984, 1985 and 1986; Economic Council of Canada 1988; North-South Institute 1987 and 1985; Pestieau 1976; Price Waterhouse 1986; and Stone 1984.)

The adjustment challenges facing the textile and clothing industries are likely to assume fresh significance in the near future, especially in the context of the Canada-U.S. Free Trade Agreement. While competition from the U.S. will be intensified, new market opportunities will be opened for Canadian producers and manufacturers in the United States. There will continue to be debate on the magnitude and nature of the impact of changing trade patterns on these and other vulnerable sectors, but there appears to be agreement on the need for well designed labour adjustment programs which will better meet the needs of workers with demographic characteristics that have traditionally been perceived as problematic.

The paper consists of four parts. Part 1 focuses on a description of the demographic characteristics of the labour force associated with the textile and clothing industries, with emphasis on the clothing industry. This incudes a discussion of the differences in the labour force of the clothing industry in Quebec, Ontario and the remainder of Canada. The analysis is based on 1986 Census data and the variables include gender, immigrant/non-immigrant status, place of birth, age, level of education and official language ability. Part 2 focuses on a description and evaluation of the labour adjustment programs provided to the textile and clothing sectors. This evaluation points to the possible relevance of the fragile nature of the labour force in these industries. Part 3 examines in more detail the relationship between demographic characteristics of workers and their capacity to adjust, including the utilization of labour adjustment programs. Finally, Part 4 discusses the need for more effective labour adjustment policies and programs which are designed to meet the needs of the labour force of the clothing industry, particularly those of immigrant women.

Demographic Characteristics of the Clothing Industry's Labour Force

As shown in Table 1, the labour force in the textile and clothing industries represented 9.6 percent of the total Canadian manufacturing labour force in 1986. The largest industry within this group is clothing, representing 6.5 percent of the total manufacturing labour force.

Women are over-represented in the textile and clothing industries, accounting for 65.7 percent of the labour force compared to only 29.2 percent in total manufacturing. The predominance of women is especially marked in the clothing industry, where they account for 76.7 percent of the labour force (Table 1).

A larger proportion of immigrants are employed in the textile and clothing industries (41.6 percent) than in manufacturing as a whole (25.4 percent). In these industries, larger numbers of female immigrants (63,505) than male immigrants (23,930) are employed. The opposite is the case for manufacturing as a whole, where almost twice as many male immigrants as female immigrants are employed (Table 1).

The predominance of immigrants is most marked in the clothing industry, where they constitute 48.9 percent of the labour force. Immigrant women (54,380) significantly outnumber immigrant men (15,625), and represent almost one-half of the female labour force in the clothing industry, a proportion significantly higher than in any other parts of the textile and clothing sectors, or in manufacturing as a whole (Table 1).

The clothing industry is highly concentrated in the central provinces. Quebec and Ontario account for 59.4 percent and 28.2 percent respectively of the Canadian labour force in the clothing industry. The remainder of Canada employs only 12.5 percent of the total clothing labour force. The clothing indus-

TABLE 1

Labour Force 15 Years and Over by Selected Industry,
Sex and Immigrant Status, for Canada, 1986 Census

Industry	Total	Selected industries as a percentage of all manufacturing %	Non-immigrants Male	Non-immigrants Female	Immigrants Male	Immigrants Female	Women as a percentage of the labour force %	Immigrants as a percentage of the labour force %	Immigrant women as a percentage of the female labour force %
Total Manufacturing Industries	2,196,745	100.0	1,186,140	453,720	368,945	187,940	29.2	25.4	29.3
Other Manufacturing Industries (1)	1,986,420	90.4	1,138,035	378,930	345,015	124,435	25.3	23.6	24.7
Total Textile and Clothing Industries (2)	210,325	9.6	48,110	74,785	23,930	63,505	65.7	41.6	45.9
Primary Textile Industries (3)	26,455	1.2	14,935	7,085	2,540	1,895	33.9	16.8	21.1
Textile Products Industries (4)	40,845	1.9	15,430	12,420	5,755	7,225	48.1	31.8	36.8
Clothing Industries (5)	143,025	6.5	17,745	55,275	15,625	54,380	76.7	48.9	49.6

[1] "Other Manufacturing Industries" includes all manufacturing industries except those in textiles and clothing, as defined in the Standard Industrial Classification (SIC). 1980.
[2] SIC Major Groups 18, 19 and 24.
[3] SIC Major Group 18.
[4] SIC Major Group 19.
[5] SIC Major Group 24.

Source: Statistics Canada, Special Tabulations, 1986 Census.

try represents 13.8 percent of the labour force in all manufacturing in Quebec, compared to only 3.8 percent in Ontario and 3.5 percent in the remainder of Canada.

There are considerable regional variations in the place of birth of the female labour force in the clothing industry. As shown in Table 2, a higher proportion of the female labour force is foreign-born in Ontario (69.3 percent) and the remainder of Canada (65.7 percent) than in Quebec (36.0 percent). In Canada as a whole, the largest groups of foreign-born women are from Southern Europe and Asia, representing 21 percent and 16.3 percent respectively of the female labour force in the clothing industry.

TABLE 2

Female Labour Force 15 Years and Over in the Clothing Industry[1] by Place of Birth and Region, 1986 Census

Place of Birth	Quebec		Ontario		Remainder of Canada		Canada Total	
	(number)	(% of total)	(number)	(% of total)	(number)	(% of total)	(number)	(% of total)
Canada	40,745	64.0	9,820	30.7	4,780	34.2	55,345	50.5
North America	280	0.4	130	0.4	105	0.8	520	0.5
Southern Europe	12,290	19.3	9,555	29.8	1,160	8.3	23,005	21.0
Other Europe	1,505	2.4	2,530	7.9	960	6.9	5,000	4.6
Subtotal Europe	13,795	21.7	12,085	37.7	2,125	15.2	28,010	25.5
Southern Asia	595	0.9	1,425	4.5	640	4.6	2,655	2.4
South East Asia	2,160	3.4	2,090	6.5	3,210	23.0	7,460	6.8
Other Asia	1,605	2.5	3,395	10.6	2,795	20.0	7,790	7.1
Subtotal Asia	4,365	6.9	6,910	21.6	6,645	47.6	17,915	16.3
Africa	515	0.8	370	1.2	60	0.4	945	0.9
Caribbean and Bermuda	2,835	4.5	1,075	3.4	60	0.4	3,975	3.6
Central and South America	1,095	1.7	1,595	5.0	150	1.1	2,845	2.6
Oceania and Other	35	0.1	30	0.1	35	0.3	105	0.1
Subtotal Foreign-born	22,920	36.0	22,195	69.3	9,180	65.7	54,310	49.5
TOTAL	63,670	100.0	32,020	100.0	13,965	100.0	109,655	100.0

Totals may not add to 100 due to rounding.

[1] SIC Major Group 24.

Source: Statistics Canada, Special Tabulations, 1986 Census.

Interesting changes have occurred in the place of birth of the female labour force of the clothing industry in Canada between 1981 and 1986 (Table 3). The proportion of foreign-born has increased from 46.9 percent in 1981 to 49.5 percent in 1986. And, while women from Southern Europe comprised 24.2 percent of the female labour force in 1981, this proportion had fallen to 21.0 percent

TABLE 3

Female Labour Force 15 Years and Over in the Clothing Industry[1] by Place of Birth, for Canada, 1981 and 1986 Census

Place of Birth	1981		1986	
	(number)	(% of total)	(number)	(% of total)
Canada	53,270	53.1	55,345	50.5
U.S.	425	0.4	520	0.5
Southern Europe	24,240	24.2	23,005	21.0
Other Europe	4,425	4.4	5,000	4.6
Subtotal Europe	28,665	28.6	28,010	25.5
Asia	11,875	11.8	17,915	16.3
Other	6,085	6.1	7,870	7.2
Subtotal Foreign-Born	47,050	46.9	54,310	49.5
TOTAL	100,315	100.0	109,655	100.0

[1] SIC Major Group 24.

Source: Statistics Canada, *1981 Census of Canada. Population. Labour force-industry by cultural characteristics.* Catalogue no 92-922 (Ottawa: Supply and Services, 1984), Table 1; Statistics Canada, Special Tabulations, 1986 Census.

TABLE 4

Female Immigrant Labour Force 15 Years and Over in the Clothing Industry[1] by Period of Immigration and Place of Birth, for Canada, 1986 Census

Period of Immigration	Southern Europe		Asia		Other		Total immigrants	
	(number)	(% of total)	(number)	(% of total)	(number)	(% of total)	(number)	(% of total)
Before 1946	50	0.2	–	–	345	2.6	415	0.8
1946-1955	2,105	9.2	170	0.9	1,290	9.6	3,565	6.6
1956-1966	11,550	50.2	1,060	5.9	1,935	14.4	14,545	26.7
1967-1977	8,285	36.0	5,575	31.1	5,585	41.5	19,435	35.7
1978-1980	475	2.1	4,905	27.4	1,630	12.1	7,010	12.9
1981-1983	345	1.5	3,875	21.6	1,730	12.8	5,960	11.0
1984-1986	195	0.8	2,325	13.0	920	6.8	3,445	6.3
TOTAL	23,000	100.0	17,905	100.0	13,470	100.0	54,380	100.0

Totals may not add up to 100 due to rounding.

[1] SIC Major Group 24.

Source: Statistics Canada, Special Tabulations, 1986 Census.

by 1986. By contrast, the proportion of Asian-born women increased from 11.8 percent in 1981 to 16.3 percent in 1986.

These changes in the proportion of Southern European and Asian women between 1981 and 1986 may be explained, at least in part, through an examination of differences in the period of immigration for these two groups. Table 4 indicates that the vast majority of Southern European women in the clothing industry immigrated during the periods 1956-1966 (50.2 percent) and 1967-1977 (36.0 percent). Only 2.3 percent arrived during the recent periods 1981-1983 and 1984-1986. By contrast, over one-third (34.6 percent) of Asian women arrived between 1981 and 1986. In absolute numbers, there were 6,200 in recent Asian arrivals in the clothing industry, compared to only 540 from Southern Europe.

The level of education in the clothing industry is much lower than in manufacturing as a whole, and there are marked differences in level of schooling by place of birth. As shown in Table 5, 8.5 percent of the female labour force in the clothing industry has less than grade 5 education, compared to 3.4 percent for all manufacturing. The proportion who have grades 5 to 10 education is 45.4 percent in the clothing industry, much higher than in manufacturing as a whole (30.9 percent). By contrast, the proportion of the female labour force with more than grade 10 education is lower in the clothing industry than in all manufacturing.

Southern European women in the clothing industry have lower levels of education than any other birth place group. Over one quarter of Southern European women have less than grade 5 education, and an additional 59.1 percent have completed only 5 to 10 years of schooling. As will be seen below, these low levels of education among Southern European women are exacerbated by limited official language skills and an older age structure.

The situation is more complex for Asian women. A slightly higher proportion of Asian women (10.7 percent) than the total female labour force in the clothing industry (8.5 percent) has less than grade 5 education. However, the proportion of Asian women with grades 5 to 10 education (41.6 percent) is lower than that for all women in the clothing industry (45.4 percent). Also, a higher proportion of Asian women have grades 11 to 13 and university education than is the case for the total female labour force.

There are significant differences among women from different parts of Asia. Southern Asian women have higher levels of education than women from South East Asia and other Asian areas. Indeed, educational levels of Southern Asian women tend to be higher than that of the total female labour force in the clothing industry. For example, over 20 percent of Southern Asian women have a university education, compared to only about 5 percent of the total female labour force.

The average age of the female labour force in the clothing industry (37.3) is higher than in manufacturing as a whole (35.9). Within the clothing industry itself, there is considerable variation in age structure by place of birth. As was

TABLE 5

Female Labour Force 15 Years and Over in Selected Industries, by Place of Birth and Highest Level of Schooling, for Canada, 1986 Census

Place of birth	Total		Less than Grade 5[1]		Grades 5-10		Grades 11-13[2]		Trades Certificate[3]		University[4]	
	Manu-facturing %	Clothing %	Manu-facturing %	Clothing %	Manu-facturing %	Clothing %	Manu-facturing %	Clothing %	Manu-facturing %	Clothing %	Manu-facturing %	Clothing %
Canada	100.0	100.0	0.7	1.5	28.8	43.9	33.7	31.7	25.0	17.9	11.8	5.0
North America	100.0	100.0	0.3	—	13.8	18.3	29.4	43.3	20.4	16.3	36.2	22.1
Southern Europe	100.0	100.0	22.1	25.6	54.4	59.1	13.1	8.9	8.2	5.5	2.3	0.8
Other Europe	100.0	100.0	1.1	3.0	20.9	29.6	33.5	28.2	30.9	29.9	13.5	9.2
Sub-total Europe	100.0	100.0	12.9	21.6	39.8	53.9	22.0	12.3	18.1	9.9	7.2	2.3
Southern Asia	100.0	100.0	5.4	4.9	28.4	32.5	25.9	27.1	15.7	15.0	24.7	20.1
South East Asia	100.0	100.0	7.4	9.3	33.5	40.3	27.0	27.2	13.1	11.3	19.1	11.8
Other Asia	100.0	100.0	11.0	13.9	34.5	45.8	27.8	27.2	13.1	8.6	13.6	4.5
Sub-total Asia	100.0	100.0	8.2	10.7	32.6	41.6	27.0	27.2	13.7	10.7	18.5	9.9
Africa	100.0	100.0	3.4	7.9	19.8	29.5	25.8	25.3	27.7	23.7	23.2	14.2
Caribbean and Bermuda	100.0	100.0	3.6	6.9	30.0	38.2	28.6	25.2	30.5	25.7	7.2	3.9
Central and South America	100.0	100.0	3.1	5.1	34.3	37.5	28.6	27.8	23.6	23.4	10.4	6.5
Oceania and Other	100.0	100.0	1.6	—	19.7	33.3	30.6	23.8	30.1	19.0	18.1	28.6
Sub-total Foreign-Born	100.0	100.0	10.0	15.6	35.8	47.0	24.4	19.5	18.6	12.3	11.3	5.6
Total	100.0	100.0	3.4	8.5	30.9	45.4	31.0	25.7	23.1	15.2	11.7	5.3

Totals may not add to 100 due to rounding.

[1] Includes responses: "no schooling or attended kindergarten only" and "grades 1-4".
[2] Includes responses: "grades 11-13" and "secondary school graduation certificate".
[3] Includes responses: "trades certificate or diploma" and "other non-university education only".
[4] Includes responses: "some university" and "university completion".

Source: Statistics Canada, Special Tabulations, 1986 Census.

seen with respect to education, there are sharp contrasts in age structure between Southern European and Asian women, and significant differences among different groups of Asian women. The average age of Southern European women in the clothing industry is 43.5, much higher than that of Asian women (36.3). Within the Asian population, the youngest group is from Southern Asia (average age 32.7), and the oldest group was born in other Asian areas (average age 39.8).

Older workers (defined here as those aged 45-54 and 55-64) represent 28.8 percent of the female labour force in the clothing industry, compared to 23.8 percent of the female labour force in all manufacturing. Almost one half of Southern European women are older workers, while only 23.0 percent of Asian women fall into this category.

A higher proportion of the female labour force in the clothing industry (8.4 percent) than in all manufacturing (2.9 percent) speaks neither English nor French (Table 6). As with other variables examined above, there are sharp contrasts by place of birth. However, in this case, Asian women are more disadvantaged than Southern Europe women. Over one quarter (25.3 percent) of Asian women do not speak either official language, compared to 17.7 percent of Southern European women. The higher proportion of Asian women without official language ability can be explained, at least in part, by the relatively large numbers of recent arrivals within the Asian labour force. What is perhaps more surprising is the existence of a significant proportion of Southern European women without knowledge of either official language, given the fact that the vast majority of these women (over 85 percent) have been in Canada for at least 10 years, and some as long as 30 years (recall Table 4). Assuming that many of these women have long attachments to the clothing industry, this suggests the hypothesis that women working in ethnolinguistic ghettos such as the clothing industry have limited opportunity to learn an official language. Within the Asian labour force there appears, once again, to be considerable heterogeneity. Whereas only 7.0 percent of Southern Asian women speak neither official language, 40.6 percent of other Asian women fall into this category.

Labour Adjustment Assistance to the Textile and Clothing Industries

The federal government provides two types of labour adjustment programs. The first category of programs, referred to as "framework policies" by the Economic Council of Canada (1988), are universally available to all workers in all industries, and are designed to assist workers in adjusting to economic change. These include unemployment insurance, as well as training, skills development and job creation initiatives provided through the Canadian Jobs Strategy (CJS). In addition the Canadian Employment and Immigration Commission's (CEIC's) Industrial Adjustment Service (IAS) provides a mechanism whereby manage-

TABLE 6

Female Labour Force 15 Years and Over in Selected Industries by Place of Birth and Official Language Ability, for Canada, 1986 Census

Place of Birth	Total		English Only		French Only		Both English and French		Neither English nor French	
	Manu-facturing %	Clothing %	Manu-facturing %	Clothing %	Manu-facturing %	Clothing %	Manu-facturing %	Clothing %	Manu-facturing %	Clothing %
Canada	100.0	100.0	60.4	23.6	20.1	56.6	19.4	19.7	–	0.1
North America	100.0	100.0	78.6	57.7	2.0	5.8	19.1	34.6	–	–
Southern Europe	100.0	100.0	65.7	48.0	9.0	18.0	10.5	16.3	14.8	17.7
Other Europe	100.0	100.0	87.2	76.5	1.8	5.8	9.9	14.1	1.1	3.6
Sub-total Europe	100.0	100.0	75.1	53.1	5.9	15.8	10.2	15.9	8.9	15.2
Southern Asia	100.0	100.0	90.2	89.5	0.2	–	3.0	3.4	6.7	7.0
South East Asia	100.0	100.0	71.7	62.6	9.5	16.0	4.8	5.3	14.0	16.1
Other Asia	100.0	100.0	61.8	53.3	1.9	2.4	5.5	3.9	30.7	40.6
Sub-total Asia	100.0	100.0	72.8	62.5	4.6	7.8	4.6	4.4	18.0	25.3
Africa	100.0	100.0	60.7	40.2	8.2	22.2	30.2	35.4	0.6	1.6
Caribbean and Bermuda	100.0	100.0	71.0	36.5	21.4	53.5	7.3	9.6	0.2	0.4
Central and South America	100.0	100.0	77.9	60.6	8.5	19.7	7.1	10.4	6.5	9.1
Oceania and Other	100.0	100.0	92.7	76.2	1.6	–	5.2	19.0	–	–
Sub-total Foreign-Born	100.0	100.0	74.3	55.2	6.7	16.1	9.2	11.9	9.8	16.7
Total	100.0	100.0	64.5	39.3	16.2	36.5	16.4	15.8	2.9	8.4

Totals may not add to 100 due to rounding.

Source: Statistics Canada, Special Tabulations, 1986 Census.

ment and labour can work together in "consultative committees" to find solutions to labour adjustment problems caused by technological and economic changes.

The second category of labour adjustment assistance is provided as a component of special sectoral adjustment assistance programs aimed at industries particularly threatened by import competition. This section focuses on the latter category of labour adjustment programs provided to the textile and clothing industries.

During the 1970s, special labour adjustment assistance to the textile and clothing industry consisted of a pre-retirement benefit program which provided income support to displaced older workers (54-65) who had a long attachment to the industry (at least 10 of the previous 15 years) and little prospect of being re-employed. The income assistance amounted to two-thirds of workers' insurable earnings, payable after their unemployment insurance payments had been exhausted.

The pre-retirement benefits program was the only form of sector-specific labour adjustment assistance available to the textile and clothing sector during the 1970s. During the period 1981-1986, by contrast, labour adjustment assistance included not only a continuation and liberalization of the pre-retirement benefits program of the 1970s, but also provided enriched training and mobility assistance, as well as the regular labour adjustment programs provided by the CEIC. In other words, labour adjustment programs in the 1980s were designed both to provide pre-retirement benefits to older workers, and to assist workers in finding re-employment.

The pre-retirement benefits program of the 1980s was different from its predecessor in several respects. Most significantly, the age of eligibility as an "older" worker was lowered to 50-53 in 1982, and further liberalized in 1983 so that workers as young as 47 could be eligible, assuming that they had long experience in the industry. Also, during the 1980s, older workers were permitted to volunteer for redundancy. These changes may have been responsible, at least in part, for substantial utilization of pre-retirement programs during the 1980s, as discussed below.

Labour adjustment assistance in the 1980s also provided re-employment programs of two types. First, textile, clothing and footwear workers had access to CEIC's regular labour adjustment programs such as institutional training, mobility assistance and job creation. Second, enriched features of some of these programs were provided for workers who had been permanently laid-off in the textile and clothing sectors. These enriched features included increased mobility assistance, a portable wage subsidy to help laid-off workers over 45 to find new employment, and increased training allowances.

Evaluations of the sectoral labour adjustment programs of the 1980s have revealed two important findings (Ahmad 1988; CEIC 1984 and 1985; Economic Council of Canada 1988; North-South Institute 1985 and 1987). First, while textile and clothing workers made some use of regular programs offered by

CEIC, they made very little use of the enriched features designed to assist displaced workers. In the period 1981/82 to 1985/86, $57.5 million was spent by CEIC on labour adjustment programs for the textile, clothing, footwear and tanning industries. Of this amount, 99 percent was spent on regular CEIC programs and only 1 percent ($300,000) was spent on enriched re-employment programs (Economic Council 1988, 110). The second major finding was that the most popular form of labour adjustment assistance during the 1980s was the pre-retirement benefits program for older workers. In 1985-86 alone, there were 5,199 active claims for this type of assistance in textiles and clothing (Economic Council of Canada 1988, 108).

The relatively high utilization of the pre-retirement program and the relatively low utilization of the enriched re-employment programs can be explained, in part, as a function of demographic characteristics of the labour force in these industries. As discussed in Part 1 of this paper, the clothing industry — which constitutes the largest employer in the textile and clothing sectors — is characterized by an older labour force than is evident in manufacturing as a whole. It is not surprising, therefore, that large numbers of workers would claim pre-retirement benefits.

There is also a demographic logic to the low utilization of enriched re-employment programs provided by CEIC. The evaluations of the labour adjustment programs of the 1980s referred to above have hypothesized that the labour force of the textile, clothing and footwear industries, which is characterized by low levels of education and skills, and a predominance of women, is unlikely to be able to take advantage of enriched mobility and training provisions.

The Relationship Between Demographic Characteristics of the Labour Force and Labour Adjustment: Evidence from Labour Tracking Studies

The suggestion that demographic characteristics of a labour force are related not only to adjustment difficulties, but also to the likelihood that workers will take advantage of labour adjustment programs, is based on a growing body of literature (e.g., Akyeampong 1987; Industry, Trade and Commerce Canada 1979; Cohen 1987; Ontario Ministry of Labour 1984; North-South Institute 1985; Picot 1986 and 1987; Picot and Wannell 1987; and Statistics Canada 1986). While the scope of this paper does not permit a consideration of all of these studies, it is useful to summarize the major findings of two labour tracking surveys — one conducted in 1977 and the other in 1986.

The Labour Force Tracking Project (Industry, Trade and Commerce Canada 1979) included a 1977 survey that assessed the labour adjustment experience of workers displaced during the period 1974-76 from industries with numerous layoffs, due to plant shut-downs or permanent reductions in production. These industries included the clothing, primary textiles and electrical/electronics sectors. The results summarized below are based on the experience of displaced workers in the clothing industry:

- A larger proportion of females (29 percent) than males (13 percent) left the labour force after being displaced from their employment. Also, a larger proportion of older workers aged 55 and over (47 percent) than younger workers under 55 (23 percent) left the labour force.

- Almost twice the proportion of women (21 percent) compared to men (10 percent) who were displaced during 1974-76 still were unemployed at the time of the survey. The same trend was true of older workers (44 percent) compared to workers under 55 (15 percent).

- The average duration of unemployment for displaced workers was longer for women (31 weeks) and older workers (36 weeks) than for men (21 weeks) and younger workers (27 weeks). In the case of women, married females experienced longer periods of unemployment than unmarried females.

These results were confirmed by the 1986 survey of the labour adjustment experience of workers who were permanently laid-off during the period 1981-84 (Picot and Wannell 1987). The study, based on a special Labour Force Survey, analysed the incidence of job loss and the labour market experience of workers in the economy as a whole. Unlike the 1977 survey, the 1986 survey also assessed the utilization of labour adjustment programs, especially training and mobility assistance, by workers with different demographic characteristics. For the purposes of this paper, the key findings can be summarized as follows:

- At the time of the survey (January 1986), the unemployment rate among workers laid-off between 1981 and 1984 was 25 percent. It was especially high for those aged 55 and over (34 percent) and those with only an elementary education (43 percent).

- "Although the unemployment rate was not dramatically different between men and women (26% and 23% respectively), women were much more likely to leave the labour force. More than a quarter (26%) of women losing jobs had left the labour force by January 1986 compared to only 12% of the men" (Picot and Wannell 1987, 97).

- Approximately 6 percent of the unemployed had not held a job since being laid off. This long-term unemployment was most marked for certain groups, including workers aged 45 and over, those with only elementary school education, and residents of Quebec.

- Among those who were most successful in finding new employment were those aged 20-44, those with a post-secondary education, and those losing jobs in Ontario, Manitoba, Saskatchewan and Alberta.

- The length of job search was greater for older workers, those with less education, and those who had lost jobs in the Atlantic region, Quebec and British Columbia — i.e., those provinces with the highest unemployment rates during the 1981-84 period.

- 17 percent of laid-off workers moved to another geographic location to find work. Of these, only 8 percent took advantage of government mobility assistance. A higher proportion of men (19 percent) than women (11 percent) moved, and a larger proportion of younger people aged 20-34 (20 percent) compared to older workers aged 55 and over (9 percent) moved to find work.

- Following permanent lay-off, 17 percent of workers took some type of training, only 28 percent of which involved government financing. In effect, only about 5 percent of all laid-off workers took advantage of government-financed training.

- Participation in training varies according to the demographic characteristics of workers. Those with high participation rates included younger workers, the more highly educated, and those in highly qualified occupations. Those with low training rates included workers aged 55 and over (7 percent) and those with only an elementary education (6 percent).

The results of these studies confirm that demographic characteristics of the labour force are important determinants of the ease or difficulty of adjustment faced by workers who have been displaced from employment. These variables are also related to the extent to which workers take advantage of labour adjustment programs such as training or mobility assistance. The most disadvantaged groups are women — especially married women, older workers, workers with low levels of education and those who are in regions — such as Quebec — which, at least during the time the above surveys were undertaken — were characterized by high unemployment levels and limited alternative employment opportunities.

Implications for More Effective Labour Adjustment Programs for the Clothing Industry

The clothing industry is a classic example of a sector that is vulnerable to import competition and, at the same time, is characterized by a fragile labour force with demographic features generally associated with labour adjustment difficulties. The future of the Canadian clothing industry will depend, in large part, on whether federal governments will continue to protect the industry.

But even with some degree of continued protection, the evidence seems to suggest that job insecurity and rapid turnover will remain important features of the clothing industry. This poses enormous challenges for labour adjustment strategies. The analysis of labour tracking data in this paper provides sobering evidence regarding the adjustment difficulties experienced by displaced workers with characteristics similar to those of the clothing industry labour force. Perhaps most striking was the finding that a minority of displaced workers take advantage of government training and mobility assistance, and that participation rates are lowest for women (especially married women), older workers and workers with low levels of education.

A number of official reports have suggested that many workers are unable to take advantage of training programs provided by the Canadian Jobs Strategy because they lack literacy skills and are in need of basic academic upgrading (Canada, House of Commons 1988; Canada, Senate 1987). A recent national survey on literacy conducted by Southam Press found that 4.5 million Canadians, representing 24 percent of the adult population 18 and over, are illiterate in English or French (Calamai 1987, 7). According to the Council of Ministers of Education, of this number, 1.5 million are illiterate in the traditional sense, i.e., they lack basis literacy and numeracy, and 3 million are "functionally illiterate," i.e., they "possess simple literacy abilities but at a level that is inadequate for the requirements of an industrialized, technological society" (CMEC 1988, 5). In most cases, persons who are illiterate in the traditional sense have less than a grade 5 education and those who are functionally illiterate have less than a grade 9 education. The survey also found that 35 percent of foreign-born residents are functionally illiterate, compared to 24 percent of all Canadian residents 18 years and older (Calamai 1987, 22; *The Citizen* 1987). Perhaps most significantly, 29 percent of the foreign-born in the survey who claimed some university education tested as functionally illiterate, compared to only 6 percent of the Canadian-born (Calamai 1987, 22; *The Windsor Star* 1987). This is undoubtedly related to the poor official language skills of many immigrants.

This discussion suggests that basic and functional illiteracy are particularly serious problems in the clothing industry. As we saw in Part 1 of this paper, a relatively large proportion of the female labour force in the clothing industry has less than grade 5 education or only 5-10 years of education. This is especially marked for women from Southern Europe. Also, it is possible that many Asian women with higher levels of education may also be functionally illiterate due to their limited official language ability. This points to the need for greater attention to literacy training and basic academic upgrading, as well as official language training, as fundamental aspects of labour adjustment programs for the clothing industry and other industries with similar labour force characteristics.

Literacy training and basic academic upgrading are generally considered to be provincial responsibilities, since problems in these areas are presumed to be related to deficiencies in elementary and secondary education systems. School boards play a major role in the delivery of functional literacy programs, and Seward has suggested that the elementary and secondary school system has the potential to expand even further its mandate in such adult education activities (Seward 1988a). Since these areas are under provincial jurisdiction, the Canadian Jobs Strategy does not offer upgrading below the high school level within its Basic Training for Skill Development program. However, the House of Commons Standing Committee on Labour, Employment and Immigration, in its recent review of the CJS, has made the following recommendations:

> That, as soon as possible, the federal government call a federal-provincial conference of Education/Training Ministers to formulate and implement a cost-shared plan to seriously address the issue of illiteracy, functional illiteracy and the problems of those who need basic upgrading.

> That more funds be allocated to basic upgrading programs under the Job Development and Entry/Re-entry Programs (Canada, House of Commons 1988, 10-11).

Closely related to the issue of literacy training and basic academic upgrading is the need for more accessible and effective language training for immigrants. The analysis in Part 1 of this paper revealed that a relatively large proportion of the female labour force in the clothing industry has no knowledge of either official language. This is particularly marked for recent arrivals from Asia (especially for "other" Asian areas) but is also true for nearly one fifth of Southern European women, the vast majority of whom have been in Canada for 10 to 30 years. A number of studies have addressed the problem of universal access to high quality language training programs offered by CEIC and Secretary of State (Arnopoulos 1979; Boyd 1987; Estable 1986; and Seward and McDade 1988). According to Seward and McDade, "there are many positive features of the language training provided by Secretary of State, including flexibility, and in some cases, integration of child care, as well as more informal, community-based programs with a multi-cultural preschool component" (Seward and McDade 1988, 22). However, there are serious problems of access. First, the programs do not provide living and travel expenses, costs which can exclude low-income women. And, second, there is unequal provision of these programs in different provinces, thereby placing particular groups at a disadvantage. Even if immigrants are fortunate enough to gain access to Secretary of State language training, it has been suggested that the length of the programs is too short to teach basic literacy, even if the participants develop some oral proficiency (*The Citizen* 1987).

Language training provided by CEIC is not available to immigrant women in the clothing industry, since potential participants must demonstrate that their lack of fluency in an official language acts as barrier to their employment. Since it is not essential for workers in the clothing industry or in certain other types of low-skill sectors to speak one of the official languages, they are not eligible for CEIC language training (Seward and McDade 1988). This would appear to be a very short-sighted policy, since lack of language skills is clearly a key factor limiting occupational mobility and the utilization of labour adjustment programs. Since the federal government has for several years placed priority on providing labour adjustment assistance to the clothing industry, it does not seem logical that workers are excluded from CEIC language training programs (Seward 1988b).

The mobilization of sufficient resources to mount a literacy/language training program which would assist workers such as those in the clothing industry would involve considerable political will. However, even if such programs could be developed, there are many workers who might not be prepared to invest a significant amount of time in such upgrading. A case in point might be older workers who may feel that "retraining is not a rational choice, since they have relatively few years of work left to accrue the benefits" (Picot and Wannell 1987,105). This may account for the relatively large numbers of older workers who took advantage of the pre-retirement benefit program provided during the 1980s. As discussed in Part 2 above, these benefits were available not only to displaced older workers, but also to older workers who volunteered for redundancy in firms which had a labour surplus. The problem with the latter option is that it permitted older workers to leave, and encouraged younger, more mobile workers to enter, and remain in, declining industries. It would probably have been better to retain older workers as long as possible, in order to keep them productively employed, and to encourage younger workers — who have less difficulty in securing new jobs — to move to more buoyant parts of the economy. In other words, the pre-retirement program should have been restricted to older workers who were involuntarily, and permanently, laid off (Economic Council of Canada 1988).

The pre-retirement benefits program for the clothing industry wound down with the termination of special sector adjustment assistance to the industry in 1986. Since the proposed federal-provincial Program for Older Worker Adjustment (POWA), to be available to all sectors of the economy, has not yet been established, there is currently no program available for older workers. This is a serious problem, given the special difficulties faced by older workers in labour adjustment. In fact, the Standing Committee on Labour, Employment and Immigration has recommended that older workers should be "identified for targeted assistance under the Canadian Jobs Strategy (at least until the program for Older Worker Adjustment becomes operational)" (Canada, House of Commons 1988, 14).

The combination of literacy and basic academic upgrading, language training and pre-retirement income assistance for older workers would assist many workers in the clothing industry. However, the provision of training, by itself, is not a guarantee of successful re-employment. As we have seen, displaced workers in industries which are concentrated in regions with high unemployment rates and limited alternative employment opportunities experience greater difficulties in labour adjustment. Therefore, the provision of training to workers must be accompanied by appropriate macroeconomic policies as well as regional employment programs. The key federal government initiative of this type is the Community Futures program in the Canadian Jobs Strategy, which provides job creation funds and related assistance to communities adjusting to the downside effects of structural and economic change. However, as reported by a Senate Standing Committee on Social Affairs, Science and Technology, "Only two of the 39 communities selected as participants in this program have received funding" (Canada, Senate 1987).

Inevitably, a number of displaced workers will face unemployment for short or longer periods. For these workers, unemployment insurance and social welfare assistance provide income maintenance. A number of proposals have been developed for the reform of unemployment insurance (see for example, Canada, Commission of Inquiry 1986; Canada, Royal Commission 1985; Courchene 1987; and Newfoundland, Royal Commission 1986). While it is not possible in the scope of this paper to review these proposals in detail, three general aspects of the proposed reforms are worth noting. First, most of the proposals suggest that training activities should be built into the provision of unemployment insurance. Second, several of the reports recognize that job creation activities are essential. And, third, at least some of the proposals call for a guaranteed annual income for the long-term unemployed and the working poor. Interestingly, recent federal-provincial initiatives in the social welfare area are also experimenting with approaches to easing the transition from welfare to paid work, through the provision of training and employment opportunities.

Conclusion

The characteristics of the labour force in the clothing industry pose significant problems in terms of labour adjustment. Disproportionate numbers of immigrant women with limited official language skills, low levels of education and an older age structure necessitate innovative approaches to labour adjustment programs which go beyond the boundaries of traditional programs and have relevance for both federal and provincial governments. It is the contention of this paper that such approaches are essential, given the limited impact of more traditional programs on workers with the demographic features such as those which characterize the clothing industry.

A multifaceted labour adjustment program, as discussed in this paper, will require considerable financial resources. However, the alternatives — continuing protection and public assistance to the industry, or high levels of unemployment — also involve considerable costs. It would seem that the long-term benefits associated with a better-educated and more highly skilled labour force would more than offset the immediate costs involved in a comprehensive labour adjustment program.

Notes

1. The research for this paper was completed in July 1988, and reflects the status of public policy initiatives at that time.

19. THE INCOME OF CARIBBEAN IMMIGRANTS IN CANADA[1]

Anthony H. Richmond

This paper examines some of the factors determining the total income and earnings of Caribbean immigrants, compared with the Canadian-born and immigrants from other countries.[2] The majority of West Indians in Canada were recent arrivals at the time of the 1981 Census. Table 1 shows the numbers admitted to Canada as landed immigrants 1968-1980, from Jamaica, Haiti, Trinidad, Guyana and the rest of the Caribbean region. The linguistic, ethnic and religious backgrounds were diverse. There were 211,205 Caribbean-born persons enumerated in Canada in 1981. The large majority had arrived after 1971 and lived in metropolitan Toronto (57 percent), or Montreal (21 percent). Altogether, 85 percent were Anglophone, 11 percent Francophone and 4 percent had a mother tongue that was not one of the official languages of Canada. Half reported their religion as Protestant, a third Catholic and 16 percent as another religion, including Hindu. Ten percent reported an "Asian" ethnic origin. Although many indicated "British," "French" or multiple ethnic origins, the majority constituted a "visible minority," one of several groups that a *Special Committee* of the House of Commons (chaired by Bob Daudlin, M.P.) identified as potential victims of racism. That committee indicated that "the government must now consciously choose to remove all roadblocks preventing the full participation of all citizens in the cultural, social economic and political life of the country." If it is to be successful, such a policy must be based upon an understanding of the dynamics of immigrant adaptation and the particular experiences of specific minorities.

Other studies have examined the economic experience of immigrants in Canada in 1981, providing broad comparisons between countries and regions of origin, or have described the characteristics of selected groups, such as those from Asia (Beaujot, et al. 1988; Basavarjappa and Verma 1985). This report focuses on Caribbean immigrants because there is reason to believe some of this group, particularly those who are of Afro-Caribbean origin, may be subject

TABLE 1

Caribbean Immigrants: 1968-1980 by Country of Last Permanent Residence

	Haiti	Jamaica	Trinidad	Guyana	Rest	Total
1968	444	2,886	2,419	823	1,965	8,537
1969	550	3,889	5,631	1,865	3,194	15,129
1970	840	4,659	4,790	2,090	2,383	14,762
1971	989	3,903	4,109	2,384	1,954	13,339
1972	936	3,092	2,739	1,976	1,578	10,321
1973	2,178	9,363	5,138	4,808	2,827	24,314
1974	4,857	11,286	4,802	4,030	2,928	27,903
1975	3,341	8,211	3,817	4,394	2,570	22,333
1976	3,061	7,282	2,359	3,430	2,117	18,249
1977	2,026	6,291	1,552	2,472	2,058	14,399
1978	1,702	3,858	1,190	2,253	1,480	10,483
1979	1,268	3,213	786	2,473	1,094	8,834
1980	1,633	3,161	953	2,278	1,294	9,319
TOTAL	23,825	71,094	40,285	35,276	27,442	197,922

Source: Manpower and Immigration/Employment and Immigration Canada, Annual Statistical Reports.

to more prejudice and discrimination in Canada than other immigrants who are "visible minorities." Studies of prejudice, social distance and discrimination have consistently shown the Black population to be among the least favoured when compared with other ethnic minorities and immigrant groups (Berry, et al. 1977; Henry 1978).

If effective programs to assist the process of economic and social integration of recent immigrants are to be designed, the importance of such factors as the demographic characteristics of a group, the length and location of residence, gender and language differences and other factors which influence occupational status and income, must be understood first. Data from the 1981 Census show that Caribbean immigrants were generally in the young adult age groups with a slight majority of females (55 percent). Educational levels compared favourably with other foreign- and Canadian-born persons. Labour force participation rates were above average. There was a relative concentration of Caribbean immigrants in "processing and fabricating," "professional and technical" and in "service" occupations. Nevertheless, unemployment levels were above those of the Canadian-born, even after standardization for age (for details see Richmond 1989).

The large majority of Caribbean immigrants arrived in Canada between 1970 and 1979. Comparisons between the total income from all sources of this cohort are shown in Tables 2 and 3, for males and females respectively. The tables compare the average income of Caribbean immigrants with those born in Italy, the United Kingdom, other European countries, Asia and remaining regions, after controlling for level of education. An index is calculated, using the mean income of the Canadian-born of the same sex and educational level, as a base for comparison. In the case of males, the mean income of the Caribbean-born is only 81 percent of the Canadian-born, lower than that of any other birthplace. When level of education is taken into account this disadvantage persists and is greatest for those with university education.

The situation of Caribbean women is somewhat different. The overall average total income is the same as that for Canadian-born women and those with secondary education, or less, actually have total incomes above the average for Canadian-born females. However, those with post-secondary and university education are relatively disadvantaged, but to a lesser degree than their male counterparts, or Italian women of similar educational attainment. The latter probably have a language barrier to overcome that the majority of Caribbean women do

TABLE 2

Total Income, by Birthplace and Education Immigrant Males, 15 Years and Over who Immigrated Between 1970-1979

| Birthplace | Elementary | Secondary | Post Secondary | | Total |
			Non-University	University	
			Average ($)		
Caribbean[1]	11,535	11,604	14,491	16,222	13,348
Italy	14,048	14,288	15,994	20,991	14,941
United Kingdom	11,058	16,238	22,605	30,556	21,950
Other Europe	14,375	13,867	17,785	22,987	16,548
Asia	10,655	11,782	15,404	18,267	15,058
Other Regions	11,962	12,040	15,521	23,251	17,449
Total Immigrants	13,007	12,972	17,260	21,409	16,580
			INDEX[2]		
Caribbean	91	78	82	65	81
Italy	111	96	90	84	90
United Kingdom	87	110	128	123	132
Other Europe	114	94	100	92	100
Asia	84	80	87	73	91
Other Regions	95	81	88	93	105
Total Immigrants	103	88	97	86	100

[1] Caribbean includes Guyana.
[2] Base = All males born in Canada, 15 years ad over, by education.

Source: Statistics Canada, 1981 Census of Canada, special tabulations.

TABLE 3

Total Income, by Birthplace and Education
Immigrant Females, 15 years and over
Immigrated 1970-1979

| Birthplace | Elementary | Secondary | Post Secondary | | Total |
			Non-University	University	
			Average ($)		
Caribbean [1]	6,876	7,379	9,287	10,487	8,324
Italy	6,419	6,874	3,628	9,562	6,407
United Kingdom	5,145	7,202	9,493	12,812	8,632
Other Europe	7,169	7,468	8,900	11,602	8,212
Asia	5,937	7,033	9,499	10,946	8,625
Other Regions	6,263	6,559	8,775	11,489	8,787
Total Immigrants	6,577	7,115	9,150	11,293	8,469
			INDEX [2]		
Caribbean	120	102	98	81	100
Italy	112	95	38	74	77
United Kingdom	90	99	100	99	104
Other Europe	125	103	94	89	99
Asia	104	97	100	84	104
Other Regions	109	90	93	89	106
Total Immigrants	115	98	96	87	102

[1] Caribbean includes Guyana
[2] Base = All females born in Canada, 15 years and over, by education

Source: Statistics Canada, 1981 Census of Canada, special tabulations.

not face, but the relative advantage of West Indian women compared with men is a more complex question. Total income is influenced by labour force participation rates, weeks worked per annum and hours worked weekly, all of which were relatively high for immigrant women generally and Caribbean women particularly, compared with Canadian-born women. Furthermore, Caribbean women were likely to be employed in hospitals and other services where there was a demand for labour, whereas Caribbean males were more likely to experience unemployment than women.

Further confirmation of the disadvantage of Caribbean immigrant men is provided in Tables 4 and 5, where age and period of immigration are controlled, as well as education. Only in the case of the very few males who arrived in Canada before 1960 (some as children or students) is the total income above the Canadian-born male average. The most recently arrived (1975-79 and

1980-81) have total incomes that are only 73 and 32 percent of the Canadian-born male average, respectively. There is a marked tendency for those with higher education to be the most relatively disadvantaged. This tendency is also evident for Caribbean women, although the degree of income deficiency — compared with Canadian-born women — is less than that for males in same sex comparisons. Caribbean immigrant women who arrived before 1970 have a more favourable income experience, with the exception of those having university education. For both men and women it is evident that the return on education is less than that for equivalent Canadian-born persons, raising questions about the recognition of credentials and the possibility of discrimination.

TABLE 4

1980 Income, by Year of Immigration and Education

Females, 25-34 years

Birthplace	Elementary	Secondary	Post Secondary Non-University	University	Total
			Average ($)		
Born in Canada	5,545	8,309	10,410	13,982	10,050
All Immigrants	7,357	8,705	10,016	13,982	9,896
Born in Caribbean	6,923	8,645	9,810	11,578	9,391
Immig. < 1960	8,936	9,394	9,201	14,912	10,416
Immig. 1960-69	9,126	9,946	11,992	13,036	11,503
Immig. 1970-74	7,672	8,954	9,855	11,613	9,543
Immig. 1975-79	6,318	7,591	8,614	8,931	8,042
Immig. 1980-81	2,931	4,983	4,950	8,101	4,808
			INDEX[1]		
Born in Canada	100	100	100	100	100
All Immigrants	133	105	96	100	98
Born in Caribbean	125	104	94	83	93
Immig. < 1960	161	113	88	107	104
Immig. 1960-69	165	120	115	93	114
Immig. 1970-74	138	108	95	83	95
Immig. 1975-79	114	91	83	64	80
Immig. 1980-81	53	60	48	58	48

[1] Base = Canadian-born.

TABLE 5

1980 Income, by Year of Immigration and Education

Males, 25-34 years

Birthplace	Elementary	Secondary	Post Secondary		Total
			Non-University	University	
			Average ($)		
Born in Canada	12,579	16,719	18,496	21,419	18,055
All Immigrants	14,989	16,777	18,268	20,209	18,167
Born in Caribbean	11,035	13,676	15,199	16,378	14,742
Immig. < 1960	12,310	15,491	19,503	20,605	18,896
Immig. 1960-69	11,703	16,414	17,177	19,387	17,493
Immig. 1970-74	12,323	14,284	15,484	15,819	15,029
Immig. 1975-79	10,013	12,432	14,048	14,377	13,250
Immig. 1980-81	3,992	6,102	4,946	6,759	5,718
			INDEX[1]		
Born in Canada	100	100	100	100	100
All Immigrants	119	100	99	94	101
Born in Caribbean	88	82	82	76	82
Immig. < 1960	98	93	105	96	105
Immig. 1960-69	93	98	93	91	97
Immig. 1970-74	98	85	84	74	83
Immig. 1975-79	80	74	76	67	73
Immig. 1980-81	32	36	27	32	32

[1] Base = Canadian-born.

Multivariate Analysis of Employment Income

In order to introduce a further level of control into the analysis, the employment income of Caribbean immigrants who worked mainly full time, for 40 weeks or more in 1980 was examined. It has been shown elsewhere that, overall, Caribbean males ranked 14th and Caribbean females 13th out of 15 birthplace categories compared (Beaujot et al. 1988, 66). The average employment income in 1980, by place of birth and sex, is shown in Table 6.

After standardizing for both age and education, Caribbean males earned 82 percent, and females 89 percent, of comparable Canadian-born persons of the same sex. The most disadvantaged were Francophone males born in the Caribbean who had only elementary education. The latter earned only 67 percent

TABLE 6

Average Employment Income[1] in 1980
by Place of Birth and Sex, Canada, 1981

Place of Birth	Average $	
	Males	Females
Canada	20,802	13,248
Outside Canada	21,830	13,007
Caribbean [2]	18,224	12,142

[1] Excluding zero income
[2] Includes Guyana

Source: Statistics Canada, special tabulations, 1981 Census.

of the income of all Canadian-born males with elementary education (Richmond 1989, Table 34).

The level of employment income of Caribbean immigrant men and women was influenced by a number of factors among which gender, age, mother tongue, education, qualifications, occupation, period of immigration to Canada and location of residence were important. To determine the relative weighting of these variables, and the relationship between them, a multivariate analysis using multiple regression was performed. A special micro-database was created for the purpose and the analysis undertaken, using SPSS-X procedures. Qualifications were defined on a scale from 0-2, in which a university degree scored "2" and a non-university qualification "1". A special classification of occupations was adapted for the purpose which provided a score ranging from "1" (high) to "15" (low) status. (Further information concerning this occupational classification prepared by Statistics Canada is included in the Appendix.) The variables were entered in the equation in a predetermined order according to approximate temporal causal sequence. Ascribed characteristics such as sex and age were entered first, followed by mother tongue. Achievement factors (years of education and qualifications) followed. Years of residence in Canada, whether resident in Montreal or in other parts of Canada, and occupation were entered last, in that order, so that their effects could be measured after ascribed attributes, and after other characteristics, were controlled.

The central hypotheses to be tested were:

- that education, qualifications and occupation would be the main determinants of employment income but that, in view of the gender variations noted above, the precise relationship would be different for men and women;

- that having English as a mother tongue would be positively advantageous, increasing employment income "when other things were equal;"
- that employment income would increase with length of residence in Canada, but there would be gender variations in this regard; and
- as the overall level of employment income, for the economically active population, was lower in Montreal than in Toronto, it was hypothesized that residence in Montreal would have a disadvantageous effect in level of employment income of Caribbean immigrants, but the extent of difference would vary by gender.

Because the number of weeks worked in 1980 and whether the employment was part-time or full-time would have an obvious effect on the level of employment income reported, the analysis was limited to those who reported in the census that they worked mainly full-time and for 40 weeks or more. This approach had the advantage of eliminating immigrants who had lived and worked in Canada for only a short time in 1980, who may have experienced prolonged unemployment during the first year in the country. It also excluded all those who, whether on a voluntary or involuntary basis, were not employed for a large part of the year, together with those who were employed mainly part-time. In this way a better understanding could be gained concerning the determinants of employment income for most labour force participants and a fairer comparison made between men and women. (The resulting number of cases in the equation was 95,034).

Given the importance of age in determining both occupational status and income, a dummy variable was also used in the regression equations, identifying the age group 35-54 years as a separate category (compared with all others over 15 years), because younger and older persons have on average lower incomes. Zero order correlations between the variables entered in the equation and the occupational scores and employment income are shown in Table 7. Years of education had the highest correlation with employment income, followed closely by the occupational status score and qualifications. (Given the direction of the occupation's status scale, a high score indicating low status, the correlation with income was negative.) Education and qualifications, were also the most powerful determinants of the occupational status score itself.[3] Together they showed that, for Caribbean immigrants as for the population generally, education and qualifications were the major influence on occupational status, which in turn was an important determinant of employment income.

Zero order correlations between gender and the occupational status score were low but indicated a slightly higher status for women, although this was accompanied by a significant negative association with income. This confirms the findings of other labour force studies which show that, depending on the measures used, full-time women workers may have higher occupational status than men, and significantly lower incomes (Boyd, 1986). Being in the "middle age" category was only weakly correlated with occupational status but more strongly

Occupational Score and Employment Income Zero Order Correlations for Caribbean[1] Immigrants

	Occ. Score	Emp. Inc
Sex (female)	− .058	− .305
Age (35-54 yrs)	− .095	.178
Mother Tongue (English)	− .071	.035
Years of education	− .534	.373
Qualification [2]	− .495	.355
Length of residence	− .259	.281
CMA (Montreal)	.068	− .061
Occupational score [3]	1.000	− .357
Employment income [4]	− .357	1.000

[1] Caribbean includes Guyana

[2] None = 0; Non-university = 1; Degree = 2

[3] Occupational score: 1 = high status, 15 = low status

[4] Employment income for persons employed mainly full-time 40 weeks or more in 1980

Number of cases = 95,034

Source: Statistics Canada, 1981 Census of Canada, special tabulations.

with income. Length of residence in Canada was positively associated with improved occupational status and higher income. Mother tongue (English) had only a very low correlation with either occupational status or income.

Regression Analyses

The results of the multiple regression analysis of employment income, for males and females combined, is shown in Table 8. "B" represents the increment or decrement of income relative to the constant and "s.e." the standard error of the estimate. (To be statistically significant "B" must be at least twice the standard error.) The variables used in the equation explained 31 percent of the variance in income, years of education being the largest single component of R square. Measured by the standardized Beta coefficient (− .285), gender had the strongest direct effect on income "when other things were equal," indicative of the disadvantaged position of women in the labour force. Being female reduced mean employment income by an average of $6,069.00 and this disadvantage was only slightly reduced (to $5,680.00), when all other factors such as age, language, education, qualifications, period of immigration, location of

TABLE 8

Multivariate Analysis of Employment Income[1]
Stepwise Multiple Regression, Caribbean Persons

		1	2	3	4	5	6	7	8	Beta
Sex	B	-6,068.95	-5,973.46	-5,997.45	-5,259.34	-5,196.52	-5,212.09	-5,205.99	-5,680.48	-.29
(female)	s.e.	61.57	60.61	60.59	56.90	56.32	55.06	54.99	54.67	
Age	B		3,368.87	3,354.29	3,111.57	3,150.35	2,251.22	2,252.43	2,089.24	.10
(35-54 yrs)	s.e.		60.52	60.48	56.50	55.91	56.31	56.24	55.35	
Mother Tongue	B			1,283.35	1,309.20	1,576.19	1,072.53	148.34	-182.29	-.01
(English)	s.e.			96.51	90.09	89.34	87.67	106.13	104.47	
Years of Education	B				949.98	592.27	544.13	534.47	340.58	.12
	s.e.				8.02	11.23	11.00	11.01	11.32	
Qualification	B					2,936.59	2,671.78	2,695.48	1,944.95	.12
(Non-Uni/Degree)	s.e.					65.19	63.85	63.79	64.03	
Years of Immigration	B						299.09	302.22	254.70	.16
	s.e.						4.51	4.51	4.51	
CMA	B							-1,333.54	-1,207.50	-.05
(Montreal)	s.e.							86.54	85.08	
Occupational Status	B								-467.97	-.20
(1-15 = low)	s.e.								8.09	
Constant	B	18,058.69	16,331.19	15,208.11	2,681.67	4,763.46	3,193.38	4,322.07	12,299.19	
	s.e.	42.35	51.96	99.13	140.56	146.56	145.22	162.49	211.03	
R Square		.09	.12	.12	.24	.25	.28	.29	.31	

[1] Only those employed mainly full-time
40 weeks or more in 1980

s.e. = standard error

Source: Statistics Canada, 1981 Census of Canada, special tabulations.

residence and occupational status, were taken into account (see column 8 of Table 8).

Initially, being 35-54 years of age adds an average of $3,369.00 to income but this benefit is reduced to $2,089.00 when all other factors are controlled. Having English as mother tongue appears at first to be advantageous but the positive increment disappears when location of residence and occupational score are entered into the equation, when the difference becomes statistically insignificant. In other words, mother tongue, as such, was not an important determinant of income for Caribbean immigrants.[4] Residence in Montreal reduced average income by $1,207.00, when other variables were controlled and this was commensurate with the employment income differential for the population as a whole. Each year of residence in Canada added an average of $255.00 to the employment income of Caribbean immigrants, when other factors were controlled.

Each year of education added $950.00 to income until the effects of other variables were controlled when it appeared that having a qualification was also important, and the effects of both were modified by length and location of residence.[5] When "other things were equal," each year of education added $341.00 to income and each of the two points on the measure of qualifications raised income by $1,945.00. Finally, after controlling for all the preceding factors, each step down on the occupational status scale (1 being a high score and 15 the lowest status) reduced income by an average of $468.00.

Gender Differences

Separate regressions were run for males and females. The results are summarized in Tables 9 and 10. After excluding gender, the remaining variables in the equations explained 24 percent of the variance in employment income for Caribbean males, and 29 percent for females. The occupational status score had the strongest direct effect when "other things were equal," with standardized Beta coefficients of -0.21 and -0.24, respectively. Although the relative effect of age was similar, the absolute advantage for men aged 35-54 years was much greater (adding $2,736.00 compared with $1,402.00), when other variables were taken into account. For both sexes the initial advantage of having English as mother tongue disappeared when other factors were controlled. The slight negative effect was not statistically significant. Each year of education added $329.00 to male income and $330.00 to those of women but, given the overall lower income of women, it meant that education was relatively more important to them as shown by a standardized Beta coefficient of 0.17, compared with 0.10 for men. However, having a formal qualification was more advantageous to Caribbean men than women. In absolute terms each of the two steps on the scale added $2,168.00 to male incomes and $1,456.00 to those of women. Each step on the occupational scale made a larger absolute difference to employment income for men ($573.00 compared with $374.00), but, as noted, the direct effect was

TABLE 9

Multivariate Analysis of Employment Income[1]
Stepwise Multiple Regression, Caribbean Males

		1	2	3	4	5	6	7	Beta
Age (35-54)	B	4,402.25	4,394.61	3,894.14	3,854.00	2,932.09	2,905.94	2,735.84	.12
	s.e.	101.37	101.25	95.13	94.18	93.73	93.53	92.07	
Mother Tongue (English)	B		1,763.40	1,830.25	2,149.88	1,508.09	51.45	-144.92	.00
	s.e.		156.26	146.52	145.39	142.46	172.00	169.20	
Years of Education	B			1,075.39	650.44	585.47	568.89	328.68	.10
	s.e.			12.96	18.47	18.07	18.07	18.69	
Qualification (Non-Uni/Degrees)	B				3,417.77	3,044.73	3,087.42	2,168.43	.12
	s.e.				106.85	104.54	104.34	104.99	
Years of Immigration	B					356.79	360.87	305.76	.18
	s.e.					7.12	7.11	7.12	
CMA (Montreal)	B						-2,169.76	-2,072.02	-0.07
	s.e.						144.27	141.89	
Occupational Status (1-15 = low)	B							-572.98	-.21
	s.e.							13.86	
Constant	B	15,801.29	14,251.77	154.33	2,727.69	960.83	2,789.71	12,371.15	
	s.e.	72.59	155.27	223.78	235.69	232.68	262.08	346.60	
R Square		.04	.04	.15	.17	.21	.21	.24	

[1] Only employed mainly full-time
40 weeks or more in 1980

s.e. = standard error

Source: Statistics Canada, 1981 Census of Canada, special tabulations.

relatively more important for women. By far the largest single difference between men and women was the consequence of living in Montreal. This reduced average male employment income for Caribbean immigrants by $2,072.00 compared with a reduction of only $150.00 for women, but this differential was similar to that experienced by Canadian-born men and women in the two Census Metropolitan Areas (CMAs).

Not all of the original hypotheses were confirmed by the multivariate analysis. As expected, education and qualifications were strongly associated with occupational status which, in turn, was the most important determinant of employment income. Notwithstanding a slightly higher occupational status than men, Caribbean women were similar to most women in the labour force in not earning incomes commensurate with their status, when compared with men. This was probably due to their clustering in "traditional" female occupations such as nursing and other service occupations that are generally poorly paid. Each year of education, and the possession of a degree or other qualification, added less in absolute terms to female incomes than to male, but the relative importance of education was more important to women. Each year of residence in Canada added less to women's employment income, but the effect of location of residence was barely significant for women although, when other things were equal, living in Montreal reduced Caribbean male income by more than $2,000.00. Contrary to the original hypothesis, having English as mother tongue had no significant effect at all when other variables were controlled and the same was true when "official language" was used as a predictor. In other words, employment income differentials *between Anglophone and Francophone Caribbean immigrants* were explained by variation in their education, qualifications, occupations, length of residence, etc., and by the fact that the majority of Francophones were resident in Montreal; therefore language problems do not explain the income disadvantage of Caribbean immigrants.

Conclusion

An analysis of 1981 total income data for Caribbean immigrants in Canada shows there was a systematic disadvantage compared with other immigrants and the Canadian-born, even after controlling for sex, age, period of immigration and educational level. The disadvantage was relatively greater for Caribbean men than for women. The relative deprivation persisted when the employment income of those working full-time, 40 weeks or more in 1980, was examined. The multivariate analysis of employment income shows that education and qualifications determined occupational status which, in turn, was the most important determinant of income. Employment income improved with length of residence in Canada but this was a more important factor for men than women. Mother tongue had no effect on income when other variables were controlled but, for Caribbean males, living in Montreal was a disadvantage relative to residence

TABLE 10

Multivariate Analysis of Employment Income[1]
Stepwise Multiple Regression: Caribbean Females

		1	2	3	4	5	6	7	Beta
Age (35-54 yrs)	B	2,217.37	2,203.73	2,187.67	2,280.87	1,542.83	1,547.20	1,401.76	.11
	s.e.	59.68	59.68	54.45	53.83	55.07	55.08	53.73	
Mother Tongue (English)	B		711.02	689.72	879.27	552.82	346.22	−99.33	.00
	s.e.		99.12	90.42	89.46	87.76	106.67	104.28	
Years of education	B			773.86	513.62	485.25	483.33	330.47	.17
	s.e.			8.13	11.09	10.86	10.88	11.04	
Qualification (Non-Uni/Degrees)	B				2,202.45	2,052.60	2,057.53	1,456.32	.13
	s.e.				64.79	63.43	63.44	62.98	
Period of Immigration	B					213.99	214.83	173.94	.16
	s.e.					4.70	4.71	4.66	
CMA (Montreal)	B						−286.39	−149.71	−.01
	s.e.						84.07	81.92	
Occupational Status (1-15 = low)	B							−374.15	−.24
	s.e.							7.58	
Constant	B	10,915.56	10,282.74	630.01	2,116.32	893.38	1,138.79	7,306.54	
	s.e.	41.54	97.50	134.90	140.19	139.68	157.15	197.58	
R Square		.03	.03	.19	.21	.25	.25	.29	

[1] Only those working mainly full-time 40 weeks or more in 1980

(s.e. = standard error)

Source: Statistics Canada, 1981 Census of Canada, special tabulations.

elsewhere in Canada, but this income differential was similar to that experienced by Canadian-born males and other immigrants. It does not explain the absolute level of disadvantage of Caribbean males.

The analysis of census data alone cannot prove the existence of discrimination against Caribbean immigrants but the evidence does support the view that there was a systematic disadvantage in employment and in income, relative to Canadians and to other immigrants. This disadvantage was comparatively more serious for men than for women and it was greatest for Caribbean males resident in Montreal. The findings must be interpreted in the light of other research which provides more direct evidence of discrimination against visible minorities in Canada and with government sponsored studies that have documented the existence of racism in Canada (Henry and Ginzberg 1984; Abella 1984, 1985; Daudlin 1984; Driedger 1987; Richmond 1988). The census data lend support to the findings of those studies and reports. There is no doubt that "Canada will be the ultimate loser if we do not take advantage of the skills and abilities which visible minorities have to offer" (Daudlin 1984, 1).

Notes

1. The author wishes to thank Statistics Canada for permission to publish special tabulations and analyses from the 1981 Census, and Dr. Ravi Verma and Mr. G. Ouellette of the Demography Division of Statistics Canada for assistance in the preparation of the micro-database and the computer runs. The author is solely responsible for the analysis and conclusions.
2. For purposes of this paper "Caribbean" includes Guyana.
3. As would be expected there were high intercorrelations between years of education, qualifications and the occupational score. Although the measure of occupational status took into account the educational levels of the incumbents, the association was not spurious. There is a logical sequence between years of education, which are a prerequisite for obtaining a qualification, which in turn is required before a person obtains a given occupation. After controlling for sex, age and mother tongue, the partial correlation between the occupational status score and years of education was $-.55$ and with qualification $-.25$, which reduced to $-.21$ when education was also controlled.
4. The substitution of "knowledge of English" as an official language did not alter the conclusion that language as such was not an important determinant of income for Caribbean persons.
5. A problem of multicolinearity can arise when two or more "independent" variables, such as education, qualifications and occupational status, are highly correlated. Slight changes in sampling or measurement error can influence the partial correlation and lead to spurious conclusions (Blalock, H.M., *Causal Influences in Non-Experimental Research*, New York: Norton, 1964, pp. 87-90). However, in this study the analysis was conducted with a constructed universe of 95,000 cases based on a 20 percent sample of the total population of Caribbean immigrants. Therefore, it is reasonable to assume that the sampling and measurement errors were small and that multicolinearity did not create problems of interpretation in this case.

Appendix

Classification of Occupations and Calculation of Occupational Status Score

The 15-point scale of occupational status was adapted from a classification developed by Statistics Canada. Using Information derived from the CCDO (Canadian Classification and Dictionary of Occupations) and the Classification of Professions, a formula using the average level of education and training of persons 25-45 years, in each of the four-digit occupational classifications was calculated. The scores ranged from a high of 84.88 to a low of 30.70. The occupations were then grouped into descriptive categories and a mean score for each category was computed. Between categories there was some overlapping of individual occupational scores and, in the original listing, the categories were not in a hierarchical order of means. Therefore, for purposes of the multivariate analysis reported in this study the categories were re-ordered as follows:

		Number of Occupations	Score Range	Mean
1.	Professionals	52	64-84	67.53
2.	Higher Managerial	10	63-73	67.16
3.	Semiprofessionals	14	63-67	65.51
4.	Technical	33	44-67	59.49
5.	Middle management	15	53-62	58.56
6.	Skilled, commercial, office	38	49-67	54.19
7.	Supervisors	52	42-62	53.00
8.	Skilled manual, secondary industries	40	49-56	52.56
9.	Skilled manual, primary industries	4	49-52	51.59
10.	Semiskilled, office	25	42-48	45.28
11.	Semiskilled, secondary industries	72	42-48	44.74
12.	Semiskilled, primary industries	10	42-47	44.53
13.	Unskilled, secondary industries	100	30-41	38.41
14.	Unskilled, primary industries	12	35-41	38.07
15.	Unskilled, office and service	18	32-41	37.75

IV

THE MULTIETHNIC CHALLENGE FOR DEMOGRAPHERS

20. THIRD WORLD IMMIGRATION AND MULTICULTURALISM[1]

T. John Samuel

From the landing of Samuel de Champlain and the first European settlers, Canada has been a nation of immigrants. In the past 200 years, people from around the world have come here to begin new lives. Since the beginning of the century more than 10 million immigrants have landed on its shores, contributing to the richness and diversity of the Canadian mosaic. Immigration has been a major source of population growth for Canada. As pointed out by Beaujot, "since the turn of the century the net migration to Canada has exceeded 4 million and this amounted to 21.2 percent of the population growth that occurred. The contribution of immigration to population growth peaked in 1901-1911 with 44.1 percent, while in 1971-81 decade it was 28.7 percent" (1987, 3).

Canada's immigration policy underwent a major change in the early 1960s when ethnicity was removed as one of the filters used in screening out potential immigrants. The changes were formalized in 1967 when the new immigrant selection criteria were introduced. Consequently, the past quarter century or so has seen tremendous changes in the composition of Canada's immigration flows. These changes heralded the birth of an "M and M" Society as Burnet (1975, 2) would say — Multicultural and Multiracial — of which the B and B Commission — Bilingualism and Biculturalism — was the midwife. In 1971 the policy of multiculturalism was officially adopted and in 1988 a multiculturalism bill was passed.

This paper will overview Canadian immigration trends in general with special attention to Third World immigration and explore its impact on multiculturalism and ethnicity. Some of the issues related to these developments such as labour market discrimination and employment equity, immigrant adaptation, immigration as a substitute for falling fertility levels, and the international implications of immigration will also be examined. However, the paper does not attempt to investigate alternative models of integration, pluralism or assimilation to situate Third World immigration, multiculturalism and ethnicity in such a context. For an excellent discussion of some of these issues see Driedger (1987).

Data used in this paper include both flow data from immigration statistics (Tables 1 and 2) maintained by Employment and Immigration Canada and stock data based on the latest available census (Table 3). Census data useful for the analysis include those on foreign-born (usually referred to as immigrants), or based on ethnicity. The ethnicity data also include the native-born of the relevant ethnic origin. However, the analysis of these data, in comparison with previous census years, is rendered difficult by changes in the census questions posed in 1986. For the first time in 1986 the census questionnaire allowed respondents to write in up to three ethnic origins not included in the marked boxes. Furthermore, the wording of the question itself changed.

A Change in Immigration Patterns

The face of Canadian immigration is changing rapidly. This can be seen from the dramatic changes in the source countries of immigration in the post-war period, as seen in Table 1. Before World War II, most immigrants came from Europe. In the 1950s, 84.3 percent of Canadian immigrants were born in Europe. By the 1980s, this proportion had dropped to 28.6 percent. Most immigrants in the 1980s have come from Asia: immigration from Asia rose from less than 1 percent of total immigration in the 1945-50 period to 42.2 percent in the 1980-86 period. At the same time, Canada began to receive immigrants from Africa, South America and the Caribbean. Immigration from these three areas

TABLE 1

Immigration by Place of Birth, 1945-1986

Area	1945-50 %	1951-60 %	1961-70 %	1971-80 %	1981-86 %
Europe	79.75	84.31	68.04	36.16	28.57
Africa	0	0	3.15	5.28	4.58
Asia	.73	1.80	9.89	30.11	42.16
U.S.	12.55	5.58	10.57	11.04	6.54
South and Latin America	0	0	1.52	6.31	9.23
Caribbean	0	0	4.63	9.20	7.46
Australia	0	.79	20.27	1.03	1.37
Not Stated	6.97	7.51	.32	1.21	.07
TOTAL	100.00	100.00	100.00	100.00	100.00

went from zero percent in the postwar era to 4.6, 9.2 and 7.5 percent respectively in the 1980s. During the years 1981-86, the country of birth for 63.5 percent of immigrants to Canada was a Third World country.

Until the end of the sixties, Europe was the dominant immigrant source, though within the region the importance of Britain declined steadily, with Eastern Europe and later Southern Europe taking up the position of major suppliers of immigrants. The dominance of Southern Europe continued in the seventies.

In 1986, visible minorities (the term refers to people who are identifiably non-white and/or non-Caucasian but excludes the native peoples) were estimated to be 1.4 million, 5.6 percent of the Canadian population (Samuel 1987a, 12).

The impact of immigration has been geographically uneven, even when the widely different shares of the regions and metropolitan areas in Canada's total population are recognized. During the post-war years, when Ontario continued to receive half the immigrants, the share bound for Quebec and the Prairies fluctuated, that for British Columbia, Yukon and Northwest Territories rose, while that of the Maritimes declined, as seen in Table 2. The main magnets for immigrants to the regions appear to be a strong economy, a favourable climate and family ties. Available evidence indicates that the internal migration of international migrants after arrival further complicated the picture. Such migration enhanced the share for Ontario and British Columbia and weakened the shares of the other regions (Da Costa undated, 3).

TABLE 2

Immigrant Settlement Intentions by Region 1945-86

Province	1945-50 %	1951-60 %	1961-70 %	1971-80 %	1981-86 %
Maritimes	5.7	2.2	2.7	1.9	2.3
Quebec	17.1	20.9	20.4	16.0	17.6
Ontario	49.4	53.1	53.4	51.0	45.9
Prairies	17.7	13.7	11.4	14.5	18.4
British Columbia and Territories	10.1	10.0	12.4	15.4	15.4
TOTAL	100.00	100.00	100.00	100.00	100.00

Immigration policy, until 1986, despite the significant role assigned to demographic factors in the 1976 Immigration Act, was directed primarily by non-demographic concerns, especially by labour market considerations (Samuel 1988a). As noted by Tepper, ''the effects of immigration on basic demography including ethnicity seems largely unintended'' (Tepper 1986, 16).

Looking at the census stock figures, the ethnic composition of Canada has changed significantly since Confederation. In 1871 the percentages of the population of British and French ethnic origins were 60.5 and 31.1 respectively (Ray 1988, 4). In 1981, these percentages were 40.2 and 26.7. In 1981, other major ethnic groups with 2 to 5 percent of the population were German, Italian, Ukranian, Dutch and native peoples. Scandinavians, Poles, Jews, South Asians, Chinese, Greek, and Balkans individually ranged between 0.5 to 1.5 percent. Among the above groups, more than half of the Balkans, Chinese, Greeks, South Asians and Italians were foreign-born in 1981 (Ray 1988, 5), indicating the relative recency of their arrival.

With 33.1 percent in 1981, those of non-British and non-French ethnic origin, often called "Other," became the second most important group in Canada. If current immigration trends continue, this group will surpass the British origin group, as it already did the French, before the end of the 20th century. The Mcdonald Royal Commission noted: "it seems likely that in future years, a substantial proportion of newcomers will be attracted from non-European nations, and these new Canadians will continue to expand the diversification of our cultural and ethnic mix. These important changes in Canada's racial and ethnic composition will continue to transform our economic and political life in the coming decades. They are also likely to generate a certain amount of social conflict, and future generations of Canadians will need to invent new policies and techniques for coping with the stresses of a vibrant and dynamic multicultural society" (Royal Commission on the Economic Union and Development Prospects for Canada 1985, 660).

Looking at the foreign-born segment, according to 1986 Census the foreign-born represented 15.6 percent of the country's population, down slightly from 16.0 percent in 1981. However, they comprised one fifth of the labour force in the eighties. In 1986, 62 percent of the 1986 foreign-born population had been born in Europe, 18 percent in Asia, 7 percent in the U.S., 5 percent in the Caribbean, 4 percent in South and Central America, 3 percent in Africa and 1 percent in Oceania. More than half of the foreign-born settled in Ontario. British Columbia claimed a quarter of them and Alberta one sixth. All the other provinces had less than the national average and Newfoundland had the lowest percentage, two percent. Over half of the foreign-born lived in Toronto, Montreal and Vancouver. Though born abroad, close to four out of five of those eligible for Canadian citizenship had taken it by 1986 (Statistics Canada 1988), showing their willingness to make a firm commitment to Canada.

What do all these numbers mean? How is Canadian society responding to the changes indicated by these numbers? How is Canadian society facing the challenges offered by these changes? What do these changes mean for multiculturalism and ethnicity?

Changing Immigration and Multiculturalism

These changes occurred while multiculturalism itself has been both attacked and defended vigorously by scholars. The most serious critic of multiculturalism has been John Porter in his famous work, *The Vertical Mosaic*. Porter considered that Canada's bilingualism and multiculturalism contribute to a vertical mosaic and argues "that the 'entry status' of certain ethnic groups in Canada, such as those from Eastern, Central and Southern Europe, would be perpetuated beyond the first generation of immigrants and give rise to a differential distribution of occupational status and income by ethnic origin" (as quoted by Basavarajappa and Verma 1985, 21). Porter's thesis was formulated in the early 1960s when bilingualism and multiculturalism were in their pre-Trudeau era, and visible minorities and multiracialism were not as important as they are today. It is interesting to speculate whether Porter would have built his vertical mosaic with reinforced steel if he were to write today!

It can be argued whether Porter's vertical mosaic is still a free-standing structure or has collapsed, since minority groups can overcome their disadvantages through education as argued by Boyd et al. (1985). Any number of positions between the vertical and horizontal are conceivable. As stated by Beaujot "...the reality is complex, more complex than any one model can properly portray" (Beaujot 1988, 12).

Among the defenders of multiculturalism are Keyfitz, who said "Recognition of imperfection indicates modesty with respect to one's culture and to oneself. If men are imperfect and their cultures are imperfect then the last thing one wants is that they should all be the same. The most one can hope for is that in the competition of culture traits there will be a natural selection of good features" (Keyfitz 1976, 78). Another staunch supporter of multiculturalism observed: "There are a number of reasons to welcome a more diverse Canada. Sustained economic growth and enhanced cultural richness are sufficient reasons" (Tepper 1986, 11). The theme of enhanced cultural richness is very popular, as made clear in the following letter to the editor of the *Toronto Star*. The letter described the experience of a Hungarian refugee in Toronto and concluded: "Is there anywhere else a city in the world where an Indonesian, two Japanese, two Hindus, a Ukrainian, an Irishman, two Englishmen, a Pole and a Hungarian could get together in an Egygtian restaurant and discuss the merits of Mogan David wine?" (Vincent D3).

One might legitimately ask: Did Canada have a choice but to be multicultural? The answer seems to be "no." A comparison between Canada and her neighbour to the South in immigrant integration would show that one of the fundamental differences between the two countries is that Canada's cultural dualism made the melting pot (whether the melting pot succeeded in doing what it was supposed to do, is another question) approach impossible. "If the British had to tolerate and respect the French, and the French the British, then there was no basis for treating other ethnic or religious communities differently" according to Thorburn (1987, 2). He continues: "This fact, so remote in the past and so apparently unrelated to the subsequent multiculturalism policy, established the fundamental relationship that defines Canada... namely toleration of and respect for other cultural and linguistic communities."

The new dimension that multiculturalism has now acquired — multiracialism — is a much more fundamental change than the pre-1960s migration flows have produced. Burnet refers to the "inadequacy of the policy" of multiculturalism, in view of the arrival of immigrants belonging to visible minorities who are disadvantaged (Burnet 1987, 71). When the Irish, the Eastern Europeans and the Southern Europeans came to a Canadian society dominated by the Anglo-French cultures, their acceptance and adaptation were hindered by differences in culture and language, not by racial differences. After a generation, whatever obstacles were present have practically vanished and they have become integrated inconspicuously into Canadian society. Unless their last names were known, it was very hard to discriminate against them. Under multiracialism this is no longer true. Despite being in Canada for generations, the newer ethnic groups — the people of colour — will continue to remain distinct and conspicuous, at least in the short run. In the long run, however, depending upon the extent of intermarriages they may "melt" into the mainstream of society. However, the million dollar question is: Will skin pigment be considered a trait that will mark them as different and render them unworthy of equality of opportunity in their own, or their parents' new land? Culturally, there will be little difference between the progeny of the newer wave of immigrants and those of the earlier settlers.

Canada has always been multiracial. After all, the native people were here long before the Europeans arrived. Despite this, significant changes in the racial composition of Canadian society came about only after changes in immigration policy. By 1981, the number of visible minorities in Canada, excluding the native population, had reached 1.13 million. This number is projected to more than double, to 2.5 to 2.8 million (between 8.7 percent and 9.6 percent of the Canadian population by the year 2001 (Samuel 1987b, 15). The increase in the number of visible minorities by 2001 compared to 1986 would be between 56 percent, and 75 percent depending upon the level of immigration.

To put the above numbers in perspective, it is worth mentioning that in 1986, the total number of visible minorities exceeded the individual population sizes of 6 out of the 10 Canadian provinces (i.e., of P.E.I., Newfoundland, New Brunswick, Nova Scotia, Saskatchewan and Manitoba) and equalled the combined populations of P.E.I., Newfoundland and New Brunswick.

Consequences of Changing Immigration Patterns

The M and M society has had an impact on all levels of government and on virtually all areas of social policy. One of the most significant areas needing examination is the discriminatory treatment of minorities, be they racial minorities (e.g., visible minorities) or ethnic minorities (e.g., Southern Europeans). Evidence of such treatment abounds in Canadian society.

The degree of acceptance of persons whose ethnic origins are non-British and non-French as equals is reflected in the social standing of ethnic and racial groupings. The existence of social ranking of ethnic and racial groups within English and French Canada was established by Pineo (1977). He ranked the social standing of ethnic and racial groups based on a national survey. The main ethnic groups in origin categories were grouped into charter group members and related groups, Western and Northern European, Mediterranean and Central European and Non-Caucasion groups. The mean rank for the charter group ranged from 56.1 for French Canadians to 83.1 for English Canadians, with Irish, Scots and British in between. Among the principal groups of Western and Northern Europeans, the score ranged between 48.7 for the Germans to 58.7 for the Dutch. The Russians received a score of 53.8 and the Austrians obtained a mean rank of 49.6 in the Mediterranean and Central European group. Last came the non-Caucasian groups with Blacks at the bottom (25.4) and Japanese (34.7) at the top. Canadian Indians received 28.3 and Chinese 33.1, while another major group, South Asians, was not ranked.

Lately in Canada the least accepted ethnic group has been the South Asians. A 1975 Gallup poll asked if Canadians would be inclined to restrict or oppose immigration from any particular country. "Of those who favoured such restrictions, 23 per cent specifically mentioned India or Pakistan, seven per cent countries in the Caribbean, and five per cent "coloured immigrants in general" (Richmond 1975, 12). The same was revealed 10 years later in Toronto when the *Toronto Star* conducted a series of surveys. When the Anglo-Saxons, the principal gate keepers of power with 45 per cent of the city's population were asked, what ethnic groups, if any, are more subject to prejudice and discrimination than others, two thirds referred to South Asians (*Toronto Star* 1985, A15). Next were Blacks with 44 percent and Chinese with 18 percent.

Public opinion polls on immigrants from Third World countries provide further evidence to support the above. Examining such polls on immigration between 1947 and 1973, Tienhara concluded that "negative attitudes to immigration are based on perceived — not necessarily real — actual or potential threats to individual well being, be it economic, social, cultural or political" (Tienhara 1974, 29). A 1982 Gallup poll on racial attitudes by the Minister of State (Multiculturalism) showed that the proposition "I would cut off all non-white immigration to Canada" was answered in the affirmative by 12 percent of the population. The same percentage agreed with the proposition that "the people of this country are looking less and less Canadian'' and that they would ''cut off all non-white immigration to Canada.'' Curiously enough 14 percent said ''racial mixing violates the teaching of the Bible''; 19 percent believed ''riots and violence increase when non-whites are let into a country''; 28 percent would not mind non-whites but would ''rather see them back in their own country''; 31 percent ''would support organizations that worked towards preserving Canada for whites only''; and 58 percent ''would limit non-white immigration and those who were let in would have to prove themselves before they were entitled to government support services'' (Howith 1988, 12).

There are a number of national studies that point to discrimination in the labour maket against visible minorities. *Equality Now*! (House of Commons 1984) recognized this aspect of the Canadian labour market and suggested approaches to increasing the employment opportunities of visible minorities in the private and public sectors. The Abella Commission report showed that in 1981 visible minorities such as Indochinese, Blacks, Central and South Americans and particularly native people, had higher unemployment rates than the general population. The Commission concluded that visible minorities face institutionalized or systemic discrimination. However, minority groups with higher than average levels of education did not suffer as much from unemployment (Abella 1984), perhaps supporting Boyd's view of the vertical mosaic as stated earlier.

Discrimination in the labour market against visible minorities can also be seen by looking at their income levels after controlling for important variables such as age and education. Beaujot et al. showed that if male immigrants from developing regions of the world to Canada had the same age distribution and education as Canadian-born persons in the labour force in 1981, they would have had incomes that were 9 to 22 percent below the Canadian-born; female immigrants would have had incomes 5 to 14 percent lower (Beaujot et al. 1987, 67-68). Another study based on a large sample (15,000) that collected data from the same cohort longitudinally for a three-year period in early 1970s found that ''both occupational and income rankings are clearly segregated according to traditional and non-traditional source countries,... [and] there exists income discrimination on the basis of country of origin, despite controlling for differences, and despite a trend towards less occupational dissimilarity between ethnic groups'' (Satzewich and Li 1987, 239).

An important development whose impact is not easily discernible was the coming into force of the Canadian Charter of Rights and Freedoms in 1982. Under Section 15 of the Charter, ''which holds great promise for many disadvantaged groups in Canada'' (Pentney 1987, 4), ''every individual is equal before and under the law and has the right to the equal protection and equal benefit of the law without discrimination and, in particular, without discrimination based on race, national or ethnic origin, colour, ...'' Furthermore Section 27 says: ''This Charter shall be interpreted in a manner consistant with the preservation and enhancement of the multicultural heritage of Canadians.''

The legal framework for race relations in Canada also needs to take into consideration the federal Employment Equity Act, which obliges certain corporate employers to develop affirmative action plans to redress the under-representation in the workforce of target groups, including visible minorities.

Equality of opportunity in the labour market has been accepted in principle by all levels of government and major private sector employers. Since it is recognized that "equality of opportunity ought not to be subject to ethnic ownership by the so-called founding races any more than water, sun or air" (Samuel 1988, 9), efforts are being initiated by all levels of government to see that equality of opportunity does not remain an elusive dream. The federal government, for instance, has acted on a number of recommendations contained in *Equality Now!* and the Abella Commission report. The Employment Equity Act was proclaimed on August 14, 1986. The Standing Committee of the Canadian Parliament on Multiculturalism (Mitges 1987) has come up with a number of recommendations in the same area. The Multiculturalism Bill just enacted has taken into consideration some of the recommendations of these studies. Also realizing that the federal civil service should reflect the multiracial character of the society it serves, a visible minority employment program to increase the groups' representatiton in the civil service has been introduced. (Currently the visible minority component of the civil service is no more than 1.7 percent, compared to a share of the Canadian population of 5.6 percent in 1986.) The RCMP has asked a national recruiting team to attract personnel to meet force (police) priorities, and to "ensure the equitable participation of Francophones, females, visible minorities, indigenous Canadians as peace officers..." (Inkster 1988, 5). Furthermore, a national advisory committee to assist the RCMP in this regard has been formed.

Some of the provincial and municipal levels of government have also got into the act. Though several provincial governments have human rights programs (e.g., Ontario, Alberta, Nova Scotia) which look into the labour market aspect as well, specific employment equity programs for visible minorities are being considered by only a few of them. The municipal governments in numerous metropolitan areas have appointed committees to advise municipal politicians on policies and programs that could effect specific minority groups. Such committees, often chaired by the mayor, exist in the Ontario municipalities of Ottawa, Toronto, Hamilton, North York, Windsor, Scarborough, Peterborough, Mississauga, Sudbury, Kitchener, Brantford and Pickering. Outside Ontario, Montreal, Vancouver, Richmond, Burnaby, Moose Jaw and Winnipeg also have such committees. At the same time, the Department of Secretary of State has funded the Federation of Canadian Municipalities to develop programs to assist municipalities in the area of race relations.

A number of school boards across the country have initiated multiculturalism committees to develop policies to sensitize their students to the changing nature of Canadian society. This approach is likely to be particularly effective "since social scientists have found that getting more information through an educational institution results in lessening of prejudice in about 2/3 of cases" (Samuel 1977, 6). The same point is made by Ramcharan when he says that "the educational institution is the main instrument in the transmission of societal values, and as such has a pivotal role to play in the creation of an egalitarian society" (Ramcharan 1987, 7).

It is educational to look at the situation south of the Canadian border to see how the affirmative action program of the U.S., which was started long before Canada's, is doing. As seen in a U.S. national survey of 4,078 employers (Braddock and James 1987), equal occupational opportunities do not exist in the employment process because of exclusionary barriers. For instance, segregated networks at the candidate stage that prevent them from "finding out about those vacancies and becoming part of a pool of candidates" (p. 7) prevent qualified minority groups from competing while closed internal labour markets that require entering "the firm in jobs that have training opportunities and are tied to upward career ladders" (p. 20) deny equality of opportunity in the labour market. Though no Canadian study is available on this aspect, it is unlikely that the situation in Canada is any different; it may indeed be much worse, given Canada's somewhat more rigid social structure.

Curiously enough, at times the labour market discrimination against minorities (be they visible or non-visible) seems to have resulted in more of the minorities being self-employed. For instance, in an analysis of family class immigrants, it was discovered that those with higher rates of unemployment had higher rates of self-employment as well (Samuel 1987, 19). This explains in part why some of the so-called non-charter ethnic groups seem to have done well in self-employment. The number of self-employed in 1981 per 1,000 Canadian population 15 and over was 62.7 per thousand (Multiculturalism Canada 1986, 3). For the British and French groups the rates were 59.1 and 48.6 respectively. On the other hand, above-average rates of self-employment, between 73 and 100, were recorded for those of Chinese, Russian, Ukrainian, Czechoslovakian, Hungarian, and West Asian origin. The rates were 103 to 150 for German, Scandinavian, Dutch, Far East Asian, Greek and Jewish ethnic groups. Most of the other groups had below average rates. To a certain extent these rates are influenced by the proportion of professionals among the groups, the employment barriers they faced, the language difficulties they experienced and the amount of discrimination in the labour market.

Discrimination against certain ethnic groups is not restricted to the labour market alone. It also extends to social, cultural and political areas. Such discrimination is often harder to measure and record, though efforts have been made in attitudinal surveys to capture the basic nature of such prejudice and the consequent discrimination.

There is little doubt that racial prejudice and discrimination against visible minorities are major obstacles to their achievement of economic and social integration. As observed by Richmond, "if policies of multiculturalism are to be meaningful to these groups, major efforts to eliminate racism will be needed"

(Richmond 1982, 122). He states further that "It is unlikely that changes favourable to racial and ethnic minorities will occur without strong leadership and clearly articulated protest".

Efforts to reverse the effects of past discrimination through employment equity or affirmative action programs have received a mixed reception from social scientists. For instance, Thorburn (1987: 8) observes: "When the previously favoured groups find themselves actively discriminated against in order to produce the desired ethnic, cultural, colour and linguistic balance, they may well resent this discrimination which they have been taught to see to be wrong; and this resentment might well become directed at the new beneficiaries of this reverse discrimination". (It is interesting to observe that gender is not included

TABLE 3

Visible Minorities as a Proportion of Total Population and of Single Ethnic Origin, by Metro area, 1986

	Total population %	Single Ethnic Origin %
St. John's	0.7	1.0
Halifax	3.4	5.8
Saint John	1.2	2.0
Chicoutimi	0.2	0.2
Quebec	0.8	0.8
Sherbrooke	0.9	1.0
Trois-Rivières	0.4	0.4
Montreal	5.8	6.4
Ottawa-Hull	5.1	7.4
Oshawa	2.1	3.4
Toronto	13.6	18.8
Hamilton	3.3	4.9
St. Catharines-Niagara	1.7	2.6
Kitchener	4.0	6.3
London	3.0	4.9
Windsor	4.6	7.2
Sudbury	1.2	1.8
Thunder Bay	1.2	2.1
Winnipeg	6.6	10.4
Regina	3.6	6.2
Saskatoon	3.2	5.7
Calgary	8.9	15.1
Edmonton	7.7	12.9
Vancouver	14.5	22.4
Victoria	4.1	6.8

Source: Calculated from Statistics Canada, *Census of Canada, 1987, Summary Tabulations of Ethnic and Aboriginal Origins*, 1987: Table 1.

among the factors mentioned above.) While there is some truth in this statement, especially regarding resentment against the new beneficiaries, one could argue that this is a policy area where one has to choose between the lesser of two evils. If left without interference, the imbalance will continue for a very long time, as is demonstrated by the prejudice towards women in the labour force for centuries and against French Canadians for decades. Such injustice perpetrated for too long is not only a waste of never-to-be-regained human resources, but is not in the least productive. As long as the policy assumes certain basic levels of qualification and competence for those who benefit from such programs, there seems to be little justification to shy away from employment equity or affirmative action programs.

The need for improved policies that work at all levels of government is obvious from the composition of the populations of various metropolitan areas. The following table shows the proportion of visible minority population of major metropolitan areas in 1986. Table 3 shows this group as a percentage of those with only one ethnic origin (78 percent did so) as well as the total population, i.e., including those who gave multiple ethnic origins.

Adaptation of New Immigrants

Another major challenge to the changing face of Canada through immigration is related to the adaptation of immigrants. Since the newer waves of immigrants are different, there will be greater problems of adaptation, be they economic, social, cultural or political. The question that needs attention is: Would it take longer for visible minorities to become adapted to their new country in non-economic areas as a result of labour market discrimination against them? The first generation, which is culturally different, would probably take longer to adapt, though one hopes that some of the positive values they bring with them such as strong family ties, hard work and enterprise will not be lost in the process of adaptation. These values have much to commend them and they are often the cornerstone of a stable, progressive and productive society.

Visible minority immigrants in general have been more eager than other immigrants to take Canadian citizenship — a sure indication that they want to make a binding commitment to Canadian society. Looking at the major immigration countries recently, the average number of years to take citizenship since immigration has been 7 for persons from France, 11 for the U.K., 12 for Greece and Portugal, 14 for the U.S., 15 for Germany and 19 for Italy. On the other hand, the time span to citizenship after immigration has been 8 years for those from Jamaica, 6 for India, 5 for Korea, the Philippines and China and 4 for Hong Kong, Iran and Haiti (Department of the Secretary of State 1986, 24-25).

An equally important aspect of the adaptation of the new wave of immigration from the Third World has been the attitude of Canadians in general to those of such origins in their midst. The ease with which such immigrants are accepted facilitates their adaptation to Canadian society. This acceptance is partly hastened by their economic contributions. Lately, an argument that used to be raised against immigration — that immigrants add to unemployment — has been discredited by American, Australian and Canadian studies. In Canada, Samuel and Conyers showed through a balance sheet approach how immigrants add to the total labour supply and demand and in the process make more jobs than they take (Samuel and Conyers, 1986). A similar finding was reported by DeVoretz and Akbari (1987). Roy (1987, 10) added further support to the view that immigrants do not displace the Canadian-born in the labour market.

The Importance of Immigration to Canada

International migration is of importance to Canada since Canadian fertility fell and remains below replacement levels. A careful look at factors affecting fertility in Canada (Romaniuc 1984; Samuel 1983) shows that Canadian fertility is likely to remain low. Major factors that keep Canadian fertility low include high and rising female labour force participation rates, the improving status of women, the high economic and psychological cost of children, the decline in the degree of religiousness, the high rate of urbanization, higher levels of education, the relatively high age of marriage, marriage breakups, cohabitation without marriage, legalized abortion and the effective use of contraception.

The Canadian fertility rate, currently at 1.67, may continue to fall if Canada emulates Quebec, where the fertility rate is as low as 1.4 similar to some of the European countries such as W. Germany and Denmark, with fertility levels at 1.3 and 1.4 respectively. With below replacement fertility, should Canada want to retain its population at a stable level, a significant level of immigration will be required. Furthermore, should Canada want to have a population growth rate of 1 percent per annum (the observed rate in the early 1980s has been 1.1) while the fertility rate probably falls further to about 1.4 in the 1990s, assuming the same levels of emigration as in the past, the number of immigrants required every year would exceed 240,000 in the early nineties and would gradually rise to 332,000 by the year 2001 (Basavarajappa and George 1983, 82). A demographic review currently underway in Health and Welfare Canada may point to the need for a Canadian population policy and the role of immigration, when it reports in the spring of 1989.

Canada's share of the world population is half of one percent, while the country is the second largest in the world. The world population, which now exceeds 5 billion, is expected to grow by another billion by the close of the century and will exert great pressures on Canada's borders in one form or another. As remarked by the former Minister of State (Immigration), the Honourable Gerry Weiner, "The combination of continuing extremely low fertility rates and increasing pressures for people to migrate to industrialized countries is probably going to make many of us develop explict demographic policies by the end of the century" (Weiner 1986, 8).

The international importance to Canada of the new wave of immigration has not been properly analysed, understood or appreciated. For better or worse, this new wave of immigration is bound to tie Canada closer to the countries from which the immigrants come. In most instances it is likely to be for the better, though the newcomers' habit of bringing their former country's political battles to Canadian soil is often a matter of concern.

While multiculturalism and ethnicity received a boost through immigration, immigration in return has been the subject of an enthusiastic lobby by the multi-cultural (normally considered to be non-English, non-French) communities. This is quite evident from the briefs which Employment and Immigration Canada receives at the time of its annual immigration levels consultations. The non-governmental organizations that lend enthusiastic support to larger levels of immigration are primarily ethnic associations and employer groups.

It is only too well known that immigrants from the Third World have added a new dimension to the Canadian cultural mosaic and that such an enrichment of Canadian culture has been beneficial to Canada. Apart from such cultural benefits, Third World immigration has opened up Canadian products and services to sending countries and has also stimulated imports from these countries. Immigration from Third World countries has also led to accusations that Canada is stealing brains from less developed countries which can ill afford to lose them (Majava 1987). On the other hand, explanations have been offered that the emigration of skilled migrants from the Third World is not to be considered as something that only damages the sending countries (Samuel 1988). Instances abound where such migrations have provided the sending countries with a safety valve to avoid potentially explosive political situations, produced badly needed foreign exchange and brought much-appreciated skills which the migrants had learned in their countries of settlement for use in their countries of origin. The best one can say about the situation is that the phenomenon of the "brain drain" depends on the country of origin and on the occupations concerned.

In this context it needs to be mentioned that no aspect of Canadian society will remain untouched by immigration and no nation can maintain its sovereignty if there is no orderly and controlled process of admitting immigrants, if the sovereign nation decides to do so. This means that the immigrant groups have a heavy responsibility if the process of legal immigration is to continue. "Only if they adopt policies of peaceful integration and avoid claiming more than their fair share of advantage will the present generous immigration policy survive" (Thorburn 1987). Often a problem arises in defining what is a "fair share," or what "fairness" is.

Another issue of relevance to the future of multiracialism is the likely impact of the Free Trade Agreement with the U.S. Ujimoto makes the important and interesting point that "Race relations as currently practised in the United States may eventually filter across the border into Canada as we may no longer be able to afford the luxury of concentrating our studies on multicultural songs and dances'' (Ujimoto 1987, 2). Undoubtedly the sociopolitical implications of the Free Trade Agreement needs careful study.

Conclusion

Third World immigration to Canada has added a new dimension to the policy of multiculturalism. Such immigration is likely to continue in view of the economic, social and demographic benefits it brings to Canada. Institutions at all levels need to become aware of the changes that are occurring and take appropriate measures to see that the integration of Third World immigrants to Canadian society takes place in an orderly manner realizing that the quintessence of multiculturalism is ''its major emphasis on cultural freedom, social justice and equality of opportunity for all within the existing political system'' (Hawkins 1988, 11). Finally, such immigration will significantly influence Canada's standing in the international community of nations.

Notes

---

1. The views expressed in this paper are those of the author and do not necessarily represent the views of the Government of Canada.

21. ETHNIC RESIDENTIAL SEGREGATION IN METROPOLITAN CANADA

T.R. Balakrishnan and K. Selvanathan

The ethnic composition of Canada has been changing substantially since the Second World War primarily through immigration patterns. Not only has the number of immigrants fluctuated from year to year but so has their ethnic origin. The shift has been from Western European to Southern and Eastern European in the 1950s and 1960s and in the last two decades from European to Third World origins. The impact of these trends on Canada's cities has not yet been well understood. Immigrants to the metropolitan areas are selective in terms of their ethnic background, language skills, occupation and educational attainment. Their adaptation to a new city will be influenced not only by the economic opportunities there but by the social and cultural characteristics of the population already resident there. This study does not claim all the ramifications of the ethnic factor in Canadian urban life, but rather looks at one aspect, namely residential segregation among the ethnic groups. Residential segregation is a manifestation of the extent to which the ethnic groups are assimilated in Canadian society. This project is an extension of earlier studies conducted by one of the authors on the 1961 and 1971 census data on ethnic residential segregation in Canadian cities (Balakrishnan 1976, 1982) and another on 1981 Census data on visible minorities in the three largest cities (Balakrishnan and Kralt 1987). As such it will draw heavily from these earlier studies. The present study however focuses primarily on the 1981 Census data and covers a larger number of metropolitan areas, as well as a different set of ethnic groups.

The main objectives of this paper are:

- to measure ethnic residential segregation in the 14 largest metropolitan areas of Canada and examine its relation to such factors as population size, ethnic diversity and regional location

- examine similarities and dissimilarities in the residential concentrations of ethnic groups in the context of social distance among them;
- investigate the influence of social class in ethnic segregation using areal data at the census tract level; and
- provide explanations to the extent possible for the observed patterns.

Theoretical Considerations

The theoretical framework is stated in detail in the earlier papers referred to above (Balakrishnan 1982; Balakrishnan and Kralt 1987). Briefly our position is that distinct patterns in residential segregation by ethnic groups can be noticed in the various metropolitan areas for a number of reasons. First, at the city level, factors such as population size as a whole and of ethnic groups in particular can affect segregation patterns as certain threshold sizes may exist for ethnic concentrations to develop. In other words, sociocultural and economic viability of an ethnic neighborhood may require certain necessary conditions. As cities increase in population size, it is likely that the number and size of ethnic groups will also increase and produce the "critical mass" necessary for the formation of ethnic neighbourhoods and institutions (Fischer 1976; Blau 1970; Darroch and Marston 1984). Even if a city has a sizeable ethnic population to satisfy the "critical mass" criterion, if they are dispersed spatially they will have less of an impact than if they were concentrated in a small area. Darroch and Marston suggest a model where ethnic residential concentration is a primary intervening variable in a process in which the demographic parameters affect ethnic pluralism (Darroch and Marston 1984). Second, to the extent segregation is determined by the homogeneity of an ethnic group, one can expect recent immigrants who are likely to be disadvantaged in terms of economic resources, official language facility and knowledge of the Canadian way of life to be more residentially segregated. Third, social distance among ethnic groups continues to persist and is apt to manifest itself in residential location patterns. Fourth, residential segregation among the ethnic groups is partly due to their social class differences. Choices of residential location is to a considerable degree determined by the economic resources as house prices and cost of transportation vary substantially within any city. Those in the lower social class will have less of a choice and hence are more likely to be segregated compared to those in the middle and upper classes. Dependence on census data precludes the testing of the above hypotheses in any rigorous way. This study is more modest and investigates some of the above themes indirectly, using 1981 Census data at the small area level.

Data and Methods

The data on which this analysis is based were drawn from the enumeration area computer tapes of the 1981 Census of Canada. These tapes contain information on the ethnic composition of the population in each enumeration area. Apart from the advantage of machine readability, the ethnic classification is uniform, whereas in the published bulletins they are grouped differently for the various metropolitan areas making comparisons impossible. The 14 largest metropolitan areas with populations over 200,000 and with at least 50 census tracts were selected for this study. They were Halifax, Montreal, Ottawa-Hull, Toronto, Hamilton, St. Catharines-Niagara, Kitchener-Waterloo, London, Windsor, Winnipeg, Calgary, Edmonton, Vancouver and Victoria. Another condition of selection was that there must be at least 500 persons in each ethnic category. Thus places such as St. John's, Newfoundland, Quebec City and Chicoutimi were excluded as they were very homogeneous and would make the constructed indices unstable. The enumeration areas in the selected metropolitan areas were aggregated to the census tract level, which form the basic unit of analysis. A very small number of census tracts with small populations and/or missing data on ethnic compositions were excluded from the analysis.

The 1981 Census question on "ethnicity" was "To which ethnic or cultural group did you or your ancestors belong on first coming to this continent?" For the first time, multiple responses were allowed. In Canada as a whole the percentage of multiple responses amounted to 7.6 percent. In the 14 metropolitan areas in the study the corresponding percentage was 8.0 percent. The population giving multiple response has been excluded in this study, which is thus based only on single responses for the following groups: British, French, Dutch, German, Scandinavian, Italian, Polish, Ukrainian, Native, Other single origins.

The measure of ethnic residential segregation employed is the "index of dissimilarity." This index is the sum of either the positive or negative differences between the proportional distributions of two ethnic populations. The index ranges from zero to unity, indicating complete similarity or dissimilarity in the residential distributions of the two ethnic populations. These indices of dissimilarity are referred to as segregation indices in this paper.

Mean Segregation Indices for the Metropolitan Areas

The mean indices of segregation for the 14 metropolitan areas are presented in Table 1. For each city, two types of indices were calculated. Index 1 is the simple arithmetic mean of indices of dissimilarity among all possible pairs of ethnic groups of single origin. Multiple origins were excluded as there is no reasonable way of handling them in this index. For our purposes the elimination of multiple origins is not considered too serious as they are not likely to alter

TABLE 1

Mean Segregation Indices for the Selected Metropolitan Areas of Canada, 1981

Metropolitan Area	Number of Census Tracts	Index[1] 1	Index[2] 2
Halifax	62	.386	.268
Montreal	657	.574	.507
Ottawa-Hull	177	.426	.345
Toronto	602	.433	.331
Hamilton	146	.377	.275
St. Catharines-Niagara	73	.383	.278
Kitchener-Waterloo	62	.331	.240
London	71	.333	.234
Windsor	56	.352	.253
Winnipeg	134	.386	.294
Calgary	115	.253	.177
Edmonton	139	.299	.219
Vancouver	245	.331	.250
Victoria	53	.282	.208

[1] Mean based on all possible pairs (all single origins only)
[2] Mean based on each group with the rest of the population.

Rank correlation between indices 1 and 2 = .96.

the basic patterns and magnitudes of the indices. Thus if there are "n" ethnic groups, Index 1 is the mean of n(n-1)/2 indices of dissimilarity. In the present case it is the mean of 9 × 10/2 or 45 indices. Index 2 is the simple average of 10 indices of dissimilarity, one for each ethnic group from all other ethnic groups. Though the values of the two indices are different they are highly correlated as shown by the rank correlation, which was .96. The rest of this paper will therefore be concerned only with Index 1.

Segregation is highest in Montreal, with the value for the mean index being .574. Apart from the ethnic factor, language probably plays a large part in the high segregation in Montreal and to a lesser degree for the high segregation in Ottawa-Hull. Next to Montreal, Toronto had the highest index at .433. In general the segregation indices seem to be somewhat lower in the western metropolitan areas. In Calgary the mean index is only .253.

Some of the relationships of segregation indices to characteristics of metropolitan areas can be examined in Table 2. Because of the small number of cities, their distinctive historical development and topography, generalizations are hazardous to make. However, there seems to be a moderate association between size and level of segregation, the rank correlation coefficient between size and the segregation index being 0.41. It may well be that larger populations provide the threshold necessary for ethnic concentrations. It is also possible that

TABLE 2

Selected Characteristics of Metropolitan Areas and Rank Correlations with Mean Indices of Segregation, 1981

Metropolitan Area	Population Size ('000s)	Percentage[1] Non-British or French	Ethnic Diversity Index	Mean Index of Segregation
Halifax	276	22.3	.41	.386
Montreal	2,792	22.8	.49	.574
Ottawa-Hull	712	25.2	.67	.426
Toronto	2,975	50.8	.79	.433
Hamilton	538	41.1	.67	.377
St. Catharines-Niagara	302	43.0	.71	.383
Kitchener-Waterloo	285	50.5	.72	.331
London	280	32.5	.57	.333
Windsor	243	42.8	.76	.352
Winnipeg	578	56.1	.83	.386
Calgary	587	46.8	.73	.253
Edmonton	650	55.0	.80	.299
Vancouver	1,251	48.1	.74	.331
Victoria	229	30.5	.53	.282

[1] Percentage who did not report single origin British or French.

Rank Correlation between
    Mean Segregation Index and Population Size   = .41
    Mean Segregation Index and Percent Non-
       British or French   = − .26
    Mean Segregation Index and Ethnic Diversity   = − .16

higher visibility through numbers may promote greater discrimination against certain ethnic groups in the larger cities. It was hypothesized that ethnic diversity will promote residential segregation. To test this, a measure of ethnic diversity was constructed for each metropolitan area. The measure was $1-\Sigma p_i^2$, where the p_i represents the proportion of total population in the ith ethnic origin. The range for the index is 1 to 1.

Given that the two charter groups of British and French form the majority of the Canadian population, one can also look upon the proportion who are neither British or French as an indicator of ethnic diversity. Table 2 shows that both of these measures are only weakly correlated with the segregation index and not in the predicted direction, the rank correlation between ethnic diversity and mean segregation index being only − 0.16. Ethnically diverse cities do not tell us much about the residential segregation prevalent in those cities. Montreal with a low ethnic diversity of .49 has a high mean segregation index of .574. Toronto with a high ethnic diversity index of .79 has also a high segregation index of .433. On the other hand, Edmonton with a high ethnic diversity index of .80 has a low segregation index of .299 and Victoria with a low ethnic diversity index of .53 has also a low segregation index of .282.

Segregation by Ethnicity

The main purpose of this paper is to investigate residential segregation by ethnic origin. Though the segregation patterns vary by metropolitan area it may be worthwhile first to examine them by aggregating over the cities to get some idea of the overall magnitude. Table 3 presents the mean indices of ethnic group segregation from every other ethnic group averaged over the 14 metropolitan areas. The British have the lowest at .293 followed by Germans at .314. At the other extreme, Natives have the highest mean segregation index of .491 with the Italians being the second highest at .439. The other European groups as well as the charter group of French fall in between. It is unfortunate that the composition of the various ethnic groups from Asia, Africa and Latin America are not available in the small area census tapes nor of certain European groups such as Portuguese or Greek as no doubt many of these ethnic groups must have very different residential patterns.

Segregation indices for the various ethnic groups by metropolitan areas are presented in Table 4. Substantial differences exist among the metropolitan areas. The British were most segregated in Montreal (.480) and least segregated in Calgary (.195). French segregation indices vary a great deal, from .603 in Ottawa-Hull to .231 in Calgary. Ottawa-Hull is however a special case because of the natural boundary and provincial differences between the Ottawa and Hull

TABLE 3

Mean Index of Segregation of Ethnic Group from Every Other Ethnic Group, 1981 (averaged over the 14 CMAs)

Ethnic Group	Index of Segregation
British	.293
French	.354
Dutch	.373
German	.314
Italian	.439
Native	.491
Polish	.353
Scandinavian	.377
Ukrainian	.342
Other single origins	.341

TABLE 4

Mean Index of Segregation for Ethnic groups, 1981

Metropolitan Area	British	French	Dutch	German	Italian	Native	Polish	Scandinavian	Ukrainian	Other Single
Halifax	.291	.297	.350	.319	.453	.522	.439	.367	.473	.347
Montreal	.480	.585	.603	.497	.675	.615	.524	.647	.553	.562
Ottawa-Hull	.327	.605	.420	.349	.484	.530	.385	.408	.393	.363
Toronto	.342	.360	.436	.355	.560	.532	.460	.441	.427	.416
Hamilton	.299	.320	.440	.328	.418	.535	.360	.416	.330	.322
St. Cath.-Niag.	.298	.406	.404	.357	.435	.528	.341	.434	.307	.314
Kitchener	.268	.266	.324	.311	.360	.449	.303	.415	.327	.290
London	.254	.275	.361	.278	.366	.476	.330	.375	.334	.283
Windsor	.273	.335	.342	.287	.357	.545	.334	.412	.306	.322
Winnipeg	.329	.462	.366	.331	.428	.520	.358	.345	.347	.374
Calgary	.195	.231	.247	.200	.355	.386	.240	.225	.218	.231
Edmonton	.247	.266	.302	.274	.420	.383	.270	.264	.270	.298
Vancouver	.271	.294	.328	.275	.488	.439	.305	.278	.271	.359
Victoria	.227	.256	.298	.231	.342	.412	.292	.242	.229	.288
Mean	.293	.354	.373	.314	.439	.491	.353	.377	.342	.341

portions of the metropolitan area. Similarly the high index for Winnipeg is due to the historical French settlement in St. Boniface. Outside of Montreal, Ottawa-Hull and Winnipeg, French are not highly segregated. Apart from the Italians and Natives, the intermetropolitan differences for the various ethnic groups follow more or less the same pattern.

Italians and Natives deserve special mention. Their segregation indices are not only higher than the other ethnic groups in almost all the metropolitan areas, but do not seem to follow the same patterns. For example, the Italians have a high index in Vancouver (.488) where all the other ethnic groups have much lower segregation indices. In Toronto and Montreal also they are the most segregated group, even more so than the Natives. There is not a single metropolitan area where the segregation index for the Italians falls below .340. There are probably a number of causes, such as official language facility, occupational specialization, recency of immigration and cultural background to explain the high concentration. Of course there are other ethnic groups on whom we do not have information here who are even more segregated than the Italians such as Portuguese, Greeks and Jews (see Balakrishnan and Kralt 1987).

Natives have not only the highest mean segregation index (.491), but also the highest in 9 out of the 14 metropolitan areas. The indices range from a low of .383 in Edmonton to a high of .615 in Montreal. The relative positions of the ethnic groups were not too different in the various metropolitan areas. In most of the areas, the Natives and Italians had the highest segregation indices and the British and Germans the lowest. This indicates that there is not a significant interaction between metropolitan area and ethnicity, a finding consistent with the earlier analysis of 1971 data (Balakrishnan 1982).

Ethnic Segregation and Social Distance

Among the many factors that cause segregation among the ethnic groups is social distance (Driedger and Church 1974; Guest and Weed 1976; Kantrowitz 1973). While economic resources will influence the residential location, it is the thesis of this paper that social distance is equally important in explaining ethnic segregation in Canadian cities. The rationale is that social distance will reflect itself to some extent in residential segregation. For example, a survey done in Toronto in 1978-79 showed that British Canadians expressed a preference not to live next door to persons of other specific ethnic groups, the proportions varying according to the social prestige of these groups (Reitz 1988). It may well be that some of these attitudes will be reflected in their behaviour when it comes to their residential choice. Ethnic groups that are culturally similar to each other are less likely to be segregated among themselves compared to other ethnic groups. Though we do not have a strict social distance scale, based from the earlier works on social distance, we venture to classify our ethnic groups in order of increasing social distance from the British as follows: British; Northern

406

TABLE 5

Mean Segregation Indices of Ethnic Groups, 1981 (14 CMAs)

	German	French	Scandinavian	Dutch	Polish	Ukrainian	Italian	Native	Other Single
British	.175	.255	.262	.252	.294	.270	.399	.471	.259
German		.297	.293	.261	.305	.281	.427	.492	.294
French			.375	.346	.353	.338	.439	.448	.322
Scandinavian				.351	.379	.356	.483	.520	.374
Dutch					.372	.359	.485	.538	.376
Polish						.264	.418	.481	.315
Ukrainian							.404	.485	.305
Italian								.537	.360
Native									.448

and Western Europe (French, German, Dutch, Scandinavian); Eastern Europe (Polish, Ukrainian); Southern Europe (Italian); and Native (Driedger and Peters 1977; Pineo 1977). "Other single," comprising all other single origins cannot be placed on the social distance scale.

Mean segregation indices between ethnic groups averages over the 14 metropolitan areas are presented in Table 5. There seems to be support for the social distance hypothesis. The mean segregation index between British and German is only .175. The indices of British with Dutch, Scandinavian and French are about the same around .255, and increases to .294 for Polish. The index of British with Italian is much higher at .399 and even higher with Native Indians at .471. The pattern is consistent for the other ethnic groups as well, except the Native Indians.

The Natives have the highest indices of dissimilarity with every other ethnic group, the values being not too different, indicating that the social distance of Natives is uniformly high from all of the ethnic groups considered here, ranging from .448 to .538. Had there been other ethnic categories low in social prestige such as Asiatic or Black, it is possible that indices of dissimilarity between Natives and these groups may have been lower. Unfortunately the published data do not allow these investigations.

To test the robustness of the social distance hypothesis, the indices of dissimilarity among the ethnic groups are examined in the three cities of Montreal, Toronto and Calgary, representing high, medium and low overall segregation and different regional locations (Table 6). The pattern is less clear in Montreal where all the indices are very high, but quite apparent in Toronto and Calgary. For example, in Toronto, the index between British and German is only .162, with Dutch it is .272, with Polish .429, with Italian .541 and with Natives .483. Similar increasing patterns can be noticed for the other ethnic groups as well, except for Italians and Natives who have uniformly high segregation indices from every other ethnic group. In Calgary, where all the indices are lower, the pattern of social distance is still evident. The low segregation of Ukrainians from the charter groups of British and French and the Western Europeans in Calgary is probably due to their large numbers, early settlement and relatively better position in Western Canada.

Ethnic Segregation and Social Class

It has often been argued that ethnic segregation is largely due to social class differences among the ethnic groups and not because of the ethnic factor itself. Occupational, educational and income composition of the ethnic groups differ and segregation patterns observed are a manifestation of these basic class differences. The assumption is that persons of the same social class are less likely to be residentially segregated even though they may belong to different ethnic groups. In Canada ethnic composition has primarily been determined by waves

Mean Segregation Indices of Ethnic Groups-Montreal, Toronto and Calgary, 1981

	German	French	Scandinavian	Dutch	Polish	Ukrainian	Italian	Native	Other Single
Montreal									
British	.300	.532	.471	.439	.417	.459	.664	.554	.481
German		.511	.515	.450	.459	.516	.678	.575	.473
French			.751	.661	.561	.585	.585	.484	.598
Scandinavian				.535	.636	.665	.830	.747	.674
Dutch					.593	.629	.791	.696	.635
Polish						.399	.624	.593	.430
Ukrainian							.595	.615	.517
Italian								.670	.642
Native									.605
Toronto									
British	.162	.180	.297	.272	.429	.375	.541	.483	.343
German		.245	.310	.281	.410	.367	.536	.518	.370
French			.345	.335	.433	.393	.544	.436	.329
Scandinavian				.387	.496	.461	.635	.576	.460
Dutch					.518	.470	.600	.587	.473
Polish						.252	.576	.588	.437
Ukrainian							.543	.568	.410
Italian								.589	.476
Native									.444
Calgary									
British	.116	.162	.141	.166	.174	.124	.324	.375	.158
German		.191	.146	.185	.183	.139	.299	.366	.171
French			.218	.221	.213	.206	.374	.323	.175
Scandinavian				.193	.209	.176	.320	.408	.213
Dutch					.238	.220	.368	.395	.239
Polish						.199	.352	.368	.224
Ukrainian							.329	.391	.176
Italian								.465	.343
Native									.382

of immigration which have been selective in terms of ethnic background. A particular wave of immigrants may lack the economic resources, educational background or occupational skills and may take some time before improving their social class status in Canada. Some previous studies, however, have shown that even when social class is controlled ethnic segregation persists (Darroch and Marston 1971; Balakrishnan 1982). Where aggregate data at the census tract level are used as here, only a crude indirect method can be employed to test the relationship between ethnic segregation and social class. For the two largest metropolitan areas of Montreal and Toronto, the census tracts were grouped

TABLE 7

Mean Segregation Indices by Socioeconomic Level of Census Tracts for Montreal and Toronto, 1981

Ethnic Group	Montreal SES Index of Census Tracts			
	< 40	40.0-44.9	45.0-54.9	55.0 +
British	.634	.559	.444	.370
French	.551	.606	.547	.535
Dutch	.720	.720	.573	.459
German	.560	.561	.458	.378
Italian	.694	.683	.589	.451
Native	.643	.614	.552	.590
Polish	.604	.584	.478	.417
Scandinavian	.825	.833	.619	.465
Ukrainian	.631	.596	.510	.422
Other Single Origins	.589	.590	.527	.490
Mean	.634	.635	.530	.458
Number of tracts	124	189	208	108
	Toronto			
	< 45	45.0-52.9	53.0-59.9	60.0 +
British	.347	.316	.312	.299
French	.370	.333	.339	.306
Dutch	.416	.431	.402	.338
German	.372	.323	.318	.307
Italian	.559	.494	.442	.377
Native	.460	.463	.553	.579
Polish	.501	.453	.418	.380
Scandinavian	.476	.410	.392	.370
Ukrainian	.437	.416	.401	.381
Other Single Origins	.388	.395	.389	.420
Mean	.433	.403	.397	.376
Number of tracts	135	174	168	109

410

into four categories according to the socioeconomic status (SES) level of the residents in those tracts. Since socioeconomic status at the individual level, cross-classified by ethnic status was not available, aggregate measures at the tract level are used as an indicator. The SES level of a census tract was determined by the education, occupation and income distribution of the population in the tract. An index was constructed combining percentage of adults with high school or higher education, percentage of males in higher status occupations and percentage of families with more than $20,000 annual income. The index was further standardized to have a mean of 50 and a standard deviation of 10. Ethnic residential segregation indices were calculated separately for these groups of census tracts (Table 7). If persons of higher social classes are less likely to be segregated one would expect segregation indices to decrease with increasing SES of the tracts. Table 7 provides qualified support for this hypothesis. In Montreal, the overall mean segregation index decreases from .634 in the poorer areas to .458 in the high SES areas, and in Toronto from .433 to .376. The decline can be noticed for most ethnic groups, the notable exception being Natives. Irrespective of the SES of the census tracts, they are highly segregated.

Summary and Conclusions

This paper examined the residential segregation patterns of ethnic groups in Canadian metropolitan areas using data from the 1981 Census. It was largely a replication of an earlier study done on the 1971 Census. The changes in the measurement and classification of ethnic groups make direct comparison impossible. Still, it can said that, by and large, the same findings hold 10 years later. Larger cities seem to have higher ethnic segregation and cities in the West lower levels. Overall ethnic diversity of a city appears to have little effect on the extent of segregation within the city. It may well be that the larger cities also have larger ethnic populations which facilitate the creation of ethnic neighbourhoods which result in greater spatial segregation patterns (Darroch and Marston 1984). Darroch and Marston also emphasize how ethnic residential segregation in turn can increase ethnic pluralism in an urban community. An interesting speculation about the cause for low ethnic segregation in the Western cities such as Calgary and Edmonton is that these cities grew rapidly in the late 1960s and 1970s, especially through migration, both internal and international of various ethnic groups. Unlike some of the cities in the East, they did not experience waves of immigrants of different ethnic origins spread over a long period of time, enabling the formation of distinct neighbourhoods.

There is considerable support for the social distance hypothesis. Western and Northern European groups are least segregated, Eastern Europeans more segregated, and Italians and Natives most segregated. The lack of data on the Portuguese, Greek, Jewish, Asiatic, Black and other Third World ethnic groups for all the metropolitan areas is a serious limitation of this paper as it is exactly these groups who are making the greatest impact on the Canadian urban scene in terms of residential patterns. A study limited to the three largest cities of Montreal, Toronto and Vancouver found that the most segregated groups in these three cities were Jews, Greeks and Portuguese (Balakrishnan and Kralt 1987). The consistently high segregation of Natives from all other ethnic groups deserves further scrutiny. Though census data is inadequate to investigate in depth the causes of ethnic segregation and its implications, this paper shows that ethnicity continues to be an important facet of Canadian society.

Notes

1. We gratefully acknowledge the financial support from the Demographic Review, Health and Welfare Canada, without which this study could not have been completed.

22. THE EMERGENCE OF MULTIETHNICITIES IN THE EIGHTIES

Karol J. Krótki and Dave Odynak

Statisticians Respond to Social Reality

After a century of reasonably consistent adherence to the Canadian definition of ethnicity a mild change took place during the 1981 Census. Then radical departure in the definition of ethnicity was instituted during the 1986 Census. Details of the minor departures from and changes in the Canadian definitions were given earlier in this volume by John Kralt. For our purposes it is sufficient to recall that the Canadian definition required going back to the ethnic or cultural origin of one's ancestor on the paternal side right to the time of his (not hers, by definition) first arrival on these shores.[1]

Except for Amerindians and the Inuit, it was, therefore, impossible for anyone else to report an ethnicity as Canadian or American, notwithstanding the fact that at each census 50,000 or 100,000 sturdy individuals insisted on writing in "Canadian" or "American." There was, of course, no pre-printed provision for such entries. Canada was, thus, possibly the only country in the world where a citizen could not declare himself or herself as a national of the country. This anomaly was one of the criticisms levied against the definition, though not the most important one.

Another criticism was that being limited to one, and often a long past, ethnicity did violence to the reality of the situation. For example, a fourth generation Canadian had to label him/herself by the ethnicity that might have been responsible for one sixteenth of his/her blood, if the first arrival and his progeny did not marry within the original ethnicity. Even in less extreme cases, with the passage of time and generations, the labelling required by the Canadian definition became less and less realistic and even less message-conveying. Still, the society could be meaningfully broken up by the Canadian definition of ethnicity into distinct groups, as was the case, for example, with the use of the

415

child-woman ratio for the study of ethnic fertility. There was life in the old dog for a long time to come, notwithstanding the continuous criticism levied at it in academic circles. It was easy to point out disadvantages of the definition, more difficult to say what could be put in its place.[2]

Over time census-takers changed: and a considerable number of respondents in 1981 spontaneously began writing in more than one ethnicity. Close to two million people out of 24 million, or 8 percent, had multiple ethnic origins entered on their census forms.[3] By 1986, census-takers turned this spontaneity into census instruction. This new instruction opened the alternative to anybody inclined to use it. We are now confronted with an entirely new ball game. Academicians who like the comfort of a one-to-one correspondence between reality and available data will open a sniping campaign against these new results. Still, adequate provisions must be made for this variable of ethnic origin. There is too much sociopolitical pressure behind this variable for it to be ignored and social scientists benefit from the provisions made to satisfy this demand. Statisticians and census-takers do not engage in social engineering, they merely try to measure social reality.[4]

> The purpose of this chapter is to report what use the 24 million Canadian respondents made of the new freedom to report their ethnicities and to attempt to develop analytic means of drawing conclusions from the reported multiethnicities.

The Canadian Definition: Static and Inflexible

In the previous section we said that the inadmissability of the declaration "Canadian" on the census form was one of the criticisms levied against the definition. Another criticism must have been the fact that it did not allow for the assimilation of ethnic groups one into another or for the assimilation of the minority groups into the predominant culture. Every respondent was stuck with whatever was the ethnic origin of the paternal ancestor at the time of first arrival on these shores.

Obviously, the Canadian definition was static and was not able to reflect the process of assimilation, subtle perhaps to begin with, but eventually resulting in radical changes and extreme transformations, such as the virtual disappearance of entire ethnic identities. Yet, in a formal sense and under the strict application of Canada's definition, the ethnicities of Canada would survive forever (unless dying out through low fertility) and with progressive assimilation, as purely formal structures and meaningless identities.

One cannot pretend at this early stage to be certain how these new data arising in 1981 and 1986 will affect the relevant analytical outcomes. However, it must be clear already, that the inputs will not be static and that they will be flexible. Multiethnicities will measure assimilation by definition: the greater the admixture the more obvious the emergence of the melting pot.

By definition, multiethnicities are the outcome of intermarriages. In themselves, intermarriage can be viewed as the opening step to cultural assimilation. The marriage partners may use both languages, if the languages of the two ethnic groups are different, interchangeably, or they may settle for the use of one language, or, most likely, they opt for the language of the majority. Opting for the language of the majority may appear particularly convenient, if there are children around, as was the case until recently with most couples. The data on multiethnicity will alert the social scientist to developments taking place, though they alone will not be able to disclose which solution the couple adopted. Nor will they alone be able to identify uniethnic couples who switch to the language of the majority under no particular compulsion. The social scientist may also be alerted through the multiethnicity data to the possibility that intermarriage may have been facilitated by structural assimilation.

Thus, the emergence of a possible way to measure intermarriage through multiethnicities provides us with a central and pivotal point of passage leading possibly from structural assimilation to, more certainly, cultural assimilation.

Assimilation, Intermarriage and Multiethnicity

A major question facing us throughout this paper will be whether we view intermarriage as leading to a loss of ethnic identity or as acting as a means of recruitment for ethnic groups. We view the issue as one of interpreting the data as a battleground for some endogamous losses but more on the level of exogamous gains (see definitions in a later section). Canadian evidence has tended to emphasize and support the explanation that a loss of ethnic identity occurs through intermarriage (Goldstein and Segall 1985).

According to the assimilationist perspective, intermarriage can be a form of "structural assimilation" whereby minority groups gain entrance into the major institutions of society (Gordon 1964). Under this theoretical perspective once marital assimilation takes place other forms of assimilation occur. Structural assimilation is dependent on the degree of primary group-type relations. "The primary group is a group in which contact is personal, informal, intimate, and usually face-to-face, and which involves the entire personality, not just a segmentalized part of it" (Gordon 1964, 31). Primary group relations for an ethnic group can be characterized by high intragroup contact, and endogamous marriages where both relatives and close friends are from the same ethnic group.

"Cultural assimilation" as opposed to structural assimilation refers more to the adaptation processes of ethnic groups to "everyday" norms of the host culture. Under cultural assimilation one begins a remarkable transformation from Ukrainian to Ukrainian-Canadian, Italian to Italian-Canadian and so forth. Secondary group relations predominate for the culturally assimilated where members of different ethnic groups participate in less personal spheres of activity. According to Gordon (1964, 32) "...[a] secondary group is a group in which contacts tend to be impersonal, formal or casual, non-intimate, and segmentalized; in some cases they are face-to-face, in others not." An overriding feature of the assimilationist perspective is that there are clear "losers" from intermarriage among participating ethnic groups because of the erosion of primary group relations focused within the ethnic group.

From our perspective some ethnic groups are endogamous losers and some are exogamous gainers. No emphasis is placed on the possibility that the intermarriage can lead to a one-sided victory that is so complete that an Italian becomes a Ukrainian whose primary relations are entirely focused on the Ukrainian community. Such instances are rare. On the one hand, there may be continual erosion of the primary group relations centred on an ethnic group when endogamous marriages within an ethnicity are lost. On the other hand, exogamous gains can be expected for an ethnicity not so much at the primary group level but at the secondary level. A major question arises whether we lament the loss of endogamous marriages that perpetuate particular forms of primary group relations for an ethnic group or look to the gains of prestige resulting from intermarriage.

In this paper we do not need to give answers and take sides. We concentrate on the new tool of multiethnicity to measure the process.

Once ethnicity becomes a random element in marriage selection and determination, the biological basis for the preservation of ethnicities will disappear. The need for ethnicity questions and the related demands will be gone. We are probably on our way to such a state, but in the meantime the matter is lively and topical. Apparently ethnic groups take part in the process with considerable differences in pace, quantity and possibly quality, a subject taken up in the next section.

The Measurement of Interethnic Differentials in Multiethnicity

For the comparison of single origins with multiple origins for each ethnic group several indices come to mind and the easiest is to contrast the numbers of singles with the number of multiples. Other things being equal, an ethnic group beginning with large numbers would have opportunities correspondingly large for intermarrying; a small group would have more limited opportunities. The assumption of "other things being equal" is heroic for a number of reasons, including a formal one. Depending on dispersion, small groups should proportionately intermarry more: their "boundaries" are larger in comparison with their "areas." Some of the assimilation hypotheses that have been found useful in the literature are listed in this chapter's appendix.

To begin with, let us take, somewhat arbitrarily, equality in numbers between the singles and the multiples as the dividing line: if for any ethnic origin, multiples are greater than singles, then we call them exogamous gainers; if less,

TABLE 1

Selected Ethnic Origins Showing Single and Multiple Origins, Canada, 1986

Selected Ethnic Origins	Single Origins	Multiple Origins	(3) as% of (2)	Selected Ethnic Origins	Single Origins	Multiple Origins	(7) as% of (6)
English	4,742,040	4,561,910	96	Greek	143,780	33,530	23
Irish	699,685	2,922,605	418	Italian	709,585	297,325	42
Scottish	865,450	3,052,606	353	Maltese	15,345	8,925	58
Welsh	23,395	126,890	542	Portuguese	199,595	37,590	19
French	6,087,310	2,027,945	33	Spanish	57,125	56,045	98
Austrian	24,900	49,745	200	Jewish	245,860	97,650	40
Belgian	28,395	46,395	163	Armenian	22,525	4,865	22
Dutch (Netherlands)	351,765	530,170	151	Iranian	13,325	2,420	18
German	896,715	1,570,340	175	Arab, n.i.e.	27,275	10,230	38
Swiss	19,135	41,145	215	Egyptian	11,580	4,135	36
Finnish	40,566	50,775	125	Lebanese	29,345	15,685	53
Danish	39,950	79,105	198	East Indian, n.i.e.	220,630	40,810	18
Icelandic	14,470	39,285	271	Pakistani, n.i.e.	24,880	6,770	27
Norwegian	61,575	182,100	296	Punjabi	10,870	4,680	43
Swedish	43,340	160,535	370	Chinese	360,320	53,720	15
Scandinavian, n.i.e.	12,375	19,440	157	Japanese	40,240	14,260	35
Estonian	13,200	7,330	56	Korean	27,680	2,020	7
Latvian	12,620	7,380	58	Filipino	93,285	13,780	15
Lithuanian	14,725	12,225	83	Cambodian	10,370	1,425	18
Czech	20,385	19,255	94	Vietnamese	53,010	9,980	19
Czechoslovakian	18,830	24,605	131	Other Latin/Cen Amer	14,660	6,025	41
Slovak	16,320	11,385	70	Haitian	10,865	6,140	56
Hungarian (Magyar)	97,850	91,145	93	Jamaican	11,210	8,505	76
Polish	222,260	389,840	175	Other West Indian	24,665	15,620	63
Romanian	18,745	32,590	174	Black	170,340	83,770	49
Russian	32,085	71,585	223	Inuit	27,290	9,175	34
Ukrainian	420,210	541,000	129	Metis	59,745	91,865	154
Croatian	35,120	9,055	26	Amerindians	286,230	262,730	92
Macedonian	11,366	5,915	52	Other origins	178,065	2,675	2
Yugoslav, n.i.e.	51,200	33,375	65				

Source for cols. (2), (3), (6) and (7): *Appendum to The Daily*, Statistics Canada, December 3, 1987, Table 2.

n.i.e. = not included elsewhere.

they are endogamous losers. For the 59 ethnic groups chosen for the exercise in the five geographic areas in Tables 1, 2 and 3, we have the following numbers of endogamous losers in terms of ethnic groups: Canada 35, Quebec 41, Ontario 34, Manitoba 30, Alberta 25.

Ceteris paribus, what these numbers suggest is that as we move westwards the exogamy becomes greater as more and more ethnic group members marry someone from outside their ethnic group.

Later we will show that to get above the threshold of 100, one third of a given ethnic group's members need to intermarry, perhaps an unduly relaxed requirement.

If we wish to go beyond mere numbers of ethnic groups, proportionate changes need to be considered. Obviously, an ethnic group with multiples equal to 105 percent of its singles is very different from one with 500 percent. The Irish and the Scottish seem to beat everybody; they have been here longest, except for the French.

A perusal of the varying ratios of multiples to singles in Tables 1, 2, and 3 provokes a number of speculative thoughts. The British are not monolithic. The English marry outside their ethnic group to an extent four and five times less than the Irish, the Scottish and the Welsh. On the face of it, the finding would suggest consistency with two of the hypotheses suggested in the appendix, namely (i) and (iv), though the Irish and the Scottish are not exactly small groups.

The French are heavily endogamous at the national level (33) and extremely so in Quebec (6), but are exogamous in Ontario (162), Manitoba (161) and even more so in Alberta (282), supporting hypotheses (i) and (iii), but not (ii).

The "older" or traditional immigrants in Table 1 from Austrians to Scandinavians, and from Poles to Ukrainians have high exogamy. Small groups tend to be endogamous losers (they intermarry less) contrary to hypothesis (ii) in the appendix, because apparently hypothesis (i) is more influential or more realistic. The "younger" groups are the more recent immigrants with little exogamy. The same picture is repeated with few exceptions due to small numbers at the four provincial levels in Tables 2 and 3. The three Baltic ethnic groups (Estonian, Latvian and Lithuanian) keep to themselves at the national level (40 years after coming to Canada?), in Quebec and in Ontario, but are outgoing in Manitoba and Alberta. It is not clear why hypothesis (i) from the appendix would not work throughout, because these three groups are small whatever the geographic dimension. Could it be that it is the nature of the host society that affects intermarriage (open in Manitoba and Alberta, closed in Quebec and Ontario?), more than features of the ethnic group concerned. Hypotheses (iii), (v) and (vi) cannot be tested until relevant data become available.

This paper is being written in the absence of cross-classifying variables. Once such variables become available, it might be possible to arrive at a typology of differential pace and nature of the adoption of multiethnicities among ethnic groups in Canada. Figure 1 is an attempt at such a typology using endogamy-

TABLE 2

Selected Ethnic Origins Showing Single and Multiple Origins, Quebec and Ontario, 1986

Selected Ethnic Origins	QUEBEC			ONTARIO		
	Single Origins	Multiple Origins	(3) as % of (2)	Single Origins	Multiple Origins	(6) as % of (5)
English	203,065	222,855	110	2,194,405	2,112,455	96
Irish	74,555	148,930	200	317,810	1,389,875	473
Scottish	41,195	104,520	254	389,775	1,394,510	358
Welsh	555	3,180	573	9,750	48,360	496
French	5,011,500	293,805	6	531,215	859,050	162
Austrian	1,645	2,135	130	10,480	16,885	161
Belgian	6,480	5,430	84	12,175	16,140	133
Dutch (Netherlands)	6,365	11,430	180	171,155	224,555	131
German	26,780	43,510	162	285,160	615,810	216
Swiss	3,425	3,630	106	7,600	15,275	201
Finnish	810	905	112	26,530	27,265	103
Danish	895	1,505	168	10,950	19,585	179
Icelandic	100	320	320	1,270	5,436	428
Norwegian	745	2,230	299	5,170	22,425	434
Swedish	640	2,120	331	7,465	30,620	410
Scandinavian, n.i.e.	165	400	242	1,900	3,290	173
Estonian	655	390	60	10,045	4,185	42
Latvian	905	366	39	9,545	4,060	43
Lithuanian	2,195	1,120	51	10,265	6,665	65
Czech	1,530	890	58	9,070	6,535	72
Czechoslovakian	1,160	1,005	87	8,945	9,070	101
Slovak	1,400	680	49	10,895	7,135	65
Hungarian (Magyar)	8,550	4,390	51	51,255	39,085	76
Polish	18,835	14,810	79	117,580	151,510	129
Romanian	3,315	1,990	60	7,385	10,655	144
Russian	1,820	3,355	184	5,780	18,355	318
Ukrainian	12,220	10,190	83	109,705	150,875	138
Croatian	920	270	29	26,755	6,050	23
Macedonian	30	50	167	11,175	5,625	50
Yugoslav, n.i.e.	3,740	1,705	46	32,215	18,485	57
Greek	47,450	5,490	12	80,320	18,185	23

TABLE 2 (cont'd)

Selected Ethnic Origins	QUEBEC			ONTARIO		
	Single Origins	Multiple Origins	(3) as% of (2)	Single Origins	Multiple Origins	(6) as% of (5)
Italian	163,880	34,635	21	461,375	167,960	36
Maltese	150	245	163	14,330	7,530	53
Portuguese	29,700	3,680	13	139,225	22,980	17
Spanish	16,605	7,815	47	28,005	24,620	88
Jewish	81,195	17,035	21	127,025	49,510	39
Armenian	10,810	1,700	16	10,750	2,370	22
Iranian	3,205	505	16	5,825	985	17
Arab, n.i.e.	9,190	3,600	39	12,705	4,250	33
Egyptian	6,155	1,840	30	4,195	1,660	40
Lebanese	8,270	3,165	38	11,820	6,695	57
East Indian, n.i.e.	12,120	2,955	24	111,775	23,105	21
Pakistani, n.i.e.	2,750	725	26	14,910	3,975	27
Punjabi	320	190	59	2,860	1,155	40
Chinese	23,205	3,550	15	156,170	24,790	16
Japanese	1,280	615	48	16,155	4,450	28
Korean	1,230	75	6	17,200	1,225	7
Filipino	5,115	925	18	44,195	6,015	14
Cambodian	5,165	615	12	3,160	505	16
Vietnamese	15,865	1,565	10	17,155	4,210	25
Other Latin/Cen. Amer.	5,685	1,150	20	6,135	3,080	50
Haitian	10,455	5,640	54	290	405	140
Jamaican	660	350	53	8,980	6,685	74
Other West Indian	1,515	1,430	94	19,870	11,015	55
Black	36,785	14,610	40	108,710	46,795	43
Inuit	6,470	890	14	675	2,285	339
Metis	5,705	5,740	101	3,720	14,565	392
Amerindians	37,150	26,435	71	51,150	99,555	195
Other origins	25,745	415	2	70,005	1,055	2

Source for cols. (2), (3), (6) and (7): *Addendum to The Daily*. Statistics Canada. December 3. 1987. Table 2.

n.i.e. = not included elsewhere.

TABLE 3

Selected Ethnic Origins Showing Single and Multiple Origins, Manitoba and Alberta, 1986

Selected Ethnic Origins	MANITOBA			ALBERTA		
	Single Origins	Multiple Origins	(3) as% of (2)	Single Origins	Multiple Origins	(6) as% of (5)
English	158,190	208,745	132	438,950	567,655	129
Irish	24,235	126,055	520	60,790	352,750	580
Scottish	40,825	150,450	369	88,645	392,420	443
Welsh	1,050	6,360	606	3,780	22,135	586
French	55,605	89,660	161	77,430	218,185	282
Austrian	1,665	3,490	210	3,165	9,165	290
Belgian	4,255	7,075	166	1,755	5,945	339
Dutch (Netherlands)	27,875	29,500	106	55,920	83,330	149
German	96,165	88,815	92	182,870	297,950	163
Swiss	595	1,725	290	2,475	8,220	332
Finnish	720	1,550	215	2,625	6,015	229
Danish	1,395	3,845	276	11,610	23,680	204
Icelandic	6,980	13,565	194	1,650	6,020	365
Norwegian	2,515	9,025	359	18,395	57,560	313
Swedish	3,335	12,455	373	10,995	43,495	396
Scandinavian, n.i.e.	615	1,140	185	3,875	6,140	158
Estonian	55	90	164	580	900	155
Latvian	400	635	159	545	890	163
Lithuanian	345	415	120	840	1,655	197
Czech	1,110	1,110	99	3,105	4,050	130
Czechoslovakian	900	1,545	172	3,445	5,680	165
Slovak	760	455	60	1,685	1,580	94
Hungarian (Magyar)	3,225	3,660	113	12,780	16,065	126
Polish	22,015	46,530	211	28,500	76,720	269
Romanian	640	1,715	268	2,795	6,920	248
Russian	1,755	4,545	259	4,185	15,185	363
Ukrainian	79,940	79,385	98	106,760	132,210	124
Croatian	670	245	37	1,990	730	37
Macedonian	0	0	–	105	120	114
Yugoslav, n.i.e.	1,195	1,045	87	4,525	3,975	88
Greek	2,025	735	36	4,030	2,810	70

TABLE 3 (cont'd)

Selected Ethnic Origins	MANITOBA			ALBERTA		
	Single Origins	Multiple Origins	(3) as% of (2)	Single Origins	Multiple Origins	(6) as% of (5)
Italian	8,230	6,970	85	23,635	26,395	112
Maltese	100	60	60	175	255	146
Portuguese	7,340	1,085	15	6,285	2,505	40
Spanish	1,180	1,825	155	5,285	5,975	113
Jewish	13,875	4,400	32	7,945	7,160	90
Armenian	75	75	100	105	195	186
Iranian	180	90	50	800	200	25
Arab, n.i.e.	275	190	69	3,145	1,030	33
Egyptian	115	25	22	640	305	48
Lebanese	170	390	229	5,010	1,425	28
East Indian, n.i.e.	6,000	1,250	21	24,635	3,780	15
Pakistani, n.i.e.	625	265	42	3,245	750	23
Punjabi	500	145	29	1,160	375	32
Chinese	8,730	2,010	23	49,210	7,550	15
Japanese	1,050	495	47	5,300	2,690	51
Korean	565	35	6	3,385	300	9
Filipino	15,815	1,525	10	10,265	1,500	15
Cambodian	315	15	5	1,025	160	16
Vietnamese	2,060	455	22	9,625	2,015	21
Other Latin/Cen. Amer.	520	155	22	1,240	700	56
Haitian	40	10	25	35	45	129
Jamaican	280	105	338	875	715	82
Other West Indian	905	520	57	1,395	1,280	92
Black	3,665	2,525	69	7,235	6,205	86
Inuit	185	515	278	295	830	281
Metis	14,270	19,015	133	16,880	23,250	138
Amerindians	40,965	14,990	37	34,490	34,475	100
Other origins	12,520	110	1	25,815	480	2

Source for cols. (2), (3), (6) and (7): *Addendum to The Daily*, Statistics Canada, December 5, 1987, table 2.

n.i.e. = not included elsewhere.

424

exogamy and early-recent period of immigration. Judging from the strange bedfellows in the cells of the figure, a 2 times 2 classification, as occurred to us, may not be sufficient for the study of multiethnicities. The typology might in turn lead to the evolution of a theory of differential change into multiethnicities. Without such a typology one would not know where and how to begin: the higher the education the faster the transformation? Does higher education increase the probability of intermarriage similarly to widening employing opportunities and increasing long-distance migration? Or is it that high education provides a cultural base sufficiently strong for the preservation of language and culture, almost independent of the endogamy-exogamy syndrome?

At the provincial level (Tables 2 and 3) the numbers are getting smaller, but the Czechoslovakian line behaves in the four provinces as at the national level. Yugoslavians behave anarchistically, but their numbers are quite small. The three native groups behave as they do at the national level, unless the numbers in any one province are small.

FIGURE 1

Endogamy, Exogamy and Time of Immigration

IMMIGRATION

	Early	Recent
ENDOGAMY	English Amerindian Inuit French	Portuguese Spanish Chinese Iranian Korean Croatians Japanese Greek
EXOGAMY	Scottish Irish Welsh Metis Armenian	Czechoslovakian Yugoslavian

The Cost of Multiethnicity in Terms of Single Origins

Multiethnicities are created and reported at the expense of single ethnicities. The actual procedure is of some significance for the understanding of the new data. It is described in this section.

The exogamous gains discussed earlier are double gains in comparison with the single origins as customarily reported under the previous Canadian definition. Both ethnicities in an intermarriage gain a "one" with each offspring (in the current Canadian practice of census analysis). If each and every Canadian reported no more than the lowest multiple, that is two ethnic origins, then the number of multiples would be 50 million for a country of 25 million people. In such a case singles would have disappeared altogether. We are far from this state, but Tables 4 through 8 show the losses experienced by singles between 1971-81, between 1971-86 and jointly between 1981-86. Tables 4 through 8 contain a different arrangement of ethnic groups than Tables 1 through 3. For Table 4 through 8 the given ethnic group had to be reported in all three censuses. For Tables 1 through 3 it only had to have a minimum number of 10,000 singles reported in 1986.

Out of the ethnic groups selected for the exercise at the national level in Table 4, we have three ethnic groups who are endogamous losers *par excellence* (shown here as gainers in singles), Portuguese, Spanish, Chinese. The Croatians, the Japanese and the Greek show much smaller gains in singles, that is, endogamous losses. These gains in singles were all experienced in 1971-81, rather than 1981-86, as if the inexorable progress of exogamy took off in 1981-86 even in the case of the hitherto stubborn endogamists. All other ethnic groups show losses in singles. These losses in singles must have meant multiple counterpart gains; in the nomenclature suggested earlier they were described as endogamous gainers; once big enough, the concerned ethnic groups presumably become exogamous gainers above the 100 threshold suggested in the discussion of Table 1 through 3.

In the previous definition, to become an exogamous gainer an ethnic group had to have at least as many multiples as reported singles. For each single respondent lost while becoming a multiple, through the outside intermarriage of the father, such an ethnic group, on the assumption of *ceteris paribus*, gained a multiple, another multiple having gone to another, intermarrying ethnic group. So, the ethnic group needs to lose only 33 percent singles who on becoming multiples are equal to half the remaining 67 percent singles. The other half of the remaining 67 percent, gained *ceteris paribus* another multiple from other singles. The two multiples together are equal to 67 percent of the singles in the given ethnicity. Moving in due course above the two multiples (or 67 percent in singles) gives the ethnic group the status of exogamous gainers. Thus, to become an exogamous gainer an ethnic group needs to lose just slightly more than 33 percent of its singles. In Tables 4 through 8 we see that the encour-

TABLE 4

Selected Ethnic Origins According to Single Origins Intercensal Changes 1971-81, 1981-86, 1971-86 Canada

Origin	1971	1981	1986	Percentage Change 81-71	86-81	86-71
British	9,624,115	9,674,250	8,332,725	0.52	− 34.54	− 34.20
French	6,180,120	6,439,100	6,093,160	4.19	− 5.37	− 1.41
Austrian	42,120	40,630	24,900	− 3.54	− 38.72	− 40.88
Belgian	51,135	42,270	28,395	− 17.34	− 32.82	− 44.47
Dutch	425,945	408,235	351,765	− 4.16	− 13.83	− 17.42
German	1,317,200	1,142,365	896,720	− 13.27	− 21.50	− 31.92
Finnish	59,215	52,315	40,565	− 11.65	− 22.46	− 31.50
Estonian	18,810	15,915	13,200	− 15.39	− 17.06	− 29.82
Latvian	18,810	16,145	12,615	− 14.17	− 21.86	− 32.93
Lithuanian	24,535	18,240	14,725	− 25.66	− 19.27	− 39.98
Hungarian	131,890	116,395	97,850	− 11.75	− 15.93	− 25.81
Polish	316,425	254,485	222,260	− 19.57	− 12.66	− 29.76
Romanian	27,375	22,485	18,745	− 17.86	− 16.63	− 31.53
Russian	64,475	49,430	32,080	− 23.33	− 35.10	− 50.24
Ukrainian	580,660	529,615	420,210	− 8.79	− 20.66	− 27.63
Croatian	23,380	34,765	35,115	48.70	1.01	50.19
Yugoslavian	67,295	64,835	51,205	− 3.66	− 21.02	− 23.91
Greek	124,475	154,360	143,780	24.01	− 6.85	15.51
Italian	730,820	747,970	709,590	2.35	− 5.13	− 2.90
Portuguese	96,875	188,105	199,595	94.17	6.11	106.03
Spanish	27,515	53,540	57,125	94.58	6.70	107.61
Jewish	296,945	264,020	254,855	− 11.09	− 3.47	− 14.17
Chinese	118,815	289,245	360,320	143.44	24.57	203.26
Japanese	37,260	40,995	40,245	10.02	− 1.83	8.01
Czechoslovakian	81,870	67,700	55,535	− 17.31	− 17.97	− 32.17
Slovenian	7,305	6,395	5,890	− 12.46	− 7.90	− 19.37
Scandinavian	384,790	282,795	171,715	− 26.51	− 39.28	− 55.37
Total	20,880,175	21,016,600	16,684,885	0.65	− 20,62	− 20.10

agement to report multiethnicities in 1981 was still slight. However, due to stronger encouragement in 1986, in the once quinquennial period of 1981-1986, the overall losses in single ethnicities were already considerable with 21 percent for Canada, 26 percent for Ontario, 28 percent for Manitoba and 30 percent for Alberta. In short, and with the exception of the 5 percent in Quebec, Canada is already on its way through intermarriages to reaching the indicator of 100 in the realm of multiethnicities.

Let us compare Tables 1, 2 and 3 with Tables 4 through 8 and see whether the two lots of exogamous gainers are the same. Ontario in Table 6 behaves

TABLE 5

Selected Ethnic Origins According to Single Origins Intercensal Changes 1971-81, 1981-86, 1971-86 Quebec

Origin	1971	1981	1986	Percentage Change		
				81-71	86-81	86-71
British	640,045	487,385	319,550	−23.85	−34.44	−50.07
French	4,759,350	5,105,670	5,015,565	7.28	−1.76	5.38
Austrian	2,500	2,275	1,645	−9.00	−27.69	−34.20
Belgian	8,220	6,465	6,485	−21.35	0.31	−21.11
Dutch	12,590	8,055	6,365	−36.02	−20.98	−49.44
German	53,870	33,770	26,780	−37.31	−20.70	−50.29
Finnish	1,865	1,140	810	−38.87	−28.95	−56.57
Estonian	1,440	745	655	−48.26	−12.08	−54.51
Latvian	1,415	1,170	905	−17.31	−22.65	−36.04
Lithuanian	3,990	2,745	2,195	−31.20	−20.04	−44.99
Hungarian	12,570	9,750	8,545	−22.43	−12.36	−32.02
Polish	23,970	19,755	18,835	−17.58	−4.66	−21.42
Romanian	2,920	2,785	3,315	20.04	19.03	42.89
Russian	4,060	2,945	1,815	−27.46	−38.37	−55.30
Ukrainian	20,325	14,640	12,225	−27.97	−16.50	−39.85
Croatian	1,100	1,550	920	40.91	−40.65	−16.36
Yugoslavian	4,950	4,365	3,735	−11.82	−14.43	−24.55
Greek	42,870	49,420	47,450	15.28	−3.99	10.68
Italian	169,655	163,735	163,880	−3.49	0.09	−3.40
Portuguese	16,555	27,370	29,700	65.33	8.51	79.40
Spanish	10,825	15,460	16,605	42.82	7.41	53.39
Jewish	115,990	90,360	81,190	−22.10	−10.15	−30.00
Chinese	11,905	19,260	23,205	61.78	20.48	94.92
Japanese	1,745	1,395	1,285	−20.06	−7.89	−26.36
Czechoslovakian	6,725	4,845	4,085	−27.96	−15.69	−39.26
Slovenian	425	260	245	−38.82	−5.77	−42.35
Scandinavian	8,820	4,225	2,540	−52.10	−39.88	−71.20
Total	5,931,285	6,077,315	5,797,990	2.46	−4.60	−2.25

by and large like the whole country in Table 4, but it is useful to note some differences in detail. The French are single endogamous losers like "everybody else," though they were just about holding their own at the whole country level in Table 4. Croatians gain about the same as in Canada, as do Greeks, Portuguese, Spanish, Chinese and Japanese.

Manitoba in Table 7 and Alberta in Table 8 have features of their own. In Manitoba with the single exception of the Germans every ethnicity loses more (or gains less) than it did in Canada as a whole. In the nomenclature previously

TABLE 6

Selected Ethnic Origins According to Single Origins Intercensal Changes 1971-81, 1981-86, 1971-86 Ontario

Origin	1971	1981	1986	Percentage Change 81-71	86-81	86-71
British	4,576,010	4,487,800	2,912,830	− 1.93	− 35.09	− 36.35
French	737,360	652,905	531,580	− 11.45	− 18.58	− 27.91
Austrian	15,765	15,145	10,475	− 3.93	− 30.84	− 33.56
Belgian	19,955	17,910	12,180	− 10.25	− 31.99	− 38.96
Dutch	206,940	191,125	171,150	− 7.64	− 10.45	− 17.29
German	475,320	373,390	285,155	− 21.44	− 23.63	− 40.01
Finnish	38,515	33,400	26,530	− 13.28	− 20.57	− 31.12
Estonian	13,730	11,800	10,045	− 14.06	− 14.87	− 26.84
Latvian	13,045	11,735	9,550	− 10.04	− 18.62	− 26.79
Lithuanian	15,365	12,070	10,265	− 21.44	− 14.95	− 33.19
Hungarian	65,695	59,140	51,255	− 9.98	− 13.33	− 21.98
Polish	144,415	122,945	117,575	− 14.87	− 4.37	− 18.59
Romanian	9,255	8,170	7,385	− 11.72	− 9.61	− 20.21
Russian	12,580	8,715	5,780	− 30.72	− 33.68	− 54.05
Ukrainian	159,880	133,995	109,705	− 16.19	− 18.13	− 31.38
Croatian	16,860	24,640	26,760	46.14	8.60	58.72
Yugoslavian	42,085	41,435	32,215	− 1.54	− 22.25	− 23.45
Greek	67,025	85,955	80,320	28.24	− 6.56	19.84
Italian	463,095	487,310	461,375	5.23	− 5.32	− 0.37
Portuguese	63,145	129,000	139,220	104.29	7.92	120.48
Spanish	10,330	25,185	28,000	143.80	11.18	171.06
Jewish	135,195	131,320	127,030	− 2.87	− 3.27	− 6.04
Chinese	39,325	118,640	156,170	201.69	31.63	297.13
Japanese	15,600	16,685	16,150	6.96	− 3.21	3.53
Czechoslovakian	40,770	33,025	28,910	19.00	− 12.46	− 29.09
Slovenian	5,635	5,040	4,720	10.56	− 6.35	− 16.24
Scandinavian	60,225	40,335	26,755	33.03	− 33.67	− 55.57
Total	7,402,895	7,238,480	5,372,330	− 2.23	− 25.79	− 27.43

defined these are the actual or potential exogamous gainers. In Alberta out of the 27 ethnic groups available, as many as 16 have losses smaller (or gains greater) than at the national level. Apparently Manitobans intermarry with greater enthusiasm than Albertans. Or is it that all the ethnic groups in Alberta had greater in-migration and immigration? Multiethnicities, like other measures in social sciences require the "holding constant" or standardization of such variables so as to increase comparability (to compare like with like).

TABLE 7

Selected Ethnic Origins According to Single Origins Intercensal Changes 1971-81, 1981-86, 1971-86 Manitoba

Origin	1971	1981	1986	Percentage Change 81-71	86-81	86-71
British	414,125	373,995	224,375	− 9.69	− 40.01	− 45.82
French	86,510	74,045	55,720	− 14.41	− 24.75	− 35.59
Austrian	3,200	3,155	1,665	− 1.41	− 47.23	− 47.97
Belgian	9,055	6,455	4,255	− 28.71	− 34.08	− 53.01
Dutch	35,300	33,875	27,875	− 4.04	− 17.71	− 21.03
German	123,065	108,140	96,160	− 12.13	− 11.08	− 21.86
Finnish	1,450	1,060	720	− 26.90	− 32.08	− 50.34
Estonian	185	180	55	− 2.70	− 69.44	− 70.27
Latvian	840	580	400	− 30.95	− 31.03	− 52.38
Lithuanian	820	515	340	− 37.20	− 33.98	− 58.54
Hungarian	5,405	4,160	3,230	− 23.03	− 22.36	− 40.24
Polish	42,705	28,445	22,015	− 33.39	− 22.61	− 48.45
Romanian	1,375	900	640	− 34.55	− 28.89	− 53.45
Russian	4,040	3,765	1,755	− 6.81	− 53.39	− 56.56
Ukrainian	114,410	99,795	79,940	− 12.77	− 19.90	− 30.13
Croatian	610	685	665	12.30	− 2.92	9.02
Yugoslavian	1,990	2,060	1,195	3.52	− 41.99	− 39.95
Greek	2,095	2,385	2,025	13.84	− 15.09	− 3.34
Italian	10,445	9,600	8,230	− 8.09	− 14.27	− 21.21
Portuguese	3,815	7,930	7,335	105.24	− 6.32	92.27
Spanish	640	1,470	1,180	129.69	− 19.73	84.38
Jewish	20,010	14,950	13,870	− 25.29	− 7.22	− 30.68
Chinese	3,430	7,065	8,730	105.98	23.57	154.52
Japanese	1,335	1,300	1,055	− 2.62	− 18.85	− 20.97
Czechoslovakian	4,760	3,590	2,770	− 24.58	− 22.84	− 41.81
Slovenian	360	305	120	− 15.28	− 60.66	− 66.67
Scandinavian	35,105	25,175	14,835	− 28.29	− 41.07	− 57.74
Total	891,975	790,305	566,320	− 11.40	− 28.34	− 36.51

The Particular Case of Quebec

In the previous section we have already indicated that Quebec uses multiethnicities less sensationally than other parts of Canada. In this section we attempt to see to what extent multiethnicities in Quebec can be employed usefully.

In Table 5 for Quebec, the French are neutral, as they were at the national level in Table 4: they do not intermarry to become exogamous gainers, and they do not gain by immigration to become endogamous losers. The gains in singles

TABLE 8

Selected Ethnic Origins According to Single Origins Intercensal Changes 1971-81, 1981-86, 1971-86 Alberta

Origin	1971	1981	1986	Percentage Change		
				81-71	86-81	86-71
British	761,665	962,785	592,345	26.41	− 38.48	− 22.23
French	94,665	111,865	77,585	18.17	− 30.64	− 18.04
Austrian	6,310	6,405	3,170	1.51	− 50.51	− 49.76
Belgian	4,265	4,125	1,755	− 3.28	− 57.45	− 58.85
Dutch	58,565	64,090	55,920	11.14	− 14.09	− 4.52
German	231,005	233,180	182,870	0.94	− 21.58	− 20.84
Finnish	3,590	4,130	2,625	15.04	− 36.44	− 26.88
Estonian	845	790	580	− 6.51	− 26.58	− 31.36
Latvian	1,010	980	545	− 2.97	− 44.39	− 46.04
Lithuanian	1,845	1,255	840	− 31.98	− 33.07	− 54.47
Hungarian	16,240	15,170	12,780	− 6.59	− 15.75	− 21.31
Polish	44,325	37,660	28,500	− 15.04	− 24.32	− 35.70
Romanian	4,670	3,800	2,790	− 18.63	− 26.58	− 40.26
Russian	10,235	7,715	4,185	− 24.62	− 45.76	− 59.11
Ukrainian	135,510	136,710	106,760	0.89	− 21.91	− 21.22
Croatian	1,130	2,375	1,990	110.18	− 16.21	76.11
Yugoslavian	5,720	5,995	4,525	4.81	− 24.52	− 20.89
Greek	3,250	4,815	4,030	48.15	− 16.30	24.00
Italian	24,805	26,610	23,635	7.28	− 11.18	− 4.72
Portuguese	2,385	6,125	6,280	156.81	2.53	163.31
Spanish	1,305	4,945	5,280	278.93	6.77	304.60
Jewish	7,320	9,460	7,945	29.23	− 16.01	8.54
Chinese	12,905	36,770	49,210	184.93	33.83	281.33
Japanese	4,460	5,230	5,295	17.26	1.24	18.72
Czechoslovakian	12,970	11,195	8,235	− 13.69	− 26.44	− 36.51
Slovenian	290	285	410	− 1.72	43.86	41.38
Scandinavian	98,425	78,565	46,525	− 20.18	− 40.78	− 52.73
Total	1,451,285	1,705,465	1,190,085	11.75	− 30.22	− 18.00

of the nationally prominent groups are much more modest in Quebec (the Portuguese, etc.). Not much is happening in Quebec in terms of interethnic exchanges. On the face of things, it looks as if Quebec has managed to preserve its 19th century ethnic balance.

There are, however, important, qualitative changes taking place within the society. Some of the immigrants are from the Third World and as such are more visible. Internal migration contributes to linguistic polarization. On balance, internal migration benefits Francophones (Lachapelle 1986, 121), but insufficiently to make up the losses through linguistic transfers. Well documented language transfers take place between censuses. These are of no concern to this paper, but being more difficult to analyse in themselves than ethnic transfers, they make ethnic transfers, which are of interest in this paper, more plausible as an explanatory factor (Lachapelle 1988a).

Due to past high fertility, Quebecers still have an age distribution favourable to fertility, hence for a while their disappearance from this continent will be slowed down (Lachapelle 1987, 5; Lachapelle and Henripin, 1980, 1982; Thermote and Gauvreau 1988). Furthermore, what the Quebecers lose linguistically *vis-à-vis* the English, they make up with gains from third languages (Lachapelle 1987, 6), but the fertility losses are not made up (Lachapelle, 1988b).

It is apparent from the chapter by Choinière and Robitaille in this volume that our Quebec colleagues are conscious of the considerable influence of inter-ethnic switches, more elegantly called by these authors "ethnic mobility." This feature of the French ethnic group has been reported in the past (e.g., Henripin, 1974; see also the numerous writings of Charles Castonguay on this topic, e.g., 1985).

Should such ethnic mobility be taking place with any magnitude, it will affect the reported singles as losses in one case and gains in the other, without bringing in the multiples. This is quite apart from the fact that persons reporting a given ethnicity do not necessarily identify with that ethnicity.[5] The low proportion of the French multiples would suggest that "they" (the erstwhile French singles), do not become French multiples, but singles of another ethnic group, presumably English.[6] Such transfers, from ethnicity to ethnicity, on common sense grounds must be "easier" for the individual concerned than transfers from one mother tongue to another; yet the latter have been reported upon the basis of detailed analysis (e.g., Lachapelle 1988, Table 7; Henripin 1985).

Some ambitious Measurement in the Future

An alternative title to this section could be "A solution to the fact that a single is not equal to a multiple." Here we stop over the fact that Statistics Canada added up as "one" each reported multiethnicity, irrespective of the number reported by a respondent. We would like to propose that the weight of "one" is heavy and illogical, though the obvious and immediate way out in this new situation. It would be more appropriate to give weights of 0.5 to each ethnicity when two are reported, 0.333 to each of three, 0.25 to each of four, and so on. More generally, and algebraically, the proposed weighting is as follows:

$$w_{ei} = 1/k \qquad (1)$$

where w_{ei} is the weight given to an individual respondent i for each of the multiethnicities e reported by him/her; and

k is the number of multiethnicities reported by a given respondent i.

This suggestion is not a complete solution to the problem of weights, because 0.333 is illogical in itself for three reported ethnicities. It should be some such combination as 0.5, 0.25 and 0.25, if that type of exercise were practical for a census questionnaire. Imposing 0.333 does violence to reality, but even 0.5 with two ethnicities could be untrue. Peter Lougheed, the ex-premier of Alberta liked to boast that he is part-Métis, the indiscretion having been committed presumably in the distant past, say, four generations ago, not among his immediate parents. Then, if he reported two ethnicities, the true weight would be 1/16 and 15/16. Still, the suggested weights of 0.5 and 0.5 are a truer reflection of reality than "one" and "one."[7]

We know that 6,986,345 respondents gave multiple ethnicities for a grand total of 17,920,235 multiethnicities. To arrive at the latter total, we have added up all the 59 ethnic groups appearing in Tables 1 through 3. The results have been compared with the total singles in each area:

$$M_s = \frac{\Sigma\, M_{a_e}}{\Sigma\, S_{a_e}} \times 100 \tag{2}$$

where M_s is the ratio of all multiples reported in the given area a by all respondents to the total of singles reported by all respondents in the same area;

M_{a_e} are multiples reported in the given area for ethnicity e, each multiple counted as "one"; and

S_{a_e} are singles reported in the given area for ethnicity e.

For Canada, the provinces and territories the ratios of multiples to singles are shown in the second column of Table 9. These averages are interesting in themselves and can be treated as an "longevity index of intermarriage." The reason why we use the word "longevity" in the description of the index, is that the greater the reported admixture, the longer into the past must it have been taking place.

Another attempt to come to grips with these new data is made in the third column of Table 9. For Canada, each province and each territory a ratio has been calculated:

$$M_a \text{ per } R = M_a/(P_a - S_a) \tag{3}$$

where M_a stands for multiples in the given area a;

R_a stands for respondent;

P_a stands for population size of the given area a; and

S_a stands for singles in the given area a.

Thus, $(P_a - S_a)$ equals the number of respondents in the given province/territory reporting multiples and the ratio gives the number of multiples reported by an average respondent reporting multiples. It is not possible to calculate these ratios for ethnic groups at the present stage of our understanding of these data because we do not have P_{ae}, population size for ethnic origin e in area a.

The small differences among provinces and territories will probably surprise colleagues working in the area. Quebec has, as it should, a low average (2.330), but it is second lowest to Newfoundland, (2.316) understandable with its ethnic monolithicity. Do we stop to notice the difference between Nova Scotia and New Brunswick? Their ethnic groups were there for about the same stretch of time, their absolute population sizes are about the same, their Englishness is about the same. Could the Acadians be responsible for the slightly lower figure in the case of New Brunswick? From Ontario westward everything is over, and well over, two and a half. Intermarriage has only begun (for individual problems along the way see Harding and Riley 1986).

TABLE 9

Average Multiple Ethnicities Canada, Provinces and Territories, 1986

	Multiple Ethnicities	
	As percentage of single ethnicities[1]	Reported by an average respondent
Canada	99.4	2.565
Newfoundland	46.2	2.316
Prince Edward Island	169.2	2.469
Nova Scotia	155.4	2.537
New Brunswick	97.8	2.497
Quebec	17.2	2.330
Ontario	131.1	2.559
Manitoba	139.9	2.594
Saskatchewan	170.0	2.623
Alberta	180.1	2.633
British Columbia	163.1	2.634
Yukon	220.0	2.694
Northwest Territories	78.1	2.593

[1] Total reported multiples as a percentage of total reported singles.

Data Requirements for Ideal Measurements of Multiethnicity

For purposes of measuring the immediate cause of multiethnicity, which is intermarriage, one would like to hold constant all intervening variables. Demographically, we would like all ethnic groups to have the same fertility

434

and the same mortality, and consequently the same age distribution. Ecologically, we would like them to be dispersed with the same density, though if they were not the same population size with some trade-offs could be negotiated with regard to size to make up for differences in density and distribution. Economically, we would like them to be of similar economic status, similar education, and similar cultural endowments. Finally, we would like each ethnic group to receive similar proportionate injections of immigrants possibly with similar immigration points acquired.

With ethnic groups that are similar, any differences in multiethnicity and in losses of singles would then be a purely ethnic phenomenon. Frankly, one would not expect many differences among ethnic groups in such circumstances, though there still could be the influence of origin, colour, race, religion and language, all variables identified customarily with ethnicity.

The above is a tall order: the recency and size of immigration streams and influence can probably be assessed by academicians. The more ambitious qualifications can probably be assessed only by those with unlimited resources.

Multiculturalism and the Emerging Multiethnicity

Multiculturalism and exogamy do not go together. There are some brides who learn the language of the bridegroom and of his family, and *vice versa*, but numerically these are small. By and large exogamy implies eventual disappearance of a given ethnic origin, sometimes both origins and molding into a third category (the melting pot). Complete exogamy means complete disappearance of multiculturalism, including most types of pluralism.

In this perspective, multiculturalism is a temporary and passing phenomenon. Multiethnicities thanks to the change in the Canadian definition provide means of measuring its demise. By the time respondents report, say, eight ethnic origins and the value of each will be computed as .125, multiculturalism will have little significance.

Notes

1. With a strict application of the Canadian definition there was no space for Métis. If fathered by a German or Frenchman with an Amerindian mother, the Métis offspring ought to be classified as German or French. If fathered by an Amerindian male with a European mother, the offspring ought to have been recorded as Amerindian. It required illogical departures from the Canadian definition to make space on the questionnaire for Métis, as was the case in 1941. At the time they were still called half-bloods, in itself probably an indication of the persistence of colour consciousness among the Anglo-Saxons, and possibly a reason why there are few reported Métis among the French.
2. Norman Ryder counts interest in the Canadian definition of ethnicity among his minor pursuits (Ryder 1988). For 36 years Ryder thought the definition should be changed. He was speechless for quite a while when he learned of the 1986 introduction of multiethnicity.
3. Statisticians were not prepared for this development. Lachapelle (1988a) reports that for the purposes of tabulations multiple answers were distributed proportionately over single answers, a procedure adequate as an immediate measure with the small numbers of 1981, but obviously begging for a more thorough solution in the long run. The multiple answers were preserved on the family/household file of the public use sample tape (PUST) and are available for analysis (see Kalbach and Richard 1985).
4. Not only do census-takers not engage in social engineering, but they have to foresee data requirements arising out of new legislation and the introduction of new public policies. There is a federal act on fairness in employment, specifically aiming at the protection of four groups: the disabled, women, visible minorities and aboriginal peoples. Discrimination and fairness can be ascertained objectively only when data are collected for the denominator. And if the new need collides with another cherished requirement, that of confidentiality protection, who wins?
5. This point is often stressed by Warren E. Kalbach (e.g., 1975, Kalbach and Richard 1985).
6. Obviously, shifters diminish their original singles and increase the receiving singles; consequently, the shifters lower the losing ethnicity and the proportions of multiples required to qualify for the status of exogamous gainers (just like the French) and increases it for the gaining ethnicity to qualify for the status of endogamous losers (just like the English).
7. In the eyes of the authors of the proposed arrangement, a Métis out of a union of Amerindian and, say, English should have weights 0.5 and 0.5. The offspring then marrying again with an English person should have weights of 0.25 for the Indian part and 0.75 for the English parts. This is not suggested as a serious census exercise, but it is to point out the logical difficulty with the ethnic origin of multiples called "Métis" given in our source, a situation that could have arisen only due to the inherent racism in an Anglo society, where a person once touched with métism, remains Métis forever. In other societies, less fragile, a Métis would soon pass out of the Indian connection and into the general society.

Appendix

Hypotheses for Emergence of Multiethnicities

The purely arithmetical exercises in this paper provide considerable insights into the differential behaviour of ethnic groups under the impact of the new census definition inviting respondents to record their ethnicity in terms of multiples. These exercises also suggest the working of various influences that could usefully be isolated. The following hypotheses are offered for consideration:

(i)   The larger the ethnic group the less intermarriage experience, if only for arithmetical or geometric reasons.

(ii)   The longer the ethnic group had been in Canada, on average, the more intermarriage experience.

(iii) The less dispersion or the more concentration, the less intermarriage experience.

(iv)   In-groups because of their supreme confidence have less intermarriage than out-groups with their anxiety to conform (or is it "more" because the in-groups are more desirable and out-groups are good at seducing?)

(v)   Current age distribution (average age, proportion of young, etc.) is irrelevant to past experience of intermarriage and the interethnic differences are too small to affect our measurements, currently crude.

(vi)   Most of these are left with 40 or 50 (or even 70?) percent of unexplained variability. In fact, practising sociologists begin to talk in terms of multicollinearity, when the proportion explained becomes too high.

APPENDICES

Appendix A

Instructions and Questions for the Ethnic Origin Data, 1871-1986

Ethnic or Racial Origin as Defined in Enumerator's Manuals Between 1871 and 1971

1871   COLUMN 13. Origin is to be scrupulously entered, as given by the person questioned; in the manner shown in the specimen schedule, by the words English, Irish, Scotch, African, Indian, German, French and so forth.

1881   COLUMN 13. Origin is to be scrupulously entered, as given by the person questioned; in the manner shown in the specimen schedule by the words English, Irish, Scotch, African, Indian, German, French and so forth.

1891   Racial origin not asked.

1901   53.   Among whites the racial or tribal origin is traced through the father, as in English, Scotch, Irish, Welsh, French, German, Italian, Scandinavian, etc. Care must be taken, however, not to apply the terms "American" or "Canadian" in a racial sense, as there are no races of men so called. "Japanese," "Chinese" and "Negro" are proper racial terms; but in the case of Indians the names of their tribes should be given, as "Chippewa," "Cree," etc. Persons of mixed white and red blood — commonly known as "breeds" —will be described by addition of the initial letters "f.b." for French breed, "e.b." for English breed, "s.b." for Scotch breed and "i.b." for Irish breed. For example: "Cree f.b." denotes that the person is racially a mixture of Cree and French; and "Chippewa s.b." denotes that the person is Chippewa and Scotch. Other mixtures of Indians besides the four above specified are rare, and may be described by the letters "o.b." for other breed. If several races are combined with the red, such as English and Scotch, Irish and French, or any others, they should also be described by the initials "o.b." A person whose father is English, but whose mother is Scotch, Irish, French or any other race, will be ranked as English, and so will any others — the line of descent being traced through the father in the white races.

1911   100.   RACIAL OR TRIBAL ORIGIN. The racial or tribal origin, column 14, is usually traced through the father, as in English, Scotch, Irish, Welsh, French, German, Italian, Danish, Swedish, Norwegian,

Bohemian, Ruthenian, Bukovinian, Galician, Bulgarian, Chinese, Japanese, Polish, Jewish, etc. A person whose father is English but whose mother is Scotch, Irish, French or other race will be ranked as English, and so with any of the others. In the case of Indians the origin is traced through the mother, and names of their tribes should be given, as "Chippewa," "Cree," etc. The children begotten of marriages between white and black or yellow races will be classed as Negro or Mongolian (Chinese or Japanese), as the case may be.

1921   94.   COLUMN 21. RACIAL OR TRIBAL ORIGIN.The racial or tribal origin is usually traced through the father, as in English, Scotch, Iris, Welsh, French, German, Italian, Danish, Swedish, Norwegian, Bohemian, Ruthenian, Bukovinian, Galician, Bulgarian, Chinese, Japanese, Polish, Jewish, etc. A person whose father is English but whose mother is Scotch, Irish, French or other race will be ranked as English, and so with any of the others. In the case of Indians the origin is traced through the mother, and names of their tribes should be given, as "Chippewa," "Cree," etc. The children begotten of marriages between white and black or yellow races will be classed as Negro or Mongolian (Chinese or Japanese), as the case may be. The words *"Canadian" or "American" must not be used for this purpose, as they express "Nationality" or "Citizenship" but not a "Race or people."*

1931   122.   COLUMN 21: RACIAL ORIGIN.The purpose of the information sought in this column is to measure as accurately as possible the racial origins of the population of Canada, i.e., the original sources from which the present population has been derived.

In the case of distinct stocks, involving differences in colour (i.e., the black, red, yellow or brown races) the answer will be Negro, Indian, Japanese, Chinese, Hindu, Malayan, etc., as the case may be.

In the case of persons deriving from European stocks, the proper answer will in many cases be indicated by the country or portion of the country from which the family of the person originally came, for example, English, Scotch, Irish, Welsh, French, but certain stocks may be found in more than one European country. In such cases the country of birth or the country from which they came to Canada may not indicate their racial origin. For example the Ukrainians (Ruthenians) may have immigrated to Canada from Poland, Russia, Austria, Hungary but they should not be classed as Poles, Russians, Austrians, Hungarians, but as Ukrainians. Similarly many immigrants from Russia are of German origin. The enumerator should make specific inquiry and should not assume that the country of birth discloses origin. A German born in France is not French by origin although he may be a citizen of France.

1931   123.   ORIGIN IS TO BE TRACED THROUGH THE FATHER. A person whose father is English and whose mother is French will be recorded as of English origin, while a person whose father is French and whose mother is English will be recorded as of French origin, and similarly with other combinations. In the case of the aboriginal Indian population of Canada, the origin is to be traced through the mother, and the names of their tribes should be given as Chippewa, Cree, Blackfoot, etc. The children begotten of marriages between white and black or yellow races will be recorded as Negro, Chinese, Japanese, Indian, etc., as the case may be. The object of this question is to obtain a knowledge of the various constituent elements that have combined from the earliest times to make up the present population of Canada.

1941   100.   COLUMN 25 RACIAL ORIGIN.
1.   *What is racial origin?* The word "race" signifies — "descendants of a common ancestor."
a.   It is imperative to understand that a person's racial origin, and nationality very often are different, for instance the Canadian nationality comprises many different racial origins, e.g., English, French, Irish, Scottish, Welsh, Italian, German, etc.
b.   The name of a country from which a person came to Canada gives no indication of that person's racial origin. e.g., a person may have come to Canada from Austria, but may be Polish, or German, or Italian, etc. A striking example are the Ukrainians (Ruthenians). They have no Ukrainian (Ruthenian) nationality, but have come to this country from the nations of Poland, Russia, Austria, Hungary, and other nations of Europe through which they are dispersed. No matter what country they come from, their racial origin is "Ukrainian".
c.   The word CANADIAN does not denote a racial origin, but a nationality; the same applies to the word AMERICAN.
d.   It is therefore necessary for the Enumerator to ascertain a person's racial origin separately from his country of birth, or nationality.
2.   WHAT DETERMINES RACIAL ORIGIN? As a general rule a person's racial origin is to be traced through his father, e.g., if a person's father is English and his mother French the racial origin shall be entered as English, while a person whose father is French and whose mother is English shall be entered as French, and similarly for other combinations.

a.   CANADIAN ABORIGINES. For the Canadian aborigines, the entry will be Indian or Eskimo as the case may be. For a person of White and Indian blood, the entry shall be "Half-Breed".

b.   COLOURED STOCKS. For persons belonging to stock involving difference in colour (i.e., the black, yellow, and brown races) the entry shall be Negro, Japanese, Chinese, Hindu, Malayan, etc., respectively, thus indicating the branch within the distinct ethnic stock, to which such persons belong.

c.   MIXED BLOOD. The children begotten of marriages between white and black or white and Chinese, etc., shall be entered in the Column as Negro, Chinese, etc., as the case may be.

1951   17. ORIGIN

It is important to distinguish carefully between "citizenship" or "nationality" on the one hand, and "origin" on the other. Origin refers to the cultural group, sometimes erroneously called "racial" group, from which the person is descended; citizenship (nationality) refers to the country to which the person owes allegiance. Canadian citizens are of many origins — English, Irish, Scottish, Jewish, Ukrainian, etc.

For Census purposes a person's origin is traced through his father. For example, if a person's father is German and his mother Norwegian, the origin will be entered as "German."

You will first attempt to establish a person's origin by asking the language spoken by the person (if he is an immigrant), or by his paternal ancestor *when he first came to this continent*. For example, if the person replies that his paternal ancestor spoke French when he came to this continent, you will record the origin as "French". However, if the respondent should reply "English" or "Gaelic" to this question, you must make further inquiries to determine whether the origin is English, Irish, Scottish, or Welsh.

If the respondent does not understand your first question, or you cannot establish the person's origin from the answer you receive, you will ask "Is your origin in the male line English, Scottish, Ukrainian, Jewish, Norwegian, North American Indian, Negro, etc.?"

Ordinarily, persons born and bred in Canada or the United States will report some European origin, such as English, French, or Spanish. However, if a person *insists* that his origin is Canadian or American, you are to accept that answer and write it in the space provided.

Do not confuse Question 12 (Language first spoken in childhood) with this question. Above all, do not assume that the answer given to Question 12 establishes the answer to the question on origin.

For persons of mixed white and Indian parentage, the origin recorded will be as follows:

a. For those living on Indian reserves, the origin will be recorded as "Native Indian."

b. For those not on reserves the origin will be determined through the line of the father, that is, by following the usual procedure.

If a person states that, because of mixed ancestry, he really does not know what to reply to the question on origin, you will mark the oval "Unknown."

1961   66.   QUESTION 10 — ETHNIC OR CULTURAL GROUP

          10.   To what ethnic or cultural group did you or your ancestor (on the male side) belong on coming to this continent?

Australian	Belgian	Czech	Danish	English	Estonian	Finnish	Native Indian
French	German	Greek	Hungarian	Icelandic	Irish	Italian	Band Member
Jewish	Lithuanian	Negro	Netherlands	Norwegian	Polish	Roumanian	Non-Band
Russian	Scottish	Slovak	Swedish	Ukrainian	Welsh	Yugoslavic	

If not listed, write here:
Mark ONE SPACE only.

It is important to distinguish carefully between "citizenship" or "nationality" on the one hand and "ethnic" or "cultural" group on the other. "Ethnic" or "cultural" group refers to the group from which the person is descended; citizenship (nationality) refers to the country to which the person owes allegiance. Canadian citizens belong to many ethnic or cultural groups — English, French, Irish, Jewish, Scottish, Ukrainian, etc.

For Census purposes a person's ethnic or cultural group is traced through his father. For example, if a person's father is German and his mother Norwegian, the entry will be "German."

If the respondent does not understand the question as worded on the questionnaire, you will ask the language spoken by him on arrival if he is an immigrant, or by his ancestor on the male side on first coming to this continent. For example, if the person replies that his ancestor on the male side spoke French when he came to this continent, you will record "French."

However, if the respondent should reply "English" or "Gaelic" to this question, you must make further inquiries to determine whether the person is English, Irish, Scottish or Welsh.

If the respondent does not understand the question as worded on the questionnaire or you cannot establish the ethnic or cultural group through the language of the ancestors, you will ask "Is your ethnic or cultural group on the male side English, French, Jewish, Negro, North American Indian, Norwegian, Scottish, Ukrainian, etc.?"

PROCEDURE FOR PERSONS REPORTING BRITISH ISLES:
If a person reports "British Isles" but does not know if he is English, Irish, Scottish, or Welsh, enter "British Isles" in the write-in space.

PROCEDURE FOR PERSONS REPORTING NATIVE INDIAN:

1. If a person reports "Native Indian" ask an additional question: "Is your name on any Indian Band membership list in Canada?" If the answer is "Yes," mark the space for "Band member." If "No" mark "Non-band."
Note that "Treaty Indians" should be marked "Band member."
2. If the person is of mixed white and Indian parentage:
    a. Consider those living on Indian reserves as "Indian" and determine Band status as outlined above.
    b. For those not on reserves, determine the ethnic or cultural group through the line of the father.

PROCEDURE FOR PERSONS REPORTING "CANADIAN," "U.S.A." or "UNKNOWN":

Since this question refers to the time when the person or his ancestors came to this continent, the answer should refer to the ethnic groups or cultures of the old world. However, if, in spite of this explanation, the person insists that his ethnic or cultural group is "Canadian" or "U.S.A.," enter his reply in the write-in space. If the person states that he really does not know what to reply to this question, enter "Unknown."

1971   QUESTION 15 — ETHNIC OR CULTURAL GROUP
From Questionnaire

15. To what ethnic or cultural group did you or your ancestor (on the male side) belong on coming to this continent?

English	Native Indian	Polish
French	—Band	Scottish
German	Native Indian	Ukrainian
Irish	—Non-band	
Italian	Netherlands	
Jewish	Norwegian	_____

Other, write here

447

From Instruction Booklet

15.   Ethnic or cultural group refers to descent (through the father's side) and should not be confused with citizenship. Canadians belong to many ethnic or cultural groups — English, French, Irish, Scottish, German, Ukrainian, Jewish, Native Indian, Negro, Chinese, Lebanese, etc.

Use as guide if applicable in your case:

1.   The language you spoke on first coming to this continent, if you were born outside Canada.
2.   If born in Canada, the language spoken by your ancestor on the male side when he came here.

From Content Manual

Additional Information
1.   It is important to distinguish carefully between "citizenship" or "nationality" on the one hand, and "ethnic" or "cultural" groups, on the other. "Ethnic" or "cultural" group refers to the group from which the person is descended; citizenship (nationality) refers to the country to which the person owes allegiance.
2.   For census purposes, a person's ethnic or cultural group is traced through his father. For example, if a person's father is German and his mother Norwegian, the entry will be "German."
3.   If the ethnic origin of an adopted child is not known, ethnic origin of the adoptive father may be reported.
4.   Procedure for persons reporting British or British Isles: If a person is of "British Isles" but does not know if he is English, Irish, Scottish, or Welsh, he should enter "British Isles" in the "Other" space.
5.   Procedure for persons reporting "Canadian," "U.S.A." or "Unknown":
     Since this question refers to the time when the person or his ancestors came to this continent, the answer should refer to the ethnic groups or cultures of the Old World except for Native Indians and Eskimos. However, if, in spite of this explanation, the person insists that his ethnic or cultural group is "Canadian" or "U.S.A.," he should mark the circle for "Other" and write "Canadian" or "U.S.A." in the space provided. If the person states that he really does not know what

to reply to this question, he should write in ''Unknown'' in the space provided for ''Other.''

Why We Ask This question

(i) The main purpose of this question is to provide an indication of the cultural or ethnic composition of Canada's people, for example, those of British Isles descent, those of French descent, and those whose forebears came from the many other cultural groups.

(ii) Statistics from this question are used extensively by many groups of people, such as sociologists (for studies of living standards or degrees of cultural intermingling), government officials (for studies related to the Indian or Eskimo population), embassy officials (for information related to ethnic groups associated with their particular country), politicians (for factual data on the ethnic composition of their ridings), advertisers and market researchers (for the promotion of certain types of products), and ethnic societies (for statistical data related to their particular ethnic group).

(iii) Although a number of ethnic or cultural groups can be identified by the question on language, the one-to-one relationship is only partial, since many new immigrants soon acquire English or French as their working language. Furthermore, certain important groups, such as Negroes, Jews, Irish and Scottish cannot be identified on the basis of language, hence the need for data on ethnic or cultural groups.

1981   From the Questionnaire

26. To which ethnic or cultural group did you or your ancestors belong on first coming to this continent?
(See Guide for further information.)

	Native Peoples
25 ☐ French	
26 ☐ English	37 ☐ Inuit
27 ☐ Irish	38 ☐ Status or registered Indian
28 ☐ Scottish	39 ☐ Non-status Indian
29 ☐ German	40 ☐ Métis
30 ☐ Italian	
31 ☐ Ukrainian	
32 ☐ Dutch (Netherlands)	
33 ☐ Polish	
34 ☐ Jewish	
35 ☐ Chinese	
36 ☐☐ Other (specify)	

449

From *The Guide*

Question 26

Ethnic or cultural group refers to the "roots" of the population, and should not be confused with citizenship or nationality. Canadians belong to many ethnic or cultural groups — English, French, Irish, Scottish, Ukrainian, Native Indian, Chinese, Japanese, Dutch,, etc.

If applicable in your case, a guide to your ethnic origin may be the language which you or your ancestors used on first coming to this continent, e.g., Dutch, Japanese. Note, however, that in cases where a language is used by more than one ethnic group, you should report the specific ethnic group, e.g., Austrian rather than German.

For Native Peoples, the phrase "on first coming to this continent" should be ignored.

Métis are descendants of people of mixed Indian and European ancestry who formed a distinct socio-cultural entity in the 19th century. The Métis have gone on to absorb the mixed offspring of Native Indian people and groups from all over the world.

1986   From the Questionnaire

17.   To which ethnic or cultural group(s) do you or did your ancestors belong? (*See Guide*)

Mark or specify as many as applicable

25 ☐ French
26 ☐ English
27 ☐ Irish
28 ☐ Scottish
29 ☐ German
30 ☐ Italian
31 ☐ Ukrainian
32 ☐ Dutch (Netherlands)
33 ☐ Chinese
34 ☐ Jewish
35 ☐ Polish
36 ☐ Black
37 ☐ Inuit
38 ☐ North American Indian
39 ☐ Métis

Other ethnic or cultural group(s). *For example, Portuguese, Greek, Indian (India), Pakistani, Filipino, Japanese, Vietnamese. (specify below)*

40 ☐☐☐
        Other *(specifcy)*

41 ☐☐☐
        Other *(specify)*

42 ☐☐☐
        Other *(specify)*

From *The Guide*

Question 17

Ethnic or cultural group refers to the "roots" or ancestral origin of the population and should not be confused with citizenship or nationality. Canadians belong to many ethnic and cultural groups, such as Inuit, North American Indian, Métis, Irish, Scottish, Ukrainian, Chinese, Japanese, East Indian (from the subcontinent of India), Dutch, English, French, etc.

Note that in cases where you use language as a guide to your ethnic group, you should report the specific ethnic group to which you belong, e.g., Haitian rather than French; Austrian rather than German.

The ethnic origin question will provide information which is used extensively by the many ethnic or cultural associations in Canada to study the size, location, characteristics and other aspects of their respective groups.

Appendix B

Selected Ethnic Origin Data for 1981 and 1986

APPENDIX B: Table 1:

Numeric and Percentage Distribution of British, French, Other, Canada and Provinces, 1981

	Total Population	Total British Origins	Total Responses British Only	Total British Multiple Response	% Total Pop'n with British	Percent of Total British which are		Percent of Total Multiples		
						Single	Multiple	British and French	British, French, Other	British and Other
Canada	24,343,180	11,150,670	9,674,245	1,476,425	45.81%	86.76%	13.24%	29.14%	8.70%	62.15%
Newfoundland	567,685	535,045	519,620	15,425	94.25%	97.12%	2.88%	66.42%	4.99%	28.56%
Prince Edward Island	122,505	101,705	93,345	8,360	83.02%	91.78%	8.22%	63.46%	5.74%	30.80%
Nova Scotia	847,440	672,990	608,685	64,305	79.41%	90.44%	9.56%	43.01%	7.97%	49.03%
New Brunswick	696,405	406,290	369,125	37,165	58.34%	90.85%	9.15%	61.42%	6.42%	32.18%
Quebec	6,438,405	582,080	487,385	94,695	9.04%	83.73%	16.27%	65.76%	9.07%	25.17%
Ontario	8,625,105	5,145,850	4,487,795	658,055	59.66%	87.21%	12.79%	30.61%	8.95%	60.45%
Manitoba	1,026,245	442,615	373,995	68,620	43.13%	84.50%	15.50%	18.07%	8.42%	73.51%
Saskatchewan	968,315	436,220	366,085	70,135	45.05%	83.92%	16.08%	12.97%	7.55%	79.48%
Alberta	2,237,725	1,167,335	962,785	204,550	52.17%	82.48%	17.52%	17.11%	9.10%	73.79%
British Columbia	2,744,470	1,634,955	1,385,165	249,790	59.57%	84.72%	15.28%	17.20%	8.82%	73.98%
Yukon	23,190	12,825	10,060	2,765	55.30%	78.44%	21.56%	19.53%	10.49%	70.16%
North West Territories	45,705	12,760	10,200	2,560	27.92%	79.94%	20.06	22.27%	10.35%	67.38%

	Total Population	Total French Origins	Total Responses French Only	Total French Multiple Responses	% Total Pop'n with French	Percent of Total French which are Single Responses	Percent of Total French which are Multiple Responses	Percent of Total Multiples French and British	Percent of Total Multiples French, British, Other	Percent of Total Multiples French and Other
Canada	24,343,180	7,138,350	6,439,100	699,250	29.32%	90.20%	9.80%	61.53%	18.38%	20.09%
Newfoundland	567,685	26,855	15,355	11,500	4.73%	57.18%	42.82%	89.09%	6.70%	4.22%
Prince Edward Island	122,505	20,785	14,765	6,020	16.97%	71.04%	28.96%	88.12%	7.97%	3.90%
Nova Scotia	847,440	107,835	71,350	36,485	12.72%	66.17%	33.83%	75.80%	14.05%	10.15%
New Brunswick	696,405	278,370	251,075	27,295	39.97%	90.19%	9.81%	83.62%	8.74%	7.64%
Quebec	6,438,405	5,202,095	5,105,670	96,425	80.80%	98.15%	1.85%	64.58%	8.91%	26.51%
Ontario	8,625,105	963,010	652,905	310,105	11.17%	67.80%	32.20%	64.95%	18.98%	16.07%
Manitoba	1,026,245	102,245	74,045	28,200	9.96%	72.42%	27.58%	43.97%	20.48%	35.55%
Saskatchewan	968,315	70,515	46,920	23,595	7.28%	66.54%	33.46%	38.55%	22.44%	39.03%
Alberta	2,237,725	186,815	111,865	74,950	8.35%	59.88%	40.12%	46.69%	24.83%	28.47%
British Columbia	2,744,470	174,715	92,310	82,405	6.37%	52.83%	47.17%	52.13%	26.75%	21.13%
Yukon	23,190	2,155	1,080	1,075	9.29%	50.12%	49.88%	50.23%	26.98%	22.33%
North West Territories	45,705	2,960	1,760	1,200	6.48%	59.46%	40.54%	47.50%	22.08%	30.00%

	Total Population	Total Other Origins	Total Responses Other Only	Total Other Multiple Responses	% Total Pop'n with Other	Percent of Total Other which are Single Responses	Percent of Total Other which are Multiple Responses	Percent of Total Multiples Other, British, French	Percent of Total Multiples Other and British	Percent of Total Multiples Other and French
Canada	24,343,180	7,799,575	6,612,920	1,186,655	32.04%	84.79%	15.21%	10.83%	77.33%	11.84%
Newfoundland	567,685	22,465	16,805	5,660	3.96%	74.81%	25.19%	13.60%	77.83%	8.57%
Prince Edward Island	122,505	9,090	5,800	3,290	7.42%	63.81%	36.19%	14.59%	78.27%	7.14%
Nova Scotia	847,440	139,750	99,390	40,360	16.49%	71.12%	28.88%	12.70%	78.12%	9.18%
New Brunswick	696,405	53,380	36,950	16,430	7.67%	69.22%	30.78%	14.52%	72.79%	12.69%
Quebec	6,438,405	783,080	725,090	57,990	12.16%	92.59%	7.41%	14.81%	41.10%	44.09%
Ontario	8,625,105	3,282,995	2,776,530	506,465	38.06%	84.57%	15.43%	11.62%	78.54%	9.84%
Manitoba	1,026,245	565,805	499,560	66,245	55.13%	88.29%	11.71%	8.72%	76.15%	15.13%
Saskatchewan	968,315	546,215	475,965	70,250	56.41%	87.14%	12.86%	7.54%	79.35%	13.11%
Alberta	2,237,725	1,128,080	937,190	190,890	50.41%	83.08%	16.92%	9.75%	79.07%	11.18%
British Columbia	2,744,470	1,224,035	999,790	224,245	44.60%	81.68%	18.32%	9.83%	82.41%	7.76%
Yukon	23,190	11,510	9,040	2,470	49.63%	78.54%	21.46%	11.74%	78.54%	9.72%
North West Territories	45,705	33,175	30,825	2,350	72.59%	92.92%	7.08%	11.28%	73.40%	15.32%

APPENDIX B: Table 2:

Numeric and Percentage Distribution of British, French, Other, Canada and Provinces, 1986

	Total Population	Total British Reported	Total Responses British Only	Total British Multiple Responses	% Total Pop'n with British	Percent of Total British which are		Percent of Total Multiples		
						Single Responses	Multiple Responses	British and French	British and Other	British, French, Other
Canada	25,022,005	12,371,485	8,406,555	3,964,930	49.44%	67.95%	32.05%	28.74%	57.06%	14.20%
Newfoundland	564,005	542,110	501,770	40,340	96.12%	92.56%	7.44%	60.20%	31.33%	8.47%
Prince Edward Island	125,090	109,560	86,410	23,150	87.58%	78.87%	21.13%	65.55%	25.85%	8.60%
Nova Scotia	864,150	729,035	542,190	186,845	84.36%	74.37%	25.63%	43.14%	43.59%	13.27%
New Brunswick	701,855	442,295	329,305	112,990	63.02%	74.45%	25.55%	61.83%	27.04%	11.13%
Quebec	6,454,490	649,335	380,265	269,070	10.06%	58.56%	41.44%	64.76%	20.53%	14.71%
Ontario	9,001,170	5,644,440	3,944,950	1,699,490	62.71%	69.89%	30.11%	30.16%	55.46%	14.38%
Manitoba	1,049,320	508,660	310,935	197,725	48.48%	61.13%	38.87%	17.95%	66.57%	15.48%
Saskatchewan	996,695	524,030	297,555	226,475	52.58%	56.78%	43.22%	12.26%	73.88%	13.86%
Alberta	2,340,265	1,372,490	805,475	567,015	58.65%	58.69%	41.31%	15.93%	69.45%	14.63%
British Columbia	2,849,585	1,818,265	1,190,315	627,950	63.81%	65.46%	34.54%	16.94%	68.89%	14.17%
Yukon	23,360	14,505	7,780	6,725	62.09%	53.64%	46.36%	17.47%	66.84%	15.69%
North West Territories	52,020	16,730	9,580	7,150	32.16%	57.26%	42.74%	20.70%	60.49%	18.81%

	Total Population	Total French Reported	Total Responses French Only	Total French Multiple Responses	% Total Pop'n with French	Percent of Total French which are		Percent of Total Multiples		
						Single Responses	Multiple Responses	French and British	French and Other	French, British, Other
Canada	25,022.005	8,127.155	6,099.095	2,028.060	32.48%	75.05%	24.95%	56.18%	16.06%	27.76%
Newfoundland	564.005	39.835	11.320	28.515	7.06%	28.42%	71.58%	85.17%	2.86%	11.98%
Prince Edward Island	125.090	28.730	11.145	17.585	22.97%	38.79%	61.21%	86.30%	2.39%	11.32%
Nova Scotia	864.150	165.845	53.420	112.425	19.19%	32.21%	67.79%	71.70%	6.25%	22.05%
New Brunswick	701.855	319.575	233.855	85.720	45.53%	73.18%	26.82%	81.50%	3.83%	14.68%
Quebec	6,454.490	5,310.095	5,019.055	291.040	82.27%	94.52%	5.48%	59.87%	26.53%	13.60%
Ontario	9,001.170	1,392.150	531.870	860.280	15.47%	38.20%	61.80%	59.58%	12.01%	28.41%
Manitoba	1,049.320	145.780	55.770	90.010	13.89%	38.26%	61.74%	39.43%	26.56%	34.00%
Saskatchewan	996.695	118.425	33.585	84.840	11.88%	28.36%	71.64%	32.72%	30.27%	37.00%
Alberta	2,340.265	296.650	77.690	218.960	12.68%	26.19%	73.81%	41.25%	20.88%	37.88%
British Columbia	2,849.585	301.595	69.095	232.500	10.58%	22.91%	77.09%	45.75%	15.97%	38.28%
Yukon	23.360	3.420	770	2.650	14.64%	22.51%	77.49%	44.34%	15.85%	39.81%
North West Territories	52.020	5.050	1.515	3.535	9.71%	30.00%	70.00%	41.87%	20.08%	38.05%

	Total Population	Total Other Reported	Total Responses Other Only	Total Other Multiple Responses	% Total Pop'n with Other	Percent of Total Other which are		Percent of Total Multiples		
						Single Responses	Multiple Responses	British and Other	French and Other	Other British, French
Canada	25,022.005	9,377.015	6,225.770	3,151.245	37.48%	66.39%	33.61%	71.80%	10.33%	17.87%
Newfoundland	564.005	26.625	9.755	16.870	4.72%	36.64%	63.36%	74.93%	4.83%	20.24%
Prince Edward Island	125.090	12.360	3.965	8.395	9.88%	32.08%	67.92%	71.29%	5.00%	23.70%
Nova Scotia	864.150	187.935	74.670	113.265	21.75%	39.73%	60.27%	71.91%	6.20%	21.89%
New Brunswick	701.855	68.830	22.420	46.410	9.81%	32.57%	67.43%	65.83%	7.07%	27.11%
Quebec	6,454.490	880.910	708.895	172.015	13.65%	80.47%	19.53%	32.11%	44.88%	23.01%
Ontario	9,001.170	4,011.770	2,721.505	1,290.265	44.57%	67.84%	32.16%	73.05%	8.01%	18.94%
Manitoba	1,049.320	647.120	460.980	186.140	61.67%	71.24%	28.76%	70.71%	12.85%	16.44%
Saskatchewan	996.695	637.800	413.400	224.400	63.99%	64.82%	35.18%	74.56%	11.45%	13.99%
Alberta	2,340.265	1,366.775	844.365	522.410	58.40%	61.78%	38.22%	75.37%	8.75%	15.88%
British Columbia	2,849.585	1,483.805	925.085	558.720	52.07%	62.35%	37.65%	77.42%	6.65%	15.93%
Yukon	23.360	13.630	7.660	5.970	58.35%	56.20%	43.80%	75.29%	7.04%	17.67%
North West Territories	52.020	39.450	33.070	6.380	75.84%	83.83%	16.17%	67.79%	11.13%	21.08%

REFERENCES

Abella, Rosalie Silberman
  1984   *Equality in Employment: A Royal Commission Report.* Ottawa: Minister of Supply and Services Canada.

Abu-Zeid, H.A.H., K.K. Maini and N.W. Choi.
  1978   "Ethnic Differences in Mortality from Ischemic Heart Disease: A Study of Migrants and Native Populations." *Journal of Chronic Diseases* 31: 137-146.

Action Committee on Immigrant and Visible Minority Women
  n.d.   "Preliminary Report: Reconvening of Consultation, September 19-22, 1986." Unpublished document.

Ahmand, Jaleel
  1988   *Trade-Related, Sector-Specific Industrial Adjustment Policies in Canada: An Analysis of Textile, Clothing and Footwear Industries.* Discussion Paper No. 345. Ottawa: Economic Council of Canada.

Akyeampong, Ernest B.
  1987   "Older Workers in the Canadian Labour Market." *The Labour Force.* Statistics Canada Catalogue no. 71-001 (November). Ottawa: Supply and Services, December: 85-120.

Alba, Richard D. and Reid M. Golden
  1986   "Patterns of Ethnic Marriage in the United States." *Social Forces* 65: 202-223.

Almquist, Elizabeth M.
  1975   "Untangling the Effects of Race and Sex: The Disadvantaged Status of Black Women." *Social Science Quarterly* 56: 129-142.

Almquist, Elizabeth M.
  1977   "Women in the Labour Force." *Signs* 2: 843-855.

Almquist, Elizabeth M. and Juanita Wherle-Einhorn
  1978   "The Doubly Disadvantaged: Minority Women in the Labor Force." In Ann Strombery and Shirley Harkness (Eds.), *Women Working.* Palo Alto: Mayfield Publishing Co.

459

Anderson, Alan
1972 "Assimilation in the Bloc Settlement of North-Central Saskatchewan: A Comparative Study of Identity Change Among Seven Ethno-Religious Groups in a Canadian Prairie Region." Ph.D. Dissertation, University of Saskatchewan.

Anderson, Alan and James Frideres
1981 *Ethnicity in Canada: Theoretical Perspectives.* Toronto: Butterworths.

Anderson, B.A.
1986 "Regional and Cultural Factors in the Decline of Marital Fertility in Western Europe." In A.J. Coale and S.C. Watkins (Eds.), *The Decline of Fertility in Europe*. Princeton: Princeton University Press.

Antunes G., C. Gordon, C.M. Gaitz and J. Scott
1974 "Ethnicity, Socio-Economic Status, and the Etiology of Psychological Distress." *Sociology and Social Research* 58: 361-368.

Armstrong, P. and H. Armstrong
1984 *The Double Ghetto*. Toronto: McClelland and Stewart.

Arnopoulos, Sheila McLeod
1979 "Problems of Immigrant Women in the Canadian Labour Force." Ottawa: Canadian Advisory Council on the Status of Women.

Axworthy, Lloyd
1981 "Multiculturalism: The Immigrant Woman in Canada: A Right to Recognition." *The Immigrant Women in Canada. Part I*. Report of the Proceedings of the Conference. Ottawa: Minister of Supply and Services Canada.

Bakan, A.B.
1987 "The International Market for Female Labour and Individual Deskilling: West Indian Women Workers in Toronto." *Canadian Journal of Latin American and Caribbean Studies* 24: 69-85.

Balakrishnan, T.R.
1976 "Ethnic Residential Segregation in the Metropolitan Areas of Canada." *Canadian Journal of Sociology* 1: 481-498.

Balakrishnan, T.R.
1982 "Changing Patterns of Ethnic Residential Segregation in the Metropolitan Areas of Canada." *Canadian Review of Sociology and Anthropology* 19: 92-110.

Balakrishnan, T.R., J.F. Kantner and J.D. Allingham
1975 *Fertility and Family Planning in a Canadian Metropolis*. Montreal and London: McGill-Queen's University Press.

Balakrishnan, T.R., G.E. Ebanks and C.F. Grindstaff.
1979   *Patterns of Fertility in Canada, 1971*. Ottawa: Statistics Canada.

Balakrishnan, T.R. and John Kralt
1987   "Segregation of Visible Minorities in Montreal, Toronto and Vancouver." In Leo Driedger (Ed.), *Ethnic Canada*. Toronto: Copp Clark Pitman.

Balakrishnan, T.R. and J. Chen
1988   "Religiosity, Nuptiality and Reproduction in Canada." Presented at the Annual Meetings of the Population Association of America, New Orleans.

Ball, R. and L. Robbins
1986   "Marital Status and Life Satisfaction Among Black Americans." *Journal of Marriage and the Family* 48: 389-394.

Barrera, Manuel, Jr.
1986   "Distinctions Between Social Support Concepts, Measures and Models." *American Journal of Community Psychology* 14: 413-445.

Basavarajappa, K.G. and Ravi B.P. Verma
1983   "The Future Growth and Structure of Canada's Population: Results and Implications of Some Demographic Simulations." In *Demographic Trends and Their Impact on the Canadian Labour Market*. Ottawa: Statistics Canada.

Basavarajappa, K.G. and Shiva S. Halli
1984   "Ethnic Fertility Differences in Canada, 1926-71: An Examination of the Assimilation Hypothesis." *Journal of Biosocial Science* 16: 45-54.

Basavarajappa, K.G. and Ravi B.P. Verma
1985   "Asian Immigrants in Canada: Some Findings from the 1981 Census." *International Migration* 23: 1.

Basavarajappa, K.G. and S.S. Halli
1986   "Fertility Levels of Asian Indians in Canada." In S. Chandrasekhar (Ed.), *From India to Canada*. LaJolla, California: A Population Review Book.

Bean, Frank D. and John P. Marcum
1978   "Differential Fertility and the Minority Group Status Hypothesis: An Assessment and Review." In Frank D. Bean and W. Parker Frisbie (Eds.), *The Demography of Racial and Ethnic Groups*. New York: Academic Press.

Beaujot, Roderic
1979   "A Demographic View on Canadian Language Policy." *Canadian Public Policy* 5: 16-29.

Beaujot, Roderic
   1982   "The Decline of Official Language Minorities in Quebec and English
          Canada." *Canadian Journal of Sociology* 7: 367-389.

Beaujot, Roderic
   1986a "Dwindling Families." *Policy Options* 7: 3-7.

Beaujot, Roderic
   1986b *The Relative Economic Situation of Immigrants in Canada: Reviews
          of Past Studies and Multivariate Analysis on 1981 Data.* London,
          Ontario: University of Western Ontario.

Beaujot, Roderic
   1988   *Income of Immigrants in Canada: A Census Data Analysis.* Ottawa:
          Minister of Supply and Services Canada.

Beaujot, Roderic
   1988   "The Family in Crisis." *Canadian Journal of Sociology.*

Beaujot, Roderic P., Karol J. Krotki and P. Krishnan
   1977   "The Effect of Assimilation on Ethnic Fertility Differentials." Paper
          presented at the annual meeting of the Population Association of
          America, St. Louis, Missouri.

Beaujot, Roderic P., K.J. Krotki and P. Krishnan
   1982   "Analysis of Ethnic Fertility Differentials Through the Consideration
          of Assimilation." *The International Journal of Comparative
          Sociology* 23: 62-70.

Beaujot, Roderic, K.G. Basavarajappa and Ravi B.P. Verma
   1988   *Income of Immigrants in Canada, 1980.* Ottawa: Statistics Canada.

Beaujot, Roderic and J. Peter Rappak
   1988   "The Role of Immigration in Changing Socio-Demographic
          Structures." Report prepared for the Review of Demography and its
          Implications for Economic and Social Policy.

Becker, G.
   1976   *The Economic Approach to Human Behaviour.* Chicago: University
          of Chicago Press.

Bégin, Monique
   1982   *Canadian Government Report on Aging.* Ottawa: Department of
          National Health and Welfare.

Bernardo, Felix M.
   1967   "Kinship Interaction and Communications Among Space-Age
          Migrants." *Journal of Marriage and Family* 29: 541-553.

Berkman, L.F. and Syme, S.L.
   1979   "Social Networks, Host Resistance and Mortality: A Nine-Year
          Follow-up Study of Alameda County Residents." *American Journal
          of Epidemiology* 109: 186-204.

Berneche, Francine
  1983 "Immigration et Espace Urbain. Les Regroupements de Population la Tienne dans la Région Métropolitaine de Montréal." *Cahiers Québécois de Démographie* 12: 295-324.

Berry, J.W., R. Kalin and D.M. Taylor
  1977 *Multiculturalism and Ethnic Attitudes in Canada*. Ottawa: Supply and Services.

Besanceney, Paul H.
  1970 *Interfaith Marriages: Who and Why*. New Haven, Conn.: College and University Press.

Bibby, Reginald
  1979 "Religion in Canada." *Journal for the Scientific Study of Religion* 18: 1-17.

Bibby, Reginald
  1987 *Fragmented Gods: The Poverty and Potential of Religion in Canada*. Toronto: Irwin Publishing.

Blalock, H.M.
  Social Statistics. Toronto: McGraw-Hill.

Blau, Peter
  1970 "A Formal Theory of Differentiation in Organizations." *American Sociological Review* 35: 201-218.

Blau, Peter, Terry C. Blum and Joseph E. Schwartz
  1982 "Heterogeneity and Intermarriage." *American Sociological Review* 47: 45-62.

Blau, Peter, Carolyn Becker and Kevin M. Fitzpatrick
  1984 "Intersecting Social Affiliations and Intermarriage." *Social Forces* 62: 585-606.

Blau, Zenith S., G.T. Oser, and R.C. Stephens
  1979 "Aging, Social Class and Ethnicity." *Pacific Sociological Review* 22: 501-525.

Bogue, D.J.
  1959 "Internal Migration." In P.M. Hauser and O.D. Duncan (Eds.), *The Study of Population*. Chicago: The University of Chicago Press.

Bogue, Donald
  1969 *Principles of Demography*. New York: John Wiley and Sons.

Bourbeau, Robert
  1983 "Quelques Tendances Démographiques et Socio-Économiques au Québec, d'après le Recensement de 1981." *Revue Desjardins* 49: 16-22.

Boyd, Monica
    1975   "The Status of Immigrant Women in Canada." *Canadian Review of Sociology and Anthropology* 12: 406-416.

Boyd, Monica
    1976a "Immigration Policies and Trends: A Comparison of Canada and the United States." *Demography* 13: 84-102.

Boyd, Monica
    1976b "Occupation of Female Immigrants and North American Immigration Statistics." *International Migration Review* 19: 73-79.

Boyd, Monica
    1982a "Sex and Generational Achievement: Canada." Paper read to the International Sociological Association World Conference, Mexico City.

Boyd, Monica
    1982b "Sex Differences in the Canadian Occupational Attainment Process." *Canadian Review of Sociology and Anthropology* 19: 1-28.

Boyd, Monica
    1985a "At a Disadvantage: The Occupational Attainments of Foreign Born Women in Canada." *International Migration Review* 18: 1091-1119.

Boyd, Monica
    1985b "Immigration and Occupational Attainment in Canada." In M. Boyd, J. Goyder, F.E. Jones, H.A. McRoberts, P.C. Pineo and J. Porter (Eds.), *Ascription and Achievement: Studies in Mobility and Status Attainment in Canada*. Ottawa: Carleton University Press.

Boyd, Monica
    1986a "Immigrant Women in Canada." In Rita James Simon and Caroline B. Brettel (Eds.), *International Migration: The Female Experience*. Totowa, New Jersey: Rowman and Allanheld.

Boyd, Monica
    1986b "Socio-Economic Indices and Sexual Inequality: A Tale of Scales." *Canadian Review of Sociology and Anthropology* 23: 457-480.

Boyd, Monica
    1987a "Migrant Women in Canada: Profiles and Policies." Paper prepared for the OECD Sub-panel on Migrant Women, Paris, April 6-7.

Boyd, Monica
    1987b *Migrant Women in Canada: Profiles and Policies*. Country Report from Canada, Monitoring Panel on Migrant Women, OECD. Ottawa: Employment and Immigration, Public Affairs Inquiries and Distribution.

Boyd, Monica
  1988a "Family Migration and Living Arrangements: The Case of Elderly
          Canadian Immigrants." Paper presented at the Population
          Association of America annual meeting, New Orleans.
Boyd, Monica
  1988b "Immigration and Income Security Policies: Implications for Elderly
          Foreign Born Women." *Population Research and Policy Review* 7:
          5-24.
Boyd, Monica
  1989   *Migrant Women in Canada: Profiles and Policies.* Ottawa:
          Employment and Immigration Canada. Public Affairs Inquiry and
          Distribution.
Boyd, M., J. Goyder, F. Jones, H. McRoberts, P. Pineo and J. Porter
  1985   *Ascription and Achievement: Studies in Mobility and Status
          Attainment in Canada.* Ottawa: Carleton University Press.
Boyd, Monica and Chris Taylor
  1989   "Canada: International Migration Policies, Trends and Issues." In
          Charles Nam, William Serow, David Sly and Robert Weller (Eds.),
          International Handbook on International Migration. Westport,
          Connecticut: Greenwood Press.
Braddock, I.I., H. Jamillo and James McPortland
  1987   "How Minorities Continue to be Excluded from Equal Employment
          Opportunities: Research on Labour Market and Institutional
          Barriers." *Journal of Social Issues* 43: 1.
Brahimi, M.
  1980   "La Mortalité des Etrangers en France." *Population* 35: 603-622.
Breton, Raymond
  1973   "Institutional Completeness of Ethnic Communities and the Personal
          Relations of Immigrants." In B.R. Blishen, F.E. Jones, K.D.
          Naegele and J. Porter (Eds.), *Canadian Society: Sociological
          Perspectives.* Toronto: MacMillan.
Buechley, R.W.
  1950   "Mortality Differentials Among Immigrants." M.A. Thesis.
          University of Washington.
Burch, T.K.
  1987   "Babel Revisited: The Role of Ideas in Explanations of Human
          Behaviour." Discussion Paper, Population Studies Centre, University
          of Western Ontario.
Burch, T.K.
  1988   "Sex-Role Homogeneity, Female Status, and Demographic
          Change." Discussion Paper for Conference on Women's Position

and Demographic Change in the Course of Development. Asker
(Oslo). Norway. June 15-18. 1988.

Burchinal. Lee G.
 1964   "The Premarital Dyad and Love Involvement." In Harold T.
        Christensen (Ed.). *Handbook of Marriage and the Family*. Chicago:
        Rand McNally.

Bureau de la Statistique du Québec
 1986   *La situation démographique au Québec. Édition 1985* Quebec
        Government.

Burma. John H.
 1963   "Interethnic Marriage in Los Angeles.1948-1959." *Social Forces*
        42: 156-165.

Burnaby. B.. M. Holt. N. Steltzer and N. Collins
 1987   *The Settlement Language Training Program: An Assessment*. Ottawa:
        Employment and Immigration Canada. Immigration Group. Policy
        and Program Development Branch. Research Division.

Burnet. Jean
 1975   "The Definition of Multiculturalism in a Bilingual Framework." The
        Conference on Multiculturalism and Third World Immigrants in
        Canada. Edmonton: The University of Alberta.

Burnet. Jean
 1987   "Multiculturalism in Canada." In Leo Driedger (Ed.) *Ethnic
        Canada*. Toronto: Copp Clark Pitman Ltd.

Burvill. P.W.. M.G. McCall. N.S. Stenhouse and T.A. Reid
 1973   "Deaths from Suicide. Motor Vehicle Accidents and all Forms of
        Violent Deaths Among Migrants in Australia. 1962-66." *Acta
        Psychiatrica Scandinavica* 49: 208-250.

Calabresi, M.
 1945   "The Relation of Country of Origin to Mortality from Various Causes
        in New York State." *Human Biology* 17: 340-367.

Calamai, Peter
 1987   "Broken Words. Why Five Million Canadians are Illiterate."
        Toronto: Southam Communications Limited.

Caldwell, J. and P. Caldwell
 1987   "The Cultural Context of High Fertility in Sub-Sahara Africa."
        Population Development Review 13: 409-438.

Canada Commission of Inquiry on Unemployment Insurance
 1986   *Report*. Ottawa: Supply and Services.

Canada, Department of the Secretary of State
 1987   *Multiculturalism... being Canadian*. Ottawa: Minister of Supply and
        Services Canada.

Canada Employment and Immigration Commission, Program Evaluation Branch Strategic Policy and Planning
    1984   "A Preliminary Assessment of the Role of Federal Labour Market Adjustment Measures Under the Canadian Industrial Renewal Program." Ottawa.

Canada Employment and Immigration Commission, Labour Market Planning and Adjustment Branch, Labour Adjustment Programming
    1985   "Canadian Industrial Renewal Program. Labour Adjustment Measures. Annual Report 1984-1985." Ottawa.

Canada House of Commons
    1988   *A Review of the Canadian Jobs Strategy*. Second Report of the Standing Committee on Labour, Employment and Immigration. 2nd Session, 33rd Parliament. Ottawa.

Canada Industry, Trade and Commerce
    1979   "A Report on the Labour Force Tracking Project/Costs of Labour Adjustment Study." Ottawa.

Canada Royal Commission on the Economic Union and Developments Prospects for Canada.
    1985   *Report. Volume Two*. Ottawa: Supply and Services.

Canada Senate Standing Committee on Social Affairs, Science and Technology
    1987   *In Training, Only Work Works*. Report of the Sub-Committee on Training and Employment. Ottawa: Queen's Printer.

Canada Textile and Clothing Board
    1986   *Report on Textiles and Clothing 1986*. Ottawa: Supply and Services.

Canada Textile and Clothing Board
    1987   *Report on Textiles and Clothing*. Ottawa: Supply and Services.

Canadian Association on Gerontology
    1981   *Two Percent Sample Tape of the 1981 Census, Aged 55 and Over*.

Canadian Industrial Renewal Board
    1982   *Report of the First Year of Activities, October 1981-October 1982*. Montreal.

Canadian Industrial Renewal Board
    1984   *Second Annual Report, November 1, 1982-October 31, 1983*. Montreal.

Canadian Industrial Renewal Board
    1985   *Third Annual Report, November 1, 1983-October 31, 1984*. Montreal.

Canadian Industrial Renewal Board
    1986   *Fourth and Final Annual Report, November 1, 1984-October 31, 1985*. Montreal.

Cassel, J.
1974   "Psychological Processes and Stress: Theoretical Formulations."
        International Journal of Health Services 4: 471-482.

Castonguay, Charles
1977   "La Mobilité Ethnique au Canada." *Recherches Sociographiques*
        18:431-450.

Castonguay, Charles
1979   "Exogamie et Anglicisation chez les Minorités Canadiennes-
        françaises." *Revue Canadienne de sociologie et d'anthropologie* 16:
        21-31.

Castonguay, Charles
1985   "Transferts et semi-transferts linguistiques au Québec d'après le
        recensement de 1981." *Cahiers québécois de démographie* 14:
        59-85.

Chamie, Joseph
1976   "Religious Fertility Differentials in Lebanon." Ph.D. Dissertation,
        University of Michigan, Ann Arbor.

Choi, N.W.
1968   "Ethnic Distribution of Gastrointestinal Cancer in Manitoba."
        American Journal of Public Health 58: 2067-2081.

Choi, N.W., D.W. Entwistle, W. Michaluk and N. Nelson
1971   "Gastric Cancer in Icelanders in Manitoba." *Israel Journal of
        Medical Sciences* 7: 1500-1508.

Choinière, Robert, Marco Levasseur and Norbert Robitaille
1988   "La mortalité des Inuit du Nouveau-Québec de 1944 à 1983:
        évolution selon l'âge et la cause de décès." *Recherches amérindien-
        nes au Québec* 18: 29-37.

Choinière, Robert and Norbert Robitaille
1988   "La fécondité des Inuit du Nouveau-Québec depuis 1931: passage
        d'une fécondité naturelle à une fécondité contrôlée." *Population*.
        (Forthcoming)

The Citizen (Ottawa)
1987   "Large Influx of Immigrants Has Boosted National Illiteracy Rate."
        September 14.

Clatworthy, S.J.
1980   "The Demographic Composition and Economic Circumstances of
        Winnipeg's Native Population." *Indian Demographic Workshop:
        Implications for Policy and Planning*. Department of Indian Affairs
        and Northern Development and Statistics Canada.

Cleland, J. and C. Wilson
1987   "Demand Theories of the Fertility Transition: An Iconoclastic
        View." *Population Studies* 41: 5-30.

Coale, A.J. and S.C. Watkins
1986   *The Decline of Fertility in Europe*. Princeton: Princeton University Press.

Cobb, S.
1976   "Social Support as a Moderator of Life Stress." *Psychosomatic Medicine* 38: 300-314.

Cohen, J.B. and J.A. Brody
1981   "The Epidemiologic Importance of Psychosocial Factors in Longevity." *American Journal of Epidemiology* 114: 451-461.

Cohen, Marjorie Griffin
1987   *Free Trade and the Future of Women's Work: Manufacturing and Service Industries*. Toronto: Garamond Press.

Cohen, Rita
1986   *Cinderella in the House: Deprivation and Management of Deprivation Feelings Among Non-White Domestics*. Ph.D. Thesis. Department of Sociology, York University, Toronto.

Cordasco, Francesco
1985   *The Immigrant Women in North America: An Annotated Bibliography of Selected References*. Methuen, N.J. and London: Scarecrow Press.

Council of Ministers of Education, Canada (CMEC)
1988   *Adult Illiteracy in Canada: Identifying and Addressing the Problem*. Statement of the Council of Ministers of Education, Canada. Toronto: CMEC.

Courchene, Thomas J.
1987   *Social Policy in the 1990s: Agenda for Reform*. Toronto: C.D. Howe Institute.

Cowgill, Donald O.
1974   "Aging and Modernization: A Revision of the Theory." In J.F. Gubrium (Ed.), *Late Life*. Springfield, Illinois: Charles C. Thomas Publisher.

Coy, P.S., S. Grzybowski and J.F. Rowe
1968   "Lung Cancer Mortality According to Birthplace." *Canadian Medical Association Journal* 99: 476-483.

Cueller, I.
1981   "Service Delivery and Mental Health Services for Chicano Elders." In M. Miranda (Ed.), *Chicano Aging and Mental Health*. Washington, D.C.: DHHS Publication # (ADM) 81-952.

DaCosta, Ronald
n.d.   *Socio-Economic Characteristics of Recent Immigrants*. Ottawa: University of Ottawa, Mimeo.

Damon, Albert
  1969 "Race, Ethnic Group and Disease." *Social Biology* 16: 69-80.

Darroch, G.A.
  1979 "Another Look at Ethnicity, Stratification and Social Mobility in Canada." *Canadian Journal of Sociology* 4: 1-25.

Darroch, G.A. and W.G. Marston
  1972 "The Social Class Basis of Ethnic Residential Segregation: The Canadian Case." *American Journal of Sociology* 77: 491-510.

Darroch, G.A. and W.G. Marston
  1984 "Patterns of Urban Ethnicity: Towards a Revised Ecological Model." In Noel Iverson (Ed.), *Urbanism and Urbanization: Views, Aspects, and Dimensions*. Leiden: E.J. Brill.

Daudlin, Bob
  1984 *Equality Now: Participation of Visible Minorities in Canadian Society*. Ottawa: Queen's Printer.

Denis, Ann
  1978 "The Relationship Between Ethnicity and Educational Aspirations of Post-Secondary Students in Toronto and Montreal." In M.L. Kovacs (Ed.), *Ethnic Canadians: Culture and Education*. Saskatoon: Modern Press.

Department of Secretary of State
  1988 *Canadian Citizenship Statistics*. Ottawa: Minister of Supply and Services.

DeRuyter, B.
  1976 "Ethnic Differentials in Age at First Marriage: Canada, 1971." *Journal of Comparative Family Studies* 7: 159-166.

Desjardins, Bertrand and Jacques Légaré
  1977 "Le vieillissement de la population du Québec: faits, causes et conséquences." *Critère* 16: 143-169.

DeVoretz, D. and S.A.H. Akbari
  1987 *The Substitutability of Immigrants in Production*. Vancouver: Simon Fraser University.

De Vries, John
  1974 "Net Effects of Language Shift in Finland, 1951-1960: A Demographic Analysis." *Acta Sociologica* 17:140-149.

De Vries, John
  1977 "Explorations in the Demography of Language: Estimation of Net Language Shift in Finland, 1961-1970." *Acta Sociologica* 20: 145-153.

De Vries, John
  1985 "Some Methodological Aspects of Self-Report Questions on Language and Ethnicity." *Journal of Multilingual and Multicultural Development* 6: 347-368.

De Vries, John and Frank Vallee
  1980 *Language Use in Canada*. Ottawa: Minister of Supply and Services.

Dohrenwend, B.P. and B.S. Dohrenwend
  1967 "Toward the Development of Theoretical Models: Part I." *Milbank Memorial Fund Quarterly* 45: 155-162.

Dominion Bureau of Statistics
  1929 *Origin, Birthplace, Nationality and Language of the Canadian People (A Census Study Based on the Census of 1921 and Supplementary Data.)* Ottawa: The Kings Printer.

Dominion Bureau of Statistics
  1956 *Ninth Census of Canada, 1951, Volume*. Ottawa: The Queen's Printer.

Driedger, Leo
  1975 "In Search of Cultural Identity Factors: A Comparison of Ethnic Students." *Canadian Review of Sociology and Anthropology* 12: 150-162.

Driedger, Leo
  1987a "Alternative Models of Assimilation, Integration and Pluralism." Conference on Canada 2000: Race Relations and Public Policy in Ottawa.

Driedger, Leo
  1987b *Ethnic Canada: Identities and Inequalities*. Toronto: Copp Clark Pittman.

Driedger, Leo and Glenn Church
  1974 "Residential Segregation and Institutional Completeness." *Canadian Review of Sociology and Anthropology* 11: 30-52.

Driedger, Leo and Jacob Peters
  1977 "Identity and Social Distance: Towards Understanding Simmel's 'The Stranger'." *Canadian Review of Sociology and Anthropology* 14: 158-173.

Driedger, Leo, Charlene Thacker and Raymond Currie
  1982 "Ethnic Identification: Variations in Regional and National Preferences." *Canadian Ethnic Studies* 14: 57-68.

Driedger, Leo and Peter Hengstenberg
  1986 "Non-Official Multilingualism: Factors Affecting German Language Competence, Use, and Maintenance in Canada." *Canadian Ethnic Studies* 18: 90-109.

Driedger, Leo and Neena Chappell
1987   *Aging and Ethnicity: Toward an Interface.* Toronto: Butterworths.

Duchesne, Louis and Yolande Lavoie
1975   "Les tables de mortalité canadiennes et québécoises, 1970-1972."
        Population et Famille 35: 107-125.

Duncan, O.D. and S. Lieberson
1959   "Ethnic Segregation and Assimilation." *American Journal of
        Sociology* 64: 304-374.

Dublin, L. I. and C. W. Baker
1920   "The Mortality of Race Stocks in Pennsylvania and New York."
        Quarterly Publication of the American Statistical Association 17: 13.

Dufour, Desmond and Yves Péron
1979   *Vingt ans de mortalité au Québec. Les causes de décès, 1951-1971.*
        Montreal: University of Montreal Press.

Dunt, D.R.
1982   "Recent Mortality Trends in the Adult Australian Population and its
        Principal Ethnic Groups." *Community Health Studies* 6: 217-222.

Economic Council of Canada
1988   *Adjustment Policies for Trade-Sensitive Industries.* Ottawa: Supply
        and Services.

Edwards, E.D.
1983   "Native-American Elders: Current Issues and Social Policy
        Implications." In R.L. McNelley and J.L. Colen (Eds.), *Aging and
        Minority Groups.* Beverly Hills, CA: Sage Publications.

Eichler, M.
1983   *Families in Canada Today.* Toronto: Gage.

Employment and Immigration Canada.
1986   *Your Rights and Canada's Immigration Law.* Ottawa: Minister of
        Supply and Services.

Epstein, Cynthia
1973   "The Positive Effects of the Multiple Negative." *American Journal
        of Sociology* 78: 912-935.

Estable, Alma
1986   *Immigrant Women in Canada-Current Issues.* Background paper
        Canadian Advisory Council on the Status of Women.

Featherman, David L.
1971   "The Socioeconomic Achievement of White Religio-ethnic
        Subgroups: Social and Psychological Explanations." *American
        Sociological Review* 36: 207-222.

Finnås, Fjalar
  1986   *Den finlandssvenska befolkningsutvecklingen 1950-1980.* Helsinki: Svenska litteratursallskapet i Finland.

Fischer, Claude S.
  1976   *The Urban Experience.* New York: Harcourt, Brace.

Fishbein, Martin
  1972   "Toward an Understanding of Family Planning Behaviours." *Journal of Applied Social Psychology* 2-3: 214-227.

Fraumeni, J.F. Jr.
  1975   *Persons at High Risk of Cancer: An Approach to Cancer Etiology and Control.* New York: Academic Press.

Frideres, James S.
  1983   *Native People in Canada: Contemporary Conflicts.* Second Edition. Scarborough, Ontario: Prentice-Hall.

Frisbie, Parker W. and Frank D. Bean
  1978   "Some Issues in the Demographic Study of Racial and Ethnic Populations." In Frank D. Bean and W. Parker Frisbie (Eds.), *The Demography of Racial and Ethnic Groups.* New York: Academic Press.

Gannagé, Charlene
  1986   *Double Day, Double Bind: Women Garment Workers.* Toronto: Women's Press.

Gardner, R. and R. Kalin
  1981   *A Canadian Social Psychology of Ethnic Relations.* Toronto: Methuen.

Gelfand, Donald E. and A.J. Kutzik
  1979   *Ethnicity and Aging: Theory Research and Policy.* New York: Springer Publishing.

George, M.V.
  1970   *Internal Migration in Canada: Demographic Analyses.* Ottawa: Dominion Bureau of Statistics.

Gerber, Linda M.
  1977   "Community Characteristics and Out-Migration from Indian Communities: Regional Trends." Ottawa: Paper Presented at the Department of Indian Affairs and Northern Development.

Gibbon, John Murray
  1938   *Canadian Mosaic.* Toronto: McClelland and Stewart Ltd.

Gibbs, Jack P. and Walter T. Martin
  1962   "Urbanization, Technology and the Division of Labour." *American Sociological Review* 26: 667-677.

Giles, Wenona
    1987   "Language Rights are Human Rights: A Discussion Paper."
            Prepared for Equality in Language and Literacy Training: A
            Colloquium on Immigrant and Visible Minority Women, Toronto.

Gittler, Joseph B.
    1956   *Understanding Minority Groups.* New York: John Wiley and Sons.

Glazer, Nathan and Daniel P. Moynihan
    1975   *Ethnicity: Theory and Experience.* Cambridge: Harvard University
            Press.

Goldscheider,C.
    1971   *Population, Modernization and Social-Structure.* Boston: Little,
            Brown and Co.

Goldscheider, C. and P.R. Uhlenberg
    1969   "Minority Group Status and Fertility." *American Journal of
            Sociology* 74: 361-372.

Goldstein, Jay and Rita Bienvenue
    1980   *Ethnicity and Ethnic Relations in Canada.* Toronto: Butterworths.

Goldstein, Jay and Alexander Segall
    1985   "Ethnic Intermarriage and Ethnic Identity." *Canadian Ethnic Studies*
            17: 60-90.

Gordon, Milton M.
    1964   *Assimilation as a Way of Life.* New York: Oxford University Press.

Graham-Cumming, G.
    1967   "Health of the Original Canadians, 1867-1967." *Medical Services
            Journal Canada* 23: 115-166.

Grindstaff, C.F.
    1988   "Adolescent Marriage and Childbearing: The Long-Term Economic
            Outcome, Canada in the 1980s." *Adolescence* 23: 45-58.

Grindstaff, C.F. and Frank Trovato
    1988   "Junior Partners: Women's Contribution to Family Income in
            Canada." Unpublished paper. London, Ontario: The University of
            Western Ontario.

Guest, A.M. and J.A. Weed
    1976   "Ethnic Segregation: Patterns of Change." *American Journal of
            Sociology* 81: 1088-1111.

Gunderson, M.
    1980   *Labour Market Economics: Theory, Evidence and Policy in Canada.*
            Toronto: McGraw-Hill Ryerson.

Gunderson,M.
    1981   *Sex Discrimination in the Canadian Labour Market: Theories, Data
            and Evidence.* Ottawa: Women's Bureau, Labour Canada.

Guttentag, Marcia and Paul F. Secord
  1983   *Too Many Women? The Sex Ratio Question.* Beverly Hills: Sage
         Publications.
Haenszel, William
  1961   "Cancer Mortality Among the Foreign-Born in the United States."
         Journal of the National Cancer Institute 26: 37-132.
Haenszel, William
  1975   "Migrant Studies." In J.F. Faumeni Jr. (Ed.), *Persons at High Risk
         of Cancer: An Approach to Cancer Etiology and Control.* New York:
         Academic Press.
Haenszel, William and M. Kurihara
  1968   "Studies of Japanese Migrants, I. Mortality from Cancer and Other
         Diseases Among Japanese in the United States." *Journal of the
         National Cancer Institute* 40: 43-68.
Hagey, Janet
  1987   *1986 Census Data Quality Note on Question 7 (Aboriginal Status).*
         Ottawa: Statistics Canada (Mimeographed).
Halli, S.S.
  1987   *How Minority Status Affects Fertility.* Westport, Conn.: Greenwood
         Press.
Harding, Edith and Philip Riley
  1988   *The Bilingual Family. A Handbook For Parents.* Cambridge,
         Cambridge University Press.
Harris, J. and R. McCullough
  1988   *Health Indicators Derived from Vital Statistics for Status Indian and
         Canadian Populations, 1978-1986.* National Health and Welfare.
Hawkins, Freda
  1988   "Canada's Multiculturalism: The Policy Explained." In A.J. Fsy
         and Ch. Forceville (Eds.), *Canadian Mosaic: Essays on
         Multiculturalism.* Amsterdam: Free University Press.
Hendrix, L.
  1976   "Kinship, Social Networks and Integration Among Ozark Residents
         and Out-Migrants." *Journal of Marriage and the Family* 38: 97-104.
Henripin, Jacques
  1972   *Trends and Factors of Fertility in Canada.* Ottawa: Statistics Canada.
Henripin, Jacques
  1974   *Immigration and Language Imbalance.* A report commissioned by
         the Canadian Immigration and Population Study. Ottawa: Manpower
         and Immigration.

475

Henripin, Jacques
  1985   "Les Québécoises dont la langue est flottante et la mobilité linguistique." *Cahiers québécois de démographie* 14: 87-99.

Henry, Frances
  1978   *The Dynamics of Racism in Toronto: Research Report*. Toronto: York University.

Henry, Frances and E. Ginzberg
  1983   *Who Gets the Work? A Test of Racial Discrimination in Employment*. Toronto: Social Planning Council and Urban Alliance on Race Relations.

Herberg, Will
  1955   *Protestant, Catholic, Jew: An Essay on American Religious Sociology*, New York: Doubleday and Company (Anchor Books).

Hertel, B.R. and M. Hughes
  1987   "Religious Affiliation, Attendance and Support for 'Pro-Family' Issues in the United States." *Social Forces* 65: 858-882.

Hostetler, J.A. and G. Huntington
  1967   *The Hutterites in North America*. New York: Holt, Rinehart and Winston.

Hurd, B.W.
  1937   "The Decline in Canadian Birth Rate." *The Canadian Journal of Economics and Political Science* 3: 40-57.

House of Commons
  1988   *Equality Now!* Report of the Special Committee on Visible Minorities in Canadian Society. Ottawa.

Houseknecht, S., S. Vaughan and A. Statham
  1987   "The Impact of Singlehood on the Career Patterns of Professional Women." *Journal of Marriage and the Family* 49: 353-366.

Howith, Harry
  1988   *Postwar Canadian Attitudes to Immigration*. Ottawa: Employment and Immigration Canada, Mimeo.

Hughes, E.C.
  1950   "Preface." In Robert Ezra Park (Ed.), *Race and Culture*. New York: Free Press.

Hull, D.
  1979   "Migration, Adaptation and Illness." *Social Science and Medicine* 13A: 25-36.

Inkster, Norman
  1988   "Multiculturalism and Policing." Speech at the Conference on Multiculturalism and Policing, Richmond, B.C., January 1, 1988.

Innis, Hugh R.
  1973   *Bilingualism and Biculturalism.* An abridged version of the Royal
         Commission Report. Toronto: McClelland and Stewart.

Isajiw, W.
  1980   "Definitions of Ethnicity." In Jay Goldstein and Rita Bienvenue
         (Eds.), *Ethnicity and Ethnic Relations in Canada* (First Edition).
         Toronto: Butterworths.

Isajiw, W.
  1981   "Ethnic Identity Retention." *Research Paper No. 125.* Toronto:
         Centre for Urban and Community Affairs Studies.

Ishwaran, K.
  1980   *Canadian Families: Ethnic Variations.* Toronto: McGraw-Hill
         Ryerson.

Ishwaran, K.
  1983   *The Canadian Family.* Toronto: Gage.

Jacobson, P.H.
  1963   "Mortality of the Native and Foreign-Born Population in the United
         States." *Proceedings, International Population Conference,* IUSSP,
         New York, 1961. Volume 1: 667-674.

Jarvis, George K. and Menno Boldt
  1980   "Death Styles Among Canada's Indians." Discussion paper No. 24.
         Population Research Laboratory, University of Alberta.

Johnson, Laura and Robert E. Johnson
  1982   *The Seam Allowance: Industrial Home Sewing in Canada.* Toronto:
         Women's Educational Press.

Johnson, Nan E.
  1979   "Minority Group Status and Fertility of Black Americans, 1979: A
         New Look." *American Journal of Sociology* 84: 1386-1400.

Joy, Richard J.
  1972   *Languages in Conflict.* Toronto: McClelland and Stewart.

Kalbach, Warren E.
  1970   *The Impact of Immigration on Canada's Population.* Census
         Mongraph, 1961 Census of Canada. Ottawa: Dominion Bureau of
         Statistics.

Kalbach, Warren E.
  1975   "Demographic Aspects of Ethnic Identity and Assimilation." In Paul
         Migus (Ed.), *Sounds Canadian: Languages and Cultures in Multi-
         Ethnic Society.* Vol. 4 in Canadian Ethnic Studies Association series.
         Toronto: Peter Martin Associates Limited.

Kalbach, Warren E.
  1983   "Propensities of Intermarriage in Canada, as Reflected in Ethnic
          Origins of Husbands and Their Wives: 1961-1971." In K. Ishwaran
          (Ed.), *Marriages and Divorce in Canada*. Toronto: Methuen.

Kalbach, Warren E and Wayne W. McVey
  1979   *The Demographic Bases of Canadian Society*. Toronto:
          McGraw-Hill.

Kalbach, Warren E. and Madeline A. Richard
  1980   "The Differential Effects of Ethno-Religious Structure on Linguistic
          Trends and the Economic Achievement of Ukrainian Canadians."
          In W.R. Petryshyn (Ed.), *Changing Realities: Social Trends Among
          Ukrainian Canadians*. Edmonton, Alberta: The Canadian Institute
          of Ukrainian Studies.

Kalbach, Warren E. and Madeline A. Richard
  1981   "The Ethno-Religious Dimension of Language Retention and
          Economic Achievement: A comparative Analysis." A paper pre-
          sented at the Sixth Biennial Conference, Canadian Ethnic Studies
          Association, Edmonton, Alberta.

Kalbach, Warren E. and Medeline A. Richard
  1985   "Multiple Origins and Ethnic Exogamy: Clues to Assimilation and
          Socio-Economic Integration of Families in the 1981 Census of
          Canada." Paper presented to the annual meeting of the Canadian
          Sociology and Anthropology Association, University of Montreal.

Kalbach, Warren E. and Madeline A. Richard
  1987   "Retention of Ethnicity and Social and Economic Status
          Achievement of Non-British Minority Groups in Canada." A paper
          presented for the Ninth Biennial Meeting of the Association for
          Canadian Studies in the United States, Montreal.

Kalbach, Warren E. and Madeline A. Richard
  1988   "Alternative Mobility Patterns for Canadian Immigrants: The Ethnic
          Church, Canadian Church and no Church." Revision of a paper pre-
          sented to the Population Association of America Annual Meeting,
          New Orleans.

Kantrowitz, N.
  1973   *Ethnic and Racial Segregation in the New York Metropolis*. New
          York: Praeger.

Kasl, S.V. and L. Berkman
  1985   "Health Consequences of the Experience of Migration." *Annual
          Review of Public Health* 4: 69-80.

Kerr, D.
  1988   "The Traditional Quebecois Family: A Selective Review of the
          Historical Evidence in Light of Emmanuel Todd's Typology of

Family Structure." Unpublished manuscript, Population Studies Centre, University of Western Ontario.

Keyfitz, Nathan
1976 "How the Descendants of English Speakers See the Speakers of Other Languages and Their Descendants." In *Multiculturalism as State Policy*. Ottawa: Canadian Consultation Council on Multiculturalism.

Kim, P.K.H.
1983 "Demography of the Asian-Pacific Elderly: Selected Problems and Implications." In R.L. McNeely and J.L. Colen (Eds.), *Aging in Minority Groups*. Beverly Hills, CA: Sage Publications.

King, H. and W. Haenszel
1973 "Cancer Mortality Among Foreign and Native-Born Chinese in the United States." *Journal of Chronic Diseases* 26: 623-646.

King, H. and F.B. Locke
1980 "Cancer Mortality Risk Among Chinese in the United States." *Journal of the National Cancer Institute* 65: 1141-1148.

Kitagawa, E.
1977 "On Mortality." *Demography* 14: 381-389.

Kitagawa, E. and P.M. Hauser
1973 *Differential Mortality in the United States*. Cambridge: Harvard University Press.

Kliewer, Erich
1979 "Factors Influencing the Life Expectancy of Immigrants in Canada and Australia." Ph.D. Dissertation, The University of British Columbia.

Kliewer, Erich and R.H. Ward
1988 "Do Immigrant Suicide Rates Converge to Rates in Destination Country?" American Journal of Epidemiology 127: 640-653.

Kloss, Heinz
1966 "German American Language Maintenance Efforts." In J.A. Fishman (Ed.), *Language Loyalty in the United States*. The Hague: Mouton.

Kmet, Janet
1970 "The Role of Migrant Population in Studies of Selected Cancer Sites: A Review." *Journal of Chronological Disorders* 23: 305-324.

Kobrin, F.E. and C. Goldscheider
1978 *The Ethnic Factor*. Boston: Little and Brown.

Kobrin, F.E. and A. Speare Jr.
1983 "Out Migration and Ethnic Communities." *International Migration Review* 17: 425-444.

Kralt, John
  1977   *Ethnic Origins of Canadians, 1971 Census of Canada Profile Studies.*
         Ottawa: The Queen's Printer.

Kralt, John
  1980   "Ethnic Origin in the Canadian Census, 1871-1981." In Roman
         Petryshyn (Ed.), *Canadian Realities: Social Trends Among
         Ukrainian Canadians* Edmonton; The Canadian Institute of Ukrainian
         Studies.

Kralt, John
  1980   *A User's Guide to 1976 Census Data on Mother Tongue.* Working
         Paper Number 3-DSC 79, Ottawa: Minister of Supply and Services.

Kralt, John and Benjamin Teitlebaum
  1983   *Examination of Visible Minority Ethnic Origins by Place of Birth,
         1981.* Evaluation done for the Department of the Secretary of State,
         Ottawa (Unpublished).

Kralt, John, Pamela White and Warren Clark
  1983   *Evaluation of the 1981 Census Data on Métis, Non-Status Indians,
         Status Indians and Inuit.* Ottawa: Statistics Canada (unpublished
         paper).

Krickus, M.A.
  1980   "The Status of East European Women in the Family: Tradition and
         Change." In *Conference on the Educational and Occupational Needs
         of White Ethnic Women.* Washington, D.C.: National Institute of
         Education.

Kruger, D.E. and I.M. Moriyama
  1967   "Mortality of the Foreign Born." *American Journal of Public Health*
         57: 496-503.

Labov, Teresa and Jerry A. Jacobs
  1986   "Intermarriage in Hawaii, 1950-1983." *Journal of Marriage and
         the Family* 48: 79-88.

Lachapelle, Rejean
  1987a "The Strengthening of Majority Positions: Recent Developments in
         the Language Situation." In Jean Dumas (Ed.) *Report on the
         Demographic Situation in Canada 1986* by Jean Dumas, Ottawa,
         Ontario: Minister of supply and Services.

Lachapelle, Rejean
  1987b "L'avenir démographique du Canada et les groupes linguistiques."
         Discussion paper on the Demographic Review, 87.A.8. Studies in
         Policy. Ottawa: The Institute for Research on Public Policy.

Lachapelle, Rejean
  1988a "L'immigration et le caractère ethnolinguistique du Canada et du Québec." *Documents de recherche No. 15.* Ottawa: Direction des études analytiques, Statistique Canada.

Lachapelle, Rejean
  1988b "Changes in Fertility Among Canada's Linguistic Groups." *Canadian Social Trends* 10: 1-8.

Lachapelle, Rejean and Jacques Henripin
  1980 *La situation démolinguistique au Canada: évolution passée et prospective.* Montreal: Institute for Research on Public Policy.

Lachapelle, Rejean and Jacques Henripin
  1982 *The Demolinguistic Situation in Canada: Past Trends and Future Prospects.* Translated by Diedre A. Mark. Montreal: The Institute for Research on Public Policy.

Langdon, S.W.
  1978 *Industrial Adjustment and Trade Relations with Less-Developed Countries.* Prepared for the Economic Council of Canada, Conference on Industrial Adaptation. Ottawa: Supply and Services.

Lansing, J.B. and E. Mueller
  1973 "The Geographic Mobility of Labor." The University of Michigan: Survey Research Center, Ann Arbor.

Lee, E.S.
  1966 "A Theory of Migration." *Demography* 3: 47-57.

Li, P.
  1980 "Income Achievement and Adaptive Capacity: An Empirical Comparison of Japanese and Chinese in Canada." In K. Ujimoto and G. Hirabayashi, (Eds.), *Visible Minorities and Multiculturalism: Asians in Canada.* Toronto: Butterworths.

Lieberson, Stanley
  1970 *Languages and Ethnic Relations in Canada.* New York: John Wiley.

Locke, F.B. and H. King
  1980 "Cancer Mortality Risk Among Japanese in the United States." *Journal of the National Cancer Institute* 65: 1149-1156.

Loh, S.
  1986 "Mortality Differences Between the Portuguese Immigrant and Native-Born Populations in Canada, 1971 and 1981." Unpublished manuscript. Department of Sociology, The University of Alberta.

Lum, D.
  1983 "Asian-Americans and Their Aged." In R.L. McNeely and J.L. Colen (Eds.), *Aging in Minority Groups.* Beverley Hills, CA: Sage Publications.

481

Lutz, W.
  1986   "Culture, Religion, and Fertility: A Global View." Working Paper
          86-34. IIASA, Laxenburg, Austria.

MacDonald, J.S. and L.D. MacDonald
  1964   "Chain Migration, Ethnic Neighborhood Formation and Social
          Networks." *Milbank Memorial Fund Quarterly* 42: 82-97.

MacLean, Michael J. and R. Bonar
  1983   "The Ethnic Elderly in a Dominant Culture Long-Term Care
          Facility." *Canadian Ethnic Studies* 15: 51-59.

Majava, Alti
  1987   *Trends and Current Situation in Revenue Transfer of Technology.*
          Geneva; United Nations Conference on Trade and Development.

Marmot, M.G. and S.L. Syme
  1976   "Acculturation and Coronary Heart Disease in Japanese-
          Americans." *American Journal of Epidemiology* 104: 225-247.

Marmot, M.G., A.M. Adelstein and L. Bulusu
  1983   "Immigrant Mortality in England and Wales." *Population Trends*
          33: 14-17.

Marmot, M.G., A.M. Adelstein and L. Bulusu
  1984a   "Immigrant Mortality in England and Wales 1970-78. Causes of
          Death by Country of Birth." Studies on Medical and Population.
          Subjects No. 47. HMSO, London, England.

Marmot, M.G., A.M. Adelstein and L. Bulusu
  1984b   "Lessons from the Study of Immigrant Mortality." *Lancet* 1:
          1455-1457.

Marshall, Katherine
  1987   *"Who Are the Professional Women?"* Catalogue no. 99-951.
          Ottawa: Statistics Canada, Ministry of Supply and Services.

Marshall, Katherine
  1987   "Women in Male-Dominant Professions." *Canadian Social Trends*
          Winter 1987.

Massey, D.S. and F. Garcia Espana
  1987   "The Social Process of International Migration." *Science* 14:
          733-738.

Mata, Fernando
  1985   "Latin American Immigration to Canada: Some Reflections on the
          Immigration Statistics." *Canadian Journal of Latin American and
          Caribbean Studies* 10: 27-42.

Mathews, Georges
  1974   "Le Québec n'a que faire d'une politique nataliste et a le temps de
          voir venir." *Bulletin de l'Association des Démographes du Québec*
          3: 14-21.

McCarroll, B. and W. Bradley
1966 "Excess Mortality as an Indicator of Health: Effects of Air Pollution." *American Journal of Public Health* 56: 1933-1942.

McInnis, R.M.
1981 "A Functional View of Canadian Immigration." Paper presented at the annual meetings of the Population Association of America, Denver.

McMichael, A.J.
1982 "A Social and Epidemiological Study of the Health of Southern European Migrants in Australia." C.S.I.R.O. Division of Human Nutrition, Adelaide.

McMichael, A.J., M.G. McCall, J.J. Hartshorne and T.L. Woodings
1980 "Patterns of Gastrointestinal Cancer in European Migrants to Australia: The Role of Dietary Change." *International Journal of Cancer* 25: 431-437.

McMichael, A.J. and A. Bonett
1981 "Cancer Profiles of British and Southern-European Migrants." *Medical Journal of Australia* 1: 229-232.

Miles, Caroline
1975 "Adjustment Assistance Policies: A Survey." In *Adjustment for Trade: Studies on Individual Adjustment Problems and Policies.* OECD Development Centre. Paris: OECD.

Mitges, G.
1987 *Multiculturalism: Building the Canadian Mosaic.* Ottawa: House of Commons.

Morrison, B.J.
1983 "Sociocultural Dimensions: Nursing Homes and the Minority Aged." In G.S. Getzel and M.J. Mellor (Eds.), *Gerontological Social Work Practice in Long-Term Care.* New York: The Haworth Press.

Multiculturalism Canada
1986 *Highlights of Self Employment of Ethnocultural Groups in Canada.* Ottawa: Teega Research Consultants Inc.

Murdock, Alan I.
1980 *Mortality Rates in Indian and Inuit Population — Changes in Trends and Recent Experience, Indian Demographic Workshop: Implications for Policy and Planning.* Department of Indian Affairs and Northern Development and Statistics Canada.

Nasca, P.C., P. Greenwald, W.S. Burnett, S. Chorost and W. Schmidt
1981 "Cancer Among the Foreign Born in New York State." *Cancer* 48: 2323-2328.

Neal, Rusty and Virginia Neale
  1987   "As Long as You Know How to Do Housework: Portuguese-
        Canadian Women and the Office Cleaning Industry in Canada."
        *Resources for Feminist Research/Documentation sur la recherche
        féministe* 16: 39-41.
Newfoundland. Royal Commission on Employment and Unemployment
  1986   *Final Report. Building On Our Strengths.* St. John's: Queen's
        Printer.
Nett, Emily
  1988   *Canadian Families Past and Present.* Toronto: Butterworths.
Newman, W.M.
  1973   *American Pluralism: A Study of Minority Groups and Social Theory.*
        New York: Harper and Row.
Noivo, Edite
  1984   *Migrations and Reactions to Displacement: The Portuguese in
        Canada.* M.A. Thesis. Ottawa: Carleton University, Department of
        Sociology and Anthropology.
Ng, Roxanna and Tania Das Gupta
  1981   "Nation Builders? The Captive Labour Force of Non-English
        Speaking Women." *Canadian Women's Studies* 3: 83-89.
Ng, Roxanna and Judith Ramirez
  1984   *Immigrant Housewives in Canada.* Toronto: The Women's Centre.
Norris, Douglas A. and Edward T. Pryor
  1985   "Demographic Changes in Canada's North." Proceedings of an
        International Workshop on Population Issues in Arctic Societies.
Norris, M.J.
  1985   "Migration Patterns of Status Indians in Canada, 1976-1981." Paper
        prepared for the session, Demography of Northern and Native Peoples
        in Canada, Statistics Canada.
Norris, M.J.
  1985   *Migration Projections of Registered Indians, 1982 to 1996.* Indian
        and Northern Affairs Canada.
North-South Institute
  1985   *Women in Industry: North-South Connections.* Ottawa: North-South
        Institute.
North-South Institute
  1987   *Canadian Adjustment Policy: Beyond the Canadian Industrial
        Renewal Board.* Background Paper and Proceedings of a North-South
        Institute Research Workshop. Ottawa: North-South Institute.
O'Bryan, K.G., J.C. Reitz and O. Kuplowska
  1976   *Non-Official Languages: A Study in Canadian Multiculturalism.*
        Ottawa: Department of the Secretary of State.

Ontario Ministry of Labour
  1984   "Labour Market Experiences of Workers in Plant Closures: A Survey
          of 21 Cases." Toronto.

Parai, Louis
  1965   *Immigration and Emigration of Professional and Skilled Manpower
          During the Post War Period.* Ottawa: Queen's Printer.

Paredes, Milagros
  1987   "Immigrant Women and Second Language Education." *Resources
          for Feminist Research/documentation sur la recherche féministe* 16:
          23-27.

Parkman, Margaret A. and Jack Sawyer
  1967   "Dimensions of Ethnic Intermarriage in Hawaii." *American
          Sociological Review* 32: 593-607.

Pentney, William F.
  1987   "Race Relations: The Legislative Base." Paper presented at
          Conference on Canada 2000: Race Relations and Public Policy.
          Ottawa: Carleton University.

Perreault, J., L. Paquette and M.V. George
  1985   *Population Projections of Registered Indians, 1982 to 1996.* Indian
          and Northern Affairs Canada.

Pestieau, Caroline
  1976   *The Canadian Textile Policy: A Sectoral Trade and Adjustment
          Strategy?* Montreal: C.D. Howe Institute.

Piché, V. and M.V. George
  1973   "Estimates of Vital Rates for the Canadian Indians, 1960-1970."
          Demography 10: 367-382.

Picot, Garnett
  1986   "The Participation in Training by Women, the Unemployed, and the
          Educationally Disadvantaged." Research Paper Series No. 24. Social
          and Economic Studies Division. Ottawa: Statistics Canada.

Picot, Garnett
  1987   "Unemployment and Training." Research Paper No. 2. Social and
          Economic Studies Division. Ottawa: Statistics Canada.

Picot, Garnett and Ted Wannell
  1987   "Job Loss and Labour Market Adjustment in the Canadian
          Economy." *The Labour Force.* Statistics Canada. Ottawa: Supply
          and Services.

Pineo, Peter C.
  1977   "The Social Standing of Ethnic and Racial Groupings." *Canadian
          Review of Sociology and Anthropology* 14: 147-157.

Porter, John
1965 *The Vertical Mosaic*. Toronto: University of Toronto Press.
Preston, S.H.
1987 "Changing Values and Falling Birth Rates." In K. Davis, M.S. Berstam and R. Richard-Campbell (Eds.), *Below-Replacement Fertility in Industrial Societies: Causes, Consequences, Policies. Population and Development Review*. Supplement to 12: 176-195.

Price Waterhouse
1986 "Canadian Industrial Renewal Board. An Evaluation Study of the Sector Firms Program and the Business and Industrial Development Program." Ottawa.

Priest, G.E.
1981 *Aboriginal Youth in Canada: A Profile Based Upon 1981 Census Data*. Ottawa: Statistics Canada.

Pryor, Edward T.
1984 *Profile of Native Women: 1981 Census of Canada*. Ottawa: Statistics Canada.

Ram, Bali and A. Romaniuc
1985 *Fertility Projections of Registered Indians, 1982 to 1996*. Indian and Northern Affairs Canada.

Ramcharan, Subhas
1987 "The Role of Education in Multiracial Canada." Conference on Canada 2000: Race Relations and Public Policy. Ottawa: Carleton University.

Rao, G.L., A.H. Richmond and J. Zubrzycki
1984 *Immigrants in Canada and Australia*. Volume One. Toronto: York University Institute of Behavioural Research.

Ray, B.
1988 *Ethnicity and Migration in Canada*. Kingston: Queen's University, Mimeo.

Reed, D., D. McGee, J. Cohen, K. Yano, S.L. Syme and M. Feinleib
1982 "Acculturation and Coronary Heart Disease Among Japanese Men in Hawaii." *American Journal of Epidemiology* 115: 894-905.

Reitz, Jeffrey G.
1980 *The Survival of Ethnic Groups*. Toronto: McGraw-Hill Ryerson.

Reitz, Jeffrey G.
1982 "Ethnic Group Control of Jobs." *Research Paper 133*. Toronto: Centre for Urban and Community Studies, University of Toronto.

Reitz, Jeffrey G.
1988 "The Institutional Structure of Immigration as a Determinant of Inter-Racial Competition: A Comparison of Britain and Canada." *International Migration Review* 22: 117-146.

Rhoads, E.D.
1984   "Reevaluation of the Aging and Modernization Theory: The Samoan Evidence." *The Gerontologist* 24: 242-250.

Richmond, Anthony H.
1967   *Post War Immigrants in Canada*. Toronto: University of Toronto Press.

Richmond, Anthony H.
1975   "Black and Asian Immigrants in Britain and Canada: Experiences of Prejudice and Discrimination." Paper presented at a Conference on Multiculturalism and Third World Immigrants in Canada. Edmonton: University of Alberta.

Richmond, Anthony H.
1988   *Immigration and Ethnic Conflict*. London: Macmillan.

Richmond, Anthony H.
1989   *Caribbean Immigrants in Canada*; Ottawa, Statistics Canada.

Richmond, Anthony H. and Ravi P. Verma
1978   "The Economic Adaptation of Immigrants: A New Theoretical Perspective." *International Migration Review* 12: 3-38.

Richmond, Anthony H. and Warren Kalbach
1980   *Factors in the Adjustment of Immigrants and Their Descendants*. Ottawa: Statistics Canada.

Richmond, Anthony and Darla Rhyne
1982   *Ethnocultural Social Indicators for Canada: A Background Paper*. Ottawa: Department of the Secretary of State (Social Trends Analysis Directorate).

Richmond, Anthony H. and Jerzy Zubryzycki
1984   *Immigrants in Canada and Australia: Vol. II, Economic* Adaptation. Toronto: York University.

Rioux, Marcel
1971   *Quebec in Question*. Toronto: James Lewis and Samuel.

Roberts, R.E. and C. Askew Jr.
1972   "A Consideration of Mortality in Three Subcultures." *Health Service Reports* 87: 262-270.

Robitaille, Norbert, Robert Bourbeau and Marc Tremblay
1985   *Profil démographique et socio-économique des anglophones et francophones du Québec, 1971 et 1981*. Study for the Secretary of State.

Robitaille, N. and Robert Choinière
1985   *An Overview of Demographic and Socio-Economic Conditions of the Inuit in Canada*. Indian and Northern Affairs Canada, Ottawa.

Robitaille, N. and Robert Choinière
1987   *Projections de la Population Inuit du Canada.* Montréal:
        Département de démographie, Université de Montréal, pour les
        affaires indiennes et du Nord Canada.

Romaniuc, A.
1984   *Fertility in Canada; From Baby-Boom to Baby-Bust.* Ottawa:
        Statistics Canada. Minister of Supply and Services Canada.

Romaniuc, A.
1987   "Transition from Traditional High to Modern Low Fertility: Canadian
        Aboriginals." *Canadian Studies in Population* 14: 69-88.

Romaniuc, A.
1981   "Increase in Natural Fertility During the Early Stages of
        Modernization: Canadian Indians Case Study." *Demography* 18:
        157-172.

Rosenthal, Carolyn J.
1983   "Aging, Ethnicity and the Family: Beyond the Modernization
        Thesis." *Canadian Ethnic Studies* 15: 1-16.

Rosenweike, I.
1984   "Mortality Among the Puerto Rican Born in New York City."
        American Journal of Epidemiology 119: 177-185.

Rosenweike, I. and D. Shai
1986   "Trends in Cancer Mortality Among Puerto Rican-born Migrants to
        New York City." *International Journal of Epidemiology* 15: 3-35.

Rowe, G. and M.J. Norris
1985   *Mortality Projections of Registered Indians, 1982 to 1996.* Indian
        and Northern Affairs Canada, Ottawa.

Roy, Arun
1987   "An Analysis of Substitutability and Complimentarity of Immigrants
        and Canadian-Base Work Force." *Labour Market Bulletin.* Ottawa,
        EIC: 4, 9.

Roy, Laurent
1974   "Conséquences socio-économiques d'une stabilisation des taux de
        fécondité au niveau de 1971." *Bulletin de l'Association des
        Démographes du Québec* 3: 54-73.

Royal Commission on Bilingualism and Biculturalism
1970   Report, Book IV. *The Cultural Contribution of the Other Ethnic
        Groups.* Ottawa: The Queen's Printer.

Royal Commission on the Economic Union and Development Prospects
        for Canada
1985   *Report, Volume 2.* Ottawa: Minister of Supply and Services Canada.

Ryder, Norman B.
  1955   "The Interpretation of Origin Statistics." *Canadian Journal of Economics and Political Science* 21: 466-479.

Ryder, Norman
  1989   A paper submitted to the Committee on Demographic Statistics and Studies, Advisory to the Chief Statistician of Canada, Ottawa.

Samuel, T. John
  1977   "Third World Migration, Multiculturalism and Education." Paper presented at the Conference on Canadian Immigration Policy and the Third World Community. Regina, Saskatchewan.

Samuel, T. John
  1983   "Canadian Fertility Trends." Demographic Trends and Their Impact on the Canadian Labour Market. Ottawa: Statistics Canada.

Seward, Shirley B.
  1988a "Demographic Change, the Economy, and Public Education." Paper presented at the Canadian Teachers' Federation, Conference on Trends and Issues in Education Finance and Teacher Bargaining, Ottawa.

Seward, Shirley B.
  1988b "Discussant." In Glenn Drover (Ed.), *Free Trade and Social Policy*. Ottawa: Canadian Council on Social Development.

Seward, Shirley B.
  1989   "Challenges of Labour Adjustment: The Case of Immigrant Women in the Clothing Industry." Ottawa: Institute for Research on Public Policy (forthcoming).

Seward, Shirley B.and Kathryn McDade
  1988   "Immigrant Women in Canada: A Policy Perspective." Background Paper. Ottawa: Canadian Advisory Council on the Status of Women.

Seward, Shirley B. and Marc Tremblay
  1989   "Immigrants in the Canadian Labour Force: Their Role in Structural Change." Discussion Paper 89.B.2. Ottawa: Institute for Research on Public Policy.

Seydegart, K. and G. Spears
  1985   *Beyond Dialogue: Immigrant Women in Canada, 1985-1990*. Ottawa: Secretary of State, Multiculturalism.

Sidlofsky, S.
  1969   "Post-War Immigrants in the Changing Metropolis with Special Reference to Toronto's Italian Population." Unpublished Ph.D. Thesis, University of Toronto.

Siggner, A.J.
  1977   "Preliminary Results from a Study of 1966-71 Migration Patterns Among Status Indians in Canada." Mimeographed, Department of Indian Affairs and Northern Development.

Siggner, A.J.
  1986   "The Socio-Demographic Conditions of Registered Indians." *Canadian Social Trends*, Statistics Canada.

Simon, R.J. and C.B. Brettell
  1986   *International Migration, The Female Experience*. New Jersey: Rowman and Allanheld.

Simpson, George E. and J. Milton Yinger
  1972   *Racial and Cultural Minorities: An Analysis of Prejudice and Discrimination*. 4th Edition. New York: Harper and Row.

Simpson, George E. and J. Milton Yinger
  1983   *Racial and Cultural Minorities*. New York: Harper and Row.

Staszewski, J.
  1976   *Epidemiology of Cancer of Selected Sites in Poland and Polish Migrants*. Cambridge, Mass.: Ballinger.

Statistical Society of Canada
  1988   "Statistics in the Capital: News from Statistics Canada." *Bulletin Liaison* 2: 36. Ottawa: Statistical Society of Canada.

Statistics Canada
  1981   *Public Use Sample Tapes: User Documentation*. Ottawa.

Statistics Canada
  1982   *1981 Census Directory*. Ottawa: Minister of Supply and Services Canada.

Statistics Canada
  1983   *The Daily*. February 1. Ottawa: Minister of Supply and Services Canada.

Statistics Canada
  1984   *1981 Census of Canada. Population and Labour Force — Industry by Cultural Characteristics*. Ottawa: Minister of Supply and Services.

Statistics Canada
  1984   *The Elderly in Canada*. Ottawa: Minister of Supply and Services.

Statistics Canada
  1985   "Marriages and Divorces." *Vital Statistics* Vol. II. Ottawa: Minister of Supply and Services.

Statistics Canada
  1985   *Women in Canada: A Statistical Report*. Ottawa: Statistics Canada.

Statistics Canada
  1986   *Special Tabulations, 1986 Census*.

Statistics Canada
   1986   "Workers Experiencing Permanent Job Loss. A Survey of Their
          Labour Market Experiences 1981-84." Survey conducted by
          Household Surveys Division for Policy and Program Analysis
          Branch, Employment and Immigration, Ottawa.

Statistics Canada
   1987   *1986 Census of Canada — Summary Tabulations of Ethnic and
          Aboriginal Origins.* Ottawa: Statistics Canada.

Statistics Canada
   1987   *The Daily.* March 12. Ottawa: Minister of Supply and Services
          Canada.

Statistics Canada
   1987   *Addendum to the Daily,* December 3. Ottawa: Minister of Supply
          and Services Canada.

Statistics Canada
   1988   *The Daily.* April 20. Ottawa: Minister of Supply and Services
          Canada.

Samuel, T. John
   1987a "Visible Minorities in Canada." In P. Krishnan and F. Trovato
          (Eds.), *Essays in Honour of Karol J. Krotki: Methodological and
          Substantive.* Population Research Laboratory, University of Alberta,
          Edmonton.

Samuel, T. John
   1987b *Immigration and Visible Minorities in the Year 2001: A Projection.*
          Ottawa: Centre for Immigration and Ethnocultural Studies, Carleton
          University.

Samuel, T. John
   1988b *Immigration, Visible Minorities and the Labour Force in Canada:
          Vision 2000.* Paper presented at The Canadian Population Society
          Meeting. Windsor, Ontario.

Samuel, T. John
   1988c Comments on "Trends and the Current Situation in Reverse Transfer
          of Technology." Geneva: UNETAD.

Samuel, T. John and T. Conyers
   1986   *The Employment Effects of Immigration: A Balance Sheet Approach.*
          Ottawa: Employment and Immigration Canada, Population Working
          Paper No. 2.

Samuel, T. John and M. Jansson
   1988a *Canada's Immigration Levels and the Economic and Demographic
          Environment.* Ottawa:Employment and Immigration Canada.
          Population Working Paper No. 8.

Sandlund, Tom
  1980   *Ethnicity and Mobility. Description of a Project.* Abo: Språkgrupp
         och Mobilitet, Research Report No. 1.
Saturday, Star The
  1985   "Most Metro Anglos Born Here, Survey Shows." Toronto: Dec. 15.
Satzewich, Victor and Peter S. Li
  1987   "Immigrant Labour in Canada: The Cost and Benefit of Ethnic Origin
         in the Job Market." *Canadian Journal of Sociology* 12: 229-241.
Sauer, H.I.
  1962   "Epidemiology of Cardiovascular Mortality, Geographic and
         Ethnic." *The American Journal of Public Health* 52: 94-105.
Schermerhorn, R.A.
  1970   *Comparative Ethnic Relations: A Framework for Theory and
         Research.* New York: Random House.
Schmitt, Robert C.
  1965   "Demographic Correlates of Interracial Marriages in Hawaii,"
         Demography 2: 463-473.
Stawszeski, J. and W. Haenszel
  1965   "Cancer Mortality Among the Polish-born in the United States."
         Journal of the National Cancer Institute 35: 291-297.
Stenhause, N.S. and M.G. McCall
  1970   "Differential Mortality from Cardiovascular Disease in Migrants
         from England and Wales, Scotland and Italy, and Native-born
         Australians." *Journal of Chronic Diseases* 23: 423-431.
Stone, Frank
  1984   *Canada, the GATT and the International Trade System.* Montreal:
         The Institute for Research on Public Policy.
Stone, L.O.
  1974   "What We Know About Migration Within Canada: A Selective
         Review and Agenda for Future Research." *Internation Migration
         Review* 8: 267-281.
Strong, C.
  1984   "Stress and Caring for Elderly Relatives: Interpretations and Coping
         Strategies in an American Indian and White Sample." *The
         Gerontologist* 24: 251-256.
Sturino, F.
  1980   "Family and Kin Cohesion Among Southern Italian Immigrants in
         Toronto." In K. Ishwaran (Ed.), *Canadian Families: Ethnic
         Variations.* Toronto: McGraw-Hill Ryerson.
Syme, S.L. and L.F. Berkman
  1976   "Social Class, Susceptibility and Sickness." *American Journal of
         Epidemiology* 104: 1-8.

Tan, Boon-Ann
    1981   "Fertility Differences in Peninsular Malaysia: The Ethnic Factor."
            Ph.D. Dissertation, University of Michigan, Ann Arbor.

Taylor, Chris
    1979   *The Métis and Non-Status Indian Population, Numbers and
            Characteristics.* Native Citizens Directorate, Department of the
            Secretary of State.

Taylor, Chris
    1987   *Demography and Immigration in Canada: Challenge and
            Opportunity.* Ottawa: Employment and Immigration Canada.

Tepper, Elliot
    1986   *Demographic Change and Pluralism.* Ottawa: Carleton University,
            Mimeo.

Termote, Marc and Danielle Gauvreau
    1988   *La situation démolinguistic du Québec.* Quebec City, Quebec:
            Conseil de la langue française.

Terry, G.
    1975   "Rival Explanations in the Work-Fertility Relationship." *Population
            Studies* 29: 191-205.

Thomas, B.
    1972   *Migration and Urban Development.* London: Methuen.

Thomas, C.B. and K.R. Duszynski
    1974   "Closeness to Parents and the Family Constellation in a Prospective
            Study of Five Disease States: Suicide, Mental Illness, Malignant
            Tumor, Hypertension and Coronary Heart Disease." *Johns Hopkins
            Medical Journal* 134: 251-270.

Thorburn, Hugh G.
    1987   "The Political Foundations of Canada's Pluralist Society."
            Conference on Canada 2000: Race Relations and Public Policy.
            Ottawa: Carleton University.

Tienhara, Nancy
    1974   *Canadian Views on Immigration and Population.* Ottawa: Canadian
            Immigration and Population Study.

Tinker, John N.
    1982   "Intermarriage and Assimilation in a Plural Society: Japanese
            Americans in the United States." In Gary A. Crester and Joseph J.
            Leon (Eds.), *Intermarriage in the United States.* New York: Haworth
            Press.

Todd, E.
    1985   *The Explanation of Ideology: Family Structures and Social Systems.*
            London: Basil Blackwell.

Tomes, Nigel
  1983 "Religion and the Rate of Return on Human Capital: Evidence from Canada." *Canadian Journal of Economics* 16: 122-138.

Toney, M.B.
  1976 "Length of Residence, Social Ties, and Economic Opportunities." *Demography* 13: 297-309.

Tremblay, Marc
  1983 *Analyse de la mortalité et de la fécondité selon le groupe linguistique, Québec, 1976-1981.* M.A. Thesis, Département de démographie, University of Montreal.

Trovato, Frank
  1981 "Canadian Ethnic Fertility." *Sociological Focus* 14: 57-73.

Trovato, Frank
  1983 "Mortality Differences Among the Native and Foreign-born Populations in Canada, 1951-1971." Ph.D. Dissertation. Department of Sociology, The University of Western Ontario.

Trovato, Frank
  1984 "Mortality Differences Among the French, British, and Native Indian Indigenous Populations of Canada, 1950-52 to 1970-72." Paper presented at the Canadian Population Society Meetings, Guelph, Ontario.

Trovato, Frank
  1985 "Mortality Differences Among Canada's Indigenous and Foreign-born Populations, 1951-1971." *Canadian Studies in Population* 12: 49-80.

Trovato, Frank
  1986 "Suicide and Ethnic Factors in Canada." *The International Journal of Social Psychiatry* 32: 55-64.

Trovato, Frank
  1987 "The Interurban Mobility of the Foreign Born in Canada, 1976-81." *International Migration Review* 22: 59-86.

Trovato, Frank
  1988 "A Macrosociological Analysis of Change in the Marriage Rate: Canadian Women, 1921-25 to 1981-85." *Journal of Marriage and the Family* 50: 507-521.

Trovato, Frank and T.K. Burch
  1980 "Minority Groups Status and Fertility in Canada." *Canadian Ethnic Studies* 8: 1-18.

Trovato, Frank and C.F. Grindstaff
  1986 "Economic Status: A Census Analysis of Thirty-Year-Old Women in Canada." *Canadian Review of Sociology and Anthropology* 23: 569-587.

Trovato, Frank and Shiva S. Halli
  1983   "Ethnicity and Migration in Canada." *International Migration Review* 17: 245-267.

Trovato, Frank and George K. Jarvis
  1986   "Immigrant Suicide in Canada: 1971 and 1981." *Social Forces* 65: 433-457.

Turner, Jean E. and Alan B. Simmons
  1987   "The Caribbean-Canadian Family: Change, Stress and Adaptive Strategies." Paper presented to the Conference on Caribbean Migration and the Black Diaspora sponsored by the Institute of Commonwealth Studies, University of London.

Uhlenberg, P.
  1973   "Noneconomic Determinants of Nonmigration: Sociological Considerations for Migration Theory." *Rural Sociology* 38: 296-311.

Ujimoto, K. Victor
  1986   "The Ethnic Dimension of Aging in Canada." In V.W. Marshall (Ed.), *Aging in Canada*. Don Mills, Ontario: Fitzhenry and Whiteside.

Ujimoto, K. Victor
  1987   "Theories of Race Relations: An Overview." Conference on Canada 2000: Race Relations and Public Policy. Ottawa: Carleton University.

Ulman, R. and J.D. Abernethy
  1975   "Blood Pressure and Length of Stay in Australia of Italian Immigrants in the Australian National Blood Pressure Study." *International Journal of Epidemiology* 4: 213-215.

United States Bureau of the Census
  1973   *The Methods and Materials of Demography*, revised edition. Henry S. Shryock, Jacob S. Siegel and Associates (Eds.). United States Government Printing Office. Washington, D.C.

Vallin, J.
  1985   "La mortalité des immigrés en Angleterre et Galles." *Population* 1: 156-161.

Veevers, J.
  1977   *The Family in Canada*. Profile Studies, Vol. 5, Part 3. Ottawa: Statistics Canada.

Veltman, Calvin
  1984   "Testing the Effects of Language as Measured by the Canadian Census." Paper presented at the meeting of the Association International de Linguistique Appliqué. Brussels.

Veltman, Calvin
  19886 "The Interpretation of the Language Questions of the Canadian
       Census." *Canadian Review of Sociology and Anthropology* 23:
       412-422.

Verma, R., K. Chan and L. Lam
  1980 "The Chinese-Canadian Family: A Socio-Economic Profile." In K.
       Ishwaran (Ed.), *Canadian families: Ethnic Variations*. Toronto:
       McGraw-Hill Ryerson.

Vincent, Peter
  1988 "Hungarian Refugee Will Remember Mr. Reid for Ever." *The
       Toronto Star*, May 8.

Webb, M.L.
  1973 Parliamentary Enquiry 724 — *Maternal and Child Health, Indian
       and Eskimo*. Ottawa.

Weeks, J.
  1986 *Population*. Third Edition. Belmont, California: Wadsworth
       Publishing.

Weiner, Gerry
  1986 *Immigration to the Year 2000: A Canadian Perspective*. Washington:
       An address to the Georgetown Leadership Seminar.

Weinreich, Uriel
  1952 *Languages in Contact*. New York: Linguistic Circle of New York.

Wesley-King, S.
  1983 "Service utilization and the Minority Elderly: A Review." In R.L.
       McNeely and J.L. Colen (Eds.), *Aging in Minority Groups*. Beverly
       Hills, CA: Sage Publications.

White, Pamela
  1987 *1986 Census Ethnic Origin: Note on Comparability, Single and
       Multiple Responses* Ottawa: Statistics Canada (mimeo).

Wilson, S.J.
  1986 *Women, The Family and The Economy*. Toronto: McGraw-Hill
       Ryerson.

Windsor Star, The
  1987 "Immigration Adds to Illiteracy." September 14.

Yancey, William L., E.P. Ericksen and R.N. Juliani
  1976 "Emergent Ethnicity: A Review and Reformulation." *American
       Sociological Review* 41: 391-403.

Yeung, W.
  1988 "The Reciprocal Effects of Female Labour Force Participation and
       Fertility." Discussion Paper No. 53. Population Research

Laboratory, Department of Sociology, The University of Alberta. Edmonton.

Yinger, Milton
1985   "Ethnicity." *Annual Review of Sociology* 11: 151-180.

Printed in Canada
by Les Editions Marquis
Montmagny, Québec